T0339997

THE ROUTLEDGE COMPANION TO ANTHROPOLOGY AND BUSINESS

Interest in anthropology and ethnography has been an ongoing feature of organizational research and pedagogy; this book provides a key reference text that pulls together the different ways in which anthropology infuses the study of organizations, both epistemologically and methodologically.

The volume hosts key scholars and experts within the fields of Organizational Anthropology, Organizational Ethnography, Organizational Studies and Qualitative Research.

The book provides a combination of methodological guidelines, exemplars and epistemological reflection. It includes methodological viewpoints, ethnographic journeys within organizations as well as beyond organizations, and individual reflections on challenges faced by organizational ethnographers.

This book is aimed at PhD, master and advanced undergraduate students and researchers across disciplines, especially those who are engaged with general management, organizational behaviour, strategy and anthropological/ethnographic issues.

Raza Mir is the Seymour Hyman Professor of Management at William Paterson University, USA. He serves as the co-Editor-in-Chief of the journal *Organization*. His research primarily deals with the strategic management, transfer of knowledge across national boundaries in MNCs, and power, exploitation and resistance in organizational settings.

Anne-Laure Fayard is Associate Professor of Innovation, Design and Organization Studies in the Tandon School of Engineering at New York University, USA. She is an ethnographer studying work and collaboration at the intersection between organizations, technology and people. Her work has been published in several leading journals such as *Administrative Science Quarterly* and *Organization Science*.

ROUTLEDGE COMPANIONS IN BUSINESS, MANAGEMENT AND MARKETING

Routledge Companions are prestige volumes which provide an overview of a research field or topic. Surveying the business disciplines, the books in this series incorporate both established and emerging research themes. Compiled and edited by an array of highly regarded scholars, these volumes also benefit from global teams of contributors reflecting disciplinary diversity.

Individually, *Routledge Companions in Business, Management and Marketing* provide impactful one-stop-shop publications. Collectively, they represent a comprehensive learning and research resource for researchers, postgraduate students and practitioners.

Published titles in this series include:

The Routledge Companion to Nonprofit Management
Edited by Helmut K. Anheier and Stefan Toepler

The Routledge Companion to Inclusive Leadership
Edited by Joan Marques

The Routledge Companion to Accounting History, 2nd Edition
Edited by John Richard Edwards and Stephen Walker

The Routledge Companion to Managing Digital Outsourcing
Edited by Erik Beulen and Pieter Ribbers

The Routledge Companion to Happiness at Work
Edited by Joan Marques

The Routledge Companion to Anthropology and Business
Edited by Raza Mir and Anne-Laure Fayard

The Routledge Companion to International Hospitality Management
Edited by Marco A. Gardini, Michael C. Ottenbacher and Markus Schuckert

The Routledge Handbook of Critical Finance Studies
Edited by Christian Borch and Robert Wosnitzer

For more information about this series, please visit: www.routledge.com/Routledge-Companions-in-Business-Management-and-Marketing/book-series/RCBUS

THE ROUTLEDGE COMPANION TO ANTHROPOLOGY AND BUSINESS

Edited by Raza Mir and Anne-Laure Fayard

Routledge
Taylor & Francis Group

NEW YORK AND LONDON

First published 2021
by Routledge
52 Vanderbilt Avenue, New York, NY 10017

and by Routledge
2 Park Square, Milton Park, Abingdon, Oxon OX14 4RN

Routledge is an imprint of the Taylor & Francis Group, an informa business

© 2021 Taylor & Francis

The right of Raza Mir and Anne-Laure Fayard to be identified as the
authors of the editorial material, and of the authors for their individual
chapters, has been asserted in accordance with sections 77 and 78 of the
Copyright, Designs and Patents Act 1988.

British Library Cataloguing-in-Publication Data
A catalogue record for this book is available from the British Library

Library of Congress Cataloging-in-Publication Data
A catalog record has been requested for this book

ISBN: 978-1-138-49642-2 (hbk)
ISBN: 978-0-367-51138-8 (pbk)
ISBN: 978-1-003-05245-6 (ebk)

Typeset in Bembo
by Swales & Willis, Exeter, Devon, UK

CONTENTS

Contents

Contents

CONTRIBUTORS

Chahrazad Abdallah is Associate Professor in Business at Singapore University of Social Sciences, Singapore. Her research focuses on qualitative research approaches, critical ethnography and ethnographic writing, and on strategy as an ambiguous discursive practice. Chahrazad's most recent publications appear in *Standing on the Shoulders of Giants: Traditions and Innovations in Research Methodology*, *The Routledge Companion to Qualitative Research in Organization Studies* and the *SAGE Handbook of Qualitative Business and Management Research Methods*.

Sadaf Ahmad is an Associate Professor of Anthropology in the Department of Humanities and Social Sciences, Lahore University of Management Sciences (LUMS), Pakistan. She is the author of *Transforming Faith: The Story of Al-Huda and Islamic Revivalism among Urban Pakistani Women*. Her work focuses on gender and includes studies on Pakistani policewomen, gender and Pakistani cinema, gender-based violence and movements for gendered change in Pakistan.

Eric J. Arnould is a Postdoctoral Researcher at Aalto University Business School, Finland. Dr. Arnould's research on consumer culture, cultural strategy, services marketing and marketing and development appears in major social science and managerial periodicals and books. He has helped legitimize post positivist inquiry in marketing scholarship and codify consumer culture theory. Current interests include sustainable business practice, sustainable consumption, collective consumer creativity, human branding and digital mobility. He has recently coedited a collective text on consumer culture theory.

Hari Bapuji is a Professor in the Department of Management and Marketing, Faculty of Business and Economics, The University of Melbourne, Australia. His research and teaching broadly cover strategic management and international business, with a specific focus on the relationship between economic inequality in society and organizations.

Mary Yoko Brannen, Professor at Copenhagen Business School, Denmark, is an organizational anthropologist specializing in cultural complexity. She is a Fellow of the Academy of International Business and Consulting Editor of the *Journal of International Business Studies*. She has an Honorary Doctorate from Copenhagen Business School and currently sits on the International Advisory Board of the Stockholm School of Economics.

Snehanjali Chrispal is currently pursuing her doctorate within the Faculty of Business and Economics at the University of Melbourne, Australia. Her research interests focus on caste, gender and gender-based violence. Using critical perspectives and qualitative research methodologies, she explores institutions, inequality, power and emotions.

Stephanie Decker is Professor of History and Strategy at the University of Bristol School of Management, UK, and visiting Professor in African Business History at the University of Gothenburg, Sweden. Her work lies at the intersection of organization studies and historical research, with a focus on the use of historical methodology in organization research. She has published in *Academy of Management Review*, *Journal of Management Studies*, *Organization* and the major business history journals and is currently serving as the joint Editor-in-Chief of *Business History*.

Mark de Rond is Professor of Organizational Ethnography at the Cambridge Judge Business School, UK. A recurring feature in his work is the experience of being human in (relatively) extreme contexts. His fieldwork has involved extended periods with Boat Race crews, doctors and nurses at war, adventurers, peace activists and, most recently, paedophile hunters.

Frank den Hond is the Ehrnrooth Professor in Management and Organisation at Hanken School of Economics (Helsinki, Finland) and affiliated with Vrije Universiteit (Amsterdam, the Netherlands). His research interest is in the broad area of business in society. He is a past Editor of *Organization Studies*.

Anne-Laure Fayard is Associate Professor at New York University, USA. She is an ethnographer studying work and collaboration at the intersection between organizations, technology and people. Her work has been published in several leading journals such as *Administrative Science Quarterly* and *Organization Science*. She is also the co-author of *The Power of Writing in Organizations*.

Fabrizio Ferraro is Professor of Strategic Management at IESE Business School, Spain. His research explores the emergence and mainstreaming of responsible and impact investing in the financial sector. His work has been published in *Administrative*

Science Quarterly, Academy of Management Review, Academy of Management Journal, Organization Science and *Organization Studies* among others.

Johan Fischer is Associate Professor in the Department of Social Sciences and Business, Roskilde University, Denmark. His work focuses on human values and markets. More specifically, he explores the interfaces between class, consumption, market relations, religion and the state in a globalized world. Currently, he is working on a research project that explores the relationship between vegetarian and non-vegetarian (food) markets in India.

Yuiko Fujita is Professor of Sociology at the School of Commerce, Meiji University, Tokyo. Her research interests include culture, media, globalization, and gender, and her current research focuses on the globalization of fashion and restaurant organizations. She is the author of *Cultural Migrants from Japan: Youth, Media, and Migration in New York and London*.

Emmanouil (Manos) Gkeredakis is Assistant Professor at IESE Business School, Spain. He studies how organizations exploit new opportunities for digital innovation with a focus on crowdsourcing. He is interested in the management and ethical challenges that crowd-based organizations face. He employs a variety of qualitative methods and uses multiple sources of online and offline field observations, interviews and archival data.

Robert Jackall is the Willmott Family Professor, Emeritus, of Sociology and Public Affairs at Williams College, USA. He is the author of many books, including *Moral Mazes: The World of Corporate Managers; Wild Cowboys: Urban Marauders and the Forces of Order* and *Street Stories: The World of Police Detectives*.

Stéphane Jaumier is Assistant Professor in Management Control at Grenoble Ecole de Management, France. His research interests include questions of organizational democracy and, more generally, those of power, control and resistance within alternative organizations. He focusses in particular on worker cooperatives, to which he applies theoretical perspectives and methods drawn from anthropology.

Lise Justesen is Associate Professor at the Department of Organization, Copenhagen Business School, Denmark. Her research interests include the interplay between management technologies and organization, public sector digitalization and actor-network theory. She has published in journals such as *Accounting, Organizations and Society* and *Organization* and she is the co-Editor of the volume *Making Things Valuable*.

Nahoko Kameo is Assistant Professor of Sociology at New York University, USA. Her research interests include organization theory, science and technology studies, economic sociology, and qualitative methods. She is currently writing a book about the changes in how Japanese university bio-scientists commercialize their inventions.

Mikkel Krenchel works at the intersection of social science and business strategy. As the head of ReD Associates' North American business, he advises executives from some of the world's largest technology, media and financial services companies on how to make sense of the people they serve and make better bets on human behaviour. He also heads ReD's emerging practice in integrated social- and data-science.

Mikaela Krohn is a Postdoctoral Researcher at Hanken School of Economics, Finland. Her research interests include visual management studies and in particular the use of new media in strategic change. Her research builds on ethnographic methodology in order to understand the lived experiences in people's relations with new technology.

Heinrich Liechtenstein is Professor of Financial Management at IESE Business School, Spain. Professor Liechtenstein holds a PhD in Managerial Science and Applied Economics from The Economics School of Vienna, a Master's degree in Business Administration from IESE Business School, and a BSc in Business Economics from the University of Graz. He specializes in entrepreneurial finance, management of wealth and governance of entrepreneurial families.

Christian Madsbjerg is Professor of Applied Humanities at The New School in New York City, USA, a Senior Fellow at The Berggruen Institute and co-Founder of the pioneering global consultancy ReD Associates. Christian Madsbjerg is the author of *Sensemaking – The Power of the Humanities in the Age of the Algorithm* and co-author (with Mikkel B. Rasmussen) of *The Moment of Clarity*, both books translated into more than 10 languages. Christian Madsbjerg's work has been featured in outlets such as the BBC, WSJ, *The Economist* and NHR Japan.

Alice Mascena is a PhD candidate at IESE Business School, Spain. She has been interested in dual purpose and hybrid organizations, in particular those that combine elements of business and social impact. She is presently researching impact investment funds and accelerators in Europe.

Stefanie Mauksch is a Postdoctoral Researcher at Leipzig University, Germany. She has conducted ethnographic research to explore practices around social entrepreneurship, primarily focusing on themes of power, such as enchantment, subjectivity and utopianism, and questions of social improvement. She has published in the journals *Organization, Business & Society and the Social Enterprise Journal*.

Alan McKinlay is Professor of HRM at Newcastle University Business School, UK. He has published extensively on business, management and labour history, including books and articles on Ford Motor Company, Motorola and knowledge management. He draws heavily upon the social theory of Michel Foucault, particularly the idea of governmentality. He is currently researching the changing nature of work, employment and careers in the creative industries.

Nanna Mik-Meyer is Professor at Copenhagen Business School, Denmark. She has an MA in Anthropology and PhD in Sociology, both from the University of Copenhagen. Her research interests are identity work in organizations, micro-sociology, qualitative methodology and processes of marginalization in public and private organizations. She has published books with SAGE, Routledge and MUP and approximately 25 peer-reviewed articles in journals such as *Human Relations*; *Work, Employment & Society*; *Sociology of Health and Illness*; *Gender, Work and Organization* and *British Journal of Sociology*.

Elisabeth Naima Mikkelsen is Associate Professor of Organizational Psychology at the Department of Organization at Copenhagen Business School, Denmark. Her research interests are in the areas of conflict, sensemaking and power in organizational settings. She is currently leading a research project on the organizing of police encounters with victims of crime.

Raza Mir is the Seymour Hyman Professor of Management at William Paterson University, USA. He serves as the co-Editor-in-Chief of the journal *Organization* and is the co-author of the forthcoming book *Philosophy and Management*. His research primarily deals with the strategic management, transfer of knowledge across national boundaries in MNCs, and power, exploitation and resistance in organizational settings.

Mette Mogensen works as a Postdoctoral Researcher at the Department of Organization at Copenhagen Business School, Denmark. Her research revolves primarily around the organization and management of the psycho-social work environment with a particular interest in visual methods and the role of the material. She has recently been involved in projects on leadership and leadership development and has co-authored a book on paradoxes and paradox management.

Fiona Moore is Professor of Business Anthropology at Royal Holloway, University of London, UK. Her research on identity in German multinational corporations has been extensively published in academic and popular journals. She has written a monograph on German expatriates in London, with a second forthcoming monograph on Taiwanese expatriates in London and Toronto. More information is available at www.fiona-moore.com.

Terry Mughan is Associate Professor of International Business at the Royal Roads University, Canada. His research interests are in the areas of intercultural communication in and across organizations and associated issues of language use and strategy. He is currently leading a 15-country transnational study of the international student experience (ISE).

Ursula Plesner is Associate Professor at the Department of Organization at Copenhagen Business School, Denmark. She is the author of *Digital Organizing – Revisiting Themes in Organization Studies*, and her research revolves around organizational impacts of digitalization. Together with Lise Justesen, she leads a project on the value of invisible work in digitalized organizations.

Melea Press is Associate Professor of Marketing at SKEMA Business School, France. She researches the socio-cultural contexts that affect how marketing strategy is developed in changing markets. Her current focus is on critiquing epistemologies of sustainable business practices and developing strong sustainability strategies for business.

Craig J. Thompson is the Churchill Professor of Marketing at the University of Wisconsin-Madison, USA. Craig's research addresses the socio-cultural shaping of consumption practices, the gendering of consumer culture, and relations of power and resistance that are contested through the marketplace. Craig is a Fellow of the Association of Consumer Research.

Tom P. Vandebroek holds a PhD in Management from IESE Business School, Spain.

John Van Maanen is the Erwin Schell Emeritus Professor of Organization Studies in the Sloan School of Management at MIT, USA. He is an ethnographer of occupations and organizations and the author of numerous articles and books including *Tales of the Field* and, with Edgar Schein, *Career Anchors*.

Mikko Vesa is Associate Professor of Management Studies at the Hanken School of Economics, Finland. He has diverse research interests but is particularly known for his research in organizational gamification, strategy as practice and technological change. His research has been published in, for example, *Academy of Management Review, Organization Studies* and *Journal of Business Ethics*.

Natalya Vinokurova is Assistant Professor of Management at the University of Pennsylvania, USA. Her research spans the intersection of the domains of business history and strategy, focusing on decision-making in fragmented systems with a particular interest in the antecedents of the 2008 mortgage crisis. She has received the designation of Top 40 Business Professors under 40 by Poets and Quants.

John Weeks is Professor of Leadership and Organizational Behavior at IMD (Lausanne, Switzerland). He is an organizational ethnographer and the author of *Unpopular Culture: The Ritual of Complaint in a British Bank*. In his book and articles, he studies how cultures evolve in ways that are both intended and unintended by their members.

Hendra Raharja Wijaya is Assistant Professor in the Department of Strategic Management and Entrepreneurship at the Rotterdam School of Management, Erasmus University, the Netherlands. His intellectual interest lies in understanding how values and emotions function in institutional processes. Drawing on qualitative methods, primarily ethnography, his investigation is focused on the lived experiences of actors in highly exclusive and secretive environments. His work has been published in *Organization Studies*.

Heung-wah Wong is Acting Head of the School of Modern Languages and Cultures, University of Hong Kong. His interest lies in the globalization of Japanese popular culture, anthropology of business, and cultural policies in East Asia. He is the author of *Japanese Bosses, Chinese Workers: Power and Control in a Hong Kong Megastore*.

Héla Yousfi is Assistant Professor in the Department of Management and Organization at the PSL-Université Paris Dauphine, DRM (UMR CNRS 7088) (France). She specializes in the field of sociology of organizations. She has conducted research and published on the topic of political culture and management practices transfer in Arab countries. Her other areas of interest include institutional change and economic development, postcolonial studies of management and social movements. She is the author of *Trade Unions and Arab Revolutions: The Tunisian Case of UGTT*.

Patrizia Zanoni is Professor at the Faculty of Business Economics at Hasselt University, Belgium, where she leads SEIN – Identity, Diversity & Inequality Research – and is holder of the chair in Organization Studies at the School of Governance of Utrecht University. Relying on various qualitative methodologies including ethnography, her work critically investigates diversity, control and resistance, and alternative organizing in and against contemporary capitalism. Since January 2020, she has been the co-Editor-in-Chief of the journal *Organization*.

Tammar B. Zilber is located at the Jerusalem School of Business, Hebrew University, Israel. Using qualitative methodologies, she explores the microfoundations of institutions, and how individual, organizational and field-level dynamics involve meanings, emotions and power relations that construct and maintain institutional realities.

1

ANTHROPOLOGY AND ORGANIZATIONAL STUDIES

A Symbiotic Connection

Raza Mir and Anne-Laure Fayard

Interest in anthropology has been an on-going feature of organizational research and pedagogy. We felt that the time was ripe to develop a single volume that pulls together the different ways in which anthropology infuses the study of organizations, both epistemologically and methodologically. We believe that the academic community in business schools will welcome a volume that links organizational studies to classical and current contemporary anthropological concerns, and makes explicit how these linkages can inform and enrich organizational research.

Motivations

This volume was motivated by observations of the field as well as personal experience. While it has been argued that qualitative research has produced some of the most interesting research in organizational studies (Bartunek, Rynes & Ireland, 2006; Rynes & Bartunek, 2015), it is still under-represented when it comes to research published in leading academic journals. Moreover, our experience as reviewers and our conversations with students or colleagues made us realize that qualitative research often seems "simple" and merely a matter of good storytelling. We can relate to Diana Forsythe reporting how her colleagues in medical computing asked her for the "just one article" they needed to read to be able to do ethnographic work, all sharing the belief that in the end "anyone can do ethnography – It's just a matter of common sense!" (Forsythe, 2001, p. 135). Yet, like Forsythe, we believe that ethnography is more than a set of techniques and that "anthropology's strongest technique is its philosophical stance" (ibid. p. 136). Therefore, we thought it was important to go back to one of the sources of inspiration of qualitative research, anthropology, as well as its methodology of choice, ethnography, and explore how they have influenced and still influence organizational studies in a generative manner.

As organizational researchers with over two decades of experiences in the field, we each have unique, and hopefully complementary approaches to organizational anthropology.

Raza chose ethnography as the methodology of choice in his doctoral dissertation. He experienced loneliness in his initial journey, and had to rely on colleagues in anthropology and other social sciences to discuss his ideas. Much later, he connected with other organizational ethnographers who shared his methodological focus, and mitigated his sense of isolation. His entry point into ethnography was critical, visualizing culture as a tool of ideology, normalization of inequalities, imperial colonialism, and global capitalism. In the field of anthropology, he was influenced by works such as James Clifford's *The Predicament of Culture* (Clifford, 1988), George Marcus and Michael Fischer's *Anthropology as Cultural Critique* (Marcus & Fischer, 1986) and Arturo Escobar's *Encountering Development: The Making and Unmaking of the Third World* (Escobar, 1995), and hoped to translate those ideas into the realm of management scholarship. For him, this book continues that journey.

Anne-Laure came to ethnography via a non-conventional route: she trained in philosophy, did a PhD in Cognitive Science, and discovered ethnography as she was working as a research assistant on a participatory design project; her first four and a half months on the project were spent observing a team of air traffic controllers. She read Hutchins' *Cognition in the Wild* (1995), Suchman's *Plans and Situated Actions* (1987), Julian Orr's *Talking about Machines* (2016) and discovered ethnomethodology, video ethnography, and conversational analysis. As she joined INSEAD Business School as an assistant professor she had the chance to meet John Van Maanen and have John Weeks as a colleague. These encounters opened up new perspectives, the field of organizational studies, many more readings – Goffman, Becker, Geertz, etc. – and lots of productive conversations which had continued over the years with her co-authors. Her own multidisciplinary journey has convinced her of the necessity of fluid boundaries across disciplines and the fecundity of mixing different perspectives. It is in this spirit that she accepted Raza's invitation to co-edit this volume.

Together, we hope we have been able through this book to collect ideas, theories and methodological discussions that will make the hitherto solitary sojourns of our fellow researchers with an interest in organizational anthropology more of a collective journey, imbued with multiplicities of interests, yet interweaved with a common language to discuss methodologies, epistemologies, and practical concerns.

It might be useful at this juncture to clarify our position on what we mean by organizational anthropology. The field of anthropology is after all a social science in its own right, incorporating a spectrum of sub-fields, from the physiobiological to the linguistic, the cultural to the archeological, and beyond. The purpose of our definition is to provide some loose and porous boundaries around which we have structured the arguments of this book, with an explicit understanding that these boundaries are ripe to be spanned. We define organizational anthropology as *the cultural study of human behavior in organizational settings*. This is a simple definition, which at the same time offers the possibility of incorporating insights from other social sciences.

Organizational Anthropology: An Incomplete History

Interest in anthropological analysis by organizational researchers has a long and distinguished history. It is not our intention in this chapter to provide a comprehensive history of organizational anthropology. Readers interested in the same can consult other works that have attempted such a history (e.g. Baba, 2012; Bate, 1997; Wright, 1994). But it is worth recalling that the Hawthorne experiments conducted by Elton Mayo and W. Lloyd Warner in the 1930s had a decidedly anthropological orientation (Roethlisberger & Dickson, 1934). Bate (1997) recalls that the first book on organizational behavior was written by a social anthropologist (Whyte, 1969). A book-length treatise written in 1951 by Elliot Jaques titled *The Changing Structure of a Factory* deployed the language and tools of anthropology to examine and develop the concept of corporate culture (Jaques, 1951). The term "business anthropology" came into the field in the 1950s (Nash, 1959, see Baba, 2012 for a detailed history). Barry Turner's analysis of cultural patterns in organizations allowed him to formulate patterns of cultural continuity that became enshrined as "organizational subculture" (Turner, 1971). Turner himself was following the traditions of Joan Woodward, whose sociological studies of organizational contingency had a strong anthropological component (Woodward, 1970). For social scientists working in the organizational realm, organizations were studied less as economic entities and more as collectivities where humans engaged in acts of culture making, and eventually developed deeply coded ways of thinking, doing, and being.

Over time, organizational anthropology began to stake its claim as a sub-discipline in the field of management research. John Van Maanen's book *Tales of the Field* (Van Maanen, 1987) has become a signpost for all organizational anthropologists and ethnographers. Van Maanen provided ways in which organizational theorists and management researchers could use methodological insights from earlier anthropological works to explore the terrain of work. Many of his students, his students' students and other researchers who were influenced by his work have shaped the field of organizational anthropology and organizational ethnography.

Subsequently, anthropology-themed books like Joanne Martin's *Organizational Culture: Mapping the Terrain* (Martin, 2001) have provided a roadmap for viewing organizations through a cultural lens. Book-length accounts of anthropological journeys such as Gideon Kunda's *Engineering Culture* (Kunda, 1986) and John Weeks' *Unpopular Culture* (Weeks, 2004) have made an explicit connection between organizational studies and anthropology. Recent ethnographies of organizations such as Catherine Turco's *The Conversational Firm* (Turco, 2016) or Michel Anteby's *Manufacturing Morals* (Anteby, 2013) show the enduring fertility of anthropological research in 21st-century settings. Some papers using ethnographic methods such as Steve Barley's *Technology as an Occasion for Structuring* (Barley, 1986), Wanda Orlikowski's *Knowing in Practice* (Orlikowski, 2002) and Beth Bechky's *Sharing Meaning Across Occupational Communities* (Bechky, 2003) are heavily cited in organizational studies and management.

Organizational ethnographies also contributed to theoretical development. Interpretive scholars rescued the idea of culture from the iron cage of positivism (Smircich, 1983). Feminist critical analysts had provided newer methodological templates to view power relations, such as Dorothy Smith's concept of "institutional ethnography" (Smith, 1986). Marxists and critical ethnographers had shown how anthropology and ethnography needed to guard against being the unwitting and occasionally conscious agent of economic exploitation (Clifford, 1988). Postcolonial anthropologists had offered subaltern subjectivities to theorize their own predicaments, rather than become subjects of Western anthropology's unconscious and conscious practices of cultural imperialism (Escobar, 1995). In such a formulation, the corporation can be visualized and critiqued as nothing more than a colony situated in in the realm of work (Mir & Mir, 2009). Armed with these new tools, a new generation of organizational ethnographers and anthropologists began to discuss research that broke new grounds, both theoretically and empirically, and showed that in the new economic atmosphere, an anthropologist was a neat colleague to have, someone who studied not just the leaves but the roots, and saw rhythms and patterns in organizational life that other perspectives had unwittingly passed by.

In the last two decades, organizational ethnography appears to have become more self-assured, arguing for incorporation into mainstreams of organizational research. When Anne-Laure Fayard and John Weeks analyze informal interactions and space in organizations (Fayard & Weeks, 2007), Karen Ho reports on her ethnography on downsized workers in Wall Street (Ho, 2009), or Alexandra Michel discusses the way overworked bankers in New York treat their bodies as problematic entities in their overworked state (Michel, 2011), they do so without feeling the need to justify their methodological choices to their business school peers. One could argue that organizational anthropology has truly come to a stage of maturity in the 21st century. Be it the world of social media or high finance, artificial intelligence or multi-firm ecosystems, an anthropological focus has the potential to add value to our understanding of organizational theories and processes.

Organizational Ethnography: Today and Tomorrow

Many recent ethnographic studies in organizational studies and management reflect changes in the phenomena that organizational ethnographers study nowadays and the associated methodological concerns. As illustrated by empirical chapters in this volume, organizational ethnographers have to play and experiment with traditional ethnography in order to develop rich understandings of new phenomena they want to study. For instance, while ethnographers would traditionally spend an extended amount of time in one single location (Van Maanen, 2011), "the field" has expanded and multiplied across multiple organizations and/or geographies and culture is not always the main focus. Even within one organization, technology is making a lot of the work invisible (Riopelle, 2013). Recent developments with algorithms and machine learning are making these tensions even more salient while also stressing the need for deep and rich studies of the use and impact of AI on work and occupations. This is evidenced by the multiple ethnographies-in-progress presented at the Academy of Management, as well as a few already published (e.g. Beane, 2019; Beane & Orlikowski, 2015; Shestakofsky, 2017). Grand challenges constitute another important and complex phenomenon that requires the deep and detailed understanding provided by ethnographic approaches (Ferraro, Etzion & Gehman, 2015). While such studies might raise complex ethical issues as noted by de Rond (Chapter 25 in this volume), an ethnographic approach can be generative and provide important contributions for researchers and practitioners (for example, Mair, Wolf & Seelos, 2016; Nanna Mik-Meyer, Chapter 17 in this volume; Goffman, 2014).

To adjust to the changes in the phenomena they study, ethnographers have been experimenting – tweaking traditional methods or creating new ones: doing video ethnography (Heath & Hindmarsh, 2002), engaging in contract ethnography (Fayard, Van Maanen & Weeks, 2016), taking a consultant role (Nahoko Kameo, Chapter 6 in this volume) or performing insider ethnography (Brannen, Mughan, and Moore, Chapter 15 in this volume). One could argue that some of these studies cannot be categorized as ethnographies because they do not solely rely on ethnography's characteristic fieldwork. However, as argued by Anne-Laure, "ethnography is more than a set of methods; it is an epistemic stance that can be enacted through different practices. What makes a study ethnographic is not so much the methods but the stance that the researcher enacts" (Fayard, 2017, p. 141).

If one embraces a creative approach to methods, with the intent to stay grounded to the phenomena and understand them in context, avoiding dichotomies and willing to do the work (tedious at times, often confusing, exciting in the end) to unpack everyday interactions and practices in their complexity and subtleties, then, we argue, there is a role for an ethnographic approach. In consequence, this volume presents "different strokes" (Van Maanen, 1998) of qualitative research from ethnography to interview-based research, photo-ethnography, and historical analysis; while using different methods for data collection and analysis, all authors favor an inductive, interpretative approach.

The notion of organizational ethnography traverses a broad philosophical and methodological spectrum, and in this volume, we have been inclusive. All chapters have made their own positions clear, and can be read as stand-alone pieces, reflecting the authors' expertise and perspective. Each chapter in this volume stands alone as exploring some facet of organizational research, but it is our hope that this volume as a whole provides an analysis of this sub-field, exploring nuances and variations in various methodological, philosophical, and contextual underpinnings.

Structure of the Book

We embarked upon the task of putting an edited book together, based on an extensive review of the literature, our own experiences in this area, and an understanding of the emergence of organizational anthropology as a confident sub-discipline in its own right. We felt that an effective volume would not just provide a history of research and reflection in this field, but would chart out directions for vibrant futures in organizational anthropology, in the areas of theory-development, innovative and effective methodologies, and new philosophical approaches toward organization and management.

Our first task herein was to identify experts in the field and invite contributions. In this regard, we have been fortunate beyond our expectations. All the contributors to this book have had impressive experience of doing anthropological research at the organizational level. In inviting contributions, we chose to not give our authors too much direction, but rather asked them to choose their topics based on their research interests and their own reflections on organizational anthropology. We conceived our role as that of facilitators initiating open-ended discussions with them on the directions they wished to take their chapters, and articulating thematic and narrative continuities between the chapters. We played a constructive but minor role in the actual production of chapters, encouraging authors to build on the themes that emerged in their work, asking for various clarifications, and ensuring that the chapters were methodologically transparent, developmental to new scholars, future-focused, and reflective of the authors' own contributions.

In our approach, we valued different perspectives and were respectful of leaving authors their own personal positions. We both believe in the value of debate, yet debate that is actually constructive. For example, one can be critical of postmodernism, activist research, or auto-ethnography, but these critiques need to engage thoughtfully and thoroughly with their criticisms of realist ethnography. We recognize that true debate is a difficult exercise. Thus, in a spirit of inclusion, we present perspectives that we do not necessarily share.

As the chapters emerged and were refined, we made sure that they mapped what we felt was the entire spectrum of the field. We then placed them into four subgroups, which we have titled *Methodological Viewpoints*, *Ethnographic Journeys*, *Beyond Organizations*, and *Reflections*.

Methodological Viewpoints

This section focuses on contributions that reflect on the various methodological traditions that have informed organizational anthropology. The term *methodology* is much broader than mere *method*. A method is a tool or a technique that is used in the process of inquiry. Methodological considerations are broader, and closely associated with ontological and epistemological positions. Chapters in this section reflect specifically on various methodological approaches and associated tools; in some cases, they propose new ways of doing organizational ethnography.

In their chapter "Archival Ethnography," Stephanie Decker and Alan McKinlay describe a methodology of research based on organizational archives – public and private, focusing on how they can be considered sites for fieldwork. They suggest that such an approach entails an ethnographic sensibility that focuses on observation of quotidian details as well as a focus on practice and what is not immediately obvious.

In "A History of Markets Past: The Role of Institutional Memory Failure in Financial Crises," Natalya Vinokurova explores how historical analysis can enrich our understanding of the relationship between institutional memory and financial crises by analyzing the security structures in three markets for mortgage-backed securities (MBS) in the United States in the 1880s, 1900s, and 1970s and showing how they are informative of the 2008 crisis. Vinokurova, while recognizing some similarities between anthropology and history, differentiates the two perspectives: anthropology focuses on understanding the market participants' practices whereas history offers a window into the co-evolution of these practices and market institutions.

In "What Good Is the Ethnographic Interview?" John Weeks makes a case for interviews as a fundamental element of ethnographic methodology. He argues that the distinction between participant observation and ethnographic interviews is not as straightforward as it might seem, particularly when each is done well. In contrast to the traditional view that ethnography relies mostly on observations, Weeks concludes that ethnographic interviews can produce rich insights as long it is not used as a shortcut to being in the field.

In "Frames of the Field: Ethnography as Photography," Mikko Vesa, Mikaela Krohn, and Frank den Hond use photography as an analogy to ethnography, as a way to focus attention on the recording of research materials during ethnographic fieldwork. Through this analogy, they highlight an under-explored dimension of ethnography, namely how the production of ethnographic data may contribute to a misplaced belief in the facticity of ethnography.

In "Ethnography Air-conditioned," Nahoko Kameo considers the methodological and pragmatic concerns that organizational ethnographers face (for example trying to gain access to the field) when doing ethnography "close to home," and discuss the solutions they may use and the potential consequences of such solutions.

In "Consumer Culture Theory: An Anthropological Contribution to Consumption Studies," Eric Arnould, Craig Thompson and Melea Press introduce consumer culture theory as a field of inquiry that unravels the complexities of consumer culture. They locate their work in anthropology, cultural sociology and cultural studies, and argue for a greater incorporation of consumer studies in business schools and schools of media and communication.

In "The Creative Use of Insider Ethnography as a Means for Organizational Self Investigation: The 'Essence of Tesco' Project," Mary Yoko Brannen, Terry Mughan and Fiona Moore describe what they call an insider ethnography: an innovative action research project, where managers from the Asian subsidiaries of the British multinational retailer Tesco Plc worked in concert with an academic team to generate cultural data about their own organization through ethnographic research. They highlight the advantages of insider ethnography in providing multiple perspectives and strategically valuable insights for the global firm.

In "Contextual Analytics: Using Human Science to Strengthen Data Science Approaches in the Development of Algorithms," Mikkel Krenchel and Christian Madsbjerg discuss the features of ethnography and data science that make collaboration between the two more valuable than the sum of their respective parts.

They present a methodology that makes collaboration between the two possible in practical terms and generate critical discussion through an examination of their practitioner experiences.

Ethnographic Journeys

This section of the book regroups ethnographies of various styles and flavors. By presenting empirical work they have done and by locating their discussion in a particular project, authors in this section are able to explain certain specific opportunities and constraints associated with the use of anthropological methods in management.

In "Managing Meat and Non-meat Markets in Contemporary India," Johan Fischer discusses his ethnographic fieldwork in South India, where he explores how manufacturing companies understand and manage "green" and "brown" standards. He argues that while existing studies of vegetarianism overwhelmingly explore micro-social aspects such as the everyday consumption among Hindu groups, they miss "the bigger institutional picture" that frames such consumption, production, and regulation. Fischer's work provides a useful template to follow a research project from design to completion, and can be seen as a potential set of guidelines for researchers embarking on a project of their own.

In "'How Do I Like Being a Policewoman? I'm Very Happy!' Pakistani Policewomen and the Challenge of Presentational Data," Sadaf Ahmad uses her experiences to illustrate why presentational data is a particular problem when studying a bureaucratic, hierarchical, and ill-reputed organization like the police. She shows how spending time in "the field" and participant observation, both of which lie at the heart of ethnographic research, can be critical in combating an important challenge; that field access in itself does not guarantee forthcoming respondents or their presenting anything but presentational data.

In "Impact Quantification and Integration in Impact Investment," Tom Vandebroek, Fabrizio Ferraro, Alice Mascena and Heinrich Liechtenstein discuss an ethnographic study based on a three-month participant observation in a pioneer impact-investing fund in the UK. At a methodological level, they demonstrate how an ethnographic approach allows researchers to delve deep into everyday practices, and uncover interactions that could not have been revealed through other methodologies. They find that contrary to the commonly held assumption that quantification decontextualizes objects, numbers are used to contextualize qualitative matters and that these numbers actually come to represent qualities.

In "Exploring the Accomplishment of Inter-organizational Collaboration: The Value of Thick Descriptions," Emmanouil Gkeredakis presents his fieldwork in the English healthcare sector, where he explored the local accomplishment of inter-organizational collaboration revolving around the collective production and agreement of formal document-contract specifications. He reflects on how organizational ethnographers have long paid attention to the role of documents in social practices, and attempts to build and extend on their insights by exploring the embeddedness of face-to-face interactions within a nexus of documentary practices.

In "A Multi-sited Approach to Policy Realization and Managerial Work," Ursula Plesner and Lise Justesen explore the digital transformation of public sector organizations in Denmark through a multi-sited ethnography. Reflecting on their experience, they argue and illustrate how multi-sited ethnography represents a methodological alternative to policy implementation studies and single-site studies and offers new insights into managerial work.

In "Still a Man's World: Finding Gender Issues in Tokyo Fashion Week," building upon her ethnographic research into the world of Tokyo's fashion industry, Yuiko Fujita reflects on how the gender of the ethnographer affects the process of ethnographic fieldwork. She discusses how a researcher negotiates entry into organizations that are not predisposed to accept them.

Finally, in "What Makes Resilience? An Ethnographic Study of the Work of Prison Officers," Mette Mogensen and Elisabeth Naima Mikkelsen, describe an ethnographic study of a Danish prison, where they make sense of the manner in which resilience is made and negotiated in the work practices and work relationships. They conclude that engaging as researchers in sensory ethnography allows for a study of contextual and ambiguous constructs such as resilience, and helps the researcher move it beyond trait-and-factor thinking.

Beyond Organizations

Organizations are imbedded in their socio-cultural environments in an organic way, and to study them holistically, organizational anthropology must by necessity bleed out of the boundaries of the organization itself, and locate some of its concerns in the macro environment. The idea of studying organizations at multiple levels is applicable to most research traditions, but perhaps more explicitly and consciously so in anthropology. In this section, we group those chapters that primarily locate their research in extra-organizational domains, though their concerns are of importance to organizations.

In "Organisational Dilemmas, Gender and Ethnicity: A Video Ethnographic Approach to Talk and Gestures in Homeless Shelter Consultations," Nanna Mik-Meyer demonstrates how video recordings of real-time interactions between homeless individuals and service providers can illuminate the many organizational dilemmas that affect the relationship between professionals and clients. She suggests that in many organizations, people actively reproduce the practices from which they explicitly distance themselves, and contends that an ethnographic analysis can be used to understand this phenomenon.

In "Capturing the Microfoundations of Institutions: A Confessional Tale of the Glorified Field," Hendra Wijaya reflects on the ontology and epistemology of microfoundations. Using a confessional mode of writing, he offers institutional fieldworkers, who are often under time and budget constraints, some recommendations on entering the field, collecting and handling data, and managing personal battles.

In "Five Ways of Seeing Events (in Anthropology and Organization Studies)," Stefanie Mauksch asks what ethnographers see when they study "events." She suggests that as representations, events bring to surface invisible principles of social ordering. In agentic depictions, they evolve as a space-time-bound context in which powerful change-makers meet, compete, and shape their cultural worlds.

In "Tweeting the Marginalized Voices: A Netnographic Account," Snehanjali Chrispal and Hari Bapuji suggest that netnographic research allows researchers to study the cultures and behavior of online communities through a multitude of ways and opens pathways to study communities that are often difficult to access or navigate in the real world.

In "What Are We Missing? Exploring Ethnographic Possibilities beyond MOS Conventions," Patrizia Zanoni and Tammar Zilber draw on four ethnographic monographs published in other social sciences to illustrate alternative, inspiring ways to craft ethnography. They make a plea for loosening current conventions concerning the crafting of ethnography and encourage early researchers to engage with ethnography in other disciplines to move the collective debate forward within our own.

In "Why Does the Study of Alternative Organizations (So Badly) Need Anthropology?" Stéphane Jaumier suggests that anthropology has a major role to play in the understanding of alternative organizations, and the acts of imagining new ones. He contends that anthropology offers a unique window on the actual making of alternative organizations because it tends to lean towards local meanings and everyday experiences of organizational members, and has a field-rather than theory-driven manner of problematizing.

Finally, in "Crisis Ethnography: Emotions and Identity in Fieldwork during the Tunisian Revolution," Hela Yousfi and Chahrazad Abdallah describe an ethnographic journey in a crisis context, using data from the Tunisian revolution that marked the beginning of the Arab Spring of 2011. Their research coincided with a period of tumult and crisis in the region, and in this chapter, they attempt to explore the challenges facing researchers who study social movements in a crisis context. They argue that in a crisis situation, the researcher is emotionally involved in the setting, and the only way forward is to accept that these emotions become a resource for the researcher to understand the socio-political transformations under study.

Reflections

The final section of this book has four chapters where scholars reflect on their own personal journeys into the world of ethnography. The value of reflecting on a body of work and seeing contingent patterns therein is the primary focus of this section.

In "It Is Not that All Cultures Have Business, but that All Business Has Culture," Heung-wah Wong advances the claim that business is either culture, or it is nothing. He suggests that culture should be seen fundamentally as an independent variable in the sociological chain. He advances the idea that ethnography is an effective method to capture the meaning of human phenomena, because it is a commitment to "thickness," the contextualization of human phenomena.

In "Ethnography and the Traffic in Pain," Mark de Rond, reflecting on the growing interest in grand societal challenges, uses examples from photojournalism to ask questions about the moral ambiguities that underlie fieldwork, those of exploitation, complicity, voyeurism, and anesthetization. The chapter does not aim to provide any solutions or resolutions, as these only emerge in practice, for a specific context. De Rond invites researchers keen to pursue fieldwork in the context of societal grand challenges to be reflective and aware of the issues they will face. More broadly, he reminds us that doing fieldwork always involves an element of ambiguity and potential moral dilemma.

In "Fieldwork in Work Worlds," Robert Jackall reflects on decades of anthropological experience, and concludes that the true fieldworker is the "compleat observer," the documenter. Jackall argues that fieldwork always started for him with reframing an intellectual problem, and this reframing continues as opportunities for empirical work arise and as the researcher makes sense of the data.

In our final chapter, "Withdrawal Pains and Gains: Exiting from the Field," John Van Maanen argues that while much has been written about "getting in" (gaining access), "getting out" (exiting) is rarely discussed. While methodologically and theoretically underspecified, exiting can and should be – argues Van Maanen – problematized. Expressing "indifference" and even "disdain" for the continuous calls for methodological or theoretical rigor in social science, Van Maanen hopes for more artistry and improvisation, something that has characterized his own work for decades.

References

Anteby, M. (2013). *Manufacturing morals: The values of silence in business school education*. Chicago, IL: University of Chicago Press.

Baba, M. (2012). Anthropology and business: Influence and interests. *Journal of Business Anthropology, 1*(1), 20–71.

Barley, S. R. (1986). Technology as an occasion for structuring: Evidence from observations of CT scanners and the social order of radiology departments. *Administrative Science Quarterly, 31*(1), 78–108.

Bartunek, J. M., Rynes, S. L., & Ireland, R. D. (2006). What makes management research interesting, and why does it matter? *Academy of Management Journal, 49*(1), 9–15.

Bate, S. (1997). Whatever happened to organizational anthropology? A review of the field of organizational ethnography and anthropological studies. *Human Relations, 50*(9), 1147–1175.

Beane, M. (2019). Shadow learning: Building robotic surgical skill when approved means fail. *Administrative Science Quarterly, 64*(1), 87–123.

Beane, M., & Orlikowski, W. J. (2015). What difference does a robot make? The material enactment of distributed coordination. *Organization Science, 26*(6), 1553–1573.

Bechky, B. A. (2003). Sharing meaning across occupational communities: The transformation of understanding on a production floor. *Organization Science, 14*(3), 312–330.

Clifford, J. (1988). *The predicament of culture*. Cambridge, MA: Harvard University Press.

Escobar, E. (1995). *Encountering development: The making and unmaking of the third world*. Princeton, NJ: Princeton University Press.

Fayard, A.-L. (2017). Bricolage in the field: Experimenting in ethnography. In R. Mir, & S. Jain (Eds.) *Routledge companion to qualitative research in organizational studies*. London: Routledge, pp. 141–153.

Fayard, A.-L., & Weeks, J. (2007). Photocopiers and water-coolers: The affordances of informal interaction. *Organization Studies*, *28*(5), 605–634.

Fayard, A.-L., Van Maanen, J., & Weeks, J. (2016). Corporate ethnography in corporate settings: Innovation from entanglement. In K. D. Elsbach & R. M. Kramer (Eds.) *Handbook of qualitative research*. New York: Routledge, pp. 45–53.

Ferraro, F., Etzion, D., & Gehman, J. (2015). Tackling grand challenges pragmatically: Robust action revisited. *Organization Studies*, *36*(3), 363–390.

Forsythe, D. (2001). *Studying those who study us: An anthropologist in the world of artificial intelligence*. Stanford, CA: Stanford University Press.

Goffman, A. (2014). *On the run: Fugitive life in an American City*. Chicago, IL: University of Chicago Press.

Heath, C., & Hindmarsh, J. (2002). Analysing interaction: Video ethnography and situated conduct. In T. May (Ed.) *Qualitative research in practice*. London: Sage Publications, pp. 99–121.

Ho, K. (2009). *Liquidated: An ethnography of Wall Street*. Durham, NC: Duke University Press.

Hutchins, E. (1995). *Cognition in the wild*. Cambridge, MA: MIT Press.

Jaques, E. (1951). *The changing culture of a factory*. London: Routledge.

Kunda, G. (1986). *Engineering culture: Control and commitment in a high-tech corporation*. Philadelphia, PA: Temple University Press.

Mair, J., Wolf, M., & Seelos, C. (2016). Scaffolding: A process of transforming patterns of inequality in small-scale societies. *Academy of Management Journal*, *59*(6), 2021–2044.

Marcus, G., & Fischer, M. (1986). *Anthropology as cultural critique: An experimental moment in the human sciences*. Chicago, IL: University of Chicago Press.

Martin, J. (2001). *Organizational culture: Mapping the terrain*. Thousand Oaks, CA: Sage Publications.

Michel, A. (2011). Transcending socialization: A nine-year ethnography of the body's role in organizational control and knowledge workers' transformation. *Administrative Science Quarterly*, *56*(3), 325–368.

Mir, R., & Mir, A. (2009). From the corporation to the colony: Studying knowledge transfer across international boundaries. *Group and Organization Management*, *34*(1), 90–113.

Nash, M. (1959). Applied and action anthropology in the understanding of man. *Anthropological Quarterly*, *32*(1), 67–81.

Orlikowski, W. J. (2002). Knowing in practice: Enacting a collective capability in distributed organizing. *Organization Science*, *13*(3), 249–273.

Orr, J. E. (2016). *Talking about machines: An ethnography of a modern job*. Ithaca, NY: Cornell University Press.

Riopelle, K. (2013). Being there: The power of technology-based methods. In B. Jordan (Ed.) *Advancing ethnography in corporate environments*. Walnut Creek, CA: Left Coast Press, pp. 38–53.

Roethlisberger, F. J., & Dickson, W. J. (1934). *Management and the worker: Technical vs. social organization in an industrial plant*. Cambridge, MA: Harvard University Press.

Rynes, S. L., & Bartunek, J. M. (2015). It just keeps getting more interesting! In K. D. Elsbach, & R. M. Kramer (Eds.) *Handbook of qualitative organizational research: Innovative pathways and methods*. New York: Routledge, pp. 9–23.

Shestakofsky, B. (2017). Working algorithms: Software automation and the future of work. *Work and Occupations*, *44*(4), 376–423.

Smircich, L. (1983). Concepts of culture and organizational analysis. *Administrative Science Quarterly*, *28*(3), 339–358.

Smith, D. (1986). Institutional ethnography: A feminist method. *Resources for Feminist Research*, *15*(1), 6–13.

Suchman, L. A. (1987). *Plans and situated actions: The problem of human-machine communication*. Cambridge: Cambridge University Press.

Turco, C. J. (2016). *The conversational firm: Rethinking bureaucracy in the age of social media*. New York: Columbia University Press.

Turner, B. (1971). *Exploring the industrial subculture*. London: Macmillan International Higher Education.

Van Maanen, J. (1987). *Tales of the field: On writing ethnography*. Chicago, IL: University of Chicago Press.

Van Maanen, J. (1998). Different strokes: Qualitative research in the *Administrative Science Quarterly* from 1956 to 1996. In J.Van Maanen (Ed.) *Qualitative studies of organizations: The Administrative Science Quarterly series in organization theory and behavior*. London: Sage, pp. ix–xxxii.

Van Maanen, J. (2011). Ethnography as work: Some rules of engagement. *Journal of Management Studies, 48*(1), 218–234.

Weeks, J. (2004). *Unpopular culture: The ritual of complaint in a British bank*. Chicago, IL: University of Chicago Press.

Whyte, W. F. (1969). *Organizational behavior: Theory and application*. London: Richard Irwin.

Woodward, J. (1970). *Industrial organization: Behaviour and control*. Oxford: Oxford University Press.

Wright, S. (Ed.) (1994). *Anthropology of organizations*. London: Routledge.

PART I

Methodological Viewpoints

2

ARCHIVAL ETHNOGRAPHY

Stephanie Decker and Alan McKinlay

Introduction

The use of archives as a site for data collection remains somewhat unusual in management and organization studies, where qualitative researchers prefer data 'generated in the course of the organizational research' (Strati, 2000: 133–134). Documents drawn from archives may have been used to support the analysis of interviews or provide background information (e.g. Rojas, 2010). Arguably this has been changing in recent years, with more and more articles published that are based entirely on archival research (Decker, 2010; Hampel and Tracey, 2017; Maclean et al., 2018; McKinlay, 2002; Mutch, 2016; Wadhwani, 2018). In a recent *Academy of Management Journal* editorial, Bansal et al. (2018: 4) highlighted that the ongoing 'historic turn' has led to a greater appreciation for the 'key principles of historical analysis,' including a 'preference for authentic archival data over retrospective material.'

However, there are relatively few methodological and reflective pieces about how to approach archival research for organizational scholars (Barros et al., 2019; Decker, 2013; Mills and Helms Mills, 2011), nor can archival research be simplistically understood as a method that is disconnected from the kind of historical narrative scholars seek to produce. An objectivistic corporate history will approach an archive differently to a realist analytically structured history (Rowlinson et al., 2014). Our focus here is on interpretive approaches such as ethnographic history, which provide a deep and empathetic understanding of events and processes from the perspective of the actors involved (Vaara and Lamberg, 2016). This requires an approach to archives as a site of ethnographic fieldwork, which we call archival ethnography. Not only has there been an ongoing exchange of ideas between ethnography and history over the years, exemplified by microhistory (Ginzburg, 1992; Levi, 1988) and other historical traditions (Stoler, 2009), but ethnographers frequently draw on archives and historical sources. Most importantly, ethnographers' conception of fieldwork focuses on how researchers engage with the site, rather than the site itself. Okely (2007: 360) maintains that 'the field can never be just a physical site. It is in the head, whole body and beyond one designated locality.' Archival ethnography requires researchers to conceive of the archive as a site for fieldwork, but one that reflects and filters sources from historical sites that are no longer accessible to direct observation (Mills et al., 2013).

We will outline the relationship between fieldwork and ethnography, and its relevance to archival research before we fully develop our methodological approach that casts archives as sites for historical fieldwork. Here we focus on the opportunities and limitations inherent in working with archives, especially organizational archives, and the way in which they are important mediating sites for historical investigations. In particular, we draw on the distinction between narrative sources and social documents (Rowlinson et al., 2014) and the way in which the researcher's (and archivist's) presence co-constructs the archive. Finally, we draw on historical traditions such as microhistory and Laura Stoler's history in the subjunctive as inspiration for the kind of archival ethnographies that can be written from organizational sources.

Ethnography and History

Deep archival research is the hallmark of 'good' history. More than this, deep archival research is essential to the identity of the historian as a historian. In large part, the authority of the historian rests on the range and volume of archival sources cited in their footnotes. This is about establishing both the novelty and the legitimacy of their account; original sources are also a subliminal signal to other historians that much archival dust has been ingested. Archive fever, it would seem, afflicts all historians alike. Similarly, in no small measure, the ethnographer's legitimacy rests on the experience of the researcher: just how long and immersive was their time in the field (Van Maanen, 1988: 46). Just as fieldwork confirms the professional identity of the anthropologist, so the individual becomes a historian in the archive. In both cases, simply being there is crucial to the research process and to the making of the researcher.

Yet one would search in vain for the most obvious rules about how to do ethnography. The fieldwork rules that do exist are prosaic: take notes quickly, certainly within twenty-four hours; keep a reflective diary. Of course, this also means that there are few methodological rules for historical ethnography to break. Nor are the methodological advantages necessarily skewed towards the contemporary ethnographer. Unlike the fieldwork ethnographer, in the archive, documents can be checked for accuracy and context, interpretations confirmed in ways that are impossible for the fieldwork ethnographer.

Ethnographers and historians share an approach to research that requires, to some extent, the immersion in the 'lifeworld' of others. For Paul Willis (2000), the ethnographic imagination entails a radically different research process from the linearity of large-scale survey work. Here, only the researcher is active, constructing order and meaning. There is nothing of this detachment in the deep, immersive fieldwork of ethnography. There is, though, a sense of loss, then detachment, in Michael Agar's (1980) famous description of the returning anthropologist as a 'professional stranger.'

Ironically, given his rejection of any claim to scientificity, Willis suggests that ethnographic research involves experimentation in the fullest sense. Ethnography necessarily collapses the distinct phases of thinking, testing, and writing into a single messy and improvisational process. Indeed, the implication is that the messiness of the research process is not something that has to be accepted, with regret or apology, but celebrated as the hallmark of ethnography itself. More than this, the ethnographic project entails working conceptually during fieldwork and thinking empirically when writing up. The making of meaning, then, is accepted as a shared capacity of researcher and respondents alike. The ethnographer's practice is a heightened, more quizzical version of the ethnographic imagination everyone exercises to make sense of their social world. The ethical and intellectual responsibility of the ethnographer is to relay this sensemaking as naturally, as faithfully as possible. Perhaps there is – or can be – more to Thomas Osborne's (1999: 52) metaphoric aside that 'for those who work in the historical disciplines, the archive is akin to the laboratory of the natural scientist.'

The ethnographer watches and listens, shares – somewhat vicariously – in the lifeworld of others. In this sense, archival ethnography is, by definition, non-participant observation. No doubt, the reliance on text, perhaps leavened by some images, means a loss of being able to observe gesture or the tone of conversations. Some of this loss can be offset, perhaps, if the researcher has personal experience of a similar situation.

The lengthy, solitary fieldwork of the anthropologist mirrors the immersion of the historian in the archives. Both are distinct activities, personally and professionally transformative, performed in spaces that are both found and made. Both types of professional strangers experience dislocation from their normal family and professional lives, sometimes discomfort, and often isolation. For the historian, the archive as a place refers more accurately to the search room, a kind of ante-room to the private, secure shelves where documents are stored. Documents are requested by – and delivered to – the historian. Search rooms vary from oak-lined opulence through to the shabby functionalism of local government offices. The historian works at tables under the eye of an archivist and, occasionally, roaming security personnel who protect documents from autograph hunters. Search aids range from sophisticated online catalogues to much-thumbed index cards packed just *too* tightly in filing drawers.

Experiences of corporate archives vary. Sometimes the historian is given no access to in-house digital systems and has to rely upon the kindness of an archivist who must, then, engage their own ethnographic imagination to figure out what sort of files might be relevant. Where they are given access to catalogues, the peculiarities of organizational evolution as much as the interpretation of organizational change by the cataloguing archivists can make finding the right files difficult without help by the archivists. The documents are produced to a schedule dictated by where documents are stored, or delivered en masse on one or more trolleys, only to overwhelm. Other archive users, by no means all historians – genealogists, architects, and enthusiasts of all kinds – are a source of easy distraction: wondering what they are searching for, their sudden movements or preternatural stillness.

All historians, whether positivist or postmodern narrativist, stoop over their files, *all* share something of an addiction to archive dust. Even Foucault was not immune to archival fever (Foucault, 2004: 4–5). The documents themselves come in all shapes and sizes, all the more difficult to handle or turn pages quickly when one is wearing cotton or neoprene gloves provided not to protect you from the dangers of archival dust, but to preserve the files from human contamination. The natural rhythm of archival research must be slow and deliberate, even if the pace is hurried by budgets or travel schedules, or the abiding anxiety that the next file, the one that might be missed, would provide the lodestone (Steedman, 2002). The physical form of the 'document' can be another reason for archival anxiety. For example, the voluminous case papers of a major British employers' organization, the Engineering Employers' Federation, were transferred onto film stock in the mid-sixties. On the side of each box is a warning that the film will deteriorate within ten years; that is, some forty years ago. The film-reader is temperamental and awkward to use; the images are often upside down or even require a mirror to read. The task is physically draining, essential, and feels oddly urgent. Perhaps this is the allure of the archive: the sense that one is becoming privy to secrets untold and conversations never intended to reach beyond a few ears.

Hand copying documents exactly is the 'artisanal task' that constitutes the historian's archival labour process. This, the distinguished historian of pre-revolutionary France, Arlette Farge, argues, is not a task that should be resented but treated with reverence as the process through which 'meaning is discerned' (Farge, 2013: 17). This is far removed from any sense of data capture through the lens of a digital camera, or smartphones, which are increasingly the standard of contemporary archival researchers. Farge is not embarrassed to concede that there are no general rules about how documents are selected or rejected, but uses a simile that alludes to the practice of micro-historian Carlo Ginzburg:

> To be honest, there is no ideal way to do this, nor are there any strict rules to follow when one is hesitating over the selection of a particular document. The historian's approach is similar to a prowler's; searching for what is buried away in the archives, looking for the trail of a person or event, while remaining to that which has fled, which has gone missing. Both presence and absence from the archive are signs we must interpret in order to understand how they fit into the larger landscape. When travelling this unmarked trail, you must always guard yourself against … the imperceptible, yet very real, way in which a historian is only drawn to things that will reinforce the working hypotheses she has settled on.
>
> *(Farge 2013: 70–71)*

Archival work does not apply theory to data, can only rarely formally test hypotheses. Farge conveys the sense of the provisional nature – 'working hypotheses' – of the historian's fieldwork that, if done well, develops their ethnographic imagination through their labour. Geoffrey Jones, a leading business historian, concludes that the reason for the abiding, perplexing marginality of business history is 'fundamentally methodological' (Friedman et al., 2014: 61). What is required, argues Jones, is that the business historian's deep archival research has to be 'translated sufficiently into convincing general propositions and concepts.' Yet very few grand theories survive a close encounter with an archive.

Narrativist historians evade the question completely by focusing exclusively on the finished product at the expense of methods sections (Bryant, 2000: 496; Durepos et al., 2017; Rowlinson, 2004; Yates, 2014). Archival research can produce counter-examples, questions, and qualifications but only rarely the type of generalizable propositions that would satisfy the positivist. We agree that methodological work is necessary but see archival work as contributing to knowledge in more ways than just theory building or testing. Moreover, we are concerned that this preserves the distinction between 'the archive' and 'theory,' ignoring the interactions between them. 'Theory' can also be more than just generalizable propositions and concepts, for example, critical theory. Rowlinson et al. (2014) define ethnographic history as inherently theoretical and analytical, but assuming a self-consciously angular theoretical approach (see also Megill, 2007: 110–111). They challenge van Maanen's assumption (1988: 76) that 'ethnographers have to construct their texts from the field, whereas the texts used by historians and literary critics come prepackaged.' Instead, historians laboriously construct narratives on the basis of a deep engagement with the archival source material, interconnecting theory and data not just through the way they interpret sources, but how they go about finding them in the first place.

Archival research lends itself more easily to exploratory research approaches. Carolyn Steedman (2002: 70) refers to the archival moment as a strange professionalized kind of transubstantiation of neglected, dusty files into a narrative driven by the historian's sense that they have acquired a deep empathy with their subjects. This strange exercise in the ethnographic imagination takes place through an elaborate process of transcription. If Farge is correct, then this mundane, yet strangely profound act of copying serves to transform the archive into a liminal space, that is neither fully empirical nor yet more than provisionally theorized. It takes time to make the liminal space that is fieldwork. This is no less true of the archive than it is of a Moroccan hill village. There are striking similarities between Farge's description of her painstaking work in the judicial archives of Paris to James Clifford's writing up his notes in the field as 'this moment of initial ordering, the making of a neat record' as crucial to the anthropologist's fieldwork process:

'Good data' must be materially produced: they become a distanced, quasi-methodical corpus, something to be accumulated, jealously preserved, duplicated, cross-referenced, selectively forgotten or manipulated later on.

A precious, precarious feeling of control over the social activities of inscription and transcription can result from creating an orderly text. This writing is far from simply a matter of mechanical recording: the 'facts' are reflected, focused, initially interpreted, cleaned up.

(Clifford, 1990: 63)

The physical act of copying, of glancing back and forth from the document to the notepad, compels the historian to assess the importance, typicality, and the meaning of *this* particular document to achieve a kind of 'critical intimacy' (Spivak, 1999). Hand-written copies are categorized thematically, linked to secondary texts also categorized thematically, with open questions recorded. The historian-archivist is producing their own filing system, which links data across time, place, and theme. Producing a series of intermediate archives, each a different liminal space, both physically and temporally one more step away from the original ethnographic site. The historian's 'finished' narrative, then, entails the translation of their own archival ethnography as well their production of text (Moore et al., 2017: 39). Farge stresses the craft-like nature of this work that the basic operations are prosaic, but the capacity to make fine judgements is based on experience. In a very real sense, by imagining 'being there,' the historian is painstakingly constructing a different archive, also geared to knowledge production, even if the specifics of that knowledge remains tantalisingly elusive during this moment (Comaroff and Comaroff, 1992: 35).

Historical imagination, the counterpart of ethnographic imagination, has long been recognized as an important element of historical work since R.G. Collingwood:

The historical imagination differs … in having as its special task to imagine the past: not an object of possible perception, since it does not now exist, but able through this activity to become an object of our thought.

(Collingwood, 1946: 242)

Historical imagination is necessary to reconstruct an image of the past, as it does not exist in present experience. This image needs to be tied to the evidence (archival and otherwise), but it will never come as close to the past as 'a photograph to its original because the historian's likeness is drawn from unorganized and mostly incomplete features, haphazardly surviving' (Little, 1983: 27). Collingwood likens this to a 'web of imaginative construction stretched between certain fixed points,' though he cautions that these fixed points provided by evidence require critical investigation rather than passive acceptance as authoritative statements. Thus seeking to reconstruct an account of past events needs to be a critical endeavour and draw on the knowledge not just of the past but also of the present. These accounts should be coherent and consilient (comprising all the available evidence in an explanation) (Whewell, 1840), which makes historical narratives similar to ethnographic accounts that seek to provide 'thick description.'

Implicit in Clifford Geertz's notion of 'thick description' is that this is an inherently, necessarily theorized account, and *not* a neutral atheoretical deductive process.

To abuse one of Geertz's aphorisms: historians study archives, good historians study processes in and through archives (Rabinow, 2008: 35). The archive becomes, to paraphrase Donald McKenzie, an engine, not a camera (MacKenzie, 2008). Here we are speaking of the modern archive. That is, the archive not just a repository of information, but the archive as a place of knowledge *production*. From the late nineteenth century, state papers were not retained and stored but actively used: first, to ensure systemic and personal accountability; second, to ensure relevant information was available; third, to produce knowledge upon which to base and evaluate policy.

The rapidity and scale of bureaucratic information growth triggered all manner of innovations in filing systems (Cole, 1913). This was accompanied by detailed instructions that covered how to file in date order, how to allocate alpha-numeric codes that signified the file's relative importance and allowed cross-referencing (Moss, 2005: 584–585). The humdrum work of filing clerks was to produce the impossible archive: a system of knowledge that aspired to becoming comprehensive: 'the sense that knowledge was singular and not plural, complete and not partial, global and not local, that all knowledges would ultimately turn out to be concordant in one great system of knowledge' (Richards, 1993: 6–7). The archive became the laboratory of bureaucracy. To be a modern state was to form an archive. We can go further: to be a modern organization was to form an archive. The fantasy of linked files producing infinite knowledge and endlessly extending power was not confined to the hubristic imagination of the British empire (Richards, 1993). Organizations of all kinds aspired to know more about their employees and customers, not just how they had behaved in the past but how they were likely to behave in the future. Such ambitions were no less evident in the frustrations of British employers attracted to scientific management but who were thwarted by the complexity and sheer scale of administration required to track the costs of tasks and workers producing highly diverse products. Today, big data has taken up the mantle from the pre-digital catalogued archive.

If we accept the existence of the archive as a specifically modern form, then our interlocutors are also moderns. We must also jettison any notion that documents are nothing more than 'relics' with an analogous status to the accidental survival of statuary or papyrus. Rather, the archive records the project of knowing and making modern individuals and populations (Manoff, 2004). Archivists become co-producers of the historian's text. Archivists are often courteously thanked for their help in locating documents, but rarely acknowledged as members of the collective architect of the archive itself.

Archives as Fieldwork

Even though archives are significant resources for research in their own right, they are not discussed as a standard in textbooks covering management and organizational research methods (Bryman and Bell, 2011; Silverman, 2011; Symon and Cassell, 2012). Where they are discussed, it is to highlight the limitations of organizational archives, which are 'collected, processed and expounded according to the organization's criteria and for the purposes of social legitimation' (Strati, 2000: 158). This is in contrast to the centrality of archives in other fields such as history, and literary and communication studies among others (Castellani and Rossato, 2014; Combe, 2010; Ramsey et al., 2010). From this stem vastly different definitions of what an archive 'is,' and how one can work with it (Manoff, 2004). Discussions of archives in organization research, however, have remained rare (Barros, 2016) as has guidance on how to work with it (Decker, 2013).

Documents drawn from archives are different from many of the documents commonly used in organizational research, in that they are often not published, not in a serial format, and only exist as a single unique copy in one archive, frequently only on paper and not digitized. These documents have been sifted and catalogued by archivists, and as many organizational archives are private, archivists both formally (through access negotiations) and symbolically (through the way these are catalogued) control the access of researchers to these documents. These documents (or images, artefacts, recordings) survive as traces from the past and are curated as part of the archive, which becomes the site for fieldwork focused on the past. While the past is ontologically inaccessible, epistemologically the archive offers a window into past events. This view on the past is not unproblematic, as it is clearly mediated by both the site (the archive) and the (historical) researcher. As the historian Richard Evans paraphrased, we see the past 'through a glass, darkly' (Evans, 1999).

Something of this was recognized some fifty years ago in Harold Garfinkel's (1967) account of the intractable difficulties encountered in transforming hospital records into a form that would allow quantitative analysis. Initially frustrated by what appeared to be the wilful incompleteness of what were supposed to be standard hospital forms, Garfinkel concluded that these documents were better regarded as elements of a conversation between knowledgeable strangers who might never meet but who shared profound forms of technical and organizational tacit knowledge. 'We start,' Garfinkel (1967: 200–201) insists,

> with the fact that when one examines any case folder for what it actually contains, a prominent and consistent feature is the occasional and elliptical character of its remarks and information. In their occasionality, folder documents are very much like utterances in a conversation with an unknown audience, which, because it already knows what might be talked about, is capable of reading hints. … the *folder contents much less than revealing an order of interaction, presuppose an understanding of that order for a correct reading.* [Emphasis in original.] The understanding of that order is not one, however, that strives for theoretical clarity, but is one that is appropriate to a reader's pragmatic interest in the order.

Following Garfinkel, then, archives can be read for discrete pieces of data but, more productively, as ways of eavesdropping on tacit conversations between insiders which assume tacit knowledge to convey meaning. For the ethnographer, the moments where those tacit meanings are unpacked, clarified, or challenged are potentially the most revealing about that wider conversation. Importantly, Garfinkel reminds us that archival ethnography is neither novel nor unusual. In common with the ethnographic project more generally, understanding and translating tacit knowledge inscribed in otherwise cryptic asides or flawed entries in a records system is something most knowledge workers do most days in organizations. In short, the shortcomings and ambiguities of any complex record system that entails a major effort to recode data, if not to render the exercise fatally flawed, becomes an opportunity for ethnography: why did those categories – so clear-cut in principle – become ambiguous in practice? What other tacit knowledge was being produced in the silences and ambiguities of incomplete forms? Symbols are read as performative, not constative: in terms of what they do, how they operate, and whom they marginalize and exclude.

Archival sources, nevertheless, have certain advantages over retrospective interviewing, which suffer from hindsight bias and sensemaking when it comes to an empirical account of past events (Wolfram Cox and Hassard, 2007). Archival documents frequently offer more accounts of how events unfolded that are more attentive to details, as they were produced closer in time to the events they refer to. While this is known as a primary source, we instead draw on the distinction between *social documents* and *narrative sources* (Howell and Prevenier, 2001) as these offer a more substantive differentiation than just primacy. Any archival ethnography depends on gaining access to an archive rich in social documents, as these are key in facilitating 'fieldwork' in the past, rather than a problem on account of their lack of uniformity.

Social documents are 'nonintentional' historical sources, produced in the process of running an organization. Examples would include minutes of meetings, business correspondence or email, reports and handover notes. These are inherently valuable to any archival ethnography because they are less susceptible to incorporating a narrative about the past. *Narrative historical sources*, on the other hand, are emplotted – that is, they tell a story (Dobson and Ziemann, 2009: 10) – and therefore it is difficult to avoid the problem of 'narrative contagion' (Alvesson and Sköldberg, 2009: 115), whereby the plot from narrative sources is imported into the construction of a historical narrative (Rowlinson et al., 2014). Historical sources can be immensely helpful in interpreting social documents that may otherwise be difficult to understand, similar to secondary historical literature. However, archival ethnography ultimately seeks to gain a relatively direct access to the processes and concerns of actors in the past, rather than the narrative sensemaking that occurred with the benefit of hindsight.

Ethnographic History

Ethnographic history, according to Rowlinson et al. (2014) is a distinct narrative strategy distinguished from corporate history by ethnographic sensibilities, an angular theoretical stance, and a conscious refusal to emplot the sources with an over-arching 'meta-narrative.' Reading sources 'against the grain' is the methodological corollary of this approach, and we see archival ethnography as a way to unpack these statements and get closer to what we actually do when we work in an archive. Archival ethnography is ethnographic fieldwork in the past, as it can be vicariously experienced through historical sources, especially those social documents high in immediacy and a holistic understanding of the archive as a 'made' and 'processed' collection with its silences and volubility. Theoretically, this approach is influenced by Foucault, Bakhtin, and critical theory more generally. The influence of ethnography not just as an approach but as a perspective and a style of presentation is also significant. In history, this has been most noticeable in microhistory and 'subjunctive history', and these approaches offer rich methodological guidance.

Microhistory is a historical tradition, which focused on the lesser known past, on individuals that did not make it into the history books, dissenters and sometimes persecuted groups and minorities (Ginzburg, 1992; Le Roy Ladurie and Bray, 1981; Levi, 1988). By painstakingly following individuals through various archives (Ginzburg and Poni, 1991) and reading the records of the inquisition like ethnographic fieldnotes (Ginzburg, 1989, 1992), they opened up an alternative understanding of the past that challenged existing narratives (Iggers, 2005; Magnússon and Szijártó, 2013).

Methodologically this kind of work requires an attitude of bracketing off the researcher's perspective in favour of first understanding the historical setting (Ginzburg, 2012; Ginzburg et al., 1993; Levi, 2012). Only after the researcher has gained some insight into the life worlds of historical subjects should we switch back to considering theories, present-day attitudes, and contextual information. In this, the microhistorians have perhaps been most explicit in what they consider 'reading against the grain' to mean. They seek to interpret the unintended content of historical sources. For this, contextual knowledge not accessible to the people at the time is necessary, as well as the knowledge that comes from hindsight, i.e., knowledge of outcomes. Finally, an angular theoretical perspective that stops researchers from taking sources at face value, while simultaneously being able to challenge some present-day assumptions about the past.

In outlining how this can be done, Carlo Ginzburg, one of the foremost microhistorians, draws on the ethnographic notion of balancing the emic and etic dimension (Ginzburg, 2012). While emic refers to an insider's perspective, etic is a more comparative perspective, that of a more distant observer, also reflecting the temporal positions of historical subjects in the past and historical researchers in the present. Archival ethnography may start from etic questions but will be challenged by emic answers, which transforms our initial interest into a richer understanding of the past, without abandoning the theoretical and conceptual insights of the present (Ginzburg, 2012: 107–111). This distinction between the particular as the emic and empirical, and the etic and general as theoretical, makes archival ethnography an approach that balances critical conceptual work with rich archival insights.

The other major methodological discussion relevant to archival ethnography is Ann Lara Stoler's (2009) reflection on writing 'history in the subjunctive' in the archives of the Dutch East India Company. The 'subjunctive' refers to epistemic anxieties, i.e., fear of what might happen, but also the hopes for a specific kind of future that never occurred. This requires that archives should not be approached with an 'extractive attitude' but 'ethnographic sensibilities' (Stoler, 2009: 92–99). Stoler problematizes technical instruments so that official accounts are read as the products of complex labour processes that establish, modify, and extend the categories that are used to understand and manage populations (Scott, 1990: 84–85). She also highlights that an interest in certain research topics 'gets you nowhere, unless you know how they mattered to whom, when, and why they did so (Stoler, 2009: 9–10).' To read 'with the grain' is to read the *form* of the archive as well as its substance: to read the archive as a process of knowledge production. The danger of the archive being treated as a meta-narrative is avoided by Stoler who looks at where knowledge production hits the sand and delivers inconsequential or unsatisfactory results. The knowledge produced – much as Garfinkel observed fifty years ago – *always* overflows the formal procedures, the immediate need for knowledge (Blouin and Rosenberg, 2012: 119; Stoler, 2009: 50). The taken-for-granted is rarely written down and even more rarely challenged epistemologically.

Ethnographic history treats archival sources as texts for the interpretation of culture, seeking to gain an impression of 'what it was like to be there' (Stone, 1979: 14). Thus, texts are not used to report on the issues that they were ostensibly written about (the constative), but rather what they tell us about commonly held assumptions and intentions (the performative):

> I ask what insights into the social imaginaries of colonial rule might be gained from attending not only to colonialism's archival content but to the principles and practices of governance lodged in particular archival forms. The ... focus is on archiving-as-process rather than archives-as-things. Most importantly it looks to archives as condensed sites of epistemological and political anxiety rather than skewed and biased sources.
>
> *(Stoler, 2009: 20)*

Clearly, this kind of research focus requires approaching archives with a flexible direction to research, and open to serendipity. Stoler emphasizes the importance of 'dissonant sources,' the occasional evidence of dissent and resistance in organizational archives that enable researchers to go beyond the constative and read other sources against the grain. Stoler highlights the importance of non-events – what could be imagined but which did not occur – as another way of understanding how archives can reveal choices *not* made and potential options that were not realized.

Archival Ethnographies in Practice

Both authors have experimented with archival ethnographies, especially when interpreting the (often unexpected) visual materials (photographs, cartoons, doodles) in business archives. One of us considered the way in which organizations ascribed meaning to their corporate architecture in the past, and reflected on how this was shaped by the subjunctive history of hope and aspirations embedded in the promise of colonial independence and economic development (Decker, 2014). Tropical modernist architecture was seen as a beacon heralding a brighter future, and business archives revealed how seriously foreign firms engaged with it. Other types of architectural creations, such as colonial bank branches or the later postmodern headquarters or mock-colonial offices, were not accompanied by such an extensive production of brochures, photographic collections, and other public relations activities. The fact that modernist corporate architecture was heavily promoted emphasized the importance of these buildings in the minds of their creators. This is where archival ethnography's reflection on why material exists on some topics and not others makes use of what is absent as much as what is present in an archive (Spivak, 1988; Trouillot, 1995: 48–49). It also requires an understanding of what kind of archive one is dealing with, and in how far the structure of the collection and the location of sources permits one to draw conclusions about the structure and intentions of the organization (Decker, 2013; Stoler, 2009: 9–10, 20). The modern, or modernizing, archive reflected organized methods of collecting and codifying information, of making data, of understanding populations and markets. The modern archive is organized hierarchically, not thematically, and this powerfully suggests causation, agency, and effect. Alfred Chandler's famous aphorism that 'structure' follows 'strategy' implies that business history *should* be written from the vantage point of corporate headquarters. Ethnographic history, on the contrary, focuses on the bureaucratic labour processes tagged as 'structure,' the better to understand how managing was imagined, and how being managed was experienced.

Unexpected and 'dissonant sources' (Stoler, 2009: 181–185, 252) can also reveal what is important in more circumspect ways:

> discrepant stories provide ethnographic entry into the confused space in which people lived, to the fragmented knowledge on which they relied, and to the ill-informed and inept responses that knowledge engendered. Coherence is seductive for narrative form, but disparities are, from an ethnographic perspective, more compelling. It is the latter that opens onto competing conventions of credibility about what and where evidence could be trusted and those moments in which it could not.
>
> *(Stoler, 2009: 185)*

As some companies were beginning their modernist building programme in West Africa in the 1950s, various sources recounted how an unpopular regional manager was deceived about the date of an important branch opening celebration. Organizational politics and intrigue highlighted how new modernist architecture was a status symbol inside and outside the firm, and structured relationships and management practices.

Decker's (2014) 'Solid Intentions' piece also provided an opportunity to reflect on the limitations of archival ethnography. Comparing the material found in different business archives study can be challenging because these collections reveal idiosyncratic patterns of organization, documentation, and communication within different firms (Decker, 2014: 168). As an in-depth research approach that requires sometimes oblique search methods to discover the unexpected, it is effectively impossible to claim to have searched large archives comprehensively. Similar to any ethnographic study, as researchers we can never claim to have observed everything or to present a representative sample. These constraints of archives are much the same as any other form of participant or non-participant observation. A researcher visiting an organization will only ever gain a partial impression, may find certain areas withheld from view, and will be faced with misrepresentations or situations she can only imperfectly interpret. Working with archival documents, researchers face very similar problems in terms of which documents were created and survived, by whom, for what purpose, etc. However, in contrast to ethnographers, they cannot physically interact with the people and places they study. Material that is absent, or confusing and misleading, often cannot be reconciled or explained, and there can be no follow-on questions to ask for clarification. Gaps or silences in the evidence cannot easily be bridged, and can derail a research project's direction, as conceptual development is driven by what archival sources are available and accessible.

Another example of this serendipity is the 'Dead Selves' piece (McKinlay, 2002). Banking archives exemplify the governmentalist logics embedded in mundane practices. Rapid expansion of retail branch networks from the closing decades of the nineteenth century triggered centralization and innovation. All branches operated as miniature replicas using uniform procedures, operated by staff rotated through the network as their careers progressed. Local conformity was assured through snap inspections. The very idea of the career as a tournament in which individuals competed on merit rather an as a reward for long service, was developed in the 1890s (McKinlay, 2002). Careers were logged in bound ledgers, a material form that made tracking cohorts or the systematic comparison of individuals all but impossible. The form itself suggests the deep uniformity of banking careers, on the one hand, and yet the capacity for the intense scrutiny of an individual, especially a suspect individual, on the other (McKinlay, 2013: 142–143, 2015). Over time, even though there was no attempt to develop numerical scoring, the ledgers' lexical system gained depth and nuance even as the commentaries they recorded became more economical. The archival form attests to the career system's focus on the individual as they made key transitions: the point of entry; their first promotion; their capacity to deal with different types of task and clients. After a decade, for all save highly specialist functions, the 'bankman' was assessed on his conformity to an ideal type of reserved masculinity, polite but never deferential, clear but rarely assertive.

Buried among innumerable folio-sized ledgers, all embossed with a gold 99 on their spines, was one that concealed more than a decade of cartoons drawn by one low-flying clerk, William Shirlaw, to entertain himself and a small group of confidantes, who had similarly low expectations of their career progression. Evidently, the careers of this group of clerks had stalled: none were transferred to gain managerial experience. Several hundred cartoons speak of mild subversion and a caustic humour exercised at the expense of their peers and, especially, their superiors. This was the hidden world of the Victorian bank clerk, standing at least one remove from the idealized 'bankman' and sceptical about the promotion of procedural justice as the trade for their daily bureaucratic drudgery. But even their choice of where to hide their irreverent cartoons was revealing. Ledger 99 was the suspense account used to record shortfalls that prohibited daily accounts to be reconciled. Such shortfalls were highly unusual, and Shirlaw and his co-conspirators knew that they would not be discovered easily by even the most sharp-eyed inspector. Understanding the labour process of bank administration allows us to understand not just how inspection operated but the bureaucratic nooks-and-crannies it did not reach. The form of the archive was not devised for the benefit of historians but reflected the ways that the bank managed itself as an organization and how it imagined its officers, as 'bankmen' who embodied the bank's values.

Conclusion

Archival ethnography opens up a new research site for fieldwork, one that offers a tentative and intriguing view of organizational pasts. Just as fieldwork remains *the* rite of passage for the anthropologist, so the archive is where the historian was made. The social documents maintained in many organizational archives provide rich perspectival material to research with ethnographic sensibilities if they are approached not with a presentist, theory-driven mindset but rather an inductive, emic and exploratory attitude. Ethnographic fieldwork is not just a metaphor for this kind of research, but rather a good guide as to how we can approach archives as research sites that allow us access to the past. This access to past events is neither unproblematic nor unlimited, nor is archival ethnography the only way in which archives can be used for historical research. As an intellectual and political project, ethnography intends to give voice to the otherwise voiceless, especially those at the very margins of mainstream society. In this respect, ethnography overlaps with microhistory and history from below, the political project to reinstall the experience of ordinary people otherwise excluded from historical narratives.

What this approach offers is deeper understanding of how actors understood events and processes at the time, and what their fears and expectations of the future were. This rich reading of a time and place is value-laden and perspectival, and opens up different kinds of research topics and questions, for example, the use of images and artefacts. It also allows a better understanding of how processes unfold over time, such as symbolic representation through architecture or the emerging notion of careers as a disciplining force. This approach integrates the use of archives into organizational ethnography, and management and organizational research more broadly.

Acknowledgements

The authors would like to thank Michael Moss and Divya Jyoti for their helpful comments. We also benefitted from colleagues' feedback when we presented our research at the Using History, Valuing Archives workshop at Henley Business

School in 2019, British Academy of Management Annual Conference 2018, and the Association of Business Historians' Annual Conference 2018, the Academy of Management Annual Conference 2017, and the ESRC-funded Seminar in Organizational History in 2016.

References

Agar M (1980) *The Professional Stranger*. New York: Academic Press.

Alvesson M and Sköldberg K (2009) *Reflexive Methodology: New Vistas for Qualitative Research*. 2nd ed. Los Angeles, CA and London: Sage.

Bansal P, Smith WK and Vaara E (2018) From the Editors: New Ways of Seeing through Qualitative Research. *Academy of Management Journal* 61(4): 1–7.

Barros A (2016) Archives and the "Archive": Dialogue and an Agenda of Research in Organization Studies. *Organizações & Sociedade* 23(79): 609–623.

Barros A, Carneiro A de T and Wanderley S (2019) Organizational Archives and Historical Narratives: Practicing Reflexivity in (Re)constructing the Past from Memories and Silences. *Qualitative Research in Organization and Management* 14(3): 280–294.

Blouin F and Rosenberg W (2012) *Processing the Past: Contesting Authority in History and the Archive*. Oxford: Oxford University Press.

Bryant J (2000) On Sources and Narratives in Historical Social Science: A Realist Critique of Positivist and Postmodernist Epistemologies. *British Journal of Sociology* 51(3): 489–523.

Bryman A and Bell E (2011) *Business Research Methods*. 3rd ed. Oxford: Oxford University Press.

Castellani P and Rossato C (2014) On the Communication Value of the Company Museum and Archives. *Journal of Communication Management* 18(3): 240–253.

Clifford J (1990) Notes on (Field)notes. In: Sanjek R (ed.) *Fieldnotes: The Making of Anthropology*. Ithaca, NY: Cornell University Press.

Cole E (1913) *Filing Systems: Their Principles and Their Application to Modern Office Requirements*. London: Pitman.

Collingwood RG (1946) *The Idea of History*. Oxford: Oxford Paperbacks.

Comaroff J and Comaroff J (1992) *Ethnography and the Historical Imagination*. Boulder, CO: Westview Press.

Combe S (2010) *Archives interdites: l'histoire confisquée*. Paris: La Decouverte.

Decker S (2010) Postcolonial Transitions in Africa: Decolonization in West Africa and Present Day South Africa. *Journal of Management Studies* 47(5): 791–813.

Decker S (2013) The Silence of the Archives: Business History, Post-colonialism and Archival Ethnography. *Management & Organizational History* 8(2): 155–173.

Decker S (2014) Solid Intentions: An Archival Ethnography of Corporate Architecture and Organizational Remembering. *Organization* 21(4): 514–542.

Dobson M and Ziemann B (2009) *Reading Primary Sources: The Interpretation of Texts from Nineteenth- and Twentieth-century History*. Abingdon: Routledge.

Durepos G, McKinlay A and Taylor S (2017) Narrating Histories of Women at Work: Archives, Stories, and the Promise of Feminism. *Business History* 59(8): 1261–1279.

Evans R (1999) *In Defense of History*. New York: W. W. Norton & Co.

Farge A (2013) *The Allure of the Archives*. New Haven, CT: Yale University Press.

Foucault M (2004) *Society Must Be Defended: Lectures at the College de France, 1975–76*. London: Penguin.

Friedman W, Galambos L, Godelier E, et al. (2014) Opinions: Business History and Anthropology. *Journal of Business Anthropology* 3(1): 15–78.

Garfinkel H (1967) *Studies in Ethnomethodology*. Englewood Cliffs, NJ: Prentice-Hall.

Ginzburg C (1989) Clues: Roots of an Evidential Paradigm. In: *Clues, Myths, and the Historical Method*, trans. *John and Anne C. Tedeschi*. Baltimore, MD: John Hopkins University Press, pp. 96–214.

Ginzburg C (1992) *The Cheese and the Worms: The Cosmos of a Sixteenth Century Miller.* Baltimore, MD: Johns Hopkins University Press.

Ginzburg C (2012) Our Words, and Theirs: A Reflection on the Historian's Craft, Today. In: Fellman S and Rahikainen M (eds) *Historical Knowledge: In Quest of Theory, Method and Evidence*. Newcastle upon Tyne: Cambridge Scholars, pp. 97–120.

Ginzburg C and Poni C (1991) The Name and the Game: Unequal Exchange and the Historiographic Marketplace. In: Muir E and Ruggiero G (eds) *Microhistory and the Lost Peoples of Europe*. Baltimore, MD: John Hopkins University Press, pp. 1–10.

Ginzburg C, Tedeschi J and Tedeschi AC (1993) Microhistory: Two or Three Things that I Know about It. *Critical Inquiry* 20(Autumn): 10–35.

Hampel CE and Tracey P (2017) How Organizations Move from Stigma to Legitimacy: The Case of Cook's Travel Agency in Victorian Britain. *Academy of Management Journal* 60(6): 2175–2207.

Howell M and Prevenier W (2001) *From Reliable Sources: An Introduction to Historical Methods.* Ithaca, NY and London: Cornell University Press.

Iggers GG (2005) *Historiography in the Twentieth Century : From Scientific Objectivity to the Postmodern Challenge.* 2nd ed. Middletown, CT: Wesleyan.

Le Roy Ladurie E and Bray B (1981) *Montaillou: Cathars and Catholics in a French Village, 1294–1324.* Harmondsworth: Penguin.

Levi G (1988) *Inheriting Power: The Story of an Exorcist.* Chicago, IL: University of Chicago Press.

Levi G (2012) Microhistory and the Recovery of Complexity. In: Fellman S and Rahikainen M (eds) *Historical Knowledge: In Quest of Theory, Method and Evidence*. Newcastle upon Tyne: Cambridge Scholars, pp. 121–132.

Little V (1983) What Is Historical Imagination? *Teaching History* 36: 27–32.

MacKenzie D (2008) *An Engine, Not a Camera: How Financial Models Shape Markets.* Cambridge, MA and London: MIT Press.

Maclean M, Harvey C, Suddaby R and O'Gorman K. (2018) Political Ideology and the Discursive Construction of the Multinational Hotel Industry. *Human Relations* 71(6): 766–795.

Magnússon SG and Szijártó IM (2013) *What Is Microhistory? Theory and Methods.* Abingdon: Routledge.

Manoff M (2004) Theories of the Archive from across the Disciplines. *Portal: Libraries and the Academy* 4(1): 9–25.

McKinlay A (2002) 'Dead Selves': The Birth of the Modern Career. *Organization* 9(4): 595–614.

McKinlay A (2013) Following Foucault into the Archives: Clerks, Careers and Cartoons. *Management and Organizational History* 8(2): 137–154.

McKinlay A (2015) Banking, Bureaucracy and the Career: The Curious Case of Mr Notman. *Business History* 55(3): 431–447.

Megill A (2007) *Historical Knowledge, Historical Error: A Contemporary Guide to Practice.* Chicago, IL and London: University of Chicago Press.

Mills AJ and Helms Mills J (2011) Digging Archaeology: Postpositivist Theory and Archival Research in Case Study Development. In: Piekkari R and Welch C (eds) *Rethinking the Case Study in International Business and Management Research*. Northampton, MA: Edward Elgar, pp. 342–360.

Mills AJ, Weatherbee TG and Durepos G (2013) Reassembling Weber to Reveal The-Past-As-History in Management and Organization Studies. *Organization* 21(2): 225–243.

Moore N, Saleter A, Stanley L and Tamboukou M (2017) *The Archive Project: Archival Research in the the Social Sciences.* London: Routledge.

Moss M (2005) The Hutton Inquiry, the President of Nigeria and What the Butler Hoped to See. *The English Historical Review* 120(487): 577–592.

Mutch A (2016) Bringing History into the Study of Routines: Contextualizing Performance. *Organization Studies* 37(8): 1171–1188.

Okely J (2007) Response to George E. Marcus 1. *Social Anthropology* 15(3): 357–361.

Osborne T (1999) The Ordinariness of the Archive. *History of the Human Sciences* 12(2): 51–64.

Rabinow P (2008) *Reflections on Fieldwork in Morocco.* Berkeley, CA: University of California Press.

Ramsey AN, Sharer WB, L'Eplattenier B, et al. (2010) *Working in the Archives: Practical Research Methods for Rhetoric and Composition.* Carbondale, IL: Southern Illinois University Press.

Richards T (1993) *The Imperial Archive: Knowledge and the Fantasy of Empire.* London: Verso.

Rojas F (2010) Power through Institutional Work: Acquiring Academic Authority in the 1968 Third World Strike. *Academy of Management Journal* 53(6): 1263–1280.

Rowlinson M (2004) Historical Analysis of Company Documents. In: Cassell C and Symon G (eds) *Essential Guide to Qualitative Methods in Organizational Research.* Thousand Oaks, CA: Sage, pp. 301–311.

Rowlinson M, Hassard J and Decker S (2014) Research Strategies for Organizational History: A Dialogue between Historical Theory and Organization Theory. *Academy of Management Review* 39(3): 205–274.

Scott J (1990) *Domination and the Arts of Resistance: Hidden Transcripts.* New Haven, CT: Yale University Press.

Silverman BS (2011) *Qualitative Research.* 3rd ed. Thousand Oaks, CA: Sage.

Spivak GC (1988) Can the Subaltern Speak? In: Nelson C and Grossberg L (eds) *Marxism and the Interpretation of Culture.* Champaign, IL: University of Illinois Press, pp. 271–313.

Spivak GC (1999) *A Critique of Postcolonial Reason: Towards a History of the Vanishing Present.* Cambridge, MA: Harvard University Press.

Steedman C (2002) *Dust: The Archive and Cultural History.* New Brunswick: Rutgers University Press.

Stoler AL (2009) *Along the Archival Grain: Epistemic Anxieties and Colonial Common Sense.* Princeton, NJ: Princeton University Press.

Stone L (1979) The Revival of Narrative: Reflections on a New Old History. *Past & Present* 85: 3–24.

Strati A (2000) *Theory and Method in Organization Studies.* Thousand Oaks, CA: Sage.

Symon G and Cassell C (2012) *Qualitative Organizational Research: Core Methods and Current Challenges.* Thousand Oaks, CA: Sage.

Trouillot M-R (1995) *Silencing the Past: Power and the Production of History.* Boston, MA: Beacon Press.

Vaara E and Lamberg J-AJ (2016) Taking Historical Embeddedness Seriously: Three Historical Approaches to Advance Strategy Process and Practice Research. *Academy of Management Review* 41(4): 633–657.

Van Maanen J (1988) *Tales of the Field: On Writing Ethnography.* Chicago, IL: University of Chicago Press.

Wadhwani RD (2018) Poverty's Monument: Social Problems and Organizational Field Emergence in Historical Perspective. *Journal of Management Studies* 55(3): 545–577.

Whewell W (1840) *The Philosophy of the Inductive Sciences, Founded upon Their History.* 2nd 1847. London: John W. Parker.

Willis P (2000) *The Ethnographic Imagination.* Cambridge, UK: Polity Press.

Wolfram Cox J and Hassard J (2007) Ties to the Past in Organization Research: A Comparative Analysis of Retrospective Methods. *Organization* 14(4): 475–497.

Yates J (2014) Understanding Historical Methods in Organization Studies. In: Bucheli M and Wadhwani RD (eds) *Organizations in Time: History, Theory, Methods.* Oxford: Oxford University Press, pp. 265–283.

3

A HISTORY OF MARKETS PAST

The Role of Institutional Memory Failure in Financial Crises

Natalya Vinokurova

The cyclical nature of the management field's interest in the methods of anthropology and history vis-à-vis the methods of management's dominant disciplines—economics, sociology, and psychology—leads to a tendency to lump together the contributions of anthropology and history under the broader heading of qualitative methods. This tendency fosters the illusion of the two disciplines' interchangeability. This chapter uses a historical case study of financial markets to argue that the differences in methods brought by anthropologists and historians to the study reflect the different questions anthropologists and historians ask and answer. These differences point to complementarity rather than interchangeability of the contributions of anthropology and history to the study of financial markets and to the management field.

Specifically, I argue that economic crises force management as a field to develop an appreciation for fine-grained observations, rendering the methods used by anthropologists and historians particularly relevant. In this chapter, I show how historians' questions and methods differ from those of the anthropologists by comparing these questions to those of anthropologists studying financial markets and methods to those of anthropologists working with archival data. Using a historical case study to explore the connection between financial crises and the failure of institutional memory to inform the re-emergence of financial instruments, I illustrate the argument with a study of the antecedents of mortgage-backed securities (MBS), one type of securities implicated in the 2008 crisis. My study demonstrates how historical analysis can enrich the management scholars' understanding of financial crises beyond the notable contributions made by anthropologists.

Taking the 2008 financial crisis as the latest economic crisis to bring about an epistemic crisis for the field of management, I provide an overview of how anthropology and history contributed to unpacking the financial market practices in the lead-up to the 2008 financial crisis. To show the value of history's differential contribution I then lay out a detailed case study of how a historical analysis of the markets for MBS that emerged in the U.S. in the 1880s and 1900s informs our understanding of the MBS market that emerged in the 1970s and culminated in the 2008 crisis. My analysis has implications for how management scholars conceptualize the relationship between institutional memory and financial crises.

Epistemic Crises and Disciplinary Commitments

Arguably, the management field's interest in applying different research methods goes through epistemic cycles alternatively dominated by scholars closely observing phenomena and generating theory. The first phase of such an epistemic cycle entails researchers accumulating fine-grained observations of empirical reality. The contributions of anthropology and history to the management field are particularly evident during the accumulation of observations phase of the epistemic cycle. For instance, anthropologists played an important role in shaping the Hawthorne studies that laid the foundation for the development of management as a discipline (Morey and Luthans, 1987). Similarly, historical analysis of the emergence of the M-form corporation (Chandler, 1962) drew on detailed archival records to inform management theory. These contributions leverage anthropologists' and historians' interest in understanding the contexts that shape human behavior, be they aspects of a society's culture or evolution of its institutions.

In the second phase of the epistemic cycle, after enough data are accumulated, management field's interest in the case particulars wanes and the careful images painstakingly drawn by the original researchers are replaced first by outlines and then by outlines of the outlines, i.e., the stylized "facts."[1] This theory-generation phase of the cycle draws heavily on economics, sociology and psychology, relying on tools of what Abbott (2004) termed "standard causal analysis." These dominant disciplines seek to sketch out generic patterns of human behavior invariant to space, time, and cultural context. An example of the first two phases of such an epistemic cycle is the evolution in the disciplinary orientation at university business schools from closely observing the phenomena and collecting facts on individual cases to generating theories that draw on the dominant disciplines (Khurana, 2010).

Epistemic crises—significant events for which the theories fail to account—restart the epistemic cycles. By demonstrating the limitations of assumptions inherent in the prevailing theories, epistemic crises disrupt the theories' dominance, generating greater interest in the context. The evidence of the theories' limitations points to the need to understand the individuals' cultural beliefs and histories of the institutions that shape them, stimulating management scholars' interest in the study of anthropology and history, and thus the start of a new cycle of inquiry. After the crisis, this accumulation of observations gives rise to theories that abstract away from the particulars until the next crisis restarts the cycle.[2]

Economic crises play an important role in the epistemic cycles for management studies. As an applied field of inquiry, management is committed to the study of reality—a commitment that turns economic crises into epistemic crises for the field. The aftermath of economic crises—events that force the field to recognize the limitations of existing theories—brings to the fore the questions overlooked by the field's dominant disciplines. This recognition points to the inadequacy of the prevalent theories, and the need to collect more data and critically evaluate the interpretations of the data already collected.

In the aftermath of economic crises, management scholars are called upon to account for the gap between what the theory says and what managers do. Offering this account is central to the management field's contribution to the broader body of knowledge. Anthropology and history shape this contribution at moments of crisis by collecting and making sense of observations that help explain this gap.

From Proximate to Distant Antecedents of the 2008 Financial Crisis

The 2008 mortgage crisis represents an opportunity for sensemaking brought about by the limitations of both academic (Krugman, 2009) and practitioner theories (MacKenzie, 2011) in accounting for the event. The massive foreclosures on residential real estate in the United States affected millions of families, bringing about bankruptcies of major financial firms and protracted unemployment. The need to make sense of the 2008 crisis produced an interest in understanding the work practices of financial market participants, energizing the social studies of finance as an emergent discipline (MacKenzie and Millo, 2003; Poon, 2009). This analytical lens built on ethnographic accounts of the financial services that emerged in the work of academics (Abolafia, 1996; Ho, 2009; Knorr Cetina and Bruegger, 2002; Zaloom, 2006), journalists trained in anthropology (Tett, 2009), and practitioners (Lewis, 1990, 2010).

In exploring the evolution of the securities implicated in the financial crisis, scholars taking a historical lens focused on the role played by innovations in security design and the practices surrounding such innovations (Funk and Hirschman, 2014; MacKenzie, 2011; Vinokurova, 2018, 2019a). These accounts leveraged the relative recency of the 2008 crisis to excavate the immediate antecedents of the securities in question, supplementing archival sources with practitioner interviews. However, they did not take advantage of the wider lens afforded by the historical method in interrogating the more distal ancestors of the securities in question. In this chapter, I contribute to filling this gap by analyzing the connections between mortgage-backed securities (MBS), which were one type of securities widely used in the lead-up to the 2008 crisis and the prior U.S. MBS markets that emerged in the 1880s and 1900s. In so doing, I highlight the differential contribution of history to the study of financial markets.

Learning from Prior Markets

In this chapter, I consider the connections between the 1880s, 1900s, and 1970s MBS markets in the United States. The emergence and re-emergence of these markets offer insights into the role played by institutional memory in the MBS market development. The U.S. MBS markets are of particular interest because of the discontinuities in their operations. Other countries' forays into mortgage securitization exhibit evolutionary change—the markets in Germany, France, and Denmark span centuries.[3] By contrast, the U.S. markets emerge, disappear after a crisis, and reemerge.

My analysis focuses on securities offered to U.S. investors backed by residential real estate. This focus rules out the securities of U.S. mortgage companies created in the 1870s that targeted European investors (Brewer, 1976), the shares of commercial mortgages offered by bond houses in the 1920s (Snowden, 1995), and the farm mortgage lending system created by the U.S. government in 1915 (Sparks, 1932). The three markets that I consider in this chapter are for the debentures backed by western mortgages issued in the 1880s and 1890s, the mortgage participation certificates issued between the 1900s and 1930s, and different types of MBS issued in the most recent market from the 1970s through 2008.

Focus on Financial Instruments

Economic historians have argued that the connection between the MBS market meltdowns of the 1890s and 1920s is that the U.S. mortgage lenders missed the important institutional lessons of the European securitization experience. For instance, Snowden (1995) contrasts the lack of a centralized regulator for mortgage lending and the issuance of MBS in the United States with the highly centralized regulation of mortgage banking in Europe. Other scholars have similarly pointed to private market competition as contributing to the U.S. MBS crises (Simkovic, 2013). These accounts have stopped short of comparing and contrasting the structures of the securities issued across the three markets.

Comparing and contrasting the security structures across the three markets is important because such analysis can document the institutional memory (or lack thereof) in the U.S. MBS markets and the financial system more broadly. Since all three MBS markets ended in crises, comparing the security structures could inform debates about whether and what market participants learn from financial crises. Persistence of the security structures would suggest that MBS market participants failed to learn not just from the overseas experience with mortgage securitization, but also from the experience of their U.S. predecessors. Furthermore, evidence of persistence in mortgage securitization practices would lend further credence to the argument that the regulators shape the scope of action available to the financial markets participants (Funk and Hirschman, 2014).

Accounts of the MBS market development in the lead-up to the 2008 crisis have focused on recent past, thus leveraging the complementarities in the methods of anthropologists and historians. Taking a longer historical perspective allows me to highlight the differential contribution of history.

Sources and Methods

In tracing the history of MBS across the three markets, I collected more than 500 printed primary sources. The primary sources consisted of MBS issuers' advertisements in newspapers and magazines,[4] the discussion of the mortgages and MBS in the trade press, the reports of the authorities supervising the markets,[5] as well as the market post-mortem reports of the relevant investigating bodies.

Each source offered its own specific lens on MBS. The advertisements placed by the MBS issuers offered a repository of claims made about the securities including the structure of the securities, the rate of interest, and the targeted audience. The persistence of advertising as a medium provides an opportunity to compare and contrast the rhetoric of the MBS issuers across the three markets. The trade press discussions of mortgages and MBS reflect the market participants' views on MBS and the evolution of these views across the markets. The regulator reports offer insights into regulatory decision-making with respect to the MBS issuer activities. The post-mortem reports of the three markets contain the lessons learned by both the private actors and the policy makers about the markets in question. I supplemented these primary materials with academic accounts of the three markets, including both contemporaneous accounts of the MBS issuers' activities and the analyses of the markets following each market's collapse.[6]

My analytical lens reflects three key aspects of a historical approach to collecting and analyzing archival sources (Kipping, Wadhwani, and Bucheli, 2014): source criticism, triangulation, and hermeneutics. Source criticism entails the need to establish both the authenticity (time and source of production) and validity (the reliability of the informants producing the documents) of the sources. Triangulation suggests that drawing on multiple written sources can help the historian establish a more accurate understanding of the relevant context, overcoming the biases in the individual sources. Finally, hermeneutics requires that an understanding of how the production of the source material fit into the historical context informs the historian's interpretation of the sources.

This approach has important similarities and differences to how an anthropologist might approach analyzing archival sources. For instance, in their analysis of how writing affects distributed collaboration, Fayard and Metiu (2014) analyze two sets of letters. Their analysis focuses on iteratively reading and coding the archival materials, using extant theory to inform their coding, and presenting their findings in relation to the relevant theories. A historian approaching the same set of materials would start by iteratively reading the primary source documents (in this case the letters) and contemporaneous secondary or tertiary sources, including academic accounts. The historian's "coding" of the letters would then be informed by their relationship to other archival sources and other historians' accounts of the period. The historian would then present the findings in relation to what is known about the period in question.

In presenting my findings, I begin with an overview of the structures of MBS to provide the reader with a basis for comparing the securities in the three markets. I then offer brief descriptions of the three markets in turn. Following these descriptions, I compare and contrast the structures of the securities across the three markets. For each market, I consider the lessons the market participants drew from their experience and investigate the extent to which the subsequent MBS market participants learned from the experience of their predecessors. I conclude my analysis by discussing how this comparison informs our understanding of the relationship between institutional memory and financial crises.

MBS across Time

Before comparing the security structures across the three markets, I offer an overview of MBS as a financial instrument. As illustrated in Figure 3.1, the starting point in MBS issuance is the assembly of individual mortgages into a pool. The MBS issuers then use the mortgages in the pool as the securities' collateral using the cash flows from the mortgages in the collateral to pay the securities' investors.

Depending on the structure of an individual issue, the MBS may represent either a debt obligation of the issuer or partial ownership of a pool of mortgages. In the former case, for the purposes of the issuer's balance sheet, the mortgage pool appears as an asset and the securities appear as a liability of the issuer. In the latter case, the issuer sets aside the mortgages by either depositing them with a trustee or setting up a separate entity to issue the securities and selling the mortgages to that entity.

There are three key assumptions underlying the issuance of MBS. First is that the quality of the mortgages entering the mortgage pool is comparable to the quality of the mortgages sold individually. This assumption undergirds the comparability of yields and risk profiles of MBS to those of the individual mortgages. Second, is that the quality of underlying mortgages does not change within markets. This assumption allows for the comparability of yields of MBS issued at different points in time. Third is that the standardization of inputs (mortgages) enables the standardization of outputs (securities).

Insight into MBS market development in the U.S. is constrained by the lax regulatory framework and fragmentation of the supervisory authority governing

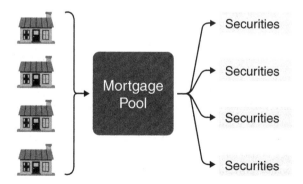

Figure 3.1   Structure of mortgage-backed securities.

mortgage lending and MBS issuance. The laxity encompasses an absence of uniform standards for mortgage underwriting and recording, lack of uniform licensing standard for mortgage underwriters and MBS issuers, as well as a dearth of requirements for transparency into the securities collateral. The fragmentation stems from a multitude of regulators governing different aspects of mortgage lenders' activities. These features of the regulatory framework make it difficult to judge how well the assumptions implicit in the MBS structure compare to reality.

MBS: 1880s–1890s

In the mid-1800s, investors from the east coast of the United States were an important source of mortgage financing for farm and city property in Midwestern and Western states. In the 1880s, the western mortgage companies started financing the mortgages they originated by issuing debentures to cater to investors who lacked sufficient capital to buy individual mortgage loans. These securities gave investors the option to invest in western mortgages by buying obligations of the mortgage lenders, collateralized by the mortgage loans the companies deposited with a trustee. The mortgage lenders collected borrower payments, passed them on to investors, and offered a guarantee of principal and/or interest repayment on the mortgages they originated. The guarantees allowed investors to forgo the expense of researching the quality of individual mortgage loans.

Figure 3.2 displays one of the earliest advertisements for western mortgage debentures published in *Christian Union*—a nondenominational general interest publication. The advertisement was accompanied by text explaining the security's features:

> These debentures are obligations of the company, who are responsible for the prompt payment of both interest and principal. They are secured by first mortgages on improved farms, and for each series of $50,000 an equal amount of these mortgages are on deposit with the Metropolitan Trust Co. of New York, and do not represent in the aggregate more than 50% of the value of the property. The Treasurer of the company, William G. Clapp, 7 Nassau Street, New York, will send a pamphlet explaining more fully their debenture system, or give any further information that may be desired.
>
> *(Christian Union, 1886, p. 30)*

The advertisement and the accompanying text suggest that in structuring its debentures, the Fidelity Loan and Trust Company of Storm Lake, Iowa had opted for issuing the securities as its debt obligations, while at the same time depositing the mortgages with a trustee to create the appearance of separation between the issuer and the securities' collateral. The securities' description also offers assurances of the quality of mortgages—the amount of the loan was not to exceed 50%. The description of the mortgaged properties as "improved farms" in the ad is meant to reassure the prospective investors that the mortgaged property in the securities' collateral

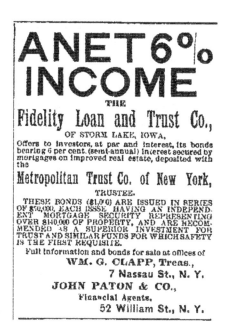

Figure 3.2 An advertisement of Western mortgage debentures offered by Fidelity Loan &
Trust Co. of Storm Lake, Iowa.

Source: *Christian Union*, Advertisement 15, October 21, 1886, p. 29.

did not include vacant land. Of note in the text above is the idiosyncratic nature
of the securities in question—the readers are advised to contact the company for a
description of the company-specific debenture issuance system.

In addition to the above description of the securities, the text accompanying the
ad provides some background on factors motivating the issuance of the securities:

> The immense and increasing demand in the agricultural districts of the
> West for Eastern capital to improve and stock newly purchased farms has
> led to great improvement in the method of negotiating Western farm
> mortgages. The debentures issued by the Fidelity Loan & Trust Co. of
> Stone Lake, Iowa, advertised on another page, belong to a system for
> which many advantages are claimed, and is worthy of the careful investi-
> gation of any one interested in this class of investments.
>
> *(Christian Union, 1886, p. 30)*

The above text suggests that the farmers' demand for capital drove the issuance of
the new securities. The quote also frames the debentures as a better way to invest
in western mortgages.

The operation of western mortgage companies issuing debentures proceeded
with no regulatory oversight until the early 1890s when bank supervisors in the

eastern states in which the companies recruited investors started issuing licenses conditional on examining firms' finances (Bogue, 1955). The regulators were careful to explain that the licensing for operation did not constitute endorsement:

> While farm mortgages, or debenture bonds based upon them, are undoubtedly safe investments when the business is *honestly* and *capably* managed, we wish it to be understood that the mere appearance of the statement of any company in this report does not, of necessity, carry with it the endorsement of the Commissioners, as for want of time and the fact that many companies were late in qualifying, some of them have not yet been examined. Neither statute law nor State supervision can give to the investor absolute protection; he must, to a great extent, rely on his own judgment and caution.
>
> *(Griswold and Goodrich, 1890, Report of the Bank Commissioners*
> *of the State of Connecticut, p. 17)*

In keeping with the regulators' caveats in the above quote, in their advertisements, the mortgage companies sought to project the image of care in their lending. These claims included lending to good borrowers, on perfect titles, in amounts not exceeding 40% of the property value (e.g., *Philadelphia Inquirer*, 1886). While the regulators were careful to avoid the appearance of endorsing the companies, the companies advertised their products as comparable in safety to government bonds (see for instance the Equitable Mortgage Company ad in the *Christian Union*, 1886, p. 29).

A piece of evidence consistent with the claims that the debentures were a safer means of investing in western mortgages, the companies advertised a lower interest rate for their debentures than for individual mortgages they sold, as seen in the Farmers' Trust Company ad in Figure 3.3.

The 1% difference in annual interest rates between the debentures and the individual mortgages in Figure 3.3 indicates greater safety claimed for the debentures.

Farmers' Trust Co.

Ohicago Office, 111 Dearborn-st.

6 Per Cent Savings Bonds.
6 Per Cent Registered Debentures.
7 Per Cent Western Farm Mortgages.

Denominations to suit Investors or Savings Depositors.

Figure 3.3   Advertisement of western mortgages and debentures offered for sale by the Farmers' Trust Co.

Source: *Chicago Daily Tribune*, 1887. "Display Ad 4", July 14, p. 12.

In appealing to investors, MBS issuers advertised the risk-diversification benefits of investing in multiple mortgages as offering protection for the investment's performance compared to buying individual mortgages. For example:

> The advantages of the debenture system are that the investor is not compelled to stand or fall with one mortgage or one piece of real estate. Each debenture bond is, in a sense, insured by all the rest of the series.
>
> *(Gleed, 1890, p. 104)*

Eastern regulators cited diversification as a rationale for licensing companies whose capital was less than one-sixth of the mortgages they guaranteed:

> Forty-three companies, organized under the laws of other States or of territories, have placed themselves under the supervision of the commissioners. Sworn reports, showing the condition of such companies on the first day of October last, will be found following the reports of the home companies. The capital stock represented by these companies is $9,171,771.26, and they have an aggregate liability for debenture bonds of $9,851,568.86, with a still further liability of $45,342,413.43, for outstanding guaranteed loans negotiated and sold by them. These liabilities amount to more than six times the amount of capital represented; but, in justice to the companies, it should be stated that **they consider the risk to be governed by the law of average and in the nature of an insurance** [emphasis added].
>
> *(Landers and Noble, 1888, Report of the Bank Commissioners of the State of Connecticut, p. 15)*

The benefits of the risk diversification that the companies claimed hinged on the assumption that the quality of the mortgages in the debentures' collateral was comparable to the quality of mortgage loans sold individually—an assumption that was at odds with the practice of the securities' issuers.

Indeed, market observers suggested that in the absence of close regulatory supervision, mortgage companies selected lower quality collateral for the securities compared to the individual loans they sold to other investors:

> The chief objection to what is called the debenture system is that **companies are likely to secure their debentures by a poorer class of mortgages**. The trustee never vouches for the character of the securities upon which debenture bonds are based. He only certifies the face value. Bad securities taken for large commissions are likely therefore to be put into the hands of the debenture trustee. There is nobody to inspect or to criticise [emphasis added].
>
> *(Gleed, 1890, p. 96)*

As this quote suggests, the trustees who held the debentures' collateral played a passive role in the issuance of securities—attesting to the face value of the mortgages placed in the trust rather than the quality of the mortgages.

Eastern bank examiners urged investors to pay attention to the securities' collateral:

> No supervision, however, can protect the investor unless he uses good judgment in the selection of the company with which he deals and carefully scrutinizes each investment, if it be a loan, to study its locality and all its conditions from the memoranda furnished for that purpose, and if it be a debenture bond, to be sure that it states clearly the security [collateral] on which it is based.
>
> *(Landers and Noble, 1889, Report of the Bank Commissioners*
> *of the State of Connecticut, p. 19)*

The regulators' guidance was particularly salient because even reputable lenders like J.B. Watkins in Kansas used the mortgage loans they could not sell individually to back the debentures. These loans had shorter terms, smaller amounts, and higher risk compared to the mortgages that were sold as individual loans (Bogue, 1955). Further compounding the problem of collateral quality was the fact that in addition to selecting lower quality mortgages to begin with, the security issuers could also replace the loans held by the trustees on the investors' behalf at the issuers' discretion.

In the lead-up to the panic of 1893, several developments contributed to the collapse of the market for western mortgages. One of these was overlending. The abundance of capital led to the lowering of mortgage interest rates as well as to unsafe lending practices. As the below quote suggests, the easy availability of capital staved off foreclosures by turning delinquent loans into new mortgages:

> A Western farm mortgage on which over a year's interest was in default was sent from the East to a Chicago firm for collection, and by it sent to a Western correspondent, who reported the borrower "badly on the down grade." A few days later word came that it would be paid, and a little later full payment was received. Being a little curious on the subject, further inquiry was made, and a reply came that a Western mortgage company had made delinquent a new loan for 40% more than the old one—adding, for which a round commission was paid.
>
> *(New York Evangelist, 1886, p. 7)*

As this quote suggests, the easy availability of capital contributed to a reduction in the quality of the loans in the debentures' collateral. The crop failures of the late 1880s resulted in defaults of many western mortgages. The concerns about farm mortgage performance in light of crop failure curtailed the flow of capital to western mortgages, reducing opportunities for refinancing. By the mid-1890s, most of the mortgage companies failed, unable to honor their guarantees due to insufficient capitalization.

MBS: 1900–1930s

As the issuance of debentures backed by western mortgages wound to a close in the 1890s, securitization reemerged as an important financing source for urban mortgage lending. Specifically, the companies originally formed to insure the validity of property titles in American cities expanded their businesses into insuring the repayment of mortgages and mortgage lending. Like the western mortgage companies before them, the title insurance companies offered investors both individual mortgage loans and securities backed by mortgage loans. However, instead of issuing debentures that constituted debt obligations of the western mortgage companies, they sold mortgage participation certificates—securities that represented partial ownership of the mortgage loans these companies originated.

Figure 3.4 offers three advertisements representative of the claims made by the certificates' issuers.

The claims in the mortgage certificate ad in Figure 3.4a echoed the claims made by the western mortgage companies in the 1800s. The issuers advertised the mortgage certificates as an improvement over prior methods of investing in mortgages, promising the mortgage holders a stream of income without having to concern themselves with investigating the details of mortgage lending practices.

An Improvement

Do you know the latest development of the guaranteed mortgage—The First Mortgage Certificate?

It is a share in a mortgage on a definite piece of property. You have all the protection of the guaranteed mortgage but there are no bulky papers to care for—we do that for you. You hold the certificate—we do all the rest and your interest reaches you each six months.

Just now they pay 5% and you can get them in any amount, odd or even, small or large. They are due in from three to five years.

Try them the first time you have money to invest.

We have guaranteed $692,-000,000 in the past 27 years and no investor has ever lost a dollar.

BOND & MORTGAGE GUARANTEE CO.

Capital and Surplus, $10,000,000

176 Broadway, New York
175 Remsen St., 196 Montague St., B'klyn
350 Fulton St., Jamaica
67 Jackson Ave., Long Island City

Can You Save ? $3.72 a Month •

ON payments as low as $3.72 a month you can buy a 5½% Guaranteed First Mortgage Certificate—and each payment will draw full 5½% interest.

These Certificates are issued under rigid State regulations. They make you actual part owner in absolute First Mortgages on selected real estate.

These mortgages are never taken for over 50% of valuation and the appraiser is appointed by the State. These mortgages are also covered by Policies of Mortgage Insurance backed by a $2,500,000 Capital.

Certificates in $100 multiples. Ask for Booklet "B."

UNDER STATE SUPERVISION

MORTGAGE GUARANTEE CO.

Fully-Paid Capital $2,500,000

626 So. Spring

Guaranteed-Certified

It makes a great difference when you invest your money whether you, yourself, take the risk of ever seeing it again or whether its return is guaranteed by someone able to 'make good his' guarantee.

When you buy a bond you do not get such a guarantee. The risk is yours. When you buy a Guaranteed First Mortgage Certificate you are certified that the risk is wholly on the Bond & Mortgage Guarantee Company.

During the past twenty-eight years more than $750,000,000 of this class of security has been bought in reliance on such guarantee, without the loss of one dollar of principal to an investor or one day's delay in payment of interest.

Bond & Mortgage Guarantee Co.

176 Broadway, New York City
175 Remsen Street, Brooklyn

Figure 3.4   Three advertisements of guaranteed mortgage certificates.

Source: New York Times, Display Ad 5, Jan. 17, 1916, p. 5; Los Angeles Times, Display Ad 47, Jun. 25, 1915, p. 118; New York Times, Display Ad 94, Jan. 11, 1921. p. 19.

As with the farm debentures in the 1880s, the issuers of the mortgage certificates targeted individual investors and, more specifically, smaller individual investors. The advertisements in Figure 3.4 show a variety of claims made by the MBS issuers to assure investors of the securities' safety. The ad in Figure 3.4a cites the investors' prior experience with guaranteed mortgages suggesting that no investor ever lost money on the securities. Of particular interest in Figure 3.4b are the appeals to state regulation and supervision as a means to assure the investors of the safety of the securities. The Mortgage Guarantee Company claimed to issue the securities both "under rigid state regulations" and "under state supervision." These claims created an illusion of government supervision if not endorsement of the securities.

As indicated in Figure 3.4c, the issuers of guaranteed mortgage certificates emphasized the value of the guarantee, arguing that the guarantee made their securities superior to other securities, lacking such guarantees, e.g., the unguaranteed [real estate] bonds. A 1923 *Wall Street Journal* article summarized the discussion of the relative merits of the guaranteed mortgage certificates and the unguaranteed real estate bonds, issued to help finance large commercial building, as the following dialogue between the issuers of the two security types shows. The mortgage insurance companies emphasized the role of guarantees and the high rates of interest offered by their products: "An Investor should choose his bond by noting whether the mortgage company will put all its resources as a guarantee behind the issue it sells, and by the rate of interest which these bonds bear" (*Wall Street Journal*, 1923, p. 5). Representing the views of the real estate bond issuers, the same article asked (p. 5): "In the final analysis, what does your guarantee amount to? Considering your guaranteed mortgages to be contingent liabilities, are your assets sufficient to meet them?" The skepticism of the guarantees expressed in the article proved to be well founded.

While the firms issuing the mortgage certificates claimed to focus on residential mortgages, their mortgage lending activities also included higher-risk lending on commercial real estate and vacant land (Alger, 1934). The mortgage participation certificates issued by the mortgage insurance companies in the 1900s were similar to debentures of the 1880s in that the mortgage insurance companies also designated certain mortgages on their books as backing specific mortgage certificates. However, instead of depositing the documentation for the mortgages backing these certificates with independent trustees, the certificate issuers used their own subsidiaries as both trustees for the mortgage documentation and depositories for collecting the interest and principal payments from the mortgage borrowers (Alger, 1934).

As with the debentures of the 1880s, the MBS issuers exercised control over which mortgages would be included in the certificates' collateral. This control allowed the issuers to select lower quality mortgages (e.g., mortgages on vacant land or commercial properties) as collateral for the certificates. Using practices that echoed those of J.B. Watkins in the 1880s, one criterion that marked mortgages for inclusion in the certificates' collateral was whether investors interested in buying individual mortgages rejected the loans in question. In the words of a vice-president of Long Island Title Guarantee Company:

> When a mortgage couldn't be sold or I had certain objections given me on a certain mortgage, why then the next time a certificate request came in I would check a certificate against it, or if there were any vacant land mortgages, they would undoubtedly be put in certificates.
>
> *(Alger, 1934, p. 95)*

Furthermore, after issuing the securities, the issuers removed higher-quality mortgages from the securities' collateral and replaced them with lower-quality ones. Such replacement would occur when other investors expressed interest in buying the specific loans or when the guaranteeing firms needed to post high-quality collateral to borrow money from the Reconstruction Finance Corporation (RFC)—a federal entity created to provide relief from the Great Depression (Alger, 1934, pp. 118–120).

As with the western mortgage companies of the 1880s, the mortgage insurance companies operated with few regulatory constraints. In theory, the New York State Department of Insurance had regulatory authority over the title insurance companies, issuing guaranteed mortgage certificates in New York. In practice, the department lacked the resources necessary to offer effective supervision and even when the department's inspectors identified problems with the companies' operations, they lacked the authority to order corrective action.

The real estate downturn of the Great Depression resulted in bankruptcies of the vast majority of the mortgage insurance companies and losses for the certificate holders. In a situation reminiscent of the 1880s market, the availability of mortgage financing before the crisis led to a relaxation of lending standards and overlending. As in the 1880s, the amount of mortgages the companies guaranteed dwarfed the companies' capital. Exacerbating the problem of insufficient reserves, the MBS issuers' failure to diversify their investments away from real estate hampered their ability to honor the guarantees.

In both the 1880s and the 1900s, MBS issuers invested the reserves designated for honoring mortgage repayment guarantees in real estate. The lack of diversification away from real estate made the issuers' guarantees and solvency vulnerable to downturns in real estate prices. In both the 1890s market crisis and the Great Depression, as the real estate prices dropped, the companies' assets invested in mortgages depreciated rapidly, thus rendering the companies unable to honor the guarantees embedded in the securities. This combination of issuer insolvency and lower mortgage quality in the securities' collateral translated into losses for MBS investors.

In the aftermath of the Great Depression, the federal government responded to a drop in residential mortgage lending activity by creating a host of government institutions to stabilize and inject liquidity into the mortgage market. These institutions included the Home Owners Loan Corporation (HOLC)—an entity that bought and restructured defaulted loans; the Federal Housing Administration (FHA)—an agency that offered mortgage insurance backed by the federal government; and the Federal National Mortgage Association (FNMA or Fannie Mae)—an agency tasked with buying mortgages from mortgage lenders, thus creating a secondary market for mortgages.

MBS: 1970s Onward

The third MBS market grew out of government efforts to shift the mortgage-market stabilization efforts to the private sector. To this end, in 1968 the U.S. Congress authorized the issuance of MBS bearing the full-faith and credit guarantees of the federal government. The 1968 Housing and Urban Development Act authorized the Government National Mortgage Association (GNMA or Ginnie Mae—an agency of the U.S. government) to guarantee the repayment of MBS collateralized by loans, the repayment of which was either insured by the Federal Housing Administration (FHA) or backed by the Veterans Affairs (VA) administration. The Act left open the exact structure of the securities to be issued: "Securities issued under this subsection may be in the form of debt obligations or trust certificates of beneficial interest, or both" (Housing and Urban Development Act of 1968, [82 STAT], Section 804).[7]

The securities issued under the Act took two forms—mortgage-backed bonds (MBBs), which represented a debt obligation of their issuers, thus resembling the debentures of the 1880s, and pass-through certificates, which represented partial ownership in a pool of mortgages sold by the issuer, thus resembling the mortgage participation certificates of the 1900s. Over time, as both types of securities struggled to attract investors, the line between the debt obligation status of the MBBs and sale of assets status of pass-through certificates became increasingly blurred.

In 1975, savings and loan associations started issuing MBBs not backed by the government guarantees. Purchasing these securities required faith in the credit quality of the issuers. To develop such faith, the MBS issuers posted collateral that exceeded the face value of securities and agreed to replenish the mortgage collateral as borrowers repaid the underlying mortgages. These efforts at collateral management did little to assuage investor concerns about the link between the mortgage collateral and the issuers' balance sheet. In the first two MBS markets, control over the securities' collateral allowed the issuers to replace the higher-quality loans with lower-quality loans, thus diluting the quality of the collateral. In the third MBS market, investors worried that in the event of the issuers' bankruptcy other creditors would claim the cash flows from the high-quality collateral backing the securities.

To address this concern, MBBs issuers separated the securities' collateral from their balance sheets in the next generation of MBBs by setting up shell corporations—separate legal entities to issue the securities. The savings and loan associations transferred the mortgage collateral to the shell corporations; the shell corporations issued the securities and transferred the proceeds of such issuance back to the savings and loan associations. While this move protected the investors from other claimants on the mortgage collateral cash flows, it fully transferred the risks associated with the mortgage collateral to the investors. Thus, effectively, the securities still labeled bonds stopped being the debt obligations of the original mortgage lenders, becoming closer in form to the 1970s pass-through certificates and the mortgage participation certificates of the 1900s.

The pass-through certificates issued in the 1970s represented shares in pools of mortgages and derived their name from passing through the principal and interest payments on mortgages to the investors. The mortgage loans backing the certificates in the 1970s differed from their pre-Depression predecessors. Specifically, the 1970s mortgages featured longer maturities, no prepayment penalties, and monthly payments of principal and interest rather than the semi-annual interest payments and a single payment of principal made by pre-Depression borrowers.[8] This combination of features made the purchase of individual mortgage loans less attractive to both individual and institutional investors.[9] The changes in the mortgage features meant that the certificates conveyed to the investors a stream of monthly payments of principal and interest in unpredictable amounts.

Responding to the concerns of the institutional investors used to processing fixed semi-annual bond interest payments, in 1975 Federal Home Loan Mortgage Corporation (FHLMC or Freddie Mac, a quasi-government agency created to develop the MBS market) introduced pay-through certificates—securities that represented shares in a pool of mortgage assets, but made semi-annual interest and annual principal payments. Freddie Mac's proprietary name for the pay-through certificates was Guaranteed Mortgage Certificates—a name that matched the generic name of the mortgage participation certificates of the 1900s. Echoing the practices of the MBS issuers in the first two MBS markets, Freddie Mac claimed that its securities represented both improvement and novelty, as the ad in Figure 3.5 indicates.

The 1970s pay- and pass-through certificates were structured using inheritance law to avoid the double taxation of the interest and principal received from the mortgage collateral backing the securities. The double taxation would arise if the borrowers' payments counted as taxable income for both the trustee holding the mortgages and the investors holding the certificates. To avoid this situation, the certificates' issuers deposited the mortgages backing the securities into passive trusts— an arrangement that precluded the certificate issuers from changing not just the composition of the collateral, but also the distribution of the cash flows associated with the securities. This structure safeguarded the collateral from the issuers' or the trustees' interference; however, it also passed on the inconveniences associated with investing in mortgages directly to the certificates' investors. These inconveniences included the inability to predict the timing of the mortgages' repayment, making it difficult for the investors to anticipate both the amount of time the securities would remain outstanding and the yield on the securities.[10]

MBS issuers worked around the unpredictability problem by directing the principal payments received by the trustee at different times to different classes (or tranches) of investors. Unable to obtain the desired tax treatment for the resultant securities when issued as pay-through certificates, Freddie Mac opted to issue them as debt obligations—with the security name changing from guaranteed mortgage

Six questions
from institutional investors
and The Answer

The Federal Home Loan Mortgage Corporation
announces the Guaranteed Mortgage Certificate. It's a new kind
of mortgage security. From a pool of residential mortgages.
It's for the institutional investor.

Question No. 1: What institutions will be interested?

The Answer: Pension Funds. Trust Funds. Banks. Insurance Companies. And Thrift Institutions.

Question No. 2: What will make the institutions interested?

The Answer: Several things.
1) The yield is competitive.
2) The return of principal provides cash flow.
3) You get principal returned once a year. This makes it easy to handle.
4) You may hold it for 15 years. Or, depending on the market, you may opt to hold it for the life of the mortgages which is 30 years or less. *It's your option.*

Question No. 3: How safe are Mortgage Certificates?

The Answer: The Federal Home Loan Mortgage Corporation unconditionally guarantees principal and interest on the underlying mortgages.
It also unconditionally warrants the timely payment of interest and minimum annual return of principal on the Mortgage Certificates regardless of the status of any individual mortgage loan.
And, the underlying mortgages are of high quality. They represent large numbers of conventional residential mortgages throughout the United States.

Question No. 4: How does the Mortgage Certificate differ from other mortgage instruments?

The Answer: It pays interest semiannually. It returns principal once a year. You can sell it back to the Federal Home Loan Mortgage Corporation in 15 years, at your option.
If held 15 years, the maximum average life of the investment is 10.5 years.
And it's been tailored for the institutional investor.

Question No. 5: Will it help the economy?

The Answer: Sure. The sale of Mortgage Certificates will provide additional money for mortgages and help those industries heavily dependent on housing.

Question No. 6: Is it "The Answer" to all my institutional money problems?

The Answer: Certainly not. But it was designed for you. It didn't just occur. It was engineered for those institutions that can profitably use cash flow. And the once-a-year principal payment is easy to administer.

● For more information please call your Securities Dealer or send for our brochure and prospectus.

Federal Home Loan Mortgage Corporation
311 First Street, N.W.
Washington, D.C. 20001

Figure 3.5 Advertisement of a Guaranteed Mortgage Certificate issued by the Federal Home Loan Mortgage Corporation (FHLMC or Freddie Mac).

Source: *Wall Street Journal*, Display Ad 72, February 5, 1975, p. 17.

certificates to collateralized mortgage obligations (CMOs). The issuance of CMOs in 1983 blurred the debt obligation line between MBBs and pass-through certificates. The Tax Reform Act of 1986 created Real Estate Mortgage Investment Conduits—a type of MBS that offered investors the tax benefits of investing in debt securities independently of whether the securities' issuer treated the issuance as a debt obligation or as a sale of assets. Effectively, the Act severed the connection between the issuer's accounting treatment of the securities and the tax treatment of the investors (Vinokurova, 2019b).

The issuance of Collateralized Mortgage Obligation (CMO)—a security accepted by the bond investors (Vinokurova, 2018)—was a culmination of a process in which over time, the more bond-like MBS retained the bond label while acquiring more mortgage features. The MBS issuers transferred the tranching tools introduced to increase the predictability of the securities' cash flows in the 1980s to default risk in the 1990s, contributing to the development of a market for non-government insured MBS. Thus, in the third market, the application of private risk management tools that leveraged diversification of risk replaced government guarantees. This market crashed in 2008 because of overlending, which rendered the tranching tools ineffective at protecting investors from default risk (Vinokurova, 2019a).

Similarities across Three MBS Markets

To explore the role played by the failure of institutional memory in the development of the three markets, I will focus my analysis on three important features of the markets—the security design with respect to the securities' debt obligation status, the guarantees offered by the securities' issuers, and the failure to recognize the role played by systemic risks in unraveling the three markets.

Did Securities Constitute Debt Obligations?

The debentures issued by the western mortgage companies in the 1880s differed from the companies' sales of individual mortgage loans inasmuch as the sales of individual loans represented sales of assets, with the loans assigned to the individual investors in the local land records. By contrast, the debentures represented debt obligations of the mortgage companies that were collateralized by mortgages deposited with the companies' trustees. The New York State Superintendent of Banks characterized the debt obligation status of the securities issued by the western farm mortgage companies as follows:

> The form of securities most largely dealt in by the investment companies are mortgages secured by real estate—either farm or city property—and debentures. These latter are securities issued by the company as a personal, direct obligation, the payment of which is secured by depositing with certain persons or corporations, securities in trust, with power in

the trustee to sell and convert these securities into money and apply the money towards the payment of the debentures or the interest thereon, whenever the company fails to meet such payments when due.

(Preston, 1891, p. 9)

The debt obligation status of the securities meant that if the companies failed to make timely payments on the debentures, the creditors could lay claim to the assets of the mortgage companies.

In contrast to the clarity around the debt obligation status of the 1880s debentures, ambiguity surrounded the contractual form of the mortgage participation certificates in the 1900s. The language describing the rights of mortgage certificate investors lacked clarity and varied across the certificates. The ambiguity allowed room for categorizing the certificates either as a sale of assets entitling the investors to fractional ownership of the underlying mortgages, or a secured debt obligation of the issuers (*Columbia Law Review*, 1934, pp. 675–676).

The ambiguity in the 1920s certificates shaped the lessons drawn by the contemporaries from the market's meltdown. Specifically, one lesson drawn from the aftermath of the issuers' bankruptcies was about the undesirability of selling mortgage participations no matter their contractual form. A New York State legislature committee charged with proposing reform of the mortgage banking system attributed the system's failure to the dangers associated with the practice of selling MBS:

> The public investments issued by the mortgage bank are to be general obligations of the bank and not shares or participations in individual mortgages or groups thereof. This is a fundamental requirement of future mortgage financing. *Our experience has shown that the practice of selling shares or participations in individual mortgages or groups, or of selling bonds secured by an individual mortgage or group, is unfair, calculated to deceive the public, and fraught with great danger* [emphasis added].
>
> *(Barker, 1936, p. 6)*

This conclusion points to two important commonalities between the first two MBS markets. First, despite the differences in the debt obligation status, in both markets the securities' issuers exercised control over the composition of the securities' collateral after the security issuance. This control meant that investors could not be certain that the mortgages that originally constituted the collateral of the securities they invested in would remain in the collateral. Second, like the sale of debentures in the first MBS market, the sale of certificates in the second market allowed the issuers to keep the profits from selling the securities on the balance sheet without acknowledging the costs associated with meeting the guarantees of loan performance.

The MBS issuers in the three markets varied in their approaches to whether the securities constituted a debt obligation of the issuers. The western mortgage companies of the 1880s issued debentures—securities that represented obligations of their issuers backed by mortgage collateral. The mortgage insurance companies of the 1900s issued certificates that represented participations in mortgage pools, leaving ambiguous the exact status of the security on the debt obligation dimension. The distinction between whether the securities represented a sale of assets or an obligation of the issuer preoccupied the MBS designers in the third market for almost 18 years, between 1968 and 1986. In all three markets, the distinction was important to the financial health of the securities' issuers who sought to remove the risks associated with the mortgages from their balance sheets.

Role of Repayment Guarantees in Market Development

In all three markets, the issuers sought to assuage investor concerns about risks associated with the mortgages in the securities' collateral by guaranteeing the performance of the loans in the securities' collateral. These guarantees of loan performance played an important role in the investors' decision-making. Promoters of western mortgage investments conceptualized investors' due diligence research as needing to focus on picking the right company and then trusting its guarantees:

> The investor has only one duty to perform, withal a very important one,—viz., *to determine once for all whether the company he is dealing with, by virtue of the character and ability of its officials, its established methods of business, the amount of its capital, and the availability of its assets, is able to give him a good and sufficient guarantee.* That there are such companies, is shown by the fact that hundreds of millions of dollars have been thus invested, without the loss of a dollar of principal or interest; and each year the examinations of these companies made by the Bank Commissioners of the Eastern States, whose savings-banks buy so largely of these loans, and which therefore insist upon these examinations, make this sole duty of the investor a comparatively simple and easy one [emphasis added].
>
> *(McGeorge, 1890, p. 431)*

In the 1900s, MBS issuers framed the guarantees they offered as a form of insurance. Most of the companies offering the participation certificates were originally licensed to sell title insurance and were regulated by the New York State Department of Insurance. However, the market's crash made obvious that the guarantees offered by the companies had little in common with other lines of insurance:

> Guaranteeing payment of principal of a mortgage has been enormously profitable, but *although it was considered to be a form of insurance, there was absolutely no actuarial basis upon which it rested.* There were no restrictions whatsoever in the law limiting the size of the guarantee of an individual mortgage in relation to total capital funds, and there was no requirement that total guarantee liability should be restricted to a certain number of times capital funds [emphasis added].
>
> *(Weil, 1933, p. RE1)*

The guarantee of interest and principal payments offered by the issuers tied the mortgage participation certificates to the financials of the mortgage insurance companies.

Although some experts were aware of the guarantees' limitations, the guarantees also played an important role in shaping the investor decision-making in the 1920s. The degree of disillusionment with the promise of guarantees attests to the public's prior faith in the instruments:

> The public has learned that there is no magic in the fact that a mortgage certificate was guaranteed. *There was an extraordinary amount of misunderstanding of the value as an investment of a guaranteed mortgage participation certificate.* There were many who believed that it was a legal investment for trust funds and infants because it was guaranteed. This is not the law. Such an investment was legal because it represented a first mortgage on unencumbered real estate and not because it was guaranteed. An unguaranteed mortgage certificate would be legal for trust funds provided the mortgage did not exceed two-thirds of the appraised value of the mortgaged property. A mortgage certificate would not be legal for trust funds, even though guaranteed, it the mortgage exceeded two-thirds of the appraised value of the mortgaged property [emphasis added].
>
> *(Weil, 1933, p. RE1)*

As this quote suggests, investors erroneously saw the guarantee as a prerequisite to making certificates a legal form of investment in the second MBS market.

Mortgage repayment guarantees were an important factor for attracting investors to MBS in the third market. The discussion of security design prior to the securities' issuance recognized the value of a government guarantees: "A Federally guaranteed debenture would overcome all of these problems and prove attractive to all lenders" (President's Committee on Urban Housing, 1968, p. 132). The MBS market that emerged in the 1970s originally relied on the default risk guarantees offered by the federal government. Chuck Graham, the treasurer of California employees' pension funds, described his interest in GNMA pass-through certificates as follows: "I like them because they have virtually a double guarantee. The underlying mortgages are guaranteed by the FHA or the VA, and interest and principal are guaranteed by the U.S. government" (Clowes, 1978, p. 19).

While the federal government offered investors protection from default risk of the securities in the third market, there was no protection from prepayment risk—the risk that mortgage borrowers would repay their loans before maturity date.[11] To help protect investors from this risk, the market participants developed tranching—a set of tools that directed the cash flows from the collateral to different groups of investors. These tools took on an important role in the development of the MBS market, first by attracting bond investors' capital to MBS and then in creating the market for non-government-backed MBS in which tranching tools replaced government guarantees for default risk. The replacement of government guarantees with private guarantees played an important role in the unraveling of the third MBS market.

Failure to Recognize the Systemic Risk

Tranching tools that protected investors from risks inherent in MBS from 1980s onwards relied explicitly on risk diversification to offer investors protection first from prepayment and then from default risk. These tools failed first in 1994 and then in 2008 because they relied on the assumption that the borrower behavior was subject to idiosyncratic rather than systemic risk (Vinokurova, 2019a). Systemic risk in these markets stemmed from the development of MBS markets inducing a high degree of correlation in borrower behavior and real estate prices.

A growth in this correlation translated into systemic risks that played an important role in unraveling all three markets. The development of all three markets followed the same trajectory. First, the mortgage securities attracted capital to financing mortgages. Then, easier access to mortgage financing drove competition among lenders, leading to overlending that triggered real estate price inflation and speculation. Overlending resulted in riskier mortgages that were more sensitive to downturns in housing prices, rendering the securities less safe. Recognition of the risks inherent in the securities led to investor flight out of the markets and a downturn in the housing prices.

In all three crises, those who tried explaining what happened framed the problem as the actions of individuals rather than the system as a whole. In the first market, this problem was framed as one of reckless practices by individual companies:

> Those who have investigated the matter for themselves, however, well know that the companies referred to have failed, *not because of any inherent weakness in the system itself,* but because of the reckless practices of the companies concerned, which were brought to light in the investigations which followed their default [emphasis added].
>
> *(McGeorge, 1890, pp. 432–433)*

The focus on the individuals precluded market observers from diagnosing the systematic weaknesses and the potential for systematic remedies to such weaknesses.

The extent to which contemporaries of the first market pointed out the needed improvements, they saw listing the securities on an exchange as a way to draw the scrutiny of institutional investors:

> And the bonds themselves are not as attractive as investments as the railroad loans, because they are not listed, and so are not readily convertible into cash. Nor can it be doubted that the listing of the bonds has the effect of directing the attention of the bondholders to the affairs of the companies far more effectively than when each bond owner is acting singly for himself. It is after all a very simple matter to investigate the affairs of a loan company. Having a list of the borrowers from the trustees, the

examination of a few of the loans will soon show how these have been made. The expense is the only obstacle, at present, preventing the holder of one or two bonds from doing this for himself, an expense which would be nominal when many bondholders participated. The recent failure of a few well known American companies must largely be attributed to speculation by the managers, which they would never have dared to commence in case their bonds had been subject to the vigilant scrutiny of the Wall Street speculators.

(Frederiksen, 1894, pp. 216–218)

This quote suggests that the failure to list the debentures on public exchanges made the securities less attractive not just compared to individual mortgages, but also to other securities listed on the exchanges.

In discussing improvements to the safety of the system, observers of the second MBS market cited individual companies' experience of adopting safeguards in issuing guarantees as insufficient to secure the system:

A negligible number of companies pursued certain rules based on an arbitrary ratio [of outstanding mortgage guarantees to the company's capital] and not on experience. One of the largest companies limited its total guarantee liability to twenty times its capital funds, but beyond that there was no basis for the formulation of rules.

(Weil, 1933, p. RE1)

The above quote highlights the few security issuers' attempts at self-imposed safeguards in contrast to the lack of care exercised by the other MBS issuers.

As the issuance of private-label, non-government-backed securities took on a greater role in the lead-up to the 2008 crisis, the credit ratings assigned to the resultant securities created an impression of equivalence between guarantees issued by private parties and the federal government (MacKenzie, 2011). This equivalence obscured from view an important difference between the two types of guarantee: private guarantees suitable for protecting investors from idiosyncratic risk and government guarantees capable of withstanding systematic risks.

In the first two MBS markets, the mortgage companies invested the assets that were supposed to back the mortgage payment guarantees they provided in land, mortgages, and real estate, underappreciating the systemic nature of the risk associated with a downturn in real estate markets. In the third market, the risk-management models assumed low correlation in default risk among the mortgages in the pools backing the securities and across the pools (MacKenzie, 2011). In all three markets, the possibility of creating private insurance solutions for systematic risks outlived the securities in question. Rather than convincing fellow entrepreneurs of the impossibility of such insurance, 1890 saw proposals for creating an insurance company to insure these risks (*American Hebrew*, 1890) and tranching—a form of private insurance— outlived the 2008 market (Vinokurova, 2019a).

Discussion and Conclusion

The structures of the MBS securities in the three markets described above share important commonalities that point to a lack of institutional memory in the system. Despite the crises following each of the three markets, the MBS issuers persisted in their experiments with the debt obligation status of the securities, claiming that the diversification inherent in the mortgage pool lowered the risks associated with MBS, and leveraging the illusion of government supervision in issuing the securities. Furthermore, the securities' issuers persistently failed to recognize the systemic risks inherent in real estate lending and investing.

Indeed, MBS issuers' persistence in structuring the securities is remarkable, given important changes in the institutional environment that took place in the period between the disappearance of the second MBS market and the appearance of the third. These included changes in the structure of the dominant mortgage loan from a 3–5 year non-amortizing loan with semi-annual payments to a 30-year amortizing loan with monthly payments, the targeting of institutional rather than individual investors, and, finally, complete turnover of the MBS issuers—no MBS issuer was active in any two of the three markets. Arguably, these changes in the structure of the institutional environment make it difficult to make the case that the MBS markets benefited from the existence of an institutional memory.

If not institutional memory, what then explains the persistence of the MBS structures across the three generations of the securities? One important aspect of the institutional environment that remained unchanged across the three markets is the lax regulation of mortgage lending and MBS issuance in the U.S. and fragmented regulatory structure that lacked either a centralized exchange or a single regulatory authority. Management scholars have hypothesized that regulatory regimes make room for individual market participants' actions (Funk and Hirschman, 2014). The analysis above is consistent with Snowden's (1995) and Simkovic's (2013) suggestion that the regulatory regime of the U.S. MBS markets may account for the persistence of the MBS issuers' practices. The coordination mechanisms missing from the state institutional framework provided were not made up by private coordination efforts.

The absence of coordination mechanisms contributed to the crises that ended the MBS markets on two levels. On one level the lack of coordination among MBS investors hindered both the effective monitoring of the MBS issuance practices and the resolution of mortgage defaults in the collateral. In the absence of institutions facilitating collective action such as the listing of the securities on an exchange, investors across the three markets were not able to observe and put a halt to the deterioration in the lending standards. In case of security default, triggered by defaults of mortgages in the securities' collateral the existence of multiple investors in the same pool of mortgages hindered the speedy resolution of the foreclosures—a collective action problem that became more evident as the mortgage defaults multiplied. Following a period of lackluster crops western mortgagors defaulted *en masse* leading the observers of the 1880s markets to comment that "the investor under the debenture system is without speedy remedy. He is part of a series. He cannot move independently" (Gleed, 1890, p. 105). To address the collective action problem associated with the widespread foreclosures in the aftermath of the Great Depression, the New York State Superintendent of Insurance formed the Mortgage Protection Corporation that coordinated the actions of the multiple holders of the certificates (Weil, 1933). Such collective action problems were also evident in the aftermath of the 2008 crisis, when loan securitization status affected homeowners' ability to obtain mortgage modifications.

The second level of a missing coordination mechanism is between the primary (mortgage lending) and secondary (MBS issuance) markets. Coordination at this level could have informed the investors about how changes in the secondary market affect the practices of the participants in the first. Investing in MBS required investor faith in the MBS issuers' efficacy of managing the risks associated with mortgage lending. The MBS issuers' efforts to manage the risk relied on risk diversification stemming from the securities collateral consisting of multiple loans. As more investor capital poured into MBS, this influx increased the availability of lending capital. The availability of lending capital led to real estate speculation and riskier lending— thus, lowering the overall quality of borrowers and raising the level of systemic risk in the system. The mortgage portfolio diversification that was effective in insuring against the idiosyncratic risk of the individual mortgages could not overcome this rise in systemic risk. In all three markets, the MBS market development drew capital to the mortgage market, leading to changes in the lending standards, overlending, and the subsequent crises.

Exacerbating the absence of coordination mechanisms in the system was MBS issuers' reliance on the illusion of government oversight. Investors interpreted the issuers' claims of government oversight as stringent governmental controls that could have provided the coordination mechanisms described above. In the western farm mortgage market, the banking regulators of eastern states started auditing the western mortgage companies soliciting investors in their state. While the regulators disavowed any knowledge of the quality of the underlying mortgages, their work lent credibility to the securities issuers by creating the impression of government scrutiny of the mortgage companies' operation. In the second MBS market, the title insurance companies operated under the supervision of the New York State Department of Insurance. Despite the companies advertising such supervision, the insurance department lacked the staff and the expertise necessary to conduct regular audits of the companies. The participation of (quasi-)government agencies including Ginnie Mae, Fannie Mae, and Freddie Mac in the third market similarly translated the agencies' status into an illusion of government oversight.

Implications for the Study of Financial Markets

The analysis of the similarities and differences across the three MBS markets allows insight into the role played by the failure of institutional memory in the development of financial instruments. The three markets share institutional similarities— most importantly a collective action problem facing MBS investors due to a lack of a centralized exchange for trading the securities, lack of transparency of the securities' collateral, and limited government oversight over security issuance. These similarities led to the persistence of the security structures this chapter documents. Moreover, it is not clear that the market participants in the second and third markets were aware of the prior experiments with securitization. The market participants in the third market who knew about the drastic reductions in house price values during the Great Depression framed the recurrence of such reductions as an unlikely event. The decision-making of the firms and regulators devising the new securities for the third market reflects no awareness of the MBS issuance in the 1880s or 1920s (Ross, 1989).

One of the issues raised by this account is whether investing in MBS offers better returns compared to investing in either individual mortgage loans or other, publicly listed securities. In the first two markets, more sophisticated investors opted for holding individual loans instead of the securities on offer (Alger, 1934; Frederiksen, 1894). In the third market, a combination of federal guarantees and risk management tools grounded in risk diversification attracted institutional investors to the market. The presence of these sophisticated investors did not resolve the issues that plagued the earlier MBS markets.

My analysis identifies two challenges faced by market participants in learning from the crises: 1) drawing the right lessons and 2) remembering the lessons drawn. The re-emergence of the MBS markets in the U.S. is symptomatic of failure on both fronts. All three markets suffered from a lack of regulatory supervision, lack of transparency into the security collateral, and lack of appreciation for the systemic risks inherent in MBS issuance. The former two issues were evident to market contemporaries in the first two markets, but not remedied in the third market. The third issue continues to affect the market.

This analysis suggests that memory plays a crucial role for preventing the recurrence of financial crises. Even if the right lessons are drawn, without memory for what lessons triggered institutional change in the crisis aftermath, this change can be reversed, allowing for crisis recurrence. The repeal of the Glass–Steagall Act in 1999 is an example of what happens when the passage of time erases the memory of why institutional change was necessary. Persistence of institutional change in the aftermath of financial crises requires a combination of institutional change and a means to preserve the memory of the connection between the change and the events the change is meant to forestall.

The case examined in this chapter illustrates the relationship between institutional memory and financial crises. Failure to identify, remedy, and memorialize the connection between the financial instrument and its consequences in the aftermath of a crisis enables institutional forgetting and, consequently, crisis recurrence. The conditions that enable the re-emergence of financial instruments and the associated crises are the persistence of the institutional framework and a failure of institutional memory for the instruments' prior performance. Absent changes in the institutional setting, the re-emergence of securities that failed in previous markets will produce the same failure. The failure of memory allows the financial instruments that failed in the past to reemerge. Treating the re-emergence of these instruments as innovations forgoes and forecloses learning from the past, setting the stage for the next crisis.

Finally, this chapter has implications for the role played by anthropology and history in the study of management. Specifically, historical analysis offers lessons with the benefit of hindsight, uncovering the process of institutional evolution over time. The cyclical nature of the management field's attention to collecting facts and the extent to which crises trigger such attention is part of a self-reinforcing mechanism. Forgetting the events of the past results in re-emergence of practices that brought about past crises. An appreciation for the role of history could forestall such crises. Arguably, a similar dynamic holds for the study of anthropology. Abstractions from a nuanced understanding of market participants' beliefs and practices embedded in the theories of human behavior lead to practices that rely on assumptions hidden in the theories. Crises highlight these limitations, reestablishing the value of anthropological research in the management field.

Acknowledgements

I am grateful to Zack Kertcher for many productive conversations about this chapter, Anne-Laure Fayard, Mary O'Sullivan, Neil Trenk, Marc Ventresca, the participants of the 2019 Business History Conference and the 2019 Smith Entrepreneurship Research Conference for helpful suggestions, to Lynn Selhat for editorial assistance and to Thomas Splettstoesser for his help with the graphics.

Notes

1 The process of abstraction from facts to stylized facts has been documented in sociology (Mizruchi and Fein, 1999), economics (Coase, 2000), and the work of management consultants (McKenna, 2009). In the case of history and anthropology, such abstraction contributes to the erasure of an appreciation of the disciplines' contributions.

2 My discussion of epistemic cycles is distinct from Kuhn's (1962) analysis of paradigm shifts. Kuhn focuses on the emergence and decline of theories, while the epistemic cycles I describe focus on methods of inquiry. A change in the popularity of methods can occur without new theory emergence. For instance, the popularity of experimental methods in economics is yet to produce a new theoretical paradigm (Quiggin, 2010). My conceptualization of an epistemic cycle is closer to Fleck's (1979) idea that theories cycle from postulation to justification and back.

3 Snowden (1995) argued that such continuity had to do with the European governments stepping in to relieve the crises that occurred in the markets in a way that preserved the integrity of mortgage lending institutions.

4 These periodicals ranged from religious and regional newspapers in the earlier periods including *American Hebrew*, *Chicago Daily Tribune*, *Christian Union*, *Los Angeles Times*, *New York Evangelist*, and *Philadelphia Inquirer* to national newspapers in later periods, i.e., *New York Times*, *Wall Street Journal*, and *Washington Post*. For the third market, I supplement my analysis of the structure of the securities with reading the securities' prospectuses or offering circulars filed with the Securities and Exchange Commission (SEC) and the Federal Home Loan Bank Board (FHLBB).

5 In the 1880s, these included the reports of the Connecticut, Massachusetts, and New York banking regulators. In the 1900s, these were the Banking and Insurance Departments of the State of New York. In the 1970s, these included the FHLBB, SEC, the Office of the Comptroller of the Currency (OCC), the Office of Thrift Supervision (OTS), the Federal Reserve, and the Federal Deposit Insurance Corporation (FDIC), among others.

6 The discussion of the 1880s market draws on Frederiksen (1894), Bogue (1955) and Snowden (1995); the 1900s—Alger (1934); and 1970s onwards—my own research (Vinokurova, 2018, 2019a, 2019b).

7 The act reflected the challenges to the Johnson administration's issuance of participation certificates in assets of various federal agencies including Fannie Mae to get around the debt ceiling (Quinn, 2010). Members of the U.S. Congress challenged these attempts, observing that the federal government remained liable for the risks associated with the assets while raising funds more expensively than if the obligations were issued by the U.S. Treasury.

8 The government institutions created in the wake of the Great Depression popularized changes in the structure of residential mortgages.

9 Individual investors who provided 50% of the funding for residential mortgages before the Great Depression were almost entirely out of the market by the 1950s.

10 This inconvenience also affected investors in pay-through bonds. Once the mortgage collateral moved off the balance sheet of the issuer, the timing of the securities' repayment and, consequently, their yield, was guesswork.

11 This risk was less problematic for the first two MBS markets because of shorter maturities of the mortgages and the availability of prepayment penalties.

References

Abbott, A. D. (2004), *Methods of Discovery: Heuristics for the Social Sciences*, W.W. Norton & Co., New York.

Abolafia, M. (1996), *Making Markets: Opportunism and Restraint on Wall Street*, Harvard University Press, Cambridge, MA.

Alger, G. (1934), *Report on the Operation, Conduct, and Management of Title and Mortgage Guarantee Corporations*, State of New York, Albany, NY.

American Hebrew. (1890), "Insurance", May 9, p. 17.

Barker, W. P. (1936), *Why Mortgage Banks?* Lyon, Albany, NY.

Bogue, A. G. (1955), *Money at Interest: The Farm Mortgage on the Middle Border*, Cornell University Press, Ithaca, NY.

Brewer, H. P. (1976), "Eastern money and western mortgages in the 1870s", *Business History Review*, Vol. 50, No. 3, pp. 356–380.

Chandler, A. D. (1962), *Strategy and Structure: Chapters in the History of American Industrial Enterprises*, MIT Press, Cambridge, MA.

Christian Union. (1886), "Debenture bonds", Oct. 21, p. 30.

Clowes, M. (1978), "Funds like mortgage-backed securities even with their funny names", *Pensions & Investments*, Jun. 5, pp. 19, 33.

Coase, R. H. (2000), "The acquisition of Fisher Body by General Motors", *Journal of Law and Economics*, Vol. 43, No. 1, pp. 15–32.

Columbia Law Review. (1934), "Present problems in New York guaranteed mortgages", Vol. 34, pp. 663–706.

Fayard, A. L., and Metiu, A. (2014), "The role of writing in distributed collaboration", *Organization Science*, Vol. 25, No. 3, pp. 1391–1413.

Fleck, L. (1979), *Genesis and Development of a Scientific Fact*, trans. F. Bradley & T. J. Trenn, University of Chicago Press, Chicago, IL.

Frederiksen, D. M. (1894), "Mortgage banking in America", *Journal of Political Economy*, Vol. 2, No. 2, pp. 203–234.

Funk, R. J., and Hirschman, D. (2014), "Derivatives and deregulation: Financial innovation and the demise of Glass–Steagall", *Administrative Science Quarterly*, Vol. 59, No. 4, pp. 669–704.

Gleed, J. W. (1890), "Western mortgages", *Forum*, Mar., pp. 94–105.

Griswold, C., and Goodrich, S. (1890), *Report of the Bank Commissioners of the State of Connecticut to the Governor*, Press of the Case, Lockwood, and Brainard Company, Hartford, CT.

Ho, K. (2009), *Liquidated: An Ethnography of Wall Street*, Duke University Press, Durham, NC.

Khurana, R. (2010), *From Higher Aims to Hired Hands: The Social Transformation of American Business Schools and the Unfulfilled Promise of Management as a Profession*, Princeton University Press, Princeton, NJ

Kipping, M., Wadhwani, R. D., and Bucheli, M. (2014), "Analyzing and interpreting historical sources: A basic methodology", in Bucheli M. and Wadhwani R. D. (Eds), *Organizations in Time*, Oxford University Press, Oxford, pp. 305–329.

Knorr Cetina, K., and Bruegger, U. (2002), "Global microstructures: The virtual societies of financial markets", *American Journal of Sociology*, Vol. 107, No. 4, pp. 905–950.

Krugman, P. (2009), "How did economists get it so wrong?", *New York Times*, Sept. 6, MM36.

Kuhn, T. S. (1962), *Structure of Scientific Revolutions*, University of Chicago Press, Chicago, IL.

Landers, G. M., and Noble, C. H. (1888), *Report of the Connecticut Bank Commissioners*, Press of the Case, Lockwood, and Brainard Company, Hartford, CT.

———. (1889), *Report of the Bank Commissioners of the State of Connecticut to the Governor*, Press of the Case, Lockwood, and Brainard Company, Hartford, CT.

Lewis, M. (1990), *Liar's Poker*, Penguin Books, New York.

———. (2010), *The Big Short: Inside the Doomsday Machine*, W.W. Norton & Co., New York.

MacKenzie, D. (2011), "The credit crisis as a problem in the sociology of knowledge", *American Journal of Sociology*, Vol. 116, No. 6, pp. 1778–1841.

———, and Millo, Y. (2003), "Constructing a market, performing theory: The historical sociology of a financial derivatives exchange", *American Journal of Sociology*, Vol. 109, No. 1, pp. 107–145.

McGeorge, W., Jr. (1890), "Western mortgages", *Lippincott's Monthly Magazine*, Mar., pp. 426–435.

McKenna, C. (2009), "Mementos: looking backwards at the Honda Motorcycle case, 2003–1973", in Clarke S. H., Lamoreaux N. R., and Usselman S. W. (Eds), *The Challenge of Remaining Innovative: Insights from Twentieth-Century American Business*, Stanford University Press, Palo Alto, CA, pp. 219–242.

Mizruchi, M. S., and Fein, L. C. (1999), "The social construction of organizational knowledge: A study of the uses of coercive, mimetic, and normative isomorphism", *Administrative Science Quarterly*, Vol. 44, No. 4, pp. 653–683.

Morey, N. C., and Luthans, F. (1987), "Anthropology: The forgotten behavioral science in management history", *Academy of Management Proceedings*, No. 1, pp. 128–132. Academy of Management, Briarcliff Manor, NY.

New York Evangelist. (1886), "Farmer's department: Western farm mortgages", Oct. 7, p. 7.

Philadelphia Inquirer. (1886), "Equitable mortgage company", Jun. 22, p. 8.

Poon, M. (2009), "From New Deal institutions to capital markets: Commercial consumer risk scores and the making of subprime mortgage finance", *Accounting, Organizations and Society*, Vol. 34, No. 5, pp. 654–674.

President's Committee on Urban Housing. (1968), *The Report of the President's Committee on Urban Housing: A Decent Home*, U.S. Government Printing Office, Washington, DC.

Preston, C. M. (1891), *First Annual Report of the Superintendent of the Banking Department Relative to Foreign, Mortgage, Loan, Investment and Trust Companies*, James B. Lyon, State Printer, Albany, NY.

Quiggin, J. (2010), *Zombie Economics*, Princeton University Press, Princeton, NJ.

Quinn, S. L. (2010), *Government Policy, Housing, and the Origins of Securitization, 1780–1968* (Doctoral dissertation, UC Berkeley).

Ross, W. B. (1989), "The evolution of mortgage-backed securities", in Lederman J. (Ed.), *Mortgage Banking*, Probus Publishing, Chicago, IL, pp. 307–318.

Simkovic, M. (2013), "Competition and crisis in mortgage securitization", *Indiana Law Journal*, Vol. 88, pp. 213–271.

Snowden, K. A. (1995), "Mortgage securitization in the United States: Twentieth century developments in historical perspective", in Bordo M. D. and Sylla R. E. (Eds), *Anglo-American Financial Systems: Institutions and Markets in the Twentieth Century*, Irwin Professional Publishing, Burr Ridge, IL, pp. 261–298.

Sparks, E. (1932), *History and Theory of Agricultural Credit in the United States*, Thomas Y. Crowell Company, New York.

Tett, G. (2009), *Fool's Gold: How Unrestrained Greed Corrupted a Dream, Shattered Global Markets and Unleashed a Catastrophe*. Hachette, London.

Vinokurova, N. (2018), "How mortgage-backed securities became bonds: The emergence, evolution, and acceptance of mortgage-backed securities in the U.S. 1960–1987", *Enterprise and Society*, Vol. 19, No. 3, pp. 610–660.

———. (2019a), "Failure to learn from failure: The 2008 mortgage crisis as a déjà vu of the mortgage meltdown of 1994", *Business History*, Vol. 61, No. 6, pp. 1005–1050.

———. (2019b), "Reshaping demand landscapes: How firms change customers' preferences to better fit their products", *Strategic Management Journal*, Vol. 40, No. 13, pp. 2107–2137.

Wall Street Journal. (1923), "Realty mortgage bond rivalries: Guaranteed mortgage certificates", Dec. 12, p. 5.

Weil, F. I. (1933), "Mortgage business put on a new basis", *New York Times*, Aug. 13, p. RE1.

Zaloom, C. (2006), *Out of the Pits: Traders and Technology from Chicago to London*, University of Chicago Press, Chicago, IL.

4

WHAT GOOD IS THE ETHNOGRAPHIC INTERVIEW?

John Weeks[1]

Introduction

In 1979, James Spradley (1979) published a small book entitled *The Ethnographic Interview*. In the past 40 years, it has been cited nearly 15,000 times by researchers who, for one reason or another, wanted to distinguish the interviews they have done as being ethnographic. What have we learned in that time about the sense in which interviews can be more or less ethnographic and about the relationship between participant observation—generally recognized as the ethnographic method par excellence (Van Maanen 2006, 14)—and interviewing? Are we in danger of the label "ethnographic" losing its descriptive power and becoming merely an honorific in qualitative research in organizations (Gans 1999, 541)? Or is the bigger risk that, haunted by the ghost of Bronislaw Malinowski (Forsey 2010a, 65), we unfairly malign some very good interview-based studies of culture in organizations by superstitiously insisting they can't be called ethnographies? Much is riding on this in the sense that what we gain in time and flexibility by doing even extensive interviewing, rather than devoting a continuous year or more full-time in the field, is enormous and should not be underestimated. For academics who are neither graduate students nor on sabbatical, the question of whether interviews and short observations can count as sufficient field work to serve as the basis of ethnography may be the question of whether ethnography can be done it all. Yet I will argue in this chapter that cleanly distinguishing participant observation and ethnographic interviewing is not as straightforward as it might seem, particularly when each is done well. It is when they are done poorly that the differences between the two methods are most evident but also least interesting.

What Is an Ethnographic Interview?

Spradley (1979) doesn't precisely define *ethnographic interview*—or, seen another way, he devotes an entire book to very precisely explaining what an ethnographic interview is by giving examples and showing the reader how to do one. He is pithy, though, when defining *ethnography*. "Ethnography is the work of describing a culture" (Spradley 1979, iii). We can infer that an ethnographic interview with a member of a culture is an interview that helps us to describe that culture. This way of defining ethnography is important. There are many different definitions of ethnography and they fall into two types. There are definitions that conflate the product and the method of cultural study and those that treat them separately (Hockey and Forsey 2012, 69). If you define doing ethnography as living among the natives for a year or more and writing about their culture, then the idea of ethnographic interviews is oxymoronic. If, however, like Van Maanen (1988, 1), you define an ethnography as "written representation of a culture (or selected aspects of a culture)," then we can have an interesting discussion about the possibilities of ethnographic interviewing. "Ethnography," Van Maanen (1988, 4) argues,

> is the result of fieldwork, but it is the written report that must represent the culture, not the fieldwork itself. Ethnography as a written product, then, has a degree of independence (how the culture is portrayed) from the fieldwork on which it is based (how culture is known).

This is in line with Geertz, who puts it this way:

> From one point of view, that of the textbook, doing ethnography is establishing rapport, selecting informants, transcribing texts, taking genealogies, mapping fields, keeping a diary, and so on. But it is not these things, techniques and received procedures, that define the enterprise. What defines it is the kind of intellectual effort it is: an elaborate venture in, to borrow a notion from Gilbert Ryle, "thick description."
>
> *(Geertz 1973, 6)*

Famously, Ryle (2009 [1968]) compared the thin description of two boys rapidly constricting their eyelids with the thick description of one boy with an involuntary twitch and another boy who is winking. Ethnography as thick description is a "construction of other people's constructions of what they and their compatriots are up to" (Geertz 1973, 9). Or, as Van Maanen explains, organizational ethnography aims "to uncover and explicate the ways in which people in particular work settings come to understand, account for, take action, and otherwise manage their day-to-day situation" (Van Maanen 1983, 39). The question then becomes: to what extent is it possible to do this uncovering and explicating and thick describing on the basis of interviews?

A Comparison of Participant Observation and Interviewing

"The most complete form of the sociological datum, after all, is the form in which participant observation gathers it," Becker and Geer (1957, 28) wrote in their seminal comparison of participant observation and interviewing.

> An observation of some social event, the events which precede and follow it, and explanations of its meaning by participants and spectators, before, during, and after its occurrence. Such a datum gives us more information about the event under study than data gathered by any other sociological method.
>
> *(Becker and Geer 1957, 28)*

Their definition of participant observation makes clear why they find it so obvious that participant observation is more complete than interviewing:

> By participant observation we mean that method in which the observer participates in the daily life of the people under study, either openly in the role of researcher or covertly in some disguised role, observing things that happen, listening to what is said, and questioning people, over some length of time.
>
> *(Becker and Geer 1957, 28)*

Participant observation includes questioning people. It includes too, as Becker and Geer (1958, 39) add in a rejoinder published a year later, "private conversations with members of the group under observation [that are] in many ways the functional equivalent of an interview and can be used to get the same sort of information."

This makes sense. As Van Maanen (1983, 43) puts it, "fieldwork, despite the best intentions of the researcher almost always boils down to a series of endless conversations intersected by a few major events and a host of less formidable ones." Participant observation is mainly conversation. In both anthropology and sociology, most participant observation data is gathered through informal interviews and supplemented by observation (Lofland and Lofland 1995, 18). Fieldworkers "collect droppings of talk" (Moerman 1988, 8) and then fertilize their ethnographies with quotes. Forsey (2010a, 74), describing the results of his study showing that ethnographers report more of what they hear in the field than what they observe, argues that "engaged listening" is as important as, and maybe a better label than, "participant observation."

Participant observation, then, includes interviewing. It is bigger than interviewing. Interviewing is impoverished by comparison. Interviewing could have no advantage over participant observation because whatever advantage it might have—aside from a savings of time and energy—would automatically accrue to participant observation as well. From this point of view, researchers should limit themselves to interviewing only as a second choice imposed by force of circumstance

(Hockey 2002, 209). Framed this way, Becker and Geer's (1957, 28) argument that "participant observation can thus provide us with a yardstick against which to measure the completeness of data gathered in other ways, a model which can serve to let us know what orders of information escape us when we use other methods," is unassailable (Atkinson and Coffey 2003, 418).

Advantages of Conducting Interviews in the Context of Participant Observation

The value of participant observation, then, at least in part, is that it allows us to do interviewing better. Fieldworkers gain three advantages from conducting their interviews in the context of participant observation: they are able to ask better questions, get better answers, and better interpret the answers they get.

First, doing participant observation allows interviewers to ask better questions because being there, "living with and living like those who are studied" (Van Maanen 1988, 2), they see things to ask about. Ethnography is about attending to mundane detail. "Usually of most interest is what is unremarkable to participants" (Silverman 2014, 447). The participant observer sees things, and can ask about things, that would never occur to the interviewee to volunteer. Describing his study of the police, Van Maanen says:

> informants are sometimes totally unaware of certain aspects underlying many of their own activities. Like fish who are presumably unaware of the water in which they swim, there are things associated with police work that all policemen take more or less for granted and therefore have a hard time articulating.
>
> *(Van Maanen 1983, 47–8)*

These are things that won't come up in response to "grand tour" questions recommended by Spradley (1979, 87) for ethnographic interviews, like, "Could you describe a typical night at Brady's Bar?" The interviewer has to know to ask about them.

Second, participant observation helps the interviewer get better answers because fieldwork provides the time and opportunity to build rapport with those being studied. Spradley (1979, 51) says about ethnographically interviewing an informant, "at a minimum, it will take six to seven one-hour interviews, so it is important to estimate whether a potential informant has adequate time to participate." This is long, longer than found in most interview studies. Longer even than what Jackall (1988) did in his excellent interview-based ethnography, *Moral Mazes*. Jackall interviewed 143 people, with each interview lasting between two and three hours, some much longer (Jackall 1988, 205). He re-interviewed more than a quarter and many of those a third and fourth time. It takes time for an interviewee to feel comfortable enough to open up and lower their defenses. It takes time for the interviewee to explore with the researcher the meanings they place on events in their world. Participant observation affords time with informants because you are living with them. Informal interviews can be done here and there as activities permit. And asking an informant to take time for a private, more formal interview, may not be such a big request when they have already accepted your presence as a participant observer.

Much has been written about the third advantage of doing interviews in the context of participant observation: a better ability to interpret what interviewees say. This interpretative advantage comes in two forms: a sensitivity to what the interviewee is trying to say and an ability to compare what interviewees say with what they do. Becker and Geer (1957, 29) note the peculiar difficulty that is created by studying groups close to home: the researcher speaks the language. Anthropologists going off to study a people whose language they have to learn before they can possibly interview anybody are aware of the likelihood of misunderstanding.

> But in speaking American English with an interviewee who is, after all, much like us, we may mistakenly assume that we have understood him and the error be small enough that it will not disrupt communication to the point where a correction will be in order.
>
> The interview provides little opportunity of rectifying errors of this kind where they go unrecognized. In contrast, participant observation provides a situation in which the meanings of words can be learned with great precision through study of their use in context, exploration through continuous interviewing of their implications and nuances, and the use of them oneself under the scrutiny of capable speakers of the language.
>
> *(Becker and Geer 1957, 29)*

Becker and Geer give the example from their ethnography of medical students, *Boys in White* (1961), of the word "crock," which was a derogatory term for a patient who complains of many symptoms but has no discoverable organic pathology. They do admit that a skillful interviewer might have been able to uncover the use of the word "crock," its subtle meaning, and its significance in a culture of medical school students who see patients primarily as objects from which they can learn. Indeed, Spradley (1979, 21) says that *The Ethnographic Interview* is, in a sense, "a set of instructions for learning another language," and gives a very similar example from his interview ethnography of skid-row men. He had to learn what "making a flop" meant for these men and, in so doing, came to understand that they don't consider themselves to be homeless. When asked by a naïve interviewer what is their address, these men—who know the language of researchers and social workers—will respond that they don't have a home. But to each other, Spradley (1979, 19) learned, they speak instead of having made a good flop last night or about how they used to jungle up down by the waterfront. In his book, Spradley (1979) aims to teach interviewers how to learn such language from interviewees, how to be taught by them, and thus to learn about the culture of the speakers. Becker and Geer's point is that participant observation makes this work easier.

The "participant" part of participant observation plays a role too in tuning the researcher to be more sensitive to what interviewees are trying to say, trying not to say, and what they might be feeling. Goffman puts it this way:

> I feel that the way this is done is to not, of course, just listen to what they talk about, but to pick up on their minor grunts and groans as they respond to their situation. When you do that, it seems to me, the standard technique is to try to subject yourself, hopefully, to their life circumstances, which means that although, in fact, you can leave at any time, you act as you can't and you try to accept all of the desirable and undesirable things that are a feature of their life. That "tunes your body up" and with your "tuned-up" body and with the ecological right to be close to them (which you've obtained by one sneaky means or another), you are in a position to note their gestural, visual, bodily response to what's going on around them and you're empathetic enough—because you've been taking the same crap they've been taking—to sense what it is they're responding to.
>
> *(Goffman 1989, 125–6)*

Organizational ethnographers should be cautious about taking this too far. We typically observe much more than we participate in the organizations we study. We most often go home each night. We seldom truly take the same crap taken by the people we study because the organizational stakes are so different for us than for them. But, by remaining close enough to the people taking that crap that we can smell it and get some of it on our shoes, we may understand better what they tell us in response to our questions.

"In essence," Van Maanen (1983, 37–8) writes, "ethnographers believe that separating the facts from the fictions, the extraordinary from the common, and the general from the specific is best accomplished by lengthy, continuous, firsthand involvement in the organizational settings under study." Speaking about his own ethnography of police, he says that "only by observing the phenomena firsthand and questioning the police about the actions they had just taken (or not taken) was I able to corroborate and elaborate upon what my informants were telling me" (Van Maanen 1983, 41). Goffman (1989, 131) is more blunt: "I don't give hardly any weight to what people say, but I try to triangulate what they are saying with events." What we get from interviews are accounts, "researcher-provoked data" as opposed to "naturally occurring data" (Silverman 2014, 357). This point is central for Becker and Geer:

> Participant observation makes it possible to check description against fact and, noting discrepancies, become aware of systematic distortions made by the person under study; such distortions are less likely to be discovered by interviewing alone.
>
> *(Becker and Geer 1957, 31)*

Dean and Foote Whyte (1958) argue in their famous article, "How Do You Know If the Informant Is Telling the Truth?" that separating fact and fiction and detecting distortion is possible too in an interview study without participant observation especially when, as in the case of ethnographic interviewing, the study involves lengthy interviews and many of them, not simply one. This gives the interviewer the opportunity to compare an informant's account with other things he or she has said and with the accounts given by other informants. Over the course of repeated interviews, and as part of the process of building a relationship and rapport with informants, the researcher will also make inferences about their relative reliability, openness, and truthfulness. Nevertheless, participant observers, seeing and hearing the people they study in many different situations, will have an even better basis for making such inferences and, as Becker and Geer (1958, 40) conclude, "the inference can never be more accurate than the observation and may be less so."

Ethnography Always Involves Interviewing

Presumably no one is arguing that a study consisting of only interviews done with no participant observation whatsoever is ever preferable if the goal is to create ethnography. This chapter is about whether it is possible; I take for granted that it is never preferable, only sometimes necessary and often convenient. Even if we were interested in doing an ethnography of the culture of people who volunteer to be interviewed by ethnographers, we might profitably observe them waiting to be interviewed and also sit in the interview chair ourselves to see how it feels. Certainly, this is not something that Spradley is claiming for the ethnographic interview:

> I want to discuss ... the interaction that goes on *during* interviews. In doing this, however, we should not lose sight of the wider context of field work. Most ethnographers will conduct participant observation at the same time, thus encountering key informants when they are working, visiting friends, enjoying leisure time, and carrying out ordinary activities.
>
> *(Spradley 1979, 79)*

As Agar (2008, 156) points out, framing the question—participant observation or interviewing—as if it were a choice between a) listening to people in an isolated room, or b) observing them without ever listening to what they say about what they do, is absurd. What I am arguing is that ethnography always involves interviewing and that this interviewing benefits from participant observation. Once I have established that, the remaining question is how much of that special benefit, if any, is needed to create good ethnography.

In his "Comment on 'Participant Observation and Interviewing: A Comparison,'" published in *Human Organization* next to Becker and Geer's piece, Trow (1957) makes the argument that we can't claim advantages for participant observation or interviewing as method in general.

The alternative view, and I would have thought this the view most widely accepted by social scientists, is that different kinds of information about man and society are gathered most fully and economically in different ways, and that the problem under investigation properly dictates the methods of investigation.

(Trow 1957, 33)

If we accept that this view is as widely accepted as Trow claims, then it means that to understand what methods might be appropriate for ethnography, we need to take a step back and consider what is the "problem under investigation" in the case of ethnography. Interviewing is central to ethnography because to learn how people understand and account for their day-to-day situation, to learn what they think they are up to, we should ask them. To ask them and simply take their response at face value is naïve. But to not ask them at all is ethnographic malpractice. If, as Van Maanen (1983, 52) argues, "the essential ethnographic question" is "what it is to *be* rather than to *see* a member of the organization," and if we are appropriately modest about the extent to which we, as researchers, even after a year or more of fieldwork, can feel confident that we experienced firsthand what it is like to be an actual member of the organization, then we have no choice but to ask people and make what sense we can of the accounts they give. Also, ethnographers care about things that they cannot observe. This includes accounts of what people are thinking and how they are feeling, but also historical events, infrequent events, and events that happened elsewhere that are context for the current situation. This is why, as Bernard says, "unstructured interviewing is the most widely used method of data collection in cultural anthropology" (Bernard 1994, 208).

Decentering Participant Observation

Observing and participating are, in contrast to interviewing, decentered in organizational ethnography. As Agar (2008, 9) says, "observation is subordinate to what one learns in interviews. Observations are ways to test out what you have learned, ways to complicate and contradict the encyclopedia, and develop additional interviews and conversations based on these problems." Agar is exaggerating here, but in many organizational ethnographies, observation is most important for the ways, described above, that it helps the researcher do better interviews. The trope that observation is important because observations represent the "facts," the "naturally occurring data" as opposed to the mere "accounts," the "researcher-provoked data," provided by interviews is suspect on two counts. First, it succumbs to two of the "Ten Lies of Ethnography" identified by Fine (1994). As participant observers we don't observe everything, not even everything that happens while we are present. We also don't capture in our fieldnotes everything we observe, and we capture nothing in our fieldnotes exactly as it happened. Second, the reflexive turn in ethnography has made unqualified claims by researchers of determining the fact of the matter to compare with accounts given by informants seem fairly quaint (Atkinson and Coffey 2003, 426).

The importance of the participation part of participant ethnography has always been problematic, suffering from what we might call the Yogi Berra problem, after his famous quote that "nobody goes there anymore, it's too crowded" (Berra 1997, 16). Participant observers—aside from those writing autoethnography—are always both participating not enough to really experience what the people under study are experiencing and participating too much to avoid influencing the scene under study. In my experience, the more important of the two problems is usually that we do too little participating. The organizational ethnographer doesn't have the advantage of doing what Malinowski called "open-air ethnography" in the Trobriand Islands (Stocking 1983, 111). The people we are studying don't live outdoors in situations of low privacy. We are lucky if we are able to find a role to be able to work among them; we seldom live among them in their homes. Our access, as Kunda (1992, 236) notes, is typically inversely related to hierarchical level since one indicator of power in organizations is often the ability to preserve privacy. Kunda's (1992) book, *Engineering Culture*, is one of the best organizational ethnographies written. By his own account, with top managers he had to content himself for the most part with formal interviews, and with his main contacts—engineers and middle managers—he observed more than he participated, and he observed less than he would have liked (Kunda 1992, 233–7). This echoes my own experience doing the fieldwork for *Unpopular Culture* (Weeks 2004) where "participation" most of the time meant shadowing someone and asking endless questions about what they were doing: in essence, interviewing them. Unobtrusive participant observation of a back-office bank clerk working alone on his or her computer is not very illuminating. Easier were aspects of work that were more "open-air" such as meetings, customer visits, conferences, and internal training programs. In other words, aspects of work where people talk to each other.

Apropos of the decentering of participant observation, the inveterate fieldworker, Geertz, says:

> There is a certain value, if you are going to run on about the exploitation of the masses, in having seen a Javanese sharecropper turning earth in a tropical downpour or a Moroccan tailor embroidering kaftans by the light of a twenty-watt bulb. But the notion that this gives you the thing entire (and elevates you to some moral vantage ground from which you can look down upon the ethically less privileged) is an idea which only someone too long in the bush could possibly entertain.
>
> *(Geertz 1973, 22)*

When your audience is a group of people many of whom may well have been long in the bush, it may be that, even more than its role in enhancing interview quality, the most important thing about participant observation is the credibility, the face validity, that a year or more of participant observation affords your ethnography. Goffman calls it the justification and warrant:

> I think you should spend at least a year in the field. Otherwise you don't get the random sample, you don't get a range of unanticipated events, you

don't get deep familiarity. It's deep familiarity that is the rationale—that plus getting material on a tissue of events—that gives the justification and warrant for such apparently "loose" things as fieldwork.

(Goffman 1989, 130)

A year is clearly arbitrary and yet Sanday (1983, 20) notes that most ethnographers would agree that at least a year of participant observation is required to do serious ethnographic work. That is to say, I suspect, that most ethnographers who themselves did at least a year of participant observation would agree that at least a year of participant observation is required to do serious ethnographic work. It is a rite of passage as much as a research method.

Ethnographic Interviews and the Interview Ethnographies

Organization studies has many examples of excellent ethnographies which are based primarily on interview data and which did not involve a year of participant observation. I have mentioned already Jackall's (1988) *Moral Mazes*. The 143 intensive interviews he did were complemented by "attendance at some management meetings, informal conversations and discussions over meals, coffee, and drinks and participation at a range of social events," as well as "two seminars for up-and-coming managers in that company, each lasting several days" (Jackall 1988, 206). Hochschild's (1983) *The Managed Heart* is another example of excellence. Fine (1994) calls *The Managed Heart* "estimable" and "one of the most influential ethnographies of the past decade," but also "not richly ethnographic" because her methods are not primarily participant observation. In fact, those methods include an open-ended questionnaire handed out to 261 of her Berkeley students as well as interviews with flight attendants, union representatives, airline officials, advertising agents, bill collectors, the public relations people assigned by the airline to handle her, and a sex therapist with ten years of experience treating flight attendants as clients. The participant observation she did consisted of attending training sessions for flight attendants and having lunch and, once, dinner with trainers, observing the recruitment interviews of flight attendants, a guided tour of an airplane and a two-hour visit to an airplane galley (Hochschild 1983, 12–17). To choose one more, Nippert-Eng's (1996) *Home and Work* is correctly singled out by Van Maanen (2006, 15) as a "wonderful" example of multi-site ethnography. Her sources were:

Seventy-two, two- to six-hour hour interviews with employees at "the Laboratory," or "the Lab," a research laboratory in the Northeast United States. (A copy of the interview schedule I developed is included as an appendix to this text.) I also incorporate observations made on-site while conducting the interviews. Six pretest interviews and dozens of less formal discussions with family, acquaintances, and other members of the Laboratory supplement the formal interviews.

(Nippert-Eng 1996, Kindle Locations 492–5)

In sociology, the tradition of interview ethnography goes all the way back to the Chicago School under the leadership of former newspaperman Robert Park. As Van Maanen (1988, 19) explains, a good part of this work was interview based with the interviews being intensive and repeated and accomplished in natural settings that provided the opportunity for observation.

So, it is possible to do interview ethnography, at least in sociology and organization studies. In anthropology, the stakes are higher because ethnography is so important to the discipline that it is often identified with it in the sense that, for an anthropologist, not having done ethnography is a source of status deprivation and not having done at least a year of participant observation means not having done real ethnography (Marcus 2009). Hockey describes graduate students in anthropology "reluctant to describe their rich qualitative interviews as ethnography, fearful that an external examiner might judge their methods inadequate when measured against this term" (Hockey 2002, 209).

> As a discipline, we may have become less apologetic about the study of locally produced "exotica," but participant-observation continues to occupy the methodological high ground.
>
> *(Hockey 2002, 209)*

Agar describes similar apprehensions among applied anthropologists:

> The applied anthropologists have obsessed for years about research opportunities that offered them *less* time than a year. Their intuitions—I'm guessing—were that the opportunity shouldn't be tossed away; you could learn *something* important in a shorter period of time. But they were embarrassed about it, because by the old one-year standard it only added to the stereotype of applied work as somehow deficient.
>
> *(Agar 2008, 38)*

Enthusiasts of participant observation in sociology and organization studies more often see the opposite problem: that "empirical ethnography is now a synonym for virtually all qualitative research except surveys and polls" (Gans 1999, 541).

> Why ethnography has gained widespread acceptance among social researchers to become the label of choice for much of the qualitative/ descriptive work currently being reported remains something of a mystery. Whether ethnography is the appropriate label for some of this work is even more questionable.
>
> *(Wolcott 1995, 79)*

Protecting and defending the boundaries of the territory that "real ethnography" is allowed to occupy holds more than academic interest to academics. It is a matter also of identity and status.

It is possible, of course, to do interview studies that are not ethnography. The name for this is "qualitative research." Interview studies make up the vast majority of qualitative research (Denzin and Lincoln 2018, 577), and it is not hard to sympathize with researchers who, having invested dozens or scores of hours in intensive and serial semi-structured interviews, conducted with the "ethnographic imaginary" (Forsey 2010b, 569), "that definitionally-elusive ethnographic sensibility" (Yanow 2009, 194), want to distinguish their work from the mass of thinner descriptions based on other, presumably easier, interview techniques.

> Among the biggest problems faced by researchers who rely heavily on semi-structured interviews are boredom and fatigue. Even a small project requires 40 to 60 interviews to generate sufficient data to be worthwhile. Most anthropologists collect their own interview data and asking the same question over and over again can get pretty old.
>
> *(Bernard 1994, 221)*

Ethnographic interviewing is efficient compared to participant observation, but it is time- and energy-consuming compared to other types of interviews. This is part of its definition:

> Thus, both the time factor—duration and frequency of contact—and the quality of the emerging relationship help distinguish ethnographic interviewing from other types of interview projects by empowering interviewees to shape, according to their world-views, the questions being asked and possibly even the focus of the research study.
>
> *(Heyl 2001, 369)*

It is even part of the name of interview techniques synonymous with ethnographic interviewing: "the long interview," (McCracken 1988), "the active interview" (Holstein and Gubrium 1995). Ethnographic interviewers are as concerned with the size of their N (number of hours of interviews and pages of transcriptions) as are participant observers (number of days of fieldwork and pages of fieldnotes).

What Is a Good Ethnographic Interview?

If we agree with Van Maanen (1988, 1) that ethnography is a product, an account of a culture, or selected aspects of a culture, and if we agree with Clifford (1986) that ethnographic truths are inherently partial—committed and incomplete—then we should evaluate how ethnographic an interview study is on the basis, not of its N, but of how well it succeeds as an account. How well does it help the reader "to understand themes of the lived everyday world from the subjects' own perspectives" (Brinkmann and Kvale 2015, 31)? How well does it translate "the meaning of actions and events to the people we seek to understand" Spradley (1979, 5) to the reader? How convincingly does it manage to interpret "presentational data"—those data which concern the appearances that informants strive to maintain (or enhance) in the eyes of the interviewer or fieldworker, as well as colleagues and even themselves (Van Maanen 1983, 42). How well does it account for all the things that the interview situation may represent to the interviewees, shaping the narratives they construct with the interviewer: the interview as identity work, as political action, as local accomplishment, as a cultural script, and so on (Alvesson 2003). How well does it cope with the challenges of reflexivity and grasp the opportunity that interviews don't simply (and sometimes don't at all) collect information about non-observable or unobserved actions, or past events, or private experiences: "interviews generate accounts and narratives that are forms of social action in their own right" (Atkinson and Coffey 2003, 424)? Does it produce "new concepts, concepts that take you closer to the world that is the object of research than previous understandings could have," (Agar 2008, 40) and does it draw upon sufficient data from numerous different sources, all of which support its conclusions in a "massive over-determination of pattern" (Agar 2008, 37)?

I suspect that it is because these aspects of quality are loose and hard to assess that we so often fall back to the size of the N. The time we invested and the paper trail we created in collecting data for the study is, as Goffman (1989, 130) said, our warrant to justify to ourselves and our readers that we have gathered enough data to credibly claim that we have learned something about the culture of the people we are studying, that we have escaped a little bit the gravitational pull of postmodern doubt that we can learn anything from interviews except how people behave in interviews and that we can learn anything in participant observation except how biased, subjective and human we are, that all ethnography is autoethnography. Yet, the truth of the sentiment that ethnographies are inherently partial (Clifford 1986, 7), that cultural analysis is inherently incomplete (Geertz 1973, 29), should lead us away from grandiose pronouncements of what can and cannot be counted as ethnography—the academic equivalent of peeing on fence posts to mark the territory of ethnography—and away from pulling out our Ns to compare sizes and assign status. Gans (1999, 544) is surely right to lament the fact, if it is a fact and not just nostalgia, that participant observation is in decline because it fits less well into today's academic economy. Brinkmann and Kvale (2015, 337) are equally right to point out that not everything should be geared toward minimizing time. If we want to understand other people, we have to spend time with them. On the other hand, as every ethnographer knows, after a certain point, more data as often overwhelms as much as edifies. Reserving the label "ethnography" as some sort of reward to motivate scholars to spend more time in the field seems to me distasteful and unhelpful and—in the case of organization studies, if not anthropology—fairly hypocritical given that the methods underpinning many of our best ethnographies fall conspicuously short of a continuous year or more of participant observation in the field.

As Agar (2008, 64) notes, the opposition between participant observation and interviewing has been with us since the birth of modern anthropology and the time of its founding fathers.

Franz Boas stressed the interview as he tried to get descriptions of disappearing American Indian cultures from older informants; Bronislaw

> Malinowski pitched his tent among the natives, learning their language
> and sharing their lives.
>
> *(Agar 2008, 64)*

The close relationship between the two approaches has been apparent for that long too, however. For Malinowski, what was to be studied was a "long conversation" taking place among the people we are studying, a conversation in which we inevitably join (Bloch 1977, 278). It was Boas, "stepping off the boat in an Eskimo village, with his suitcase in hand, preparing for a long stay in residence," that established the paradigm of fieldwork in American anthropology (Wallace 1972, 469).

Interviewing, by which I mean some mix of informal questioning, conversation and formal unstructured interviews, is a central part of participant observation and it is where most ethnographic data comes from. Participant observation is the preferred method of ethnography in large part because of the advantages that interviewing done in the context of participant observation has over interviewing done without that benefit. Participant observation is not the same as ethnography, however, and it is not essential for it. We have seen in this chapter good examples of ethnographic interviewing and its product, interview ethnography. Ethnographers who cite Spradley (1979) would do well to read him too and imitate exemplary interview ethnographies. Ethnographic interviewing is difficult and time consuming to do well. It requires a substantial commitment of time and energy (and, *pace* Bernard (1994), apparently a high boredom threshold), albeit a commitment that conveniently doesn't require continuous time away from work, family and other obligations. If some readers and reviewers are suspicious of the very idea of interview ethnography, it may be in reaction to papers that claim to be based on "ethnographic interviews" but read as if what their authors meant by that method was "interviews requiring little preparation." In this case, we should keep in mind Sturgeon's Law. Science fiction writer Theodore Sturgeon (1957) noted, in response to claims that so much science fiction is of poor quality, that "90% of science fiction is crap, but 90% of everything is crap." There is plenty of bad ethnography of all kinds, the difference with interview ethnography is mainly that it can be done badly more quickly. The similarity with participant observation ethnography is that it can also be done well.

Note

1 I would like to thank Martin Kralik for his help.

References

Agar, Michael H., 2008, *The Professional Stranger: An Informal Introduction to Ethnography*, 2nd edition, Bingley: Emerald.

Alvesson, Mats, 2003, "Beyond Neopositivists, Romantics, and Localists: A Reflexive Approach to Interviews in Organizational Research," *Academy of Management Review*, 28:1, 13–33.

Atkinson, Paul and Amanda Coffey, 2003, "Revisiting the Relationship between Participant Observation and Interviewing," in James A. Holstein and Jaber F. Gubrium, eds., *Inside Interviewing*, Thousand Oaks: Sage, 801–814.

Becker, Howard S. and Blanche Geer, 1957, "Participant Observation and Interviewing: A Comparison," *Human Organization*, 16:3, 28–32.

Becker, Howard S. and Blanche Geer, 1958, "'Participant Observation and Interviewing': A Rejoinder," *Human Organization*, 17:2, 39–40.

Becker, Howard S., Blanche Geer, Everett C. Hughes and Anselm Strauss, 1961, *Boys in White: Student Culture in Medical School*, Chicago: University of Chicago Press.

Bernard, H. Russell, 1994, *Research Methods in Anthropology: Qualitative and Quantitative Approaches*, Thousand Oaks: Sage.

Berra, Yogi, 1997, *The Yogi Book*, New York: Workman Publishing.

Bloch, Maurice, 1977, "The Past and the Present in the Present," *Man*, 12:2, 278–292.

Brinkmann, Svend and Steinar Kvale, 2015, *InterViews: Learning the Craft of Qualitative Research Interviewing*, Thousand Oaks: Sage.

Clifford, James, 1986, "Partial Truths," in James Clifford and George E. Marcus, eds., *Writing Culture: The Poetics and Politics of Ethnography*, Berkeley: University of California Press, 1–26.

Dean, John P. and William Foote Whyte, 1958, "How Do You Know if the Informant Is Telling the Truth?" *Human Organization*, 17:2, 34–38.

Denzin, Norman K. and Yvonne S. Lincoln, 2018, *The Sage Handbook of Qualitative Research*, 5th edition, Thousand Oaks: Sage.

Fine, Gary A., 1994, "Ten Lies of Ethnography," *Journal of Contemporary Ethnography*, 22:3, 267–294.

Forsey, Martin G., 2010a, "Ethnography and Myth of Participant Observation," in Sam Hillyard, ed., *New Frontiers in Ethnography*, Volume 11, Bingley: Emerald, 65–79.

Forsey, Martin G., 2010b, "Ethnography as Participant Listening," *Ethnography*, 11:4, 558–572.

Gans, Herbert, 1999, "Participant Observation in the Era of 'Ethnography'," *Journal of Contemporary Ethnography*, 28:5, 540–548.

Geertz, Clifford, 1973, *The Interpretation of Cultures*, New York: Basic Books.

Goffman, Erving, 1989, "On Fieldwork," *Journal of Contemporary Ethnography*, 18:2, 123–132.

Heyl, Barbara S., 2001, "Ethnographic Interviewing," in Paul Atkinson, Amanda Coffey, Sara Delamont, John Lofland, Lyn Lofland ed., *Handbook of Ethnography*, Thousand Oaks: Sage, 369–383.

Hochschild, Arlie R., 1983, *The Managed Heart*, Berkeley: University of California Press.

Hockey, Jenny, 2002, "Interviews as Ethnography? Disembodied Social Interaction in Britain," in Nigel Rapport, ed., *British Subjects: An Anthropology of Britain*, Oxford: Berg, 209–222.

Hockey, Jenny and Martin Forsey, 2012, "Ethnography Is Not Participant Observation: Reflections on the Interview as Participatory Qualitative Research," in Jonathan Skinner, ed., *The Interview: An Ethnographic Approach*, London: Bloomsbury, 69–87.

Holstein, James A. and Jaber F. Gubrium, 1995, *The Active Interview*, Thousand Oaks: Sage.

Jackall, Robert, 1988, *Moral Mazes: The World of Corporate Managers*, Oxford: Oxford University Press.

Kunda, Gideon, 1992, *Engineering Culture: Control and Commitment in a High-Tech Organization*, Philadelphia: Temple University Press.

Lofland, John and Lyn H. Lofland, 1995, *Analyzing Social Settings: A Guide to Qualitative Observation and Analysis*, Belmont: Wadsworth.

Marcus, George E., 2009, "Notes Towards an Ethnographic Memoir of Supervising Graduate Research through Anthropology's Decades of Transformation," in James D. Faubion and George E. Marcus, eds., *Fieldwork Is Not What It Used to Be: Learning Anthropology's Method in a Time of Transition*, Ithaca: Cornell University Press, 1–34.

McCracken, Grant, 1988, *The Long Interview*, Thousand Oaks: Sage.

Moerman, Michael, 1988, *Talking Culture: Ethnography and Conversation Analysis*, Philadelphia: University of Philadelphia Press.

Nippert-Eng, Christina, 1996, *Home and Work: Negotiating Boundaries through Everyday Life*, Chicago: University of Chicago Press.

Ryle, Gilbert, 2009 [1968], "The Thinking of Thoughts: What Is 'Le Penseur' Doing?," in Julia Tanney, ed., *Col-lected Essays 1929–1968: Collected Papers*, Volume 2, London: Routledge, 494–510.

Sanday, Peggy R., 1983, "The Ethnographic Paradigm(s)," in John Van Maanen, ed., *Qualitative Methodology*, Thousand Oaks: Sage, 19–36.

Silverman, David, 2014, *Interpreting Qualitative Data*, 5th edition, Thousand Oaks: Sage.

Spradley, James P., 1979, *The Ethnographic Interview*, Belmont: Wadsworth.

Stocking, George, 1983, "The Ethnographer's Magic: Fieldwork in Anthropology from Tylor to Malinowski," in George Stocking, ed., *Observers Observed: Essays on Ethnographic Fieldwork, History of Anthropology*, Volume 1, Madison: The University of Wisconsin Press, 70–120.

Sturgeon, Theodore, 1957, *Venture*, 49.

Trow, Martin, 1957, "Comment on 'Participant Observation and Interviewing: A Comparison'," *Human Organization*, 16:3, 33–35.

Van Maanen, John, 1983, "The Fact of Fiction in Organizational Ethnography," in John Van Maanen, ed., *Qualitative Methodology*, Thousand Oaks: Sage, 37–56.

Van Maanen, John, 1988, *Tales of the Field: On Writing Ethnography*, Chicago: University of Chicago Press.

Van Maanen, John, 2006, "Ethnography Then and Now," *Qualitative Research in Organizations and Management*, 1:1, 13–21.

Wallace, Anthony F. C., 1972, "Paradigmatic Processes in Culture Change," *American Anthropologist*, 74, 467–478.

Weeks, John R., 2004, *Unpopular Culture: The Ritual of Complaint in a British Bank*, Chicago: University of Chicago Press.

Wolcott, Harry F., 1995, "Making a Study 'More Ethnographic'," in John Van Maanen, ed., *Representation in Ethnography*, Thousand Oaks: Sage, 79–111.

Yanow, Dvora, 2009, "Organizational Ethnography and Methodological Angst: Myths and Challenges in the Field," *Qualitative Research in Organizations and Management*, 4:2, 186–199.

5

FRAMES OF THE FIELD

Ethnography as Photography

Mikko Vesa, Mikaela Krohn
and Frank den Hond

Introduction

Anthropological studies of organization and work were at the roots of the study of organizations. But anthropology and the study of organization and work drifted apart, only to be slowly reconnected from the 1970s onward. With ethnography's newfound and ascending – but contested (Bate, 1997) – legitimacy in the field of management and organizations studies, it is timely to examine the process of anthropological knowledge creation. This is important on two grounds. First, the relative novelty of organizational ethnography, and even its current status of being somewhat fashionable, is overshadowed by a lack of reflexivity regarding the particularities of the ethnographic knowledge creation process, notably the recording of research materials. Second, because it studies a powerful actor, the capitalist corporation, organizational ethnography is potentially a contested practice itself, implicated in the reproduction of the ideologies and power relations of its research subject. It is our primary intention here to develop the former, but we will also present some observations on the latter.

In this chapter, we use photography as an analogy to ethnography in order to focus attention on the recording of research materials during ethnographic fieldwork. With "recording" we refer to the capturing of lived life in a format that lends itself for later systematic reproduction and analysis. Although attention has been drawn to some defining characteristics of ethnography – e.g., to the nature of the ethnographic text as a synthetic composition (Van Maanen, 1995, 2011 [1988]), to how one can think about ethnographic data as encountered by the fieldworker (Van Maanen, 1979), and to the subjectivity of the ethnographer (Clifford & Marcus, 1986) – we still have an insufficient understanding of the recording itself. In the legacies of Van Maanen, Clifford and Marcus, and others, organizational ethnography has largely been about writing, reading and text, but less so about the recording of lived life.

Yet, according to Flusser (2000 [1983], p.7), after a first fundamental turning point in human culture – the invention of linear writing, around the middle of the second millennium BCE – a second one has been observed: the invention of the making of technical images through apparatuses. Our highlighting of this second fundamental turning point allows for a dual reflection on the process of ethnographic knowledge creation: on the use of the visual recording in ethnography, and on viewing ethnographic method itself as an apparatus. Although ethnographers have recognized for some time now that interviews, for example, produce a co-constructed narrative instead of an objective and true account of the facts and meaning of lived life (e.g., Alvesson, 2003), we have not yet fully grasped how the technique of the method may frame the research material. By virtue of research materials being recorded, all observational field notes, interviews and visual objects are inherently framed at the very moment of their inception, not only in the sense of them being socially constructed, but also in a *technical* sense, which is independent from the subjectivity of the ethnographer as a "fieldworker" or a "tale worker." This latter framing has been insufficiently recognized, yet it is likely to affect the post-fieldwork reading of research materials. We can only analyze what we have previously framed.

The Essence in the Field: Data, Knowledge and the Knowledgeable

With the publication of Van Maanen's (2011 [1988]) *Tales of the Field*, the reflexive turn that went through anthropology in the 1980s reached management and organization studies. In spite of a number of prominent champions of the ethnographic approach in the field of management and organization studies, ethnography still seems to occupy a rather specific niche. Rather than being seen as the crafting of cultural inscriptions, ethnography is equated, within management and organization studies, with qualitative fieldwork conducted in order to generate data, understood broadly. Management and organization studies is a domain in which leading journals and publishers are heavily focused on the dissemination of both general and generalizable organization theory.

It is thus often understood that data, regardless of their nature, refer to essences of people, objects, or situations (e.g., Lune & Berg, 2017), *quod non*. This essence, in turn, is subjected to different kinds of queries. The deductive query poses the data against existing theory, typically seeking quantified essence for verification or falsification of theoretical claims and thereby filling in missing corners of an existing paradigm (Sutton & Staw, 1995). Conventionally juxtaposed to deduction is the inductive approach, often case-based, in which typically qualitative approaches are used to unearth novelty (Eisenhardt, 1989). More pragmatically, both approaches often involve abduction between theory (as knowledge) and data (as essences) (Corbin & Strauss, 2008) in a search for breakdowns between assumptions and impressions (Alvesson & Kärreman, 2007). We should not assume, however, that this somewhat idealized deduction-induction-abduction triad reflects accurately what researchers actually do when developing theory (Mantere & Ketokivi, 2013).

Still it is interesting to observe that these three approaches to doing research, whilst assuming that the researcher does different things, in fact do put the researcher in the same posture. In one hand s/he has data, in the other theory. What is different among these approaches is how s/he relates these two assumedly independent entities. S/he might be the inductive explorer, the deductive judge or the abductive detective, but whichever the researcher's role, (s)he stands untouched and independent behind the analytical lens. In either case, it is by building a bridge between the essence of data and the knowledge of theory that the researcher crafts a contribution.

In this vein, ethnographic data, supposedly capturing the essences of the world, are treated as objects; they were conquered for scrutiny, mined, transported, and sometimes even made publicly available. Thus it appears as if some sleight of hand takes place: when the researcher leaves the field, raw data get "processed" for query and all the more so as the analytical process proceeds, to be finally cemented in the formal publication. In this understanding, data are and remain neutral, objectively correct capturings of the essences of the field. But are they?

If not, the question becomes, what does it mean to know something like management in an ethnographic manner? Many concepts attempt to express this; emic knowledge, lived experience, participation, and the ethnographic moment of insight. There is a clear distinction between ethnographic knowing of management and simply examining management using general qualitative methods. General theory builds from data in attempting to create a knowledge *of* something, but the ethnographer is a knowledge worker who is also worked upon by the knowledge itself; and knowledge is never something simply discovered but also something yielded for a purpose. Hence, data refer back to the subject-position of knowledge workers in the network of relations in the field in which they are located. To record something is therefore to record it from a particular position, but not only so, it is also to record it through the use of an apparatus. "All images are socially *and technically* constructed" (Harper, 1994, p.406, as cited in Ray & Smith, 2012, p.290, emphasis added). Fieldwork implies framework: the use of an apparatus in the production of ethnographic data, which we explore next in this chapter.

Beyond the Objective: Fieldwork as Framework

But DATA, which turn interesting details into autonomous compositions, which transform true colours into bright colours, provide new, irresistible satisfactions. The destiny of ETHNOGRAPHY has taken it far beyond the role to which it was originally thought to be limited: to give more accurate reports on reality (including ORGANIZATION). ETHNOGRAPHY is the reality; the real object is often experienced as a letdown. DATA make normative an experience of ORGANIZATION that is mediated, second-hand, intense in a different way.

(adapted from Sontag, 2005 [1973], p. 115)[1]

We begin our exploration about the nature of ethnographic data analogically by turning to the long-standing debate on the nature of photography, seeking for serendipity in the idea that the generation of ethnographic data is analogous to the making of photographic pictures: they are purposefully generated and recorded using a technical medium, an apparatus. In this spirit, we carefully read some of the classical works on photography and substituted the language of ethnography for that of photography. As in the quote at the beginning of this section, the photographer becomes the ethnographer, photographs data, the camera ethnographic method, etcetera.[2] We discuss John Berger and Susan Sontag on how they understand the artifact of the photograph. We present Henri Cartier-Bresson and Diane Arbus to exemplify two radically distinct approaches to photography. We highlight how Vilém Flusser considers the photograph as a technical image that is produced with an apparatus that both constrains and affords the photographer. And we reflect on Ariella Azoulay, who gives the people in front of the camera a subject position. We use this analogy as a methodological tool (Ketokivi, Mantere, & Cornelissen, 2017) that enables us to serendipitously focus on the often overseen technical nature of ethnographic data; at times we even engage in playful hypothetical monologues of the photographer lecturing the ethnographer.

Our exercise turns around the well-established but misleading distinction between "something given" ("data," from the Latin root *dare*) and "something made" ("fact," from the Latin root *fare*). Ethnographic data are not "given" but "made," just as photographs require action on the part of the photographer to create them in the first place. In contrast to data being made, "facts" are inalterable "givens," like yesterday's rain or today's sunshine, or, indeed, the flowers in the field, awaiting to be taken by the collector. In order to play their role in ethnographic research, facts are and need to be transformed into data by recording them. Likewise, operating a camera transforms facts into data; Sontag pointed out the violence that may be involved in this transformation.[3]

We build up our argument by analytically separating and highlighting individual elements of the photographic constellation: the picture itself, the photographer, the camera as an apparatus, and its subject, and then we discuss the public use of photographs. This separation allows us to start a discussion of the nature of ethnographic data and to stimulate reflexivity on their recording. Further, it bears emphasizing that despite using the analogy of photography, our concern for the nature of ethnographic data is not limited to visual methods or visual ethnography (cf. Becker, 1974; Pink, 2007; Rose, 2016). Rather, we include all types of recorded data, from field notes and interview recordings to pictures and videos in our analysis, thus also speaking to, but not exclusively so, the field of visual ethnography.

The mores of academic writing in the social sciences require us to state that, of course, this analogy, like all analogies, is in many ways limp, imperfect. If it were perfect, there would be no point in making the analogy in the first place. Therefore, we accept and acknowledge any critique on how we are wrong in representing ethnography by reducing it to the simile of photography. But that is not the point. The point is that we hope to stimulate reflection on the recording of data during ethnographic fieldwork and on the uses of these data in ethnographic research in general, and in organizational anthropology in particular, by taking an unusual lens – literally so – on the "frames of the field."

Ethnographic Photography

The magical fascination of DATA can be observed all over the place: The way in which they put a magic spell on life, the way in which we experience, know, evaluate and act as a function of these DATA. It is therefore important to enquire into what sort of magic we are dealing with here.

(Flusser, 2000 [1983], p. 16)

Explicit knowledge of organizations – as in organization theory – emerged in the late 19th century as a parallel development to the emergence and proliferation of the organizations of modernity, particularly in the form of the corporation. An interesting observation in this regard is that the same can be said for one of the most defining gadgets of this emerging modernity, the camera, which became widely accessible after the late 19th century, with the invention of the Eastman Kodak Brownie camera that allowed the making of snapshots. But even before the turn of the century, photography was practiced in anthropological expeditions and ethnographic inquiries (Pink, 2007). The first widely known use of this equipment was, arguably, the Torres Straits expedition of 1888, on which a young Cambridge graduate named Anthony Wilkins was hired to act as the expedition's camera recorder (Philp, 2004). He was not the only one.

All over the world during the 19th century, European travelers, soldiers, colonial administrators, adventurers, took photographs of 'the native', their customs, their architecture, their richness, their poverty, their women's breasts, their headdresses, and these images, besides provoking amazement, were presented and read as proof of the justice of the imperial division of the world. The division between those who organized and rationalized and surveyed, and those who were surveyed.

(Berger, 2013b [1982], p. 70)

Photography was also used to attest to the scientific objectivity of the ethnography (Pink, 2007), and it did so until well into the 20th century. For example, *Argonauts of the Western Pacific* extensively employed photographs; the book came "WITH 5 MAPS, 65 ILLUSTRATIONS, AND 2 FIGURES" (Malinowski, 1922, p.iii). Limited by the camera technology of the day, his pictures follow a certain way of framing. What is depicted is the cultural and the social: scenes from village life, the conduct of rituals, and arranged photographs of the natives. Every single picture appears as "a sight which has been recreated or reproduced. It is an appearance, or a set of appearances, which has been detached from the place and time in which it first made its appearance" (Berger, 2008 [1972], pp. 9–10).

One can only begin to speculate what Malinowski's use of photography might imply. Certainly, the pictures bear witness to a fundamental transformation of the ethnographic practice; in its aspiration to become a science, it was firmly pushed out of the splendid isolation of distant University halls into the very midst of the native life that it sought to document. And thus, as already noted by Malinowski, there was a constant need to develop the ways in which ethnographic fieldwork is conducted. The camera offered something that appealed to the spirit of this emerging modernity, to which ethnography, too, could not be immune. The camera was novel. The magic to which Flusser points in the quote that begins this section is now at its most powerful. Mediated by the camera, something entirely novel was brought from the field to the eyes of distant audiences. The camera goes beyond words, and with its novelty, the scenes of native village life – exotic beachside villages, strange magic-invoking rituals, and savage women with exposed breasts – brought along a sensation that would be improper to part in the ethnographic text itself. The picture was the ethnographer's sensation; that which will be gossiped about.

As noted by Clifford (1986, p.112), this representational approach was legitimated by the need to salvage a vanishing world by recording it. Malinowski, for example, predicted that in a generation or two there would be nothing left of these "primitive" cultures. Therefore, he saw himself almost as an archeologist of a decaying, biological world. The cultures and people that he studied were about to vanish, to be washed onto the pages of history, unless the ethnographer captured a final shot of the dying breed. This built into the dominant scientific mood of the era, one in which the only empirical approach to research rested on the pure ideal of the exact natural sciences. For Malinowski, whilst acknowledging degrees of impurity in the pursuit of ethnography, this was still the first purpose of ethnographic fieldwork:

> 1. The organization of the tribe, and the anatomy of its culture *must be recorded in firm, clear outline. The method of* concrete, statistical documentation *is the means through which such an outline is to be given.*
> *(Malinowski, 1922, p.24, original emphasis)*

Thus, the perception of the camera's promise of exactness fed directly into Malinowski's pursuit of the recordable. It was assumed that pictures do not lie and that the camera just captures what it faces as it is. It is only once this recording and dissection of culture of which Malinowksi spoke is done that more qualitative touches should be added to the ethnographic endeavor. In the arsenal of the early 20th century educated gentleman-cum-scientist-cum-fieldworker, the camera became the mark of his profession. The doctor had a stethoscope, the clerk a typewriter, and the ethnographer a camera. But let us leave Malinowski on the beach of Nu'agasi and ask where are we now, a good century later?

It would be wrong to claim that there has not been a reflection over the use of visual methods in ethnography, over the image's ability to replicate reality. The notion of pure images is no longer viable in visual ethnography (Becker, 1974; Crawford, 1992; Pink, 2007). The field has acknowledged that images come with their own ontological assumptions (LeBaron, Jarbakowski, Pratt & Fetzer, 2018). Yet, in some quarters, visual methods are still celebrated as offering "rigorous and authentic representations" (Schembri & Boyle, 2013, p.1251) that capture detailed accounts of complex organizational phenomena (Zundel, MacIntosh & Mackay, 2018) and work practices (Hindmarsh & Llewellyn, 2018). Nevertheless, as Sontag (2005 [1973], p.14) reminds us:"it is never *ethnographic* evidence which can construct – more properly, identify – events; the contribution of *ethnography* always follows the naming of the event."

Yet what does it mean to view photographs as *re*-presentations rather than as representations? Because that which is recorded is re-presented; but can data re-present, say, the corporation? Because for certain, the corporation and its re-presentation are not the same thing. But, then, what are they if not representations? Photographs are two-dimensional images, referring in some way, yet to be discussed, to the four-dimensional world we experience. Depth is lost – but for our knowledge of optics and perspective; an imaginary depth steps in to compensate for this loss – and the passing of time is lost in the closing of the shutter.

> ETHNOGRAPHY is much more than what is printed IN A PUBLICATION, trans-forming any event into DATA. ETHNOGRAPHIC DATA bear the seal of the event itself, and reconstructing that event requires more than just identify-ing what is shown in the DATA. One needs to stop looking at the DATA and instead start watching it.
>
> *(Azoulay, 2008, p.14)*

There is a seduction in the image, a magic that seems self-explanatory.Yet, a picture is not just what it shows. It is a "persistent myth that the camera simply records whatever is in front of it" (Becker, 1974, p.3). Thus, "*data*, which cannot themselves explain anything, are inexhaustible invitations to deduction, speculation, and fan-tasy" (Sontag, 2005 [1973], p.17).

Enter the Photographer

> An image [is] a record of how X had seen Y.
>
> *(Berger, 2008 [1972], p.10)*

> [The camera] will make the picture ... look just the way the photographer thinks it should look.
>
> *(Becker, 1974, p.11)*

Fine, Morrill and Surianarain (2009) point out a tension in the work of ethnogra-phers that stems from their "focus on obtaining the perspectives of participants as they enact their 'natural' routines" (p.612). Ethnographers are supposed not to play "too great a role in defining and organizing the setting" (p.612) in which they do their fieldwork, because if they did, the observed behaviors would no longer be "real": "The behavior studied should be that of the participants, not that of the researcher. The traditional model for ethnographic research is for the participant observer to remain passive, observing the scene as might 'a fly on the wall'" (p.612). Yet, as Fine et al. acknowledge, ethnographers typically have a research agenda for the fieldwork, and not interfering in the research setting may imply that "the content of the observations are haphazard and not entirely focused on the researcher's concerns, compromising the focus or the generalizability of the observations" (p.612).

This ideal of the ethnographer's invisibility in the field of study is thus both a practical impossibility and a desired accomplishment. It reifies the supposed "realness" of the recordings as much as it obscures the actual recording. As a fly on the wall, s/he can choose the wall from which to record data. S/he can also assume various roles and methods to record her data – any textbook on ethnographic methods explains several such roles and methods. Yet, the actual recording remains underexposed.

We only see what we look at. To look is an act of choice.

(Berger, 2008 [1972], p.8)

In his first photography book, *The Decisive Moment/Images à la sauvette*, from 1952, Henri Cartier-Bresson details his looking. It is striking how much the photographer personifies the traditional model of the ethnographer. In his early years as a photographer, Cartier-Bresson prowled the streets of Marseille, feeling "very strung-up and ready to pounce, determined to 'trap' life – to preserve life in the act of living. Above all," he continued, "I craved to seize, in the confines of one single photograph, the whole essence of some situation that was in the process of unrolling itself before my eyes" (Cartier-Bresson, 1952). This seizing or capturing the "essence of the situation" remained Cartier-Bresson's approach. To an audience of ethnographers, he might have confessed an inclusive partnership of sorts.

> We ETHNOGRAPHERS deal in things that are continually vanishing, and when they have vanished, there is no contrivance on earth that can make them come back again. We cannot develop and print a memory. ... for ETHNOGRAPHERS, what has gone is gone forever. From that fact stem the anxieties and strength of our profession.

Out in the field there is "such an abundance of material that an ETHNOGRAPHER must guard against the temptation of trying to do everything. It is essential to cut from the raw material of life – to cut and cut, but to cut with discrimination." This selection is a two-stage project, as Cartier-Bresson would explain to Fine's traditional ethnographer:

> there are two kinds of selection to be made, and either of them can lead to eventual regrets. There is the selection we make when we look through

the view-finder at the subject; and there is the one we make after the DATA have been TRANSCRIBED and printed. After TRANSCRIPTION and printing, you must go about separating the DATA which, though they are all right, aren't the strongest.

Such a selection is permitted, according to Cartier-Bresson, as it maintains the integrity and authenticity, the "real-ness" of the situation. Nevertheless, "We must neither try to manipulate reality while we are shooting, nor manipulate the results in THE OFFICE." Further, the ethnographer should be as unobtrusive as possible.

> In whatever picture-story we try to do, we are bound to arrive as intruders. It is essential, therefore, to approach the subject on tiptoe ... A velvet hand, a hawk's eye – these we should all have. It's no good jostling or elbowing. ... Unless AN ETHNOGRAPHER observes such conditions as these, he may become an intolerably aggressive character.

Cartier-Bresson (1952) also discusses details of photographic technique that bear upon interviewing.

> The ETHNOGRAPHER's eye is perpetually evaluating. An ETHNOGRAPHER can bring coincidence of line simply by moving his head a fraction of a millimeter. He can modify perspectives by a slight bending of the knees. By placing the QUESTION closer to or farther from the subject, he draws a detail – and it can be subordinated, or he can be tyrannized by it. But he composes THE DATA in very nearly the same amount of time it takes to click the shutter, at the speed of a reflex action.

Moreover, and irrespective of the taboo on manipulation, Cartier-Bresson emphasizes the importance of the final analysis and writing, when the ethnographer is no longer in the field but back home, in the office.

> During the process of enlarging, it is essential to re-create the values and mood of the time the DATA were taken; or even to modify the DATA so as to bring it into line with the intentions of the ETHNOGRAPHER at the moment he shot it. It is necessary also to re-establish the balance which the eye is continually establishing between light and shadow. And it is for these reasons that the final act of creating in ETHNOGRAPHY takes place AT A DESK IN THE OFFICE.

In this account, there is a strong and interesting parallel to Van Maanen's distinction between first-order and second-order concepts: "first-order concepts are the 'facts' of an ethnographic investigation and the second-order concepts are the 'theories' an analyst uses to organize and explain these facts" (Van Maanen, 1979, p.540).

But let us go back to the field. The photographer cannot be omnipresent in the field of study, everywhere, all the time. Hence the dual needs of engaging in prolonged periods of fieldwork and becoming an "insider," to "go native," in order to make up for not being able to be everywhere all the time. Thus, when Diane Arbus was documenting nudist camps in the early 1960s, "she had to be a participant observer: she had to agree to be naked, too" (Warburton, 1992, p.402).

Arbus' photography is premised on ideas opposite to those of Cartier-Bresson. Warburton offers an interesting interpretation of one of the pictures from the nudist camp series. "In this photograph of the retired nudists, Arbus is showing us something very specific about particular individuals and the gap between how they want to be seen and how actually we do see them" (Warburton, 1992, p.402).[4] This gap is something that Arbus actually sought to create by making her subjects pose in front of the camera. According to Sontag,

> Arbus wanted her subjects to be as fully conscious as possible, aware of the act in which they were participating. Instead of trying to coax her subjects into a natural or typical position, they are encouraged to be awkward – that is, to pose.
>
> *Sontag (2005 [1973], p.29)*

Hers is not the lucky and artful capturing of the "decisive moment"; "There is no decisive moment [in Arbus' photography]" (Sontag, 2005 [1973], p.29). Instead, there is a breach of the ordinary (Garfinkel, 1967). Arbus is such a renowned photographer because she is able to make visible the dramatization of the situation, not just by her mastery of technique, but even more so by her mastery of the situation.

In Van Maanen's terms, Cartier-Bresson privileges *operational* data, whereas Arbus privileges *presentational* data, as the main source of expressive power in their pictures. "[O]perational data deal with observed activity (behavior per se) and presentational data deal with the appearances put forth by informants as these activities are talked about and otherwise symbolically projected within the research setting" (Van Maanen, 1979, p.542). Nonetheless, in spite of their different approaches to photography, neither Cartier-Bresson nor Arbus produces pictures that are "mechanical records" of "what really happened." "Data are not, as is often assumed, a mechanical record. Every time we look at data, we are aware, however slightly, of the ethnographer selecting that sight from an infinity of other possible sights" (Berger, 2008 [1972], p.10). Becker (1974, p.11) details some of this selection when he discusses how "the photographer exerts enormous control over the final image and the information and message it contains" and when he quotes Saul Warkov, one of his photography teachers at the San Francisco Art Institute, to have said that "The camera is a wonderful mechanism. It will reproduce, exactly, what is going on inside of your head."

However different in their approaches, Cartier-Bresson and Arbus practice their skills through well-developed theories-in-use. But what remains and what results, when ethnographers hand out their cameras – literally so – to their research participants, such that *they* make the recordings? Or when ethnographers become flies on the wall – literally so – as they start to rely on recordings from fixed cameras?

Hindmarsh and Llewellyn (2018) offer an example of the latter situation. They discuss the use of video recording using a fixed camera to investigate socio-materiality in micro-interactions. There is little discussion of the camera itself. Obviously, there are choices to be made regarding the number of cameras to be used and their positioning, direction and focus (p.417). But once in place, the setup allows for the automatic collection of data with little or no further inference by the researcher. Beyond these considerations, Hindmarsh and Llewellyn acknowledge that "the limitations of a camera lens mean that some aspects of the scene will not be in view," only to assert that "this simply demands that the analyst refines the scope of the analysis to consider only practices that are visible on the video materials at hand" (p.418). This points to how the camera's angle of vision reifies the researchers' *a priori* assumption that all there is, is in the interaction itself; the camera itself has become a non-human agent in the inquiry by making non-existent and therefore irrelevant everything that is out of its focus.

Handing over the camera to research participants, such as in collaborative and participatory methods for recording data, too, has been argued to strengthen research by its ability to provide insights that researcher-led data recordings are unable to uncover (Rose, 2016; Slutskaya, Game & Simpson, 2018). It can be used as a strategy of data collection in situations when the organizational site under scrutiny is dispersed or virtual, for example, and therefore inaccessible through traditional ethnographic methods (Slutskaya, Game, & Simpson, 2018). It is therefore of no surprise that participant recordings appeal to organizational ethnographers who seek in-depth understanding of the native's point-of-view without affecting the site too much (Fine, Morrill, & Surianarain, 2009).

But what does the ethnographer obtain? It can be argued that when relying on participant-led data collection, s/he essentially obtains a set of "selfies": pictures that the self takes of the self (and/or of situations in which the self finds itself), to show the self to the rest of the world. That is, a set of "*re*-presentations of self in everyday life" (cf. Goffman, 1959), "records of how X had seen X" (cf. Berger, 2008 [1972]). The production of the image has thus shifted from the mere showing of an object or situation – "see this, here, now" – to a situated performance – "see me showing you me" (Frosh, 2015, p.1610). It is well known that selfies produce idealized visual representations of oneself, used for impression management (Lobinger & Brantner, 2015; Senft & Baym, 2015). The ethnographer's request on the research participant, to record whichever is of significance to him/her, makes the thing recorded by the research participant part of his or her self. We may, of course, turn this around and consider the recording by the ethnographer in a similar light; the ethnographer, too, is a participant in her/his own research. It begs the question whether "the behavior studied" in ethnography can be anything else but "that of the researcher" (cf. Fine, Morrill, & Surianarain, 2009, p.216).

The Apparatus

To put it another way: In the act of photography the camera does the will of the photographer but the photographer has to will what the camera can do.

(Flusser, 2000 [1983], p.35)

Berger (2008 [1972], p.8) proposed that the very way in which we see things is affected by what we know or believe, but this way of seeing is also affected by the apparatus used to record the seeing. We produce images (DATA) to "recreate or reproduce" (p.9) what we saw. Before the invention of the camera, traditional images – drawings, oil paintings, sculptures – were "record[s] of how X had seen Y" (p.10). After the invention of the camera, images became *technical* images, produced by an apparatus (Flusser, 2000 [1983]) and seen as mere "records of Y." Whereas drawings, oil paintings and sculptures invite us to reflect over the artist's choices of technique, composition, expression, embedded meanings, etcetera – all of which find their origin in the confrontation of the artist and his/her subject (Berger, 2008 [1972], p.15) – the photograph dissects the image from its source. Consequently,

> through DATA, the world becomes a series of unrelated, freestanding particles; and history, past and present, a set of anecdotes and *faits divers*. ETHNOGRAPHIC METHOD makes reality atomic, manageable, and opaque. It is a view of the world which denies interconnectedness, continuity, but which confers on each moment the character of a mystery.
>
> *(Sontag, 2005 [1973], p.17)*

Recognition of the apparatus (Flusser, 2000 [1983]) – in its first approximation: the camera, the recording device – is crucial to understanding this fragmentation of "the world" through the recording thereof.[5] Whereas "traditional images signify phenomena, ... technical images signify concepts" (p.14). In the case of traditional images, there are the creator-artists who encode – "in their heads" (p.15) – the world when they produce their images. In the case of technical images, however, the encoding takes place in an apparatus. In this "black box" (p.16) "scientific statements and equations [i.e., a program] [translate the world out there] into states of things, i.e. images" (p.19). In this way,

> [technical images] are metacodes of texts which ... signify [the scientific-technical] texts [on the base of which they were produced by the apparatus], not the world out there. The imagination that produces them involves the ability to transcode concepts from texts into images; when we observe them, we see concepts – encoded in a new way – of the world out there.
>
> *(p.15)*

This is somewhat complicated language to say that an apparatus, such as the camera, is unlike any ordinary tool or machine. Ordinary tools and machines were invented as simulations (and extensions) of the "teeth, fingers, hands, arms, legs" of human beings (Flusser, 2000 [1983], p.23), useful in "tearing objects from the natural world and informing them, i.e. changing the world" (p.25). Apparatuses, however, were invented with the intention "to change the *meaning* of the world" (p.25, emphasis added) by simulating (and extending) specific thought processes: "thinking expressed in numbers" (p.31). In this sense, "all apparatuses ... are calculating machines ..., the camera included, even if their inventors were not able to account for this" (p.31). They are designed according to a program, and they can be operated by following its program. In this way, "an 'apparatus' [is] a thing that lies in wait or in readiness for something ... The photographic apparatus lies in wait for photography; it sharpens its teeth in readiness" (p.21), and in a similar way, "the ETHNOGRAPHIC METHOD is a tool whose intention is to produce ETHNOGRAPHIC DATA" (p.21).

The program of the apparatus is the set of possibilities it affords its operator, just as the rules of chess can be seen as the program of the game (Flusser, 2000 [1983], p.30). This program is vast and rich, "practically inexhaustible" (p.36) but "nevertheless finite" (p.26). It offers its operator – the ETHNOGRAPHER as its "functionary" (p.27) – a great number of possibilities to explore, and hence operating the apparatus is like playing, not with it "but against it" (p.27), in the "endeavor to exhaust the ETHNOGRAPHIC METHOD by realizing all their possibilities" (p.26).

Belonging to the species of *Homo ludens* (Flusser, 2000 [1983], p.27, *cf.* Huizinga, 1949 [1938]),

> ETHNOGRAPHERS attempt to find the possibilities not yet discovered within it [the apparatus]: They handle the ETHNOGRAPHIC METHOD, turn it this way and that, look into it and through it. If they look through the ETHNOGRAPHIC METHOD out into the world, this is not because the world interests them but because they are pursuing new possibilities of producing information and evaluating the ETHNOGRAPHIC program. Their interest is concentrated on the ETHNOGRAPHIC METHOD; for them, the world is purely a pretext for the realization of ETHNOGRAPHIC possibilities.
>
> *(p.26)*

For sure, functionaries – the photographer, the ethnographer – can control the apparatus from the outside, but they do not really know what is going on inside of it.

> They know how to feed the ETHNOGRAPHIC METHOD ..., and likewise they know how to get it to spit out DATA ... Therefore the ETHNOGRAPHIC

METHOD does what the ETHNOGRAPHER wants it to do, even though the ETHNOGRAPHER does not know what is going on inside the ETHNOGRAPHIC METHOD.

(Flusser, 2000 [1983], pp.27–28)

Yet, because the internal functioning of the apparatus is and remains a black box, its functionary operates it under the – false – impression that it is an ordinary tool. "It looks here as if ETHNOGRAPHERS could choose freely, as if their METHODS were following intention. But the choice is limited to the categories of the METHODS, and the freedom of the ETHNOGRAPHER remains a programmed freedom" (p.35). For Flusser, this is the fundamental characteristic of apparatuses: "The functionary controls the apparatus thanks to the control of its exterior (the input and output) and is controlled by it thanks to the impenetrability of its interior" (p.27–28).

It is through this understanding of the camera/ethnographic methods as an apparatus invented to produce technical images that one cannot treat photographs/data as "windows" on the world out there (Flusser, 2000 [1983], p.15f.). Hence Berger's (2008 [1972]) insistence on how the photograph dissects the image from its source and Sontag's (2005 [1973]) concern, first, with how photography fragments the world and, second, with the violence stemming from this fragmentation. As a result, for the ethnographer, "All events are … aimed at DATA, in order to be translated into a state of things. In this way, however, every action simultaneously loses its historical character and turns into a magic ritual and an endlessly repeatable movement" (Flusser, 2000 [1983], p.20).

The Subject of the Objective

(i) The photographer chooses the event he photographs. This choice can be thought of as a cultural construction. The space for this construction is, as it were, cleared by his rejection of what he did not choose to photograph.

(Berger, 2013b [1982], pp.66–67)

(ii) A photograph arrests the flow of time in which the event photographed once existed.

(Berger, 2013b [1982], p.62)

(iii) When we find a photograph meaningful, we are lending it a past and a future.

(Berger, 2013b [1982], p.64)

As indicated by these excerpts there are a number of alternative, potentially confusing and conflicting, readings of the agency involved in the photographic endeavor and similarly in ethnographic fieldwork. Linking with the above excerpts, it could be argued that agentic primacy is attributed to various entities, respectively to:

(i) the photographer, as the operator of the camera and the one who makes the decision to trigger it (but limited by the program of the apparatus, see the previous section);

(ii) the moment, as an inseparable uniquely whole instant, of which the photograph becomes a trace (from a radical post-humanist stance about the agency of phenomena);

(iii) the interpreter, as the interpreter of the photograph, attributing and infusing it with meaning in the stream of lived experience (from a hermeneutic stance).

But it is also worth asking if the question of doing fieldwork – of which photography can be a part – can truly and satisfactorily be understood in these terms. We think it is worthwhile to pay closer attention to the subject of the objective: the manager or the corporation, for example. Because with the possible exception of some really isolated early incidents, perhaps indeed the early salvage-oriented ethno/photography of natives, we live in a world in which everyone understands what it means to be photographed. In fact, if one was to think of the reach of social media sites such as Instagram, then sometimes it almost appears as if to exist implies to be photographed! Therefore, the one photographed, the subject of the objective, has consented or even desired to be recorded, at least in the modern ethnography with its ethnical norms. This condition of the subject knowing what it means to be photographed, results in photography that is purposefully pre-infused with interpretative meaning beyond the device, the moment, and the photographer. This condition begs the question: "What is the influence of those photographed – men, women, both contextualized – on the making of a photographic account of them?" If we accept this expansion in the meaning of the photographer-cum-fieldworker, we move close to the thinking of Azoulay.

> The theory of ETHNOGRAPHY proposed in this book is founded on a new ontological-political understanding of ETHNOGRAPHY. It takes into account all the participants in ETHNOGRAPHIC acts – METHOD, ETHNOGRAPHER, ETH-NOGRAPHED subject, and spectator – approaching the DATA (and its meaning) as an unintentional effect of the encounter between all of these. None of these have the capacity to seal off this effect and determine its sole meaning.
>
> *(Azoulay, 2008, p.23)*

Not just the photograph, the photographer, and the camera, but those photographed, too, are an inalienable, autonomous element in the process of making a photograph or even in the decision to make one. In contrast to fieldworkers – ethnographers, photographers – who maintain a distinction between themselves and those photographed, Azoulay presents those photographed as co-constructors of photography. For her, there is a citizenry of photography that is open to everyone as she reaches out for photography's emancipatory potential for challenging power relations; and also points a way toward resistance to corporate forms of hegemony. It is quite possible that this "cultural construction" (Berger, 2013b [1982], p.66) may not always be a pleasant affair; it may expose the conflict and struggle implicit in the creation of meanings.

Particularly, in recording management this will be manifest because there is much which never registers on the ethnographer's film, because the typical site of recording – the corporation – does not disclose itself to the recorder. This is so because of the unique and typically privileged position that the corporation occupies in contemporary society. A corporation must be restricted; it is so because of legal demands and special interests it desires to protect, but also because it typically does not desire to join the citizenry of photography occupied by a *hoi polloi* of activists, environmentalists and champions of the disenfranchised. Access itself is through locked doors, with organizational status dictating who may go where; with critical corridors and rooms guarded by 24/7 monitoring CCTV recorders. Moreover, we are likely to find internal political conflicts and departmental boundaries that all add complications to that which is made recordable and why; all of which render the recorded data into purposefully constructed political artifacts. All this does not necessarily imply that the corporation's inability to disclose itself is a malign act, rather it stems from the utter structural inability to be something neutral and removed from society.

In Goffman's (1959) terms, privilege implies that what can be recorded is only that which is front stage in a dramaturgical sense: the facades of corporations (buildings, meeting rooms), corporate communications, executive performances, brands, social media content, mass media content, professional media content. These dramaturgical acts serve to enhance the public self-image of the corporation; they are always scripted to suit the specific time, place and values of the managers who make the corporation available for recording. They form the "can be seen" of corporations. If this is all that we can ever see, then perhaps Warburton's (1992) photographic stance is of relevance. Precisely because the front is dramatized and staged, the posture "given off" may subtly differ from the posture "given." Can the ethnographer, just like Diane Arbus, see and make visible the cracks and inconsistencies in the dramatized front? The "present absences" and the "absent presences" (cf. Knox, O'Doherty, Vurdubakis, & Westrup, 2015) of the situation?

Ethnography beyond the Lens: The Private and the Public Picture

What served in place of data, before the INVENTION OF RECORDING? The expected answer is the engraving, the drawing, the painting. The more revealing answer might be: memory. What DATA does out there in space was previously done within reflection.

(Berger, 2013a [1978], p.51)

The gathering of data in organizational ethnography is often conducted in an acquisitive mode; what is recorded is what the researcher (within some framework of decency stipulated by e.g. research ethics, research boards, or access restrictions) wills to be recorded. S/he places the camera in front of what warrants recording and pushes the red button for record. This is largely irrelevant of the kind of recording made; a film, a photograph, an interview, or even the scribbling of field notes follows a similar logic. What is valued in such recording is often somehow exceptional – be this a single unique instance of deviant behavior or an entire pattern of counter-intuitive findings. But what is important here is *for whom* the recording takes place. Although ethnographic data can be collected for the private use of the ethnographer, more often it is collected with an eye to using them to inform an external public: the academic community. Berger makes a distinction between the private and public uses of photography, cautioning us against the recording *for a public*.

> We need to return to the distinction I made between the private and the public use of ETHNOGRAPHY. In the private use of ETHNOGRAPHY, the context of the instant recorded is preserved so that the DATA lives in an ongoing continuity. … The public DATA, by contrast, is torn from its context, and becomes a dead object which, exactly because it is dead, lends itself to any arbitrary use.
>
> *(Berger, 2013a [1978], p.56)*

But the question becomes, can there be space for data which bring forth the novel or the unseen? Many ethnographers would likely agree that there is indeed such space; they see their enterprise as one of bringing out the fine details of everyday life, not unlike the photography of Diane Arbus. Yet, there is cause for skepticism because pictures that rely on simple novelty – especially of the more shocking kind – have a strange shelf life: the picture that initially shocks and tremendously energizes us, renders us, sooner or later, jaded or even cynical (Sontag, 2005 [1973], p.15). We see this effect most clearly in instances of great distress, such as the photography of war, humanitarian crisis, or abject poverty. What is an initial surge of consciousness ebbs away after some time into a distressed sense of resignation and passivity.

The problem with such photography, or fieldwork for that matter, is its production of recording simply for consumption. Even when a picture or an ethnographic inscription is recorded with an empathetic intent, it lacks force if it does not carry the wider context.

> The task will determine both the kinds of DATA taken and the way they are used. There can of course be no formulae, no prescribed practice. Yet in recognizing how ETHNOGRAPHY has come to be used by capitalism, we can define at least some of the principles of an alternative practice. For the ETHNOGRAPHER this means thinking of her- or himself not so much as a reporter to the rest of the world but, rather, as a recorder for those involved in the events ETHNOGRAPHED. This distinction is crucial.
>
> *(Berger, 2013a [1978], pp.57–58)*

Behind every picture or piece of data is a lived life. In reflexive fieldwork, the camera should mentally point away from, rather than aiming at, the subject as an object of spectacle. What is shot onto the film or recorded on a device is evidence, or a trace, of where the site positioned the ethnographer. The recording of ethnographic data should be an act of integrity towards the recorded, and not recorded (and later analytically consumed) as a decontextualized, clinical device. All recording is to perform an act of memory, though a piece of data is but a single node in a larger rhizome of remembering. It is part of a wider experience or social memory (Berger, 2013a [1978], p.59). The recording of such experiences and memories is to perform a re-placement of time from the actual to a narrative form; into something that is remembered and thus also into something collectively contextualized and empowered, because "the remembered is not the terminus of the line" (p.59). Thus, transferring Berger's sentiment to organizational ethnography implies that as such we need to go beyond recording. Recording by itself is both incomplete and decontextualized.

Conclusion

In this chapter, we pointed to ethnographic data and their recording as an underexposed topic in the literature on (organizational) ethnography. We did so by invoking photography as an analogy to ethnography. We found this analogy to be fruitful, because considerable reflection has taken place on questions such as "How to understand photographic pictures?" and "What is this practice of photography?" Such questions have been asked since the very invention of photography, in 1839. Critical thinkers such as John Berger, Susan Sontag, Vilém Flusser and Ariella Azoulay made decisive moves in rejecting the still widespread belief that photographs are objective and truthful reflections of, and hence windows on, reality, and thereby pushed the thinking about photographs and photography well beyond aesthetics and semiotics.[6]

Our chapter is timely. The attempt to highlight how ethnographic data are "framed," in a very literal sense, is of great relevance given the increasing popularity of using "visual methods" for data collection and data analysis. It adds to Van Maanen's discussion of misplaced belief in the facticity of ethnography.

> The results of ethnographic study are thus mediated several times over: first, by the fieldworker's own standards of relevance as to what is and what is not worthy of observation; second, by the historically situated questions that are put to the people in the setting; third, by the self-reflection demanded of an informant; and fourth, by the intentional and unintentional ways the produced data are misleading.
>
> *(Van Maanen, 1979, p.549)*

We add to this fourth mediation through our discussion of the recording of ethnographic data. Our argument exposes ethnographic data as "technical data" – initially building on Berger and Sontag, and fully on Flusser – to argue that seeing them otherwise is to succumb to the "magic of the image." Moreover, and extending from Azoulay, we note that in organizational ethnography, and in particular in anthropology of management, the questions of what can be data, and how data can be crafted, are negotiated with the subjects of the objective. For all these reasons, data are *re*-presentations, recorded through an apparatus. This condition needs to be understood when recording and contemplating ethnographic data. Hence our invitation, and hence our title: "Frames of the Field."

Notes

1 In this quote there are several substitutions: DATA substitutes *photographs* and *images*, ETHNOGRAPHY substitutes *photography*, ETHNOGRAPHIC METHOD substitutes *camera*, ORGANIZATION substitutes *art*. These and similar substitutions in other quotes in the chapter are printed in small caps type.

2 In making the analogy of photographs and ethnographic data, we conveniently ignore that one can discuss a single photograph when it has been printed and published, but not a single ethnographic datum, as ethnographic data are never published as such. However, for many documentary photographers, it is not the single picture that matters but the "picture story," the photographic reportage, the "telling [of] a story in a sequence of pictures" (Cartier-Bresson, 1952).

3 "To photograph is to appropriate the thing photographed. It means putting oneself into a certain relation to the world that feels like knowledge – and, therefore, like power" (Sontag, 2005 [1973], p.2). And more forcefully: "To photograph people is to violate them … it turns people into objects that can be symbolically possessed. Just as the camera is a sublimation of the gun, to photograph someone is a sublimated murder" (p.10).

4 *Retired man and his wife at home in a nudist camp one morning, NJ. 1963*, available from: http://collections.vam.ac.uk/item/O125684/retired-man-and-his-wife-photograph-arbus-diane/.

5 The "Lexicon of Basic Concepts" in Flusser (2000 [1983], p.83) offers as definition: "*Apparatus* (pl. -*es*): a plaything or game that simulates thought [*trans*. An overarching term for a non-human agency, e.g. the camera, the computer and the 'apparatus' of the State or of the market]; organization or system that enables something to function." This formulation suggests a connection to Foucault's use of *dispositif*, often translated in English as "apparatus," and the related process of subjectification (see Agamben, 2009, for an accessible introduction and background to the term in Foucault's corpus). A full treatment of the meaning of the concept of apparatus with Flusser is beyond the scope of this chapter.

6 This chapter obviously does not discuss "photo elicitation" (Collier, 1967), the technique of probing research participants to elicit comments, memories, feelings, associations, etcetera, by showing them photographs. Questions such as whether and how our chapter speaks to this technique are beyond its scope.

References

Agamben, G. (2009). *What is an apparatus? And other essays*. Stanford, CA: Stanford University Press.

Alvesson, M. (2003). Beyond neopositivists, romantics, and localists: A reflexive approach to interviews in organizational research. *Academy of Management Review*, 28(1), 13–33.

Alvesson, M. & Kärreman, D. (2007). Constructing mystery: Empirical matters in theory development. *Academy of Management Review*, 32(4), 1265–1281.

Azoulay, A. (2008). *The civil contract*. New York, NY: Zone Books.

Bate, P. (1997). Whatever happened to organizational anthropology? A review of the field of organizational ethnography and anthropological studies. *Human Relations*, 50(9), 1147–1171.

Becker, H. S. (1974). Photography and sociology. *Studies in Visual Communication*, 1(1), 3–26.

Berger, J. (2008 [1972]). *Ways of seeing*. London, UK: Penguin.

Berger, J. (2013a [1978]). Uses of photography. In G. Dyer (Ed.), *Understanding a photograph*, 49–60. London, UK: Penguin.

Berger, J. (2013b [1982]). Appearances. In G. Dyer (Ed.), *Understanding a photograph*, 61–98. London, UK: Penguin.

Cartier-Bresson, H. (1952). *The decisive moment [Images à la sauvette]*. New York, NY: Simon and Schuster (retrieved on 23 October 2018, from https://digitalphoto1sva.files.wordpress.com/2013/09/cartierbresson_the-decisive-moment.pdf).

Clifford, J. (1986). On ethnographic allegory. In J. Clifford & G. E. Marcus (Eds.), *Writing culture: The poetics and politics of ethnography*, 98–121. Berkeley, CA: University of California Press.

Clifford, J. & Marcus, G. E. (Eds.). (1986). *Writing culture: The poetics and politics of ethnography*. Berkeley, CA: University of California Press.

Collier, J. (1967). *Visual anthropology: Photography as a research method*. New York, NY: Holt, Rinehart and Winston.

Corbin, J. M. & Strauss, A. L. (2008). *Basics of qualitative research: Techniques to developing grounded theory* (3rd Ed.). Los Angeles, CA: Sage.

Crawford, P. I. (1992). Film as discourse: The invention of anthropological realities. In P. I. Crawford & D. Turton (Eds.), *Film as ethnography*, 66–82. Manchester, UK: Manchester University Press.

Eisenhardt, K. M. (1989). Building theories from case-study research. *Academy of Management Review*, 14(4), 532–550.

Fine, G. A., Morrill, C. & Surianarain, S. (2009). Ethnography in organizational settings. In D. Buchanan & A. Bryman (Eds.), *The Sage handbook of organizational research methods*, 602–619. London, UK: Sage.

Flusser, V. (2000 [1983]). *Towards a philosophy of photography (Für eine Philosophie der Fotografie)*. London, UK: Reaktion Books.

Frosh, P. (2015). The gestural image: The selfie, photography theory and kinesthetic sociability. *International Journal of Communication*, 9, 1607–1628.

Garfinkel, H. (1967). *Studies in ethnomethodology*. London, UK: Polity Press.

Goffman, E. (1959). *The presentation of self in everyday life*. New York, NY: Free Press.

Harper, D. (1994). On the authority of the image. In N. K. Denzin & Y. S. Lincoln (Eds.), *The Sage handbook of qualitative research*, 403–412. Thousand Oaks, CA: Sage.

Hindmarsh, J. & Llewellyn, N. (2018). Video in sociomaterial investigations: A solution to the problem of relevance for organizational research. *Organizational Research Methods*, 21(2), 412–437.

Huizinga, J. (1949 [1938]). *Homo ludens: A study of the play-element in culture*. London, UK: Routledge & Kegan Paul.

Ketokivi, M., Mantere, S. & Cornelissen, J. (2017). Reasoning by analogy and the progress of theory. *Academy of Management Review*, 42(4), 637–658.

Knox, H., O'Doherty, D., Vurdubakis, T. & Westrup, C. (2015). Something happened: Spectres of organization/disorganization at the airport. *Human Relations*, 68(6), 1001–1020.

LeBaron, C., Jarzabkowski, P., Pratt, M. & Fetzer, G. (2018). An introduction to video methods in organizational research. *Organizational Research Methods*, 21(2), 239–260.

Lobinger, K. & Brantner, C. (2015). In the eye of the beholder: Subjective views on the authenticity of selfies. *International Journal of Communication*, 9, 1848–1860.

Lune, H. & Berg, B. L. (2017). *Qualitative research methods for the social sciences* (9th ed.). Harlow, UK: Pearson Education.

Malinowski, B. (1922). *Argonauts of the Western Pacific*. London, UK: George Routledge & Sons.

Mantere, S. & Ketokivi, M. (2013). Reasoning in organization science. *Academy of Management Review*, 38(1), 70–89.

Philp, J. (2004). 'Embryonic science': The 1888 Torres Strait photographic collection of A.C. Haddon. In R. Davis (Ed.), *Woven histories, dancing lives: Torres Strait islander identity, culture and history*, 90–106. Canberra, Australia: Aboriginal Studies Press.

Pink, S. (2007). *Doing visual ethnography*. London, UK: Sage.

Ray, J. L. & Smith, A. D. (2012). Using photographs to research organizations: Evidence, considerations, and application in a field study. *Organizational Research Methods*, 15(2), 288–315.

Rose, G. (2016). *Visual methodologies: An introduction to researching with visual materials* (4th Ed.). London, UK: Sage.

Schembri, S. & Boyle, M.V. (2013). Visual ethnography: Achieving rigorous and authentic interpretations. *Journal of Business Research*, 66(9), 1251–1254.

Senft, T. M. & Baym, N. K. (2015). What does the selfie say? Investigating a global phenomenon. *International Journal of Communication*, 9, 1588–1606.

Slutskaya, N., Game, A. & Simpson, R. (2018). Better together: Examining the role of collaborative ethnographic documentary in organizational research. *Organizational Research Methods*, 21(2), 341–365.

Sontag, S. (2005 [1973]). *On photography*. New York, NY: RosettaBooks.

Sutton, R. I. & Staw, B. M. (1995). What theory is not. *Administrative Science Quarterly*, 40(3), 371–384.

Van Maanen, J. (1979). Fact of fiction in organizational ethnography. *Administrative Science Quarterly*, 24(4), 539–550.

Van Maanen, J. (1995). Style as theory. *Organization Science*, 6(1), 133–143.

Van Maanen, J. (2011 [1988]). *Tales of the field: On writing ethnography*. Chicago, IL: University of Chicago Press.

Warburton, N. (1992). Diane Arbus and Erving Goffman. *History of Photography*, 16(4), 401–404.

Zundel, M., MacIntosh, R. & Mackay, D. (2018). The utility of video diaries for organizational research. *Organizational Research Methods*, 21(2), 386–411.

6

ETHNOGRAPHY, AIR-CONDITIONED

Nahoko Kameo

Introduction

Unlike Malinowski who lived among the Islanders in New Guinea, I started my first fieldwork in a software engineering firm, in which I was also employed at the time. The firm believed that by having fieldworkers they would find a better way to interact with customers and also to manage software projects. In my second ethnographic work, I observed a software engineering division in another firm, this time as a consultant to the research unit of the corporation that the software engineering division was part of. I didn't travel too far for either project, nor did I have to learn a new language. Rather, my second fieldwork project, which I will draw upon in this chapter, was a convenient 30 minutes' drive from home. I would park the car and then walk right into a room that was cool and air-conditioned, with open desks (that was one of the features I was studying). The hardest part of the travel to the fieldsite was not the distance, but the gate: I got into the building with a key card granted by the upper management, and took the elevator to the organizational labyrinth.

I was interested in how organizational change – the introduction of a team-based, empowered work scheme – shaped the way engineers work and think about their workplace. I was a graduate student, and was tucked into a larger project within the firm that was trying to understand work practices and knowledge management in the firm. Software engineers were nice to me – or at the very least polite. Some thought I was tied to the senior management, and I was myself conflicted about that; it was true that I *was* tied to the management, in the sense that the whole ethnographic project was tied to the management. At the same time, no one really cared about what I was doing – who would care about the ethnographer's lengthy report when the version 2.0 of the software that was promised to customers was going to be missing the deadline?

I wrote about the ways in which engineers interpreted the management scheme that was supposed to create empowered teams, in the context that the management frequently changed managerial practices. I am confident about what I wrote in the paper (Kameo 2017), but also wondered how my paper (or a book, if I was to write a book) would be different if I actually knew software engineering, or if I actually intimately knew how the people who worked there lived their lives outside the workplace. Of course, I could assume that they probably went to the shopping malls nearby, to schools similar to those I knew, and had family lives. But I was not sure – I only saw them in the office, during a quick lunch, happy hour drinks for coworkers, and a company-sponsored family day.

For modern anthropologists, the supposed difference between "us" (rational and sensible Westerners) and "savages" (for whom we need a good amount of cultural decoding), was cause for much reflection and repentance. Ethnography in business (and other) organizations, on the other hand, is a distinctively modern development. We never assumed our interlocutors were much different than we are. As a matter of fact, in finding a new fieldsite, we don't even try and look for an unfamiliar setting; indeed we often look for a site that is familiar, that the ethnographer once worked at, or at least a site that the ethnographer has contacts outside of her ethnographer persona. Given we aren't studying "savages," the similarity between the fieldworker and the subjects is considered an asset. A designer turned ethnographer studying a design office; a former activist studying a neighborhood council; a former high school teacher studying a classroom. In some cases, it's not even that ethnographers are similar to the participants, but much like in my own biography, a participant becomes ethnographer – as ethnography gains traction in organizations, especially in the corporate world, there are increasing numbers of lay (non-academically trained) people trying to do a bit of ethnography in their own firm (Fayard et al. 2016; Suchman 2013).

Yet, much as the dangers of orientalism continue to plague modern anthropology, we need to examine the ramifications of our own genre – of the ethnography of contemporary organizational spaces – where we move through one air-conditioned space to another. The difference is not only epistemological – studying "us" instead of the "other" – but also methodological and pragmatic. In this chapter, I will focus on ethnography of a social space that is considered professional, such as corporate boardrooms, hospitals, high-tech firms and the like. In the following, I consider pragmatic concerns that organizational ethnographers may face, and the potential consequences of the solutions ethnographers may use to conduct ethnography in organizations. *Access* and *engagement in the field* discuss how organizational ethnographers are situated in the field and why it affects the way they collect and analyze data. Such specific kinds of engagement then lead the ethnographer to produce work that is unlike traditional ethnography in relation to *thick description* and *the community of inquiry*.

First, I show that the kind of access – how the ethnographer gets entry into the organization – plays a key role in what kind of research the ethnographer can conduct. Organizations aren't public spaces, and the pragmatic strategies ethnographers use affect what kind of research topic, data access, and objectivity the ethnographer can secure during and after the fieldwork. Second, the norm of thick description has to be considered in the context of organizational ethnographic research. Every ethnographer after Geertz purports to write "thick description": but how to engage with this concept when we describe an organization that is so close to home, so culturally "transparent"? Third, as the difference between organizational ethnographers and corporate culture consultants becomes blurred, the careful reflection on the communities we belong to – the community we study, and the community of inquiry that are at least part of our intended readership – allows us to both recognize the intellectual space where corporate culture experts may be useful and also the value of academic ethnographers.

Access

Getting access into a professional organizational space is not an easy thing. Many ethnographers will tell you about gaining access in their appendix (if they have a book), or will tell you a tale or two over drinks in conferences. The difficulty is not a matter of geographic distance, because the ethnographer does not even move from her own city in most cases. The difficulty is about getting the key card that opens the magic door to the organizations. Whereas more traditional sites of ethnography – neighborhood, ethnic communities, religious institutions, or social movement groups – welcome newcomers and engage with their members publicly, modern organizations exist by demarcating who the participants are, what the roles of these participants will have, what is being exchanged between the participant and organization, and what the organization does to the outside world. Instead of trying to figure out what people are doing in their community in ethnography, organizational ethnographers start with the codified, and inscribed, definition of what the organization is, what each of the organizational members do in the organization, and so on. While finding out what is going on may be the core mission of a traditional ethnographer, problematizing what we are already told is going on is often one of the hardest charges of the organizational ethnographer.

When I started the ethnography of a software engineering firm, I knew precisely who these people were – there were project managers, line managers, team managers, and software engineers, neatly described in an organization chart. In a tightly regulated space like this one, someone (an ethnographer) cannot just come in and chat. Of course, the organizational chart is infamously imprecise – as soon as the chart is passed down to the ethnographer, any organizational member would tell her that it is not accurate anymore, and that it probably wasn't accurate to start with. Nevertheless, the organization is managed by having (if not necessarily observing) tightly regulated roles, scripts, exchanges and goals that the ethnographer is spoonfed on the very first day.

Entry by Consulting

One way the ethnographer gets access to such spaces is by acting as a consultant. By labeling the ethnographer a consultant, the organization solves quite a few problems – it defines the role and status of an ethnographer, it sets itself a putative benefit from her fieldwork, and it gains some control over what she will be able to see. For an organization, a member who does not quite do anything (except hanging out) is unintelligible. Thus, even if the ethnographer initially refuses to be an official consultant for fear of curtailing their freedom of research, the people who are getting her access – most often senior managers – have their own reasons as to why they let a stranger in their midst.

Unless the ethnographer gained access by strong family or friendship network ties (which will be discussed momentarily), the managers' hope is that the ethnographer will see something that they weren't able to notice with their trained eyes as professional managerial staff. Executives are normally unaware of the training and value of an academic, who holds a Ph.D. in human/social sciences, but they do value university-produced degrees – they themselves usually have a couple of these. Oftentimes, they come up with the idea of consultancy in order to make sense of letting in an outsider – gaining some kind of professional advice sounds more sensible than having a person who does not work there simply hanging out because they want to.

There are a few practical ways to deal with this overt or covert request. The first is to agree with a condition saying that since you are a researcher, the research agenda will not necessarily coincide with the managers' interest, but (and this "but" is key) you'll be able to show them the "unbiased" findings so the managers can see what the ethnographer thought was prominent. While the ethnographer is excused from presenting something directly useful to the managers, this excuse can direct the ethnographer's core research agenda in subtle ways. What if, for example, the ethnographer found that gender relations in the corporate boardroom was the aspect her research would be focused on, and what if – as an example – the gendered compromise on the part of the female executives is ubiquitous and "functional" to the operation of smooth decision-making? Executives who think it may be useful to have an observer on a whim aren't usually excited to hear that their offices are the stage of gendered performance that reproduces heteronormativity.

If the ethnographer knows that the executives expect some findings that do not disrupt the organization and can contribute to the productivity of the organization (which would be what a manager should want, after all), then the ethnographer must either present results that will not satisfy those who took the effort to bring her in, or prepare something that is entirely different from her own research altogether. This is a practical problem inherent in doing corporate ethnography when findings are interpreted by organizational members (Suchman 2013; Fayard and Van Maanen 2015). Even if organizations are more likely to be open to – or even willing to purchase – the written texts that describe their yet-to-be-encoded culture, the ethnographer is highly unlikely to produce exactly what the managers had in mind.

The second strategy is to explicitly align the ethnographer's interest with that of managers. This seems easier than a purist academic ethnographer (who would simply refuse the consultant role) might think, because any organization has multiple groups, and even within a group, people have various ideas about what they want to know and do about the organization. The technicality of work itself helps, too – as the work in the modern corporation is complex, there are some subtypes of work where the ethnographer's interest and the organization's interest align – sales, customer service, user interface design, meeting procedures, use of certain artifacts or technologies within the organization, and so on.

The classic ethnography of this type is workplace studies, which PARC – Palo Alto Researcher Center – pioneered with the work of Orr (1996), looking at how field engineers shared their embodied knowledge of the copiers they troubleshooted. Orr was interested in the practices of technicians who fixed printing machines in offices that rented them. The corporation – Xerox – was interested in disseminating information regarding machine troubles and the techniques to fix them. Orr, himself both a former technician and an anthropologist, observed the way field technicians work and concluded that the work is fundamentally social and that talking about machines in a narrative form – sharing "war stories" about their day with colleagues – was an essential way that the engineers shared their embodied knowledge regarding the tips, quirks of the machines, and other information regarding the machines.

At a glance, there seems to be no problem in matching the ethnographer's interest and that of the corporation. Orr was a researcher in a subsidiary company of Xerox, so he was indirectly paid by the company he studied even while the status of in-house researcher allowed him a somewhat independent position in terms of the agenda of the study. Focus on technical work also at first sight may seem inherently apolitical. If the ethnographer's interest is, as an example, how the organizational members use new technologies – such as corporate wiki – or how designers work together to create user-centered GUIs – how can it possibly matter if the ethnographer is dependent on the organization or not? But technology has to be practiced, and the way organizational members get to use it for work almost always has a political aspect to it. In a reflection piece he wrote much later, Orr noted that at the time of fieldwork, he noticed that the management – the level above the field leader – did not recognize let alone value the actual ways field technicians' accumulated knowledge about machines and honed their expertise (Orr 2006). The discrepancy between what was going on at the level of the field and the management was an underlining theme of his writing, which shed light on the creative ways through which field technicians solved problems at work.

Orr (2006) suggested that the corporation remained somewhat ignorant about the field technician's work and needs – they kept trying to control or assist engineers in ways that were not helpful to them. Thus, while not discussed in his book, the organizational disjuncture was scaffolding the lively, creative and closed "talk at work" that Orr described. The ethnography – that is primarily about the group culture and knowledge sharing among engineers – quickly started to have implications regarding management and the organizational structure. So, if the organization does want the ethnographer to "contribute," the dilemma about the ethnographer's interest and the organization's expectation is a salient issue the ethnographer must solve, case by case. Again, while Orr's original work is no less illuminating for it, there were aspects of the job he worked around so that he would not be at odds with the company.

Moreover, when the ethnographer is compensated by the organization, the problem is even trickier (Jordan 2016, Fayard et al. 2016). If the ethnographer is politically savvy, she may present the findings in a way that does not offend the one who "paid" for it (although it may offend someone else in the organization), or if the ethnographer is determined to exit without needing to keep her good reputation, she may present her findings as is. But the question is not only how to present the analysis, but how the knowledge that the entry tacitly included a favorable report may affect the data collection, analysis, and presentation on the side of ethnographer.

Entry and Social Similarity

A second way that ethnographers gain entry is by leveraging their social proximity with organizational members. For example, the ethnographer in an investment bank may be a former stock trader-turned Ph.D. student (Ho 2009). The ethnographer may personally know someone who is powerful enough to get access for the ethnographer through family connections. Even when the ethnographer gains entry simply by asking enough people, the proximity of the social background is often palpable (ranging from both ethnographer and organizational members being college-educated middle class to having very similar educational and personal backgrounds).

Leveraging social proximity can sometimes afford researchers more independence from the management than coming in as an overt/covert consultant because once she gets in and blends in well enough, people in the organization tend to stop caring about her. The ethnographer effectively ceases to be the issue to be resolved. This happens especially when the ethnographer gained entry mostly by persistence and sheer luck – consistently talking to enough people in the industry often leads to someone nice and powerful enough to open the door for you (although you will most likely take a few years to encounter such luck). In any case, the virtue of this scenario is that since the access was given as a personal favor, the ethnographer often has few obligations. In these cases, the ethnographer may have to work hard to establish a position within the organization, and, unlike the official "in" as a consultant, she cannot force people to talk to her.

The social proximity between the ethnographer and the organizational members means that ethnographers are embedded in a particular structure of meanings prior to entry. In this case, acculturation was the key to access – if you are doing observations in elite places, it is your own elite status that got you in; if you are doing observation in technical places, it is your own educational and professional background. Setting aside the question of acculturation to the later section, the more pragmatic question that arises while the ethnographer is doing fieldwork is that of quality of access. The ethnographer has less official privilege to ask questions and hang out in this case than being a consultant. Entry to the field does not guarantee access to the organizational members. Who, how, and how much the ethnographer gets to hang out with varies drastically in organizational ethnography.

Engagement in the Field

The position of the ethnographer often determines whose perspectives she obtains more access to. In studies of – as an example – a religious institution, or non-profit volunteers – the ethnographer is a participant and thus expected to behave like everyone else, and see and do what everyone else does. Thus, a new person in a church (Monahan and Fisher 2015), or a new volunteer tutor for a free afterschool program (Eliasoph 2011), is expected to pray, or tutor, respectively, and have the exact same role and access as fellow participants serving the organization. To be sure, being a full-participant observer does not let one see everything – one does not have access to, for instance, management issues being discussed by higher authorities in the particular sect, or the way a non-profit founder is intermingling with local power elites to secure private funding. But oftentimes being a fellow participant allows you to know about it, by word of mouth, and know about it through the perspective of fellow church members or volunteers.

An organizational ethnographer, on the other hand, even when she is similar to her interlocutors, is clearly marked as an outsider from the beginning and therefore her data is skewed not due to the subgroups she belongs in, but due to the selection bias of who wants to talk to the ethnographer. In the cases where the ethnographer carries the stamp of approval from the higher-up, and is working as a consultant, there will be people who want to talk to you, and people who don't, which makes data collection inevitably skewed. Using an example of my own ethnography of a software engineering organization, I quickly realized that some software engineers looked a little worried when they were speaking to me. On the other hand, the senior manager who was responsible for the entire west-coast teams was very accessible, clearly because his manager – the executive – agreed to take part in this research. What was interesting was that middle managers had different responses; some seemed to understand the participation of a research team as a part of ongoing political moves within the organization. Perhaps for that reason, one line manager was quite eager to talk to me, and invited me to meetings, to show me how he was adopting the empowerment scheme I was studying in his own teams. Software engineers – the ones who were most affected by the organizational change I was observing – also had a variety of reactions. Although some were open and happy to talk, others only answered questions when asked.

Another problem is that although the organizational members may be well-meaning and intend to help the ethnographer, they are, by definition, busy working. Organizational ethnographers may encounter members politely refusing to engage with you – because they need to focus on generating ideas, writing presentations, and so on (Tavory 2019). Organizational layout and work practices may often help members "escape" interference by ethnographers, because many offices allow their employees to work in quiet stations, closed office space, or cafes outside the organization. Instead of being able to follow through the production of work, organizational ethnographers thus often have access to bits and pieces of the progress and product through windows of observation such as shadowing, attending team meetings, and attending meetings in which teams often have to report their progress to their superiors. The fact that most of the work tasks are accomplished by team work – with multiple people, and increasingly in multiple locations – makes it even harder to follow the work that organizational members are engaged in and paid for.

Similarity, in other words, isn't enough. When conducting fieldwork in organizations, the ethnographer must establish her own techniques to have enough reliable data on members' organizational lives, combining shadowing, attending various meetings, having lunch or coffee with the members, hanging out in spots where members converse (Fayard and Weeks 2007; Kellogg 2009), to gain enough inside understanding about how the organizational members live and work within the organization. Informally asking about the members' work, when they seem to be available and willing to do so, becomes a skill that ethnographers must acquire – being courteous, friendly, but also resilient.

An ethnographer may also leverage this awkward position in a couple of ways. First, of course, who is talking to the ethnographer and who isn't is itself data. In many cases of organizational change, indeed, it signals that the change isn't accepted by everyone, even at the managerial level. The ethnographer learns quickly that there are power struggles within this group, and changes in the managing techniques are seen to be an integral part of the power struggle. Second, especially in work organizations, but in most organizations – people are busy doing what they are supposed to be doing, so the ethnographer can be a "fly on the wall" in a way that is not possible in many other fieldsites. As Becker (1996) notes, the strength of ethnography is that we observe actors "in the context of what actors do on a day-to-day basis, when all the constraints of their lives are operative." In this context, actors rarely continuously modulate their action – the immediacy of their daily work-life is acute enough that after a while, they stop caring about the ethnographer.

Still, walls have partitions, closed doors, and multiple units on multiple floors, and being a fly on the wall is more challenging than it first seems. Accessing work sites beyond the communal work space – or lined-up cubicles – can be hard for multiple reasons. For example, the organizational members may simply prefer to work alone, unbothered by the ethnographer's constant questions, or forget to keep adding her to the invitation list for meetings (Tavory 2019). The social dimension – the friendship that the ethnographer manages to create with the members – becomes critical in being able to prompt them to keep giving access to the ethnographer to important meetings. In this sense, many ethnographies of corporate settings are "ethnographies of meetings" where the meetings and one-on-one interviews take center stage in the ethnography rather than members' actual work, their work interaction outside of meetings, or online conversations/emails.

Talking with Strangers

Who would want to talk to the ethnographer in the organizational setting? In my fieldwork, in addition to managers who saw it as advantageous to take the (imagined) side of the ethnographer, some other people were also friendly. First were the veteran engineers who were recognized by all members for their skill in software engineering and their knowledge about the ways the firm's old software is written (so called "spaghetti codes"). These engineers never went into management, and seemed to be very open with their criticisms and opinions about the way the organization operates and how organizational change was or should have been managed. They were not afraid of the management, because they never would become one of them at this point, and their work-life was predictable – they had been working in the organization for decades, and had gone through numerous organizational changes. The fact that they were recognized as technical experts also made them feel secure enough to criticize management. So they, more often than others, spoke critically in meetings, and also were friendly and happy to share their thoughts on what was going on in the field.

The second category of people who ethnographers might find easy is the self-defined outsiders. In Kunda's ethnography of a software firm, he found that some software engineers consciously kept a distance from their roles to prevent themselves from attaching to the corporate ideologies and "burning out" – physical and psychological collapse due to excessive work (Kunda 2009 p. 75). Kunda describes these organizational members as "sociologists." Instead of accepting the culture of the engineering firm, these "sociologists" are the ones who choose to have emotional distance from the organization – they observe and comment on how other members work from a birds-eye perspective. Thus, they are happy to comment on other workers' behavior and analyze why they act in the way they do (Kunda 2009).

The Use of Interviews

One way to circumvent the problem of access is to set up formal interviews with the organizational members. Much ethnography consists mostly of repeated in-depth interviews supplemented by some ethnographic observation, in part for the reasons described above. In the case of workplace studies, interviews tend to be used less as the primary source of data, because understanding the work process in action requires ethnographic, interactional data (see Bechky 2003). But many workplace ethnographies had relied primarily on interview data. Studying wall-street banking professionals, Ho (2009), for example, drew on her own experience working as an investment banker and on in-depth interviews among investment bankers she got to know through her stints. In my own research about Japanese university scientists, I relied on in-depth interviews with Japanese university bioscientists and archival data to analyze practice changes after Japan introduced more Americanized, formal, and aggressive policies regarding commercialization of research (Kameo 2015).

Claims about practice changes, changes in scientists' attitudes and action towards more application oriented research were made by analyzing the interview data.

Whereas in business studies and anthropology the two methods of open interview and ethnographic observation aren't clearly distinguished, methodological debates in sociology seem to highlight the epistemological differences and possible analytic concerns between the two methods. In a provocative series of papers and replies, Jerolmack and Khan (2014) argued that asserting people's practices by their verbal answers during an interview could lead to fallible understandings about how they act in actual situations (see DiMaggio 2014; Lamont and Swidler 2014; Cerulo 2014 for methodological discussions). People's attitudes – or what they say in surveys and interview situation – is "cheap" in that even if they meant what they said, there is often only a tenuous relationship between what people do and what people say they do. In particular, three analytic problems of relying on interviews have been pointed out in this methodological literature.

First, people may answer your interview questions in a more idealistic or ideological way than they would actually behave in real life (the classic work for this point is LaPiere 1934, observing that motel and restaurant owners let Chinese customers in, although they said they would refuse to accept Chinese customers in phone interviews). Second, people's accounts of their actions could be "half-truths," or a narrative that is created by vocabulary of motives (Mills 1940) which could be unaligned with the actual process through which they ended up taking the course of action they did. Lastly, without the social context and deep understanding about the life interviewees lead, interviewers may not understand what the interviewee actually meant. Drawing on the fieldwork in medical schools, Becker and Geer (1957) gave an example of the word "crocks" – patients that complain about their physical symptoms but do not exhibit any pathology. Without prior fieldwork and deep understanding of the culture of medical school where patients are valued only to the extent that medical students could learn new, hands-on, medical knowledge, understanding what the "crocks" actually meant and how it reflected the medical school culture would have been impossible.

I do not particularly think interview method and ethnography need to be compared for superiority, nor the usefulness of interview be contested. I do think reflecting upon the ways that organizational ethnography often consists of many in-depth interviews is necessary, given it is a method that is often taken for granted and not explicated. There are distinctive strengths of relying on interviews. In the organizational setting, interviews are extremely useful, particularly in mitigating the problems discussed above: given ethnographers tend to have skewed access to organizational life, complementing data from different perspectives by interviewing members who were observed less would be necessary to understand the organization.

More pragmatically, some organizational events that are essential to the organization are not easily observable because they happen infrequently. Going back to my case, when I wanted to study the change in practices of commercialization, if I observed a professor's science lab, they would be mostly running experiments, discussing scientific projects, and writing articles and grants; commercialization of research is only a small part of a scientist's daily routine, and it is not very pragmatic to observe a week of work hoping for a 20-minute conversation the professor may or may not have with an industry partner over the years to come.

Thus, organizational ethnographers should use interviews strategically – but be aware of the methodological issues depicted in the literature. For example, when an organizational ethnographer interviews members of the organization, she should know the importance of the terms or expressions she doesn't understand as they reflect the system of meaning in that particular workplace. Methodological guide-posts are available, such as *Learning from Strangers* (Weiss 1995), *Ethnographic Interview* by Spradley (2016), or Lamont and Swidler (2014). Future work on the relation-ship between ethnography and interviews, and the reflections on the methodolog-ical issues of interviews, is needed to enable organizational ethnographers to fully engage in the two methodologies.

Thick Description

Given what we know about the specific challenges of access and engagement in the field for organizational ethnographers, what are the ramifications of such challenges after the ethnographer exits the field – and writes up her ethnography? I want to take up two things that we, ethnographers, care about – the issue of *thick description*, and who are we part of – *the community of inquiry*.

In his seminal work, Geertz (1973) advocated for cultural anthropologists to engage in thick description – the narrative that ethnographers generate by fol-lowing the actions and interactions of participants. The goal of ethnography is not to abstract a set of rules for actions or to map out the system of meanings, but to understand how people in the field guide themselves to deal with their existential dilemmas of life – and to delineate the ways through which people understand their surrounding world in situ. Organizational ethnographers, perhaps more than eth-nographers of other "exotic" fieldsites, run the risk of assuming, not understanding, the ways in which organizational members understand and navigate their lives. For one, it is simply hard to take the perspective of a stranger when you know the place so well. Even if the ethnographer is a novice in that particular type of organization – let's say, a graduate student who has never worked in a corporate setting – there are so many assumptions she would make in the field so as not to embarrass herself and "stand out" in the organization. The very reason organizational ethnographers get access is their social proximity – but the ethnographer must then enter the fieldsite as a stranger-learner and "unlearn" the details they are so familiar with (Horiguchi and Imoto 2015).

But to borrow from the example of Ryle (1949; see 2009) discussed by Geertz (1973), describing the cultural contexts participants are living through requires not only deep knowledge about how people navigate their lives, but also how much one assumes the readers of the ethnography are familiar with the cultural objects under discussion. To describe a scene where "a young team leader pretended to wink to his senior manager behind his back in front of his team members to signal the discord between his team and the manager," does the ethnographer start by explaining that contracting eyelids purposefully in front of someone is called a wink, and what symbolic meaning it usually has, or does she start by assuming the readers know what a wink is?

If the ethnographer goes to a, let's say, "all-hands meeting," she may just want to describe it as an all-hands meeting, with only a brief explanation – such as "a meeting held weekly by all the team members to discuss progress on tasks"; this is obvious. But what really is an *"all hands meeting"* in this particular organization? Who is invited and who is not? What kind of governance structure does the meeting presuppose? If the ethnographer is, let's say, observing a team that is responsible for a new GUI, what, really is a GUI? Why do they have to create a team just to produce that specific graphic medium through which lay people can use computers? It may seem economical to assume that your readers know organizational settings in the modern world, but as Garfinkel (1967) amply showed us, to de-familiarize is to know the fundamental underlying assumptions of the social fabric. If the ethnographer is to assume what an "all-hands meeting" is, she will miss the fact that despite it being called such a thing, there are organizational members who are invited, not invited, trying to join by telephone or internet, and who actually speak in this seemingly participatory business meeting.

If the purpose of the ethnographer was to understand and explain the social fabric and lived experience of the members of the field as they try to solve their everyday dilemmas, there is also another simple problem. The organization, by definition, has a door that opens and closes. People come through to live part of their lives in the organization, traditionally from 9am to 5pm, and they exit the organization to move onto other parts of their lives. The ethnographer also studies the organization for its working hours – and as a consequence, she more often than not, has no real idea as to how the people in the organization live their lives outside of the organization.

Coupled with the social proximity between the ethnographer and the members, the ethnographer consciously or unconsciously supplements the understanding of organizational members' lives with her knowledge about how an "average" person with the social and economic characteristics of the participant live with little snippets about their personal information, such as where they live, what they do on weekends, their social media account, and so on. Yet again, this assumption is only an assumption, and without it the ethnographer does not have a picture of the webs of social situations and meanings the organizational members live in, and how these "other worlds" the members live in affect the way they understand and act in the organization under study (Trouille and Tavory 2019).

Community of Inquiry

Organizational ethnography may serve unorthodox purposes more often than other ethnographic sites for a couple of reasons. As already discussed, the fact that the ethnography is done in an *organization* and the ethnographer given access means that the organization – or at least some members – may expect some kind of feedback. Somewhat counterintuitively in the age of big data and sophisticated statistical analysis, ethnography gained recognition from the business world as a useful tool to understand its customers, use of technology, and the organization itself. In practice, this meant that organizational ethnography evolved in a different direction than a purely academic alternative, and scholars have discussed the ramifications of the new genre in various ways (Forsythe 1999; Jordan and Dalal 2006; Westney and Van Maanen 2011).

Although the majority of ethnographers still have institutional affiliations within academia and are generally paid by (and reliant on) their academic appointments, increasingly there are "paid" ethnographic work placements where the ethnographer is directly paid for their work by the organization of study, or even employed by the organization she studies. The issues – or potential problems – of such organizational ethnography seem to be as follows: first, the belonging of the ethnographer, or, simply put, if the ethnographer is paid by the organization to do the job; second, the quality of ethnography and the *ethnographer*; and lastly, the audience.

First, it seems that many ethnographers discuss among themselves the legitimacy of being funded by the organization that is also the fieldsite. Here, the premise of fieldwork is at stake – how can the ethnographer be sufficiently distant if she is part of it, and also, dependent on it? The ethnographer must establish a niche in which the ethnographer contributes to the corporation by unveiling their cultural practices while the ethnographer herself is embedded in the organization that she must make "exotic" – make visible the tacit cultural assumptions and work practices (Suchman 2013). The second problem discussed – that is deeply related to the first – is whether the work produced actually qualifies as ethnography, and the practitioner as an ethnographer, a qualified person to do anthropologically committed participant observation? Especially when the ethnography is on a corporate site, where the pressure for quick results is paramount and the understanding for academic needs is thin, quick observations, focus groups, and short interviews replace long-term apprenticeship, in-depth interviews, and participant observation. Jordan and Lambert (2009) showcase their experience working at Intel factories as a consultant – thus, instead of years, or months, corporate ethnographers are too often afforded a span of a few weeks to observe multiple fieldsites. Added to this is the qualification problem – that is, as business anthropology has gained traction, there are increased numbers of fieldworkers who are not trained academically in graduate school to do ethnography, and some believe that policing the boundary between appropriate ethnography and less-appropriate, corporate forms is important to maintain the legitimacy of organizational ethnography (Cefkin 2010).

And the last concern, which I argue needs to be better explicated, is *audience*. As it was discussed above, organizational ethnographers often report to the organization in addition to their academic peers in the form of academic books and articles. In some cases, the only report is to the managers of the organization – such as the case where the ethnographer is working as a consultant, or working for the organization itself. How do we, ethnographers, understand the increasing prominence of the corporate audience to the ethnographic work? Fayard et al. (2016) share their experience conducting what they termed "contract ethnography" where the ethnographers were paid *per diem* by the design firm they studied, in order for the organizational members – mainly managers – to know more about, and improve, the culture of the firm. Fayard et al. observed that the organization changed in reaction to these reports of their culture and this feedback loop then provided important data to find out more about the firm by knowing how they responded to the ethnographers' articulation of the firm's culture. Contract ethnography, they argue, can produce both entanglement and innovation – a new way to understand the culture of the organization being studied.

The concept of the "Community of inquiry" was introduced by an American pragmatist Charles S. Peirce. When scientists arrive at a conclusion about their observations, how can they be sure that what they believe is the relationship between theory and observation is true? Instead of looking for how people arrive at the "truth," Peirce emphasized the need for *community of inquiry* so that a person can reach a "belief" that her conclusion was right. The community of inquiry consists of members who apply the methods of scientific work, and the scientific methods aim for collective "belief correction" – that is, to test and modify scientific claims as new ideas are examined by exposing them to the conversation with the ideas of their peers and intellectual predecessors. Participating in a community of inquiry helps us produce insights by raising questions about the fit between the observation and the claim, plausibility of the theory, and lastly, relevance – if the finding is significant and useful to the community of inquiry (Tavory and Timmermans 2014).

Once we consider the issue of *community* the ethnographer belongs to, the problems and possibilities of organizational ethnography can be seen in a new light. The issue of payment, for example, is not about – or at least not only about – financial reliance on the organization. Rather, if the ethnographer is employed in the organization and does not belong to academic circles, then the ethnographer only reports to the organization and does not have an academic community of inquiry. The criteria for a legitimate belief are non-existent, or at least not separate from endemic organizational criteria. By employing the pragmatist's notion of how a scientist could, or should, reach the conclusion that her theory that explains the phenomena is belief-worthy, we can understand that this is not only about "trials of strength" (Latour 1987) – the tests that solidify associations between various elements such as observations and theoretical claims. An ethnographer's work – scientific inquiry into how humans act together in situations – is, in the end, a communal endeavor to reach a modicum of agreement, and the community is a vital reference point and repository for accumulated knowledge.

The problem of organizational ethnography that has few reference points other than the organization itself is, in this regard, that the work does not need to be rigorous and distilled theoretically and applicable in other organizations, and does not need to be relevant outside the organization. If the ethnographer investigates work in a factory and finds out that the tracking system that supposedly tells workers where the lot is doesn't quite show where it is, and the workers' sophisticated guess about where the missing lot actually is was essential to the operation, the ethnographer can suggest the system should include more options that accurately locate the lots (such as in the lab undergoing examination or between workstations) (Jordan and Lambert 2009) or tell the manager of the design firm about how the employees were "past oriented" in the sense of talking eagerly about the "good old days" and that changes tended to be interpreted negatively unless the employees saw the proposed changes as a return to elements of the "good old days" (Fayard et al. 2016). The ethnographers, if they were only reporting to the organization (which, to put it clearly, they weren't, and that's why we know about these studies through academic articles), could certainly help the organization – but the findings do not need to be belief-worthy to people other than those in the organization, and thus are practically a private matter.

Discussion

The politics of belonging haunt the ethnographer as well as the people in the field. In this chapter, I have identified how organizational ethnographers may solve particular pragmatic and theoretical problems when doing ethnography in organizations. Ethnography – and its approved or disapproved cousins – is popular in studies of organizations exactly because it can offer rich narratives and insights into the life in organizations, shedding light on theoretical issues in organization studies, or give a new perspective to tackle issues in the organizations for the managers. As the genre of organizational ethnography has become well established, it is perhaps time we considered the promises and pitfalls of organizational ethnography not by the ways it has been discussed – the sponsorship, the depth, the length, and the quality – but the community. Ultimately, as the ethnographer finds entanglements and nuances of meanings, actions and relationships in the field, she also finds that she is also entangled, not only with the participants in the field, but with the community that she imagines and interacts with once she finishes her observation. Ethnographers' multiple belongings – to the members of the organization, to the academic institutions, and to the academic communities – shape the ways through which they try and solve the dilemmas of organizational ethnography, for the time being.

References

Bechky, B.A. 2003. Sharing meaning across occupational communities: the transformation of understanding on a production floor. *Organization Science*, 14(3), pp. 312–330.

Becker, H. S. 1996. The epistemology of qualitative research. In Jessor, R., Colby, A., and Shweder, R. A. eds. *Ethnography and Human Development*. Chicago, IL: University of Chicago Press, pp. 53–71.

Becker, H.S. and Geer, B. 1957. Participant observation and interviewing: a comparison. *Human Organization*, 16(3), pp. 28–32.

Cefkin, M. ed., 2010. *Ethnography and the Corporate Encounter: Reflections on Research in and of Corporations*. New York: Berghahn Books.

Cerulo, K. A. 2014. Reassessing the problem: response to Jerolmack and Khan. *Sociological Methods & Research*, 43(2), pp. 219–226.

DiMaggio, P. 2014. Comment on Jerolmack and Khan, "Talk Is Cheap": ethnography and the attitudinal fallacy. *Sociological Methods & Research*, 43(2), pp. 232–235.

Eliasoph, N. 2011. *Making Volunteers: Civic Life after Welfare's End* (vol. 50). Princeton: Princeton University Press.

Fayard, A.L. and Van Maanen, J. 2015. Making culture visible: reflections on corporate ethnography. *Journal of Organizational Ethnography*, 4(1), pp. 4–27.

Fayard, A.L., van Maanen, J, and Weeks, J. 2016. Contract ethnography in corporate settings: innovation from entanglement. In Elsbach, K. D. and Kramer, R. M. eds., *Handbook of Qualitative Organizational Research: Innovative Pathways and Methods*, London: Routledge, pp. 45–53.

Fayard, A.L. and Weeks, J. 2007. Photocopiers and water-coolers: the affordances of informal interaction. *Organization Studies*, 28(5), pp. 605–634.

Forsythe, D.E. 1999. "It's just a matter of common sense": ethnography as invisible work. *Computer Supported Cooperative Work (CSCW)*, 8(1–2), pp. 127–145.

Garfinkel, H. 1967. *Studies in Ethnomethodology*. Upper Saddle River, NJ: Prentice-Hall.

Geertz, C. 1973. *Thick Description: Toward an Interpretive Theory of Culture. The Interpretation of Cultures: Selected Essays*. New York: Basic Books, pp. 3–30.

Ho, K. 2009. *Liquidated: An Ethnography of Wall Street*. Durham, NC: Duke University Press.

Horiguchi, S. and Imoto, Y. 2015. Fostering learning through unlearning institutional boundaries: a 'team ethnography' of a liminal intercultural space at a Japanese university. *Ethnography and Education*, 10(1), pp. 92–106.

Jerolmack, C. and Khan, S. 2014. Talk is cheap: ethnography and the attitudinal fallacy. *Sociological Methods & Research*, 43(2), pp. 178–209.

Jordan, B. ed., 2016. *Advancing Ethnography in Corporate Environments: Challenges and Emerging Opportunities*. London: Routledge.

Jordan, B. and Dalal, B. 2006. Persuasive encounters: ethnography in the corporation. *Field Methods*, 18(4), pp. 359–381.

Jordan, B. and Lambert, M. 2009. Working in corporate jungles: reflections on ethnographic praxis in industry. In Cefkin, M. ed. *Ethnography and the Corporate Encounter: Reflections on Research in and of Corporations*. New York: Berghahn Books, pp. 95–133.

Kameo, N. 2015. Gifts, donations, and loose coupling: responses to changes in academic entrepreneurship among bioscientists in Japan. *Theory and Society*, 44(2), pp. 177–198.

Kameo, N.A. 2017. Culture of uncertainty: interaction and organizational memory in software engineering teams under a productivity scheme. *Organization Studies*, 38(6), pp. 733–752.

Kellogg, K.C. 2009. Operating room: relational spaces and microinstitutional change in surgery. *American Journal of Sociology*, 115(3), pp. 657–711.

Kunda, G. 2009. *Engineering Culture: Control and Commitment in a High-tech Corporation*. Philadelphia, PA: Temple University Press.

Lamont, M. and Swidler, A. 2014. Methodological pluralism and the possibilities and limits of interviewing. *Qualitative Sociology*, 37(2), pp. 153–171.

LaPiere, R.T. 1934. Attitudes vs. actions. *Social Forces*, 13(2), pp. 230–237.

Latour, B. 1987. *Science in Action: How to Follow Scientists and Engineers through Society*. Cambridge, MA: Harvard University Press.

Mills, C.W. 1940. Situated actions and vocabularies of motive. *American Sociological Review*, 5(6), pp. 904–913.

Monahan, T. and Fisher, J.A. 2015. Strategies for obtaining access to secretive or guarded organizations. *Journal of Contemporary Ethnography*, 44(6), pp. 709–736.

Orr, J.E. 1996. *Talking about Machines: An Ethnography of a Modern*. New York: Cornell University Press.

Orr, J.E. 2006. Ten years of talking about machines. *Organization Studies*, 27(12), pp. 1805–1820.

Ryle, G. 2009. *Collected Essays 1929–1968: Collected Papers Volume 2*. London: Routledge.

Spradley, J.P. 2016. *The Ethnographic Interview*. Belmont, CA: Waveland Press.

Suchman, L.2013. Consuming anthropology. In Barry, A., and Borrn, G. Eds. *Interdisciplinarity: Reconfigurations of the Social and Natural Sciences.* London: Routledge, pp. 157–176.

Tavory, I. 2019. Community ethnography and the ethnography of work: a comparison of dilemmas. *Journal of Contemporary Ethnography.* Forthcoming.

Tavory, I. and Timmermans, S. 2014. *Abductive Analysis: Theorizing Qualitative Research.* Chicago, IL: University of Chicago Press.

Trouille, D. and Tavory, I. 2019. Shadowing: warrants for intersituational variation in ethnography. *Sociological Methods & Research,* 48(3), pp. 534–560.

Weiss, R.S. 1995. *Learning from Strangers: The Art and Method of Qualitative Interview Studies.* Vancouver: Simon and Schuster.

Westney, D.E. and Van Maanen, J. 2011. The casual ethnography of the executive suite. *Journal of International Business Studies,* 42(5), pp. 602–607.

7

CONSUMER CULTURE THEORY

An Anthropological Contribution to Consumption Studies

Eric J. Arnould, Craig J. Thompson and Melea Press

Introduction

Consumer Culture Theory (CCT) is a field of inquiry that seeks to unravel the complexities of consumer culture (Arnould and Thompson 2005, 2007, 2018). It refers to work in anthropology, cultural sociology, culture studies, and fellow travelers primarily with academic affiliations in business schools and schools of media and communication. It includes scholars with other academic affiliations and some consultants and anthropologist practitioners (e.g., Sunderland and Denny 2007). It has emerged in parallel to the work of social scientists working in anthropology or sociology such as Dominique Desjeux, Eva Ilouz, Daniel Miller, Richard Wilk, or Viviana Zelizer. Foundational texts co-authored by anthropologists in consumer culture theory include Belk (1991), Costa and Bamossy (1995), McCracken (1988b), and Sherry (1995).

Consumer culture theory addresses the rich mosaic of consumer culture and the ways it affects personal identity, social interactions and affiliations, and behaviors in the marketplace. Researchers examine how these interrelations are manifested across a wide range of consumption contexts and brings to light core commonalities, revealing points of distinction, that help us better understand why consumers do what they do and why consumer culture takes the forms it does. To illustrate, let us consider two different consumption contexts in which active consumption is the conduit for individuals to transcend constraints on their identities and forge meaningful connections with others. These transcendent experiences can be a result of intimate elements of engagement with an organization, as is the case with the CSA, or can be consciously driven by consumers who seek to connect with those who share common passions, as in the case of cosplay. In both cases, consumers enlist commercial products, services, experiences, and ideals towards their individual and collective ends, and in both cases the consumers themselves transform as a result of their engagements.

Community Supported Agriculture (CSA)

Community Supported Agriculture programs (CSAs) are independent operations in a de-centralized, share-based marketing system through which participating stakeholders obtain shares of farm-grown produce (Press and Arnould 2011a). CSAs were started in the US in the mid-1980s as a way to re-connect with the land and support local farmers through a new business model. CSAs are typically structured such that people join as members and prepay for their respective season of produce; members pick up their produce or "share" once a week at pre-arranged locations. The core value proposition of CSAs is the guarantee of fresh, locally grown produce, often produced by farmers trying to address the "evils" of the industrial food system (Thompson and Coskuner-Balli 2007). CSAs offer direct relationships between growers and members, opportunities to learn about local agriculture, ecosystems, and growing methods, to try new types of produce, and to engage in community-building experiences with the land, the farmer, other CSA members, neighbors, and even people in their own households (Press and Arnould 2011b).

CSAs tend to have extensive communication with their members, through websites, newsletters, interactions on the farm and at pick-up. All of these means of communication share the values of the CSA with members—through exchanging stories about produce growing in the field, a workday organized on the farm, or a meal that was shared among community members. In their longitudinal study of CSA members, Press and Arnould (2011b) follow first-time CSA members through their initial year with the CSA and beyond. They explore the process of identification formation between the members and the CSA. In their findings, Press and Arnould (2011b) show that as new members start to identify with the CSA, they experience and exhibit personal transformations in both their values and behaviors. Thus, an engineer who previously only ate junk food, said that for years he wanted to improve his health but had done nothing, and claims he hated vegetables begins eating all the produce he gets from his CSA. He starts bringing a lunch of organic produce to work and begins buying locally raised meat and dairy products. A doctor who feels guilty feeding her family "industrial food" finds a way to connect with her daughter at the farm where "their produce" comes from and finds a way to feel better about the consumption choices she makes for her family. She and her daughter bond over taking the "ugly tomatoes" and making tomato sauce from them. A low-income diabetic single mother is able to provide herself and her children with better food choices that fit into their budget and support her values by joining the CSA. A busy father who is also a workaholic stops resorting to fast food takeout as he and his wife start to cook together. He begins to prioritize family time and slowly steps back from responsibilities at work to enjoy time with his family. A young married couple who never eat together discover intimacy through the food they bring from the farm and start to cook and eat together, opening up a new dimension of their relationship. These changes happen over the course of the year that Press and Arnould (2011b) followed the CSA members, and illustrate the behavioral and material dimensions of identification formation. That is, CSA members begin to cook and eat different food, they begin to prioritize food and build and strengthen their relationships around food, family and community. Using a variety of means to build their relationship with the CSA, including the communication materials from the CSA and the produce itself, members take on specific values of the CSA, such as eating local food, buying local products, taking time for enjoying food with others.

Cosplay

All over the world, cosplay fans gather at conventions and parties to share their appreciation of and affection for anime and manga. These productive consumers, who also refer to themselves as *otaku*, wear detailed makeup and elaborate costumes modeled after their favorite anime, manga, and related video game characters. Consumer Culture Theorists Anastasia Seregrina and Henri Weijo set out to see what all the fuss was about. They learned that cosplayers are not fans, but something else. They spend immeasurable resources constructing or purchasing the components of costumes, learning their characters' signature poses and dialogue, and performing at Comics conventions and parties, as they transform themselves from "real world" identities into chosen (fictional) characters. This identity play is the essence of cosplay, or *kosupure* (Winge 2006).

In popular parlance, cosplay refers to the activities, such as masquerades, karaoke, and posing for pictures with other otaku, that are associated with dressing and acting like anime, manga, and video game characters. While cosplay encompasses various types of costumed role-playing, such as science fiction, fantasy, horror, mythology, fetish, and so forth, Japanese and North American cosplay related to Japanese anime, manga, and video games is perhaps enjoys the widest popularity (Allison 2014).

To the uninitiated, cosplay can seem like little more than a glorified costume party. But where a costume party ensemble is picked simply to amuse, many cosplayers feel a deeper connection with their chosen character that elevates the experience from mere dress-up to a more profound experience. They don't just don the same outfit as a beloved character; they adopt the same mannerisms, posture and accent, embodying the character rather than just imitating (Bastow 2014).

Researchers Seregina and Weijo found that cosplay is a highly competitive field with an almost endless supply of opportunities to accumulate social status and prestige among cosplay fans and other cosplay participants. To do so participants make complex investments in emotional labor and skill building (Seregina and Weijo 2017). Constructing costumes and expertly performing characters as well as making costumes for others as a small business, enriches the experience. Thus, cosplay is an emotionally rewarding practice that combines intrinsically pleasurable Do-It-Yourself costume crafting that combats the alienation from productivity that characterizes market capitalism (Moisio, Arnould, and Gentry 2013) with intoxicating identity play that inverts the social order or evokes utopian dreams (Kozinets 2001). Cosplay participants experiment not only with the performance of fictional entities' character but may also experiment with the performance of gender in male-to-female and female-to-male transformations into the iconic media characters.

CSA and cosplay illustrate how people identify with an organizational culture, using a variety of materials to build that relationship. They engage in different mobilizations of consumption practices to support their interest in the communities they are part of, and to support their shifting values and behaviors. Thus, in addition to outcomes, we also see process as an important part of CCT.

Consumer Culture Theory: What Is It?

Consumer culture theorists are fascinated by phenomena such as the alternative exchange model of CSA and the deep engagement of cosplay. They seek to unravel their secrets and, in so doing, provide a more robust and nuanced understanding of global consumer culture and the market-mediated society that molds our lives as consumers within this world. In the following pages, we define consumer culture theory, and outline its general contours with the help of some recent examples.

Consumer culture theory adopts perspectives inspired by Geertz's (1973) thick description and Clifford and Marcus's (1986) views of the situatedness of representation. Rather than viewing culture as a fairly homogeneous system of collectively shared meanings, ways of life, and unifying values shared by a member of society (e.g., Americans share this kind of culture; Japanese share that kind of culture), CCT explores the heterogeneous distribution of meanings and the multiplicity of overlapping cultural groupings that exist within the broader socio-historical frame of globalization and market capitalism (Arnould and Thompson 2005). From a CCT standpoint, consumer culture is a dynamic network of boundary-spanning material, economic, symbolic, and social relationships or processes. Consumer culture is what consumers do and believe rather than an attribute of character. Similarly, "being a consumer" is an identity intrinsic to market capitalism, our dominant global economic system, and the two, market capitalism and consumer subjectivity, evolve in tandem. Here there is a link to Daniel Miller's (1987) Hegelian perspective on consumption and subjectivity. Concretely, as sociologist Don Slater (1997) proposes, consumer culture denotes a social arrangement in which markets either directly affect or directly mediate the relationships between lived experiences, that is, between meaningful ways of life, and the symbolic and material resources like brands, on which they depend.

Again following Don Slater, the consumption of market-made commodities and desire-inducing commercialized symbols is central to consumer culture. At the same time, the perpetuation and reproduction of this system is largely dependent upon the internalization of belief in the exercise of personal choice in the private sphere of everyday life. That is, in consumer culture, people embrace belief in the choice to choose among commercialized offerings. Implicit here is the ontological critique of choice as a culturally and historically specific, ideological epiphenomenon of what Marshall Sahlins (1976, 2008) called "La pensée bourgeoise," and the extended critique of the sign economy offered by the cultural sociologist Jean Baudrillard (1975, 1993, 1996). In other words, consumer culture theorists are highly skeptical of the claims advanced by economists and consumer psychologists regarding the universality of individuals and of individual choice-making respectively as foundational social units. The term consumer culture also conceptualizes an interconnected system of commercially produced images, texts, and objects that groups use—through the construction of overlapping and even conflicting consumption practices, identities, and meanings—to make collective sense of their environments and to anchor and orient their members' experiences and lives.

The basic CCT framework is a heuristic mapping of four clusters of theoretical and practical interests. These common structures of theoretical interest systematically link together studies that manifest diversity in terms of methodological orientations (e.g., ethnography, phenomenology, multiple schools of textual analyses, historical methods, web-based methods). They combine diverse theoretical traditions (variously drawing from sociology, anthropology, literary criticism, critical theory, and feminist studies, to name a few). And of course, consumer culture theory is focused on explicating substantive issues emanating from the domain of consumption.

The domain of consumption may be characterized as the acquisition, use, and disposition of commercially circulated products, services, knowledge, images, and experiences by groups and individual actors. Acquisition processes include inheritance, gifting, production, appropriation, and theft. Use includes display, customization, appreciation, disposition, collecting and curation, physical or symbolic incorporation, storage, and so on. Disposition includes discard, disposal, bequest, reuse, recycling, and so on.

The four clusters of theoretical and practical interests are consumer identity projects, marketplace cultures, the socio-historic patterning of consumption, and mass-mediated marketplace ideologies. Each one is illustrated in turn below.

Consumer Identity Projects

Research on consumer identity projects aligns CCT with the cultural studies' focus on identity work and the negotiation of cultural contradictions through the marketplace, as well as the commodification of cultural rituals and emotions. Researchers ask questions like: Why is identity such an issue in consumer culture? How do consumers pursue their identity projects? How do they use commercially circulated products, services, knowledge, images, and experiences to construct identities? What meanings do consumers pursue? How does a sense of selfhood form in market-mediated societies? What problems does globalization of consumer culture pose to individuals in diverse cultural contexts?

One example is Jafari and Goulding's (2008) research in which they analyze the different meanings of consumption and consumer identities for young adult Iranians in their home country and, subsequently, in expatriate locales in the UK.

In the former case, study participants described using consumption as means to resist theocratic restrictions imposed on their identity practices. Participation in Western consumer culture became a risk-laden expression of defiance and liberty (see for instance the recent trend among Iranian women to post "uncovered" selfies on social media sites). Once ensconced in the UK, however, these immigrant consumers struggled to address the overwhelming array of "free" market choices and the unnerving obligation to construct an "authentic" identity that often conflicted with internalized Iranian moral codes. But, they also used consumption to enact a visible degree of Westernization and thereby ease suspicions that they might be a threat to the civic order. In both settings, these consumers experienced themselves as the subjects of panoptic social surveillance, though taking different ideological forms. Facing these contrasting and potentially disempowering conditions, their consumption practices sought freedom from theocratic restriction (which could afford a more expressive identity project) and, in the UK context freedom to live in anonymity, rather than as subjects of perpetual suspicion by members of the host culture.

Over time, CCT research has expanded its initial theoretical focus on consumer experiences and consumer identity construction practices, which mobilize marketplace resources. Beginning in the 1990s, CCT researchers became increasingly interested in the question of how processes of social structuration—gender and class-based socialization, collective social and cultural formations, naturalized cultural ideologies, and enduring inequities in the distribution of capital—shape and are shaped by consumption practices and consumer individual and collective identity projects. This turn towards a more institutional perspective has animated the three remaining clusters of research in consumer culture theory.

Marketplace Cultures

The interest in marketplace cultures aligns CCT with anthropological studies on material culture and the role of everyday practices and rituals in creating institutional forms of social and familial solidarity. Research on brand communities, for example, highlights the way in which technology and market structures facilitate new forms of communal organization and rituals of solidarity. Another stream of research examines consumer tribes. Consumer tribes are multiple and potentially ephemeral. Take the Lomo tribe as an example (Cova and Cova 2002). The whole tribal phenomenon around Lomo is an ephemeral joint construction of reality; a shared feeling about what is going on around the tribe supported by numerous rituals and the collective reconstruction or repossession of meanings. Because the signs appropriated from the Soviet era camera by the Lomo tribe are shared only within that tribe, their apparent secrecy lend added identity to the Lomo tribe. A later generation of studies explores specific tensions between local and global meaning systems and institutions. Researchers ask questions like: How do communities form in market-mediated society? What forms does community take in market-mediated society? How do "taste" cultures emerge? How do consumers participate in, or precipitate market emergence? How do consumers create value through collective association?

For example, Sandıkcı and Ger (2010) detail the emergence of the market for *tesettür* fashion, which involves an intersection of political Islam, familiar market channels, and the strategic use of economic and cultural capital. *Tesettür* began as metropolitan professional women appropriated a dressing practice that had formerly been associated with the impoverished and less educated rural sector of Turkish society. These formerly secular women embraced political Islam and sought to destigmatize veiling practices. Leveraging their economic capital and the cultural capital acquired through their middle class upbringing, formal education, and, most of all, lifelong immersion in the sphere of secularized consumer culture, and assisted by profit-seeking market intermediaries, these women remade the once stodgy and unflattering *tesettür* style of dress into a more urbane, appealing, and hybridized fashion style. These aestheticizing transformations led to the emergence of an upscale *tesettür* market of designers, retailers and middle-class clientele that not only legitimated this mode of public presentation but also further mainstreamed political Islam as a countervailing ideology to the secular legacy of Kemal Attaturk, the nation's founding father. Consequently, *tesettür* fashion becomes a classifying practice with multiple variations and implicit political affiliations represented.

Socio-historic Patterning of Consumption

The socio-historic patterning of consumption aligns CCT with sociological and historical research on the role of class, gender, and ethnicity as structural influences on marketplace behaviors and vice versa. Researchers ask questions like: How do consumers use consumption to express and remake sociological categories like gender, age, ethnicity & nationality? How do immigrants assimilate through consumption, or how do host cultures use consumption to resist their assimilation? How does consumption reinforce or challenge social boundaries? How does market-mediated society assimilate diverse peoples to the contemporary "consumer" template? Who or what is a consumer?

An example here is David Crockett's (2017) paper in which he investigates and illuminates the intersection of race, class, culture and consumption. He historicizes "the politics of respectability," which has been a prominent feature of middle-class African American consumer culture since post-Civil War emancipation in the 19th century. He further analyzes the contemporary influences exerted by this multifaceted ideology. Through the politics of respectability middle-class African American consumers make a claim to legitimate citizenship (and thereby seek to rebuke disparaging racial stereotypes). Their legitimating, de-stigmatizing practices of racial uplift draw from the Protestant work ethic, Christian piety, and an ethos of self-discipline that embody principles of comportment and decorum characteristic of a professional class, work milieu. Crockett further argues that this uplift strategy aligns with the twin practices of entrepreneurial self-development and oppositional respectability, whereby African Americans use the marketplace and conspicuous consumption practices to reclaim selected aspects of black culture from negative associations circulated by dominant racialized institutional discourses in popular media. For example, a *kente* cloth ribbon has become a ubiquitous element of dress among African American university graduates receiving their diplomas. Of course, originally *kente* cloth was produced and consumed only among the Ashanti people of central Ghana.

Mass-mediated Ideologies and Consumers' Interpretive Strategies

Mass-mediated ideologies and consumers' interpretive strategies form the fourth stream of research. This aligns CCT with the critical theory tradition in social theory associated with the Frankfurt School that examines the ideological bases of consumer culture and resistance thereto. It also aligns CCT with contemporary media studies research on the active and creative media user. Consumer culture theorists argue that consumers creatively and constructively rework mass media and advertising messages in ways that often run against the grain of their corporate encoded meanings. This stream of research examines how consumers exert agency and pursue identity goals through a dialogue (both practical and narrative) with the cultural frames imposed by dominant commercial ideologies. Researchers ask questions like: What are the ideological underpinnings of consumer societies? How do consumers make sense of these ideologies? How do resistant and divergent consumer ideologies form? How do such ideologies take material form in consumer goods and services? How do new technologies and markets become legitimate objects of consumer desire?

CCT studies have explored the power relations manifest in consumption and market-mediated relationships, such as the cultural discourses and systems of classification that normalize certain consumer identities and practices while casting others as problematic or deviant. Thus, some of this work looks at how body weight has become entangled with moral judgements of good and bad that deeply stigmatize some consumers. More broadly this research looks at how recent consumer ideology inculcates in us particular self-management models such that consumers who fail to take "responsibility" for their diets, physical fitness, and health are deemed to threaten the moral order and everyday standards of propriety.

Chronis, Arnould, and Hampton (2012) offer a culturally grounded theory of the consumer imagination that highlights the workings of ideology. Thus, they theorize imagination as anchored in historical storytelling, historical reenactments, intertextual associations with a variety of media, and recontextualizing historical events in the light of current events. Based on their research at the Gettysburg American Civil War battlefield historical site, they show that imagination is narratively anchored. This means imagination at Gettysburg is inseparable from the Civil War narrative. Public and private sector guides, who the authors consider cultural intermediaries and whose tales are already inflected with ideological content, stage these narratives. Narrative includes actors (i.e. participants in the battle), central plot elements, (e.g. Pickett's Charge), settings (e.g. Little Round Top hill), and evokes common narrative forms, such as drama and tragedy. At the material level, memories of the dead heroes and their paradigmatic deeds are sedimented in the land and the artifacts.

The landscape, monuments, weapons, and built environment become parts of (re)imagining a collective past, and of course, these monuments are themselves embedded in narratives of heroism, patriotism, sacrifice, nationalism, manhood, and so on. The study sheds light on the way emotional experiences infiltrate imagination, facilitate empathic connections with story protagonists, and generate associations with contemporary social dramas and emotional moments in consumers' lives. Finally, imagination at Gettysburg is anchored in cultural values exemplified in the actors' stories. Whether these stories are about unity, patriotism, dedication, or in the case of the South, lost White heritage (see Thompson and Tian 2008 for a discussion of this topic), they all inform an imaginary that is steeped in moral valuations of a collective past. Imagination generates an edifying past that tells us what we should value and instructs us what our attitude should be in the present. The authors also emphasize that ideology is a social process: people form and (re)imagine socially sanctioned narratives, through interaction, in a social context.

Mapping the diversity of empirical research into these four clusters of theoretical interest provides an orienting device. It can also help a masters or doctoral student researcher identify a subset of CCT research questions and findings that have the most relevance for his/her given study, or reciprocally to discern important questions; identify boundary conditions; re-think research contexts as venues for programmatic theoretical contribution; and more broadly, to identify domains of theoretical concern that have not been addressed by prior CCT studies.

Arnould and Thompson (2005, 2007) proposed that these four structures of common theoretical interest were interrelated and mutually implicative rather than being independent factors. As noted in the original article, a given CCT study can potentially tap into all four of these domains (see for example Holt 1997) though more typically, one or perhaps two of these domains will be the primary focus with the other remaining background or tacit considerations. For example, Crockett and Wallendorf (2004) investigated the role that normative political ideologies play in shaping African American consumers' responses to attenuated grocery store access in their urban neighborhoods. Their analysis and theoretical explications were primarily directed toward questions related to *mass-mediated marketplace ideologies and consumers' interpretive strategies* and *the socio-historic patterning of consumption* (by socialization in class-based and racial histories). Yet, implications for consumer identity projects and marketplace cultures could easily be derived from their ethnographic insights but, given the theoretical framing of the study, these implications remain tacit.

Where Did It Come From?

CCT emerged as a corrective to the overly rationalistic and utilitarian view of the consumer that predominated in business schools up until the 1980s. This conventional orientation was based on the idea that consumers were rational decision makers, most concerned with the functional benefits of goods, and maximizing subjective utility. Consumer research based on these rational-utilitarian assumptions invested considerable effort in studying how factors, such as pricing, product assortments, retailing systems and formats, and information presentation in advertising and public relations, for example, influenced consumers' decision-making strategies. This substantial body of research had little to say about what fascinated early CCT researchers: consumers' desires, the consumption experiences that arose after purchases or the ways in which consumers meaningfully integrated brands and commercial services into their personal and social lives.

For example, research conducted on American Thanksgiving Day celebrations, which is the most widely celebrated holiday in the US, uncovers a host of myths and consumer projects that mobilize vast numbers of American consumers. Research finds that through this consumption ritual people perform important ideas about American social life. They celebrate the specific beliefs about family pooling and redistribution of resources, women's nurturant role in the household, and a belief in the abundance of basic consumption opportunities for all. At Thanksgiving, family members often make heroic efforts to come together across time and space, even though members may experience considerable mutual ambivalence during most of the year. Participants vigorously recollect the past, imagine the future and negotiate their relationships in the kitchens and around the dining tables and games that bring together families and even strangers "with nowhere else to go" on Thanksgiving Day. Through cooking and following what they claim are old family recipes, people celebrate skills and in turn are celebrated. They work out their dietary preferences and establish just what a "homemade" meal actually means. They often believe they celebrate just like everyone else although researchers found a variety of distinctive ways of celebrating this holiday (Wallendorf and Arnould 1991).

In the early 1980s, the scholars who formed the nexus of what would become CCT drew on distinctive theoretical and methodological sources to address these overlooked topics (Arnould 1989; Belk 1988; Hirschman 1986; McCracken 1988a; Sherry 1983). Whereas traditional consumer and marketing research had been inspired by economic and psychological theory, the nascent consumer culture theory field drew upon anthropology, sociology, semiotics and a host of other sources (design, history, literary criticism, and social psychology for example). Owing to fundamental differences in the subject matter of interest, that is, the whole cycle of consumption, and the theoretical orientations chosen, CCT scholars pursued methods designed to understand what people were up to in their consumption activities. Thus, the approaches adopted relied on qualitative methods such as existential phenomenological inquiry if the focus was on individual action, and on ethnographic methods if the focus of interest was collective action. Through netnographic inquiry (Kozinets 2015), CCT scholars have pursued consumers into online forums. In every case, the goal is to understand how consumption experiences are shaped by webs of cultural meanings and to understand the symbolic value that consumption goods (and the practices that put them into use) serve in consumers' personal and collective projects.

Looking to the Future

Though CCT has an academic origin, its approach has found application in the managerial sphere, as brand managers realized that cultural meanings, consumer collectivities and social affiliations, and consumer identity projects are integral to the market success of brands (Atkin 2004; Cova and Cova 2002; Fournier and Lee 2009; Holt 2004; McCracken 2009). This is why nowadays anthropologists and designers inspired by cultural insights find positions in many companies and in successful consulting firms like the Practica Group, ReD Associates, Stripe Partners, or the Anthropik network. Moreover, the cultural approaches inspired by CCT have led a number of scholars to apply them to the task of reimaging marketing management from a cultural perspective as for instance in Sunderland and Denny (2007), Holt and Cameron (2010) or Madsbjerg and Rasmussen (2014). Indeed, CCT can be a powerful tool to identify myriad issues in organizations and connect such issues with appropriate strategy development, building innovation and thought leadership.

Similar to anthropologist Grant McCracken's (2009) call to institutionalize chief cultural officers in leadership positions in management, Doug Holt (2017) has proposed an approach to research that he terms Consumer Culture Strategy (CCS). His goal is to identify contextually-situated and culturally resonant approaches to address significant real-world problems—climate change, poverty, inequality, shortfalls in the distribution of health care services. Holt's consumer culture strategist would pursue his/her project by building expertise in the social problem domain, designing and conducting research that can address gaps in practice and building problem-solving models that can redress those gaps. For a CCS-oriented researcher, theory becomes a means to the larger end of combatting the larger social/policy problem. Holt (2017) also suggests that research following a CSS should be diffused through platforms such as books, blogs, think-tank white papers, and practitioner-oriented journals. A good example of this type of approach is that adopted by Linda Scott, a contributor to foundational feminist CCT scholarship (2006). In recent years, she has devoted her efforts to the promoting and publicizing of what she calls the XX economy, a gynocentric vision of economic relations, with special focus on the developing world. Her network manifests a blog, aggregates projects devoted to women's empowerment, engages in advocacy directed to governmental and inter-governmental organizations, and develops teaching cases on women's empowerment (see www.doublexeconomy.com/). The core of the position is that, unlike other strategies promoting economic development, the empowerment of women is the only proven means of broadly achieving the goal of socio-economic development in the global South. Consumer Culture Theorists may also take inspiration from the Ethnographic Praxis in Industry Conference (EPIC) group composed primarily of practitioner ethnographers and designers. EPIC has begun to develop strategic platforms such as Holt proposes (see www.epicpeople.org/). Thus, while CCT studies adopt a wide variety of theoretical and methodological perspectives, they have until recently remained focused on consumption from the consumer perspective. Holt and Scott both open the door for a CCT approach to address broader managerial perspectives and broader global issues as diverse as sustainability strategies and gendered development, using a culturally situated approach to research and application.

References

Allison, Peter Ray (2014), "Cosplay: 'It Is Fun to Be Someone Entirely Different'," *The Guardian*, www.theguardian.com/lifeandstyle/2014/may/13/cosplay-sci-fi-weekender-dressing-up-fantasy-characters

Arnould, Eric J. (1989), "Toward a Broadened Theory of Preference Formation and the Diffusion of Innovations: Cases from Zinder Province, Niger Republic," *Journal of Consumer Research*, 16 (September), 239–267.

Arnould, Eric J. and Craig J. Thompson (2005), "Consumer Culture Theory (CCT): Twenty Years of Research," *Journal of Consumer Research*, 31 (4), 868–882.

Arnould, Eric J. and Craig J. Thompson (2007), "Consumer Culture Theory (And We Really Mean Theoretics): Dilemmas and Opportunities Posed by an Academic Branding Strategy," In *Consumer Culture Theory, Vol. 11 of Research in Consumer Behavior*, eds. Belk Russell and John F. Sherry, Jr., Oxford: Elsevier, 3–22.

Arnould, Eric J. and Craig J. Thompson, eds. (2018), *Consumer Culture Theory*, London and New York: Sage Publications.

Atkin, Douglas (2004), *The Culting of Brands: Turn Your Customers into True Believers*, New York: Portfolio.

Bastow, Clem (2014), "Cosplay: It's More than Just 'A Glorified Costume Party'," *The Guardian*, www.theguardian.com/culture/australia-culture-blog/2014/jul/08/cosplay-its-more-than-just-a-glorified-costume-party

Baudrillard, Jean (1975), *The Mirror of Production*, St. Louis, MO: Telos Press.

Baudrillard, Jean (1993), *Symbolic Exchange and Death*, London: Sage.

Baudrillard, Jean (1996), *The System of Objects: Myths and Structures*, London: Verso.

Belk, Russell W. (1988), "Possessions and the Extended Self," *Journal of Consumer Research*, 15 (September), 139–168.

Belk, Russell W. (1991), *Highways and Buyways: Naturalistic Research from the Consumer Behavior Odyssey*, Provo, UT: Association for Consumer Research.

Chronis, Athinodoros, Eric J. Arnould, and Ronald D. Hampton (2012), "Gettysburg Re-Imagined: The Role of Narrative Imagination in Consumption Experience," *Consumption Markets & Culture*, 15 (3), 261–286.

Clifford, James and George E. Marcus, eds. (1986), *Writing Culture. The Poetics and Politics of Ethnography*, Berkeley and Los Angeles, CA: University of California Press.

Costa, Janeen Arnold and Gary J. Bamossy, ed. (1995), *Marketing in a Multicultural World: Ethnicity, Nationalism, and Cultural Identity*, Thousand Oaks, CA: Sage Publications.

Cova, Bernard and Véronique Cova (2002), "Tribal Marketing: The Tribalisation of Society and Its Impact on the Conduct of Marketing," *European Journal of Marketing*, 36 (5/6), 595–620.

Crockett, David (2017), "Paths to Respectability: Consumption and Stigma Management in the Contemporary Black Middle Class," *Journal of Consumer Research*, 44 (October), 554–581.

Crockett, David and Melanie Wallendorf (2004), "The Role of Normative Political Ideology in Consumer Behavior," *Journal of Consumer Research*, 31 (December), 511–528.

Fournier, Susan and Lara Lee (2009), "Getting Brand Communities Right," *Harvard Business Review*, April, 105–111.

Geertz, Clifford (1973), *The Interpretation of Cultures*, Boston, MA: Basic Books.

Hirschman, Elizabeth C. (1986), "Humanistic Inquiry in Marketing Research: Philosophy, Method, and Criteria," *Journal of Marketing Research*, 23 (3), 237–249.

Holt, Douglas B. (1997), "Poststructuralist Lifestyle Analysis: Conceptualizing the Social Patterning of Consumption in Postmodernity," *Journal of Consumer Research*, 23 (March), 326–350.

Holt, Douglas B. (2004), *How Brands Become Icons: The Principles of Cultural Branding*, Boston, MA: Harvard Business Press.

Holt, Douglas B. (2017) "Consumer Culture Strategy," www.academia.edu/15574357/Consumer_Culture_Strategy, downloaded January 25, 2018.

Holt, Douglas B. and Douglas Cameron (2010), *Cultural Strategy: Using Innovative Ideologies to Build Breakthrough Brands*, Oxford: Oxford University Press.

Jafari, Aliakbar and Christina Goulding (2008), "We are Not Terrorists!" UK-based Iranians, Consumption Practices and the "Torn Self," *Consumption, Markets & Culture*, 11 (June), 73–91.

Kozinets, Robert V. (2001), "Utopian Enterprise: Articulating the Meanings of Star Trek's Culture of Consumption," *Journal of Consumer Research*, 28 (June), 67–88.

Kozinets, Robert V. (2015), *Netnography Redefined*, 2nd ed, Thousand Oaks, CA: Sage Publications.

Madsbjerg, Christian and Mikkel Rasmussen (2014), *Moment of Clarity*, Boston, MA: Harvard Business School Publishing.

McCracken, Grant (1988a), "Diderot Unities and Diderot Effect: Neglected Cultural Aspects of Consumption," In *Culture and Consumption*, ed. G. McCracken, Bloomington and Indianapolis, IN: Indiana University Press, 118–129.

McCracken, Grant (1988b), *Culture and Consumption*, Bloomington and Indianapolis, IN: Indiana University Press.

McCracken, Grant (2009) *"Getting past Guru" and "Stealth CCO's," Excerpt from Chief Culture Officer: How to Create a Living, Breathing Corporation*, New York: Basic Books, 5–40.

Miller, Daniel (1987), *Material Culture and Mass Consumption*, New York: Basil Blackwell.

Moisio, Risto, Eric J. Arnould, and James W. Gentry (2013), "DIY Home Improvement as Men's Therapeutic Labor," *Journal of Consumer Research*, 40 (August), 298–316.

Press, Melea and Eric J. Arnould (2011a), "American Pastoralism: Linking Post-War Suburbia and Community Supported Agriculture," *Journal of Consumer Culture*, 11(2) 168–194.

Press, Melea and Eric J. Arnould (2011b), "How Does Organizational Identification Form? A Consumer Behavior Perspective," *Journal of Consumer Research*, 38 (4), 650–666.

Sahlins, Marshall (1976), *Culture and Practical Reason*, Chicago, IL: University of Chicago Press.

Sahlins, Marshall (2008), *The Western Illusion of Human Nature*, Ann Arbor, MI: Prickly Paradigm Press.

Sandıkcı, Özlem and Güliz Ger (2010), "Veiling in Style: How Does a Stigmatized Practice Become Fashionable?" *Journal of Consumer Research*, 37 (June), 15–36.

Scott, Linda (2006), *Fresh Lipstick: Redressing Fashion and Feminism*, New York: St. Martins Press.

Seregina, Anastasia and Henri A. Weijo (2017), "Play at Any Cost: How Cosplayers Produce and Sustain Their Ludic Communal Consumption Experiences," *Journal of Consumer Research*, 44 (June), 139–159.

Sherry, John F., Jr. (1983), "Gift Giving in Anthropological Perspective," *Journal of Consumer Research*, 10 (September), 157–168.

Sherry, John F., Jr., ed. (1995), *Contemporary Marketing and Consumer Behavior: An Anthropological Sourcebook*, Thousand Oaks, CA: Sage Publications.

Slater, Don (1997), *Consumer Culture and Modernity*, Malden, MA: Blackwell.

Sunderland, Patricia L. and Rita M. Denny (2007), *Doing Anthropology in Consumer Research*, New York: Routledge.

Thompson, Craig J. and Gokcen Coskuner-Balli (2007), "Countervailing Market Responses to Corporate Co-optation and the Ideological Recruitment of Consumption Communities," *Journal of Consumer Research*, 34 (August), 135–152.

Thompson, Craig and Kelly Tian (2008), "Reconstructing the South: How Commercial Myths Compete for Identity Value through the Ideological Shaping of Popular Memories and Countermemories," *Journal of Consumer Research*, 34 (February), 595–613.

Wallendorf, Melanie and Eric J. Arnould (1991), "'We Gather Together': The Consumption Rituals of Thanksgiving Day," *Journal of Consumer Research*, 18 (June), 13 31.

Winge, Theresa (2006), "Costuming the Imagination: Origins of Anime and Manga Cosplay," *Mechademia*, 1, 65–76.

8

THE CREATIVE USE OF INSIDER ETHNOGRAPHY AS A MEANS FOR ORGANIZATIONAL SELF INVESTIGATION

The "Essence of Tesco" Project

Mary Yoko Brannen, Terry Mughan and Fiona Moore

Ethnography, while having considerable value as a means of generating rich, experiential data about cultural, micropolitical and complex social phenomena in organizations, is not always used to its full potential in organizational research. In particular, the analytical perspective is usually limited to that of the researchers, who gather and analyze data about managers in an organization, ignoring or minimizing the existence of other perspectives, a practice frequently critiqued in anthropology, organizational and otherwise (see Clifford, 1986; Arnoud and Cayla, 2015). Furthermore, as Westney and van Maanen (2011) argue, there is a tendency by researchers to absorb the perspectives of managers into studies of organizations without appropriate reflexivity or contextualization, a process they deem "casual ethnography." The need to incorporate managerial perspectives in an intelligent, reflexive way that acknowledges their contribution while failing to acknowledge their particular biases is thus necessary.

This chapter describes a project, the "Essence of Tesco," which addresses this issue by involving managers from the project in the actual gathering and analysis of ethnographic data, in collaboration with a team of academic researchers, following an approach which we term "insider ethnography." We use this term following Brannick and Coghlan (2007) to mean action research that is conducted on a setting of which one is part. The resulting process has the benefit outcomes of global integration and continuous organizational renewal for the corporation, as well as a richer and fuller analytical picture for researchers.

This project adds to the theoretical literature in that it describes a methodologically innovative study, which does not treat the practitioners involved simply as a source of data, but enlists them as researchers and analysts, allowing a multi-perspective view of a complex organization. Secondly, it defines the complications that developed and the ways in which the team successfully resolved these. Thirdly, it considers ways in which this method can be more widely used and applied to different organizations. Finally, it suggests new roles for practitioners as researchers and analysts, capable of researching and gaining understanding about their own organizations, for the benefit both of researchers and themselves.

Project Background

Tesco is Britain's number one private sector employer and the world's third largest food retailer, with stores in 14 countries across Asia, Europe and North America. Tesco's international operations are diverse, including joint ventures with local partners (e.g., Samsung-Tesco Home Plus in Korea, Tesco Lotus in Thailand), reflecting Tesco's strategy of being locally responsive to host country market opportunities and policies. At the time of the study, however, it had begun to lose its competitiveness in its UK (Tesco plc financial report, April 2010) home base, while still maintaining substantial profit growth worldwide led by its six Asian subsidiaries located in Japan, Korea, China, Malaysia, Thailand and India.

As a consequence, the "Essence of Tesco" project was initiated. The challenge for Tesco lay both in identifying the global advantage for foreign subsidiaries of being part of the Tesco group, as well as in learning from them ways in which Tesco could reinvigorate its home country competitive advantage through recontextualization (Brannen, 2004): that is to say, the process through which "transferred organizational assets … take on new meanings in distinct cultural contexts" (p. 595). These challenges first involved identifying the essence of Tesco's home country advantage, and, second, assessing its robustness—that is to say, whether the essence of Tesco UK was strong or weakening, and, if the latter, in what areas was there room for improvement. The subsequent challenges included determining criteria for discriminating practices that were transferable abroad from those that were not, and then capturing and leveraging the learning from positive recontextualization (Brannen, 2004) of Tesco's practices in the foreign subsidiaries throughout its global footprint.

In the "Essence of Tesco" project we, the researchers, trained a multicultural team of nine Asian managers (here called the "Project Team") to become in-house ethnographers of Tesco UK for a 3-month period studying 52 stores in the UK with dual objectives of helping Tesco (1) to understand and evaluate the core practices that comprised the essence of Tesco's home country advantage, and (2) to identify sources of learning from Tesco's foreign subsidiaries to aid in reinvigorating its core in light of increasing competition in its home market. To arrive at this finding, we adapted and extended the ethnographic method to the operation of teams across geography and global corporate identities, developing what we term "insider ethnography."

This study develops Westney and van Maanen's concept of "casual ethnography," harnessing the reflexive element that they identify as missing in most studies involving managers as informants (2011). It does so in that a team of Asian in-house managers with no prior ethnographic skills, and English as a second language, executed the study. Our academic team (nicknamed the "A Team" by the Project Team members during the course of the project) acted as advisors, trainers and coaches to the project team at every stage of the ethnographic process. We designed an initial intensive custom-made training course including instruction in ethnographic research techniques. In addition, we put in place purpose-built group-oriented techniques to collate data gathered by a team of nascent ethnographers with unique tools for the extraction and evaluation of key themes across data from a culturally diverse group.

In the following sections, we shall, firstly, outline the wider theoretical lens through which we approached the project and developed the insider ethnography method; secondly, describe the methodology and analysis used on the "Essence of Tesco" project; thirdly, discuss the methodological contribution of the project and the key issues in implementing practitioner ethnography in an intelligent, reflexive fashion; and, finally, consider directions for future research.

The Development of Insider Ethnography in an Organization Studies Context

Insider ethnography is a methodological experiment, grounded in a long tradition of ethnographic research on organizations, in anthropology and in organization studies. The novelty of our approach is that ethnography has never before been used strategically by managers to investigate their own company. Using traditional techniques, we have developed a new method which can be used by insiders, and which can be taught to others.

Ethnographic research, defined here as a research process in which the researcher's experiences, as observer and participant, form the core of the methodology and analysis (Sanday, 1979), has been used to study culture in organizations since the 1920s (Schwartzman, 1993) and multinational corporations since the late 1970s (see Baba, 1998). Its value to organization studies has been repeatedly noted. Firstly, it allows researchers to understand the day-to-day, lived experience of working which underlies ideal-typical descriptions of work (Barley, 1996; Morris, Leung, Ames and Lickell, 1999; Moore, 2011; O'Docherty, de Cock, Rehn and Ashcraft, 2013; Bleiklie, Enders and Lepori, 2015). As Gephart (1978) notes, it can be used to "explore the micro-sociological processes which occur in situated, face-to-face interactions." Secondly, ethnography is useful for uncovering tacit (as opposed to explicit) discourses, that is to say, things which are not directly spoken about, either because they are "taken for granted" by people within the organization (van Maanen, 1979), because people are not consciously aware of them (Jeffcut, 1994; see, for instance, Brannen, 2004, O'Docherty et al., 2013), or else because the subject is taboo (Mars, 1982; Bleiklie, Enders and Lepori, 2015). Thirdly, it can be used to explore unusual aspects of organizations which are hard to capture by less experiential means (Jeffcut, 1994), such as magical thinking (Moeran, 2014) or the concept of "the uncanny" (Beyes and Steyaert, 2013), Finally, it is often used as part of a process of "triangulation," combining and comparing data obtained from qualitative and quantitative methods to obtain a balanced image of organizational culture (see Jick, 1979; Harris, 2000). All four contributions, but particularly the first two, are relevant to the Tesco case.

However, one could argue that researchers in organization studies tend to be rather conservative in terms of how they practice ethnography as a method. Ethnography in management studies has largely been restricted to the (relatively) long-term study of a single group, by a single ethnographer (as in Barley, 1983, 1990, 1996; Brannen, 1992, 1995a, 1995b; Salk, 1992; Sakai, 2000; Moore, 2005, 2011) or (as in Miles, 1979), a small team. The data gathering is largely a mix of participant observation by the researchers, with the relative proportions of participation and observation depending largely upon the setting, and in-depth interviews, with other forms of data, usually survey results or statistics, being included as required (see, for instance, Graham, 1995; Moore, 2005; Sharpe, 2006). Consequently, although insider perspectives are included, of necessity the researcher perspective dominates, and is prioritized in terms of the study's conclusions.

Furthermore, there continues to be a lack of reflexivity concerning the relationship between researcher and subject, and regarding the ways in which managers' perspectives enter into the study. Westney and van Maanen (2011) argue that researchers frequently absorb managers' perspectives in unacknowledged ways, hearing their views on the organization and incorporating them into their study without challenging or questioning them. Likewise, Arnoud and Cayla (2015) argue that the discipline of commercial ethnography is implicated in encouraging and perpetuating a more general "organizational fetishization" (p. 1362) of consumers. Organization studies thus could not only do with more creative uses of ethnography, but also more self-criticism of how it is used.

By contrast, ethnographies in social and cultural anthropology have included such genres as life history (Black Elk and Lyon, 1990; Carsten, 2000), experimental ethnography (McFeat, 1974), ethnohistory (Douglas, 1993; Holt, 2006), holistic ethnography (Mayer and Mayer, 1961; Lo, 1990), autoethnography (Moeran, 1985, 2005; Fox, 2004; Short, 2013), ethnographic metafiction (Sillitoe and Sillitoe, 2009), home-culture ethnography (Alvesson, 2009), and single-incident case study (Gluckman, 1958; Ben-Ari, 1991). Of particular note is the, relatively rare, cross-genre practice of including studies in which the "subjects" are also participants in the study, generating and analyzing data (for instance Dumont, 1978; Crapanzano, 1980; Heilman, 2000; Lassiter, 2005), or even co-authors (such as Black Elk and Lyon, 1990). Such studies have the advantage of, first, including multiple perspectives on the group or practice under study; secondly, challenging the prioritization of the academic viewpoint as the "correct" one and the hierarchical placement of researcher over subject; and, finally, allowing the development of a more holistic picture of the group. In a multi-sited, complex organization, which spans numerous national cultures, such a technique might prove particularly useful. The innovative development of including insiders as ethnographic researchers and analysts can expand the potential of ethnography and its utility in organizational research, building on innovations currently being developed in organization studies and anthropology.

The "Essence of Tesco" project is thus a methodological experiment, not only in the utility of ethnography as a means of uncovering the elements and dynamics of culture in a multinational corporation, but also of the feasibility and benefits of including managers within the organization as part of the data-gathering and analytical team. Furthermore, the use of insider-outsider research techniques has the effect not just of better understanding internal dynamics, but also of reinvigorating the organization as managers absorb and recontextualize the insights they have gained. Finally, from a practitioner point of view, such a project is more valuable to an organization than the use of external consultants, because helping insiders to understand their own organization allows them to surface tacit knowledge while at the same time integrating a more shared understanding of the organizational culture, and also because the insights gained are proprietary, and can remain within the organization's global footprint.

Research Design

The research design of this study comprised three main phases. As surfacing contextually based implicit (and often tacit) knowledge is difficult to do from within one's own context, and because Tesco's global performance was being led by strong positive performance by its Asian subsidiaries with perhaps the most to offer the home base in terms of learning, the study began with the formation of a global team of nine managers (called the "project team") chosen from Tesco's Asian operations to be trained and serve as "in-house ethnographers" of Tesco's UK operations. Two managers each were chosen from Tesco's biggest and fastest growing Asian markets—China, Korea and Japan—and one each from the remaining three countries—Malaysia, Japan and India. The selection criteria were that the managers needed to have worked for Tesco for at least three years, were work level two employees or above (there are only five work levels at Tesco), and they needed to be conversant and comfortable in reading and writing English (see Table 8.1 for full project team profiles).

In this first phase, the academic research team of four scholars, skilled in organizational and strategic field-based analysis, trained the project team in ethnographic, cultural analysis and grounded theorizing techniques. Training sessions were on topics including observation skills, note-taking methods, analysis of media and documentation, interviewing techniques, and on organizing and making sense of data through techniques of content analysis, coding, triangulation, and the comparative

Table 8.1 Project team

Country	Years of service	Role at time of study	Previous roles in Tesco	Previous roles outside Tesco	Higher education	Overseas experience	Other
Malaysia	6 years	Head of Seasonal Events and International Sourcing—Commercial	International Buying Manager Division Manager Commercial Buyer	Commercial Buyer Inventory Controller	BSc, Computer Systems Engineering Pursuing Masters at time of study	Product sourcing from China, HK & Thailand	Married; no children
Japan	3 years	Recruiting Manager	N/A	Consultant (Employment Agency)	BA degree	Singapore; consultant for 8 years	N/A
India	6 years	Regional Manager—HR	HR Manager Planning for the business Career development program project for IT team	Manager HR for south region stores	Masters in Social Work, India	None	Married Enjoys traveling
China	4 years	Communication Manager	Store manager	Marketing Project Manager Buyer	MBA, China	1 year working in Tesco UK 1.5 years working in Tesco Malaysia as store manager	Married, 1 child Enjoys travel
China	3.5 Years	Training Manager	Leadership Training Manager (China) Business HR Manager (China) Employee Relations Senior Specialist (China) Central HR Team Graduate Trainee (UK)	High Education Foundation Programme Project (UK)	MA, Industrial Relations and HRM, UK BA(Hons) English Language, Translation and Cultural Studies, UK	Educated and worked in UK (2002–2008)	Enjoys back-pack traveling

(Continued)

Country	Years of service	Role at time of study	Previous roles in Tesco	Previous roles outside Tesco	Higher education	Overseas experience	Other
Korea	9 years	Head of Brand	Market Analysis leader Product innovation E-leaflet leader Global logistics project leader Big seasons delivery project leader Primary distribution project	Carrefour Korea (1998–2002) Co-managed Inventory Project manager, Logistic operation manager	BA, S.Korea	Language course in Canada (1997–1998)	Married, two children
Korea	5 years (4 full- time, 1 part- time)	Research & Insight Manager	Capacity Manager in Online Business Analyst in Site Research Team Secretary, Property Service Group	Secretary Overseas trading personnel	MBA, Korea; MA, Australia	Singapore (elementary, middle school) Australia	Married, no children
Thailand	3 Yrs 9 Mos	Senior Operations Development Manager: OM	Senior Retail Project Manager Hypermarket Store Manager	Store Manager, Wal Mart USA Customer Service Manager, Bed Bath and Beyond USA Academic Co-ordinator, WSU USA	MA, Theory of Communications USA	Educated and worked in USA (1994–2006) Store Structure Program in UK (10 Wks)	Single
Thailand	17 years	Sr. Business Development Manager: Store Operations	Buyer Manager Hypermarket Support Office Manager Retail Operations	None	BA, PR of Communication Arts, Thailand	None	Enjoys traveling

method. This took place at a Tesco training center retreat where both the project and academic teams stayed for six full days of classes with acculturation social events in the evenings.

The ethnographic training agenda included Tesco induction sessions where Tesco UK managers conveyed basic information regarding Tesco's business context—strategy and competitive environment, Tesco UK's culture ("The Tesco Way"), leadership culture, and a current market analysis (see Table 8.2). The Tesco induction sessions also served as a practice opportunity to which the project team could apply their nascent ethnographic skills taking notes on what they learned and reflecting on their notes from their own country perspective. The academic team gave ongoing guidance and feedback throughout the week and accompanied the project team as "shadow guides" on their first in-store field visit on the final day of training.

In the second phase of the study, the project team conducted fieldwork in pairs visiting a total of fifty-two stores across the five principal grocery retail formats developed and operationalized in the UK—Tesco Express, Tesco Metro, Tesco Extra, Tesco Direct and Tesco Bank. The project team members lived in three separate apartments, cooked and ate together, and generally shared with one another their experience in the UK and their thoughts regarding the project. These informal debriefs led to another organizational effect around global learning—the project members being able to learn comparatively from each other's experiences the differences and similarities particular to their regions. During this phase, the academic team provided ongoing guidance and feedback to the project team as they conducted their fieldwork. Our emphasis during this phase was on the quality of, and routines for, note taking, and on initial and focused coding of data.

The final phase of the project comprised data analysis and recommendations. This began with the project team coding their own field notes and interview transcriptions and surfacing the major themes that emerged as the underlying practices that were the essence of Tesco in its UK context. We then met as the full research team in order to triangulate across the individually collected data to check for inter-rater reliability, shared understanding of the codes, consolidate related codes as sub-codes, and surface the main themes common across the data collected by the nine project team members. Out of thirty-four initial themes that emerged from the collective data of the project team, ten core themes that were salient, robust and common across the individual project team members' data were winnowed through a process of categorizing sub-themes and redundancies (see below for in-depth description of these themes). These were then further analyzed in order to give recommendations to Tesco around the strength of its culture, or "essence" as it was termed, and suggestions as to how Tesco UK might leverage best practices from its Asian subsidiaries to strengthen its core.

This project therefore represented an opportunity for academics to work with an in- house mixed global team, as they identified the "Essence of Tesco" through their application of fieldwork techniques, and as they operated as vectors of recontextualization between their subsidiary organizational context and the UK home context.

Table 8.2 Training week schedule

Monday	Tuesday	Wednesday	Thursday	Friday	Saturday
ORIENTATION	*Active Listening Skills*	TESCO INDUCTION PROGRAM II	*Interviewing Skills*	*Skills Practice:* CULTURE EMERSION	INTO THE FIELD
Introduction					
Overview of the Research Design: Introduction to MBI Model	*Note-Taking Skills* TESCO INDUCTION PROGRAM I	Tesco Leadership Culture Tesco Academy		Cultural simulation II	Two person research teams with academic team pairs: studying Tesco Metro, Extra, and Express
Researchers' Self-Intro	The Tesco Way Tesco In Context: Business Environment, Strategy	Other Tesco Topics			
Lunch	Lunch	Lunch	Lunch	Lunch	

SENSING CULTURE	Skills Check/Debrief	Skills Check/Debrief	TESCO BUDDIES TRIAL	Reflection
Culture Simulation I	*Document Analysis Skills*	TESCO MEDIA & DOCUMENT ANALYSIS	Joined by 5–9 TESCO employees with whom the researchers practice interviewing skills	Triangulation
Debrief on Sensing Cultures	TESCO MEDIA & DOCUMENT ANALYSIS	Skills Check/Debrief		Content Analysis
Mapping Skills	Skills Check/Debrief		Interviewing Trials:	Comparative Method (vis-à- vis their home contexts)
Mapping Culture: UK national culture, organizational culture			"Speed-dating" Semi-Structured interviews	Coding
Cross-Cultural Adaptability Assessment			Open-Ended Interview	
Bridging Skills				
			Triangulation	
Social Event			*Social Event*	

Data Analysis

Developing an Understanding of the "Essence of Tesco"

The ten themes were coded using Schein's corporate culture diagnostic (Schein, 1985) to ascertain whether they were robust and congruent across the artifact, value and assumption levels of analysis. We did this in the following way. We color-coded each of the ten thematic sets of consolidated field notes marking phrases and quotes that were indicative of the theme as an artifact—an explicit manifestation of the theme; a value—an espoused manifestation; or an assumption—a tacit expectation. We then looked at the frequency of artifacts, values and assumptions for each theme. Some of the themes were heavy on assumptions and values and lean on artifacts, thus indicating that Tesco does not deliver in these areas. For example, for the theme "opportunity to get on," employees thought that if they joined Tesco, they would have an opportunity to move up the job-levels; however, in actuality many employees complained that they were not given this option. Others were heavy on artifacts but lean on espoused values and basic assumptions, thus indicating that Tesco needs to question whether there is a shared understanding of the purpose and meaning behind these protocols, rituals and behaviors. As an example, for the theme "customer is at the heart of everything," whereas there were many slogans, signs, etc. stating that this was so, there were in fact contradictions at the value and assumption levels where employees felt caught on a tightrope having to meet key performance indicators (KPIs) at the expense of customer needs.

"The Essence of Tesco": Identification of Themes

As the aim of the project, as far as the company and multicultural management team were concerned, was to distill what was the "essence" of Tesco, what part of that essence might lend itself to global integration and what was more vulnerable to local recontextualization (Brannen, 2004) and hence an opportunity for learning and reinvigorating Tesco UK. In addition to this overarching aim, we were asked to focus on the following three areas: 1) people and culture, 2) brand management, 3) operational excellence. The identification of key themes that made up the essence of Tesco UK was achieved by adapting traditional ethnographic coding techniques to a team process. This was not an easy feat given the diverse cultural and linguistic challenges posed by a multicultural team of this sort. Each of the nine project team members was asked to code their own field notes first by using open coding considering their data in minute detail while developing initial categories, then to surface recurring themes by using selective coding around core concepts. We then pooled all of the themes that were surfaced by the nine team members. This came to an initial thirty-four themes that we then discussed, defined, and sorted, integrating themes and sub-themes until we refined the list into ten overall themes:

1 Customer at the heart of everything
2 Leadership DNA

3 Opportunity to get on
4 Teamwork and collaboration (intangibles)
5 Work environment (tangibles)
6 Embracing and implementing change
7 "It's my business"
8 Operational efficiency
9 Trusted brand
10 Respect for facts and insights

On the surface, these themes might appear to be quite generic strategic initiatives for any business. Rather, out of a plethora of initiatives generated by Tesco management, these are the ones that surfaced from the project team's field notes as being relevant and present on the shop floor. This is an important aspect of the methodology that distinguishes itself from the rather more superficial readings of organizations generated by consulting firms that are unable to leverage insider perspectives on the phenomena under study. These ten themes were derived from complex, deep bodies of in-vivo text generated by a bottom-up inductive process rather than having been given to the project team members in a top-down communication from Tesco executives. Taken in isolation by their titles the themes do not convey the full depth and meaning that the project team members were able to understand through their research. For example, the theme "Opportunity to Get On" may appear to be a key theme in any company, but in the retailing sector, especially in the UK, one of Tesco's competitive advantages in recruiting and developing staff is seen by employees as a key differentiator from other shops on the high street.

Further, after initially identifying each theme, the project team members carefully and collectively defined and clarified what comprised their essence using in-vivo quotes. For instance, the following was the descriptive essence of the theme, "Opportunity to Get On":

Variety of jobs and levels for everybody
Staff morale (also pay)
An interesting job
Career development and personal development
Talking about how to develop people in a fair way
Long-term service—employees working at Tesco for a long time (lifetime)
Personal development as well as career development
Powerful message around people development
Leadership by coaching and inclusivity
Our ability to change lives

The process of developing these themes was significant to the subsequent analysis.

When listening to induction speeches by Tesco UK management and in subsequent follow-up interviews with various UK managers, during the initial training period, the project team developed an idea of the official version of the company's values and identity. However, they also often noted that the British managers seemed to rely heavily upon Tesco's tools and rhetoric without actually engaging their teams or enacting effective people-management skills. The reflexive skills that the project team members had learned to employ in their roles as strategic ethnographers enabled them to go beyond considering the corporate values unproblematically to further analyze, triangulate, and critique them. They were thus able to consider how their reactions to the different Tesco UK managers' presentations affected how they received their opinions: for example, they would pay more attention to the presenters with whom they felt a rapport either because of a shared functional identity or point of view, and thus prioritized these managers' versions of events. The process of coming up with the themes was also subject to power relations internal to the project team, as some wanted to see the corporate values reflected in the themes, while others, having formulated different opinions during the training process, were more ambivalent. This process of discussion and debate made for a more complex image of corporate culture, and, more importantly, one incorporating contradictory discourses. Furthermore, they were able to consider the managers' views in another context—how these values were experienced at the shop level. For instance, one researcher critiqued the concept of efficiency by saying:

> I began putting some labels on products, as I wanted to experience the process for myself. The system was slow for the time given to change the labels and it can be quite frustrating when you do not find the product to match the label.

The project team members thus did not simply develop a managerial image of Tesco, but were able to conduct holistic ethnography (see Moore, 2011) to obtain perspectives on the firm from different levels of the organization.

Ethnography, Culture and Nuance: Analyzing the Themes

One significant outcome of the methodological choice was that in identifying the themes, the project team members were able to incorporate critiques, even outright contradictions, of the themes in their analysis. For instance, under "Opportunity to Get On," the project team members noted that the examples cited to them were generally of people who had risen in the company through taking their own initiative, rather than people who had been helped by the company to success. Therefore, while it was certainly true that the company was seen as a place where people could "get on" in their careers, and that the opportunity was provided, the company generally did not help employees to meet this goal.

The project team thus identified a gap between Tesco's espoused values and practices. For instance, they noted that Tesco has an official value of being a "great place to work," and yet also noted employees saying, "What's special about Tesco? Nothing much. They pay me and that's all." One of the focal espoused values of Tesco, and indeed one of their overall themes, is "customers at the heart of everything we do," meaning that the company tries to effectively manage the conflict between performance KPIs and customers' needs. An analysis of the ethnographers' field notes demonstrates that this essence is, indeed, robust at all three of Schein's levels. However, with 453 affirmative and 263 contradictory field observations, the analysis also indicates that Tesco currently has conflicting values in place around trying to achieve performance KPIs, such as sales targets, while concurrently keeping customers at the heart of the organization. In the process of placing heavy emphasis upon trying to meet and exceed performance goals, at the store level, managers and front-line staff have forgotten what it means to truly place customers first. Consider the following:

> I could not believe they would have a staff meeting on the shopping floor. Although it is a wide corridor, it is disturbing for customers. It is a huge store and they should find another place to meet.

By exploring the espoused values, and the lived experience of being members of the company, the project team members were able to acknowledge the company's self- identification, but also the ambivalences, contradictions and variations embodied in these themes, rather than taking the statements as a simple, objective and unproblematic truth about the company. The use of the ethnographic method thus allowed for a complex and dynamic analysis and understanding of the firm's culture by its managers.

Reflexivity and Comparison: The Analytic Process

Another significant factor in the process of generating and analyzing the data was the diversity of the team. Tesco's international operations are diverse, including joint ventures with local partners (e.g., Samsung-Tesco Home Plus in Korea, Tesco Lotus in Thailand), reflecting Tesco's strategy of being locally responsive to host country market opportunities and policies, and the project team members therefore came not just from different countries, but from firms which had a quite different relationship to the parent company. Some of the participants were employees of companies that were joint ventures between Tesco and a failing or weak local partner, whereas in other cases, for instance the Korean operation, the power balance between Tesco and the local partner was more equal, leading to power struggles over whose values would dominate. As ethnography is inevitably a comparative act (see Ellis and Bochner, 2000), implicitly if not explicitly, there was always an element of comparison with the project team members' home situation: for instance, one observer critiqued a store's front-of-house display by saying that it is not what she would have expected in her home country, leading her to reflect on why the differences were present. Again, the diverse backgrounds and power relations of the project team members conducting the study led to a dynamic view of the corporation's culture.

For the academic team, there was also a substantial opportunity for reflexivity both in regard to the research process around training and working with insider ethnographers as well as theory development regarding the evolution of corporate culture in global organizations. The academic team was charged with facilitating the Asian project team to carry out a number of tasks including observing the operations and behavior of people in a selection of Tesco stores across the UK, interviewing store staff, office staff and suppliers, and reviewing past reports conducted in-house or by consultancies, but not to conduct the actual in-store ethnographic research ourselves, providing opportunities to reflect on our own research practice and its strengths and weaknesses. The process did certainly, as noted, generate a more complex image of corporate culture and one that could include the ambivalences and contradictions found in organizations (as noted in Martin, 1992). However, as Burawoy (2013) notes in his critique of ethnographic methodology, it is also the case that researchers can miss important things they are not looking for; the British class system, for instance, appeared not to be very significant to the team of managerial researchers, yet this subject would feature prominently in most lectures or courses on the subject of organizations in British life (see Fox, 2004).

This study also had to overcome numerous challenges to both the academic and business viability of the project posed by language differences between headquarters and the Asian project team and indeed with the project team itself. Traditional expectations are that if the working language is English and everyone is speaking it, non-native speakers will usually be competent and motivated enough to get the job done despite native English speakers often being unaware of the difficulties they are encountering (CILT, 2005). Other research (e.g. Neeley, 2013) has indicated that fluency in the lingua franca of the organization does not necessarily determine status or performance. This project gave rise to findings that rather expand our understanding of this important language dynamic in multicultural teamwork. In fact, language competence does matter, but not necessarily in the way you would expect it to. In this project team, the three best performers—those who uncovered the most recontextualizations and offered useful insights that could be used to reinvigorate Tesco's core operations (as assessed by the academic co-leads and triangulated by the project team lead from Tesco Asia) over the entire project on all levels were the ones who had the weakest spoken English yet had the longest tenure in Tesco in their native country. This indicates that familiarity with company language and identification with the organization is a key component of communicative efficacy in global organizations. We also uncovered a significant lack of correlation between ability in spoken English and written English across the whole team, with several project team members producing field notes of much higher quality than expected based on their speaking ability. A significant attenuating factor here may be the language "strategy" of Tesco as a company which holds that simplicity and clarity with the needs of the customer (and the interlocutor) are key elements of development and behavior at all levels of the organization.

These findings draw into question some key tenets of internationally distributed research projects which do not build in control mechanisms to combat these unreliable assumptions about language competence Kubota (2011) labels under the term "linguistic instrumentalism." They also suggest that international companies that adopt a developmental approach to language in all its forms and functions may as a result obtain advantage through better, deeper communication and the production of more unifying codes which work across borders. Language policy consists of much more than selection and imposition of a lingua franca (Harzing, Köster and Magner, 2011).

Challenges in Note Taking, Fieldwork and Analysis

The design of the project generally and the training which comprised the first phase of it was driven by the express desired outcomes of Tesco plc. Working within such constraints, as well as those of time, funding and the competences of individual team members, stretched the abilities and experience of the academic team. It had to be recognized that we were not working with conventional students, and corners had to be cut with regard to the scope of the syllabus and reading time available on the part of the project team.

In the training phase, all the project team members had difficulty with the absorption of the nature of ethnographic practice, the techniques of observation and judicious participation and the painstaking technique of note taking. Whilst some of these uncertainties were eased when the academic team accompanied the project team members on pilot sessions in local stores, some key uncertainties persisted, such as the border between "objective" and "subjective" phenomena and the way in which they should be recorded. In order to help the project team focus their participant observation, we offered a simple rubric—focus on three questions: What is *familiar*? What is *surprising*? What do I want to learn *more* about? We termed these "the F, S, and M's" and asked them to mark these in their field notes. Some of the project team members were concerned about how they would be received in the stores and worried about being viewed as "Asian spies." Fortunately, Tesco already had a policy wherein all store managers and Tesco executives must spend one week per year working in the stores so as not to lose touch with the customer. We therefore counseled the project team to use this practice, termed "Tesco Week in Stores" or "TWIST" as a way of helping the Tesco UK store employees understand their presence in the stores and to explain that this was just a new global twist on this standard routine.

Some of the managers also struggled with the discipline of writing-up field notes and took more time to construct the personal routine required. Others required remedial sessions to help with decision-making and weaknesses with their English. In order to facilitate this, we devised a template for field note taking and a daily checklist. This included a left-hand column for subjective reflections, a right-hand column for objective notes, and check boxes for F, S, and M's. The team members then sent their weekly field notes to two of the academic advisors who regularly gave feedback and encouraged them to register their subjective opinions regarding their observations as much as possible. This latter point was very important for the project, because in order for Tesco to learn from insider-outsider eyes, the project team members needed to register and communicate differences between how things were done in their home context versus in the UK. These differences, as recontextualizations (Brannen, 2004) can be, as discussed above, sources of innovation and continuous sustainable improvement for Tesco plc that could distinguish it from its competitors, and it was this that they needed to identify.

Coding posed even more problems for the group. Whilst content that they were, in almost all cases, assembling sufficient field notes, they found it very difficult to stand back from their work and analyze, identify and highlight relevant sections of text. Again, remedial sessions gave the group confidence to work systematically on their burgeoning file of notes as they gradually covered the majority of the United Kingdom visiting stores and offices.

An important dimension of the project, which represented a particular challenge, is that of language (Piekkari and Zander, 2005). All the project team had differing native languages. Mandarin, Thai, Hindi, Japanese and several others all figured in the profile of the group and alongside their language identity, each manager had a strong cultural belonging to an individual nation which was further nourished by a strong desire to see Tesco in their country excel within the Asian context. In addition, the level of proficiency in English of the project team members was by no means even. In spoken English, four team members stood out as having more ability than the others because of residence, study or work experience in English-speaking countries. Three project team members were noticeably weaker than the rest in spoken English and one of them had never before visited an English-speaking country. Our knowledge of their respective abilities in writing, reading and listening was to be discovered in the course of the induction, training and field work and the gap between the more and less able turned out to be smaller in writing than in speaking.

While these issues of language proficiency and use and its relationship with ethnographic skills is not the focus of this chapter (and has indeed been discussed in more detail by Myhre [2013]) it is relevant at this stage to point out some of these key issues as they pertain to performance generally and more specifically to competence in understanding what they heard and read and their ability to conduct interviews and gather data directly from Tesco employees in a variety of scenarios. Note taking and analyzing data were of course also key tasks in the project, which relied on a good command of English. Furthermore, language proficiency affects managers' willingness to respond and candidness in making observations. Further discussion about constraints and performance stemming from the issue of language proficiency will be carried out in the relevant parts of the following sections.

Having considered the performance of the team during the project and the strengths and weaknesses of the methodology in practice, we shall now consider the implications for research and practice, and the transferability of the "Essence of Tesco" project.

Limitations and Directions for Future Research

Limitations of the "Essence of Tesco" Project

The use of practitioners as ethnographic researchers, blurring the lines between academic and research subject, raises several issues for the study of organizations. There is, for instance, the question of whether ethnography is something which should only be done by trained professionals: on the one hand, it is a practice requiring extensive training and the development of insight into social phenomena (see Fetterman, 2010). On the other, it is perfectly feasible to train non-academics in the practice, and to forbid them from learning these techniques appears rather like the sort of gatekeeping criticized by the postmodern anthropological movement (see Clifford, 1986), as well as the failure to critically examine our sources flagged up by Westney and van Maanen (2011). If ethnography is a means of gaining insider perspectives on a culture, then, the question remains, why should insiders not be allowed access, not just as sources of data, but also as generators and analyzers of data? Moeran (2005) also argues that anthropologists shape, and are shaped by, the discourses of the people who are the subjects of their ethnographies; certainly this dynamic process is well worth encouraging to help with the integration of large, geographically dispersed organizations. Also, in the case of organizations, the subjects of the research are generally well-educated, elite, "members of the academy," as it were, who may have studied the social sciences and who can present an academically informed perspective on their experiences.

The counterargument is, however, that including practitioner participants does not magically erase the power dynamics of the research process, but instead redraws the boundaries; the process of conducting the "Essence of Tesco" project did include periodic conflicts between managerial and academic members of the project over its direction and contents. Furthermore, at least one of the managers found it difficult to adopt a researcher perspective on the organization, and to treat the project as an exercise in data gathering rather than of reproducing the organization's own internal "party line." As with any skill, individuals vary in how well they are able to conduct ethnographic research. Finally, the project has the same potential to go wrong as any ethnographic project, and as such should not be undertaken lightly (see Moeran, 1985). However, these are not reasons to avoid using practitioner ethnographers, but rather guidelines to possible problems that might emerge when doing so.

Some possible points of guidance would be to insist on the involvement of trained ethnographic researchers as supervisors and mentors on similar projects. However, it might also be worth, in light of the project's findings, encouraging researchers in non-ethnographic research to find other ways of taking practitioner perspectives into account within the company under study.

Ways Forward

The project also suggests some further directions for research and practice. Integration is a key concern of multinational corporations as is the need to learn from the firm's global footprint in order to continually reinvigorate core operations. The "Essence of Tesco" methodology offers a way for both of these goals to be achieved. Utilizing global teams as insider ethnographers comparing and contrasting their home operations not only shares knowledge that is otherwise dispersed but also integrates learning across the various subsidiaries. The project's methodological achievements also suggest, as has been argued elsewhere (e.g. Birkinshaw, Brannen and Tung, 2011;

Moore, 2011; Brannen and Doz, 2012), that the disciplines of international business and organization studies could do well to make more creative and/or unusual use of ethnography, and of techniques from other disciplines, such as linguistics (as in Piekkari and Zander, 2005), to generate new theoretical insights. They also suggest seeking out practitioner knowledge, for instance through business memoirs and similar insider documents (e.g. Augar, 2000) and allowing practitioners greater access to methods based on a postmodern ability to grasp the tacit and symbolic (see Jeffcut, 1994). Crucially, they suggest ways of harnessing the "casual ethnography" observed by Westney and van Maanen (2011) and providing a rigorous, reflexive framework in which to make use of it. Areas in the "Essence of Tesco" project that need further analysis include the linguistic issues encountered by the research team, and also the role of the managers as vectors of recontextualization within the company.

Contributions and Conclusions

Contributions of the Project to Research and Practice

The "Essence of Tesco" project represents a new development in organizational research methods, building on existing practice in organization studies. In the first place, the project provides a response to the common assumption that ethnography is a tool best used for studying small groups in-depth (Miles, 1979; Sackmann and Phillips, 2004) and thus is incapable of providing a broad picture of the whole organization, in that the researchers were able to obtain thick, experiential data ranging not just across the UK, but extending into Tesco's international operations, and were able to take multiple perspectives on the organization into account. The method discussed here could thus be used to provide extensive, but manageable, qualitative data on large and/or multinational corporations.

Secondly, the project's methodology allowed the team to integrate the perspectives of managers into the study, not just as passive research subjects, but also as active contributors to the analysis (see Westney and van Maanen, 2011). This, first, challenges and breaks down the hierarchies of the research process, whereby the researcher gathers data from the research subjects on behalf of the organization's top management (or other instigating body), critiquing the divide between researcher and researched and critiquing hierarchies within the academic process. Secondly, it provides a way of dealing with reliability issues (see Sinkovics, Penz and Ghauri, 2008; Ghauri and Grønhaug, 2010), ensuring that the academic perspective is not the only one represented or given priority, that "casual ethnography" is incorporated with sufficient analytic rigor, and thus providing a way of developing research that practitioners can engage with at all stages, as well as mitigating the so-called "Rashomon effect," whereby multiple, conflicting perspectives on the data vie for dominance within an academic narrative.

Finally, the project allows practitioners to harness aspects of ethnographic research that may be helpful to them in their day-to-day working lives. A knowledge of ethnographic techniques could benefit managers working in cross-cultural management, or training, or mergers and acquisitions, among many other areas; by expanding the teaching of ethnographic techniques out of the academy, we can help managers to do their jobs better, through reflecting critically on their own organization and practices. The project also, through the identification and definition of the "Essence of Tesco," provided a final result that was of practical benefit to a specific company as well as being of theoretical benefit to the discipline of international business. Finally, the data and insights gained remain proprietary to the company, rather than subject to the interests of third parties.

Conclusions

The "Essence of Tesco" project therefore did not simply allow managers crucial insight into the nature of their own organization, but it also serves as a test case to show how ethnography, using a team of researchers and managers, can be used to generate valuable theoretical and practical insights into transnational organizations and the sort of cultural recontextualization that goes on in them. Furthermore, it suggests ways in which lesser-used forms of ethnography can be leveraged to advantage in management studies, and in which already-extant "casual" data gathering can be acknowledged and analyzed with sufficient rigor. Finally, it serves as a challenge to traditional positioning of researchers and subjects in organizational research as well as in the social sciences more generally, forming part of the body of literature critiquing the researcher's role in the research process (see Arnoud and Cayla, 2015).

For future development, the project provides a template for researchers, and practitioners, to develop practitioner-led ethnographic techniques: employing teams of managers trained in ethnographic techniques under the guidance of experienced researchers to study different organizations, thereby gaining the sort of rich data and experiential insights which more traditional methods, and which conventional researcher-led ethnography, does not provide, for both academic and practical issues. This model can be adapted to fit many different sorts of research questions, as needed. The project also expands and develops debates within the research community on the subjectivity of different research methods, and the question of how to identify and emphasize the most appropriate "voices" within the organization. The "Essence of Tesco" project is thus a development of, and contribution to, ongoing themes in organization studies.

References

Alvesson, M. (2009). At-home ethnography: Struggling with closeness and closure. In *Organizational ethnography: Studying the complexities of everyday life*, London: Sage, 156–174.

Arnoud, E.J. and Cayla, J. (2015). Consumer fetish: Commercial ethnography and the sovereign consumer. *Organization Studies*, 36(10): 1361–1386.

Augar, P. (2000). *The death of gentlemanly capitalism: The rise and fall of London's investment banks*. London: Penguin Books.

Baba, M.L. (1998). Anthropology of work in the Fortune 1000: A critical retrospective. *Anthropology of Work Review*, XVIII(4): 17–28.

Barley, S.R. (1983). Semiotics and the study of organizational cultures. *Administrative Science Quarterly*, 28(3): 393–413.

Barley, S.R. (1990). Images of imaging: Notes on doing longitudinal field work. *Organization Science*, 1(3): 220–247.

Barley, S.R. (1996). Technicians in the workplace: Ethnographic evidence for bringing work into organization studies. *Administrative Science Quarterly*, 41(3): 404–441.

Ben-Ari, E. (1991). *Changing Japanese suburbia*. London: Kegan Paul.

Beyes, T. and Steyaert, C. (2013). Strangely familiar: The uncanny and unsiting organizational analysis. *Organization Studies*, 34(10): 1445–1465.

Birkinshaw, J., Brannen, M.Y. and Tung, R. (2011). From a distance and generalizable to up close and grounded: Reclaiming a place for qualitative methods in international business research. *Journal of International Business Studies*, 42: 573–581.

Black Elk, W. and Lyon, W.S. (1990). *Black Elk: The sacred ways of a Lakota*. New York: Harper and Row.

Bleiklie, I., Enders, J. and Lepori, B. (2015). Organizations as penetrated hierarchies: Environmental pressures and control in professional organizations. *Organization Studies*, 36(7): 873–896.

Brannen, M.Y. (1992). 'Bwana Mickey': Constructing cultural consumption at Tokyo Disneyland. In J. Tobin, ed., *Remade in Japan: Everyday life and consumer taste in a changing society*. New Haven, CT: Yale University Press, 216–234.

Brannen, M.Y. (1995a). Your next boss is Japanese: Negotiating cultural change at a western Massachusetts paper plant. (PhD Doctoral Dissertation, University of Massachusetts, Amherst).

Brannen, M.Y. (1995b). Does culture matter? Negotiating a complementary culture to support technological innovation. In Liker, J.K., Ettlie, J.E. and Campbell, J.C., eds, *Engineered in Japan: Japanese technology-management practices*, Oxford: Oxford University Press on Demand, 321–345.

Brannen, M.Y. (2004). When Mickey loses face: Recontextualization, semantic fit, and the semiotics of foreignness. *Academy of Management Review*, 29: 593–616.

Brannen, M.Y. and Doz, Y.L. (2012). The languages of strategic agility: Trapped in your jargon or lost in translation? *California Management Review*, 54(3): 77–97.

Brannick, T. and Coghlan, D. (2007). In defense of being 'native': The case for insider academic research. *Organizational Research Methods*, 10(1): 59–74.

Burawoy, M. (2013). Ethnographic fallacies: Reflections on labour studies in the era of market fundamentalism. *Work Employment and Society*, 27(3): 526–536.

Carsten, J. (2000). 'Knowing where you've come from': Ruptures and continuities of time and kinship in narratives of adoption reunions. *Journal of the Royal Anthropological Institute*, 6(4): 687–703.

CILT. (2005). *Talking to the world*. London: CILT (Centre for Information on Language Teaching). London.

Clifford, J. (1986). Introduction: Partial truths. In J. Clifford and G.E. Marcus (eds.), *Writing culture: The poetics and politics of anthropology*. Berkeley, CA: University of California Press, 1–26.

Crapanzano, V. (1980). *Tuhami: Portrait of a Moroccan*. Chicago, IL: University of Chicago Press.

Douglas, M. (1993). *In the wilderness: The doctrine of defilement in the book of numbers*. Oxford: Oxford University Press.

Dumont, J.P. (1978). *The headman and I: Ambiguity and ambivalence in the fieldworking experience*. Austin, TX: University of Texas Press.

Ellis, C.S. and Bochner, A. (2000). Autoethnography, personal narrative, reflexivity: Researcher as subject. 733–768.

Fetterman, D. (2010). *Ethnography: Step-by-step* (3rd ed.). Applied Social Research Methods Series Vol. 17. London: Sage Publications.

Fox, K. (2004). *Watching the English: The hidden rules of English behaviour*. London: Hodder.

Gephart, R.P. (1978). Status degradation and organizational succession: An ethnomethodological approach. *Administrative Science Quarterly*, 23(4): 553–581.

Ghauri, P. and Grønhaug, K. (2010). *Research methods in business studies* (4th ed.). London: Financial Times Prentice Hall.

Gluckman, M. (1958). *Analysis of a social situation in modern Zululand*. Manchester: Manchester University Press.

Graham, L. (1995). *On the line at Subaru-Isuzu: The Japanese model and the American worker*. Ithaca, NY: ILR Press.

Harris, S. (2000). Reconciling positive and interpretative international management research: A native category approach. *International Business Review*, 9(6): 755–770.

Harzing, A.W., Köster, K. and Magner, U. (2011). Babel in business: The language barrier and its solutions in the HQ-subsidiary relationship. *Journal of World Business*, 46(3): 279–287.

Heilman, S.C. (2000). Ethnography and biography, or what happened when I asked people to tell me the story of their lives as Jews. *Contemporary Jewry*, 21(1): 23–32.

Holt, R. (2006). *Beneath these red cliffs: An ethnohistory of the Utah Paiutes*. Logan, UT: Utah State University Press.

Jeffcut, P. (1994). From interpretation to representation in organizational analysis: Postmodernism, ethnography and organizational symbolism. *Organization Studies*, 15(2): 241–274.

Jick, T.D. (1979). Mixing qualitative and quantitative methods: Triangulation in action. *Administrative Science Quarterly*, 24: 602–611.

Kubota, R. (2011). Questioning linguistic instrumentalism: English, neoliberalism, and language tests in Japan. *Linguistics and Education*, 22: 248–260.

Lassiter, L. (2005). *Collaborative ethnography*. Chicago, IL: University of Chicago Press.

Lo, J. (1990). *Office ladies, factory women: Life and work at a Japanese company*. London: East Gate.

Mars, G. (1982). *Cheats at work: The anthropology of workplace crime*. Winchester: George Allen & Unwin.

Martin, J. (1992). *Cultures in organizations: Three perspectives*. Oxford: Oxford University Press.

Mayer, P. and Mayer, I. (1961). *Townsmen or tribesmen: Conservatism and the process of urbanisation in a South African city*. Oxford: Oxford University Press.

McFeat, T. (1974). *Small-group cultures*. Elmsford: Pergamon Press.

Miles, M.B. (1979). Qualitative data as an attractive nuisance: The problem of analysis. *Administrative Science Quarterly*, 24(4): 590–601.

Moeran, B. (1985). *Okubo diary: Portrait of a Japanese valley*. Stanford, CA: Stanford University Press.

Moeran, B. (2005). *The business of ethnography: Strategic exchanges, people and organizations*. Oxford: Berg.

Moeran, B. (2014). Business, anthropology, and magical systems: The case of advertising. *Ethnographic Praxis in Industry Conference Proceedings*, 119–132.

Moore, F. (2005). *Transnational business cultures: Life and work in a multinational corporation*. Aldershot: Ashgate.

Moore, F. (2011). Holistic ethnography: Studying the impact of multiple national identities on post-acquisition organizations. *Journal of International Business Studies*, 42(5): 654–671.

Morris, M.W., Leung, K., Ames, D. and Lickel, B. (1999). Views from the inside and outside: Integrating emic and etic insights about culture and justice judgment. *Academy of Management Review*, 24(4): 781–796.

Myhre, K.C. (2013). The pitch of ethnography: Language, relations, and the significance of listening. *Anthropology Today*, 12(2): 185–208.

Neeley, T.B. (2013). Language matters: Status loss and achieved status distinctions in global organizations. *Organization Science*, 24(2): 476–497.

O'Docherty, D., de Cock, C., Rehn, A. and Ashcraft, K.L. (2013). New sites/sights: Exploring the white spaces of organization. *Organization Studies*, 34(10): 1427–1444.

Piekkari, R. and Zander, L. (2005). Preface: Language and communication in international management. *International Studies of Management and Organization*, 35(1): 3–9.

Sackmann, S.A. and Phillips, M.E. (2004). Contextual influences on culture research: Shifting assumptions for new workplace realities. *International Journal of Cross-Cultural Management*, 4(3): 370–390.

Sakai, J. (2000). *Japanese bankers in the city of London: Language, culture and identity in the Japanese diaspora.* London: Routledge.

Salk, J.E. (1992). International shared management joint venture teams: Their developmental patterns, challenges, and possibilities (Doctoral dissertation, Massachusetts Institute of Technology).

Sanday, P.R. (1979). The ethnographic paradigm(s). *Administrative Science Quarterly*, 24(4): 527–538.

Schein, E. (1985). *Organizational culture and leadership: A dynamic view.* San Francisco, CA: Jossey-Bass Publishers.

Schwartzman, H.B. (1993). *Ethnography in organizations.* Newbury Park: Sage Publications.

Sharpe, D. (2006). Shopfloor practices under changing forms of managerial control: A comparative ethnographic study of micro-politics, control and resistance within a Japanese multinational. *Journal of International Management*, 12(3): 318–339.

Short, N.P. (ed.) (2013) *Contemporary British autoethnography.* Rotterdam: Sense Publishers.

Sillitoe, P. and Sillitoe, J. (2009). *Grass-clearing man: A factional ethnography of life in the New Guinea Highlands.* New York: Waveland Press.

Sinkovics, R.R., Penz, E. and Ghauri, P. (2008). Enhancing the trustworthiness of qualitative research in international business. *Management International Review*, 48(6): 689–714.

van Maanen, J. (1979). Reclaiming qualitative methods for organizational research: A preface. *Administrative Science Quarterly*, 24(4): 520–526.

Westney, E. and van Maanen, J. (2011). The casual ethnography of the office suite. *Journal of International Business Studies*, 42(2): 602–607.

9

CONTEXTUAL ANALYTICS

Using Human Science to Strengthen Data Science Approaches in the Development of Algorithms

Mikkel Krenchel and Christian Madsbjerg

Introduction

The term "Big Data" has gone out of fashion. Some posit that it collapsed under the weight of lofty expectations – access to massive datasets is not, as business leaders found out, a digital panacea.[1] Others contend it was simply refashioned into less fetishizing terms like "data-driven"[2] or replaced by references to its real-world applications like machine learning.[3] Most agree, however, that big data – though no longer deserving of capitalization[4] – lives on in the ever-increasing relevance of its mission: some 80% of any company's data remains unstructured and unused, and businesses strive to make that information accessible to those with the necessary skills and tools to harness its value.[5] Increasingly, this means looking beyond the traditional methods of data analysis.

Social scientists, too, have sought to shed new light on deep and dark data lakes by combining big data analytics with qualitative observation in the form of ethnographically inflected "thick data."[6] In the proceedings of EPIC alone, discussion around collaboration between the social and data sciences has ranged from new opportunities for mixed methods research,[7] to exploring the lifecycle of a data source,[8] to understanding decision-making within data analytics processes.[9] Moreover, as Kate Crawford describes in her 2017 Keynote to the Conference on Neural Information Processing Systems, data scientists themselves are now seeking input from people with a deep expertise in human issues.[10] For example, in response to recent high-profile privacy scandals, companies like Facebook are advertising the need to look past trace data and towards "the contextual knowledge that computers lack."[11] Data and human scientists are well agreed on the opportunities of combining their respective methodologies. The question, then, is no longer whether we need to combine big and thick data – the question is how best to do it.[12]

The danger of ignoring this practical question – and simply presuming a commonsense relationship between data and human science – lies in the failure to consciously identify how these two methodologies might actually influence one another. As Nick Seaver writes, the big and thick data conversation fits within a long lineage of "neatly opposed methodological moieties."[13] In relation to methods of standardizing behavioral analysis – of which big data is far from the first – human scientists continue to rehearse established scripts about how "renewed attention to the blood and sex of daily life" might rescue or regulate formal analysis.[14] Seaver argues for pushing beyond these familiar scripts to attend more carefully to how these specific methodologies might actually interact. With Seaver, in this chapter we will explore how an understanding of social and data science processes might more meaningfully inform collaboration between the two. Consequently, we will attempt to give more "texture and specificity" to the practices of big data and interrogate the "coherence and self-evidence" of ethnography in the process.[15]

Over the last two years Cognizant – a leading technology services company with deep capabilities within Data Analytics and AI – and ReD Associates – a consulting firm that helped pioneer the use of applied ethnography – have developed a suite of offerings that leverage the best of both data and human science in the service of real client problems. We've had hundreds of conversations with Fortune 500 executives around potential services, but it has become clear that the one area where the integration of human and data science is most demanding – and potentially most impactful – is in the creation and refinement of algorithms. These algorithms increasingly make up the backbone of many businesses by automating their interactions with customers, employees, and stakeholders. Concerns about ethics and efficiency, however, have led these same businesses to seek new insights around their algorithms. In response, ReD and Cognizant developed a methodology called Contextual Analytics: a project process for uniting data analysts and social scientists under the mandate of building more effective and credible algorithms.

Simply putting data analysts and social scientists in a room together is not enough to ensure a better algorithm. Rather, our experiences point to the need to design projects in a fundamentally different way in order to overcome the methodological and philosophical challenges of integration. This chapter will begin with a short overview of existing efforts to integrate big and thick data before turning to a description of the three phases of the Contextual Analytics methodology. Drawing from insights gained while working with clients, the chapter will ultimately suggest new ways of achieving meaningful cooperation between the human and data sciences.

Integrating Data and Human Sciences

A Brief History of Big and Thick Data

Most attempts to define big data focus on the "3Vs" – volume, velocity, and variety – to demonstrate the sheer size and scope of data sources available today.[16] Other definitions include "veracity" and "value" or look to different letters altogether,[17] but the general concept remains the same: big data is the phenomenon of having massive datasets on human behavior drawn from millions of touchpoints between businesses and organizations and their customers and clients, tracked in a variety of formats. Data analysts use statistical techniques to analyze datasets, and in doing so create new ways of interpreting and classifying relationships between human and non-human actors.[18]

When the concept of big data was still nascent, social scientists recognized its potential complementarity with their own discipline. Their initial attempts to promote the use of "thick data" – a term borrowed from Clifford Geertz and used to describe deep insights into human behavior derived through ethnographic method – failed to garner much interest among data scientists.[19] In recent years, however, thick data has become an industry imperative due to shifting priorities around data privacy and ethics. Since the advent of machine learning – a fully-automated tool designed to find relationships in massive pools of data – dozens of studies have called into question the opaque decision-making of their resulting "black box" algorithms.[20] Moreover, business leaders increasingly struggle to accept the results of automated algorithms that lack a persuasive account for their findings.[21] Now that economic incentives around performance are aligned with ethical imperatives to make more transparent algorithms, interventions on behalf of social scientists for "thickening" and "socializing" the process of data analysis are increasingly cited by politicians, pundits, and industry leaders.[22]

The Evolution of Integrated Approaches

Mixed-methods approaches often structure their research in the ways most familiar to them – social science first or data science first – and use the other method as a supplement or corrective.[23] In presenting learnings on Contextual Analytics, however, we will join others who attempt a more even-keeled integration of the two. For example, while we contend that social scientists and data analysts must also participate in and internalize each other's research, we join the authors of the "blended" model by extending their recommendation that the merging of insights be rapid, iterative, and done before analysis is fully finished so that one method may help guide the other.[24]

Moreover, "Living Labs" models – which use coordinated community workshops to test technologies and services in a real world context – tell us that interaction between teams can start well before the workshop with the analysis of available trace data, subsequently enhanced through participant interaction.[25] Like Living Labs researchers, our studies suggest that, when possible, it is beneficial to start a project with "exploratory" data analysis that finds new patterns to inform subsequent ethnographic research protocols.[26] We also draw on "Collaboratory" models: one-time workshop events where ethnographers and industry data analysts come together to share their knowledge and experiences.[27] While Collaboratories focus on concept development rather than implementation, these workshops demonstrate the benefits of using ethnographic research to slow down traditional data analysis in order to explore more open-ended ways of solving a problem.[28]

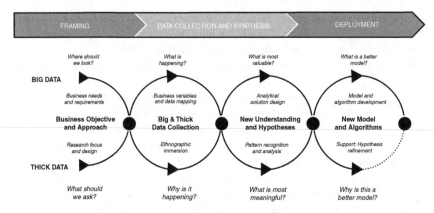

FRAMING | DATA COLLECTION AND SYNTHESIS | DEPLOYMENT

Figure 9.1 The 12AI Contextual Analytics Process. ReD Associates and Cognizant, 2018. Used with permission.

In outlining an integrated approach to algorithm development, we hope to build on existing work as well as present new learnings for what teams must do differently in a corporate setting. Drawing on this dual focus, we aligned social and data science workstreams into a process called Contextual Analytics, to which we will now turn.

The Contextual Analytics Process

Contextual Analytics was designed by ReD and Cognizant to allow data analysts, social science researchers, and client data and business teams to work together to address well-established analytics gaps (see Figure 9.1).

The process leverages quantitative and qualitative analytical techniques across three project phases – Framing, Data Collection and Synthesis, and Deployment – to build actionable insights for a company's current situation and produce improved algorithms for generating new insights going forward. Over the past year, we have applied this methodology to high-stakes corporate problems in various industries. Overall, our work suggests that there are three critical elements for integrated teams to consider:

1 *Specificity in Framing* – While strong framing is critical for any research project, there is a greater need for epistemological and logistical specificity in the planning stages when combining data science and social science teams. In order to acquire the right data sets in a timely manner and deploy teams to the right locations, ethnographers need to get specific about what they really need to know and how data analysts can help. Data analysts, in turn, need to be clear about what it will take to acquire and operationalize the necessary data sources. Doing so in a way that avoids hypothesis-driven thinking and allows for agile

redirections of the project frame requires practitioners on both sides who are experienced enough to foresee potential problems in team communication and data access.

2   *Forced Immersion in Data Collection and Synthesis* – The complementarity of social science and data science is most beneficial when a single team conducts research and analysis while in constant conversation, collaborating to share their findings and align on next steps. To do so, practitioners from each of the workstreams must understand how the other practically conducts their projects and what this means for their own work. Thus, to collect and present their data in a way that is mutually beneficial, data scientists and social scientists must briefly, but meaningfully, step into the methodological shoes of the other.

3   *Integrated Storytelling in Deployment* – The customs around good storytelling vary widely between (and among) ethnographers and data scientists. To get the most out of an integrated approach a common language is needed that borrows the best from both disciplines. Thus, integrated teams must not only produce two separate deliverables – a highly persuasive story behind insights and a model with statistically improved results – but also create meaningful links between those two deliverables. To do so requires practitioners to move out of their respective black boxes and towards a common set of mid-level theories: data analysts by opening their algorithms to tell the stories that the data represents, and ethnographers by pushing beyond grand narratives alone to connect them to testable and sizeable hypotheses.

When these elements are taken into account throughout project design and practice, the resulting collaborative efforts are not necessarily faster or cheaper, but allow for teams to jointly create algorithms that are more grounded, that have better results, and that people in the C-suite can understand. With all this in mind, our chapter will now move on to discussing Contextual Analytics in practice, outlining how the methodology can be applied in each of the three phases.

Phase One: Framing

In the first phase of a Contextual Analytics project – Framing – teams are designed to balance quantitative and qualitative methods to better direct the course of data analysis. Ideally, a project is framed so that quantitative data informs the start of an ethnographic investigation by focusing its traditionally broad scope through the statistical identification of promising markets and segments. Ethnographic immersion, on the other hand, generates rich contextual information through open-ended inquiry, and so broadens the data analytics framing process which traditionally relies on hypotheses generated from easily available data sets.

We've learned that – despite the best intentions of both teams to work collaboratively in framing – their efforts can be impeded if they don't specifically account for process silos and problems with data access. To account for the former, a strong project management team needs to ensure frequent communication between both social and data scientists so the two don't return to old ways of conducting their research independently. For the latter, teams must consider the practical constraints of data access; a particularly relevant challenge given new data protection and privacy laws like those implemented across the European Union in May of 2018. The result: well-framed projects can enrich research and speed up raw data collection, but teams must spend more time planning them upfront.

Contextual Analytics in Practice: The Project Framing Phase

In the framing phase, project goals are two-fold. First, develop research questions to guide the inquiry process: what to ask and why? Second, develop research protocols: who to meet and where? Typically, social scientists and data analysts approach these same goals from different epistemological starting points. Social scientists, with theoretical foundations in ethnographic and grounded theory approaches, frame research in a purposefully broad manner in order to approach a phenomenon without potentially misguided assumptions.[29] In this way, framing is abstract and leaves room for serendipity: go after the biggest questions, and narrow the scope based on what shows up as important along the way. Data analysts, however, follow a scientific method approach by starting with a set of hypotheses that could explain the business problem. The input for these hypotheses often comes from business leaders who provide their perspective on the issue or from prior models that explain the situation for different use cases. Thus, data analysis typically begins with a deep understanding of existing data sources and how they've been used in the past, along with the preparation of any data that hasn't been used or analyzed previously.

Despite social scientists and data scientists having different starting points when framing projects, a key value added by the Contextual Analytics process is that the integrated team continuously shares, discusses, and debates any prior analyses, hypotheses, and unknowns they may have before and during the course of the project. By integrating their analytical techniques in response to the specific demands of a given case, an integrated team has the potential to dramatically strengthen their starting point for analysis and algorithm development.

Take, for example, our project on prospect targeting for a global financial services company. Before ReD and Cognizant intervened, the financial company's data team had embarked on a project to develop new models that would increase the response rate of SMBs (small-to-medium businesses) to credit card offers received over the phone or via mail. Yet in their own words, one of their blind spots was an understanding of *why* those SMBs would be receptive to offers. As a result, their current models resulted in an astoundingly low response rate – a mere 3.5% – and in the process left countless business owners feeling spammed by irrelevant offers. Our challenge was to develop ethnographic insight into why SMBs respond or fail to respond to offers at particular times, and to develop and translate those insights into data implications and proxies for building a new, more precise, targeting model.

Working in a silo – removed from any insights that a sales team may have had from actually interacting with SMBs – the client data team had relied on a combination of intuition and evidence to frame their analysis. Their intuition led the team to start with analysis of historical data that showed predictability in offer response-rate for other populations. Then, after searching for those same correlations in their lists of SMBs, subsequent data analysis showed a small uptick in the model which gave them the evidence to justify their data use. One data analyst on the project told the ReD and Cognizant team that this framing constituted a "big creative leap" in which their hypothesis was based not on "what would cause credit card conversion now?", but rather on "there was conversion for this type of problem in the past"; all correlation, with no proof of causation.

Enter Contextual Analytics. After identifying this limitation of the existing model, the ReD and Cognizant team planned their project to start with social science research in order to move past a narrow framing based on existing knowledge – what does the data tell us about the phenomenon? – and towards framing based on open-ended analysis – what does the phenomenon tell us to look for in the data? Instead of going after existing correlations of data, our ethnographic team planned a backwards-engineered segmentation to find the underlying drivers for how financial decisions are made in SMBs; they gathered and studied businesses in different industries, with different revenue and employee size, and then searched for common factors that most affect their probability of responsiveness. This blank-slate segmentation approach allowed the whole team to think creatively around different types of data to start with, including examples of proxies like local mentality: if the business has closer ties to other institutions in their neighborhood, they were less likely to respond to an unsolicited offer. Through their combined efforts, the integrated team was able to envision a sound frame for the project that used social science to make up for a lack of guiding insights.

Where, ideally, a data analysis stream would first develop certain research protocols by sharing hypotheses from past models, in this case those hypotheses couldn't be trusted without their validation in the population that was actually being studied. That being said, machine learning is powerful, and can find corollaries in troves of data that would confound human analysis. Ethnographers learned to pay special attention to areas where data analysis said the business problem was most pressing, and where parts of research needed to happen. If framing is to succeed, conversations like the above have to happen in the context of each project, based on an honest assessment of limitations and strengths.

Key Success Criteria for the Framing Phase

A proper framing process for Contextual Analytics sets up data and human science for success by customizing interaction between the two workstreams. Yet even the best laid plans of human and data scientists are subject to practical tests within a corporate setting. Without establishing a clear process to guide the mandate of working collaboratively, we've seen that teams have a tendency to retract into silos: a data science team working in isolation with a hypothesis dictated by opportunistic data, or a social science team identifying a phenomenon and lines of inquiry unguided by existing analyses. These two silos acutely demonstrate the need to understand and account for one another's epistemologies when framing a project.

Data scientists can push beyond their normal tools and methods by thinking more carefully about what the data is *not* showing. Instead of defaulting to a focus on what is trackable – what is "happening" – this team can take inspiration from Bourdieu's concept of "social silence" and ask deeper questions about what is *not* happening. What are the silences in the inquiry that are being overlooked – what are people not saying and not doing? Why?

The social-science teams, on the other hand, need to be prepared to think more concretely about their data access much earlier in the process. Data professionals already know that they are likely to spend the majority of their time (nearly 70% of it) just getting the data and putting it into a clean, usable format. Moreover, following a spate of governmental programs on the fair and anonymized use of aggregated data, corporations are cautious when it comes to sharing their internal and private data.[30] Ethnographers are often not familiar with these lengthy data delays and they need to be plan accordingly.

In theory, an integrated approach is one where workstreams are set up to begin their data collection and analysis on an equal footing. But, in reality, that is not always possible, and it may not always be the most adaptive or prudent approach. The data is not always there to start, so quantitative and qualitative tracks will often run at different times. It is important, however, to orchestrate data collection and synthesis so that both tracks can still guide and direct each other as much as possible.

Phase Two: Data Collection and Synthesis

The integration of data and human science workstreams is most critical in the second phase of Contextual Analytics, Data Collection and Synthesis. Data collection takes place in two parallel workstreams: ethnographers observing a small sample size of respondents in the field and data analysts tracking correlations in large datasets. The former is meant to add to and explain quantitative findings, while the latter lends statistical significance to qualitative observations. We've learned, however, that synthesis cannot take place during a single event following research. Rather, data collection and synthesis occur simultaneously and iteratively so that each of the workstreams can use their findings to guide the other to new areas of inquiry. This reciprocity is especially important as data analysts guide researchers on which types of data are actually accessible.

When data collection is done independently – each team taking responsibility for only their own realm of expertise – the representation of social-science based insights in the algorithm is put at risk. Thus, collaborative projects require an element of "forced immersion" on behalf of both data analysts and social scientists, where each practitioner purposefully takes an extra step beyond their normal research. Social scientists need not become data experts (or vice versa), but we've learned that taking the time and effort to learn how the other side conducts their analysis prepares each team to pre-emptively set up their own work in ways that make it easier to merge, translate, and present findings.

Contextual Analytics in Practice: The Data Collection and Synthesis Phase

Contextual Analytics crucially relies on the use of social science research to ground possible correlations from data analysis and to identify hypotheses found outside the margins of available datasets. Take, for example, our project with a leading Nordic energy provider on improving call center performance. The provider runs a contact center that typically fields calls from two types of customers: those looking to invest in new energy solutions, and those struggling to pay their bills. The company worried that they weren't catching a significant amount of the investor population. Meanwhile, employee hours were clogged with calls to and from concerned customers discussing their hefty bills. To solve both problems, the provider desired a new predictive algorithm that could streamline operations by suggesting when employees could pre-emptively contact these different customer segmentations.

Due to the team's lack of data access, data collection began with open-ended ethnographic inquiry: how do homeowners relate to their energy? By spending time with homeowners across a wide demographic range, researchers found that the energy provider could benefit from a more general understanding of the events in the life of a homeowner. These events most often correlated with energy consumption and smart-meter data, leading the team to suggest proxies for which the home – rather than the homeowner – was the locus of analysis.

By providing proxies early and often in data collection, ethnography can help jumpstart the quantitative process of data analysis. In Contextual Analytics projects, ethnographic teams collect insights in ways that roughly map onto potential data sources. Thus, after only a few weeks of observing customer calls with the energy provider and setting up post-call interviews, ethnographers had filled their field notes with new and promising correlations. The team focused on event-based proxies – like the purchase of a new home or flat which primed "warm" homeowners to invest in energy – because they believed such insights could be tracked in easily available data. Yet while opportunistic data sources may risk showing correlation without causation, rudimentary ethnographic findings like the above run the opposite risk. After hunting for and hinting at various correlations from the field, qualitative findings need "quantitative backup" to prove their long-term value.

The term "quantitative backup," coined by one of ReD's researchers, refers to the process of having a data analyst check possible proxies against available data in order to demonstrate sufficient frequency and help prove that a particular correlation in the thick data isn't anomalous. After identifying hypotheses from the field and potential proxies for those hypotheses, the process of checking correlations requires a data analyst to assess the feasibility of translating that insight quantitatively using their knowledge of existing data sources.

By checking in with the data analysts embedded within their team, researchers studying the call center found that many of the events they identified – the installation of a solar panel, the exchange of heating information, a recent move, financial distress – had corresponding variables within existing data sources. Even without access to internal data at the time, the data analyst had the foresight and expertise to inform the team that much of the data they anticipated using existed in a large number of systems, or in datasets that they couldn't trust due to missing or incomplete fields. Thus, validation proved helpful in pointing the team towards finding new proxies to replace their rudimentary attempts.

Key Success Criteria for the Data Collection and Synthesis Phase

Quantitative and qualitative methodologies offer ways to both explore new and validate existing correlations during data collection and synthesis, but only if the two are working in concert. A forced immersion ensures proper presentation and translation of insights between the two workstreams. Ethnographers, for example, tend to underestimate the amount of time and effort it takes for data analysts to translate qualitative insights into variables that can be meaningfully included in the model. The more creative the finding, the harder it will be to unpack it. A forced immersion can help them to better assess which findings to give to the data team for testing and in what format they choose to deliver them in. It calls for ethnographers to take a stance on their data by delivering not just insights, but rudimentary proxies that take accessible data sources into account.

Data analysts, on the other hand, need to embrace the intangible nature of insights delivered from the ethnographic team. If they focus solely on the accompanying data proxies, the representation of those insights in the algorithm is put at risk. In order to make the leap from qualitative insight to quantitative proxies, data teams must get familiar with high-level insights that cannot be measured in a direct 1:1 relationship with the data sources. That is, the use of qualitative observation requires data analysts to think of the underlying human behaviors and actions behind an insight, and how both new and existing data sources can capture them in creative ways. Thus, the best data analysts are not just great mathematicians, but also have what C. Wright Mills called a "sociological imagination": the ability to pull their thinking away from the technical problem at hand, and to understand the interactions that are actually taking place between the points within a dataset and the contexts into which they will be applied.[31]

To cultivate sociological imagination, data analysts working with ethnographers likely need to take some part in the ethnographic research process when developing the first concepts of what the proxies will be. They can only make a real creative translation – taking a methodological leap of faith – when they truly understand the social-science based insights and the contexts from which they emerge.

Phase Three: Deployment

Central to the final phase of Contextual Analytics is the development of two critical deliverables: 1) the final model with a proof point that demonstrates the impact of social-science hypotheses on the algorithm, and 2) the overarching "story" that is able to explain why that algorithm actually works.

Neither the story nor the statistics, however, are particularly novel on their own. Rather, the power of a Contextual Analytics project is that collaboration between data and social scientists allows the two deliverables to be linked through a set of mid-level theories designed to balance the specificity of big data proxies and the high-level inspiration of ethnographic narratives.

Contextual Analytics in Practice: The Deployment Phase

Neither big nor thick data can be used as the sole end-point of algorithm development. Qualitative insights are often thought too small to be reliable on their own. Numbers alone, on the other hand, lack the persuasive power to enact change within an organization. Thus, after aligning on proxies, integrated workstreams show their value to the client through two mutually informative deliverables – numbers made emotional, and stories given statistical weight.

According to a 2017 Cognizant report, most corporate decision-making remains "gut-based" despite the infusion of new data collection, management, and analytical technologies.[32] This is because data analysts find it difficult to keep on top of business needs while juggling multiple algorithm development projects.[33] As a result, data teams are often technically well-prepared, but ill-equipped to demonstrate the overarching business impact of their "black box" algorithms. In response, social scientists focus on providing the "why" behind new correlations in the model.

We can see an example of this in a recent project on curbing attrition and retaining skilled employees with a technology solutions company. The company was using rich data – from exit interviews to Glassdoor reviews – to identify the segments of their workforce who had a higher historic likelihood of quitting. The company HR department had a few hunches about why particular segments were most at risk but lacked the human data that would explain why the model marked certain employee groups and departments as "attrition hotspots."

In order to gather insights on drivers of attrition (and retention) and build a predictive model from them, our approach entailed four collaborative workstreams: the continued quantitative investigation of attrition hotspots and related data proxies; deep dives with employees and those around them, including managers, colleagues, and family/friends; discourse analysis of data gathered with and from human resource teams and in employee town halls; and stakeholder interviews that clarified the cost of attrition and the benefits to solving the issue.

The data science team created a list of over 200 proxies for predicting attrition but this level of granularity meant little to the human resource officers who sought to understand why that attrition happened in the first place. Simultaneously, then, the social science team created a values framework to map onto the proxies that predict attrition and, more importantly, describe the motivations and needs of employees when it comes to their work-life ambitions. This values framework ultimately gave the HR team the explanation they needed in order to identify key employee rationales behind their choosing to stay with or leave the company. The ethnographic "big story" provides buy-in and articulates need on behalf of big data.

As applied ethnographers quickly learn while working in a corporate context, however, scale is often valued over story. Moreover, insights based on ethnographic research can run the risk of seeming anecdotal. Even if the ethnography team has a great story to tell, that story is at its strongest when coupled with statistical proof.

Key Success Criteria for the Deployment Phase

The creation of two separate, though mutually informing, deliverables provides the client with the technical tools and persuasive stories to build effective and convincing algorithms. When the integrated team separates to build different products, they default to the type of product that comes easiest to them: ethnographers developing a governing thought and data scientists focusing on specific proxies. Through all the cases, however, we saw the importance of keeping the two workstreams aligned by pushing each practitioner to embrace "mid-level theory" in their work. This concept, first developed by Robert K. Merton, is an approach to sociological theory construction that balances a focus on the overarching big idea and the particularities of various lower-level hypotheses. As Merton (1968) defines the term:

> ... what might be called theories of the middle range: theories intermediate to the minor working hypotheses evolved in abundance during the day-by-day routine of research, and the all-inclusive speculations comprising a master conceptual scheme.

In the case of Contextual Analytics, mid-level theory functions as a method by which both data and social scientists embrace the needs of the other in order to build more well-rounded deliverables.

For social scientists, embracing big data methods means achieving a level of specificity in insights that might be uncommon and uncomfortable for many ethnographers. Given rapid advances in analytics, it is no longer helpful to produce only a single, abstract overarching theory to sum up an entire project. Rather, ethnographers need to meet in the middle with data analysts by splitting their theories into more granular and focused recommendations custom-tailored for different versions of a model. This specificity is critical to ensure that the stories ethnographers tell are internalized and utilized to their maximum capacity across a company's data portfolio. By baking mid-level theory into the way that they produce deliverables, teams ensure that the collaborative spirit of Contextual Analytics extends through the project's resolution.

Conclusion

Extending Frames of Reference

In practice, the building of contextually informed algorithms calls for qualitative and quantitative studies that go beyond merely observing the complementarity of statistical analysis and ethnographic research.[34] Indeed, as we have seen, simply putting the practitioners of big and thick data together does little to enable their practical collaboration. Both social scientists and data analysts must make attempts to better understand one another's project processes in each phase – Framing, Data Collection and Synthesis, and Deployment – in order to facilitate the integration of their findings. We have learned that whether through frequent communication, forced immersion, or mid-level theory, a Contextual Analytics project relies on practitioners who are willing to move beyond their original frames of reference. We encourage continued conversations around the integration of big and thick data workstreams and the practical collaboration of their practitioners, and hope that future discussions will further engage the practicalities of Contextual Analytics processes in corporate settings.

Acknowledgements

An early draft of this chapter was published in the Proceedings of the Ethnographic Praxis in Industry (EPIC) conference in 2018, under the title "Contextual Analytics: Towards a Practical Integration of Human and Data Science Approaches in the Development of Algorithms" by Mikkel Krenchel alongside co-authors Millie Arora, Jacob McAuliffe and Poornima Ramaswamy. The authors of the present chapter would like to thank Jake, Millie and Poornima for their input and ideas to these early discussions, as well as countless colleagues at ReD Associates who through constructive discussions have helped hone key ideas since then.

Notes

1. Oremus, Will (2017, October 16). "How 'Big Data' Went Bust. And What Comes Next." Slate.
2. Dykes, Brent (2018, August 22). "Build a Data-Driven Culture, One Meeting at a Time." Forbes.
3. Burton, Besty and Hank Barnes (2017, August 11). "2017 Hype Cycles Highlight Enterprise and Ecosystem Digital Disruptions: A Gartner Trend Insight Report." Gartner.
4. Boelstorff, Tom (2015). "Making Big Data: In Theory." Tom Boelstorf and Bill Maurer (Eds.), *Data, Now Bigger and Better!* (87–108). Chicago, IL: Prickly Paradigm Press.
5. Gartner (2017). "Forecast: Internet of Things – Endpoints and Associated Services, Worldwide, 2017." Gartner; PricewaterhouseCoopers (2015): "Seizing the Information Advantage: How organizations Can Unlock Value and Insight from the Information They Hold." A PwC report in conjunction with Iron Mountain.
6. Wang, Tricia (2013, May 13). "Big Data Needs Thick Data." Ethnography Matters.
7. Rattenbury, Tye and Dawn Nafus (2018). "Data Science and Ethnography: What's Our Common Ground, and Why Does It Matter?" *Ethnographic Praxis in Industry 2017*.
8. Haines, Julia Katherine (2017). "Towards Multi-Dimensional Ethnography." *Ethnographic Praxis in Industry Conference Proceedings 2017*.
9. Kolsto, Ellen (2017). "A Researcher's Perspective on People Who Build with AI." *Ethnographic Praxis in Industry Conference Proceedings 2017*.
10. Crawford, Kate (2017). "The Trouble with Bias." *Conference on Neural Information Processing Systems (NIPS)*, Keynote Address 2017.

11 See, for example, the Facebook-funded post on the New York Times (2018) "Artificial Intelligence: How We Help Machines Learn." The New York Times Paid Post.

12 Boelstorff (2015)

13 Seaver (2015): 37.

14 Ibid.

15 Ibid.: 44.

16 Salganik, Matthew (2017). *Bit by Bit: Social Research in the Digital Age*. Princeton University Press: 18

17 Lupton, Deborah (2015, May 11). "The Thirteen Ps of Big Data." *This Sociological Life*.

18 Donoho, David (2015). "50 Years of Data Science." Princeton, NJ: Tukey Centennial Workshop.

19 Wang (2013); Geertz, Clifford (1973). *The Interpretation of Cultures: Selected Essays.* New York: Basic Books; Madjsberg, Christian (2017). *Sensemaking: The Power of the Humanities in the Age of the Algorithm*. New York: Hachette Books.

20 The data scientist Cathy O'Neil exposes some of the biased data behind opaque algorithms used to predict patterns in policing and felony – algorithms which, through their aura of ostensible objectivity, "create the reality they purport to describe." O'Neil, Cathy (2016). *Weapons of Math Destruction: How Big Data Increases Inequality and Threatens Democracy*, Crown Publishing & Random House. See also Osoba, Osonde A. and William Welser, IV (2017). "An Intelligence in Our Image: The Risks of Bias and Errors in Artificial Intelligence." Santa Monica, CA.: RAND Corporation, RR-1744-RC.

21 Brynjolfsson, Erik and Andrew McAfee (2018). "The Business of Artificial Intelligence: What It Can – And Cannot – Do For Your Organization." *Harvard Business Review*.

22 Storey, Margaret-Anne (2016, May 4). "Lies, Damned Lies and Software Analytics: Why Big Data Needs Thick Data [Webinar]."

23 Lepri, Bruno, et al. (2017). "The Tyranny of Data? The Bright and Dark Sides of Data-Driven Decision-Making for Social Good". *Transparent Data Mining for Big and Small Data*: 3–24.

24 Ibid.

25 One such example is the "Laboratorio Urbano" in Bogota, Colombia, where city government, citizens, architecture firms, and academic institutions collaborated to test out pilot plans for new mobility and safety policies in the rapidly changing city. (The Tyranny of Big Data, 16) For other creative uses of public data see: Nafus, Dawn (2016). "The Domestication of Data: Why Embracing Digital Data Means Embracing Bigger Questions." Ethnographic Praxis in Industry Conference Proceedings 2016. 384–399.

26 Smith, Adrian (2018). "Smart Cities Need Thick Data, Not Big Data." *The Guardian*. Accessed April 18, 2018.

27 Following an Anthropology of the Contemporary (ARC) model, Collaboratories examine the tactics of experts in order to interrogate their traditional methods of knowledge production. Ruppert et al. (2015) "Socialising Big Data: From Concept to Practice." CRESC Working Paper Series. CRESC, The University of Manchester and the Open University.

28 Ibid.

29 See Creswell, John W. and Cheryl N. Poth (2017). *Qualitative Inquiry and Research Design: Choosing among Five Approaches* (4th ed.)

30 Crook, Izaak (2018, April 06). "How GDPR Will Affect Data Science." Dataconomy.

31 Mills, C. Wright (1959). *The Sociological Imagination*. New York: Oxford University Press.

32 Krishnamurthy, Karthik, et al. Cognizant. (2017). "Analytical Storytelling: From Insight to Action." Cognizant White Paper: 4.

33 Kolsto (2017)

34 Venturini, Tommaso and Bruno Latour (2010). "The Social Fabric: Digital Traces and Quali-quantitative Methods." Proceedings of Future En Seine.

References

Blok, Anders and Morten Axel Pedersen. 2014. "Complementary Social Science? Quali-quantitative Experiments in a Big Data World." *Big Data & Society* 1(2): 1–6.

Boelstorff, Tom. 2015. "Making Big Data: In Theory." Tom Boelstorf and Bill Maurer (Eds.), *Data, Now Bigger and Better!* (87–108). Chicago, IL: Prickly Paradigm Press.

Bornakke, Tobias and Brian L. Due. 2018. "Big-Thick Blending: A Method for Mixing Analytical Insights from Big and Thick Data Sources." *Big Data and Society* 1: 1–16.

Bowker, Geoffrey C. 2013. "Data Flakes: An Afterward to 'Raw Data' Is an Oxymoron." Lisa Gitelman (Ed.), *"Raw Data" Is an Oxymoron* (167–171). Cambridge, MA: MIT Press.

Boyd, Danah and Kate Crawford. 2012. "Critical Questions for Big Data: Provocations for a Cultural, Technological, and Scholarly Phenomenon." *Information, Communication & Society* 15(5): 662–679.

Brynjolfsson, Erik and Andrew McAfee. 2018. "The Business of Artificial Intelligence: What It Can – And Cannot – Do For Your Organization." *Harvard Business Review*. Retrieved from: https://hbr.org/cover-story/2017/07/the-business-of-artificial-intelligence. April 12. 2020.

Burton, Besty and Hank Barnes. 2017. "2017 Hype Cycles Highlight Enterprise and Ecosystem Digital Disruptions: A Gartner Trend Insight Report." *Gartner*. August 11, 2017.

Crawford, Kate. 2017. "The Trouble with Bias." *Conference on Neural Information Processing Systems (NIPS)*, Keynote Address 2017.

Creswell, John W. and Cheryl N. Poth. 2017. *Qualitative Inquiry and Research Design: Choosing among Five Approaches* (4th ed.). Thousand Oaks, CA: Sage Publications.

Crook, Izaak. 2018. "How GDPR Will Affect Data Science." *Dataconomy*. Retrieved from: https://dataconomy.com/2018/04/how-gdpr-will-affect-data-science/. April 06, 2018.

Donoho, David. 2015. *50 Years of Data Science*. Princeton, NJ: Tukey Centennial Workshop.

Dykes, Brent. 2018. "Build a Data-Driven Culture, One Meeting at a Time." *Forbes*. Retrieved from https://www.forbes.com/sites/brentdykes/2018/08/22/build-a-data-driven-culture-one-meeting-at-a-time/#1539442f782f. April 12, 2020.

Facebook, The New York Times Paid Post. 2018. "Artificial Intelligence: How We Help Machines Learn." *The New York Times Paid Post*. Retrieved from: https://paidpost. nytimes.com/facebook/artificial-intelligence-how-we-help-machines-learn. html?tbs_nyt=2018-feb-nytnative_apmod&cpv_dsm_id=189293206.

Frank, Malcolm, Paul Roehrig, and Ben Pring. 2017. *What to Do When Machines Do Everything: How to Get Ahead in a World of AI, Algorithms, Bots, and Big Data*. New York: Wiley.

Gartner. 2017. "Forecast: Internet of Things – Endpoints and Associated Services, Worldwide, 2017." *Gartner*. Retrieved from: https://www.gartner.com/en/documents/3840665/forecast-internet-of-things-endpoints-and-associated-ser. April 12, 2020.

Geertz, Clifford. 1973. *The Interpretation of Cultures: Selected Essays*. New York: Basic Books.

Haines, Julia Katherine. 2017. "Towards Multi-Dimensional Ethnography." *Ethnographic Praxis in Industry Conference Proceedings 2017*.

Knieff, Ben and Universal Payments Aite Group. 2016. "2016 Global Consumer Card Fraud: Where Card Fraud Is Coming From." Boston, MA. Retrieved from: https://www.aitegroup.com/report/2016-global-consumer-card-fraud-where-card-fraud-coming April 12, 2020.

Kolsto, Ellen. 2017. "A Researcher's Perspective on People Who Build with AI." *Ethnographic Praxis in Industry Conference Proceedings 2017*.

Krishnamurthy, Karthik, Melissa Morello, and James Jeude. 2017. "Analytical Storytelling: From Insight to Action." *Cognizant White Paper*. Retrieved from: www.cognizant.com/whitepapers/analytical-storytelling-from-insight-to-action-codex2475.pdf.

Lepri, Bruno, Jacopo Staiano, David Sankokoya, Emmanuel Letouze, and Nuira Oliver. 2017. "The Tyranny of Data? The Bright and Dark Sides of Data-Driven Decision-Making for Social Good." *Transparent Data Mining for Big and Small Data* 3: 3–24.

Lupton, Deborah. 2015. "The Thirteen Ps of Big Data." *This Sociological Life.* Retrieved from: https://simplysociology.wordpress.com/2015/05/11/the-thirteen-ps-of-big-data/. May 11, 2015.

Madjsberg, Christian. 2017. *Sensemaking: The Power of the Humanities in the Age of the Algorithm.* New York: Hachette Books.

———. 2018. "Thanks, Robots! Now These Four Non-Tech Job Skills Are in Demand." *Fast Company.* February 23, 2018.

Margolis, Abby. 2013. "Five Misconceptions about Personal Data: Why We Need a People-Centered Approach to 'Big' Data." *Ethnographic Praxis in Industry Conference Proceedings 2013.*

Merton, Robert K. 1968. *Social Theory and Social Structure* (1968 enlarged ed.). New York: Free Press.

Mills, C. Wright. 1959. *The Sociological Imagination.* New York: Oxford University Press.

Nafus, Dawn. 2016. "The Domestication of Data: Why Embracing Digital Data Means Embracing Bigger Questions." *Ethnographic Praxis in Industry Conference Proceedings 2016.*

New York Times. 2018. "Artificial Intelligence: How We Help Machines Learn." The New York Times Paid Post.

O'Neil, Cathy. 2016. *Weapons of Math Destruction: How Big Data Increases Inequality and Threatens Democracy.* New York: Crown Publishing & Random House.

Oremus, Will. 2017. "How 'Big Data' Went Bust. And What Comes Next." *Slate.* Retrieved from: www.slate.com/articles/technology/technology/2017/10/what_happened_to_big_data.html. October 16, 2017.

Osoba, Osonde A. and William Welser, IV. 2017. "An Intelligence in Our Image: The Risks of Bias and Errors in Artificial Intelligence." Santa Monica, CA: RAND Corporation, RR-1744-RC.

Pascual, Al, Kyle Marchini, Sarah Miller, and Javelin Strategy & Research. 2017. "2017 Identity Fraud: Securing the Connected Life." Retrieved from: www.javelinstrategy.com/coverage-area/2017-identity-fraud. February 21, 2017.

PricewaterhouseCoopers. 2015. "Seizing the Information Advantage: How Organizations Can Unlock Value and Insight from the Information They Hold." *A PwC report in conjunction with Iron Mountain.*

Rattenbury, Tye and Dawn Nafus. 2018. "Data Science and Ethnography: What's Our Common Ground, and Why Does It Matter?" *Ethnographic Praxis in Industry 2017.*

Ruppert, Evelyn, Penny Harvey, Celia Lury, Adrian Mackenzie, Ruth McNally, Stephanie Alice Baker, Yannis Kallianos, and Camilla Lewis. 2015. "Socialising Big Data: From Concept to Practice." CRESC Working Paper Series. CRESC, The University of Manchester and the Open University.

———. 2015. "A Social Framework for Big Data." CRESC Working Paper Series. CRESC, The University of Manchester and the Open University.

Salganik, Matthew. 2017. *Bit by Bit: Social Research in the Digital Age.* Princeton, NJ and Oxford: Princeton University Press.

Seaver, Nick. 2015. "Bastard Algebra." Tom Boelstorf and Bill Maurer (Eds.), *Data, Now Bigger and Better!* (27–46). Chicago, IL: Prickly Paradigm Press.

Smith, Adrian. 2018. "Smart Cities Need Thick Data, Not Big Data." *The Guardian.* Retrieved from: www.theguardian.com/science/political-science/2018/apr/18/smart-cities-need-thick-data-not-big-data. May 18, 2018.

Stirrup, Ashley. 2018. "The New "V" for Big Data: Virtue." *Business 2 Community.* January 18, 2018. Retrieved from: www.business2community.com/big-data/new-v-big-data-virtue-02004798. January 31, 2018.

Storey, Margaret-Anne. 2016. "Lies, Damned Lies and Software Analytics: Why Big Data Needs Thick Data [Webinar]." *ACM SIGSOFT Webinar Series.* Retrieved from: www.

slideshare.net/mastorey/lies-damned-lies-and-software-analytics-why-big-data-needs-rich-data. May 4, 2016.

Venturini, Tommaso and Bruno Latour. 2010. "The Social Fabric: Digital Traces and Quali-quantitative Methods." *2010 Proceedings of Future En Seine.*

Wang, Tricia. 2013. "Big Data Needs Thick Data." *Ethnography Matters.* Retrieved from: http://ethnographymatters.net/blog/2013/05/13/big-data-needs-thick-data/. May 13, 2010.

Wilson, William J. and Anmol Chaddha. 2010. "The Role of Theory in Ethnographic Research." *Ethnography* 10(4): 549–564.

PART II

Ethnographic Journeys

10

MANAGING MEAT AND NON-MEAT MARKETS IN CONTEMPORARY INDIA

Johan Fischer

Introduction

During my six months of fieldwork in India in 2017, I visited one of the country's largest food manufacturing companies located in South India. The company manufactures both vegetarian, including readymade meals, and non-vegetarian (meat, poultry and seafood) food and that poses certain challenges in terms of managing vegetarian (veg) and non-vegetarian (non-veg) production. In 2011, the Indian state made it mandatory that all processed food products should bear marks to indicate whether products are vegetarian (green) or non-vegetarian (brown). The food processing complex occupies a large site in a rural area outside one of South India's major cities and the whole complex is carefully organized and managed so that green and brown production is separate according to Food Safety and Standards Authority of India (FSSAI) specifications, and FSSAI often carries out announced as well as unannounced inspections and audits to check that green/brown production compliance is properly managed.

To Hindus, food/drink is closely related to bodily substance, health, well-being and purity/pollution (Malamoud 1996; Marriott 1976), as well as to caste, class, gender and kinship. Hindu vegetarianism among different class and caste groups has always been contentious in India, but now the country finds itself at the interface of three major transformations that are fundamentally reshaping conventional forms of vegetarianism: Hindu revivalist agendas; discourses and institutions which are penetrating everyday life and reconfiguring public culture (Hansen 1999); the fact that an increasing number of companies are involved in, and must comply with, rising forms of vegetarian regulation; and the emergence of a new Hindu middle class of about 300 million consumers attentive to the crucial distinction between veg and non-veg. All my middle-class Hindu informants could classify family, friends and colleagues as "veg" or "non-veg." At the same time, long-held notions of vegetarianism as superior, healthy and spiritual are being reconceptualized, and my project unpacks these developments among South Indian Hindus who are not necessarily at the forefront of vegetarian politics or Hindu nationalism as practiced in some Indian states in the north.

In this chapter, I use "green governmentality," that is, forms of proceduralism and expert knowledge that reshape attitudes and values and interiorize forms of (self-)discipline, to capture how the management of meat and non-meat manufacturing in India is framed by much more than standardized food regulation. My motivation for studying this topic is to a large extent spurred by a larger interest in the changing relationship between religion, regulation and markets (Fischer 2008, 2011, 2015; Fischer and Lever 2019; Lever and Fischer 2018) and the Indian case allows me to explore similarities between kosher (a Hebrew term meaning "fit" or "proper"), halal (an Arabic word that literally means "permissible" or "lawful") and Hindu vegetarianism/meat-eating (Fischer 2016).

In a recent article (2019), I reviewed the literature on vegetarianism and meat-eating in India. My central aim was to explore how vegetarianism and meat-eating are addressed in existing research in order to identify gaps and pave the way for a new research agenda on the complex and changing relationship between vegetarianism and meat-eating at different levels – consumers, markets and regulators – in contemporary India. Why and how Hindus eat meat is not well understood and much of the existing literature often assumes that not only does the concept of *ahimsa* (non-injury to all living creatures), cow veneration and banning of cow slaughter prevent Hindus from eating meat, but also that the relationship between vegetarianism and meat-eating is relatively simple and stable among Hindu groups. In Hindu nationalist discourses, as well as scholarly studies, Hindu meat-eating is often seen as exceptional and/or due to spiritual, ritual or religious circumstances, rather than as an everyday practice. However, the complex and contested relationship between vegetarianism and meat-eating is as topical as ever: in 2011 when the Indian state made it mandatory that all processed food products should bear marks to indicate whether products are vegetarian (green) or non-vegetarian (brown) and with the rise of consumer culture in super/hypermarkets, these logos are ubiquitous on packaging throughout India. I argued that the above aspects have been central in the making of a powerful vegetarian ideology that has seduced much of the scholarship on vegetarianism into suggesting that vegetarianism in India is dominant among Hindus. The central research question concerned why and how a vegetarian ideology created the hegemonic view of vegetarianism as proper Hindu practice and how Hindus respond to and are affected by this over time. Thus, I use green governmentality to explore how the powerful vegetarian ideology is understood, practiced, and contested in manufacturing companies in India. More specifically, my ethnographic approach captures how business managers find themselves operating between green governance/law on the one hand and green mentality/ideology on the other that together give shape to the concept of governmentality. In doing so, I show how researchers can explore management empirically and critically between different levels of the social scale: government, business and individual understandings/practices of managers on the ground.

While the concept of *ahimsa* is central to Hinduism and Hindu vegetarianism is explored in a large literature, there is no corresponding exploration of how "green" and "brown" production is managed in contemporary India. What is more, India is a major exporter of meat and water buffalo beef in particular – including the company discussed above. Based on fieldwork in India, this article explores how manufacturing companies understand, and manage "green" and "brown" standards. I argue that while existing studies of vegetarianism overwhelmingly explore micro-social aspects such as the everyday consumption among Hindu groups, "the bigger institutional picture" that frames such consumption, production and regulation is not well understood. This chapter asks and answers this research question: how is modern green/brown production managed in contemporary India? Based on ethnographic fieldwork in India, the last part of the chapter explores green/brown regulation and management in three manufacturing companies. This exploration is part of a larger research project that explores the complex and changing relationship between veg and non-veg in India. I conclude that management based on regulation is essential to green, green/brown and brown production in contemporary India.

A Note on Methodology and Key Findings

The fieldwork for this project took place between July and December 2017 in the state of Telangana in South India. Methodologically, this study follows "the people" (veg and non-veg consumers, bureaucrats, representatives from vegan/vegetarian bodies, activists and company representatives); "the things" (the circulation of vegetarian commodities/meat as manifestly material objects of study) as well as "the metaphor" (the vegetarian/non-vegetarian embedded in particular realms of discourse, modes of thought and practices) (Marcus 1995). The basic methodological approach is qualitative in nature and I use urban India as the setting for a detailed, intensive and complex analysis by employing and combining participant observation, semi-structured interviews, informal conversations, life biographies and group discussions among state institutions, interest groups, companies and consumers. I also explore historical and contemporary quantitative data on the development of the retail sector and the market for vegetarian products to better frame the qualitative analysis. Based on fieldwork in producers and retailers (butchers and super/hypermarkets), this generated new knowledge about how these are affected by and respond to new forms of vegetarian regulation. Thus, I approached regulation, bureaucratization and classification "from below" to explore how local and foreign producers and retailers think about and practice these challenges in the context of the liberalized Indian economy. Company representatives were selected for in-depth interviewing and participant observation focusing on corporate strategies for coping with vegetarian regulation and training of staff to comply with rising vegetarian requirements. Participant observation is also used to study ways in which vegetarian certification is changing everyday work processes and strategies. This approach generates new knowledge on how producers and retailers understand and practice vegetarianism between liberalized markets and state regulation.

The initial stage of my fieldwork was quantitative in outlook. A survey conducted in late 2017 among 1000 informants above the age of 15 in and around Hyderabad in South India mapped everyday food habits with specific reference to veg and non-veg. The survey was based on stratified random sampling in locations such as markets, educational institutions, workplaces and residential areas. Respondents were asked about their familiarity with the green and brown logos issued by FSSAI, and the responses show that 75 percent are not familiar with these logos. The vast majority of Hindu respondents are meat-eaters who listed reasons such as health, taste and family for meat-eating. Thus, regardless of age, gender, education/income and caste, the idea that meat is healthy has become widespread. Moreover, eggs, onion and garlic are widely consumed not only among meat-eaters but also among vegetarians. The majority of meat-eaters consume meat on a weekly basis, and as income levels rise meat is more frequently bought in hypermarkets where respondents come into contact with the green and brown marks.

These findings suggest that the relationship between veg and non-veg is being redefined in contemporary India: the long-held idea that the more individuals and social groups follow a vegetarian lifestyle, the higher the social status they will enjoy, is breaking down. What is more, vegetarianism and meat-eating are increasingly individual lifestyle choices rather than determined by religious orthodoxy. A key question is how Hindu consumers understand, practice and contest vegetarianism and meat-eating in their everyday lives, and my ethnography challenges the idea that class/caste affiliation is inseparable from the veg/non-veg distinction: that is, that the higher the caste, the less likely Hindus are to eat meat and, conversely, the lower the caste, the more likely people are to consume meat. Paradoxically, these middle-class Hindus go about their everyday food consumption in the world's most standardized market for vegetarian products in which green/brown marks are ubiquitous and can be found on billions of products and on the facades of restaurants. In fact, my survey supports statistics showing that Telangana may be one of the least vegetarian states in India, and this project explores why and how this may the case (Fischer 2019).

Green Governmentality

FSSAI and food manufacturing in India share some characteristics such as explicit rules, a division of labor, an intent to act on or change everyday life, and a governing ethos (for example, making money or a particular management principle) (Gellner and Hirsch 2001). A central question is how businesses think about and practice green/brown production and regulation. Foucault's (1991) concept of "governmentality" describes forms of proceduralism and expert knowledge that reshape attitudes and values and interiorize forms of (self-)discipline. According to this approach, bureaucratic regulation creates compliant subjects, and auditing and risk management can be seen as the internalization of attitudes and procedures. Power (1999) argues that risk is a mode of governmentality that reveals itself in managerial forms of standards and guidance. The emergence, consolidation and expansion of an audit culture around vegetarian/green and non-vegetarian/brown practices is evident when the FSSAI regulates production by performing "on site" audits and inspections in factories. The concept of transnational governmentality grasps how new practices of government and new forms of "grassroots" politics are emerging on a global scale. Examples are new strategies of discipline and regulation, exemplified by green/brown regulation and standards, but also transnational alliances forged by activists and grassroots organizations and the proliferation of voluntary organizations supported by complex networks of international and transnational funding and personnel (Ferguson and Gupta 2002).

Another important theme is the emergence, consolidation and expansion of an audit culture around vegetarian/green and non-vegetarian/brown practice. FSSAI regulates production by performing "on site" audits and inspections in factories. Audit culture has been explored from an anthropological perspective focusing on consensus endorsing government through economic efficiency and good practice. In this form of modern accountability, the financial and the moral converge to form a culture of what are deemed acceptable forms. Audits and audit practices are discussed as descriptors applicable to all kinds of reckonings, evaluations, and measurements and as distinct cultural artifacts in the market that works as a platform for both individual interest and national politics (Strathern 2000). There is a large body of literature on the rise of an "audit society," but further scholarship is needed on the ways in which audits and inspections are understood and practiced in local contexts. The pervasiveness of an audit culture within and around veg/non-veg practices is not well understood, but, as I will show, it links veg/non-veg and markets in new ways. Audit and inspection systems are a feature of modern societies. They exist to generate comfort and reassurance in a wide range of policy contexts. To a large extent, auditing is about the cultural and economic authority granted to auditors (Power 1999). A central aspect of audit culture that is also highly relevant to the market for veg and non-veg is the call for increased control and self-control in companies to satisfy the need to connect internal organizational arrangements to public ideals (Power 1999).

Standardization processes are apparent in green/brown certification, but standardization is also market driven. Green/brown standards and standardization can mean several things. They can refer to the design and qualities of products as well as to the proper conduct of states, organizations and individuals, for example with regard to the production, preparation, handling and storage of products. But they can also be seen as instruments of control and forms of regulation attempting to generate elements of global order (Brunsson and Jacobsson 2000). Busch (2000) argues that standards are part of the moral economy of the modern world that stipulate norms for behavior and create uniformity – a relevant point when it comes to the emergence and expansion of green/brown standards. Moreover, standards are the recipes by which we create realities and they invoke the linguistic categories we use to organize the world – material as well as ideal (Busch 2013). Moral and religious behaviors are subject to standards of tolerance as they define the limits of tolerable behavior in divergent settings.

Green/brown regulation is no longer an expression of esoteric forms of production, trade or consumption, but a huge and expanding market in which transnational governmentality and standards play important roles. In sum, based on empirical data this chapter explores standards and their stories, that is, how manufacturing companies interact with standardized forms, technologies and conventions built into infrastructure (Star and Lampland 2009). Moreover, food labels are operationalized arguing that these are expressions of neoliberalization, that is, these labels signify the creation of markets, value, and regulation. Food labels are political forms of economic protection that exclude the non-certified/standardized. Moreover, labels are governed by non-transparent public–private partnerships leading to radical governance mechanisms and property rights (Guthman 2007).

Ahimsa and Meat

Ahimsa originally signified non-violence to living beings and had nothing to do with vegetarianism (Alsdorff 2010 [1962]). In the Brahmin *Lawbook of Manu*, leeks, garlic, onions and mushrooms are also forbidden as they can be considered "heating" and may arouse sexual desire. *Ahimsa* was based on a "magico-ritualistic" dread of destroying life, but the origins and source of *ahimsa* have not yet been explored satisfactorily. The author traces *ahimsa* in legal texts and in the gradual emergence and assertion of vegetarianism and cattle protection arguing that vegetarianism and the cow taboo must be separated. Historically, Buddhism and Jainism reinforced Hindu understandings of vegetarianism, but Alsdorff warns that as there are no clear answers regarding its origins, scholars should be careful to avoid "rationalist" answers and to essentialize vegetarianism as an unequivocally Hindu phenomenon.

Simoon's classic study *Eat Not This Flesh* (1994) explores various forms of vegetarianism in India throughout history: from meat-eating to strict vegetarians who reject meat, fish, and eggs as well as many other types of food. Traditionally, top social status was given to strict Jain and Hindu vegetarianism. Exceptions are Hindu Dravidians in South India (Simoons 1994), the Reddi of Hyderabad, and tribal peoples who breed pigs for sacrifice, but Hindu influence was halting this (Simoons 1994). Cow veneration in India comprises the world's most important surviving cattle cult rejection of beef as human food (Simoons 1994), even though cattle are important in Indian economic life. The origins of cow veneration and the reasons for the ban on beef are not only contested, but also dynamic and changing over time. For example, Brahmins accepted beef in early history (Simoons 1994).

The sacred cow concept gained impetus from rivalry between Muslims and Hindus at independence and the ban on cow slaughter was incorporated into the Constitution of India Article 48 leading to decades of legal controversy often involving Muslims. Lynchings of Muslims accused of slaughtering, selling and eating cows are frequent in India (Jaffrelot 2017). Today cow slaughter is banned in many Indian states. Article 48 mandates the state to prohibit the slaughter of cows and in 2005 the Supreme Court of India upheld the constitutional validity of anti-cow slaughter laws enacted by 20 out of 29 Indian states. Violators face six months jail and/or 1,000 Rupees fine. While the export of beef (cow, oxen, and calf) is prohibited the meat of buffalo, goat, sheep and birds is allowed.

India is home to the world's largest concentration of water buffalo. It is important to note the difference between water buffalo and cattle beef or zebu cows (also known as indicine cattle or humped cattle). Since the late 2000s, India's exports of water buffalo beef in particular have expanded rapidly, with the country emerging as the world's largest beef exporter in 2014. This development is due to rising demand for low-cost meat by consumers in developing countries, India's large water buffalo herd and the emergence of private sector and export-oriented Indian processors. Most of India's majority Hindu population (about 80 percent of the population in 2011) does not eat cattle beef (United States Department of Agriculture 2016). A recent survey shows that while less than 1 percent of Hindus in the Hindi heartland eat beef/buffalo meat, nationally this number is increasing – especially in the southern states (*The Hindu* 29 October 2016). However, surveys like this one are often flawed as respondents are reluctant to admit to eating beef.

Based on ethnographic studies in a village in northern India, 1958–59 and in 1977–78, Freed et al. (1981) demonstrated that belief in the sanctity of the zebu cows significantly influenced the demography of cattle and water buffalo in this village, that is, the relationship between Hindus and cows/buffalo was determined by belief and not so much a cultural-ecological and functional framework. Thus, beef in India has to be broken down into cattle beef or buffalo beef. In India cow veneration, the ban on cow beef and large-scale and growing meat production are concrete expressions of human cultural perceptions of diverse animals, their social and economic role, and their ritual purity or impurity. To Hindus, "internal pollution" is worse than "touch" pollution since "internal pollution" involves penetration of the body by pollutants, including impure foods. What is more, Hinduism was profoundly affected by the new religions that to a large extent conditioned the emergence of *ahimsa* (Harris 1977).

In November 2017, I was in the audience when the Prime Minister of India, Narendra Modi, delivered his speech at the major food fair *World Food India* held in central Delhi, which attracted more than 2,000 participants and 400 exhibitors from 20 countries. Modi, who has been Prime Minister since 2014, belongs to the Hindu nationalist Bharatiya Janata Party (BJP), is a strict vegetarian, and promotes vegetarianism as a national project, declared that *World Food India* would provide a "glimpse of the opportunities that await you in India" and the sampling of "some of our most delightful cuisine, which has stimulated taste buds across the world." Modi then went on to explain that India is the world's largest producer of milk and the second largest when it comes to rice, wheat, fish, fruits and vegetables. In a broader perspective, "India is today one of the fastest growing economies in the world. … Increasing urbanization, and a growing middle class, are resulting in an ever-growing demand for wholesome, processed food." Modi ended by saying that: "I assure you of my whole-hearted support, whenever required. Come. Invest in India. The place with unlimited opportunity from farm to fork. The place to produce, process, and prosper. For India, and for the world."

Modi failed to mention that India is also one the world's largest and fastest-growing producers of meat and water buffalo beef in particular, and that within the last couple of decades the country has witnessed a meat revolution: more and more meat is being sold and consumed throughout the country, and particularly among the urban Hindu middle class. Modi's omission points to a much larger issue, in that it sustains a vegetarian ideology, that is, India was, is and should be a vegetarian nation. Brahmin groups, the Hindu priestly caste within the *Varna* (caste/class) system, who traditionally promote vegetarianism, and the Hindu nationalist movement of which Modi is at the forefront, have carefully supported this idea, accepting at face value the notion that most Hindus are, or desire to be, vegetarians while Muslims and lower castes are not and do not wish to be. At the same time, Hindu revivalist agendas, discourses and institutions penetrate everyday life and reconfigure public culture (Hansen 1999).

"Moral consumption" among the emergent middle class is producing a new configuration of capitalism that makes recurrent reference to Hindu doctrine and practice and to the formation of a Hindu subject capable of acting and competing in a neoliberal, but still profoundly religious economic environment. Moral consumption constitutes India's contemporary "divine market" in which commodities are spiritualized and spirituality is subjected to a logic of commodification (Srivastava 2017).

The reconfiguration of veg and non-veg reflects India's "aesthetics of arrival" (as we saw in Modi's speech): namely the novelty, visibility and celebration of the post-reform landscape (Kaur and Hansen 2016). On the one hand, vegetarianism is celebrated, promoted and certified by BJP and the state, and on the other meat-eating (and its "brown" regulation) is a sign of prosperity, pluralized markets, reconfigured status/hierarchies, inclusion, social mobility, health and cosmopolitanism. Indeed, a wide range of meat is now available in expensive hypermarkets as well as in traditional butchers' shops. Within the Indian aesthetics of arrival, veg and non-veg are constantly interpreted in multiple frames – for example, the mandatory marks on food and other products can be seen as a specific disciplinary aesthetic, since all multinational companies exporting to India must brand their food products/ingredients with these marks. Meat sold in super/hypermarkets is often packaged and this is very different from the bazaar or butchers' shops.

Managing Markets

There is a large and growing literature on organizational anthropology (Caulkins and Jordan 2012; Garsten and Nyqvist 2013; Ybema et al. 2009), but how green/ brown regulation is managed is not well understood. In a notification issued by the Food Safety and Standards Authority of India (FSSAI) under the Ministry of

Health and Family Welfare (2011, 29), "Non-Vegetarian Food" is defined in the following way: "an article of food which contains whole or part of any animal including birds, fresh water or marine animals or eggs or products of any animal origin, but excluding milk or milk products, as an ingredient" whereas "Vegetarian Food" is "any article of Food other than Non-Vegetarian Food as defined in regulation" (2011, 30). Moreover, "Every package of 'Non-Vegetarian' food shall bear a declaration to this effect made by a symbol and colour code as stipulated below to indicate that the product is Non-Vegetarian Food. The symbol shall consist of a brown colour filled circle" that must have a minimum specified diameter to be "inside a square with brown outline having sides double the diameter of the circle." Conversely, "Every package of Vegetarian Food shall bear a declaration to this effect by a symbol and colour code as stipulated below for this purpose to indicate that the product is Vegetarian Food. The symbol shall consist of a green colour filled circle" that must have a minimum specified diameter to be "inside the square with green outline having size double the diameter of the circle." Finally, it is specified in detail that the size of green/brown marks must match the overall surface of products in order to be clearly visible (2011, 35). Throughout the document, specifications for packaging and labeling are detailed. Not only in India but also globally, billions of Indian products carry green or brown marks.

I locate this focus on and fascination with the "green" within the broader extension of the Indian consumer goods markets and advertising: a complex ideology or social ontology of global consumption was required. In India, the emergence of such a new ontology of consumption was felt most forcefully in the advertising of images that reflected the desire of individual consumers and simultaneously presented the national community reconceptualized as an aesthetic community (Mazzarella 2003).

Green/brown Ethnography

Green

Novozymes is the leading enzyme manufacturer globally. The company has enzyme plants in six countries, three in Denmark, two in the US, two in China, two in India, one in Brazil, and one in Canada. Novozymes has more than 6000 employees and the company makes around 900 enzyme products purchased by many different industries manufacturing detergents, foods, beverages, textiles, biofuel and animal feed among other things. The company started its operations in India in 1983 and is the largest supplier of industrial enzymes and microorganisms in South Asia. When I visit the Novozymes facility in Bangalore (November 2017), the Senior Specialist explains that Novozymes India has more than 500 employees with three sites in Bangalore that cover research/technology, manufacturing, business functions and a service center. Some of the key business areas for Novozymes India are household care, textiles, food/beverages, oils/fats, baking and beverage alcohol. The Senior Specialist has been with Novozymes for 18 years and she holds an MSc in food technology. Her main responsibility is raw materials and good manufacturing practices, including FSSAI vegetarian regulation, kosher ("fit" or "proper" in Judaism) and halal (literally, "lawful" or "permitted" in Islam) practices. I also meet the Senior Specialist at Novozymes' headquarters in Denmark. Kosher and halal are not major issues in Novozymes India whereas vegetarian regulation has a long history in the Indian context, she explains. The Prevention of Food Adulteration Act from 1954 came into existence as the first federal law to ensure safe, pure and wholesome food to consumers. The present green/brown logos enforced by FSSAI are only the latest versions of logos that indicate whether food and ingredients in India are veg or non-veg. Novozymes India is a strictly "green" company, that is, all the company's food grade products carry the green mark. However, from 2011 onwards Novozymes India had to apply for a FSSAI license. The Head of Quality Assurance explains that depending on the type, size and income of food businesses three types of licenses have to exist and Novozymes falls under a "central" one in Delhi. All details can be found on FSSAI's website. For both types of licenses there is a fee that depends on

> ... the type of unit you are putting up. The FSSAI Inspectors come for inspections. They have their federal headquarters in Delhi, but inspections and audits will be at the state level. They don't inform us when they come here. They can come down whenever they want. They have inspected us in 2016. Normally ... the person who came last time he was here for around four hours. We also have FSSAI requirements like how the plant should be established, what kind of activity should be conducted regarding veg and non-veg. Everything is outlined on the website. We never had any animal ingredients.

When we discuss why green regulation is so important in India the Head of Quality Assurance argues that "In India we have populations from Rajasthan, Gujarat and Southern India where many people are vegetarian. There are different cultural backgrounds. So, these logos make it easy to choose veg or non-veg." Most of all, she considers the logos to be symbols rather than logos of certification or standards. The green mark can be found on a multitude of Novozymes India packaging in India and elsewhere and in Novozymes India's formulation unit the relevant staff team receive training on the proper kind of labeling on each product. In sum, for Novozymes India green regulation in India is not very complex or challenging as long as the company only uses ingredients and products that are not of animal origin and there is no formal requirement in terms of staff being vegetarians themselves.

Brown

At World Food India (November 2017) I meet a representative from a major meat-producing company based in Europe. He holds a diploma in commerce and started in the meat industry in 1980. Since that time, he has focused on trading meat and training employees in Europe, the Middle East and China. About 10 years back the company started looking at the vast and expanding Indian market. The representative suggests that "a market of 1.3 billion consumers simply can't be ignored." Most of all, the company exports pork to India, but it also buys Indian water buffalo meat that is exported to other countries in Asia in particular. The company is aware that India has local pork production, but there exists little material on this – other than a photo the representative took of a pig carcass at a local and unhygienic butcher's shop.

In order for the company to export meat to India, products aimed at the Indian market are separated from "normal production" – particularly because they must bear the mandatory brown marks. At the company's headquarters in Europe this type of compliance only exists because the Indian market is seen to be vast and growing. More specifically, the company exports meat to a local Indian importer that sells the meat to hotels and restaurants. On each label this information is mandatory: the brown mark issued by FSSAI, name and details of exporter/importer, license number, type of commodity as well as expiry date.

The Indian market has proven to be challenging and the total export to India was "only" 650 tons in 2016 – "We're still waiting for the boom and one of the problems is that Belgian pork exporters were approved before us," the representative explains. These exporters sent large shipments of pork and were "first movers" in the Indian markets that only recently and slowly opened up for meat imports and pork in particular. "Being a 'first mover' in this emerging meat market for pork is absolutely essential," the representative argues. On top of that, negotiating with local importers is challenging. The company learned that large parts of Belgian pork breast are consumed by Koreans working in the Indian car industry. The company has been exporting large quantities of pork breast to Korea for decades and knows Korean preferences well, but the Indian context is challenging: as Belgian companies were first movers they set a kind informal standard in terms of pork cuts: chefs in Indian hotels and restaurants are now used to Belgian pork cuts that are cubed into 68 cubes and fried while the company's cuts are longer and offer 90 cubes and "Local chefs can't relate to that now that they're used to Belgian cuts and if we comply with the Belgian cut sizes it means that a lot of meat is wasted," the representative maintains. Altogether, Indian meat markets are still "unstandardized" and this also goes for detailed market statistics that potentially could be provided by the embassy of the company's home country in India, but this data has to be generated from scratch and this is time-consuming and expensive – "And this is unfortunate: our feeling is that this is a market in which everything is changing, but we're not sure what the trend is," the representative argues. When company representatives first went to India 10 years ago they visited Indian supermarkets in Bangalore and elsewhere such as Big Bazaar and Ratnadeep and all they found was a very narrow selection of frozen meat and fish – and no pork. Traditionally, pork products in India were Spanish Serrano ham and bacon that had to be boiled or cured to be approved by the food safety authorities. However, these authorities are often inefficient and difficult to reach – even if obtaining a certificate signed by FSSAI is the essential step in order to import. Similarly, the process of putting the brown mark on packaging is troublesome, to say the least – because the brown mark is unique to India it prevents any kind of standardized labeling that is normally unproblematic elsewhere. Altogether, the import process is bureaucratic and for every new customer headquarters has to issue new customer numbers. Even if the company is supported by agricultural organizations, the ministry of agriculture in its home country and EU representation markets opportunities in India still appear to be "untapped."

Green/brown

During fieldwork (in December 2017) I visit one of India's largest food manufacturing companies located in South India. The company's history stretches back several decades and during that time it has expanded not only in India, but also has production facilities, offices and cold storage abroad. Currently, there are about 1,500 employees and that number is growing steadily. The company produces both veg (meat, poultry and seafood) and non-veg food, including readymade meals, and that poses certain challenges in terms of managing veg and non-veg. Approved by veterinary authorities in many countries, each month the company exports thousands of tons of meat in particular to Asia and Africa. The food processing complex occupies a large site in a rural area outside one of South India's major cities. The company stresses that it does not slaughter cows, bulls or bullocks, but only buffalos and that as a "Muslim company" all slaughter is carried out according to halal guidelines. These points should be seen in the context of constant rumors that a company such as this one not only mistreats animals, but also slaughters cows, bulls or bullocks illegally.

More recently, the company has started focusing on the vegetarian market and now produces items such as frozen French fries, burgers, samosas, parathas, fruit, pulps and vegetables. More generally, the company has shifted its focus from chilled food to frozen food because of the latter's better shelf life. The General Manager explains that India is the company's major revenue contributor at 35 percent, followed by Malaysia at 25 percent and countries like the UAE, the Philippines and Japan making up the rest. Vegetarian products will see an increase and about half of the company's products are vegetarian to cater for Indian segments as well as customers looking for a healthy alternative to meat – especially among the emerging urban middle classes.

During my visit to the complex the General Manager explains to me that he has been with the company for almost 20 years and that his father and grandfather are also in the same company. As a Muslim, he explains that "If Allah allows us, I hope the future generation also serves in this business." In his own family they mostly eat non-veg, but every five to six days shift to veg. All the meat produced and exported is halal to cater for Muslim consumers – especially in import countries such as Malaysia.[1] The Manager frequently travels around India and abroad. However, the green/brown regulation is more resource demanding: FSSAI regularly does announced as well as unannounced inspections and audits in the company. A typical FSSAI visit takes an entire day and "It's different inspectors every time. Ingredients should also have that certification and FSSAI also checks for that. A large number of staff is involved in quality control because it is a big place." That goes both for halal and green/brown regulation. Green and brown logos are only necessary for the Indian market and not for exports, the General Manager explains when we look at a box of frozen halal buffalo meat product to be exported to the Philippines. However, halal logos for exports are only necessary in relation to meat and not veg. "Food authorities in the Philippines don't require any marks on the inner pack- aging, but they require branding related to Islamic rights and the slaughtering of buffalos, land registration number, production code and the name of the importer on packages." Islamic authorities often carry out inspections in the company. For example, JAKIM comes every two years whereas FSSAI come more often.

There are detailed FSSAI rules about the separation of veg and non-veg, as the General Manager explains:

> Veg and non-veg production must be in separate buildings or at least there must be a wall between veg and non-veg production. When starting food production in India FSSAI is giving a layout of how the plant must be organized. When they give the license, they also check whether or not the construction of the plan is according to the FSSAI standards. These rules are clear and makes production easier – even for companies that only produce veg.

Similarly, staff space is standardized: separate rooms for men and women in terms of changing clothes and storing their belongings: "Standardizing everything will be good for the Indian market," the General Manager argues. Unlike halal pro- duction in countries like Malaysia, "There is no requirement that Hindus have to be involved in veg production. Anybody can produce either veg or non-veg, but when they produce, it should be pure veg and non-veg." Similarly, people from all over India including Maharashtra, Orissa and Andhra Pradesh work at the complex. About 230 employees are involved in veg and the number for non-veg is about 1100 people. The General Manager makes clear that the difference between the numbers of the staff is because of the volume. Staff never shift between veg and non-veg production.

Prior to the 2011 introduction of the green/brown marks, "There was a mark for non-veg. It was round and half and colored with brown." Consequently, the company was already compliant with existing regulation and did not have to change production processes. Most certificates are valid for four years; if anything changes in relation to requirements or legislation FSSAI will let the company know so that it can adjust accordingly. When we discuss why green/brown logos were introduced in the first place the General Manager argues that it's due to "The unity of the people. According to me the main idea behind the legislation is to make sure that nobody should suffer in choosing veg and non-veg food items." Of course, hygiene is essential to a company such as this one and for example plastic containers are used in kitchens and if they leak they can be disposed of. Before we start our tour around the complex, several posters in the reception room state that the company maintains the highest level of quality assurance that delivers a hygienic production environment. Wearing protective plastic suits, this is evident as we move from the non-veg/abattoir area to the veg area in which workers produce samosas, for example. This is also where spices for veg as well as non-veg production are stored. In the veg area signs above doors state that this is a "Raw vegetables" zone only.

Discussion and Conclusion

I have shown why and how green/brown regulation conditions a nationalized form of management culture in India. Existing studies on veg/non-veg in India mostly explore individual and group food consumption and not the surrounding markets and regulation. In both political/public discourses and scholarly studies, Hindu meat-eating is often seen as exceptional and/or generated by certain ritual or religious circumstances rather than as an everyday practice. Similarly, the management of meat production and non-veg more generally are given modest attention. Given impetus by Hindu nationalism, four issues seem to condition the Hinduism and Hinduness on the one hand and vegetarianism as proper Hindu practice on the other: cow veneration; banning of cow slaughter; vegetarian regulation in the form of green/brown marks; and India being a major producer of meat and water buffalo beef in particular. However, my study shows that green/brown management also extends in biotech production, for example, and the company Novozymes was an example of that.

Meat-eating and vegetarianism alike are commercialized and standardized in contemporary India. Both veg and non-veg can function as markers of new, mobile middle-class Hindu identities and are promoted by some Hindu groups as Indian "Hindu virtues" in which veg can be associated with a proper and pure lifestyle, whereas meat signifies social mobility, prestige and nutrition. Controversies over what Hinduism is, or ought to be, are intensifying between elite/nationalist ideology and everyday practices as meat-eating is becoming more and more common and standardized. I have explored green/veg and brown/non-veg in the histories and cultures of companies. Within the last decade or so FSSAI has "disciplined" companies. In other words, in India regulatory institutions are disciplining companies with regard to green/brown understanding and practice, but companies have also become more skilled in negotiating standardized requirements. One reason for this is that green/brown standardization in Malaysia is part of the particular history of the country with its Hindu nationalism and state regulation.

A central aspect of audit culture is the pushing of control and self-control further into companies to satisfy the need to connect internal organizational arrangements with public ideals. Many companies argue that even if requirements and control have intensified, green/brown production is more professionally regulated and standardized today compared to unclear and confusing requirements of the past. Simultaneously, these companies have developed and refined technoscientific solutions to comply with FSSAI requirements. It is clear from the above that a multitude of divergent veg/non-veg understandings are now being overshadowed by processes of standardization and that companies themselves are rationalized to deal with these challenges. It is clear that green/brown as a state injunction influences the social organization of businesses, that is, how companies understand and practice veg/non-veg requirements as social organizations.

A final ethnographic example: I am in the Star hypermarket in Gachibowli, a booming IT suburb about 20 kilometers west of Hyderabad. I am looking at food products from the company discussed above that produces both veg and non-veg. The Star hypermarket opened in 2017, and as in all other stores across India, all food (except vegetables and meat), drinks, and care products carry distinctive green or brown marks. After coming to power, Modi decreed that not only all food products but also all nutraceuticals (dietary supplements), care products, and cosmetics should be labeled either green or brown. Local and multinational industry players, who have entered India in large numbers in the wake of market reforms and liberalization starting in the 1990s, filed a lawsuit arguing that the law was rushed through without any kind of consultation, resulting in high costs and highly complex implementation challenges. In the Star hypermarket, as well as hypermarkets such as Spar, a wide range of fresh meat and (live) fish are readily available for consumers to buy. And they certainly do: during my fieldwork in Hyderabad and Delhi, lines in front of the meat sections in these hypermarkets are often long, and hypermarket managers told me that the sale of meat is booming, including among new groups of consumers who were traditionally vegetarians. In the Spar hypermarket that opened in central Hyderabad in 2007, the meat/fish section is still enclosed behind a glass wall that clearly sets it off from the main shopping area. The side of the glass wall that faces the main shopping area is lined with vegetarian products from Organic India (the country's largest producer of organic products that are also marketed internationally). Thus, the division between the meat/fish on one side and the main shopping area on the other is clearly marked and "fortified" by "green" Organic India products that appeal to many middle-class consumers. In the recently opened Gachibowli hypermarkets, there is no wall between the meat/fish sections and the main shopping area, and the reason for this is twofold: first, meat and its consumption are becoming more and more accepted in India, even among Hindu groups that were traditionally vegetarian, and second, new hypermarkets are designed to accommodate the sale of meat/fish. In these hypermarkets, chicken in particular is promoted as healthy and wholesome on posters in the meat sections. The whole story is visible in the Indian hypermarkets: we see how neoliberal reforms and the intensified globalization of food markets has led to a vast pluralization of shopping desires and choices; how religious, vegetarian/vegan, and "green" protests and regulations struggle to keep up with but also legitimize production, trade, and consumption; and how large and growing numbers of middle-class Hindu consumers are confronted with all these vast changes on a daily basis. In these hypermarkets managers would often explain to me that due to green/brown regulation, FSSAI compliance is fundamental.

Note

1 For a detailed discussion of halal in Malaysia see Fischer 2008, 2011, 2015.

References

Alsdorff, L. (2010) [1962]. *The history of vegetarianism and cow-veneration in India*. London and New York: Routledge.

Brunsson, N. and Jacobsson, B. 2000. *A World of Standards*. Oxford and New York: Oxford University Press.

Busch, L. 2000. The moral economy of grades and standards. *Journal of Rural Studies* 16, pp. 273–283.

Busch, L. 2013. *Standards: Recipes for Reality*. Cambridge, MA: MIT Press.

Caulkins, D. and Jordan, A. T. (eds.) 2012. *A Companion to Organizational Anthropology*. Chichester: Wiley-Blackwell.

Ferguson, J. and Gupta, A. 2002. Spatializing states: Toward an ethnography of neoliberal governmentality. *American Ethnologist* 29(4), pp. 981–1002.

Fischer, J. 2008. *Proper Islamic Consumption: Shopping among the Malays in Modern Malaysia*. Copenhagen: Nordic Institute of Asian Studies Press.

Fischer, J. 2011. *The Halal Frontier: A Global Religious Market in London*. New York: Palgrave Macmillan.

Fischer, J. 2015. *Islam, Standards and Technoscience: In Global Halal Zones*. London and New York: Routledge.

Fischer, J. 2016. Markets, religion, regulation: Kosher, Halal and Hindu vegetarianism in global perspective. *Geoforum* 69, pp. 67–70.

Fischer, J. 2019. Veg or non-veg? From bazaars to hypermarkets in India. *International Journal of Asia Pacific Studies* 15(1), pp. 1–32.

Fischer, J. and Lever, J. 2018. *Religion, Regulation, Consumption: Globalising Kosher and Halal Markets*. Manchester: Manchester University Press.

Food Safety and Standards Agency India/Ministry of Health and Family Welfare. 2011. *Notification*. New Delhi: Ministry of Health and Family Welfare.

Foucault, M. 1991. Governmentality. In G. Burchell, C. Gordon, and P. Miller, eds. *The Foucault Effect: Studies in Governmentality*, 87–104. Chicago: University of Chicago Press.

Freed, S. et al. 1981. Sacred cows and water buffalo in India: The uses of ethnography. *Current Anthropology* 22(5): 483–502.

Garsten, C. and Nyqvist, A. 2013. *Organisational Anthropology: Doing Ethnography in and among Complex Organisations*. Chicago: University of Chicago Press.

Gellner, D. N. and Hirsch, E. 2001. Introduction: Ethnography of organizations and organizations of ethnography. In D. N. Gellner and E. Hirsch, eds. *Inside Organizations: Anthropologists at Work*, 1–18. Oxford and New York: Berg Publishers.

Guthman, J. 2007. The Polanyian way? Voluntary food labels as neoliberal governance. *Antipode* 39(3), pp. 456–478.

Hansen, T. B. 1999. *The Saffron Wave: Democracy and Hindu Nationalism in Modern India*. Princeton: Princeton University Press.

Harris, Marvin. 1977. *Cannibals and Kings. The Origins of Cultures*. New York: Random House.

Harris, Marvin. 1977. *Cannibals and Kings. The Origins of Cultures*. New York: Random House.

Jaffrelot, C. 2017. India's democracy at 70: Towards a hindu state? *Journal of Democracy* 28(3), pp. 52–63.

Kaur, R. and Hansen, T. B. 2016. Aesthetics of arrival: Spectacle, capital, novelty in post-reform India. *Identities* 23(3), pp. 265–275.

Lever, J. and Fischer, J. 2019. *Kosher and Halal Business Compliance*. New York and London: Routledge.

Malamoud, C. 1996. *Cooking the World: Ritual and Thought in Ancient India*. New Delhi: Oxford University Press.

Marcus, G. E. 1995. Ethnography in/of the world system: The emergence of multi-sited ethnography. *Annual Review of Anthropology* 24, pp. 95–117.

Marriott, M. 1976. Hindu transactions: Diversity without dualism. In B. Kapferer, ed. *Transaction and Meaning: Directions in the Anthropology of Exchange and Symbolic Behaviour*, 109–142. Philadelphia: Institute for the Study of Human Issues.

Mazzarella, W. 2003. *Shoveling Smoke: Advertising and Globalization in Contemporary India*. Durham, NC and London: Duke University Press.

Power, M. 1999. *The Audit Society: Rituals of Verification*. Oxford: Oxford University Press.

Simoons, F. J. (1994). *Eat not this flesh: Food avoidances from prehistory to the present*. Madison and London: The University of Wisconsin Press.

Srivastava, S. 2017. Divine markets: Ethnographic notes on post-nationalism and consumption in India. In D. Rudnyckyj and F. Osella, eds. *Religion and the Morality of the Market*, 94–115. Cambridge: Cambridge University Press.

Star, S. L. and Lampland, M. 2009. *Standards and Their Stories: How Quantifying, Classifying, and Formalizing Practices Shape Everyday Life*. Ithaca, NY: Cornell University Press.

Strathern, M. 2000. Introduction: New accountabilities. In M. Strathern, ed. *Audit Cultures. Anthropological Studies in Accountability, Ethics, and the Academy*, 1–18. London and New York: Routledge.

The Hindu. 2016, 29 October. More Indians eating beef, buffalo meat. Available at https://www.thehindu.com/news/national/%E2%80%98More-Indians-eating-beef-buffalo-meat%E2%80%99/article16085248.ece

United States Department of Agriculture. 2016. *From Where the Buffalo Roam: India's Beef Exports*. Washington, DC: United States Department of Agriculture.

Ybema, S. Yanow, Harry Wels and Frans Kamsteg et al. 2009. *Organizational Ethnography: Studying the Complexity of Everyday Life*. Thousand Oaks: SAGE Publications.

11

HOW DO I LIKE BEING A POLICEWOMAN? I'M VERY HAPPY!

Pakistani Policewomen and the Challenge of Presentational Data

Sadaf Ahmad

Policewoman A (in an affected tone): *Aap nai police join ki hai, aap kaisa mehsoos ker rahee hain?* (You have joined the police force, how do you feel?)

Policewoman B (replying in an equally affected tone): *Mein bohat acha feel ker rahee hun* (I'm feeling very good).

The other policewomen in the room we were all sitting in burst out laughing.

Policewoman B (continuing): *Yahan akay mainay judo seekhi, karate bhi seekhi, mein bohat acha feel ker rahee hun!* (I learnt karate here, I learnt judo here, I feel very good!).

More laughter.

The satirical exchange I witnessed during the course of my ethnographic research on policewomen in Pakistan in 2015 and 2016[1] made a mockery of the interviews these and other policewomen have had to give journalists in recent years. The media has become increasingly interested in throwing a spotlight on policewomen, framing their presence in a male-dominated profession as an act of bravery, and highlighting the obstacles they have had to overcome to get this far. The National Police Bureau (NPB) reports that policewomen only make up 1.46% of the police force in the country (Dawn, 2017). This is a jump from their being 0.89% of the police force in 2011 (Sethi, 2012), but it is still a very low figure; not only nationally but also within the region.[2] Their low numbers in an occupation that has

192

traditionally been associated with men has made policewomen the subject of many such interviews. Many policewomen enjoy the spotlight and share their personal journeys and challenges happily. Others, like the police constables quoted above, quickly tire of the attention that turn them into objects of fascination for the larger public. Their frustration is compounded by the fact that they can only give routine responses about their experience in the police. These and many other policewomen I met during the course of my research mentioned that their supervisors gave them strict directives to present the police force and their role within the department in a positive light. The result, even for those who shared their personal struggles in media interviews, was a sanitized account of their experience. Their making fun of reporters—as well as themselves as they found themselves colluding in the production of a particular kind of knowledge about themselves—through this brief, spur of the moment role play is situated within this context.

Presentational data is a particular challenge when studying the police organization. It is related to "appearances that informants strive to maintain (or enhance) in the eyes of the fieldworker, outsiders … " and is "often ideological, normative, and abstract, dealing far more with a manufactured image of idealized doing than with the routinized practical activities actually engaged in by members of the studied organization" (Van Maanen, 2007, p. 296).

In this chapter I will discuss why moving beyond presentational data is a particular challenge when studying the police, and then draw upon my ethnographic fieldwork on Pakistani policewomen to shed light on how anthropology's ethnographic method is particularly well suited for overcoming this challenge. More specifically, I will illustrate how building trust by spending time in "the field" and by participant observation, both of which lie at the heart of ethnographic research, can be useful: in accessing information that would be inaccessible otherwise, identifying new lines of inquiry, gaining unexpected insights, and understanding the various ways in which people's worldviews and an unofficial organizational culture can undermine official rules and policies. The three-dimensional, nuanced and complex knowledge that is then generated can subsequently have, as I will discuss in the conclusion, multiple benefits for theoreticians and practitioners alike, and can contribute to the existing literature on organizations in general and the police in particular.

The Ethnographic Approach

While socio-cultural anthropology has been traditionally associated with the study of "exotic" non-state societies, researchers have also used the ethnographic method to study industry in the past. Today, it has been used to study organizations as diverse as the bureaucracy, multinational organizations and corporations (Nash, 2007), as well as other public and private "organizations" such as the Freemasons (Cohen, 2007), Wall Street (Ho, 2009), hospitals (Long, Hunter, & van der Geest, 2008), and of course the police. In fact, there has been an increasing emphasis on police ethnographies by anthropologists as well as other social scientists since the turn of the century (Fassin, 2017).

The ethnographic method involves immersing oneself in the everyday lives of the subjects of one's study. Although conventional tools like interviews are a common part of the process, the ethnographic method's uniqueness lies in the researcher spending a significant amount of time with his or her subjects, engaging in participant observation. This method is a part of the larger ethnographic approach that posits that one can gain a better understanding of a world by becoming a part of it.

The ethnographic approach has many benefits associated with it. For instance, it utilizes an inductive framework which "restrains preconceived ideas or preformed judgments, since it does not suppose hypotheses to test or questions to answer, but proceeds by progressive elaboration of knowledge through the emergence of meanings" (Fassin, 2017, p. 5). This emphasis on discovery creates the conditions for an expansive understanding of the subject matter and is particularly useful in exploratory research where the aim may be to understand the culture of an organization and the dynamics among the people within it. Questionnaires, which require pre-existing knowledge for the formulation of particular questions, and which limit the production of unthought-of categories, have little utility in such a context (Gardner & Whyte, 2007).

Furthermore, questionnaires' "*a priori* assumptions and reliance on attitudes expressed out of context" do not account for the fact that behavior does not always meet professed values and beliefs. It does not capture the creative ways in which behavior shifts in different contexts (Wright, 1994, p. 3). Interviews, too, can "displace subjects and subjectivities from the relative obscurity of the everyday and in so doing potentially position them under the spotlight of the research process" (Avis, 2002, p. 197). This can facilitate prevarications or the production of presentational data. Participant observation, especially when long term, can provide a far more complex and authentic understanding of people's attitudes and behaviors by showing the slippages between discourse and practice in their daily lives.

I employed the ethnographic method to gain a comprehensive understanding of Pakistani policewomen's experience of working in an occupation that has traditionally been associated with men and "manly" characteristics, in a context in which limited ethnographic research exists on them (Taj, 2004). I was particularly interested in understanding how their experiences varied across rank and geographical space. This research thus took place across nine smaller and larger cities in the provinces of Khyber Pukhtunkhwa, Punjab, and Sindh.[3]

Semi-structured interviews were conducted with 168 policewomen. These women belonged to different ranks, ranging from the lower ranked Constables and Head Constables to the most highly ranked Pakistani policewoman, a Deputy Inspector General of Police. These policewomen either worked in the provincial police (e.g. police stations, the traffic police) or in different federal police branches (e.g. the National Highways and Motorway Police). I also engaged in a few hundred hours of observation, and in some instances, unwitting participant observation, as policewomen did their duties across a range of spaces. For instance, as they dealt with complainants in police stations and offices, patrolled and gave out tickets on the motorway, did security duty in mosques during the month of Ramadan (the Muslim month of fasting), maintained crowd control in protests, etc. Logistical practicalities meant that I was able to do research ranging from a few weeks to a few months in some cities, like Islamabad, Rawalpindi and Lahore, but spent comparatively less time in other cities like Abbottabad, Faisalabad or Karachi. Nevertheless, the ethnographic method played a critical role in helping me move beyond presentational narratives and towards a more complex account in each of these instances.

Studying the Police: The Limits of Access

While gaining permission allows a researcher to enter a "field site," access, in itself, does not guarantee forthcoming respondents (Gardner & Whyte, 2007). The first step, if wanting to do research among the provincial police, for instance, is to get permission from the office of the highest-ranking police officer in that province, the Inspector General of the Police (IG). However, this permission does not automatically translate into disclosure. Sometimes gaining physical access to a space is far more straightforward than gaining open, honest accounts from the subjects of one's study.

The concern with informants who lie, mislead or deliberately withhold information is an old one within cultural anthropology. Bronislaw Malinowski, who is popularly credited with articulating the significance of the ethnographic method for subsequent generations, documented his anger towards lying informants in the private journals he wrote while he conducted research in the Trobriand Islands during the World War I years (Wax, 1972). Anthropologists since his time have recognized that such moments create an opportunity to learn people's concerns and the webs of power within which they operate.

There are a number of reasons why informants may be reluctant to divulge personal or professional information, for instance, a legitimate "why should I bare my life to a stranger?" stance. Not fully understanding the reason for the research or what will happen once the information is shared with others can further compound this reticence. I had only been visiting a Woman Police Station[4] (WPS) in a city for a week when one of the policewomen there, perhaps sick and tired of my intrusive presence, and my asking them questions whenever they had a moment—What were they writing in that police register? What does the term *roznamcha* mean? Who is a *muharrar*?—spoke to me with some irritation. I kept seeing a woman in civilian clothes moving around the police station, silently doing chores for the policewomen. She was not cleaning staff and, curious about her position, I asked her if we could speak when she was free. She did not respond and walked away but this policewoman did, speaking curtly: "No, she cannot speak with you. What do you want to want to find out? Why are you here? I don't understand any of this." I had, of course, tried to explain my interest in learning about their experiences as they worked as a minority in this "masculine" profession. I had also brought up issues of anonymity and confidentiality and did so with everyone I met. But many policewomen did not find that convincing and merely tolerated me because they had to, frequently stonewalling my efforts to get in-depth or diverse information.

The desire for privacy, suspicion, and/or a general desire to present oneself in a positive light—it is rare for informants to admit to socially disapproved behavior (Khan, 2007; Van Maanen, 2007)—are some common reasons for informants' reticence or their misleading researchers. Organizations are often similarly wary of researchers. This wariness can stem from a concern that speaking to the researcher may fan workers' existing frustrations, or a concern over what the researcher may learn and how he or she may portray the organization (Gardner & Whyte, 2007).

There are additional reasons for reticence or misleading researchers that are particularly pertinent for the police as an organization. For instance, the police may withhold or remain silent about some aspects of their job but emphasize other aspects in an effort to maintain their "mythology," as depicted by television serials, films, and novels (Fassin, 2017, p. 7). The emphasis on chases or volatile encounters with the public may, for instance, hide the fact that the bulk of police work actually involves a lot of waiting and boredom. Burleigh B. Gardner's and William Foot Whyte's 1946 address to the American Sociological Society on "The Methods for the Study of Human Relations in Industry" offers us another reason why informants may mislead researchers or be particularly reticent in organizations like the police. They claim that in hierarchical and authoritarian organizations,

> where there is ... apprehension of authority [by low level staff members], it is always difficult to gain acceptance ... [this authority] makes everyone more wary of what he does and says, especially before the outsider who is sanctioned by management and might be a channel of communication to the top.
>
> *(Gardner & Whyte, 2007, p. 6)*

Such reticence, which other scholars have also commented upon (Hoag & Hull, 2017), is also linked with hierarchy and authority in that seniors' directives to present a positive image of the police will carry weight. Going against a senior's directives can have serious consequences such as unwanted transfers, show cause notices on minor or trumped up charges, etc.

Furthermore, concern over disclosure and representation is particularly high in organizations that may have something to hide and where "legal and normative constraints are important ... [yet] discretionary power is the rule in the street" (Fassin, 2017, p. 5). The Pakistani police is associated with high levels of corruption and a regular abuse of human rights. Hiding one's socially disapproved-of behavior and/or doing the same for one's colleagues—what has varyingly been referred to as "collective secrets" (Van Maanen, 2007, p. 299), a "code of silence" (Corsianos, 2012, p. 79), or the "norm of secrecy" (Roebuck & Barker, 1974, p. 27)—often becomes common practice in this context. The resulting misdirection or dishonesty can stem from a sense of loyalty to one's colleagues, a desire for acceptance, and/or as a strategy to ensure that their colleagues will similarly have their back. Furthermore, a public spotlight on police activities that violate police rules or criminal law embarrasses the organization. The fear of being known as the source of negative leaks and becoming vulnerable to negative repercussions can also, as indicated above, propel many to silence or misdirection.

Researchers have repeatedly turned towards the ethnographic method for the role it plays in reducing informant reticence and minimizing the acquisition of presentational data. The section below illustrates how it can play a positive role in this regard and aid the production of a more nuanced, complex account.

The Benefits of the Ethnographic Method: Moving beyond Presentational Data

"The job cannot be done in a hurry."

(Gardner & Whyte, 2007, p. 5)

Some informants are more forthcoming than others. Some are just friendly and want to be helpful. Others may have a desire to "blow off steam" (Gardner & Whyte, 2007, p. 6) or feel that sharing information could lead to better working conditions. A higher rank can also make informants feel invulnerable to potential negative consequences and translate into more open accounts. But trust in the researcher "is crucial in gaining genuine information" (Khan, 2007, p. 70) and this is especially true when the research is on sensitive topics (Ibid.). Like assurances of anonymity, trust in the researcher can also help offset the different fears, concerns and motivations mentioned in the prior section. This can increase the likelihood of informants divulging more information than they would have otherwise.

The ethnographic method is well suited to building trust. Spending considerable time with the subject of one's research, which lies at the foundation of the ethnographic method, can be a crucial tool in this context. It is "with time, [that] relations of trust develop between observer and observed, and the officers' control over themselves diminishes, giving free rein to spontaneous attitudes" (Fassin, 2017, pp. 5–6). I spent a substantial amount of time in the WPS in Islamabad, often going in the morning, when the staff who had worked the overnight shift would be preparing to leave, and spend half the day there. Alternatively, I would go later in the day and stay until late. I usually sat in a cramped room at the front of the premises. Its large glass windows overlooked the driveway and gate, and it was the complainants' first point of contact with policewomen when they entered the premises This room was the center of all daily activity. It was where women came with their complaints; where all incoming and outgoing policewomen had their "arrival" and "departure" noted; where policewomen often dropped by to exchange work-related gossip, personal news, and concerns; where duty schedules were made; where junior policewomen were scolded if they came late or fussed about not wanting to do a particular duty; and where police-related crises in the city (for instance, the suspension of a particular police officer for letting a convict escape while on duty) or current cases in the WPS were discussed.

There would be days when I would spend hours sitting in this one room, observing the rhythms of the police station, making note of all the activities and conversations happening around me. There would be other days when I would also interview the policewomen on the premises, jotting down their life histories, supplementing what I had already learnt about them through our informal conversations over the course of time. Sometimes I accompanied policewomen when they left the WPS to do duties in different vicinities.

Anthropologist Ali Khan discusses the importance of building trust via reducing the threat factor in the context of his ethnographic work on child labor in the football manufacturing industry in Pakistan. He explains, "my position as a young fieldworker helped me to reduce the distance between adult researcher and child informant" (Khan, 2014, p. 53). Similarly, I was often perceived to be younger than I actually was. This, in addition to my informal manner and insistence on not standing on ceremony, made it difficult for policewomen to see me as a threat. In fact, they would often introduce me to other policewomen by saying "*bachi thesis likh rahi hai*" (this girl is working on her thesis) despite my (often repeatedly) telling them of my professional affiliation. My being a woman also helped, automatically creating a space where policewomen felt comfortable asking me personal questions, for instance about my marital status (unmarried). My response would always be followed by a "why?" as well as arguments to convince me to change, what they called, an unfortunate state of affairs. Barriers between a researcher and interviewee can come down fast after a conversation like this, and help build rapport.

While I had limited control over how others perceived me, I did take some small steps to portray myself as less of a threat. Field researchers have written about the usefulness of not using recording devices during interviews or not taking notes during informal conversations in order to create "as relaxed an atmosphere as possible" during fieldwork (Khan, 2007, p. 70). I began to do the same over time and noticed a significant increase in policewomen's comfort level when it came to their sharing sensitive information, which they, then, shared more of.

Informal interactions, for instance in the form of sharing meals or playing sports with one's informants, can also foster a closer relationship between the researcher and his or her subjects (Gardner & Whyte, 2007; Khan, 2007). It gives them an opportunity to get to know the researcher and that helps build rapport and trust. In fact, researchers often place more importance on building relationships through such informal interactions and conversations even if they learn nothing about their topic of interest, because having a good relationship can pave the way for a richer understanding over time. I often hung out with some of the policewomen who lived on the WPS premises. Watching a television serial with them in their room in the evening, having *iftari* or "breaking the fast" with them during Ramadan, dropping them off to their duty sites if I happened to be leaving the WPS premises at the same time they were (and saving them a longer journey on public transportation) are examples of instances that created opportunities to build rapport and trust.

In addition, my spending long hours with policewomen and my willingness to face many of the challenges they did as they did their duties—such as bearing the summer heat with little food and water while doing security duties at rallies or crowd control at protests—played a particularly important role in their increasing their trust in me. This facilitated their openness and allowed me access to different experiences. PSP[5] Assistant Superintendent of Police[6] Arsla Saleem[7] was the senior most policewoman in Islamabad when I did my research there. She observed me on different occasions and began to vocalize her appreciation of my methods, connecting them to sincerity and a genuine desire to understand policewomen's experiences. For instance, she once introduced me to a colleague of hers by referring to the most recent day I had spent with them, at a doctors' protest: "She spent the whole day with us. And it wasn't like she sat in the car the whole day. She was with us all the way—on the roads, in the heat … ." My approach was in stark contrast to the brief, official trips others had made to interview policewomen previously, for research projects that were housed in different international organizations. PSP Arsla valued the difference and began to make sure I knew of other such activities when they happened, hence opening additional avenues for understanding.

Sharing intense experiences were particularly useful in those cities where I did not have the luxury of spending weeks building rapport. I was conversing with a female Station House Officer (SHO) during my first day in one such city when I learnt that a number of policewomen from this WPS were leaving to do security duty at a politician's rally. I decided to cut my conversation short and accompanied these policewomen instead. Our first stop was a police station close to the site where the rally was to take place later that day. It was the height of summer, with the temperature touching 110° F. We spent the first few hours cooped up in a small, fan-less room with only enough chairs for about half of us. This was followed by a few more hours of sitting on dusty ground underneath the blazing sun, waiting for the rally to begin. The policewomen's frustration over wasting time by being there hours before they were needed was compounded by their physical discomfort and the eventual realization that they were not even needed at the rally; the rally was only for men and as per custom, only policemen dealt with male members of the community. Going through this experience with them played an important role in bringing down barriers between us. This would not have been likely if I had only met them for a short period of time at the WPS over the course of my short stay in this city. The camaraderie we developed by virtue of our shared physical discomfort alone resulted in a shift in their narrative. The official or presentational "we are all one big happy family" narrative that many of them began with transformed into a more complex and nuanced account of their experience in the police force. Some policewomen began disclosing more information with variants of "*humari aap sai gup shup hogayee hai tau hee hum apko bata rahay hain*" (We're telling you this because we've developed a good relationship with you). Granted, speaking from a space of frustration may result in some exaggeration. But much of what they spoke of, of what hurt them or frustrated them, was similar to what emerged in other places as well.

My experience with Constable Zarina illustrates how the trust that is built over time—from getting to know the researcher and her aims, and from sharing experiences—can produce non-presentational narratives. I interviewed Constable Zarina soon after meeting her. It was during the course of this interview that she, of her own volition and completely out of the blue, began highlighting her religiosity—she fasted, she prayed—and swore by the Quran that she never abused or exploited people. The police's reputation as corrupt and violent often resulted in policewomen marking themselves as honest and moral early on in our conversations. It was with time, however, especially as I accompanied Constable Zarina to different duties and spent hours with her and other policewomen that she began to proudly regale me with tales of all the female political workers she had beaten up over the years—in the context of "crowd control" at protests, but also in other, private spaces.

It was also the deepest kind of trust, which once again, was built over time that resulted in my hearing intimate personal narratives that furthered my understanding of the webs of power that policewomen were embroiled in. Some of these narratives involved their male colleagues sexually harassing them. Others revolved around the range of ways in which some policemen made policewomen's working lives difficult if they refused their advances. A policewoman in the National Highways and Motorway Police spoke bitterly about how her male colleagues ganged up against her when she refused the sexual advances of one of them. For instance, she would be marked absent even if she was five minutes late. Absences translate into salary cuts and are thus no small matter. Other kinds of retaliatory harassment included assigning her the sole car without AC for her patrolling during the summer, or insisting that she pay for a cracked windshield when a bird crashed into it. Another policewoman narrated a similar story with equal degrees of bitterness:

> Men in the police first perceive you as a female. They just want you to become "set" with them. If you play the game you get a lot of benefits. I didn't … so they began sharing my personal information, like my phone number, with others. I would be punished a great deal if I was one minute late but someone who was an hour late wouldn't be. Others would be given extra holidays. My requests to link my monthly holiday (4 days a month) to our national holidays (like Eid) would be consistently denied. I would get a show cause notice on minor things. I can compile a book if I start putting these experiences together.

Interviewees must have a great deal of trust in the researcher in order to entrust them with the personal details of their life. Building this trust is invaluable for the role it can play in reducing their concerns, and giving the researcher access to a more authentic understanding via non-presentational accounts.

The Benefits of the Ethnographic Method: Greater Complexity and Nuance

The benefits of the ethnographic method are not limited to their role in building rapport and trust which, in turn, can lead to greater openness. These methods can also make particular kinds of information and understanding possible. For instance, some lines of enquiry can only be satisfied through observation, such as exploring the role of non-verbal communication in negotiations in different parts of the world (Community of Organizational Anthropology, n.d.; Fassin, 2017). Observing people's behavior as they carry out their daily tasks, especially on a long term basis, can also help the researcher discover an organization's dominant ideology, values, and modus operandi; things which informants may not be able to articulate because they take them for granted by virtue of being a part of that system (Van Maanen, 2007). In addition, these methods can help researchers understand what is typical or routine behavior and what is not, uncover new lines of inquiry, and offer unexpected learnings and insights (Fassin, 2017). I will expand upon some of these themes in this section and then conclude by discussing how such knowledge can benefit different stakeholders.

Unexpected Insights

I accompanied Constable Parveen and a dozen women beggars to the courts one day. Begging is against the law and these beggars, after having spent the night in a police lock-up, were now going to pay bail to avoid going to jail. We all scrambled out of the back of the police van when we reached the court and Constable Parveen hurried everyone inside, telling me to bring up the rear. The women followed her, some talking animatedly on their mobile phones, telling the people they had called to come over with money, and some having hurried conversations with the people who were already waiting for them there. Constable Parveen led us to a narrow corridor emanating a strong stench of urine, and told me to keep an eye on the women as she disappeared into an office. Some women sat down on the dirty cracked floor of the corridor and others leaned against its stained walls. Constable Parveen came out a number of times in the next hour. She sometimes sat on the sole chair in the corridor and directed an angry diatribe towards the women from there. "*Sar kha lita ai kuttiyan nai bhonk bhonk kai ... main inan de baap di naukar aan jai garmi ich aithay bethi ravan?!*" (These bitches have given me a headache with their incessant barking ... what am I, their father's servant, that I have to keep sitting here in this heat for them?!). Other moments had her huddling with the people who had come for these women. It was during one of these group interactions that she slipped some money in her bra. She had been collecting bail money from them. Not all of it went towards their bail. On the one hand, witnessing this behavior fed into the popular stereotype of the police being corrupt. On the other hand, close participant observation and the insights it provided also began challenging this simplistic image.

The entire trip took three hours. The heat was energy sapping. My throat was parched because I had taken to doing what policewomen did, i.e., not drinking outside the WPS given the lack of public toilets for women, and given that one doesn't know when one's duty will end. Parched, drained from the heat, and nauseous from the stench of urine in the corridors, I began wondering what doing this exercise day in and day out would do to me after months or years. Would I also begin cursing them loudly and openly for putting me through this ordeal on a daily basis? Would my frustration with them help me justify my exploiting them? It was an uncomfortable insight, but an important one, especially for those interested in curbing police corruption and who believe that merely adding women (whom they believe are morally superior to men) will help reduce corruption levels. Some scholars have suggested that job-based frustrations like overwork, poor working conditions and low salaries can make it easier for the police to both engage in and justify corrupt behavior. I learnt that policewomen, especially those in the lower ranks, have additional frustrations in the form of gender-based mobility issues, juggling their jobs and domestic responsibilities, a lack of flexible hours, physically challenging work conditions (e.g. not having access to toilets), etc. A "the system owes us" and "let's get what we can" attitude can thus develop as a result and can contribute to unprofessional behavior in general and the routinized nature of corruption among both men *and women* in particular.

The following example also illustrates how participant observation can offer unexpected insights. The WPS in Peshawar was set up in 1994 but it never served the role of a regular police station. Women police officers did not have the authority to register First Information reports (FIRs) and they lacked facilities like a telephone or their own car (Ahmad, 2012). The premises housed a lock-up for women and served as a congregating point for policewomen; they often left for their duties from this location. Few women complainants went there and if they did, their cases were forwarded to other police stations. Apart from the lack of facilities, the WPS's location also came in the way of women going there for advice, if nothing else. The WPS was set well within the Police Lines and I got first-hand experience of what getting there involved on my second day in Peshawar. It required getting out of a rickshaw and walking to a security check-post on the main road, where I was asked who I was, where I was going and for what purpose. I was allowed to go through the Police Line gate after I had answered the security personnel's questions and they had seen my national identity card. The ten-minute walk that followed involved some backtracking as there were no signs for the WPS anywhere. I eventually made it to another security check point, where two policemen sat behind a desk. One of them, a big bodied man in his mid-40s, began questioning me: "Where are you from?" "What business do you have here?" "Are you in touch with the SHO?" "Does anyone in the WPS know that you are coming?" I was a bit taken aback at this interrogation by a man outside a space that had been created to make women feel comfortable. However, the matter did not end there. He informed me he could not allow me inside if I did not have the SHO's permission and told me to call her from my phone and have him speak to her. He did not have a phone outside and would not use his mobile phone. The SHO did not pick up the phone, and neither did anyone from the City Police Office (CPO), from where I had received permission to do fieldwork in Peshawar. I stood there trying both numbers while the two policemen sat there, watching me do so. One of them eventually gave me a number and told me to call the WPS directly. The man who picked up the phone turned out to be an operator and he connected me to the WPS. They clearly still did not have a direct phone line. The policeman then spoke to the woman on the other side, took my national identity card and gave it to the second policeman, and accompanied me to the WPS. He, on my asking him, told me that all women had to go through this process to go to the WPS. The process, from the Police Lines entrance to the WPS, took 40 minutes, involved 2 interrogations by men, and included multiple phone calls.

My first trip to this WPS had been organized by the CPO and had taken place the day before. They organized a police car to take me there, which meant I got there, from door to door, without interacting with any policemen, or experiencing anything resembling what an ordinary complainant would were she to go there on her own. It was only by deliberately choosing to make my own way there that I got an understanding of one of the possible reasons for women's reluctance in going to the WPS for advice. Some of the policewomen I had spoken to the previous day had mentioned that the WPS's location within the city and the Police Lines, which had beefed up its security in the last few years due to the terrorist attacks in the region, had made it cumbersome for women to get there. But going through the process also shed light on its gendered dimension, underlining the need for greater gender sensitivity in the police.

Distinction between Discourse and Practice

Apart from creating opportunities for greater insights, participant observation can also help researchers move beyond presentational data by identifying discrepancies between discourse and practice. For instance, the long-standing problems associated with the WPS in Peshawar eventually led PSP Ihsan Ghani, who was serving as the IG of the police in the province of Khyber Pukhtunkhua (KP) in 2013, to set up 63 women's help desks—with two policewomen assigned to each "desk"—in different police stations all across the province that year. I met him in 2015, when he was working as the Director General of the NPB in Islamabad. He explained that he wanted to provide women with a functional alternative to the WPS, one which would improve their access to policewomen in different parts of town, and encourage them to seek the police's help.

The women's help desks in KP have received a lot of positive media attention, especially because the initiative took place in a province that is known for its conservatism. These media reports, and the policewomen and policemen I met, all spoke highly of these help desks and referred to the high number of women using them. There were eight women's help desks in Peshawar in 2016 and the police officers in the CPO office in Peshawar encouraged me to visit them, telling me that the SHO of the WPS could organize these visits for me. I asked her to do so during my first visit to Peshawar, requesting that we begin with the help desk at Sharki police station, simply because it was the closest and I did not have the time to go further that day. I learnt that one of the policewomen assigned there was on leave and the other had been assigned a general duty elsewhere; she would go home straight after. I suggested the following day and learnt that no policewoman would be available at any help desk because they were all assigned special security duties due to the local elections scheduled the next day. I went ahead and dropped by the Sharki police station during my next visit to Peshawar a few weeks later. This time the policewoman who was meant to be there was out during security duty at a Public Service Commission exam site.

Observation is crucial to helping researchers identify how an organization actually functions versus how it is reported to function, as well as what workers do in contrast to what they say they do (Britan & Cohen, 1980a; Van Maanen, 2007). No one spoke about the frequent non-availability of policewomen at these help desks and this is something I learnt because I did not go there through official, pre-arranged visits. However, having observed this, I was able to bring it up and discuss it with the police officers I subsequently met. Many policewomen who worked there or who had once worked there complained that the police station in which they were located or the WPS often sent them out to do general duties even though they were meant to work at the help desk for the entirety of their shift. This meant that their own work suffered. Insufficient women in the police force in KP (although some policewomen also blamed the situation on the mismanagement of the available personnel) was a key reason for this problem. In fact, it was because of this that the women's help desks closed down in the city of Abbottabad in KP, something I learnt when I went there in 2016.

Women's help desks are doing important work in KP but observation "confronts discursive propositions with actual facts, thus allowing for the unveiling of discrepancies" (Fassin, 2017, p. 5). This leads to a more expansive and authentic understanding of how these desks actually function as well as how they could become more effective.

Accessing the Inaccessible

Observation can provide direct access to those work-based behaviors or aspects of an organization's functioning which may not be accessible otherwise. The example of the women's help desks in Peshawar illustrates this, as does seeing some policewomen take money from complainants, or take female beggars out of the lock-up in the WPS; they were told to clean the premises. It is also observation that then provides the grounds for greater understanding as "the fact that the social scientist has witnessed such deviant practices calls for explanation, which would probably not be formulated otherwise" (Fassin, 2017, p. 6). The justification(s) provided, such as not having sufficient funds to operate the police station, adds another dimension of understanding—in this case, of the conditions under which a police station is run and which can subsequently facilitate exploitation.

Use toilets whenever you come across one in "the field" because you never know when you will find the next one, is common advice given to anthropologists embarking on their ethnographic journeys. The importance of this could not have been underlined more in this research, as toilets for women in the world of policing—as I learnt to my discomfort—were few and far between. My request to use one in the main academic block of the Police College Sihala, the biggest and most well-known police college in the province of Punjab, resulted in my learning that there was not a single toilet for female students or female instructors in the entire building. Those who wanted to use one during the course of offering or attending classes during the day had to walk 10 minutes to the girl's hostel to do so. They used to have one, I was told. This is when they had a female Deputy Superintendent of Police, whose rank gave her the authority to take over a washroom, obtain a lock for it, and ensure that only women had access to its key. However, the male clerical staff took it back when she was transferred elsewhere. This state of affairs was not unique to Sihala. I slowly learnt that most police stations and many police buildings did not have separate toilets for women. Many policewomen thus chose to not use them at all during their working hours and limited their water intake as a consequence. Others hurriedly used their male supervisor's toilet (they have their own) when said supervisor was not in the room, or sought permission to do so, something which caused them excessive embarrassment. These, I learnt, were typical on-the-job behaviors for women who were not stationed in WPSs. My desire to use one thus created the conditions whereby the policewomen hosting me *had to* explain why I had to leave the building to use one. It led them to open up about an issue they had remained silent about until then, hence giving me an unexpected insight into one of their key sources of frustration in this profession. I gained an experiential understanding of why so many of them preferred to work in WPSs, along with a growing awareness of the range of gender-based discriminations within the police force.

The Impact of Worldviews and Cultural Embeddedness

Ethnographic work reminds us of the importance of moving beyond official police rules to gain a more authentic understanding of the conceptual framework of members of the police; this, rather than official discourse, is what shapes and legitimizes their action (Van Maanen, 2007). It further reminds us that an organization is a living system that may be shaped by formal structures, rules and roles but which may not be defined by these given the presence of informal rules and the dynamics among people within the organization (Wright, 1994). These dynamics may be shaped by how people within the workplace respond to any one identity or characteristic of a worker or group of workers, such as their ethnicity or gender. "In the case of women in non-traditional occupations, their 'female' status is activated   " (Martin, 1978, p. 46). This is in contrast to the assertion that I frequently heard during fieldwork, i.e., that there are no men and women in the police organization, only police officers. The reality, of course, is that men and women are not genderless bodies who function within a cultural vacuum. Gender and gendered concerns shape their workplace behaviors. As such, "organizational dynamics [are] not the direct outcome of existing formal structure, but a complex result of social patterns, cultural understandings, and exogenous factors outside the organization's control" (Britan & Cohen, 1980b, p. 13).

To illustrate—I learnt that policewomen relied upon a variety of strategies to deal with the dilemma of engaging with their male colleagues and with men in the public arena. This was especially true if they lived in smaller towns or came from backgrounds in which interaction among unrelated men and women was looked down upon and could, therefore, ruin a woman's reputation. The strategies they employed to deal with their fear of being socially stigmatized or being sexually harassed meant that they sometimes engaged in unprofessional behavior.

I was sitting in PSP SP Ammara Athar's office one day when she got a call from a colleague who told her that the IG Punjab had seen policewomen wearing large *chadors* over their uniforms while doing their duty and that he was angry. He wanted them to speak to these policewomen about professional conduct. It was thus that I found myself attending a function in the Police Lines in Lahore in 2016. SP Ammara brought up the issue of professional attire and behavior with the policewomen who resided there. The ensuing discussion resulted in the senior policewomen in attendance realizing the extent to which these policewomen, most of whom were constables, were uncomfortable wearing their uniform in male-dominated public spaces. Pakistani policewomen used to wear the national dress, the *shalwar kameez* (baggy trousers with a knee length shirt) in the police colors until a few years ago; until senior officials in some provinces decided they should wear trousers, topped with shirts that came up to their upper thighs. Some policewomen welcomed what they called a "more professional" look. Others were uncomfortable with this change. Sexual harassment in public is a common phenomenon in Pakistan. Being a woman in a uniform makes you the subject of additional attention, which they felt was further compounded by their new uniform. Almost all policewomen, especially those in the lower ranks, therefore covered their heads and upper chests with a *dupatta* (a long, thin scarf) in the police colors, a headscarf, or covered their heads and their entire upper bodies with large *chadors*. Some even wore black colored *abayas* or gowns on top of their uniforms while doing their duty. An unprofessional attitude may explain dress code violations in some instances. However, other instances have more to do with a top-down policy that is divorced from policewomen's cultural reality. Their cultural concerns and need to navigate a gendered landscape is often far more important to them than official police policy and the latter gets ignored in this context. This also, however, results in the perpetuation of a particular gender stereotype ("policewomen are unprofessional") and contributes towards others not taking them seriously.

Ethnographic work is based on the idea that official policies and rules (cultural construct themselves) are often undermined by different cultural concerns and worldviews. The example above illustrates this and demonstrates how participant observation becomes particularly useful in capturing the "interfaces, gaps, and frictions [that result from] 'worldviews-in-action'" (Ho, 2009, p. 31). To illustrate through another example: there has been a lot of talk of the Pakistani police undergoing gender training and gender sensitization courses so that they are better equipped to deal with women who report being domestically abused or raped. My interviewees frequently mentioned taking such courses and dealing with such cases with sensitivity. Observation, however, frequently revealed that strong pre-existing beliefs shaped police attitudes and behavior. For instance, a young woman in her early twenties came to a WPS to complain that her father had raped her multiple times when she was much younger. She spoke to the media about what she had undergone as well and an FIR was filed. But the policewomen's comments to each other clearly revealed that they did not believe this girl.

> Head Constable D: "Why didn't she say something four years ago, when she said she was raped?"
>
> Head Constable E: "Yes, that's what the investigating officer also wondered."
>
> Assistant Sub-Inspector F: Only God knows what really happened. But yes, it's strange that she took four years to speak up. If something like this happens to you, you go to the police, you run away. Plus, these things only happen in small, backward areas, not in larger towns. And even if something like this did happen, what decent girl wishes to draw attention to her shame by speaking to the media?

The policewomen's skepticism was rooted in their culturally informed ideas of how rape victims—or rape victims who were worthy of help—were supposed to behave. Such ideas, beliefs and attitudes can have an impact on how complainants are spoken to, how much effort is put into their cases, as well as how those cases are handled.

Participant observation can also reveal how people in decision-making positions can use their discretion when applying organizational rules (Hoag & Hull, 2017). A senior policewoman I was sitting with in a police station one day told her junior police officer to change the details in a police report. A group of young men had been over the speed limit at night when their car hit a man on a motorbike. People gathered to help the seriously injured man and called the police. The young man who had been driving did not have a license. Believing that he had made an unfortunate mistake, had the rest of his life in front of him, and did not deserve the punishment he was likely to get if the facts were documented accurately, this policewoman directed her junior officer to change the driver's name in the report, replacing his name with one of his friends who was also in the car and had a license. She felt sorry for this young man. He was already quite shaken up over this incident, she explained. He would still be punished, she assured me, but with a lighter sentence.

A further example of "discretion" involved another senior policewoman, telling me that she once had her junior police personnel beat up a man who had sexually harassed her brother's girlfriend. The importance of one's kin and social relations, and the outrage over someone daring to violate a woman (an embodiment of a group's honor), and that too in one's inner circle, trumped rule-based police conduct. She did not believe she had done anything wrong by taking the law into her own hands and felt proud of teaching the man a lesson.

All the examples in this section illustrate the different ways people's cultural embeddedness and the worldviews they uphold shape their workplace behavior, as well as how this behavior contradicts formal police rules. Observation and the narration that comes with increasing trust in the researcher over time become important tools for identifying the different ways and varying extents to which this happens, throwing the culturally rooted practices of an organization into stark relief.

Conclusion

I have drawn upon my fieldwork experiences to illustrate how ethnographic research can help researchers move beyond presentational data, and facilitate the production of a more three-dimensional, nuanced and complex understanding of the phenomenon under study. This understanding has the potential to inform praxis and would be in line with the work that has been and continues to be done in the field of "the anthropology of organizations." Such work has often involved anthropologists generating knowledge about organizations with an interest in using that knowledge—or giving managers that knowledge—to solve organizational problems. Anthropology's emphasis on the emic perspective is useful in understanding workers' views and can be particularly useful in designing more effective policies and thoughtful interventions in the workplace (Wright, 1994).

For instance, this ethnographic research provided a comprehensive understanding of the range of gendered and non-gendered frustrations policewomen experienced. Identifying the varying sources of their frustration can help others understand why their job satisfaction reduces over time. This knowledge is significant in itself and can be used to improve women's working conditions. But this research suggests that this knowledge is also significant because ongoing frustrations can make it easier for policewomen to violate police rules. Apart from complicating policewomen's simplistic representation as unprofessional, corrupt and insensitive, knowing what work-based challenges women face can also feed into designing practical interventions and reforms that can reduce such violations. Interventions to reduce corruption levels, for instance, would be far more effective if they were designed keeping the inverse relationship between job satisfaction and corruption in mind. Addressing policewomen's daily work-based problems would play a more significant role in this regard in comparison to simply recruiting more of them as an anti-corruption strategy. Police reforms can thus have the potential to benefit both the police (by addressing the issues that frustrate them) as well as those they are meant to serve, the public (by reducing their exploitation).

Furthermore, ethnographic research can be useful in identifying the spheres in which the police require greater training or in assessing the effectiveness of the training that they have undergone. For instance, being questioned by the policeman outside the WPS in Peshawar, or witnessing policewomen's attitudes towards a rape victim in another WPS, are just two of many such instances that indicate a need for greater gender sensitization in the police, along with a need for a greater understanding of the dynamics of gender-based violence. Simply setting up a WPS is clearly insufficient. Ongoing exposure to such a discourse through different forums can possibly create the conditions whereby more women would feel comfortable approaching the police with their issues, secure in the knowledge that their trauma would not worsen because of their interaction with the police. Related to this, sexual harassment at the workplace also emerges as an area that the police administration needs to focus on. Skewed power dynamics between men and women in the larger society become worse in an organization where more men have greater formal authority over women, and thus have the ability and power to make their lives extremely difficult. These ethnographic research-based findings highlight the importance of designing interventions that focus on prevention, as well as the need to create or strengthen systems that can provide victims of sexual harassment with a recourse to justice within the organization.

Anthropology's emphasis on culturally grounded research allows for an understanding of the role particular cultural contexts play in shaping (organizational) culture and workplace behaviors. For instance, our understanding of the relationship between formal organizational rules or professional conduct, and actual police behavior, deepens through identifying the cultural ideas and values (such as the importance of kin ties or appropriate gendered conduct) that mitigate this relationship in particular places. Remembering that culture plays a critical role in shaping police behavior can serve those in decision-making positions in organizations. It can be a reminder that top-down decision making that does not consider the cultural context in which people operate, or which excludes the voices of those whom those decisions will affect, may often result in said decisions not being followed. The situation with the policewomen's new uniform is a case in point. A more inclusive approach to decision making in such instances may result in a more successful implementation of new policies.

Last but not least, anthropology's emphasis on ethnography sets the stage for cross-cultural comparative work. This not only fuels theory building and deepens our understanding of particular domains (like gendered coping strategies), but also makes it possible for practitioners to learn from case studies from different parts of the world.

All data collection methods have their advantages and disadvantages and the ethnographic method is no different. Researchers, for instance, do not always have the time that is needed to conduct such research. But its benefits are vast and it is particularly well suited to studying complex groups. Formal organizations are no different.

Notes

1 I am thankful to the Lahore University of Management Sciences (LUMS) for supporting this research through its Faculty Initiative Fund [grant number FIF-SHS-2077].
2 Policewomen in India and Bangladesh make up 6.11% and 4.63% of their police force respectively (Commonwealth Human Rights Initiative, 2015). They are 1.6% of the police force in Afghanistan (Rubin, 2015).
3 This study is a work in progress and the next phase will include research in Baluchistan and Gilgit-Baltistan.
4 Women Police Stations began being established in different cities in Pakistan from 1994. They were created for female complainants and aimed to provide them with a female-only

space where they could go and discuss their problems more comfortably and openly. Most large cities in Pakistan have at least one such police station.

5 People who succeed in their Central Superior Services (CSS) examinations become eligible to join a department in the civil service in Pakistan. The Police Service of Pakistan (PSP) is one of these departments. Those who join the PSP enter the police force directly at an officer rank, and have greater authority and status than their counterparts who (called "rankers" in police jargon) have reached the same rank through promotions.

6 The ranks mentioned in this chapter are the ranks police officers had at the time this research was conducted.

7 The names and identifying information of police officers have only been changed in those instances where disclosure could make them vulnerable within the police organization.

References

Ahmad, G. B. (2012). *Women police in Pakistan*. Islamabad: Individualland.

Avis, H. (2002). Whose voice is that? Making space for subjectivities in interviews. In Bondi, L., Avis, H., Bankey, R., Bingley, A., Davidson, J., Duffy, R. & Wood, N. (Eds.), *Subjectivities, knowledges, and feminist geographies* (pp. 191–207). Lanham, MD: Rowman and Littlefield.

Britan, G. M., & Cohen, R. (1980a). Introduction. In Britan, G. M. & Cohen, R. (Eds.), *Hierarchy and society: Anthropological perspectives on bureaucracy* (pp. 1–7). Philadelphia, PA: Institute for the Study of Human Issues.

Britan, G. M., & Cohen, R. (1980b). Toward an anthropology of formal organizations. In Britan, G. M. & Cohen, R. (Eds.), *Hierarchy and society: Anthropological perspectives on bureaucracy* (pp. 9–30). Philadelphia, PA: Institute for the Study of Human Issues.

Cohen, A. (2007). The politics of ritual secrecy. In Jimenez, A. C. (Ed.), *The anthropology of organizations* (pp. 43–64) Burlington, VT: Ashgate. (Reprinted from *Man*, 6, 1971).

Commonwealth Human Rights Initiative. (2015). *Rough roads to equality: Women police in South Asia*. Retrieved from: www.humanrightsinitiative.org/download/1449728344rough-roads-to-equalitywomen-police-in-south-asia-august-2015.pdf

Community of Organizational Anthropology. (n.d.). In *About organizational anthropology and COA: Organizational anthropology as a field of study*. Retrieved from https://www.ntnu.edu/sosant/coa/about-coa

Corsianos, M. (2012). *The complexities of police corruption: Gender, identity, and misconduct*. Lanham, MD: Rowman & Littlefield.

Dawn. (2017, April 26). Women make up less than 2pc of country's police force: Report. Retrieved from www.dawn.com/news/1329292

Fassin, D. (Ed.). (2017). *Writing the world of policing. The difference ethnography makes*. Chicago, IL: Chicago University Press.

Gardner, B. B., & Whyte, W. F. (2007). Methods for the study of human relations in industry. In Jimenez, A. C. (Ed.), *The anthropology of organizations* (pp. 3–9) Burlington, VT: Ashgate. (Reprinted from *American Sociological Review*, 11, 1947).

Ho, K. (2009). *Liquidated: An ethnography of Wall Street*. Durham, NC: Duke University Press.

Hoag, C., & Hull, M. (2017). *A review of anthropological literature on the civil service*. Policy Research Working Paper 8081. World Bank Group. Retrieved from https://openknowledge.worldbank.org/bitstream/handle/10986/26953/WPS8081.pdf?sequence=1&isAllowed=y

Khan, A. (2007). *Representing children: Power, policy and the discourse on child labor in the football manufacturing industry in Pakistan*. Karachi: Oxford University Press.

———. (2014). Power and authority in the field. In Chaudhuri, S. K. & Chaudhuri, S. S. (Eds.), *Fieldwork in South Asia: Memories, moments, and experiences* (pp. 31–69). New Delhi: Sage.

Long, D., Hunter, C., & van der Geest, S. (2008). When the field is a ward or a clinic: Hospital ethnography. *Anthropology & Medicine*, 15(2), 71–78.

Martin, S. E. (1978). Sexual politics in the workplace: The interactional world of policewomen. *Symbolic Interaction*, 1(2), 44–60.

Nash, J. (2007). Anthropology of the multinational corporations. In Jimenez, A. C. (Ed.), *The anthropology of organizations* (pp. 79–106) Burlington, VT: Ashgate. (Reprinted from *New directions in political economy: An approach from anthropology*, 1979, Rod Press).

Roebuck, J. B., & Barker, T. (1974). A typology of police corruption. *Social Problems*, 21(3), 423–437.

Rubin, A. (2015, March 1). Afghan policewomen struggle against culture. *The New York Times*. Retrieved from www.nytimes.com/2015/03/02/world/asia/afghan-policewomen-struggle-against-culture.html?

Sethi, A. (2012). *Gender strategy of police 2012–2016: Equality in perspective.* Islamabad: Deutsche Gesellschaft fuer Internationale Zusammenarbeit.

Taj, F. (2004). *Policing in purdah* (Unpublished doctoral dissertation). University of Bergen, Norway.

Van Maanen, J. (2007). The fact of fiction in organizational ethnography. In Jimenez, A. C. (Ed.), *The anthropology of organizations* (pp. 293–304) Burlington, VT: Ashgate. (Reprinted from *Administrative Science Quarterly*, 24, 1979).

Wax, M. (1972). Tenting with Malinowski. *American Sociological Review*, 37(1), 1–13.

Wright, S. (1994). 'Culture' in anthropology and organizational studies. In Wright, S. (Ed.), *Anthropology of organizations* (pp. 1–31). London: Routledge.

12

IMPACT QUANTIFICATION AND INTEGRATION IN IMPACT INVESTING[1]

Tom P. Vandebroek, Fabrizio Ferraro,
Alice Mascena and Heinrich Liechtenstein

Introduction

One key moment in our research journey studying impact investing was the conversation with one of the co-founders of Bridges Ventures,[2] the leading impact investor in Europe. As she explained their approach towards integrating impact and financials in their investment process, she joined both hands at the height of her heart, in a yin and yang motion. In this chapter, we examine how Bridges goes about integrating impact considerations into its investment decisions, and contrary to the dominant view in the commensuration literature that numbers serve primarily to decontextualize, we find that quantification of impact was used to facilitate conversations and a deeper understanding of social impact, rather than limiting it.

Impact investing is defined as the allocation of capital with the intention to generate positive social impact beyond financial return (Harji and Jackson, 2012) or as the investment made with the dual purpose of obtaining financial *and* social returns (Mair and Hehenberger, 2014). As the interest in seeking social impact alongside financial returns grows, an "ecosystem" has developed consisting of specialized intermediaries and investors (Millar and Hall, 2013). Initiatives that have helped shape and grow this ecosystem include, in the United Kingdom (UK), the Social Investment Task Force launched in 2000, and Big Society Capital, a £600 million fund launched in 2012 that aims to stimulate the development of the social investment market (Cabinet Office, 2011). The chairman of the Task Force, Ronald Cohen, together with two other co-founders (one of whom we interviewed), created Bridges Ventures in 2002, an impact-investment fund manager. With the development of the field, the discussion around impact evaluation becomes prominent for both scholars and practitioners, some of which even consider the field's definition contingent on the *measurement* of impact.

More broadly, as boundaries between the social and private sector progressively erode, organizations working towards impact find themselves in a competitive environment for resources (Lyon and Arvidson, 2011). This setting encourages the deployment of objective tools of impact measurement, which contrasts with a basic challenge: there is still not a universal agreement of how environmental or (especially) social impact is to be assessed. As methods of impact measuring become seemingly more rigorous, scholarship is turning its attention to understanding how the impact-oriented organizations will use these tools to shape their own decisions, as well as how these impact measures will be used to shape environments and influence others (Hwang and Powell, 2009). As impact measurement increasingly relies on quantitative measures and tools, practitioners and scholars alike debate the likely consequences of this quantification process.

In fields as diverse as sociology, political science, anthropology and philosophy, there is a growing number of scholars joining in the critique of "governing by numbers." The literature on commensuration and quantitative rationality brings forth significant vulnerabilities regarding quantification's reductive, disembedded character (Fourcade, 2016; Merry, 2016; Power, 2004; Townley, 2008). As the transformation of qualities into a determined set of quantities, these numbers become more taken for granted and more constitutive of what they measure (Espeland and Stevens, 1998). The seemingly objective, depersonalized quantification tool, thus, may be incorporating certain subjectivities and arbitrariness, such as thresholds or cut-off points that create differentiated categories (Fourcade, 2016).

So far, most studies on the topic have taken a more macro-sociological perspective, for which reason scholarly effort should be employed in more fine-grained studies on the impact of "rational procedures and evaluative tools on decision making" (Hwang and Powell, 2009, p. 293). Hence, this study stems from an interest in understanding everyday practices of quantification, following recent studies of quantification processes as rituals (Mazmanian and Beckman, 2018). Anthropologists have been called upon to research organizations such as investment fund managers, i.e. organizations at the "heart of capitalism" (Gusterson, 1997), but have had no access to them, with notable exceptions such as ethnographies of arbitrage trading (Beunza and Stark, 2004) and of investment banking in Wall Street (Ho, 2009). More specific to the phenomenon of impact investing, the assessment and quantification of impact in investment decisions has not been studied directly. Thus, in this study we explore how impact is conceptualized and incorporated into investment decision-making.

To answer these questions, the chapter takes on an ethnographic approach to examine Bridges, an impact investing fund manager in the UK. This setting is especially relevant as the firm is considered a pioneer in the field, making it an informed, tenured source with consolidated practices. Also, it is profoundly involved in shaping field practices, by actively engaging in dialogues with other actors and by openly spreading their impact-measuring methodologies. With this study, we contribute to our understanding of impact measurement and commensuration. We found that numbers are used to contextualize qualitative matters, as opposed to decontextualize; the numbers represent qualities which remain present in the discussion, as opposed to disappearing once being translated into a number. Impact in Bridges is integrated into investment decision-making by maintaining a separate organizational unit, whose mission is to encourage dialogue on impact, and through the iteration of quantitative and qualitative tools.

Theoretical Background

Quantification is understood as the production and communication of numbers (Espeland and Stevens, 2008), and *commensuration*, as the expression or measurement of characteristics normally represented by different units using a common metric (Espeland and Stevens, 1998). They are similar concepts and most quantification can be understood as commensuration (Espeland and Stevens, 1998). Common examples of commensuration include monetization and cost–benefit ratios, as well as utility calculations.

Commensuration has been considered a reduction of reality (Townley, 2008) which, on the one hand, facilitates communication and comparison, and on the other, is detached from reality and may carry a false sense of neutrality, even if it abides by values and reference points (including latent ones). These points will be further discussed below: we will provide a synopsis of the literature on quantification and commensuration, identifying main problematizations emerging, with special attention to commensuration applied to impact evaluation.

Commensuration as Integration

Numbers are standardized. They provide for transforming qualities that may be uncertain into proxies that are simpler to handle and compare (Espeland and Stevens, 1998). As dimensions are reduced to a common metric, i.e. they are commensurable, objects can be compared and understood in terms of "how much of one thing is needed to compensate for something else" (Espeland and Stevens, 1998, p. 317).

When it comes to societal or environmental issues, research has suggested that their quantification is a way to more efficiently integrate them into decisions; the transformation of incommensurables into numbers is a spreading practice (Davis and Kim, 2015), and has been called on by different stakeholders such as funders and regulators (Hwang and Powell, 2009). When an environmental issue is transformed into a financial figure, it is more easily integrated into financial decisions, and diverse interests are thus brought together in a commensurable manner (Crane et al., 2015). Quantification of impact also allows for external comparison, as argued by Hwang and Powell (2009): quantitative evaluations of programs allow for organizations and their audiences the ability to benchmark various organizations on common metrics.

Fourcade (2011) provides an empirical example of how readily quantifying what is qualitative may actually benefit the intangible in casu. In the context of oil spills caused by and – to a greater or lesser extent – paid for by the indicted oil companies, she found that the jurisdiction that was more comfortable with translating intangibles such as "the value of nature" into monetary amounts, viz. the American, awarded considerably higher restitution orders than the one that was much more reluctant to do so, viz. the French.

Commensuration as Decontextualization

Quantification's "reliance on numbers and quantitative manipulation minimizes the need for intimate knowledge and personal trust" and facilitates coordination and settlement of controversies across large distances (Porter, 1995, p. xi). For this reason, Porter referred to it as a "technology of distance." At the same time, the literature on commensuration and quantitative rationality brings forth significant vulnerabilities regarding quantification's reductive, disembedded character (Fourcade, 2016; Power, 2004; Townley, 2008). Qualities turned into quantities are "silenced," reduced to numbers. Anthropological studies on social indicators and rankings call attention to how commensuration may change the reality it is aiming to measure: in her study, Merry (2016) finds the use of numbers provides meaning to complex social phenomena, and binds it to those aspects of the phenomenon that get measured.

This impersonal and reductive element of commensuration has been criticized for leaving out important dimensions of what is being measured. As a decontextualizing mechanism, it can lose important features to the debate, in its preference for reducing uncertainty and focusing on definite aspects (Townley, 2008). Most notably, criticisms arise as the objectivity behind quantification is put into question: it is argued that this process always involves a degree of discretion and may, in fact, perpetuate values and power relations (Espeland and Stevens, 1998).

In the process of transforming concepts into numerical values, there is a space for making choices about what is measured and how; occasionally even values attributed to costs and outcomes are chosen (Arvidson and Lyon, 2013). These decisions are not neutral; they construct choices, that are many times taken for granted or stay latent (Townley, 2008): the criteria and standards by which social impact is measured may be anti-democratic and not very accountable when important audiences such as beneficiaries do not participate in the establishment of these measures (Hwang and Powell, 2009). Boundaries and cut-off points, as well as the definition of success and failures, are emphasized by Fourcade (2016), who argues that continuous scales are often not attainable; instead, cut-off points that produce significantly different categories are chosen. Thus, symbolic categories such as "the 1 percent" or the IQ threshold which separates gifted children are made real as cut-off points (Fourcade, 2016).

Commensuration is said to be, therefore, not an impartial approach but innately political (Maier et al., 2014). Moreover, once the choices around commensuration take place, it may change the very objects it measures; it becomes more taken for granted and constitutive of the phenomena it measures (Espeland and Stevens, 1998). Rankings, a common form of commensuration, have been shown to feed back into what has been referred to as "reactivity of rankings" (Espeland and Sauder, 2007). Altering actions towards conforming to the rank itself, this form of commensuration becomes an end in itself; a studied case is that of winemakers producing wine that is increasingly more compatible with critics' tastes (Fourcade, 2016; Lampland, 2010).

Finally, what is commensurable? Literature discusses the limits of expressing categories in terms of a common metric. An incommensurable category is defined as socially unique in that it is not considered to be comparable. It involves a "failure of transitivity"; out of two categories, no alternative is better than the other, and there could be some other alternative that is better than one of them but not the other (Espeland and Stevens, 1998).

Social Impact Measurement

For organizations exposed to conflicting demands, such as the demands to obtain simultaneously social and financial results, commensurability should be especially challenging. This applies to organizations that are in some way abiding by social and commercial or financial logics; they attempt to carry out dual purposes, and while commercial or financial performance is easier to assess, the nature of social impact has been difficult to define (Barman, 2007). There is a lack of agreement on what amounts to good social impact evidence (Arvidson et al., 2010; Hall, 2014) and measurement is especially challenging.

Although challenging, social impact measurement has been spreading, and different actors strive to find common language and practices. One earlier example of commensuration in impact measurement is the social return on investment (SROI), a ratio that conveys a cost–benefit analysis to impact; it has been a widespread tool, thus making it a protagonist in recent scholarship on social impact measurement. Although widely known in the impact measurement community, it has faced barriers and criticisms of its adoption and use. Examining SROI informs on some important issues that have surfaced on the implementation of commensuration in which objects, practices, and individuals may be given a market value represented by financial numbers or ratios (Arjaliès and Bansal, 2018). The literature on the topic has pointed out technical barriers to the implementation of commensuration tools, which should eventually be resolved as the tools develop and organizations professionalize, as well as other types of barriers, more important to the discussion in this chapter: barriers that relate to tensions in values and logics. A more recent, global initiative, the Impact Management Project ("IMP") is a "forum for building consensus on how to measure, report, compare and improve impact performance" (Impact Management Project, n.d.). IMP is a platform that is meant to be used by enterprises, intermediaries and investors and defines impact across five dimensions: what, who, how much, contribution, and risk. Although not aiming to reach a single ratio to inform investment decisions, this initiative and set of tools also incorporate language and practices of the financial logic, as illustrated in the *risk* dimension of impact.

In line with the commensuration literature discussion on numbers perpetuating privileges, studies on impact measurement tools account for decisions on what to measure and how these decisions reflect and perpetuate power relations. Available evidence points to "business-like" legitimacy being one of the main drivers towards adopting the methodology in the first place (Arvidson et al., 2010; Maier et al., 2014). Aiming for communication and marketing purposes, organizations emphasize results. This emphasis on outcomes and evidence-based performance has been said to miss out on key aspects of third sector activity (Millar and Hall, 2013), as is illustrated by the case interviews in Arvidson and Lyon's study, in which interest in results over processes guided the communication strategy of the enterprise (Arvidson and Lyon, 2013).

Recent scholarship on impact measurement hints on how the tool can transform the relationship of the organizations with the phenomena they were aiming to assess. Organizations may engage in a *strategic commensuration*, intentionally select indicators (Arvidson and Lyon, 2013) or even change the practices themselves in order to better results on indicators, using activities easy to monetize (Maier et al., 2014).

Likely because the literature on the topic has focused mostly on nonprofit organizations or social enterprises that operate mostly under a charity logic, studies report on *ideological barriers* to employing commensuration tactics. Ideological issues draw attention to how performance measurement tools may clash with the values and culture of social enterprises. Some tools, such as social audit and benchmarking, originated in the private sector and were adapted to public and nonprofit contexts. They were originally designed to focus on large business models, where rationalization, resource maximization, market growth and financial measures are the main purposes. For organizations that are hybrid, they may adopt different business ideologies, ethics and organizational structures (Ridley Duff et al., 2011). The use of financial proxies to evaluate results of social organizations has been considered, by organizations themselves, as inappropriate; they have felt that measuring intangible social outcomes using financial tools is inadequate (Millar and Hall, 2013).

As previously mentioned, these issues mostly have to do with the decision for implementation, the adoption of a particular measurement tool. As organizations that have stronger social imprinting, i.e. mission-driven organizations, the idea of quantifying at times may conflict with their principles. The commensuration literature, however, also emphasizes that even when quantification is adopted without a value conflict, there are issues to be looked at. The use and interpretation of these numbers are not a given; they are constructed. While previous literature has mostly explored this through a more macro view, this chapter will focus on more everyday uses and interpretations of commensuration.

Methods

In order to address the question of how impact is being measured and how it is incorporated into the overall decision-making for the investors, this study builds on primary data gathered through a three-month intensive *participant observation*. It also encompasses several interviews, in addition to archival data collected during this stay and received from the company. The study takes as setting the impact investing fund Bridges Ventures, which aims for social impact alongside financial return.

Research Setting

Bridges Ventures was founded in London in 2002 as a dedicated impact-investment fund manager. Its co-founders had extensive backgrounds in private equity and social investment. We came to select Bridges Ventures as a research site after several sources, knowledgeable of the social-investment space, had mentioned the firm as being a pioneering firm in the impact-investment industry, and thus one with the longest experience with this practice. Access to research sites such as these is difficult. In our case one of the authors, who had had professional interactions with the firm, brokered our access. We all participated in the interview process, and the first author was invited to join the firm as participant observer. This personal involvement with the field was exclusively used for the purpose of gaining access and we consider it to be in no way antithetical to maintaining necessary professional distance (Anteby, 2013).

The investment personnel are divided into two organizational units: the larger one is more akin to traditional private equity as it seeks commercially viable financial returns alongside social/environmental impact. The smaller, i.e. the "socially oriented fund" team, focuses on sustainable investments that will generate financial return, but not necessarily at market rate. Finally, there is a small "Impact team," assisting over twenty investment-team members, an in-house specialized consultancy function, focusing on impact considerations (as will be further explored below). This is the team that the participant observer joined. Typically, investment opportunities arrived through one of the funds. As the due diligence process initiated, the investment teams, assisted by the Impact Team, would write their reports on impact considerations alongside traditional due diligence reports.

As the firm was experiencing rapid expansion, with several new people (including interns) coming in shortly before as well as during the 3-month participant observation, office space became increasingly cramped and frequent changes would be made in the seating plan. This actually turned out to be an opportunity as the participant observer thus came to sit with both the Impact team (for the initial two weeks) and alongside the distinct investment teams (for five of the remaining ten weeks each). At the start of the study, the Impact-team members were seated together and were sharing a desk with some of the investment personnel. By the end of the observation period, the Impact team had been scattered, with all three of its members sitting at different desks. In addition to three desks for the investment personnel and the Impact team, there was one further desk with the partners that did not sit immediately among the investment personnel, another one with the personal assistants and one with the accounting department. This provided the researcher with an all-around inside view of the firm, and exposure to different organizational members.

Investment-team members at Bridges Ventures tended to be highly educated, many having earned their degrees from highly reputed British universities and some holding MBAs, mainly from top European Business Schools. Even the PAs tended to hold university degrees. The office space included a small kitchen, which would be a place where the researcher would often try to make conversations with organizational members while they were preparing their teas.

Data Collection

Participant Observation

This chapter builds on both ethnographic interviews and participant observation. The first author conducted a 3-month intensive participant observation (Spradley, 1980), from early March till early June 2014, during which he joined Bridges Ventures' Impact team as a full-time intern. Being an intern granted the researcher access to team meetings, and he was tasked with various support activities to the team, from working on presentations to researching relevant topics such as recent developments in social finance. The Impact team, as previously mentioned, was an in-house impact advisor, which would give support on impact considerations to investment analysts from the different funds Bridges had. Working days typically started at 9 am and finished around 6.30pm. While the workload was high, the participant observer would make jot notes during the working day including the weekly meeting, during which all investment-team members came together to discuss ongoing business. Following each day at the office, he would expand the jot notes into a complete field note, composed of a descriptive note and a meta-note – i.e. notes that represent some level of inference or analysis (DeWalt et al., 2010). At the end of the 3-month period, these chronologically organized field notes had accumulated to over 250 single-spaced pages.

During the 3-month ethnographic study the researcher spent a total of over 500 hours in the office, observing work practices at Bridges Ventures from the inside. Observation mainly consisted of how people were carrying out their work at their desks and breakout areas and conversations taking place in their surroundings. As everyone was co-located in the same office space, most of the work actually took place there. The participant observer also attended a weekly team meeting and some further selected meetings, including some of the largest fund's pipeline meetings and internal Impact-team meetings as well as conference calls. A main advantage of observation over a prolonged period of time was that it enabled us to assess whether Bridges "walked their talk," e.g. in relation to what they purport to be doing in their impact assessment.

In-depth Semi-structured Interviews

Overall, *three* interviews were conducted with knowledgeable individuals outside Bridges; from Bridges, *six* interviews were conducted with organizational members prior to and during fieldwork, and finally *three* more as follow-up. We interviewed these three experts in the impact space, outside of Bridges, including the then Research Director at the European Venture Philanthropy Association, and two impact investing firm managers from European countries, in order to form an understanding of the impact investing space. From Bridges, prior to joining the organization for the purpose of the participant observation, the first three authors had interviewed one of Bridges' co-founders and one of its partners.

Throughout the participant observation part of the study, we conducted three formal semi-structured interviews with selected members at Bridges. One additional interview with a Bridges investment-team member took place in a local café at the interviewee's request and could thus not be recorded. Following the participant observation and preliminary data analysis, we conducted three additional focused follow-up phone interviews with selected Bridges investment-team members. With the one café interview exception, interviews were transcribed and coded, which will be further discussed in the analysis section.

Unobtrusive Archival Data

As an intern working at Bridges, the researcher had access to deal documentation relating to all their deals, including at the different stages of evaluation and investment, including deal sheets, investment memoranda, exit papers (if applicable) and periodically reviewed impact scorecards. Prior to joining Bridges as an intern, Bridges had also made detailed and comprehensive deal documentation, concerning thirteen of their deals, available to us through a "virtual data room" (which we could access after signing non-disclosure agreements with the firm). This ensured that we were able to acquaint ourselves with the different templates used at Bridges as well as their deals prior to joining. The deal documentation in the data room also allowed us to judge its evolution by comparing early deals with more recent ones.

In addition to deal documentation, the participant observer's role as an intern at Bridges implied access to relevant internal email exchanges. Some of its key knowledge pieces, including a piece on Bridges' approach to impact, the firm makes available to the wider public.

Data Analysis

We analyzed the data in line with the customary approach to qualitative data analysis (Miles and Huberman, 1994). Our initial coding of the field notes and interview transcripts, through the qualitative data analysis software *Atlas.ti*, yielded seventy-three primary codes and twenty-four secondary codes. We met regularly to discuss and assimilate embryonic ideas and to relate emerging themes with relevant literature. In an iterative fashion, we refined the coding.

We used grounded-theory techniques (Glaser and Strauss, 1967) to induce key themes. Once we had identified emerging themes supported by the data, we elaborated memos relating these to the relevant literature. At that point, during a formal meeting with two of the authors, these preliminary themes were presented to one of the co-founders and an Impact-team member at Bridges, for the purpose of checking validity and receiving feedback. An emerging theme on the definition of "impact investing" remaining ambiguous by design, was discussed and clarified, and was thus dropped from our analysis. More broadly, the meeting helped us select themes that had broader contextual validity and an indication that the research was uncovering non-trivial findings.

Following the feedback session and an internal de-briefing session, the first author read all the coded documents anew and composed a running document of all instances that related to the themes we had shortlisted to explore. As we immersed ourselves more in the literature, we engaged in an iterative process of drafting the article, turning to the literature and going back to the data.

After finalizing a presentable, yet still more descriptive draft of the study, we went back to the company for their feedback. They had very little comments and felt so comfortable with the truth-value of our claims that they mentioned they were even contemplating making the article available to their own employees for them to learn and become more aware of their own organization. They did, however, point us to a limited number of corrections and clarifications that were due. For example, they pointed out to us that the "counterfactual" (a concept that will be further discussed in the findings section) has two elements to it: firstly, what would happen to the venture if Bridges did not invest in the venture (i.e. whether it was likely to get its funding elsewhere) and, secondly, what were the likely impact implications should the venture end up not being funded. The feedback session served mostly to make sure observations and interpretations of actions and conversations during the participation observation were accurate. Following that, we then moved forward towards a more analytical piece, and all four authors were engaged in further iterations of interpretation and analysis of the data, relating it to existing literature and narrowing down those concepts that were relevant to this study.

Findings

In order to answer the research questions, we turn to the way Bridges implements its core task of analyzing investment proposals through a combined financial and social/environmental lens. Hereto, Bridges employs what it calls an integrated approach, whereby impact considerations are blended into the overall investment analysis. The Impact team fulfills a major facilitating role herein. In this section, we present how impact was conceptualized in Bridges and the importance of impact measures, but also how the organization was able to create dialogue around numbers.

Impact Investing Conceptualization

For Bridges' Impact team, impact investing should be measurable, otherwise, it is not actual impact investing. The deals are evaluated considering financial sustainability, ESG (environmental, social and governance) and impact of service or location of the organization. The impact rationale is two-fold: not only around a potential investee, but also encompassing Bridges' *own impact as an investor*. Impact investing, then, is perceived as occurring in two layers: the investee impact – that is or will be achieved by the social enterprise – and the investor impact in terms of additionality, i.e. whether their investment represents additional impact in relation to other or traditional investments.

Bridges' approach to impact moves away from propositions in which social and financial return represent a tradeoff. The sought-after "lock-in" mode refers to when there is alignment between the financial return with the mission so that as the enterprise scales up, there will not be either/or situations and mission drift is less likely. Below, we examine further how this conceptualization is operationalized and integrated into their decision-making processes.

Impact Investing Evaluation: Creating Dialogue around Numbers

Bridges makes decisions and evaluates impact (*ex ante*) using tools such as the impact scorecard, which is part of the investment deal documentation, and an "impact radar" for impact evaluation. The impact radar is constructed for each venture being considered for an investment based on a four by two matrix: scores of one through three are given for four dimensions of impact, and each dimension is rated for risk and for return. The four dimensions are: target outcomes, ESG issues, alignment (between social and financial goals) and the difference with the counterfactual. The rates are then visually represented with an impact radar graph[3] as depicted in Figure 12.1.

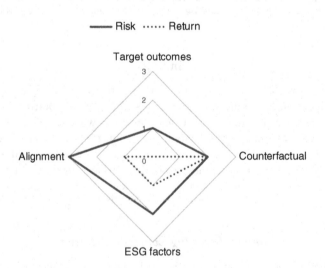

Figure 12.1   Impact radar

Impact Radar

In relation to "target outcomes," Bridges seeks to assess the potential of a venture in terms of matters such as scalability (i.e. could the scope easily be widened to include more beneficiaries?), depth of impact (i.e. to what extent is any given beneficiary positively impacted?) and systemic change (i.e. could this deal have wider-scale repercussions, e.g. in the market?). Risk on this dimension relates to the level of research evidence available that the concerned intervention or business model will deliver what it purports to. "ESG factors" refer to the impact generated by the venture beyond its main intended one, as it is understood any venture has a net impact comprised of positive and negative impacts across environmental, social and governance factors. "Alignment" relates to how aligned the venture's ability to generate impact is with its ability to generate competitive financial returns. Finally, "counterfactual" refers to what would happen to the venture if Bridges did not invest in the venture and what would the likely impact implications be should the venture end up not being funded.

Thus, this tool borrows from economics and finance language to conceptualize and consider impact in ratio terms, for risk and return. The financialization of social impact points to the discussion in social sciences of economics' emphasis on quantitative reasoning (Fourcade et al., 2015, p. 90) and the "imperialism" of economics' language, ideology and tools (Ferraro et al., 2005; Lazear, 2000). In Bridges' case, the organization carries out a dual purpose of impact *and* financial returns, but it is the dominant logic of finance that provides a means, a common language to discuss social impact, as this Impact-team member states:

> We don't all use the same clear language for impact, as people do for finance. … *when people talk about the finance side of the deal, they all use a common language*, and so you could have a very structured conversation.

While the Impact team plays a key role in carrying the social impact logic, its ideal objective is to be increasingly less necessary: "Impact+ team, we're always trying to make ourselves redundant" (Impact team member). This will happen as other all investment professionals are "imprinted" with both goals into an investment decision, as illustrated in conversations with the Head of the Impact team:

> We want them to be responsible for impact also, without us 'telling them'. … I don't want people in the world who only think with a finance hat on. Why would you ever want to have professionals doing that? It's dangerous is what we've seen. And, likewise, you wouldn't ever really want people to think with a pure impact hat on because they're not taking into account like financial sustainability and the market context. … So, *my dream is that people think in an integrated way*. But … most people aren't trained to think in both ways.

This integration was indeed observed during the fieldwork. It was possible to witness how financial and social impact considerations of potential new ventures were both considered at the same time, such as:

> Investment analyst 1: "NeXtFloor. They're break even. They produce floor tiles that generate quite some electricity when you walk on them... They are looking to raise 2 million. It currently costs 200 pounds per tile. They want to get it down to about 20 pounds per tile, which is the normal tile price... They are environmentally very interesting. I don't know what you guys think in terms of...?" ... "They raised 300k. Good board of directors, good advisory board."
>
> Investment analyst 2: "Have they got a patent?"
>
> Investment analyst 1: "Yes, not sure whether on the tile or the process. Can be used in health also, e.g. notifies you if people fall out of bed. Info can be sent with WiFi." ... "Probably worth spending time on this."
>
> CEO: "I agree."
>
> Investment analyst 1: "So far, commercially not viable... Major future cost saving would be from using recycled materials."
>
> *(FN37/3)*

Importantly, also in spontaneous, "unstructured" and "unsupervised" conversations, Bridges people tend to mix elements of business and social return. At one instance, the participant observer noticed an investment-team member ask what seemed to be a substantive question to the Head of Impact, in relation to a proposed investment. As the researcher could not tap into the full conversation as it happened, he later asked the investment-team member about it:

> Investment analyst: "It's a great opportunity (he walks to the cupboard and takes out a folder). We want to do something similar as we did here, i.e. make a property generate its own energy by means of photovoltaic solar panels. The Government tariffs have gone down, but the cost of the panels has gone down as well. And in [the one in the folder], it has worked well. *We have a 100% occupancy and it has been a major success for us. So the new deal has great opportunity in terms of carbon reductions.*"
>
> *(FN25/8)*

So, although there is already a certain degree of "individual integration," in the sense that each person at Bridges has (or is being trained to have) financial and social purposes in mind, having this team separation provides for instances of brainstorming, negotiation and subsequent adaptation of deals that strike a balance between the two purposes. To the extent that an investment-team member "embodies" one goal (financial) and another employee, an "Impact +" team member, embodies the other (social), they may engage in a dialogue that encompasses the duality, as illustrated below in a conversation about a possible deal:

> Impact-team member asked: *What would you need?* [for it to be considered for investment]
> Investment-team member said: [either] *Environmental leadership. Or that it is a site where it's hard to argue that* [something else would be done with it]

The dialogue shapes the offers towards an optimal proposition for both goals. The shaping into a proposition that fully integrates the dual purpose is the abovementioned "lock-in" stage, in which there is no perceived tradeoff between commercial gains and social impact.

Qualitative Discussions on Scores

Interestingly, the use of formal tools that borrow from a financial logic carries a degree of discretion and subjectivity. For instance, analyzing the use of Impact radar, we observe that although there is scoring from 1 to 5, there is no established cut-off point, and thresholds remain informal or flexible. There are some reference points present when using the impact tools, as evidenced in instances such as, in a discussion on the Impact radar, an Impact-team member saying that the "alignment" return is always 3 (highest) for growth funds and 2 for social sector funds deals as a kind of rule. However, the cut-offs remain flexible in the moments of decision-making. The tools, then, are not devised to be categorical, and do not establish a certain sum or ratio that has to be abided by, as expressed in the following passage in the interview with an Impact-team member:

> So, it's not the case if a deal is 2.5 impact return, and a 1, impact risk. That's now how it works. It's so that you have a structured conversation. The *scoring is just meant to lead to a structured conversation* so that you can say, 'Well, why did you score it a 3, or a 2.5? Why do you think the risk is a 2.5, but you think it's going to fall to a 1.5?' And that is what allows you to make a sensible investment decision."

Is it reasonable to assume that numbers actually worked better to *contextualize* discussions on investment decisions? An investment-team member of the socially oriented fund firmly seemed to advocate this during an informal interview:

> [The Head of Impact] revolutionized the impact assessment [through the introduction of the tools]. Before, we just had an unstructured discussion… Now, we better understand what is driving the impact. And we can do better tracking and follow-up and adjustment, if needed.
>
> *(FN69/2)*

There are more examples of instances in which there is a similar display of qualitative and quantitative not merely co-existing, but actually reinforcing one another. One is the investment memoranda, which are the internally compiled dossiers on ventures invested in. The "impact-thesis" section tends to consist of two main parts: the Impact radar and a "narrative," detailing the underlying elements and considerations in a number of paragraphs.

Therefore, even more than the tools as such, it is their particular use at Bridges that testifies to their "integrated" nature. As a prime example, the Impact radar, in itself and at first sight, could well strike an observer as an attempt to quantify what is qualitative and complex, to simplify the accounting of the investment decision. Our ethnographic study, especially through the participant observation, enabled us to realize that numbers may be integrated into qualitative discussion in a contextualizing manner. Thus, we find that, contrary to the dominant view in the commensuration literature that numbers serve primarily to decontextualize, at Bridges, rather, numbers were put onto certain crucial social dimensions so as to ensure that their underlying drivers would be treated in a satisfactory way. Rather than "silencing" a complex issue by putting a number on it, at Bridges, the number, instead, ensures that a conversation about the fundamentals will take place. During an internal meeting of the Impact team, the participant observer also observed the Head of Impact underlining the validity and importance of anything other than what is quantitative, as she mentioned that, "*the counterfactual matters, even if it's just a feeling*" (FN48/3).

Discussion

This study's ethnographic approach allowed us to delve deep into everyday practices. Could we have learned this in another way? In this case, having access to documents and investment memos alone, which would be already difficult to access for confidentiality concerns on organizations of this type, would have disclosed the quantification of impact considerations. Although deal documentation showed us early on that Bridges did account for impact in its investment decisions though different tools such as the impact scorecard, final scoring and ratios would have been observed in a static manner. The *interactions and processes* that generate the numbers, however, could only have been captured by onsite observation; the ethnographic approach has allowed us to learn how things "actually happen" (Watson, 2011) in and around these decisions. Thus, the everyday practices observed were able to shed a more nuanced light on the potential of quantification and commensuration: contrary to what prior literature maintained, quantification can be enabling, not just in the sense of making decisions easier, but also in the sense of potentially enriching matters by helping to account for context.

Recent research responds to calls for studies that aim to improve on ways to capture and report on the value of organizations that have a social impact (Peattie and Morley, 2008). As has been discussed in this chapter, quantification and commensuration alter our understanding of complex social phenomena and, consequently, how we attend to them (Merry, 2016). The literature on the topics emphasizes economics' rationality on the development of tools that measure utility for a number of fields and industries such as healthcare and program evaluation, and "its conceptual and practical influence is hard to overstate" (Espeland and Stevens, 1998). These "formal aspirations" coming from economists, however, can be said to, at times, favor "methodological and theoretical precision over real-world accuracy" (Fourcade et al., 2015, p. 93).

In this research, we focused on how commensuration is done in everyday practices, how it is used and interpreted. To this end and more concretely, we zoomed in on how Bridges Ventures, a pioneering impact-investment fund manager, practically deals with the issue of accounting for impact considerations at the heart of its investment decision-making. We came to find that the answer emerging from Bridges' practices is one of "impact integration," whereby the firm seeks to make a simultaneous consideration of both the business and the social/environmental elements that are at the firm's core "second nature" to its investment personnel. We discovered the crucial role performed hereby by a designated Impact team, which, paradoxically, has been separated out from the investment teams, on the road to integration.

Conversing with the literature on commensuration and quantification, this chapter has discussed implications of and subjectivity in measures. The practice of assessing impact investigated here, however, seems to counter some expectations set by the literature with regard to the de-contextualization of numbers. Though quantification and financial tools are used as a shared language, numbers and ratings on social impact are actively discussed qualitatively. While decisions made based solely on numbers may hold the appearance of being objective and impartial (Porter, 1995), Bridges' processes maintain subjectivity and complexity in decisions, not merely "leaving it to" the numbers to decide.

The present study follows recent empirical explorations of quantifications as human processes, that carry symbolic and instrumental aspects. In their study at a hotel management company, Mazmanian and Beckman (2018) describe how different units of the company, using various inputs, arrive at a single budget number. By analyzing budgeting as a ritual, they are able to point out how the process followed to derive the budget number legitimizes the final numerical value and people's participation in the process. They also observe how budgeting reiterates trust in numbers as an objective tool that legitimizes actions in the organization. Numbers stand on their own, granted there is a process, a ritual, that is followed to arrive at them.

Similarly, in our study, the numbers used to evaluate the impact of a potential investee are legitimized by a process in which they are discussed and agreed upon. Differently than in Mazmanian and Beckman's study (2018), however, in this case, the numbers are not meant to stand on their own. Numerical scores contextualize a discussion around impact criteria and provide reference points for future assessments of the same projects as time passes. In the view of organizational members, numbers brought about more structure and common grounds to the conversation around impact, since for the financial aspect there was always a "common language" (whereas for impact there was no common established language to start with). Impact numbers, however, are not supposed to be determinants of decisions, and they are accompanied by discussion around what these numbers mean.

Not only does this observation challenge the predominant view on numbers and their decontextualizing role in the commensuration literature, but it also stands out against findings in Slawinski and Bansal's (2015) climate change study, where "[q]ualitative tools encouraged dialogue" (p. 541). In the case of Bridges, quantitative tools, unexpectedly, encouraged dialogue. This would seem to lead to a more nuanced view on numbers and quantification vis-à-vis contextualization, i.e. of quantification being both enabling and constraining.

The apparent dilemma posed by Fourcade and colleagues between theoretical precision and real-world accuracy, thus, does not seem to apply. In measuring social impact, the tools and how they are exercised in Bridges seem to be enabling dynamic maintenance of dual logics of functioning. While a financial logic is dominant in the "means," social "ends" are present and integrated through active qualitative discussions within and between teams, thus preserving an iterative process between numbers and qualities that allows for complexity and projectivity to enrich evaluations.

Furthermore, Bridges attempts to go beyond a "mere" juxtaposition of business and the social. It rather treats them as intertwined, e.g. the Head of Impact's comment that, *"at Bridges, we never think of one aspect in isolation"* and her reprimanding an investment-team member that, *"every single person in this firm should champion both."* Rather than juxtaposing what is business and what is social, Bridges aims for – indeed – integration.

In this vein, we can recall the Bridges' co-founder's hand gesture mentioned at the beginning of this chapter, in which she illustrated Bridges' approach of integration with a "yin and yang" gesture. This integrated, holistic, view, was also instantiated by the Head of Impact's mention of the intuition behind the counterfactual. Interestingly, this also seems illustrative of the fact that Bridges' impact integration goes beyond the purely cognitive realm, that it is also a matter of feeling, intuition – indeed, a "second nature."

Conclusion

Societies are increasingly realizing that many of the main challenges we face are "wicked problems" (Rittel and Webber, 1973) and "grand challenges" (Ferraro et al., 2015). Firms – and particularly hybrid organizations that attend to multiple goals (Battilana and Lee, 2014), such as social enterprises or impact investors – have been pointed to as being able to help alleviate some of these (Holt and Littlewood, 2015). Our ethnographic study focuses on the work practices of an impact-investment fund manager, which actively seeks out "wicked problems" to tackle, in line with the social/environmental component of its mission. The insights provided into how Bridges deals in practice with marrying its financial-return objective with contributing to a better society represent important additions to our understanding of the potential role of for-profit business in resolving some of society's most intractable problems, notably in addition to the paradoxical frames put forward by Smith and Besharov (2015).

As pointed out by the literature on commensuration, organizations aiming to measure social impact may simplify complex phenomena by reducing them to quantifiable factors (Merry, 2016) and run the risk of *strategically* assigning numbers; they must thus strike a balance and set limits when encouraging discussion. Commensuration refracts power in many ways. It can enlarge decision-making or legitimate preordained decisions. It can be cynically manipulated by elites or it can limit their discretion. It can create disciplined subjectivities or arm dissenters (Espeland and Stevens, 1998). Thus, the hazard of "strategic commensuration" should be attended to, understanding its antecedents and what it is reinforcing. This issue is an interesting avenue for additional research on this topic.

Future research could further explore whether qualitative discussions can be used as a tool to maintain critical discussions on impact operationalization and the risk of impact initiatives turning to easily quantifiable outcomes. In the trend towards professionalism and increasing resource competition (Hwang and Powell, 2009), organizations promoting social impact may narrow their scope to undertaking easy to quantify (and thus simple to measure and communicate) operations. This would encourage a move by these dual-purpose organizations *away* from the attempt to solve "grand challenges" (Ferraro et al., 2015). These challenges, large and unresolved such as poverty alleviation, demand complex and concerted rather than ad-hoc discussions and responses.

Notes

1 We would like to thank Anne-Laure Fayard, Raza Mir, Irene Beccarini, Guillermo Casasnovas, Robert Gregory, Anne-Claire Pache, and Arthur Gauthier for their helpful comments on earlier versions of this chapter or insights about its subject. We also thank Bridges Fund Management (previously Bridges Ventures) for providing access to the data collected in this study. We thankfully acknowledge the European Investment Bank (EIB) financial support under the EIB Institute Knowledge Programme, and the Family Office Circle. Any errors remain those of the authors. The findings, interpretations and conclusions presented in this chapter are entirely those of the authors and should not be attributed in any manner to the EIB.

2 Bridges Ventures changed its name to Bridges Fund Management in 2017. Throughout the chapter, we will still refer to it as the name it had when data collection took place, or simply "Bridges."

3 The titles of the dimensions have changed over time, but the overall concepts behind them remain the same.

References

Anteby, M. 2013. PERSPECTIVE—Relaxing the taboo on telling our own stories: Upholding professional distance and personal involvement. *Organization Science*, 24(4), 1277–1290.

Arjaliès, D. L., and Bansal, P. 2018. Beyond numbers: How investment managers accommodate societal issues in financial decisions. *Organization Studies*, 39(5–6), 691–719.

Arvidson, M., and Lyon, F. 2013. Social impact measurement and non-profit organisations: Compliance, resistance, and promotion. *Voluntas*, 25(4), 869–886.

Arvidson, M., Lyon, F., McKay, S., and Moro, D. 2010. The ambitions and challenges of SROI. *Working paper. TSRC Third Sector Research Centre*, 49.

Barman, E. 2007. What is the bottom line for nonprofit organizations? A history of measurement in the British voluntary sector. *Voluntas*, 18(2), 101–115.

Battilana, J., and Lee, M. 2014. Advancing research on hybrid organizing – insights from the study of social enterprises. *Academy of Management Annals*, 8(1), 397–441.

Beunza, D., and Stark, D. 2004. Tools of the trade: The socio-technology of arbitrage in a Wall Street trading room. *Industrial and Corporate Change*, 13(2), 369–400.

Cabinet Office. 2011. Launch of Big Society Capital – the world's first ever social investment market builder. Retrieved from https://www.gov.uk/government/news/launch-of-big-society-capital-the-world-s-first-ever-social-investment-market-builder

Crane, A., Graham, C., and Himick, D. 2015. Financializing stakeholder claims. *Journal of Management Studies*, 52, 878–906.

Davis, G. F., and Kim, S. 2015. Financialization of the economy. *Annual Review of Sociology*, 41, 203–221.

DeWalt, K. M., DeWalt, B. R., and Wayland, C. B. 2010. *Participant Observation.* Walnut Creek, CA: AltaMira Press.

Espeland, W. N., and Sauder, M. 2007. Rankings and reactivity: How public measures recreate social worlds. *American Journal of Sociology*, 113(1), 1–40.

Espeland, W. N., and Stevens, M. L. 1998. Commensuration as a social process. *Annual Review of Sociology*, 24, 313–343.

Espeland, W. N., and Stevens, M. L. 2008. A sociology of quantification. *European Journal of Sociology*, 49(3), 401–436.

Ferraro, F., Etzion, D., and Gehman, J. 2015. Tackling grand challenges pragmatically: Robust action revisited. *Organization Studies*, 36(3), 363–390.

Ferraro, F., Pfeffer, J., and Sutton, R. I. 2005. Economics language and assumptions: How theories can become self-fulfilling. *Academy of Management Review*, 30(1), 8–24.

Fourcade, M. 2011. Cents and sensibility: Economic valuation and the nature of "nature". *American Journal of Sociology*, 116(6), 1721–1777.

Fourcade, M. 2016. Ordinalization: Lewis A. Coser memorial award for theoretical agenda setting 2014. *Sociological Theory*, 34(3), 175–195.

Fourcade, M., Ollion, E., and Algan, Y. 2015. The Superiority of Economists. *Journal of Economic Perspectives*, 29(1), 89–114.

Glaser, B. G., and Strauss, A. L. 1967. *The Discovery of Grounded Theory: Strategies for Qualitative Research.* New York: Aldine.

Gusterson, H. 1997. Studying up revisited. *PoLAR: Political and Legal Anthropology Review*, 20(1), 114–119.

Hall, M. 2014. Evaluation logics in the third sector. *Voluntas*, 25(2), 307–336.

Harji, K. and Jackson, E. T. 2012. *Accelerating Impact: Achievements, Challenges and What's Next in the Impact Investing Industry.* New York: The Rockefeller Foundation.

Ho, K. 2009. *Liquidated: An Ethnography of Wall Street.* Durham, NC: Duke University Press.

Holt, D., and Littlewood, D. 2015. Identifying, mapping, and monitoring the impact of hybrid firms. *California Management Review*, 57(3), 107–125.

Hwang, H., and Powell, W. W. 2009. The rationalization of charity: The influences of professionalism in the nonprofit sector. *Administrative Science Quarterly*, 54(2), 268–298.

Impact Management Project. n.d. Retrieved from https://impactmanagementproject.com

Lampland, M. 2010. False numbers as formalizing practices. *Social Studies of Science*, 40(3), 377–404.

Lazear, E. P. 2000. Economic imperialism. *The Quarterly Journal of Economics*, 115(1), 99–146.

Lyon, F., and Arvidson, M. 2011. Social impact measurement as an entrepreneurial process. *TSRC Third Sector Research Centre, Briefing Paper 66* (October).

Maier, F., Schober, C., Simsa, R., and Millner, R. 2014. SROI as a method for evaluation research: Understanding merits and limitations. *Voluntas*, 26(5), 1805–1830.

Mair, J., and Hehenberger, L. 2014. Front-stage and backstage convening: The transition from opposition to mutualistic coexistence in organizational philanthropy. *Academy of Management Journal*, 57(4), 1174–1200.

Mazmanian, M., and Beckman, C. M. 2018. "Making" your numbers: Engendering organizational control through a ritual of quantification. *Organization Science*, 29(3), 357–379.

Merry, S. E. 2016. *The Seductions of Quantification*. Chicago: University of Chicago Press.

Miles, M. B., and Huberman, A. M. 1994. *Qualitative Data Analysis: An Expanded Sourcebook*. (2nd ed) Thousand Oaks, CA: Sage Publications.

Millar, R., and Hall, K. 2013. Social Return on Investment (SROI) and performance measurement. *Public Management Review*, 9037(July 2015), 1–19.

Peattie, K., and Morley, A. 2008. *Social Enterprises: Diversity and Dynamics, Contexts and Contributions, a Research Monograph*. Cardiff: ESRC Centre for Business Relationships.

Porter, T. M. 1995. *Trust in Numbers: The Pursuit of Objectivity in Science and Public Life*. Princeton, NJ: Princeton University Press.

Power, M. 2004. Counting, control and calculation: Reflections on measuring and management. *Human Relations*, 57(6), 765–783.

Ridley Duff, R., Seamour, P., and Bull, M. 2011. Measuring social outcomes and impacts. In: Ridley-Duff, R. & Bull, M. (eds) *Understanding Social Enterprise: Theory and Practice*. London: Sage, 230–246.

Rittel, H. W., and Webber, M. M. 1973. Dilemmas in a general theory of planning. *Policy Sciences*, 4(2), 155–169.

Slawinski, N., and Bansal, P. 2015. Short on time: Intertemporal tensions in business sustainability. *Organization Science*, 26(2), 531–549.

Smith, W. K., and Besharov, M. L. 2015. Bowing before dual gods: How paradoxical frames sustain multiple conflicting organizational identities. *Working paper* (version June 2015).

Spradley, J. P. 1980. *Participant Observation*. New York: Holt, Rinehart and Winston.

Townley, B. 2008. *Reason's Neglect: Rationality and Organising*. Oxford: Oxford University Press.

Watson, T. J. 2011. Ethnography, reality, and truth: The vital need for studies of 'how things work' in organizations and management. *Journal of Management Studies*, 48(1), 202–217.

13

EXPLORING THE ACCOMPLISHMENT OF INTER-ORGANIZATIONAL COLLABORATION

The Value of Thick Descriptions

Emmanouil Gkeredakis

Introduction

In this chapter, I draw on Hodder's ideas on the interpretation of documents and material culture (Hodder 2003) to argue that the study of situated social interactions can greatly benefit from thick descriptions of associations among multiple pieces of mute evidence (documents, in particular). By mapping such associations that may span temporal and spatial boundaries, we can better appreciate how what is said and done in particular contexts – concrete episodes of human interactions – "fits into a more general understanding" (Hodder 2003, p. 166). Conducting such analysis can provide rich historical insights into the epistemic and deeply political work that multiple social actors – distributed in time and space – do to interpret and reinterpret texts that are valued as seminal, pursue different goals and construct the broader cultural context, within which local social interactions unfold (Yates and Orlikowski 1992).

In this chapter, I develop such thick descriptions in the context of a research project I conducted in the English healthcare sector. I explored how multiple organizations worked together to transform the delivery of healthcare services, in particular stroke services, by implementing "evidence-based recommendations". Based on fieldwork (non-participant) observations, the exploratory focus was on the local accomplishment of inter-organizational collaboration, which revolved around the collective production and agreement of a formal document – contract specifications. While inter-organizational collaboration happened predominantly through the situated doings and sayings of local actors, who acted as representatives of certain organizations, it was by trailing associations among multiple documents (referred to and used by participants) that new light was shed on the broader context, within which collaborative efforts unfolded. For the people I was observing, collaboration was meaningful primarily because it was entangled in a broader pursuit of improving healthcare services at a national, not merely local level. Reaching text-based agreement was an effortful process of drawing upon and incorporating "evidence" and standards that had been produced through distant activities. By identifying the origins of multiple "standards" and evidence, which served as the material linchpins between local and distant activities, I provide a thick description of material associations among multiple texts and highlight consequences for inter-organizational collaboration.

Theoretical Background: Studying Documents and Material Culture

Ethnographers in general and organizational ethnographers, in particular, have long paid attention to the role of artefacts in social practices (Fayard and Metiu 2012, 2014; Osterlund 2004; Østerlund et al. 2015; Shankar 2018; Shankar, et al. 2017; Yates 1989; Yates and Orlikowski 1992). Ethnography itself is a practice of producing numerous documents (fieldnotes, field reports, narratives) (Riles 2006). Organizational communicative practices become distinctive through the ongoing use of certain material objects and documents. Documentary practices are constitutive of, and perform, a material culture. "Material culture is active ... artifacts are produced so as to transform, materially, socially, ideologically" (Hodder 2003, p. 159). It is the exchange of artefacts and documents itself that constructs social relations (Bechky 2003a). Hospital records, for example, have been found to help create alliances (Raffel 2014). As another example, in her ethnographic study of a semiconductor manufacturing company, Bechky showed how objects inscribe social relations across interacting occupational communities (Bechky 2003a, 2003b). In short, "an adequate study of social interaction depends on the incorporation of mute material evidence" (Hodder 2003, p. 159). As one form of mute material evidence, documents can be an important tool for ethnographic organizational research.

The place of documents in ethnographic research is nevertheless ambivalent. On one hand, documents are described as the "most despised of all ethnographic subjects" (Latour 1988, p. 54). On the other hand, documents are regarded as paradigmatic artefacts of ethnographic research and may help us "apprehend modernity ethnographically" (Riles 2006, p. 2). For example, rich descriptions of documentary practices help us understand how documents become crucial technological elements of the bureaucratic organization (Heimer 2006), medical work (Osterlund 2004) and managerial work (Yates 1989). Documents become increasingly important as they become digitized or are digitally produced (Fayard and Metiu 2012; Shankar et al. 2017). A number of authors argue that "written documents' ethnographic centrality has increased" (Shankar 2018, p. 18).

So, how may we explore documents and documentary practices? The materiality of the documents matters both for those who produce and use them and for those who study them. For one, documents endure physically. At the same time, documents constitute "a form of artifact produced under certain material conditions (not everyone can write, or write in a certain way, or have access to relevant technologies of reproduction) embedded within social and ideological systems" (Hodder 2003, p. 157). They are artefacts entangled in social practices and inscribe social purposes, in particular, goals to document (Shankar et al. 2017), i.e. represent and communicate stuff. Of course, documents may serve other purposes as well, depending on whether they are formal and or less formal documents, e.g., personal diaries (Lincoln and Guba 1985) or memos (Yates 1989).

The organizational ethnographer needs to be particularly attentive to the particular social contexts in which documents are produced and shared, interpreted and reinterpreted differently across time and space. The "written text is an artifact, capable of transmission, manipulation, and alteration ... doing different things contextually through time" (Hodder 2003, p. 160). As a text is read and re-read in different contexts, it acquires new, often contradictory meanings. As a specific document travels across time and space, the gap between authors and readers widens. This may not only mean a physical or temporal gap, but may also pertain to distance in ideology and epistemological stances. Readers of a document produced in the past are likely to construct different social and political strategies to form an interpretation. In that sense, documents may transcend context and be symbolically enriched.

For ethnographers, documents may offer rich historical insights – how different domains of practice become more or less intentionally related, or, indeed, remain deeply disconnected. While it may be tempting to think of documents as meaning carriers, meaning does not reside in the text, but in the practices of writing and reading, or more generally, communicative practices (Fayard and Metiu 2014; Yates and Orlikowski 1992). Documents become important objects of study if we aim to untangle political aspects of certain phenomena and explore multiple and potentially conflicting voices and interacting interpretations. By tracking inter-temporal patterns and temporal variations in interpretations of documents, by moving between past and present, organizational ethnographers may decipher a "document's career" (Meehan 1986). They may find that the original meaning becomes lost, or discover continuities across participants' current narratives and past documented narratives.

In sum, documents constitute an object of ethnographic research, which offers valuable insights into organizational practices and social interactions. What needs to be better understood, however, is how face-to-face interactions (conversations constitutive of communicative practices) are complemented by, and embedded within, a nexus of documentary practices; how the co-production of a document in a local interaction setting is enveloped within a nexus of trans-local documentary practices. In what follows, I present in detail how I made extensive use of documents in my fieldwork in the context of an inter-organizational collaboration in healthcare.

Empirical Study of Inter-organizational Collaboration

Empirical Setting

In my empirical study, part of a larger research project,[1] I observed how commissioners, so-called Primary Care Trusts (hereafter PCTs), in a large geographical area in central England sought to define and jointly agree with healthcare providers (three hospitals) a set of service specifications, which would eventually become part of a new contract. My focus has been on the process of inter-organizational collaboration through which a new TIA service specification would be agreed. Since 2007, there has been a lot of emphasis in the UK on improving the management of stroke, in general, and of Transient Ischaemic Attack (TIA – colloquially known as small stroke) in particular.

A key driver for the increasing interest in stroke and TIA management and treatment in the English National Health Service (NHS) was the development of scientific knowledge. A growing number of studies showed that if stroke and TIA were treated as fast as possible, major health benefits could result. In the case of TIA, in particular, it had been shown that if patients, presenting with TIA, were treated immediately (e.g. within 1–2 days), then the risk of having a full stroke subsequently would be reduced by as much as 80% (Rothwell et al. 2007).

The project I observed was initiated by the commissioning organization (PCT). According to a report by the regional stroke networks for the PCT's geographical area, "the service for patients with TIA was not yet well-developed. Neuro-vascular assessment was not available daily. Patients with high risk TIAs therefore waited more than 24 hours for assessment … the service was not yet achieving expected targets." Sue (a senior PCT manager) described the project as "virtuous": it was about saving lives without much investment.

From the very beginning, commissioners and providers worked closely. Yet, the different groups involved were aiming to achieve different things. Commissioners sought to embed standards in their contracts and to be assured that better "value" would be extracted from standardized contracts. Providers would agree on new service specifications so long as the cost of implementation and changes required would be reasonable. Healthcare professionals (employees of providers) would agree to comply with new guidelines so long as proposed changes would not impose a burden on their practice and their jurisdictions.

A first draft of the specification was jointly written in February 2010 after a large workshop, in which clinicians, consultants, commissioners, nurses, managers of the acute trust and from the stroke network took part. As Cathryn (service improvement manager) explained to me, "agreeing the TIA pathway" was the core objective of all meetings. Through a written specification, the clinical pathway, service standards, and workforce issues would be clearly defined. The focus of my analysis was thus on the process by which the specification, as text, evolved through discussions, and its content was negotiated and agreed by stakeholders (commissioners, providers, stroke network, GPs).

I was initially sensitized by a scholarly definition of inter-organizational collaboration as "a complex set of ongoing communicative processes among individuals who act as members of both the collaboration and of the separate organizational hierarchies to which they are accountable" (Hardy et al. 2005, p. 59). I approached collaboration as an irreducibly local accomplishment, constitutive of situated discussions, modifications, amendments, and responses to the written statements of the specification.

Thick Descriptions of Situated Social Interactions

In this section, I present some of my fieldnotes taken at a series of meetings among all parties involved.

Fieldnotes from Meeting 1

Lara (Assistant Director of Commissioning, who is leading the TIA project) addresses the providers: "As commissioners we want a robust and sustainable TIA pathway … at the moment it is quite general … We need to look at the skill mix and [other] provider issues… how far away [are providers] from delivering [the pathway]? … [But] first and foremost … we [need to] get the clinical pathway right … We want to make sure the wording [in the specification] is appropriate… [we don't want] to make it so prescriptive … but we also need to specify standards … we, commissioners, try to get one specification … to describe roughly the pathway and then be able to look at the uptake … we don't intend to monitor every bit of the pathway … only the things that are sensible to monitor … We need to look at the specification … paragraph by paragraph."

Extensive discussion followed about these issues. One of most important paragraphs was the following:

"People who experience a TIA need a rapid specialist assessment at a one stop outpatient service. Such a service will ensure that referrers and patients can expect a confirmed diagnosis, relevant investigations performed, results available and interventions organised in a single visit. This assessment will be completed within 24 hours for higher risk patients and 7 days for lower risk patients. Where possible TIA Clinics should allow for same day referrals." (Excerpt from specifications)

This paragraph sparked a number of conversations.

The Stroke Consultant asks: "When does the clock start? If the patient presents with TIA to a GP [General Practitioner] and the GP refers the patient hours after the TIA, we can't be responsible!"

Lara says that "as a health economy we need to monitor from the moment they [patients with TIA] are seen by GPs … . I am saying [that's how it is defined] in the Vital Signs targets … The definition of vital signs drives the specification."

The consultant agrees, but raises the issue about providers (at times) not being responsible for delays, for example.

Lara does not want to disagree, and admits "it would be helpful to expand on that."

Alan (General Practitioner) says that "we need to be careful with targets. They might skew appropriate clinical behaviour. We need to take targets with a pinch of salt."

Sue (Service Redesign Manager) objects and says that "that [the sentence Alan referred to] comes from the National Stroke Strategy (NSS). You can't change the wording!"

Lara says that "we, as commissioners, are interested in the entire health economy…"

Another stroke consultant interrupts her: "You've talked a lot about the 'health economy'. What do you mean?"

Lara says that she means every provider in the entire area.

The first consultant adds: "In fact, the clock starts with the patient." (that is, the patient has to go to the GP or other healthcare professional.) "We need to clearly define the event in order to determine which service is needed: the 24-hour [for high risk patients] or the 7-day service [for low risk]."

Lara suggests that they leave that for the moment, as they have run out of time.

On one hand, commissioners sought to specify standards and ensure that providers would agree to comply with those standards. On the other hand, providers sought to untangle the "wording" and be assured that they would be sensibly monitored. The inter-organizational collaborative effort was thus an ongoing negotiation among commissioners, providers (representatives from three local hospitals) and healthcare professionals (doctors, nurses, GPs). In what follows, I summarize some of the key changes brought about through negotiation.

→ The first draft of the specification was updated to "reflect" the discussions that took place at the first meeting. Certain sentences were added and some wording was modified. For example, in the aforementioned paragraph of the specification it was clarified that: *"This assessment will be completed within 24 hours <u>from the point of referral</u> for higher risk patients and 7 days for lower risk patients "* (Amendment underscored)

→ Upon Lara's request, the providers (more than 2 acute hospital trusts) provided a "gap analysis" and the "position of each trust against the specification". The responses of all trusts took the form of *writing formally* to commissioners and making specific reviewer-type comments on each paragraph, for example, on workforce issues, operational procedures which are in place and demonstrate "adherence to" the requirements, KPIs, standards of access, plans to recruit more staff, tools. Responses also included written plans for how a requirement would be soon addressed, e.g. access to brain scanning.

→ Subsequently, commissioners made detailed notes and raised questions about each point in the providers' written responses. Some important points they made were the following: clarification of doctor availability, timescales of the plans, explaining that they won't pay twice for certain procedures, workforce models, highlighting "non-compliance", raising training issues. At times, this process of scrutinizing revealed some gaps in their own understanding of the specification. For example, the specification required availability of 7-day neuro-imaging and carotid ultrasound provision. The response of a trust was that they would provide 7-day CT scanning and 5-day MRI scanning. Commissioners were uncertain if that was "acceptable". They liaised with the local network of vascular surgeons (known as stroke network) to clarify that issue. Commissioners finally sent their feedback about specific elements of the specification in a *formal letter.*

→ *Formal letters,* acknowledging commissioners' feedback and issues raised, were sent by providers back to commissioners.

→ Subsequent face-to-face meetings were attended by a senior national figure invited by the stroke network. Providers gave a presentation with the topic *"Meeting the specification: staffing, access to diagnostics, delivery against KPIs and timescales for implementation".* These presentations were the updated positions of providers for key specification requirements; for example, confirming that "referral forms will be faxed directly to the TIA clinic"; "high risk patients will be seen within 24 hours", etc.

→ Discussions *reaffirmed the content of agreements* and highlighted *new disagreements.* For instance, "John (national stroke network) expressed concerns and advised that the Stroke Strategy does not specify that a Stroke Consultant must see all patients, but it does focus on the demonstrable skills and competencies of staff. He advised that commissioners need to be assured that a robust staffing model is agreed and an appropriate infrastructure needs to be available on each site. At the end of the presentation, John confirmed this was a robust proposal from Trust X and asked for Vital Signs information from all trusts." (Fieldnotes)

→ A final meeting was arranged. An updated version of the specification, which included payment arrangements (based on national tariff policy) as well as a service audit was circulated prior to the meeting. That meeting took place to "sign off" the service specification. A few amendments were made and a single referral form was circulated to everyone. After the meeting, agreed amendments were incorporated in the specs, and final confirmation of agreement followed.

The central role of textual practices is manifested throughout the process of inter-organizational collaboration. The attention and energy of all parties was channelled toward reading, writing, reviewing, commenting, negotiating, deleting and adding text, rephrasing certain sentences, etc. Verbal conversations were anchored in an evolving document. Yet, their collaborative efforts, I argue below, were also enveloped in a broader, continually morphing, nexus of textual practices.

Thick Descriptions of Associations among Official Documents

Throughout the collaborative project, references to and invocations of multiple, official and immutable documents were made. For example, commissioners repeatedly noted that, "the source of the specification is NICE guidance (2008), RCP stroke guidelines (2008), NSS Quality markers (2007), and Vital signs monitoring return". The PCT scored very low at vital signs (below 50% of Transient Ischaemic Attack (TIA) cases with a higher risk of stroke who are treated within 24 hours – 2010). A recent quality review (2010) also noted that the PCT had only met a bit more than 50% of the *quality standards for stoke and TIA*, while "there was not yet a commissioning plan for TIA services."

References to multiple official documents produced by other official organizations (the Department of Health, NICE, see below) were repeatedly made during meeting discussions. Recall the Service Designer, who ardently argued that a sentence of the draft document came from the National Stroke Strategy and that they "can't change the wording!"; and the contentious issue of "when the clock starts for a 24-hour service." Perhaps, most significantly, the project was launched, not due to pressures to better manage healthcare resources, but because "there is a clear, new evidence base for the management of TIA" (as Sarah, a Service Improvement Manager, said at the first TIA meeting). All parties accepted this as a "fact".

A number of questions then need to be further explored: How did evidence "reach" the specification, since evidence producers didn't take part in meetings? Was the claim for the evidence-basedness of the specification pretentious, masking the real interests of commissioners and other parties?

In an effort to address these questions, I examined associations and temporal patterns in the use of certain documents. I found that the consecutive production of a number of seminal publications paved the way for scientific evidence to reach the collaborative project I observed. Table 13.1 summarizes these documents.

Table 13.1 List of "seminal documents"

Document title
• Publication of the National Stroke Strategy (NSS) in 2007
• National Sentinel Stroke Audits (2007) results (published by RCP)
• Development of National Institute of Clinical Evidence (NICE) "Stroke: national clinical guideline for diagnosis and initial management of acute stroke and transient ischaemic attack (TIA)" (guideline 68) (2008). NICE was commissioned by the Department of Health (DoH) to produce this guideline
• Publication of the full version of the above NICE national guideline by the Royal College of Physicians (RCP) in 2008
• "National clinical guideline for stroke" (3rd edition) Prepared by the Intercollegiate Stroke Working Party and published by the Royal College of Physicians (RCP) in 2008

(Continued)

Table 13.1 (Continued)

Document title

- NICE quality standards for stroke (2009)
- Launch of the NHS national "Stroke Improvement Programme" and the TIA national project (2009–2010), which has been led by regional stroke clinical networks
- Development of the national "vital sign" monitoring indicator for the management of TIA patients (vital signs are targets, against which PCTs' performance is measured)
- Development of mandatory "Best Practice Tariff" (BPT) for adhering to specific clinical standards (as defined by the NSS and NICE guidelines) by the Payment by Results Group of the Department of Health in 2011.

I traced the origins and associations of these authoritative documents and sought to foreground the hidden political work that was necessary for scientific evidence to find its way in the inter-organizational collaborative project I had observed. In what follows, I first present the seminal scientific study, which attracted the attention of multiple expert, policy making and managerial groups. I then offer an account of how this original evidence was reinterpreted across time and space.

The Production of Scientific Evidence

The EXPRESS (Early use of eXisting PREventive Strategies for Stroke) study carried out by a large research team based in Oxford University (Rothwell et al. 2007) and published by the prestigious journal *Lancet* became one of the most widely cited (not only by academics, but also policy makers and clinicians) papers in research and policy making circles. The study, which "was nested within a rigorous population-based incidence study of all TIA and stroke (Oxford Vascular Study; OXVASC)", aimed to "determine the effect of more rapid treatment after TIA and minor stroke in patients who are not admitted direct to hospital" (p. 1432). This two-phased research yielded some solid findings: "Early initiation of existing treatments after TIA or minor stroke was *associated* with an 80% reduction in the risk of early recurrent stroke" (emphasis added). Scientific results from the EXPRESS and a rapidly growing number of other studies (Luengo-Fernandez, et al. 2009) indicated that early initiation of existing treatments (i.e. aspirin dose) for stroke and TIA could produce significant health benefits, i.e. without investing in expensive new technology, it was possible to significantly improve health outcomes.

The EXPRESS study publication essentially became an "immutable, presentable, readable, and combinable" artefact (Latour 1988, p. 26) that would be subsequently used to mobilize a wider network of individuals, ideas and organizations. It is important to note that research findings merely indicated the potential and simply outlined "implications" (albeit important) for improved healthcare delivery. They didn't prescribe either how exactly services should be reconfigured or what the optimum time horizon (e.g. exactly 24 hours) is for managing TIA patients. It was another group who would embark upon the task of defining precisely how the national service should respond to these important scientific findings: the Department of Health (DoH) and the National Institute for Clinical Excellence (NICE; in 2018, "NICE" stood for National Institute for Health and Care Excellence).

Reinterpreting Scientific Evidence (First Wave): The Development of a National Stroke Strategy

A document that became the catalyst for the diffusion of these widely acclaimed scientific findings by Rothwell et al. (2007) was the National Stroke Strategy (NSS) (DoH 2007). According to its authors, the NSS, which was sent to all NHS executives and clinical directors,

> has been developed by six expert project groups, comprised of representatives from the wide range of professionals who support people with stroke, people who have had a stroke, carers and voluntary associations … It sets a framework of quality markers (QMs) for raising the quality of stroke prevention, treatment, care and support over the next decade.
>
> *(p. 4)*

The then Secretary of State for Health, Alan Johnson also noted (Foreword in the NSS) that:

> this strategy presents 20 quality markers outlining the features of a good … These markers are distilled into a ten-point plan for action to guide those affected by stroke, their carers and the public in looking at the services available locally. Collectively, these markers set an ambitious agenda to deliver world-class stroke services, from prevention right through to life-long support.

The authors of the NSS argued for a much closer attention to be paid to people presenting with a transient ischaemic attack (TIA) or minor stroke in order to minimize the chances of a full stroke occurring. It suggested that:

> a more urgent response to both stroke and TIA will save lives and reduce long-term disability … Investigating and treating high-risk patients with TIA within 24 hours could produce an 80 per cent reduction in the number of people who go on to have a full stroke [citing the EXPRESS study].

The NSS then articulated specific expectations for the management of stroke and TIA patients by specifying the two main quality markers (QMs) related to TIA services (see Figure 13.1).

The authors of the National Stroke Strategy reinterpreted the published scientific evidence and created prescriptions: quality markers (QMs). QMs were not

TIA and minor stroke

QM5. Assessment – referral to specialist

Markers of a quality service

- Immediate referral for appropriately urgent specialist assessment and investigation is considered in all patients pressenting with a recent TIA or minor stroke

- A system which identifies as urgent those with early risk of potentially preventable full stroke – to be assessed within 24 hours in high risk cases; all other cases are assessed within seven days

- Provision to enable brain imaging within 24 hours and carotid intervention, echocardiography and ECG within 48 hours where clinically indicated.

QM6. Treatment

Marker of a quality service

- All patients with TIA or minor stroke are followed up one month after the event, either in primary or secondary care.

Figure 13.1   Snapshots from the National Stroke Strategy

evidence per se, but service standards, i.e. stable, identifiable and ostensive characteristics of a good service, which would hypothetically result in better health outcomes.

Reinterpreting Scientific Evidence (Second Wave): The Production of Clinical Guidelines

In conjunction with the publication of the NSS, the Department of Health (DoH) commissioned the National Institute for Clinical Excellence (NICE) to produce a national *clinical guideline*. The remit of NICE was to "develop a clinical guideline for the diagnosis and initial management of acute stroke and transient ischaemic attack (TIA)" (National Collaborating Centre for Chronic Conditions 2008). The publication of the guideline in 2008 followed that of the NSS. The development of the guideline transformed evidence into another form of information ("recommendations" and statements of clinical standards) that eventually became useable in the context of improving TIA services. According to the producers of the guideline, their aim was (Ibid. p. 5):

> to provide a user-friendly, clinical, evidence-based guideline for the National Health Service (NHS) in England and Wales that:
> – offers best clinical advice for the diagnosis and acute management of stroke and TIA
> – is based on best published clinical and economic evidence, alongside expert consensus

- takes into account patient choice and informed decision-making
- defines the major components of NHS care provision for the management of acute stroke and TIA
- details areas of uncertainty or controversy requiring further research
- provides a choice of guideline versions for differing audiences.

It is recommended that the guideline "should also be read alongside" the NSS; "however, the NICE Guideline Development Group (GDG) feel that their recommendations are based on evidence derived from all of the relevant literature as identified by systematic methodology" (Ibid. p. 4) (suggesting that their recommendations are more "robust", or, at least, of a different kind). In the full version of the guideline, the NICE GDG demonstrated that they adopted a very rigorous, transparent and robust methodology (National Collaborating Centre for Chronic Conditions 2008). The guideline comprised 12 evidence-based recommendations (see Appendix 1).

As prior research has shown, far from being a theoretical, research exercise, the production of clinical guidelines is a practical activity:

> The avowed objective of guidelines is to change healthcare practices by replacing substandard interventions. While maintaining a proactive stance, guideline developers are also aware of the fact that they need to adjust recommendations to prevailing external conditions … By evoking possible scenarios, guideline developers attempt to manage relations between recommendations, users, and other relevant stakeholders.
>
> *(Knaapen et al. 2010, pp. 690–691)*

The NICE GDG indeed asserted that their recommendations needed to be implemented by many other stakeholders (NICE also develops "implementation" guidance). The recommendations represented *carefully constructed* textual statements. "Claims are excerpted from publications … and embedded in guidelines … This is far from a mechanical transposition, but this process presupposes and depends on the upstream production of specifically formatted claims" (Knaapen et al. 2010, p. 686). Moreover, the NICE recommendations for TIA (NICE 2008) represented a series of statements, which aimed to "weed out unwarranted variation in diagnostic or therapeutic practice and to enhance the scientific nature of medical care delivered" (Berg et al. 2000, p. 766). NICE recommendations transformed evidence claims into prescriptions for clinical practice. For example, it was asserted that "people suspected with TIA *should* have the diagnosis established within 24 hours." According to its authors, the "guidelines provide clinicians, managers and service users with summaries of evidence and recommendations for clinical practice. Implementation of guidelines in practice, supported by regular audit, improves the processes of care and clinical outcome" (NICE 2008, p. 4).

In essence, apart from synthesizing scientific evidence, guidelines produced devices for regulating clinical practice and provided ready-made justifications for altering practices (Thévenot 2009). For example, NICE developed devices, such as the NICE quality standards for stroke, the NICE implementation and commissioning guides, as well as the development of a pathway "algorithm" (see Appendix 2).

Reinterpreting Clinical Guidelines (First Wave):
The Production of Performance Metrics

Following the publication of the NICE recommendations, the DoH created the following vital "monitoring" indicators:

A   *Transient Ischaemic Attack (TIA) cases with a higher risk of stroke who are treated within 24 hours*
B   *Number of people who have a Transient Ischaemic Attack (TIA) who are at higher risk of stroke*

(DoH 2010)

The so-called "Vital Sign" for TIA, which was repeatedly invoked throughout the discussions of the TIA project, defined high risk patients "in accordance with the NSS and NICE guidelines", i.e. using the $ABCD2^2$ score of 4 and above. Furthermore, it incorporated all those investigations and treatments that were recommended in NSS and NICE: blood tests, electrocardiogram, brain scan, completing of carotid imaging, commencement of treatment with aspirin, statin or control of blood pressure. All these processes, "in line with NICE clinical standards", should be completed within 24 hours for high risk patients. Commissioners were required to monitor this indicator and "return" the data to DoH. Figure 13.2 shows an example of the output of the monitoring process.

The creators of vital sign essentially transformed "clinical standards" into a different kind of device. To comply with Vital Signs monitoring standards, commissioners, providers, clinicians and all those who were involved in TIA management needed to create relevant data infrastructure. Clear rules for counting and accounting TIA patients were provided in the official DoH publication: e.g. excluding admitted patients, counting only those attending outpatient clinics. Furthermore, in their published FAQ (November 2009), the authors of the vital sign publication envisaged different scenarios of "how to count time":

> Within 24 hours of presentation, i.e. the first time an individual with a suspected TIA presents with symptoms to medical personnel. For example, for patients who dial '999' [emergency number], the 24-hour clock starts as soon as a paramedic reaches the patient; or, if a patient calls their GP, the clock starts when the GP sees the patient.

Thus, the definition of "when the clock starts", which preoccupied and was the objective of negotiation among different parties during the TIA project I observed, was also relevant to a distant set of actors – those collecting and analysing vital sign data at a local and national level.

Title: Number of Transient Ischaemic Attack (TIA) cases with a higher risk of stroke who are then subsequently treated within 24 hours
Summary: VSMR TIA is the collection of data to monitor cases with a higher risk of stroke

Period: October to December 2010
Source: Department of Health: Unify2 data collection - VSMR
Basis: Commissioner
Published: 16th February 2011
Revised: –
Status: Published
Contact: Stella Gondo - Unify2@dh.gsi.gov.uk

SHA Level Data

Year	Quarter	Code	Name	Transient Ischaemic Attack (TIA) cases with a higher risk of stroke who are treated within 24 hours	Number of people who have a Transient Ischaemic Attack (TIA) who are at higher risk of stroke	Percentage of Transient Ischaemic Attack (TIA) cases with a higher risk of stroke who are treated within 24 hours
2010–11	3	–	**England**	2,667	4,161	64.1%
2010–11	3	Q30	North East	84	114	73.7%
2010–11	3	Q31	North West	299	519	57.6%
2010–11	3	Q32	Yorkshire and the Humber	184	367	50.1%
2010–11	3	Q33	East Midlands	436	606	71.9%
2010–11	3	Q34	West Midlands	204	428	47.7%
2010–11	3	Q35	East of England	173	355	48.7%
2010–11	3	Q36	London	483	518	93.2%
2010–11	3	Q37	South East Coast	156	267	58.4%
2010–11	3	Q38	South Central	289	387	74.7%
2010–11	3	Q39	South Wes	359	600	59.8%

Figure 13.2 Vital sign monitoring indicators across England. Notably, the percentage of high risk TIA cases treated within 24 hours is much higher in London than the rest of England (probably due to easy access to acute hospitals).

Moreover, the creators of vital sign monitor indicators (the DoH stroke unit) argued that they did "not deal with clinical issues ... addressed in the relevant guidance (e.g. the RCP's National Clinical Guideline for Stroke (third edition), The National Stroke Strategy etc.)."Yet, they were decisively meddling with clinical practice by demanding that additional tasks of collecting data, codifying TIA management processes, and calculating time be carried out by healthcare professionals. They could legitimately demand these tasks since NICE and NSS had provided unambiguous, explicit definitions of what counts as clinically appropriate practice.

Reinterpreting Clinical Guidelines (Second Wave): The Production of Payment Tariffs

In 2011–2012 the DoH introduced "a mandatory Best Practice Tariff (BPT) for non-admitted services for suspected TIA (mini-stroke), aligned with quality markers 5 and 6 of the National Stroke Strategy [the authors copied and pasted the quality markers from the NSS]" (DoH 2011, p. 65). BPT was a new technology, which, according to DoH Best Practice Tariffs[3]

> represents one of the enablers for the NHS to improve quality, by reducing unexplained variation and universalizing best practice. With best practice defined as care, that is both clinical and cost-effective, these tariffs will also help the NHS deliver the productivity gains required to meet the tough financial challenges ahead. The aim is to have tariffs that are structured and priced appropriately both to incentivize and adequately reimburse for the costs of high quality care ... linking payment to (best practice) clinical characteristics.

BPTs essentially reinterpreted the NSS and NICE recommendations by creating another type of standard: currency for payment. Like the creators of vital sign indicators, the creators of the BPT relied on widely accepted specifications of what counted as legitimate clinical practice (quality care). Furthermore, they were able to point at "unexplained variation" and reprimand providers who did not adhere to best clinical practice. Interestingly, the BPT for TIA

> is aligned with the vital sign for TIAs and mini-stroke, for which the time-frame is currently defined as follows:
> (a) the clock starts at the time of first relevant presentation of the patient to any healthcare professional (e.g. a paramedic, GP, stroke physician, district nurse or A&E staff)
> (b) the clock stops 24 hours after this initial contact, by which time all investigations and treatments should be completed.

In addition to prescribing the required investigations for achieving BPT status, the BPT ensured that additional payments would be made to those who perform well in the vital sign for TIA.[4] The collaboration we observed relied heavily upon the BPT for TIA. In essence, the BPT not only encouraged practitioners to conform to NICE recommendations, but made adherence to clinical standards mandatory, if additional payment was to be secured. For adherence to be made possible, practitioners involved in the commissioning and delivering of TIA management had to produce accounting information as well as specific performance measures (vital sign). Effectively, clinical guidelines had been reinterpreted through developing a monitoring and payment infrastructure. NICE "algorithms" were also complemented with different kinds of payment algorithms (see Appendix 3).

Spreading Best Practices: A Nationally Coordinated Effort to Improve TIA Services

Significant efforts to support extended coordination for delivering improved TIA management across the country were made by NHS Improvement. The NHS Improvement, according to its website (https://improvement.nhs.uk/home/)

> … *aims to achieve sustainable effective pathways and systems, share improvement resources and learning, increase impact and ensure value for money to improve the efficiency and quality of NHS services. Working with clinical networks and NHS organisations across England, NHS Improvement helps to transform, deliver and build sustainable improvements across the entire pathway of care in cancer, diagnostics, heart, lung and stroke services.*

Accordingly, in 2009–2010, the Stroke Improvement Programme National Project 2009–10 was organised by NHS Improvement. A key component of the programme was the TIA national project, which "covers implementation of quality markers five and six of the National Stroke Strategy". The NHS Improvement TIA project was delivered at 10 NHS "demonstration sites". In 10 geographical areas, the improvement of TIA services was pursued through the active involvement of stroke networks, acute hospital trusts and (in only a few cases) commissioners. TIA improvement projects across the country were effectively multi-party collaborations, which aimed at specifying and improving TIA management in accordance with common parameters:

– Specifying the local needs to reduce time to treat TIA patients
– Setting-up a 7-day/week outpatient TIA clinic in order to improve the management of TIA patients
– Reducing the time it takes to refer, diagnose and manage TIA patients, especially high risk patients, and minimizing it within 24 hours
– Addressing the requirements of the Vital Sign Monitoring Return for TIA: "proportion of high risk patients that are treated within 24 hours" (notably, on many projects, difficulties in understanding the indicator were reported)

- Re-thinking the current and future management of TIA in terms of "points of access, staffing/competency requirements, routes the patient should take (pathway), access to imaging, referral for surgery within 2 weeks (for those indicated)"
- Differentiating among and "optimizing" pathways for high risk and low risk TIA patients. In some cases, pathways were visualized as algorithms (as per NICE algorithms)
- Enhancing communications between referrers and TIA clinic and other groups and triaging through a universal pro-forma, which uses the ABCD2 "risk assessment tool"
- Establishing "robust" data collection and "auditing" system
- Ensuring access to brain imaging within 24 hours and of carotid interventions within 2 days

The project I followed, I gradually found out, was influenced by exemplary TIA projects. Indeed, one commissioning manager had visited one demonstration site to gather more information. Most importantly, the draft service specification was "informed by the specifications" developed in other demonstration sites.

Summary

In the preceding sections, I presented an account of how text-based, multi-party collaboration was accomplished in a particular setting. A thick description of situated human interactions revealed that the collaborative task of developing and agreeing upon the content of a document (the TIA service specification) involved spelling out contractual obligations and best clinical practice, articulating in writing service standards and delivery requirements (e.g., staffing issues), creating instruments for documenting compliance with standards (e.g. service algorithms, forms) and outlining payment methods. Upon deeper investigation, I found that none of these activities would have been possible without the construction of a wider nexus of textual practices.

I developed thick descriptions of associations among different documentary practices of reporting scientific findings; reinterpreting scientific evidence to develop national strategies, quality markers, clinical recommendations, standards and algorithms; re-contextualizing such strategies and clinical recommendations to manufacture monitoring devices and payment tariffs; orchestrating a national effort to spread, through documentation, best "TIA improvement" practices. Such thick descriptions, I argued, significantly complemented and enhanced detailed observations of the situated doings and sayings of the actors that took part in the collaboration. They help me account for the embeddedness of the situated and localized social interactions in a wider nexus of textual practices.

For example, the meaning attached to the EXPRESS study by Oxford academics was enriched over time, as the study was interpreted and reinterpreted by different social actors and institutions. As Hodder insightfully noted (2003) the load of meaning invested in an artefact increased through time. Yet, re-interpretations, omissions and alterations as well as additions to the conclusions reported in that study produced multiple consequences for the entire "health economy" (to use the expression of the TIA project lead). Most significantly perhaps, the local actors taking part in the inter-organizational collaboration project had to make do with the given materials (definitions, algorithms, standards, etc.) produced within a nexus of textual practices without being able to negotiate the (material, ideological) form of such materials. For example, the NICE algorithm of TIA management represented clinical practice as a disembodied rational activity, suppressing an understanding of medicine as an embodied practical activity, in which case-based, narrative modes of reasoning are key (Montgomery 2005); these algorithms were one of the many other artefacts that served as "rationality badges" (Clarke 1999). Collaborators were constrained as well as enabled by the text(s) they inherited through a set of densely interconnected documentary practices.

Reflections and Conclusion

Documents are political, epistemic and cultural artefacts that may "strip away context" (Riles 2006, p. 9), i.e. obscure the conditions under which they were originally produced by real people and social interactions. Documents abstract, i.e. de-contextualize and transform (Muniesa et al. 2007) as well as inscribe certain meanings. At the same time, documents may *create* the context of situated local interactions. Insofar as "authoritative" and other documents, which have already been produced by distant actors (deemed stakeholders from a participant's point view of view), are persistently referenced and recurrently drawn upon in local inter-action settings, it may be ethnographically profitable to trail associations with distant documentary practices. As shown in my study, authoritative documents produced by distant actors profoundly shaped the motivations, argumentative strategies, and negotiation moves of local actors. Without exploring in detail the nexus of documentary practices that had unfolded over several years and across different places, I would have developed an impoverished image of the context, with which local interactions and negotiations took place.

Moreover, the approach suggested in this paper, i.e. to situate local social processes within trans-local documentary practices, also helps unveil the political and ideological work that documents may perform. Documents may render certain ideologies more visible than others. For example, the ideology of "regulatory objectivity" in medicine (Cambrosio et al. 2006) was made visible and dominant in discussions around TIA management. Commissioners, providers and healthcare professionals were discussing definitions, such as "when the clock starts", and statements drawn from NICE's evidence-based recommendations, which objectified medical practice, and healthcare management practice, more generally. It was telling that algorithms (see Appendices 1 and 2) were regarded as adequate representations of medical practice – even by medical professionals themselves, who were part of the negotiations. The official documents at hand prompted all parties to bracket out the messiness of "practical rationality" (Sandberg and Tsoukas 2011) and omit the lived experiences of professional medical workers. Such messiness was missing from the solidified accounts of "appropriate clinical practice" provided in the documents and algorithms, which were available to social actors. The organizational ethnographer's job then may be to unveil, through rich descriptions of documentary practices and inter-temporal associations among documents, how meanings are being excluded, consolidated as well as contested over time.

A number of research challenges may also need to be borne in mind. First of all, it may be difficult to obtain "member checks" (Hodder 2003). Some documents are mute and access to authors' doings may be well concealed. There may be no possibility of interaction with a spoken emic insider. Yet inter-temporal patterning of how documents travel over time may provide a form of check. Moreover, it may be tempting to overemphasize the role of belief, ideas and intentions in documentary practices, e.g. to assume a document was written for this or that reason. There is some risk of retrospective attribution (Tsoukas 2010). Importantly, the researcher needs to be mindful of her/his own contribution to the interpretation of salient associations among documentary practices. The ethnographer herself/himself engages in epistemic practices of defining the boundaries of a social context and potentially reifying the context within which documentary practices unfold. Hence, it is crucial that thick descriptions of associations across documentary practices are developed. This chapter offered one way by which such thick descriptions could be produced.

Notes

1 I gratefully acknowledge the generous funding from the UK NIHR SDO programme on "Management Practice" (project SDO 08/1808/244). Neither the NIHR SDO nor the UK Department of Health are responsible for the content of and the ideas expressed in this article.
2 ABCD2 score is a validated, seven-point, risk-stratification tool to identify patients at high risk of stroke following a TIA. "A", stands for "age", "B" stands for "blood pressure", "C" stands for "clinical features", first "D" stands for "duration of symptoms", and second "D" standards for "Diabetes melitius".
3 www.dh.gov.uk/en/Managingyourorganisation/NHSFinancialReforms/DH_105080
4 The tariff has a structure: (i) a base tariff of £450 (meeting minimum criteria of "best practice"), (ii) additional payment of £92 for treatment of high risk patients within 24 hours, and (iii) additional payment of £92 for using MRI.

References

Bechky, Beth A. 2003a 'Object lessons: Workplace artifacts as representations of occupational jurisdiction'. *American Journal of Sociology* 109: 720–752.
Bechky, Beth A. 2003b 'Sharing meaning across occupational communities: The transformation of understanding on a production floor'. *Organization Science* 14: 312–330.
Berg, Marc, Klasien Horstman, Saskia Plass, and Michelle Van Heusden. 2000 'Guidelines, professionals and the production of objectivity: Standardisation and the professionalism of insurance medicine'. *Sociology of Health & Illness* 22: 765–791.

Cambrosio, Alberto, Peter Keating, Thomas Schlich, and George Weisz. 2006 'Regulatory objectivity and the generation and management of evidence in medicine'. *Social Science & Medicine* 63: 189–199.

Clarke, Lee. 1999 *Mission Improbable: Using Fantasy Documents to Tame Disaster*. Chicago, IL: University of Chicago Press.

Department of Health (DoH). 2007 *National Stroke Strategy*. London: Department of Health.

Department of Health (DoH). 2010 *Vital Signs Monitoring Return (VSRM) – Commissioner Based* (version 1.11). London: DoH.

Department of Health (DoH). 2011 *Payment by Results Guidance 2011–2012*. London: DoH.

Fayard, Anne-Laure and Anca Metiu. 2012 *The Power of Writing in Organizations: From Letters to Online Interactions*. New York: Routledge.

Fayard, Anne-Laure and Anca Metiu. 2014 'The role of writing in distributed collaboration'. *Organization Science* 25: 1391–1413.

Hardy, Cynthia, Thomas B. Lawrence, and David Grant. 2005 'Discourse and collaboration: The role of conversations and collective identity'. *Academy of Management Review* 30: 58–77.

Heimer, Carol A. 2006 'Conceiving children: How documents support case versus biographical analyses'. In *Documents: Artifacts of Modern Knowledge*, A. Riles (ed). Ann Arbor, MI: University of Michigan Press, pp. 95–126.

Hodder, Ian. 2003 'The interpretation of documents and material culture'. In *Collecting and Interpreting Qualitative Materials*, N. K. Denzin and E.G. Guba (eds). Thousand Oaks, CA: Sage, pp. 155–175.

Knaapen, Loes, Herve Cazeneuve, Alberto Cambrosio, Patrick Castel, and Beatrice Fervers. 2010 'Pragmatic evidence and textual arrangements: A case study of French clinical cancer guidelines'. *Soc Sci Med* 71: 685–692.

Latour, Bruno. 1988 'Drawing things together'. In *Representation in Scientific Practice*, M. Lynch and S. Woolgar (eds). Cambridge: MIT Press, pp. 19–68.

Lincoln, Yvonna S. and Egon G. Guba. 1985 *Naturalistic Inquiry*. Thousand Oaks, CA: Sage.

Luengo-Fernandez, Ramon, Alastair M. Gray, and Peter M. Rothwell. 2009 'Effect of urgent treatment for transient ischaemic attack and minor stroke on disability and hospital costs (express study): A prospective population-based sequential comparison'. *Lancet Neurology* 8: 235–243.

Meehan, Albert J. 1986 'Record-keeping practices in the policing of juveniles'. *Urban Life* 15: 70–102.

Montgomery, Kathryn. 2005 *How Doctors Think: Clinical Judgment and the Practice of Medicine: Clinical Judgment and the Practice of Medicine*. New York: Oxford University Press.

Muniesa, Fabian, Yuval Millo, and Michel Callon. 2007 'An introduction to market devices'. *Sociological Review* 55: 1–12.

National Collaborating Centre for Chronic Conditions. 2008 *Stroke: National Clinical Guideline for Diagnosis and Initial Management of Acute Stroke and Transient Ischaemic Attack (TIA)* London: Royal College of Physicians.

NICE. 2008 *NICE Clinical Guideline 68. Stroke: National Clinical Guideline for Diagnosis and Initial Management of Acute Stroke and Transient Ischaemic Attack (TIA)*. London: NICE.

Osterlund, Carsten. 2004 'Mapping medical work: Documenting practices across multiple medical settings'. *Journal of the Center for Information Studies* 5: 35–43.

Østerlund, Carsten, Jaime Snyder, Steve Sawyer, Sarika Sharma, and Matt Willis. 2015 'Documenting work: From participant observation to participant tracing'. In Kimberly D. Elsbach and Roderick M. Kramer (eds) *Handbook of Innovative Qualitative Research*. New York: Routledge, pp. 391–400.

Raffel, Stanley. 2014 *Matters of Fact (RLE Social Theory): A Sociological Inquiry*. London: Routledge.

Riles, Annelise. 2006 *Documents: Artifacts of Modern Knowledge*. Ann Arbor, MI: University of Michigan Press.

Rothwell, Peter M., Matthew F. Giles, Arvind Chandratheva, Lars Marquardt, Olivia Geraghty, Jessica N. E. Redgrave, Caroline E. Lovelock, L. E. Binney, L. M. Bull, F. C. Cuthbertson, S. J. V. Welch, S. Bosch, F. Carasco-Alexander, L. E. Silver, S. A. Gutnikov, and Z. Mehta, Express Study. 2007 'Effect of urgent treatment of transient ischaemic attack and minor stroke on early recurrent stroke (EXPRESS study): A prospective population-based sequential comparison'. *Lancet* 370: 1432–1442.

Sandberg, Jörgen and Haridimos Tsoukas. 2011 'Grasping the logic of practice: Theorizing through practical rationality'. *Academy of Management Review* 36: 338–360.

Shankar, Kalpana, David Hakken, and Carsten Osterlund. 2017 'Rethinking documents'. In *Handbook of Science and Technology Studies*, Ulrike Felt, Rayvon Fourche, Clark A. Miller and Laurel Smith-Doerr (eds). Cambridge MIT Press.

Shankar, Kalpana. 2018 'Ethnography, documents, and big data: Reflections on teaching with David Hakken'. *Anthropology of Work Review* 39: 17–21.

Thévenot, Laurent. 2009 'Postscript to the special issue: Governing life by standards'. *Social Studies of Science* 39: 793–813.

Tsoukas, Haridimos. 2010 'Strategic decision making and knowledge: A Heideggerian approach'. In *Handbook of Decision Making*, Paul Nutt and David Wilson (eds). Chichester: John Wiley & Sons, Ltd, pp. 379–402.

Yates, JoAnne. 1989 'The emergence of the memo as a managerial genre'. *Management Communication Quarterly* 2: 485–510.

Yates, JoAnne and Wanda J. Orlikowski. 1992 'Genres of organizational communication: A structurational approach to studying communication and media'. *Academy of Management Review* 17: 299–326.

Appendix 13.1
EXAMPLE OF NICE RECOMMENDATIONS

Below is a snapshot taken from the full guidelines. It illustrates the structured approach NICE claims to have adopted in order to arrive at recommendations.

6.2.4 Clinical Evidence Statements

The proportion of patients with MR-DWI abnormalities ranged from 25 to 58 %.

Only the results of multivariate analysis are reported here:

- At 1 year, patients without a DWI abnormality were significantly more likely to have a subsequent TIA, but significantly less likely to have a subsequent stroke, than patients with a DWI abnormality (N=85).[34] **Level 3**
- Patients with a DWI abnormality were significantly more likely to have an in-hospital recurrent TIA or stroke then those without a DWI abnormality (N=146).[35] **Level 3**
- At 3 months, DWI abnormalities were a significant independent predictor of stroke (N=203).[36] **Level 3**
- The presence of a DWI abnormality in patients with TIA or minor stroke was Significantly associated with an increased risk of 90-day stroke (N=120).[37] **Level 3**
- Symptoms greater than 1 hour and DWI abnormalities were significant independent predictors of further cerebral vascular events or any vascular event (follow-up mean 389 days) (N=83).[38] **Level 3**

6.2.5 From Evidence to Recommendations

The evidence reviewed did not specifically compare CT with MR after TIA. However, it is well established that MR is more sensitive than CT in the detection of vascular lesion particularly if performed early. The consensus of the GDG was that where brain scanning was felt to be necessary following TIA, MR with DWI within 24 hours should be performed. For those patients with contraindications or unable to tolerate MR, CT Scanning should be used.

6.2.6 Recommendations

R12 People who have a suspected TIA who need brain imaging (that is, those in whom vascular territory, or pathology is uncertain) should undergo diffusion-weighted MRI except where contraindicated,[1] in which case computed tomography (CT) scanning should be used.

Appendix 13.2

THE NICE ALGORITHM FOR THE MANAGEMENT OF TIA PATIENTS[2]

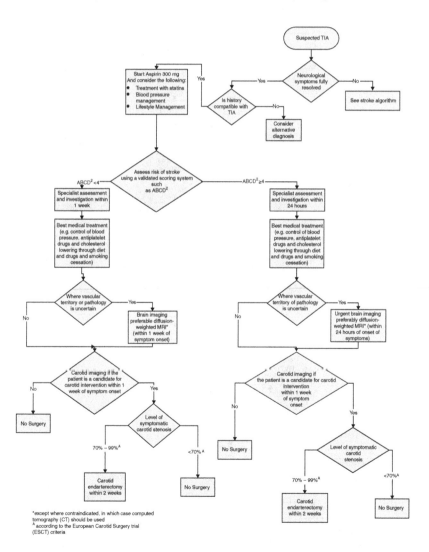

*except where contraindicated, in which case computed tomography (CT) should be used
[A] according to the European Carotid Surgery trial (ESCT) criteria

Appendix 13.3

ALGORITHM FOR BPT FOR TIA (SNAPSHOT FROM DOH GUIDANCE)

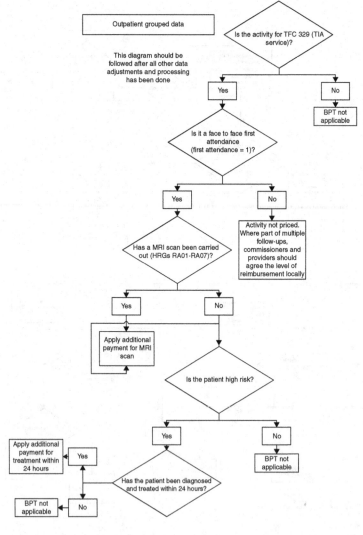

Appendix Notes

1 Contraindications to MRI include people who have any of the following: a pacemaker, shrapnel, some brain aneurysm clips and heart valves, metal fragments in eyes, severe claustrophobia.
2 http://guidance.nice.org.uk/index.jsp?action=download&o=41317.

14

MANAGERIAL WORK WITH DIGITALIZATION

A Multi-Sited Ethnographic Approach to Data and Data-Driven Management in Practice

Ursula Plesner and Lise Justesen

Introduction

Digitalization is a hot topic. Much discourse in the media and elsewhere seems based on either dystopian or utopian visions of a transformed future digitalized society. Despite the hype, relatively little attention has been paid to how digitalization transforms everyday work in organizations, including managerial work (Plesner, Justesen, & Glerup, 2018). This chapter illustrates how a multi-sited ethnographic approach can inform studies of boundary-spanning phenomena like digitalization as an organizational phenomenon requiring managerial work.

Over the course of a decade, a prominent digitalization agenda for the public sector has developed in many countries. This is also very much the case in Denmark, which is the empirical context for our study of managerial work with digitalization. Denmark has been described as a frontrunner and role model for other countries (Schou & Hjelholt, 2018). Dunleavy and colleagues refer to the steps towards digitalizing ever more work processes and services in the public sector as digital-era governance (Dunleavy, Margetts, Bastow, & Tinkler, 2011). This trend entails that managers across public sector organizations are confronted with a digitalization imperative, portraying digitalization as a means to enhance both the efficiency and quality of public service delivery. The public sector is an interesting context for studying how digitalization transforms everyday practices and managerial work in organizations because, although digitalization is changing aspects of most types of organizations, public sector organizations have no choice but to digitalize due to ambitious government reform programs requiring them to do so (Plesner et al., 2018). As such, in this context, digitalization can be understood as an agenda pushed from above by policymakers, but at the same time, it can be understood as a set of practices or enactments in particular organizations by particular managers.

Ethnography offers a set of qualitative methods for capturing the everyday practices through which managers contribute to realizing the overarching digitalization agenda. Yet, studying how digitalization influences public sector organizations and how managers partake in realizing the digitalization agenda also challenges traditional ethnographic notions of the field and the site because the phenomenon of interest spans many different localities (Wright, 2011). The in-depth, single-site ethnography can provide insights into local translations of the digitalization imperative but has less to offer in terms of understanding concerns and practices that are simultaneously crosscutting and diverse (Strathern, 2000). As an alternative, multi-sited ethnography (Marcus, 1995) represents an entry point to understanding how the digitalization agenda is realized through both managerial work *in specific sites* and the shaping of ideas and practices *across sites*. Multi-sited ethnography allows us to describe specific managerial initiatives and challenges as well as important conditions and concerns shared by public managers.

To illustrate the potential of the multi-sited ethnographic approach, we draw on a large empirical study on the realization of an ambitious digitalization agenda in the Danish public sector designed to fundamentally transform the entire sector. Denmark has had digitalization strategies for the public sector since 2001, which is when the state, the regions and local authorities initially agreed on specific digitalization projects that would cut across various public sector organizations (Jæger & Löfgren, 2010). As mentioned above, Denmark is considered a frontrunner in the area of digitalization among the EU countries. It has recently embarked on a new ambitious national digitalization strategy, the New e-Government Strategy 2016–2020 (Digi, 2018), which aims to intensify the digitalization of the public sector further by digitalizing ever more services and work processes. This intensive work on the policy level to change how public sector organizations operate makes the Danish public sector a relevant case for studying how a digitalization agenda becomes realized by managers in practice.

The chapter is structured as follows. First, we define digitalization and argue that this phenomenon should be understood as both "crosscutting and diverse" (Strathern, 2000). This definition of digitalization as an object of study invites us to go beyond single-site studies of individual technologies or organizations. Next, we present the methodological idea of multi-sited ethnography based on Marcus' (1995) work, focusing chiefly on his idea of the strategically selected ethnography. We then argue for the relevance and main features of the case. We offer an account of the methodological choices made to construct the case and to tell the story of the enactment of the digitalization agenda in practice. The chapter then illustrates the types of findings produced through the multi-sited ethnographic approach by describing a specific aspect of managers' realization of the digitalization agenda: concerns about data and data-driven management as they are enacted in three different sites. The chapter concludes with reflections on the insights gained by multi-sited ethnography in relation to the realization of the digitalization agenda and the associated managerial work.

Digitalization as an Object of Study

In her study of accountability and audit cultures, Strathern (2000) noted how mundane practices taking place across different domains have somehow come together and become a global phenomenon, although in a "multiplex" way. Similarly, digitalization can be understood as a phenomenon enacted in many sites simultaneously, but in heterogeneous ways. It has many different aspects, such as automation of routine tasks, implementation of self-service solutions, machine learning to support decision-making processes, and concerns with data and data-driven management. It is infused both with normative ideals, hopes, promises, and broader political objectives and with specific technological solutions and concrete work routines. These different aspects are, however, typically only loosely coupled. Viewed in this way, digitalization is not merely, or even mainly, a question of technology implementation, but a practice characterized by both programmatic and technological elements (Power, 1999, p. 6). Conceiving of digitalization as a practice does not imply that it is only a local phenomenon. We share Nicolini's "appreciation of the connectedness of practice and the fact that activities never happen in isolation, so that practices are always immersed in a thick texture of interconnections" (Nicolini, 2009, p. 1407).

Practices can be connected across sites in various ways. In this chapter, we pay analytical attention to the discourses and policies pushing the digitalization agenda as well as to technologies and the more practical and managerial work done with the digitalization of organizations. The discourses and everyday work connected to digitalization are at the same time "crosscutting and diverse" and elements in "a culture in the making" (Strathern, 2000). Methodologically, this understanding implies that the various instances where digitalization is enacted in organizations are not parts that add up to a whole. Rather, digitalization is realized in sites that are partially connected (Strathern, 2004), in ways that are sometimes similar, sometimes differing. Studying digitalization defined in this way calls for certain methodological considerations.

Multi-sited Ethnography as Methodology

Ethnographic methods lend themselves particularly well to studying how a phenomenon like digitalization is enacted in everyday practices. At the heart of the ethnographic study lies field work and extensive participatory observations of everyday practices, leading to thick ethnographic descriptions of these practices (Geertz, 1973). Besides observations, ethnographic studies also involve attempts to elicit how actors ascribe meaning to their practices. Informal conversations and more formal interviews give insight into actors' interpretations. Finally, as Atkinson and Coffey

(2011) pointed out, documentary realities are integral to contemporary societies and should be part of ethnographic objects of study.

Ethnography was developed in anthropology and originally deployed in studies of far-away cultures, such as the Trobriand Islands, famously studied by Malinowski in the 1920s. Since then, ethnography has been adopted as a methodology by scholars in many different fields and applied in less exotic locations. For instance, in management and organization studies, organizational ethnography has emerged as both a field and a methodology and as a way of writing up empirical accounts (Neyland, 2008; Pedersen & Humle, 2016; Watson, 2012). Relatedly, an "anthropology of policy" has developed as a distinct field where ethnographic methods are deployed to study social-cultural practices relating to policymaking and implementation (Shore & Wright, 1997, 2011). These studies direct attention to organizational and managerial workplace practices that are affected by reforms, but not in a linear, unidirectional way where organizations are seen merely as recipients of policies developed elsewhere (Plesner et al., 2018). From this perspective, policies are not reduced to "external, generalized or constraining forces" (Shore & Wright, 2011, p. 1), but are instead viewed as productive, performative aspects of socio-cultural practices that are shaped locally in various ways. We found such approaches useful because digitalization is not an easily observed everyday phenomenon. Instead, studying digitalization as defined above requires reflections on how it can be observed as enacted in practice, in this case by managers.

In the study of digitalization in public sector organizations, ethnographic methods such as participatory observations over time, along with informal and formal conversations, allowed us to work from the assumption that digitalization is a situated, everyday phenomenon and to study it in this way. But single-site ethnographic studies did not allow us to study digitalization as the type of complex, boundary-spanning phenomenon described in the previous section. In his seminal article on multi-sited ethnography, Marcus (1995) argued that new modes of ethnographic enquiry were required to deal with complex objects of study. It seems fair to argue that digitalization is precisely a complex object as described by Marcus. It involves a large number of institutions, managers, employees, technologies, policies, discourses, and so on.

To account for the crosscutting and diverse discourses and practices in relation to the digitalization of public sector organizations, we turned to multi-sited ethnography as a research methodology. Multi-sited ethnography also differs from single-site ethnography because, besides being complex, its objects of study are often "mobile." That is, their formation takes place across several different locations (Marcus, 1995, p. 99), or in our case, beyond the borders of single public organizations.

Although Marcus problematizes the anthropological tradition of seeing sites as bounded, multi-sited ethnography nonetheless maintains an emphasis on the cultural logics so central to anthropology. But in complex societies, cultural logics are produced not only locally but also at sites that, in Marcus' (1995) terminology, constitute the system, for instance, the media, state, and markets. Traditionally, ethnographic studies have paid close attention to local practices, but less so to how phenomena cut across different localities. In classical ethnographic studies, local practices have often been seen as lifeworlds that are parts of a larger system, but Marcus questions the idea of parts and wholes, stating:

> The world system is not the theoretically constituted holistic frame that gives context to the contemporary study of peoples or local subjects closely observed by ethnographers, but it becomes, in a piecemeal way, integral to and embedded in discontinuous, multi-sited objects of study.
>
> *(p. 97)*

The system is not seen as framing the lifeworld and it is not seen as an overarching set of dynamics that influence local practices. The idea that any site is "the container of a particular set of social relations" (Falzon, 2009, p. 1) to be studied and compared to other contained sites is challenged. To put it differently, ethnographic methods give insights into local practices, but these local practices should not be considered as separate from other practices. The contribution of multi-sited ethnography is to extend ethnography's usefulness to the exploration of crosscutting and diverse phenomena such as, in our case, the digitalization of public sector organizations.

The Strategically Selected Ethnography

Given that there is no clear distinction between lifeworld and system, Marcus (1995) suggested that the ethnographer should, "quite literally follow connections, associations, and putative relationships" (p. 97) between entities across sites. This idea of tracing connections to understand social phenomena by abandoning the distinction between the local and the global resonates with other relational and practice-oriented approaches to organization and management (Czarniawska & Hernes, 2005; Latour, 2005; Nicolini, 2009). Such an approach raises important issues about how to select sites to zoom in on. Since a totality can never be captured, the choice of site is as political as writing an ethnographic account. For instance, if we want to study how managers realize the digitalization agenda to learn something about the digitalization of an entire public sector, it makes an enormous difference for the story we are able to tell whether we choose organizations where managers are eager or reluctant about digitalization, where it has been possible to hire talented developers or not, where budgets allow for experimentation or not, etc. In our case, it requires a commitment to not choose extreme cases, but have an eye for where it is possible to observe shared concerns.

Although the aim of a multi-sited ethnography is not a holistic representation, the site must represent something more than itself. In Marcus' (1995) words:

> The strategically situated ethnography attempts to understand something broadly about the system in ethnographic terms as much as it does its local

subjects; It is only local circumstantially, thus situating itself in a context or field quite differently than does other single-sited ethnography.

(p. 111)

Marcus proposed to follow, for instance, the people, the thing, the metaphor, the story, the biography or the conflict to move beyond the single site (pp. 106–110). In our case, we chose to follow how a concern with data and data-driven management was articulated and enacted in practice across sites as a way of connecting to the digitalization agenda. We chose to focus on data and data-driven management because these themes were prevalent across the material. Often, when we asked about "digitalization" in interviews or more informal conversations during our fieldwork, managers would talk about "data." Taking this native translation of digitalization was useful to understand how managers make practices "hang together" – in this case the digitalization agenda and daily managerial practices.

We zoomed in on a particular organization where the concern with data gave rise to managerial practices similar to practices we had observed in other organizations. The interviews we conducted often had references to data and data-driven management and we were invited to meetings regarding these issues. This strategic choice of site was supplemented with strategic choices of other sites where the concern with data and data-driven management was articulated in slightly different ways. The combination of sites gave insight into different, but also connected, articulations and enactments of the digitalization agenda. The methods used for studying each site were not similar, but consisted in different combinations of observations, interviews, and document studies. As Marcus notes, our understanding of different sites may be produced by different means, and need to be actively brought together to "posit their relationship":

> To do ethnographic research, for example, on the social grounds that produce a particular discourse of policy requires different practices and opportunities than does fieldwork among the situated communities such policy affects [...]. *To bring these sites into the same frame of study* and to posit their relationships on the basis of first-hand ethnographic research in both is the important contribution of this kind of ethnography, regardless of the variability of the quality and accessibility of that research at different sites.
>
> *(p. 105, our emphasis)*

To sum up, in multi-sited ethnographies, not all sites need to be treated with equal attention and the same methods. Sites should be selected strategically and may be studied by different means. In our exploration of how managers realize the digitalization agenda in the Danish public sector we followed two different, but related, phenomena across sites. In the first instance, we followed digitalization, while in the second instance, we followed and accounted for a particular aspect of digitalization, namely data and data-driven management, at sites where this was particularly relevant.

Research Strategy: A Multi-sited Study of Digitalization in the Danish Public Sector

To explore how the digitalization agenda circulates and is realized in multiple sites that have both shared and different operating conditions, we spent six months doing documentary research, attending industry events and conducting qualitative interviews with more than 40 managers across various public organizations in Denmark. Such an eclectic approach in terms of data collection strategies is in line with the multi-sited ethnographic research strategy. As Marcus (2011) writes: "multi-sited projects involve ethnography of different modalities and intensities within the same frame of fieldwork" (p. 10). The documents collected (reports, strategy documents, media stories and PowerPoint presentations) provided insights into specific digitalization projects as well as the dominant discourses regarding the digitalization of public organizations. The industry events (a large conference with the participation of public managers and IT specialists and several thematic morning meetings arranged by the provider of a widely used administrative system) offered insight into pertinent managerial and technical concerns in relation to the digitalization agenda. Finally, the interviews (in, e.g., ministries, agencies, tax authorities, hospitals and local authorities) focused on current digitalization projects in specific organizations, providing insight into the multiple ways in which organizations realize centrally formulated digitalization ambitions.

Based on this broad and varied empirical material, we identified themes across different settings involving the reorganization of work in connection with digitalization and the managerial work related to this task. We saw concern with the automation of work processes, with the sharing and use of data across sectors, and with designing user-friendly digital infrastructures that put citizens in focus. These themes were all interesting from an organizational point of view, but the material collected offered little insight into everyday organizational practices and the managerial work required to realize ambitions to automate work, to grapple with data in new ways, and to establish new relationships in the interface between public servant and citizen. But our exploratory research strategy provided access to various public organizations, allowing us to select a site where the above-mentioned shared concerns seemed to be crystallized and where we could study these practices. To borrow a set of metaphors also used by Nicolini (2009), we zoomed in on an organization to be able to describe in some detail organizational practices related to data and data-driven management. We were able to supplement this with thinner, but equally relevant, descriptions by zooming out and directing our attention to two other sites that partake in the formation of digitalization in the Danish Public sector.

Nicolini (2009) presents the strategy of zooming in as a matter of choosing to focus on particular practices on the basis of a selectively chosen set of conceptual tools and perspectives. Zooming in is not only about getting closer to practice by attending to details, but also about switching lenses to bring certain aspects of practice to the fore (ibid., p. 1402). This is a useful contribution to a multi-sited research strategy, allowing us to account for a varying analytical focus across sites. In our case, when we selected policy sites for inclusion in our study, we chose to focus on the *articulations* of data prevalent in documents and interviews rather than the *practices* we studied through observations. Zooming out is a matter of connecting observations of practices to a wider horizon. As Nicolini writes:

> Paraphrasing Latour (2005, p. 44) we can state that practice is always a node, a knot and a conglomerate of many types of material and human agencies that have to be patiently untangled. For this reason, the study of practices cannot be limited to focusing on the details of their accomplishment. There is a need to integrate and alternate the zooming in movement with one which is horizon-widening and that, in accordance with the idea of zooming in, I would describe as zooming out on the texture of practice. Zooming out on practice requires thus moving between practice in the making and the texture of practices which causally connects this particular instance to many others.
>
> *(p. 1408)*

For Nicolini, zooming out is fundamental to getting an understanding of practice. In the case of managers' realization of a digitalization agenda, it seemed that the relevant entities to focus on in the zooming out moment were the discourses of policymakers and other actors who contribute to articulating the digitalization imperative and circulating it. Having chosen to follow data across sites, we directed our attention to how data was articulated in documents and interviews in sites outside of the organization where we did more traditional fieldwork and conducted participant observations for a longer period of time. In Marcus' view, such an approach implies that the research can potentially surpass dualistic accounts of, for instance, top-down formulation and implementation of policy. In the following, we describe the site selection in more detail.

Strategically Selected Sites

Throughout our research process, interviews with managers across the public sector, as well as observations at industry events, gave us an extensive understanding of several sites. We obtained a rough idea about what the shared concerns were, who the central actors were, and which discourses were being reproduced or contested in the Danish public sector. Since so many actors referred to the Danish Agency for Digitisation and the interest organization Local Government Denmark (LGDK) as central to the articulation and realization of the digitalization agenda, we did document studies as well as several interviews in both organizations. These two organizations became the first two strategically selected sites. After the first six months, we chose to zoom in on digitization in a municipal center, which became a third site. We zoomed in on this specific site because it was referred to by interviewees from other parts of the public sector, who portrayed the center as a very ambitious organization in terms of managers' efforts to digitalize services and processes. It soon became clear to us that digitalization took many forms at this site. The center was working continuously with digitalization through various new projects and its managers were highly ambitious and articulate about the work required to digitalize the organization further. When we made our initial appointments at the center, we asked for permission to follow the work there over a longer period, starting with six months. We continued our engagement with the organization for more than a year. This meant that in total, our study lasted 18 months, including the exploratory phase and the fieldwork in the center.

We were permitted to shadow employees as they went about their daily work, allowing us to study their everyday work practices. We were given access cards to come and go as we pleased. We were able to study the managerial work associated with digitalization because we had asked to be invited to relevant meetings and attended a large number of such meetings. This included weekly, lean-inspired section morning meetings, meetings of the management team, strategy meetings, coordination meetings on digitalization projects, and other types of meetings. Work practices and section meetings were easy to follow because they took place in large, open office settings. From the beginning, it was clear from our observations of meetings and everyday interactions that a reorganization of work and multiple managerial considerations related to digitalization were present in the organization. Many of the concerns we had observed in the various public organizations were voiced in this municipal center as well, so in this site, we were able to explore several themes that are central to the realization of the digitalization agenda in the public sector.

In the following, we will exemplify how we gained insight into one such theme, namely the concern and fascination with data and data-driven management. Digitalization in the public sector is multifaceted, as the term covers automation, digital self-service, and many other technical solutions to organizational problems. In that way, the concern with data is only one aspect of digitalization. However, the use of big data and data analytics has been constructed as a remarkably important aspect of the digitalization of public sector organizations (Maciejewski, 2017). As a result, the development of new organizational practices related to new ways of working with data is widely recognized as a necessity. Based on our ethnographic work conducted at the center, we provide examples of how data was enacted as an organizational concern and how managerial work with data and data-driven management became important aspects of the realization of digitalization. Let us begin, however, by describing the first site where we encountered a well-articulated concern with data.

Selected Findings: Enactments and Articulations of Data across Sites

First Site: The Agency for Digitisation and Strategies on Data

The agency is a central driver of strategies and collaboration concerning this agenda, and practically all the managers we interviewed across public organizations pointed toward the agency and the documents it produced. So as we embarked on our exploratory study, it soon became clear to us that the Agency for Digitisation was a site of relevance if we were to follow the phenomenon of digitalization in the public sector. For that reason, we zoomed in on how the concern with data was articulated at this specific site.

Here, it was relevant to examine strategy documents. In the most recent strategy (2016–2020), a main focus is on the sharing of data across public institutions (Digi, 2018). This focus area is meant to increase efficiency, transparency, and, not least, coherence across a public sector whose current state is often described as operating and thinking in silos. Data, it seemed, was key to fulfilling the programmatic ambitions inscribed in the digitalization agenda, and if we take a closer look on how data is articulated at this site, we see that it is evoked both as a foundation and a free-floating resource and as a connector across the public sector at large.

Data as a Foundation

The strategy document emphasizes the fact that the Danish public sector already has a large number of very high-quality data sets and databases. The basic data program (Digi, 2018, p. 27) is portrayed as a cornerstone of the various initiatives in the document. Basic data is the data recorded by the Danish authorities on citizens, businesses, property, addresses, etc. The document describes good quality data as the foundation of the public sector: "Much public sector basic data is now available online and free of charge for individuals, businesses and authorities alike. All of this makes up the solid *foundation* which the public sector will develop further up to 2020" (p. 13, our emphasis).

In addition to the document analysis, we interviewed managers from the agency, who also emphasized that this type of data is the foundation of digitalization. One manager told us:

> You know, we've based our entire administration [of the Danish public sector] on it [high quality, shared data], so we can exchange data and identify the same citizen in the same way in the health care system, in elderly care, and at social work centers. In that way, we can combine data across [organizations and sectors], which is internationally very unique. And that's also why we have such a well-functioning, highly digitalized society as we do.

Invoking data as the foundation for digitalization foregrounds data as a key element in the broader digitalization agenda, making it possible for data to also be the connector that ensures coherence and breaks down silos.

Free-floating Data as a Connector

The agency not only articulated data as foundation, but also as a *connector* that would bind together otherwise separate sectors because data would float freely between them. A manager from the agency used the floating metaphor in this way:

> We create common standards for how to build [data architecture] so data can float between them, because then you can begin to create really nice

user experiences. We can look up your address, we can see how many kids you have, we can see if you need to have your passport renewed – those types of extra services.

The manager also touched upon what floating data implies on the organizational level:

> … it will change the organizations, if data enters them continuously […] if we're able to learn from data, if we have the skills … You know, actually we lack these skills in the public sector; people who can read data, see the patterns and spot the tendencies and understand what that means for the product, or services from the authorities, right?

This shows that even if the agency were successful in establishing a better foundation that would enable the free floating of data, additional work is needed to ensure the connection and coherence the agency aspires to create. In other words: *People who can read data, see patterns and understand them in the relevant organizational context.* These people will typically be local managers or experts employed to help managers with this task. To study this further, we zoomed in on a different site, a municipal center, heavily influenced by the digitalization agenda, and accordingly, concerned with data.

Second Site: A Municipal Center and Data as Organizational Concerns

We decided to zoom in on the managerial practices in the municipal center because multiple initiatives were taken at this site to digitalize an increasing number of work tasks, and because managers had been both early to implement digital technologies and continued to be ambitious about the digitalization agenda. Despite a number of successful digitalization projects, which had allowed the center to work more efficiently, the center's managers were still looking for ways to make their organization more efficient and the quality of their work higher, and they were investing resources in various digitalization projects to help them realize this goal.

Data as an Entry Point to the Future

When we began our fieldwork in this organization, two temporary employees with degrees in the social sciences had just been hired to dig into the organization's data and open data to support more data-driven management. Their tasks were not specified in detail in advance, but management was interested in learning whether having data analysts work with data in new and inventive ways would add value to the center's daily work. The top manager explained to us that his new employees were superb at harvesting data: "I can't analyze data the way they can. It's amazing."

In our initial fieldnotes we highlighted that there seemed to be a concern with becoming more data-driven, but also that management had little idea about what the outcome would be yet, as both the idea of working with data exploratively and the idea of hiring employees with data skills were new at the center. The center obviously already worked with multiple data sources, but their vision was to become more creative and to use data, for instance, for predictions, for citizen profiling, and for improving the center's services in general. This was a step into unknown territory and the top manager told us that his new employees had to prove their worth. However, he believed that "they can come up with some issues that we aren't able to even consider before they inspire us."

To illustrate the potential of data and more data-driven management, the top manager showed us a PowerPoint presentation on data-driven management that he had recently given at a conference arranged by the association for municipalities (LGDK) mentioned above. Professionally made, the PowerPoint included videos, images, and technical explanations. One of the slides contained the image of a "heat map" of the city drawn up on the basis of data from the addresses of citizens in contact with the center. It used different sizes of circles to visualize where the fewest and largest number of citizens lived. But when we asked the manager how this map could inform and support decision-making or work practices, he hesitated and explained that they were not yet certain about this. He went on to speculate that future outreach activities could be based on such visualizations. Here, we could observe a tension between the imagined possibilities of data-driven management and the lack of specific goals in this project.

As we learned about more specific digitalization projects during our fieldwork, it seemed that the idea of data-driven management allowed for the allocation of resources to projects like the heat map. In these other projects, the immediate value seemed similarly unclear but held the *promise* of delivering value in entirely new ways. As the manager explained to us in a follow-up interview after our initial observations at the center:

> Right now, in relation to data-driven management, we think we've become a bit smarter, *or we can begin to act wiser in the future*. At least in some areas. [our emphasis]

When we remarked that it seemed like a very intuitive way of working with data, the manager agreed and added that this is a way of "trying to make sense together in areas that do not make sense at a first glance," and that "the best way of predicting the future is to create it yourself." Taken together, when we encountered managerial work with data in this sense, it was seen as an entry point to the *future*, as promising decision-making based on surprising patterns and predictions.

Data as Old News

Some weeks into our fieldwork, we attended a management team meeting on, as it said in the Outlook invitation, "data-driven management." One of the newly recruited employees with a background in data analytics was invited to give a presentation. She said that she had been "looking into the systems" and now she wanted to know what kind of data and statistics the management would like to dive into. She presented several options, but faced with these options, the four participating managers all looked a bit puzzled. One of them remarked that much of the data suggested by the newcomer had been available and used for years.

The group then proceeded to discuss what would be really useful to know more about. One of the managers suggested that "an informed guess" about a certain cost issue would be very useful. Her younger colleague, the newly appointed data analyst, interrupted and laughing somewhat nervously said: "I'm sorry, I'd like to stop you there. We don't do informed guessing." She returned to telling the group about what she had learned about the organization's core IT system at a recent seminar. A discussion among the managers followed. Like earlier on, one manager remarked that they already had access to and routinely discussed this type of data at management meetings.

While discussing our observation notes afterwards, we speculated if two different professional approaches to data were clashing at the meeting. The newcomer, who was supposed to be the data expert and come up with new ways of using data, had to start from the ground up, it seemed, and get acquainted with not only the systems and the datasets, but also the organizational context and existing knowledge in order to produce valuable knowledge. The managers, who had used the systems and the data for various purposes for a long time, had an intimate knowledge of both, and were often comfortable with using the data intuitively to make informed guesses. This creative, intuitive approach was not that popular with the person appointed to expand the use of data in precisely a creative and intuitive way – to experiment and produce new insights. In the early phase of her job, she stuck to well-known data and rigorous methods, which can be seen as somewhat paradoxical if she had been hired to find entirely new ways to let data inform decision-making.

These observations tell us something about the promise of data-driven management and the realization of it. There are negotiations about how data can be made more valuable, and considerations about who is best suited to do it. In the eyes of one team leader, it can add value to hire people who are detached from handling cases so they can "look at data as simply that: data." In her opinion, data experts have a more unhindered approach. But, as we observed at the meetings, the realization of the promise of data-driven management seems to be highly dependent on people who can draw on detailed organizational knowledge of data and assess their validity and newness. Otherwise, work with data can become a matter of producing old news.

Data as a Legal Concern

At the center, the concern about data was raised in connection with more than just data-driven management. For example, there was ongoing concern with the quality of data, and with legal issues relating to data. At the time of our fieldwork, the EU General Data Protection Regulation became effective. This entailed a range of meetings between managers at the center and the chief data officer of the municipality. We attended one such meeting, where the atmosphere was rather tense to begin with. We followed two managers as they marched towards the meeting room with a large print of an Excel file. With raised eyebrows and some heavy sighs, they signaled that they considered the meeting a waste of time. A legal compliance employee from the municipality waited in a meeting room, and the local manager greeted him hurriedly and jumped into an explanation of how the center handled data at the different stages of their workflows. There was quite a lot of technical discussion.

In the end, the meeting participants agreed that they now had a foundation for making risk assessments regarding data protection at the center. The atmosphere changed and the participants seemed relieved to have succeeded in going through all the technical questions. They agreed that it had been a good idea to get together and settle the details so no more back and forth was needed. After the meeting, the local manager pulled us aside and explained that they spent enormous amounts of time creating process descriptions, risk assessments and data protection measures. Seemingly, the workload associated with such procedures was part of the explanation for the initial attitude towards yet another meeting on data protection. And seemingly, this issue cannot be settled once and for all because laws, procedures and the organization of the different units in the municipality change when the political landscape changes. Even what looks like relatively small changes in how policies are administered may have consequences for the handling – and thus protection – of data.

To sum up, our observations at the center allowed us to grasp various aspects of how the digitalization agenda is realized by managers when we focus specifically on data. Zooming in on this site gave insight into a range of mundane, practical activities carried out at meetings, but it also gave us an understanding of how managers understand data as an entry point to the future, and as an important phenomenon that requires new hires and new practices. In this way, they clearly connect to both the programmatic and technological aspects (Power, 1999) of the digitalization agenda, but our ethnographic fieldwork also showed how these aspects are not easily aligned in practice. This misalignment leaves open a space for continuous managerial work.

Apart from attending to the center's work with data, the top manager also participated in meetings and knowledge sharing events about data-driven management organized by the municipalities' interest organization, which plays a role in articulating the digitalization agenda as a municipal issue. To enrich our understanding of the conditions for management in relation to digitalization, we now zoom out again and examine how data appeared at this site.

Site Three: Local Government Denmark (LGDK)

The interest organization LGDK produces advice on digitalization and is interesting in relation to digitalization in the municipal sector because they have a guiding function and an approach to digitalization that lies in-between the national, strategic level and the local level. Their mission is "to safeguard common interests of the municipalities, assist individual municipalities with consultancy services, and ensure that the local authorities are provided with up-to-date and relevant information" (LGDK, 2018). They are also a formal partner in the joint digitalization strategy formulated in a collaboration between state, regions, and municipalities. As part of our exploratory study, we visited their headquarters, carried out interviews and collected documents. In 2018, LGDK initiated a project, Municipalities' Technological Leap Forward. The project involved a large mapping of new technologies and their impact in the municipal area, as well as pilot projects experimenting with new technologies (e.g., artificial intelligence and virtual reality) in specific domains.

To our surprise, LGDK had commissioned the report from a consultancy firm, DareDisrupt, which has affiliations to the so-called singularity milieu. Singularity refers to the idea that the growth in computing power increases exponentially and that artificial intelligence will one day surpass human intelligence. A futuristic, technology deterministic view reigns in this consultancy environment. In our explorative research phase, we realized that this consultancy firm also gave talks in various municipalities with titles such as "Understand the future." We chose to examine the DareDisrupt report with a focus on the discourse relating to data that the consultants and their report made available to municipal managers and their industry association. We consider the consultancy report a relatively central document to analyze because it borrows legitimacy from a formal partner and because its advice and articulations travel widely when consultants are booked to present it in municipalities across the country. It should be noted that, although the report gave rise to heated public debate and was the object of heavy criticism, it remained part of LGDK's advisory package.

Data as Having Agency

The report produced by DareDisrupt and distributed to municipalities is more than 200 pages long and organized around five technological themes. The concept of data appears 291 times in the report and obviously has multiple meanings, depending on the context. But throughout the report, a recurrent way of framing data is to bestow it with agency. For instance, in the case of artificial intelligence, big data and robotics, a short-term future scenario states: "Large parts of our jobs today consist in processing information – computers will be able to do that for us in the future. Move data around, make simple decisions based on rules stipulated by law, and cleanse data" (DareDisrupt, 2018, p. 4). Here, algorithms and data take over our work, and do not seem to require practical, analytical or managerial work. And in the Internet of Things section, the report states:

> When we can predict maintenance and continue to receive streams of real-time data that point to the need for inspection or the location of

tasks, we will have new possibilities for organizing and tendering. When more and more decisions are generated directly by data from sensors, it is imperative to secure the quality of data at every stage.

(p. 11)

Here, again, no human agency is required; data produces decisions.

In the report and the rhetoric produced by DareDisrupt and circulated by LGDK, data acquires a new kind of agency, partly because it is described in connection with elements other than those we see in the texts produced by the Agency for Digitisation or in the practical work of managers at the center. For instance, the DareDisrupt report links data to futurist discourses on advanced artificial intelligence and the Internet of Things, where data is supposed to operate without human intervention.

Differences aside, there are also affinities between the future-oriented discourses of the report and the way data emerges in the other sites. Like we saw in both the Agency for Digitisation and the municipal center, a common concern is ensuring the quality of the data and the infrastructure where data floats freely.

Concluding Discussion

Through an analysis of three strategically selected, partially connected sites we have tried to illustrate the value of multi-sited ethnography in investigations of what is at stake when a digitalization agenda is articulated and realized in the public sector and how managerial work plays an important role in this regard. By following one key aspect of digitalization, labeled data and data-driven management, across sites we were able to describe both programmatic and technological aspects (Power, 1999) of enacting an abstract phenomenon such as digitalization in practice.

We saw that managers connect to the digitalization agenda in various ways in practice. Our multi-sited ethnography helped us see them as active participants in realizing the digitalization agenda – active in the sense that public management is not "just" about implementing legislation or executing decisions taken at a higher level, but about enacting the digitalization agenda in ways that are both connected to and different from other sites.

We shared different findings from the study to illustrate which types of insights can be gained by zooming in and out on a phenomenon such as data and data-driven management in different sites. On the basis of observations of how managers hire new data analysts and engage in meetings on data-driven management, we proposed that they view data as an entry point to a future and bestow data with the ability to drive decision-making. A similar, future-oriented narrative on data as having agency is articulated strongly in other sites, such as in the reports and events made in collaboration between the municipal interest organization and disruption consultants. The futurist discourses of digitalization are co-produced among actors spanning different sites, and this discourse has effects in practice, informing specific managerial choices about recruitment and resources spent on innovative projects. The multi-sited ethnographic research strategy helped capture this dynamic.

Another finding had to do with more everyday, practical issues relating to data. Managers have pressing concerns about the quality, underlying architecture and surrounding legal issues relating to data. These issues are also at the heart of current digitalization policies articulated by the Agency for Digitisation, which emphasizes how data needs to become a freely floating resource that connect silos and develop into a much more solid foundation for digitalization. While our study identified this common "practical" concern with data in policy language and among managers, it also identified an issue, which is rarely articulated, namely the discrepancy between the ideals about data quality and the practical work with ensuring it. Zooming in on managerial work in an organization allowed us to illustrate the large amount of resources spent on extremely mundane activities relating to the handling of data.

A final finding should be highlighted here as it points to the value of ethnographic observations of enactments of the digitalization agenda. The ethnographic observations allow us to reflect on issues that are *not* observable in policy discourse on digitalization – but maybe ought to be, because they are important in practice. In selecting a particular site to zoom in on to conduct ethnographic observations, one otherwise unobservable phenomenon relating to the realization of the digitalization policy stood out. It became clear how the knowledge managers have of the organization and the data sets produced in and by the organization was, in certain respects, superior to knowledge and suggestions provided by the data experts. Data became old news because the data analyst depicted a well-known situation, or because imprecise and useless data could only be explained by experienced managers. Policymaking on digitalization rarely articulates issues like professionalism and human expertise as crucial elements in the realization of digitalization, but these become apparent in ethnographic observation of everyday, managerial practices in organizations.

A multi-sited ethnographic approach to policy realization hence produces insights on the managerial work required in connection with a number of hopes and tasks connected to data. If the study had been based on documents or interviews only, it would not have been possible to account for the major managerial work carried out, for instance, in the many meetings where the digitalization agenda is broken down into smaller pieces like data or data-driven management (as well as automation and numerous other elements not focused on in this account). In practice, digitalization becomes a matter of engaging with data and devising organizational strategies in relation to data.

At the same time, the focus on discourses (re)produced across sites is also important because some of the crosscutting articulations connected to the digitalization policy agenda explain the urgency with which data initiatives are invented and realized in practice in an organization such as the municipal center. Several sites contribute to the articulation of data as a foundation, of data as a freely floating resource and connector and of data as an entry point to the future.

The multi-sited research design requires, as Marcus (1995) wrote: "an explicit, posited logic of association or connection among sites" (p. 105). In our case, there has been a movement between our exploratory study on digitalization across sites – in observations, interviews, and documents – and our analytical choice to focus on data as it emerges in different sites. This reduced the complexity of the phenomenon we initially studied (digitalization in the public sector), creating a narrower account of a selected part of this agenda (the realization of the policy through the engagement with data). We further narrowed our analysis by zooming in on data through traditional ethnographic observation studies in a particular organization and then by zooming out again, analyzing textual material produced by central actors. The result is a thoroughly constructed account of how the digitalization agenda is realized across multiple sites. Marcus calls such an ethnographic approach "a revival of a sophisticated practice of constructivism" (p. 105). Constructivism, here, implies that the aim is not to create a representational description of a phenomenon or account for different perspectives on the same issue, but to interrogate how a phenomenon such as digitalization of the public sector is constructed and to be explicit and transparent about how the ethnographic story of that phenomenon is constructed as well.

Our understanding of digitalization and the above attempt to define digitalization as an object of study opens up for methodological reflections regarding the various dimensions of such a complex phenomenon. Marcus (1995) suggested that complex objects of study require new modes of ethnographic enquiry, and proposed multi-sited ethnography as an approach to following "mobile" entities across sites. While multi-sited ethnography can indeed be seen as a suitable approach to study complex phenomena that are crosscutting and diverse (as we have argued throughout this chapter), it requires extra layers of methodological reflection to arrive at an understanding of what type of object is being studied or followed.

In our case, if digitalization is a complex web of technological, discursive, human, organizational and policy elements, it poses a methodological problem to break this phenomenon into entities that can be followed. There is no obvious recipe telling us which technological components, which discursive elements, or which types of organizations to study, or at which levels. Another problem concerns the ontological status of these entities. Studying a phenomenon like digitalization, it becomes difficult to follow Marcus' suggestion, to follow the people, the thing, the metaphor or the connections between such entities. We tentatively defined data and data-driven management as the entities to follow, but calling them mobile objects can be questioned. Rather than speaking of objects, which can be followed, it might make more sense to theorize them as multiple objects (Mol, 2003). The idea of multiple objects problematizes the idea of an object that can be traced. It entails an interest in how objects are "enacted," which in our case means how data is "done" in practice in multiple ways. Such reflections raise questions about the validity of the constructed stories we produce with multi-sited ethnography: By looking at discourses and practices relating to data, which we chose to do here, what do we learn about the enactment of the digitalization agenda? How much does it take to argue for their connectedness? The attempt to unpack digitalization and study how this agenda is enacted in practice by managers across the public sector raises not just methodological questions, but should also provoke us to raise more ontological questions, as indicated here.

References

Atkinson, P., & Coffey, A. (2011). Analysing Documentary Realities. In D. Silverman (ed.) *Qualitative Research: Theory, Method and Practice*. London: Sage Publications, pp. 56–75.

Czarniawska, B., & Hernes, T. (2005). *Actor-Network Theory and Organizing*. Frederiksberg: Copenhagen Business School Press.

Dunleavy, P., Margetts, H., Bastow, S., & Tinkler, J. (2011). *Digital Era Governance: IT Corporations, The State, and e-Government. Digital Era Governance: IT Corporations, The State, and e-Government*. Oxford: Oxford University Press.

Falzon, M.-A. (2009). Introduction. Multi-sited Ethnography: Theory, Praxis, and Locality in Contemporary Research. In M.-A. Falzon (ed.) *Multi-sited Ethnography: Theory, Praxis, and Locality in Contemporary Research*. London and New York: Routledge, pp. 1–24.

Geertz, C. (1973). *The Interpretation of Cultures*. New York: Basic Books.

Jæger, B., & Löfgren, K. (2010). The History of the Future: Changes in Danish e-Government Strategies 1994–2010. *Information Polity, 15*(4), 253–269.

Latour, B. (2005). *Reassembling the Social – An Introduction to Actor-Network-Theory*. Oxford: Oxford University Press.

Maciejewski, M. (2017). To Do More, Better, Faster and More Cheaply: Using Big Data in Public Administration. *International Review of Administrative Sciences, 83*(1 suppl), 120–135.

Marcus, G. E. (1995). Ethnography in/of the World System: The Emergence of Multi-Sited Ethnography. *Annual Review of Anthropology, 24*, 95–117.

Marcus, G. E. (2011). What Is at Stake–And Is Not–In the Idea and Practice of Multi-Sited Ethnography. *Canberra Anthropology, 22*(2), 6–14.

Mol, A. (2003). *The Body Multiple: Ontology in Medical Practice*. London: Duke University Press.

Neyland, D. (2008). *Organizational Ethnography*. London: Sage Publications.

Nicolini, D. (2009). Zooming In and Out: Studying Practices by Switching Theoretical Lenses and Trailing Connections. *Organization Studies, 30*(12), 1391–1418.

Pedersen, A. R., & Humle, D. M. (eds.) (2016). *Doing Organizational Ethnography*. London and New York: Routledge.

Plesner, U., Justesen, L., & Glerup, C. (2018). The Transformation of Work in Digitized Public Sector Organizations. *Journal of Organizational Change Management, 31*(5), 1176–1190.

Power, M. (1999). *The Audit Society*. 2nd Edition. Oxford: Oxford University Press.

Schou, J., & Hjelholt, M. (2018). *Digitalization and Public Sector Transformations. Digitalization and Public Sector Transformations*. Basingstoke: Palgrave Macmillan.

Shore, C., & Wright, S. (1997). Policy. A New Field of Anthropology. In C. Shore & S. Wright (eds.) *Anthropology of Policy. Critical Perspectives on Governance and Power*. London: Routledge, pp. 3–39.

Shore, C., & Wright, S. (2011). Introduction. Conceptualising Policy: Technologies of Governance and the Politics of Visibility. In C. Shore, S. Wright, & D. Peró (eds.) *Policy Worlds: Anthropology and the Analysis of Contemporary Power*. Oxford: Berghahn Books, pp. 1–26.

Strathern, M. (2000). Introduction: New Accountabilities. In M. Strathern (ed.) *Audit Cultures: Anthropological Studies in Accountability, Ethics and the Academy*. London and New York: Routledge, pp. 1–18.

Strathern, M. (2004). *Partial Connections*. Walnut Creek: AltaMira Press.

Watson, T. J. (2012). Making Organisational Ethnography. *Journal of Organizational Ethnography*, *1*(1), 15–22.

Wright, S. (2011). Introduction to Studying Policy: Methods, Paradigms, Perspectives. In C. Shore, S. Wright, & D. Peró (eds.) *Policy Worlds: Anthropology and the Analysis of Contemporary Power*. Oxford: Berghan Books, pp. 27–31.

Websites

DareDisrupt, 2018: www.kl.dk/ImageVaultFiles/id_85157/cf_202/Kommunernes_Teknologiske_Fremtid_-fuld_version-.PDF, accessed 29.10.18.

Digi, 2018: https://digst.dk/media/16165/ds_singlepage_uk_web.pdf, accessed 10.11.18.

LGDK, 2018: www.kl.dk/English/Local-Government-Denmark/, accessed 24.10.18.

15

STILL A MAN'S WORLD

Finding Gender Issues in Tokyo Fashion Week

Yuiko Fujita

Introduction

At one meeting last April, we started saying, 'Executives in our industry are all men.' Eighty percent of the customers in the fashion business industry are women. Seventy percent of the workers are women, too. Yet, there are not many women in positions making business decisions. There are a decent number of women in the middle-management class. According to a survey, conducted by *Senken Shimbun* (newspaper) last year, the percentage of female managers was slightly higher than other industries, at 10.5 percent. However, the percentage drops all the way to 3.7 percent for directors and above. This is a very regrettable matter.

(Nikkei Business, *interview with Yoko Ohara, July 18, 2014*)

Yoko Ohara, who established a women's group in the fashion world, pointed out that men were dominant in the fashion industry in Japan. This point, however, had not been problematized outside of the relatively small circle of women in the fashion industry. I noticed this gender inequality in the fashion industry, which had not been paid much attention to by either insiders or outsiders, when I conducted participant observation in the field of fashion in Tokyo.

In this chapter, I explore how the gender of the ethnographer affects the process of ethnographic research in various ways. Gender, as well as sexuality, race, ethnicity, or class, is one of the issues of the subject position faced by the researcher. As DeWalt and DeWalt (2002: 99) note, the gender of the ethnographer has an impact on several areas of the ethnographic enterprise. One very important influence relates to the "experiences" of the ethnographer during the field research. Just as men are often barred from situations in which they can know the intimate worlds of women, women ethnographers are sometimes barred from important parts of the worlds of men. Even a researcher studying sexism encounters and must deal with it during her/his research project.

However, at the same time, female ethnographers have some advantages in studying women's lives. Feminist viewpoints may challenge dominant modes of thought and discourse. In *Writing Culture*, a well-known collection of papers edited by Clifford and Marcus (1986), it is discussed that ethnographic truths are "inherently partial"—committed and incomplete. The collective message of the book's authors focused on the authority of the ethnographic text. They questioned the established modes of ethnographic writing that embodied a single authorial voice (Hammersley and Atkinson 2007); such a voice has often been made by male researchers. Clifford (1986) argues that a great many portrayals of "cultural" truths now appear to reflect male domains of experience; in recognizing such biases, it is well to recall that our own "full" versions will themselves inevitably appear partial. Female ethnographers, as Skeggs (2001) notes, have used empirical research to counter the assertions of previously taken-for-granted analyses and articulate what was previously invisible.

Based on the above arguments, in the following sections, I—a female ethnographer—describe and reflect on my field experience studying cultural organizations, especially, fashion organizations, as described in the opening paragraphs. Due to my gender, I have experienced difficulties approaching some field sites; however, I have found that I could also develop a new research question I had not yet considered at the beginning of my fieldwork. It would be impossible for me to learn about the situation, if I only conducted questionnaire surveys and formal interviews and did not enter and observe the field site. As Clifford (1986) pointed out, states of serious confusion, violent feelings or acts, important failures, changes of course, and excessive pleasures were often excluded from the published account. However, reflexivity is now taken for granted, and ethnographers need to acknowledge that we are part of the world we study (O'Reilly 2009). My story, just as much as many other ethnographic tales, may be useful to understand how the gender of the ethnographer affects ethnographic research.

Entry into Cultural Organizations: Art, Cuisine, and Fashion

First, I discuss how I managed to enter fashion organizations, comparing this process with art and culinary organizations. It is often said that entry is the most critical phase of fieldwork. If we cannot enter, we cannot conduct research. Sometimes, an organization is strongly guarded and defensive. Thus far, I have conducted field research in cultural organizations within three fields—art, cuisine, and fashion (Fujita 2009, 2011, 2017). In each, I encountered different types of difficulties in accessing field sites and continuing my field research. This is mainly because these fields have different organizational settings and people. In my fieldwork, art organizations and restaurants were open to outsiders like me. Fashion organizations, on the other hand, were strongly guarded. Thus, fashion organizations, such as luxury fashion companies and influential fashion publications, are exclusive and selective;

they do not welcome ordinary people. However, once I gained entry, the situation changed. I will describe my entry experience into these three types of cultural organizations and how my gender, as well as age, educational background, and occupation, affected the process.

Art

To research the "art worlds," in Howard S. Becker's sense (1982), I conducted fieldwork in a Tokyo art gallery and art museums in local cities in Japan. It was easy to enter these organizations. In the case of the art gallery, to get permission, I simply wrote an email that explained my desire to conduct research on some artists represented by the gallery. Gallery staff seemed familiar with these kinds of requests from academics (I was an associate professor at the time) and replied to me the next day. Curators often hold a master's degree or doctorate and have similar educational backgrounds to those of university professors and graduate students. They asked me to attend a reception to meet their artist. Once I participated in the reception and spoke with people there, the gallery staff became more cooperative. They helped me conduct interviews with their artists and introduced me to the gallery owner. I was able to enter the art museums in a similar way. I wrote emails to artists or museums, and they let me into the field sites.

Over time, however, I found that doing fieldwork in art organizations was not as easy as I had expected. I met some middle-aged men who worked for art organizations. I told them who I was and that I wanted to learn from them about people and practices in the art worlds. However, some of them occasionally took an overbearing attitude toward me, emphasizing their superior art knowledge, despite telling them my specialization was not art. It was very stressful, and often upsetting, for me. One day, a middle-aged man working part-time in an art museum said, "I have a lot of experience, but I never got a tenured position"—the art-related job market was always tight and competitive in Japan. This gave me a clue. Most likely, he was irritated by my presence in the field, as I appeared to be ignorant and kept asking him a lot of questions (but this is what ethnographers do); in addition, such a woman had told him that she was a "professor." Warren (1988) argues that women in the field have often been harassed and are sometimes barred from important parts of men's worlds. In fact, according to the *Mainichi Shimbun* (newspaper), seven female curators and staff members accused the male director of the 21st Century Museum of Contemporary Art, Kanazawa of harassing them in 2013. Japan's art world is a male-dominant society, and generally, men are in dominant positions and women in subordinate ones. Some feminist and ethnic writers argue that true rapport can only be achieved by researchers who come close to matching the informants in gender, race, and class (DeWalt and DeWalt 2002). In this case, it seemed that my gender made it difficult to build rapport with some men in the field. Later, partly because of this gender relation, I discontinued conducting participant observation in the field of art.

Cuisine

Culinary organizations, such as gastronomy restaurants, are also male-dominated field sites. According to data from the U.S. Bureau of Labor Statistics, in 2013, only 20 percent of U.S. chefs and head cooks in the culinary industry were women. The only area where women are better represented is in the pastry department (Harris and Giuffre 2015). However, it was less difficult for me to gain entry to and continue fieldwork in restaurants than it was in art organizations. I did fieldwork in restaurants in Tokyo and Paris, in order to explore how Japanese cooks specializing in French cuisine developed their transnational networks and careers. In both cities, as in the United States, most cooks were men.

There are, perhaps, some reasons why I was able to enter these sites and continue research in this field. First, the cooks and restaurant staff generally welcome strangers (i.e., customers); providing quality service and treating people nicely is part of their job. They kindly replied to my emails and let me enter their restaurants and kitchens. Second, most cooks were young and/or men without college degrees, and a middle-aged woman, like me, was not often seen as the cooking staff in restaurant kitchens. However, there were other roles in restaurants for middle-aged women with college degrees. One role is that of a food writer or journalist, as there are many food media outlets in Japan, and many food writers and journalists are women. As Fine (1996) notes, for some restaurants, as well as chefs, a good review generates business and can make a restaurant successful. When I explained the purpose of my study to my informants, I told them I was writing a book. They wanted to be covered or interviewed by the media, probably because they considered it an important part of their business. I suppose that my informants regarded me, not as a competitor, but as a possible benefactor—a kind of food writer, journalist, or critic. Namely, they thought cooperating with me might benefit their own business or careers.

Fashion

The majority of the fashion industry is comprised of women; therefore, it is likely that women can access the field sites more easily. However, fashion organizations are generally the most guarded of the three types of cultural organizations, even for female ethnographers and regardless of their gender. As Tseëlon (1995) notes, "the temple of fashion is not open to everyone, and only a carefully scrutinized set of fashion editors, photographers, buyers, distinguished clients, and celebrities are allowed into the inner sanctuary." The same is true in Tokyo. In order to conduct research on new fashion brands and their business, I emailed and called small, independent apparel companies, as well as a famous department store and a Tokyo branch of a famous global fashion magazine. I explained who I was and told them that I would like to interview buyers or editors. However, the department store and the magazine turned down my request, and some apparel companies never replied to me.

Rocamora and Entwistle (2006) conducted fieldwork at London Fashion Week. The two scholars also noted that they found themselves confronting, on a daily basis, the physical boundaries of the field and the separation of "laity" and "clergy." Academics, even if they study fashion, are basically outsiders to the fashion world. Moreover, fashion-related companies are more commercial than art museums, which view educating the public as part of their mission. Fashion companies are always busy with creating or catching up with new fashion trends and are not motivated to spend time with "ordinary people" who do not matter to their business's bottom line.

However, I persisted in trying to contact people in the field of fashion in Tokyo for several months. One day, I met someone, like Doc in the classic ethnographic study *Street Corner Society* (Whyte 1943)—a male senior executive who is an insider willing to share access and insights. I was introduced to him by an acquaintance of mine. Few people in Tokyo's fashion industry are interested in academic studies, but he was attracted to my academic project and became one of my key informants. He introduced me to many important figures of the fashion world and took me to some fashion shows in Tokyo and Paris. As Rocamora and Entwistle (2006) note, it is difficult for academics to gain access to fashion shows. Yet, if you establish connections (i.e., social capital) with insiders, such as journalists, buyers, or business people in the fashion industry, you can secure access to shows and be granted an entry "pass" through the connections. Once the door opened, it became easier for me to conduct field research. In Tokyo, the fashion community is called a "village"; insiders tend to know each other, and it is convenient to snowball. In addition, in fashion organizations, the majority of workers—clerks, designers, pattern makers, editors, journalists, and public-relations people—are women. There were many roles for a middle-aged female ethnographer to adopt, as a participant observer. In this way, I finally achieved entry into small apparel companies and showrooms and started field research in Tokyo Fashion Week.

As I have described, I encountered different types of difficulties, in each field, in accessing cultural organizations and building rapport with informants in the field sites. This was because each field had different settings, and my personal background—as a middle-aged Japanese female professor—affected the process of gaining entry and building rapport in the field. For me, it was difficult to study the field of art, as men are particularly dominant in Japan's art world. If my gender, as well as age, race, occupation, educational background, and other factors, were different (for example, if I were a senior white male professor), perhaps I would have experienced the process differently. Later, my subjective position also impacted the process of developing a research question. In the next sections, I will discuss how I found gender issues through fieldwork at Tokyo Fashion Week.

Observing in Tokyo Fashion Week

Previous ethnographic studies on fashion organizations, such as Kawamura (2004), Mears (2011), and Rocamora and Entwistle (2006), often refer to Pierre Bourdieu's concept of "field" (in French, "*champ*"; this notion is different from the notion of "field" in ethnographic methods). According to Bourdieu's theoretical model, any social formation is structured through a hierarchically organized series of fields (the economic field, educational field, political field, etc.), each defined as a structured space with its own laws of functioning. In any given field, agents occupying the various available positions engage in competition for control of the interests or resources specific to the field (Johnson 1993). As for the field of fashion, Bourdieu also discusses the French field of high fashion. He argues that those in the dominant position "are the designers who possess in the highest degree the power to define objects as rare by means of their signature, their label, [and] those whose label has the highest price" (Bourdieu 1993).

According to Rocamora and Entwistle (2006), in the fashion field, among others, the issue arises as to who belongs to the field, or what constitutes its boundaries, which are "often invisible." Such boundaries are "a stake of struggles," or a struggle to define who are its legitimate members; in fashion fields, the significant ones include designers, journalists, buyers, and others. Through the setting of these boundaries, clear limits are established between the outside world—the world of the "laity," to borrow Bourdieu's analogy, including all the hopefuls waiting outside the tents to catch a glimpse of this world—and that of the "clergy," or, as the press often calls them, "fashionistas" (Rocamora and Entwistle 2006).

As I was one of the "laity," I experienced difficulties in crossing such boundaries and getting into the field of fashion in Tokyo. However, after crossing those boundaries, I found participant observation an especially useful method to study Tokyo's fashion world, which had not been studied much previously. Additionally, few scholars entered Tokyo Fashion Week, which is the central event of the fashion industry in Japan but is not well known to outsiders.

In general, "fashion week," also called "the collections," showcases the upcoming season's prêt-à-porter clothing. Tokyo Fashion Week was started in 1985 by the Council of Fashion Designers, Tokyo (CFD, Tokyo). At that time, there were organizations for designers in fashion cities such as Paris, Milan, and New York, but none in Tokyo. The designers in Japan longed for a Tokyo collection and constantly worked to establish such an organization. Currently, the fashion week held in Tokyo is called the "Rakuten Fashion Week Tokyo." It is hosted by the Japan Fashion Week Organization and is held twice a year, in March and October. Tokyo Fashion Week consists of an exhibition of designers' work in the manner of a trade show but, also, and more famously, a series of runway shows. Most fashion shows are held at the Shibuya Hikarie and Omotesando Hills shopping complexes, as well as other locations in Tokyo. In addition to fashion shows, countless fashion exhibitions are held in Tokyo during this event. The Rakuten Fashion Week Tokyo slogan is: (1) "to become the gateway for success in the world for new designers"; (2) "to become the starting point for cooperation between designers, manufacturers, and apparel retailers"; and (3) "to make Tokyo more fashionable and enjoyable." Tokyo Fashion Week lasts for about a month, making it virtually impossible for international journalists and buyers to attend the entire event. As Kawamura (2004) notes, unlike fashion weeks in Paris or New York, Tokyo Fashion Week is rarely publicized in the Western media.

Next, ethnographic methods allowed me to closely observe the field and its inner workings. To explain in detail, my fieldwork consisted of participant observation and qualitative interviews. I mainly studied young Japanese designers working for or running small fashion companies in Tokyo. At first, I contacted some designers who were reported on in newspapers, magazines, or websites. Subsequently, I used snowball sampling by asking the informants to name Japanese designers who have been working in Tokyo or Paris. I followed them mainly during the period of Tokyo Fashion Week, as well as Paris Fashion Week. During Tokyo Fashion Week, I visited my informants' studios, exhibitions, or shops and also talked to buyers, executives, managers, publicists, journalists, editors, pattern makers, shop staffs, and fashion school staffs, among others. This information forms part of my "multi-sited ethnography" (Marcus 1995), in which I followed respondents from Tokyo to Paris and continued fieldwork with them for over two years, starting in 2014. Using the above ethnographic methods, first, I found who belonged to the "field" of Tokyo Fashion Week in Bourdieu's sense.

The Membership

Rocamora and Entwistle (2006) stated that among the key people who are recognized as players and insiders of the fashion world, those who come to London Fashion Week include designers, models, journalists, buyers, fashion stylists, and celebrities, as well as less important figures, such as fashion school students, who exist on the margins of the fashion world. When I observed Tokyo Fashion Week, people of various professions participated, in addition to the ones noted by Rocamora and Entwistle (2006). They were from organizations, such as factories, educational organizations, and government agencies. Now that informatization has advanced, bloggers and influencers were also frequently coming to the show. Furthermore, as indicated in the following field note, the same faces were repeatedly seen at multiple shows, dressed in their usual clothing:

> Looking across the seating area before the show starts, Mr. A, who runs a fashion company, is sitting in the second row in the back on the right side. He's dressed completely in black, as usual. Ms. B, who does exhibition work, and Mr. and Mrs. C, from the media, are seated in the middle of the front row. Mr. and Mrs. C are always wearing the same kinds of clothes. Mr. B is wearing a loosely shaped white top. Mr. and Mrs. C are wearing a beret and checkered jacket. It seems that people in the fashion industry have their own style and always dress in a similar style.
>
> *(An excerpt from my fieldnotes at a fashion*
> *show of a young designer's brand X)*

These insiders were always wearing the same kinds of clothes, as this relates to their membership and cultural capital in the field of fashion. Rocamora and Entwistle (2006) participated in London Fashion Week and argue that, in the fashion world, it is important to be able to articulate recognized forms of fashion capital, and develop an appropriate fashion habitus, so that one's body actually looks like it belongs. Likewise, cultural capital is critically important. This includes one's knowledge about not only the history of fashion, but also up-and-coming designers and trends. However, significant for the reproduction of one's position in the field are the objectified forms of cultural capital, in the guise of clothes and accessories from fashionable and exclusive brands, all highly dependent on one's economic capital. In addition, bodily demeanor and carriage are also part of one's performance in the field: in the field of fashion, examples would include one's weight—a thin body being a fashionable body (Rocamora and Entwistle 2006).

In fact, I heard repeatedly that the fashion industry was a "village," as noted above. They said the center consisted of people from long-established Japanese apparel companies and department stores, fashion schools, and some fashion magazines; organizations that did not specialize in fashion, such as major newspapers, and people from overseas were treated as outsiders. I also saw and heard how individuals who were considered outsiders were harshly criticized or given trouble in conflicts over this territory. Furthermore, I observed race- and gender-related characteristics among those who came to the shows in Tokyo. First of all, many people from a wide range of backgrounds went to Fashion Week in Paris and New York. However, the vast majority of those who came to the shows in Tokyo were Japanese. There were only a few non-Japanese Asians and whites. Meanwhile, the majority of models were white, and there were few Asian models. Since I am Japanese, I was included in the racial majority. The gender situation was also noteworthy: there were many men among the executives in organizations, while there were many women in the press and audience. In Paris and New York, it is said that women and men, alike, have key roles.

The power relationship was demonstrated by the seating positions at the Tokyo Fashion Week shows, just as it was at London Fashion Week. In some ways, the shows in Tokyo were different from the shows I had previously observed in Paris and New York. In Paris and New York, the seats were preassigned, and your name and organization were written on a piece of paper and taped onto your seat. You randomly formed one or two lines, as needed, before the doors opened, finding your seat once they did.

In contrast, the participants in Tokyo were instructed to form multiple lines in front of the show's venue, according to the ranking on the invitation (Figure 15.1). Then, before the show began, ushers guided people to empty seats. The ranking was indicated by the color of the sticker on your invitation (e.g., gold, silver, or green). You would not know where you were ranked until you arrived at the venue and saw how the lines were formed. The guests with a high-ranking sticker were important people, so they were led, early on, to seats closer to the runway. The guests with a low-ranking sticker waited longer in line, because they were let in last and led to seats in the back. The most important guests did not stand in line; they were escorted to the front row as soon as they arrived at the venue. The most important guests often included foreign media, national newspapers, fashion magazine

Figure 15.1 Lines in front of a show's venue at Tokyo Fashion Week
Copyright: Yuiko Fujita (author)

journalists, government agency officials, executives of large companies and famous brands, and people from major department stores.

While the show ended in about 10 minutes, the wait time was longer than the show, often lasting for 30 minutes or more. Meanwhile, the Tokyo Fashion Week visitors continued standing in line, allowing others to see where they were ranked in the fashion world. Therefore, unlike at London Fashion Week, your status in the fashion world remained on display while you were standing in line.

Since I was an outsider to the fashion industry, I was usually ranked as the least important guest, even when I received an invitation (and for popular shows, I could not obtain tickets at all). When I participated by requesting a brand to send me an invitation for their show, I was usually seated in the back. However, when I accompanied the influential individual in the fashion world who was cooperating with the study, I was escorted to the front row with him several times without an invitation. This indicates that who you know is an important factor in determining the seating for the show. In the world of fashion, social capital is extremely important. As Rocamora and Entwistle (2006) note, players in all fields are endowed with different amounts of capital, while different capitals are effective in relation to a particular field. A high amount of social capital allows one to move freely within the social network of field participants. In the field of fashion, social capital is essential to acquiring tickets to shows.

I also asked companies and PR firms that manage brands for an invitation to their show by using my title of "professor at the University of XX." At each of those shows, I observed graduate and undergraduate students, whom I knew, involved in a student-run fashion publication or fashion organizations, being allowed to enter before me and, sometimes, taken to the front seats. In general, the status of "university professor" is higher than that of graduate and undergraduate students, outside the fashion world. However, this hierarchy did not apply inside the fashion world; individuals with more fashion-society-related capital had a higher status.

In my case, it was unpleasant at times, but my purpose was research, and I considered that observing such a situation was, in itself, meaningful. Still, it was a bit painful to stand in line for a long time at each show, because there were many shows to see during Fashion Week. For many participants, the fight over seating assignments, which overtly showed this power struggle, caused emotional reactions. At one point, I observed an older woman saying, angrily to the usher, "I'm leaving if I have to take standing room!" Moreover, the following situation was observed at the show of a young designer's brand Y.

> I [the author, Y.F.] arrived at the show's venue around 10:30 a.m. Many people are already lined up. There are dozens of people, who seem like fashion school students, lined up outside Hall A [of Shibuya Hikarie], which is the venue. The guests are supposed to form two lines at the signs, one marked by a pink sticker and the other by a yellow smiley sticker. My invitation had a pink sticker. Ahead of me are three men in suits who look like office workers. I get in line behind them.
>
> One of them says, "This is different from the everyday world," and laughs. He seems to be from a different industry, having come to the show for the first time. He's wearing discolored khaki leather dress shoes, and his clothes are the kind of suits sold at mass retailers; this is not attire for an insider of the fashion industry. Around us are men and women in their 30s, all dressed in dark clothing. People with seats in the rows closest to the front bypass the lines and are allowed inside the venue ahead of others. Only a few are Westerners; I saw Mr. E, president of Company D, going inside around 11 o'clock.
>
> […] Still forced to stand in line at around 11 o'clock, one of the three men in suits in front of me says, "This is badly executed." He still sounds amused. Perhaps, he is here for the first time, does not know that guests in the back seats are forced to stand in line for a long time, and that fashion shows don't start on time.
>
> […] My line was led inside the venue last. I ended up taking standing room on the left, facing the stage. One from the trio started to get mad, saying, "Standing room? I was invited!" When he called to the usher and pleaded to be allowed to take an open seat in a row closer to the front, the usher refused, explaining that they were expecting more media people. The space for standing room on both sides of the venue was full by the time the show started.
>
> *(an excerpt from my fieldnotes at the show of a young designer's brand Y)*

As described, if you are an outsider, you are regarded as a powerless person in the fashion world, even if you have status in a different field. Since fashion-school students and lower-ranking individuals in the fashion industry belonged inside the fashion world, and knew the customs of these shows, I did not observe them expressing anger (like those who seemed to be outsiders), even when they had to stand in line for a

Figure 15.2　A Show at Tokyo Fashion Week
Copyright: Yuiko Fujita (author)

long time. On the other hand, conflicts over and awareness toward these seating situations were observed among influential people in the fashion world, as well.

As Rocamora and Entwistle (2006) argue, this is because the catwalk, or "runway," stretches out into the audience, who sits in a rectangle around it (Figure 15.2). This relationship of stage to audience allows for the "struggle for visibility" to be played out between participants who become part of the spectacle, as one's eyes are directed across the stage to the bodies seated on the other side. In such an auditorium, observing the audience becomes part of the spectacle of the show, while, in turn, one becomes keenly aware of being watched. Front-row participants are, therefore, very much part of the spectacle. The more powerful bodies are the most visible on the front row. Beyond the front row are allocated seats for less important players. The furthest reaches are designated as "standing," and this area contains those without much power or influence, such as particularly resourceful fashion students (Rocamora and Entwistle 2006). From their argument, we can understand that for some insiders, it was more important to be seen at the show than to see the show.

By gaining entry to the closed fashion community and participating in Tokyo Fashion Week, I found out who belonged to the field of fashion in Tokyo and which organizations had power. I observed that the same people were allocated the front rows in different fashion shows. Such people were from fashion publications, government agencies, major department stores, and large fashion companies. Moreover, they were mostly men, except for those from the media. In the next section, I will delineate how I developed a new research question through my fieldwork—the marginalization of women in Tokyo fashion organizations.

Finding a Research Question

The setting of a fashion week show is a visualization of the relation between power and the fashion world. I observed fashion shows at Tokyo Fashion Week and found that most of the executives in the front rows were men. As I noticed this gender imbalance, I began to pay close attention to gender aspects during my fieldwork. Then, the fact that there were few female company executives could also be confirmed from various angles. For example, the fashion magazine *WWD* featured CEOs of fashion-related companies in its 2017–2019 issues, and all the CEOs appearing on the cover were men. The most striking fact I noticed was that the executives of the Japan Fashion Week Organization (JFW)—the steering body of Tokyo Fashion Week—were also all men (Table 15.1). However, no one I met in the field questioned this inequality of gender.

Table 15.1 Japan Fashion Week Organization Board Members [June 26, 2019]

Role	Name	Occupation	Gender
Board chairperson	Masahiko Miyake	Chairman and President, TSI Holdings	Male
Vice-president	Kazushi Hashimoto	Executive Vice President, Toray Industries, Inc.	Male
Executive director	Ken Akamatsu	Chairman, Japan Department Stores Association	Male
Executive director	Nobuyuki Ota	President, MD03 Inc. (Collection Program Representative)	Male
Executive director	Minoru Kitabatake	Chairman, Japan Apparel Fashion Industry Council	Male
Executive director	Hikosaburo Seike	Executive Officer, Onward Kashiyama Co., Ltd.	Male
Executive director	Kenichi Tomiyoshi	Vice Chairman, Japan Chemical Fibers Association	Male
Executive director	Tsutomu Hagihira	Chairman, Institute for The Fashion Industries	Male
Executive director	Michio Fukuda	Chairman of The Board, Adastria Co., Ltd.	Male
Executive director	Masahiro Horie	Director and Executive Officer, Tokyu Corporation	Male
Executive director	Masahiro Morofuji	Managing Executive Officer, President, Textile Company, ITOCHU CORPORATION	Male
Auditor	Akishige Manabe	President, Japan Fashion Association	Male
Auditor	Yuji Hasegawa	President, Japan Apparel Fashion Industry Council	Male
Adviser	Akira Baba	Board chairperson, Japan Fashion Association	Male

I observed that, among all the designers participating in Tokyo Fashion Week, young designers, who continued to flourish, tended to be men. For example, Tokyo New Designer Fashion Grand Prix is an award given to outstanding young designers. Seventy percent of the winners in the professional category, between 2013 and 2017, were male.

Furthermore, it seems that men were more likely to be chosen to succeed the heads of major women's brands in Japan. For example, Yu Amatsu, who became the designer of the Hanae Mori brand, and Kei Ninomiya, who is the designer of Noir Kei Ninomiya, the collection by Comme des Garçons, are all men; although, Hanae Mori and Rei Kawakubo, of Comme des Garçons, are women. I asked one young male designer why male designers were dominant in Tokyo; he took it for granted and just said that "perhaps it was Japan's unique culture."

As described, despite the fact that women account for a large percentage of workers in the Japanese fashion industry, the number of young female designers who continued to flourish is relatively low, and the percentage of female executives is lower in apparel companies than in other industries. In other words, women who become designers or take other positions continue to have low status in the Tokyo fashion world. However, virtually no previous study has explored or analyzed the state of women in the fashion world in Japan.

One of the main reasons is that men have also been dominant in academic communities in Japan. Until recently, they have rarely been interested in the sphere of women. Many scholars still regard fashion studies as being much less important than art or architecture studies. On the other hand, I have much interest in the field of fashion and paid attention to women's situations within it. At the beginning of my research, my objective was to explore young Japanese designers' brands and their business, but I gradually became interested in gender issues in the field site. It led me to develop another research question—"How are women marginalized in the fashion world in Tokyo, where the majority of the workers are women?" As Skegges notes (2001), feminist research is often related to why and how women are oppressed, and ethnography can be used as "grounded theory," in which theories are used as examples of empirical experience.

In order to explore gender inequality in the field of fashion, I did a literature review to examine occupational issues of female workers, as this should be related to how people work in the entire fashion industry. Previous studies on labor and gender have repeatedly noted that labor in Japan involves long work hours, which has deterred women from holding long-term jobs. You have to come up with new designs, manufacture products, and advertise new products to many people in an endless stream, especially in the fashion industry, because new designs are released multiple times per year. It can be said that working long hours is a prerequisite. For example, Chitose Abe, the designer of sacai, which has now grown into a leading Japanese brand, says that what prompted her to leave her employer, Comme des Garçons, and start a brand business was her pregnancy.

Abe: Although my newborn daughter was adorable and I did not regret it, all in all, I agonized [over it] a lot. My husband is dedicated to his job. Meanwhile, I'm alone with my baby, feeling completely left behind by society, unable to join the circle of mothers or people at the park and pushing the stroller at a shrine in the neighborhood.

Reporter: The sense of unfairness at home that goes, "Why me?" I can understand that.

Abe: I mean, I used to work hard, too, until just before [the baby]. Besides, my husband and I had similar aspirations and ideals for work. But as soon as I gave birth to my child, "XYZ's mom" became my identity, and I don't even get a name. I actually told my husband over and over, "Don't you think this is unfair? Don't you think something is wrong here?"

Reporter: What was the breakthrough?

Abe: Seeing me depressed at home, my husband said at one point, "Why don't you create your own brand then?"

(Nikkei Business, *February 27, 2014*)

I also conducted informal and formal interviews with men and women in the field sites. The same stories were heard in my fieldwork, regarding this point. For example, designers and apparel company workers said the following:

That is true, once you have a child, whether you are a pattern maker or designer. Although, it might be different, if there's a supportive environment. If your parents aren't nearby, and you are kind of taking care of the child on your own, I would think it's extremely hard to continue working. (A young designer)

Actually, more and more of the people around me are married and childless, but those who aren't married and, consequently, don't have children are working extremely hard, as you might expect. They work vigorously, after all. It's impossible to compete with the amount of work they do and their dazzling footwork. (An apparel company worker)

[excerpts from my fieldnotes in fashion organizations]

In these kinds of long-hour jobs in the creative economy, women are further disadvantaged when it comes to maternity and childcare.

In addition to the long work hours, another factor discouraging women from continuing in their positions has been gender discrimination in the office (Otsuki 2015). I heard similar stories in the fashion world. They say that men are placed in sales and production management departments, while the majority of workers in the store sales and public relations departments are women. Of these jobs, they say that the ones that lead to promotion are the sales and merchandising jobs. As a result, those who are promoted to managerial positions tend to be men. Ms. F, who worked at an apparel company, explained it, as follows:

> Ms. F: Most of those in the publicity department are women. There are men, of course, but there are many women, and, in such a setting with many women, the head is also a woman. In terms of the front-end sales, women definitely outnumber men in sales and storefront. In terms of positions, store managers and supervisors are almost all women. The reason is that those are people who moved up from sales. Another profession with many women is the technical profession; there are quite a lot of female pattern makers and designers. Close to 80 percent are women at XX [company name].

> Y.F: Does everyone work for many years?

> Ms. F: When you work for many years, you do follow a path of becoming the leader of the pattern team or the leader of the designer team, but almost no one becomes the top of the brand from there. The reason is that merchandisers are very influential, since we are originally what you'd call SPA [a Specialty retailer of Private label Apparel], or a company that is supposed to handle retail and everything else. I don't want to sound rude, but they are high-ranking, so to say, and it's like becoming a merchandiser is a short cut for elites. Merchandising is also a line of work you do by crunching numbers a lot on the basis of "since the budget for buying inventory is this much, we'll place an order for this many to make this many products," and most brand merchandisers are men.

> [...] I think most of the female designers and directors with that kind of capability end up becoming independent rather than climbing up the organizational ladder. And because they end up leaving the company, they don't climb the corporate ladder.

As we can see from this account, in addition to long work hours, gender disparity in job duties has become a factor that prevents women from being promoted in the fashion world. Some women cannot work long hours in companies, become independent, and start their own brand business, in this way; however, there are circumstances where it is difficult for women to start a business or continue business as a designer. In the case of becoming an independent designer, this means that you set up a company and outsource product manufacturing to small and medium-sized companies, such as textile manufacturers and garment factories. You then present the manufactured products at the exhibitions for retail buyers to order. However, there were remarks, such as it is difficult for young women to obtain loans or participate in homosocial male networks. There are women who started a business and became successful as designers, such as Rei Kawakubo of Comme des Garçons. However, in many cases, their husbands are helping with the business aspects or taking care of all business aspects.

Concerning financial issues, my respondents, both company employees, and independent designers, often said they could not earn much money. In Japan, the average annual salary of in-office fashion designers is not high—$45,000 USD. Furthermore, Japan still has the third highest gender pay gap in the OECD (Organization for Economic Co-operation and Development)—at 25.7%, and women earn only about 75 percent of what men do. Young designers who have just launched their brand in the last few years can expect only a small amount in annual sales. Therefore, young designers usually attempt to win fashion awards offering prize money in order to support their first show at the Tokyo Fashion Week (to hold a fashion show in the Tokyo Fashion Week costs approximately $50,000 USD, at least). Young independent designers, especially women, are financially insecure, and more than a few designers I interviewed quit their brand business within a couple of years, due to financial problems.

Some women freelance, but it is very difficult for freelancers to attain a high position in the fashion world, because power in the fashion world is concentrated among the executives of large companies. For example, as Table 15.1 shows, the directors of the Japan Fashion Week Organization are executives from major apparel companies, textile manufacturers, department stores, and trading companies, making the Japan Fashion Week Organization a "boys' club" where the only members are men who have climbed the ladder at large companies.

As described above, female designers are often marginalized in the fashion world. This is related to their long work hours and the disparity in job duties. While it is difficult for young designers to stay in business, in terms of financing, female designers also face issues with the structure of the work. Although it is necessary to keep working for a long time in order to increase all types of capital, the issue is that continuing to work is, in itself, difficult for female designers. Through fieldwork, I observed, heard, and found these "truths," which are rarely seen and questioned by people in Japan's male-dominant academic worlds.

Conclusion

In conclusion, as the literature on gender and ethnography pointed out, the gender of the ethnographer affects the process of ethnographic fieldwork in various ways. Partly because of my gender, I encountered different types of difficulties in accessing cultural organizations and in building rapport with informants in the given field. In a field where the majority of workers were women, there were many roles for me, a female ethnographer, to take as a participant observer, once I managed to enter. Then, through participant observation, I was able to find who belonged to the field and who had power—the majority of the workers were women, but the powerful figures were men. This led me to focus on gender issues in the field. In this way, I developed a new research question that I did not consider at the beginning of my fieldwork—"How are women marginalized in the fashion world in Tokyo, where the majority of the workers are women?" Thus, ethnographical methods allowed me to develop a new research question. A great deal of feminist ethnography has used empirical research to articulate what was previously invisible. Without entering and observing the field, it would have been impossible for me to notice the gender issue in the fashion industry, where most insiders took for granted that it is a man's world.

References

Becker, Howard S. 1982. *Art Worlds*. Berkeley, CA: University of California Press.

Bourdieu, Pierre. 1993. *Sociology in Question*. London: Sage.

Clifford, James. 1986. "Introduction: Partial Truths." In James Clifford and George E. Marcus eds., *Writing Culture: The Poetics and Politics of Ethnography*. Berkeley, CA: University of California Press, pp. 1–26.

DeWalt, K. M., and DeWalt, B. R. 2002. *Participant Observation: A Guide for Fieldworkers*. Walnut Creek, CA: AltaMira Press.

Fine, Gary A. 1996. *Kitchens: The Culture of Restaurant Work*. Berkeley, CA: University of California Press.

Fujita, Yuiko. 2009. *Cultural Migrants from Japan: Youth, Media, and Migration in New York and London*. Lanham, MD: Lexington Books.

Fujita, Yuiko. 2011. "Fabricating Japanese-ness? the Identity Politics of Young Designers and Artists in Global Cities." *International Journal of Japanese Sociology* 20 (1), 43–58.

Fujita, Yuiko. 2017. "Transnational Japanese Fashion Designers." In Yuiko Fujita, Hiroshi Narumi and Izumi Tsuji eds., *Doing Sociology through Fashion*. Tokyo: Yuhikaku, pp. 232–253.

Hammersley, Martyn, and Paul Atkinson. 2007. *Ethnography: Principles in Practice*, 3rd ed. New York: Routledge.

Harris, Deborah Ann, and Giuffre, Patti. 2015. *Taking the Heat: Women Chefs and Gender Inequality in the Professional Kitchen*. New Brunswick, NJ: Rutgers University Press.

Johnson, Randal. 1993. "Editor's Introduction: Pierre Bourdieu on Art, Literature, and Culture." In Randal Johnson ed., *The Field of Cultural Production, by Pierre Bourdieu*. New York: Columbia University Press, pp. 1–25.

Kawamura, Yuniya. 2004. *The Japanese Revolution in Paris Fashion*. Oxford: Berg.

Marcus, George E. 1995. "Ethnography In/of the World System: The Emergence of Multi-Sited Ethnography." *Annual Review of Anthropology* 24, 95–117.

Mears, Ashley. 2011. *Pricing Beauty*. Berkeley: University of California Press.

O'Reilly, Karen. 2009. *Key Concepts in Ethnography*. London: Sage.

Otsuki, Nami. 2015. *Shokumu Kakusa (Gender Gap in Workplace)*. Tokyo: Keiso Shobo.

Rocamora, Agnès, and Entwistle, Joanne. 2006. "The Field of Fashion Materialized: A Study of London Fashion Week." *Sociology* 40 (4), 735–751.

Skeggs, Beverly. 2001. "Feminist Ethnography." In Paul Atkinson, Amanda Coffey and Sara Delamont eds., *Handbook of Ethnography*. London: Sage, pp. 426–442.

Tseëlon, Efrat. 1995. *The Masque of Femininity. The Presentation of Woman in Everyday Life*. London: Sage.

Warren, Carol A. B. 1988. *Gender Issues in Field Research*. Newbury Park, CA: Sage.

Whyte, William Foote. 1943. *Street Corner Society: The Social Structure of an Italian Slum*. Chicago, IL: University of Chicago Press.

16

WHAT MAKES RESILIENCE?

An Ethnographic Study of the Work of Prison Officers

Mette Mogensen and Elisabeth Naima Mikkelsen

Introduction

In this chapter, we show the potential of sensory organizational ethnography as it relates to future resilience research and theorizing, suggesting a wider use of sensory approaches for the study of similar, complex organizational phenomena. Confronted with the potentially dangerous setting of Danish prisons as part of our field study, our own resilience was put to the test, subsequently inspiring us to draw on our own sensory and emotional capacity as researchers (Lee-Treweek, 2000; Pink, 2015; Warren, 2002). Using visual methods, such as autophotography, and considering our own ambiguous emotions helped us realize that the ambiguity that we felt in fact mirrored the Janus-faced nature of resilience in prison work; these observations produced new and valuable insights into the phenomenon of resilience. We argue that there is a need for nuance and contextualization, not just for the phenomenon of resilience but equally for the role and potential of sensory methodologies. While romantic arguments of empathy, closeness and getting more deeply connected with the field and its habitants are often put forward, following our experiences, the potential of sensory ethnography may lie as much in the possible misfits and resistances produced in the field, including the researcher's feelings of being both different, incompetent and morally misaligned.

Taking Turns with the Phenomenon of Resilience

As complexity and instability are increasingly considered inevitable environmental characteristics of both public and private organizations, the concept of resilience has come to the fore as a suitable approach for addressing risk and the successful management of it. The focus on resilience, namely the ability of individuals, groups or organizations to respond flexibly and effectively in situations of adversity, forms part of an optimistic agenda of identifying and nurturing the positive resources of individuals and organizations (King, Newman, & Luthans, 2016; Masten, 2001; Weick & Sutcliffe, 2007). Born in child psychology, resilience research has proliferated into many subdisciplines of the humanities and social sciences. While it has been argued that we can learn much by moving beyond the dominant trait-and-factor thinking in psychological resilience research and instead study resilience as a social configuration (Walsh-Dilley & Wolford, 2015), 'what makes resilience' in specific organizational practices remains understudied. While the point of departure in organizational resilience literature was close empirical investigations of work and its organization, 'the resilient organization' is increasingly presented as a prescriptive mould relevant to fit any organization regardless of its contextual specificities (Bardoel et al., 2014; Hollnagel, 2011; Lengnick-Hall, Beck, & Lengnick-Hall, 2011; Luthans et al., 2010; Vogus & Sutcliffe, 2007; Weick, Sutcliffe, & Obstfeld, 2008). In this chapter, we respond to calls from Anderson (2015) and Kossek and Perrigino (2016) to appreciate the contextual and dynamic qualities of resilience rather than to measure and deduce its meaning beforehand. Drawing on sensory ethnography (Pink, 2015), using shadowing, autophotography and interviews across two prison settings, we study resilience by focusing on the work of prison officers and how they talk about, negotiate and enact their role(s) within the prison setting.

With a particular focus on the positive resources in work, we identify two distinct yet interdependent resources pivotal to the resilience of prison officers and simultaneously demonstrate their highly ambiguous nature: 'Relations with inmates' and 'Belonging to the officer group'. As opposed to the research field in general, this version of resilience does not measure up according to one-dimensional scales. During our fieldwork, we discovered that the positive resources in prison work do not simply act as 'protective factors'. These resources have a flip side to them, thus calling for a more ambiguous conceptualization of resilience than the one currently presented. We therefore conclude that producing resilience is not about factors to be known, audited and properly anticipated. Resilience is rather a situated and mundane accomplishment inherent to the specific social, physical and emotional 'orders' of the specific work environment.

The potential of sensory ethnography for the study of resilience and similar psychosocial phenomena such as stress or well-being is pivotal in this regard and points to more general learnings. It allows for the phenomenon to be not simply observed and measured but equally to be experienced and felt, inviting in much-needed contextualization and nuance. As we have been studying resilience in a prison setting prone to potential risk and danger, this has put resilience centre stage in a double sense. We have not only been offered the opportunity to observe in practice the resilience of prison officers but also been confronted ourselves with issues of risk and resilience as we entered the prisons. Taking on these emotional reactions as important data and deliberately involving our emotional and sensory capacity as part of the research afford the most fine-tuned and flexible scale of investigation imaginable. This 'scale' does not have to adhere to the classic Likert scale from 1–5 or settle for fixed factors beforehand. As our work suggests, engaging oneself as a researcher in sensory ethnography – even if it is from a position of incompetence, difference and occasionally moral disdain – serves to produce a much wider spectrum of data, subsequently allowing for the phenomenon under study to unfold in new and different ways.

Resilience Research

The most recent decades have seen an increased interest in the phenomenon of 'resilience' within the humanities and social sciences. Evidence of interest has emerged particularly within the field of psychology, where resilience was observed among disadvantaged children who were remarkably robust despite encountering significant adversities (Garmezy, 1993; Masten, Best, & Garmezy, 1990). Resilience is defined as '[T]he capability and ability of an element to return to a stable state after a disruption' (Bhamra, Dani, & Burnard, 2011: 5376) and refers to the ability to maintain normal functioning and performance in the face of hardships. Some researchers even relate resilience to the ability to learn and develop in the face of adversity, thus potentially returning even more strengthened and resourceful than before (Lengnick-Hall et al., 2011; Vogus & Sutcliffe, 2007).

Psychological Resilience

Since the first documentation of resilience in at-risk children, psychological resilience research has developed a core focus on protective factors to explain what makes an individual resilient. These factors are often accounted for in terms of personal strengths, specifically personality traits and abilities, such as hope, optimism, intellectual functioning, self-esteem and self-efficacy (Masten, 2001; Tusaie & Dyer, 2004) or 'competences', that foster a successful, adaptive stress response (Luthar & Cicchetti, 2000). Later, characteristics of other supportive factors present in the social network of the resilient individual have been included, such as social support and parenting quality (Jackson, Firtko, & Edenborough, 2007; Rutter, 1985).

The majority of psychological resilience research is either variable focused, which assesses linkages between the degree of risk, outcome and personal attributes that compensate the risk, or person focused, which examines case studies of resilience by comparing two groups drawn from the same high-risk population (Masten, 2001). The Kauai Longitudinal Study by Werner and Smith (1992 cited in Werner, 2005) is a classic example of this dominant trait-and-factor thinking in psychological resilience research. As research has grown, consistent themes have been intra-individual factors that strongly correlate with resilient outcomes. Several self-report instruments to quantify these resilient factors in individuals have been developed (Tusaie & Dyer, 2004), for example the Ego Resilience Scale (ER89). Although considerable psychological resilience research addresses the balance between risk and protective factors as a dynamic process between the individual and the environment, attention beyond individual traits is mostly found in other research fields.

Organizational Resilience

The growing attention to resilience in organization theorizing is found in the literature on psychological capital (Luthans et al., 2010) and positive organizational scholarship (Cameron & Spreitzer, 2011; Dutton, Glynn, & Spreitzer, 2008), where resilience research comprises a focus on the positive factors of organizational life. Set within an organizational context yet similar to psychological resilience research, the core interest is to identify factors that foster resilience in the workplace and its resultant influence on workplace outcomes, cutting across individual, team and organizational levels of analysis (King et al., 2016).

Another research area with a particular focus on organizational resilience has flourished around the study of organizations with a high-risk profile, the so-called 'high reliability organizations' (HROs). Studying procedures and coordination in organizations that operate in extremely trying conditions, such as nuclear power-generation plants, air traffic control systems and naval aircraft carriers (Bourrier, 1996; Rochlin, LaPorte, & Roberts, 1987; Weick, 1990), this area of research has sought to offer a specific organizational approach to resilience. Rather than a focus on factors and individual capabilities, the study of HROs has focused on the deliberate organization around failure rather than success. The distinguishing feature of HROs' resilience is that they have the capacity to bounce back from errors and cope with surprises in the moment as they monitor small errors and elaborate experiences of near misses (Weick, Sutcliffe, & Obstfeld, 2008).

Bourrier (1996), one of the few within resilience research to apply fieldwork methodology, explored the unusual properties of HROs by focusing on everyday organizing in two nuclear power plants. In line with the Berkeley HRO group (La Porte, 1996), she found that rather than formal hierarchy, rules and workers compliance, the resilient organization depends on the everyday structuring of tasks and coordination between workers as well as the informal 'latent' networks activated in the face of uncertainties. While Bourrier (1996) presents an example of close empirical investigation of resilient organizing, much of the HRO literature has evolved around an explicit prescriptive and generic agenda: how to best design, educate and organize for resilience (Hollnagel, 2011; Lengnick-Hall, Beck, & Lengnick-Hall, 2011; Weick & Sutcliffe, 2007; Weick, Sutcliffe, & Obstfeld, 2008). Here, the resilient organization is often presented as a concept and mould relevant to fit any organization regardless of its contextual specificities.

Stress and Resilience in Prison Officers

While numerous empirical investigations have examined work-related stress in prison officers, only limited research has focused specifically on resilience in prison officers' work. Regardless of the specific focus, however, methods often involve self-reporting questionnaires to measure variables, such as environmental characteristics, stressors, and protective factors relevant to stress or resilience. Another shared characteristic is that conclusions are often mixed and even contradictory. Several studies have demonstrated that many prison officers are satisfied with their job (Cullen et al., 1990; Leip & Stinchcomb, 2013) and have no intention of resigning; they may also simultaneously experience considerable stress on the job. This notion has been explained by officers' tough 'macho' image, which prevents them from acknowledging their stress (Cheek & Miller, 1983). Other studies have focused specifically on the sources of stress in prison officers, finding that perceived dangerousness of the job is the strongest predictor of stress in correctional work (Dowden & Tellier, 2004). Reviews of the literature on stress in correctional work additionally conclude that work environment factors are more important in shaping the well-being of prison officers than personal factors (Lambert, Hogan, & Barton, 2002; Schaufeli & Peeters, 2000). These studies distinguish between risk factors, such as the dangerousness of the job and inmate interaction, which cause stress and burnout, and positive factors, such as peer support, which has a positive effect on prison officers' well-being.

Focusing specifically on inmate interaction, most studies consider it a risk factor: one study for example found that high levels of officers' well-being were positively related to officers' social distance from inmates (Farkas, 1999), and a Danish study of burnout in prison officers similarly concluded that the emotional demands of the job (relating to inmate interaction) predict burnout (Andersen et al., 2017). By contrast, another study showed that in more human service-oriented units where officers were more positively inclined towards supporting inmates, officers reported significantly higher well-being than traditional custody-oriented officers (Hepburn & Knepper, 1993). The limited literature on resilience in prison officers has also reached different conclusions. Focusing again on inmate interaction, Johnson and Price (1981) found that prison officers who combined their custodial role with a human service role and approached inmates with a rehabilitative orientation contributed to the development of 'resilient prisons', i.e., more safe, responsive and caring prisons. By contrast Morgan, Van Haveren, and Pearson (2002) found that higher education and rank in prison officers was associated with their higher resilience to burnout, suggesting that higher ranking officers in management who do not interact with inmates are the most resilient.

Looking across the various bodies of literature reviewed in this chapter, resilience is a rather multifaceted phenomenon and has given rise to a range of different theoretical models and approaches with little conceptual or methodological consensus. What unites resilience research across disciplines, however, is a common interest in defining and measuring the positive resources and abilities of a given entity and deducing general principles for how to become more resilient. While increasingly popular as a concept as well as an overall optimistic agenda, the subject of 'what makes resilience' remains understudied in specific organizational practices. Following Kossek and Perrigino (2016) in a recent review of resilience within organization and management studies, there is a need to (re)appreciate the highly contextual and dynamic qualities of resilience to move the field forward. They argue that one way to do this is to consider the phenomenon of resilience as inseparable from the specific occupational context in which it appears.

Our ambition with this chapter is therefore to extend the literature on organizational resilience by way of a close ethnographic study of how resilience is made and negotiated in the work practices and work relationships of prison officers within a Danish prison setting. We argue that the prevailing survey instruments used and the scales developed within resilience research risk producing a both decontextualized and far too 'rigid' version of resilience. As shown above, using scales to distinguish and measure risk factors and positive factors in prison work has primarily produced a rather contradictory picture, as it is does not adequately capture the ambivalence and dynamics characteristic of the work of prison officers. By unfolding the contextual dynamics of resilience empirically and focusing specifically on the ambivalence of the positive resources in prison work, we wish to show the potential of organizational ethnography for resilience research and theorizing.

Methods

We conducted fieldwork in two prisons: a detention facility and an open prison. Both prisons are situated within the same region. The detention facility is a small yet technologically advanced facility, often housing some of the particularly hard cases. Most of the inmates are there for a short period of time as they await their sentence. Security measures are strict with little possibilities for inmates to interact. In effect, interaction between inmates and prison officers is both very frequent and demanding. The open prison is a large male facility, which holds 160 inmates and comprises self-contained wings and a special addiction treatment unit. The open prison targets prisoners who present a low risk of absconding. Security measures are therefore low with a single fence as opposed to the tall brick walls of the detention facility. Inmates go to work inside the prison and are able to socialize between themselves and efforts are generally made to make prison life as similar to life outside the prison as possible.

Methodologically, we tried to situate the phenomenon of resilience among prison officers by investigating positive and negative resources as inseparable to work and its everyday organization. We spent approximately 130 hours shadowing officers in the two prisons, covering both day and evening shifts (Czarniawska-Joerges, 2007). Comprehensive field notes were taken after each shift. Additionally, we conducted 19 interviews in total. Eleven individual interviews and three group interviews were conducted in the open prison, and four individual interviews and one group interview were conducted in the detention facility. Individual interviews covered officers' views on their primary task and its organization, their work role and their experiences of the positive as well as the negative aspects of work. As will be elaborated below, the group interviews and one single interview had a different character as they were elicited from autophotographs (Warren, 2005) and photographs taken by the prison officers themselves with reference to the overall theme: a good workday. All the interviews were audiotaped and transcribed. Our motivation for researching prison work was to contribute to a better understanding and knowledge of the demanding and often risky aspect of prison officers' work, especially the many ambiguities they face in the course of a regular workday.

Engaging with Risk and Danger in a Prison Setting

Within the field of ethnography, the notions of risk and danger have played ambiguous roles. There has been a tendency to glorify the risks and dangers experienced by the ethnographer, presenting them as 'war stories' told with enthusiasm and as signs of group membership. However, since the early 1990s, danger has been given attention as a specific methodological concern to ethnographers working within particularly dangerous settings (Lee, 1995; Lee-Treweek & Linkogle, 2000; Morgan & Pink, 2018). The article by Sluka (1990) is emblematic of this approach. Based on his close engagement with a Catholic-Nationalist ghetto in Belfast, Sluka develops a pragmatic stance towards danger as something to be anticipated in advance and acted upon in the ongoing positioning as researcher vis-a-vis the field. Sluka was situated in a high-conflict setting and therefore being identified and affiliated with one side or the other could in itself produce considerable danger.

In terms of anticipating and planning for danger before entering the prison settings, we had not given it much thought. First and foremost, we found it interesting and thrilling to be given access. The fact that we have been doing our ethnography within a Danish prison setting undoubtedly played a role in this respect. Stories about assaults on prison officers do occur in the Danish media, yet prison life in Denmark is far from the tense and conflict-driven reality of American prisons. The Danish system is known for its rather 'soft' approach based on relation building and rehabilitation as much as punishment and incarceration. However, this does not mean that we did not experience risk and danger. Similar to Sluka (1990), the risk we experienced was primarily related to our positioning in the field, namely, 'belonging' to the group of prison officers. On one hand, this affiliation was positive, as it supported our access to the field and offered us physical protection from inmates in case of trouble. On the other hand, this affiliation also produced a sense of vulnerability and risk because it 'automatically' placed us in opposition to the dangerous 'others', and the affiliation was highly precarious because we could not truly place our trust in 'our' group membership. As we elaborate further in the analysis, in the liking with the prison officers, the positive resource of belonging to the officer group, could readily show as Janus-faced, producing vulnerability and risk.

Emotional Danger and Sensory Ethnography

The dangers met and described by Sluka in the field are primarily of a physical nature. However, dangers may also be psychological and emotional in character, although this aspect is more rarely explored. The emotional distress involved in following auxiliary workers within a care home for elderly people is eloquently described by Lee-Treweek (2000). During her four weeks of observation, she becomes still more disgusted and depressed about the insensitivity displayed in the daily 'care' of the elderly. Reflecting her emotional experiences, Lee-Treweek argues that the emotional reactions of the researcher may serve as highly important methodological 'tools' in ethnography, as they serve to mirror the emotional tensions already at play in the field under study. Being attentive to emotions and being open towards a wider spectrum of sensory representations of the field is found within 'sensory ethnography' (Pink, 2015). This particular ethnographic approach is about engaging with the multisensoriality of the (work)places, inviting more varied forms of knowledge into the research of other people's experiences. As we will show in this chapter, the results of being sensitive to the multisensoriality of our experiences in the field afford new aspects and layers of knowing that enable us to challenge and enrich our current theoretical understandings of resilience.

Indeed, focusing on our personal experiences within the prison, including our emotional responses, provided valuable data not only in terms of acknowledging the health and safety aspect of our ethnographic endeavour but as input to grasp the specific dynamics of risk and resilience as experienced by the prison officers. Rather than considering the emotional responses of the researcher exclusively in terms of personal relevance, they should be treated with care as they offer a unique access to the emotion rules and the order of the social setting under study (Lee-Treweek). Emotion rules prescribe how we should feel in a given situation by marking off degrees of appropriateness of a feeling (Hochschild, 1990). Emotion rules are constructed in social interaction and they are guided by an ideological aim that covertly controls individuals (Mikkelsen & Wåhlin, 2020; Putnam & Mumby, 1993). As we show in the analysis, our personal emotional responses and our grappling with prevailing emotion rules provided us with valuable insight into the ambiguities of risk and resilience in prison work.

Combining Ethnography with Visual Methods

In addition to drawing on our own emotional responses, we also attempted to produce better access and a richer representation of the knowledge and experience of officers by combining our observations and interviews with the visual method of autophotography (cf. Pink, 2011; Schwartz, 1989). Visual methods and especially *auto*photography produce a larger sensitivity towards the empirical setting and its informants as it more profoundly engages the informants as well as the researcher, propelling Warren (2002, 2005) to present it as part of a 'sensual methodology'. We used autophotography by inviting prison officers in both prisons to take pictures of 'a good workday' and to add a small text explaining the picture and its link to the theme. After a period of 14 days during which the camera circulated among the officers, the pictures and the accompanying texts were then to be returned to the researchers and used for subsequent photoelicitation in group interviews with 3–5 officers. In our specific context, autophotography produced valuable insights into an otherwise inaccessible world of prisons and prison work; however, it also proved to be a rather difficult and in many respects a method unfit, even provocative, to the specific setting of the prison.

Following general security measures, cameras are not permitted in prisons. While this precaution is directed towards inmates and not prison officers, the mere presence of a camera, not to mention taking pictures, was considered controversial and a potential breach of security. Furthermore, as we did not have the chance to introduce the camera to the group of officers in person, we had to rely on a shop steward in the open prison and a manager in the detention facility. This proved to be decisive to the process. While the shop steward was a highly esteemed colleague who managed to positively promote the camera with her colleagues, in the detention facility the affiliation with management, which is generally mistrusted, had a negative effect on the reception among the prison officers. In the open prison, the prescribed method of circulating the camera and sending each photograph including texts via e-mail to one of the researchers was followed rather smoothly by the officers but less so in the detention facility. Here, only a couple of officers engaged in taking photographs, and they never sent their pictures to us. Instead, we found them stored in the camera with a handwritten note, which was to a large extent crafted after the fact by a daily coordinator, thus making the link between each photograph and text rather arbitrary. Thus, in our experience, introducing a camera is not a flawless method of gaining better access or 'getting closer' to the field. The potential of the method depends on its interaction with the particular context (Mogensen, 2012), which may in itself prove to be valuable data. In the strict security setting of the detention facility, the method seemed to reinforce a potential opposition between 'outsiders' – be it managers or researchers – and the prison officers. By contrast, in the rehabilitation unit of the open prison, a camera was far better aligned with the open doors, friendly chit-chat between inmates and prison officers, and the general character of prison work.

The different receptions of the camera notwithstanding, in terms of eliciting stories and involving prison officers in open conversation about their daily work, the autophotographs proved highly useful. They helped us make sure that we talked about topics that were deemed relevant to the field rather than following a list of (potentially arbitrary) themes defined by the researcher. In the following analysis, we make use of two specific photographs to serve as our analytical anchor point. They serve to visualize the two most decisive resources in prison work according to the officers: 1) *Relations with inmates,* and 2) *Belonging to the officer group.* As the analysis unfolds, we add additional resources of interview quotes and field notes to gradually expand the meaning of the single photograph. In the course of the analysis, it is made progressively obvious how these positive resources constitute core aspects of resilience in the work of prison officers. Moreover, these officers simultaneously carry negative aspects with them, thus constituting an ambiguous risk dimension.

Relations with Inmates

Figure 16.1 shows a prison officer sitting at a table by herself while making crawling pixies, a particular kind of Christmas decoration. She looks down, smiling as she is drawing something on the pixie. On the table is also a Poinsettia, a flower

Figure 16.1 Activities with inmates

characteristic of this particular season, namely Christmas time. The surroundings are dark and blurry but it is clear that this scene is set within a large room with roof lighting characteristic of a public building. However, what strikes the viewer in this scene is a uniformed officer making pixies. It seems slightly odd and surprising. It is a picture far from the general idea of prison work as something stressful and dangerous. The uniform notwithstanding, it could have been a picture of a situation playing out in a family around Christmas. Going through the pictures, there are many more like it. Some are also related to this particular time of year, showing a group of prisoners standing in the middle of a Christmas tree plantation looking happy and ready to use an axe. There is also a picture of a Christmas tree being decorated by an inmate. Then, there are the pictures of homemade sweets produced by inmates and a table set with flour and bowls, ready for baking. The common denominator across these pictures, supported by the texts accompanying them, is that they are all pictures of prison work involving inmates. Preparing for group interviews, we themed these pictures: 'activities with inmates'. Although the prison officer is captured alone with the pixies, two additional pictures taken from a different angle reveal that two colleagues also wearing uniform and four inmates are sitting around the same table, all busy preparing for Christmas. As the text explains: 'Marie and I are busy preparing Christmas decorations for Christmas time in the detention'. What is particularly noticeable, at least to outsiders such as us, is not just the fact that prison officers are engaged in activities with inmates. It is the mundane characteristic, the 'homeliness', of these activities that produce the surprise and spur our curiosity. As we interview the prison officers, it is evident that these particular activities play a highly important role for the officers and in their sense of having a good workday. Engaging with inmates and building relations act as positive resources in work and thus strengthen officers' resilience.

Dynamic Security

Across the detention facility and the open prison, the prison officers explain the pictures of these mundane activities with inmates as being closely related to fulfilling the double task of prison officers. In a popular yet official version, it is described as the ability 'to balance the hard and the soft'. On one hand, these activities ensure that law and order are fulfilled, keeping inmates incarcerated following the terms of their sentence. On the other hand, the goal is to work to rehabilitate inmates to reduce the risk of recidivism. In the Danish Prison Service this particular combination carries the name of 'dynamic security'. Interacting and building relations with inmates is key in this respect. Trying to figure out this particular 'construct', the dialogue played out as follows between the interviewer and a group of officers in the open prison. Regarding the pictures of Christmas trees, John and Karen elaborate as follows:

> John: You are together in a whole different way, and because of that you can have a better relation and you can pass on information to your colleagues, right: where they are at the moment, whether they are in the middle of a bad period, if the girl friend has just left or other things. So, all the way round, it offers you something that you have this specific angle to it, right.
>
> Interviewer: But it is funny … to me it sounds as if 'dynamic security' becomes a bit instrumental. It is good that they are happy, because then there is peace and quiet, or how?
>
> Karen: Well, that's also about it.

Being with the inmates in 'this way', referring to the informal setting framed by the activity of cutting down trees, baking, or making crawling pixies, gives the prison officers a unique opportunity to establish a relationship with inmates, subsequently gaining access to valuable knowledge that might be relevant in terms of security. If an inmate is pressured due to personal issues, this may jeopardize security. However, if this is already known among the officers, they are able to anticipate potential negative reactions. As the interviewer comments, this relationship comes across as instrumental. They are interested in relating to inmates since this will make their jobs easier and less risky. Talking to another group of officers in the open prison as they are commenting on the same happy picture of inmates from the plantation, this interpretation is confirmed. Putting it concisely, one officer states: 'If there is harmony, then there is also less trouble and everything runs better and security is higher.' If inmates are happy, this will make everyday routines run more smoothly, i.e., without any trouble, which subsequently creates a good and less risky workday.

While relationship building carries an implicit, rational goal orientation across the majority of the prison officers, the quality of the relationship and the opportunity to get to know the inmates in a different way also carries a different value. The mundane homely activities provide an opportunity to inmates and officers to become someone else. This is experienced as highly meaningful to the officers, both in terms of being able to help inmates become better people but also in terms of expanding their own role.

Becoming Someone Else

Offering inmates an alternative setting to prison life brings out alternatives to the identity of the tough and rough criminal normally at the forefront in prisons. As we talk about the picture of pixies, one of the officers recalls a certain experience he once had in another prison. The image is of a big, tough, tattooed biker known from the tabloid press as a psychopath, sitting at a table all concentrated on painting a 'Hello Kitty' for his five year-old daughter's birthday. He sums up this experience as follows: 'it is about going beyond their own boundaries'. It is about allowing for different aspects of the inmates to become visible to others, even if it may compromise their image. The same transformation is addressed in relation to the picture of happy inmates in front of the Christmas tree plantation. As they were caught up in finding the best and biggest tree, in the eyes of the prison officers, the inmates all of sudden turn into a bunch of enthusiastic five-year-olds. Witnessing this transformation and seeing the little boys behind the tough group of criminals or the sensitive father in the hardcore biker give the officers a sense of meaning: the feeling that they are making a difference to these people.

Thus, bringing inmates out of the ordinary prison setting and out of their role as criminals also offers the prison officers a new position. As another officer put it: 'It's cool to get out and be able to be together as human beings.' A role quite different from what was depicted in this quote came from the same officer: 'being parked behind the wrong side of the counter, saying "yes" or "no" to paroles'. When baking, playing volleyball, going on trips or making crawling pixies with inmates, the role of the traditional bureaucrat officer is replaced or at least expanded with another and more human and personal approach. This is also why activities among prison officers and inmates are associated with autonomy and variation in work. Certainly, there are limits to the activities offered within the prison depending on whether it is the open prison or the more restricted setting of the detention facility. Nevertheless, within those limits, the officers have the liberty to buy into the activities that they personally find the most appealing. Allowing officers to relate more freely and personally to inmates serves as a core resource in the work of prison officers as they are building relations and doing 'dynamic security'. However, the very same individualized relations pop up as a constant source of quarrel and dispute, thus representing a flip side to them.

Hardliner or Laissez-faire?

In the day-to-day routines, the personal approach of the prison officers is at the root of many of the controversies that appear during a normal workday. Differences in officers' approaches to inmates often spur conflict as it positions officers against each other. A young officer working in the detention facility suggests a scale by which to characterize the individual prison officer. On the one end you find 'the hardliner', and on the other 'the laissez-faire-like'. He explains as follows:

> We are different as persons, and some are very like: 'Well, yes that is fine', meaning laissez-faire-like. Whereas others, they go very strictly by the book, and this creates problems, and this is what I know from the inmates. They know. They get to know us very quickly. They know who runs it very tightly and who doesn't.

Illustrating the hardliner and laissez-faire approaches, the prison officer gives an example of handling the daily workout. Every morning, before 8.30 am, inmates should sign up for workout later in the day. They are then placed on a list that organizes who can go when. If an inmate then asks at approximately 10 am if he can sign up, responses are likely to be quite different. According to this officer, he would not mind. He would be flexible: 'If there's room on the list, I do not lose anything' he argues. However, he is well aware that one of his colleagues – a real hardliner – would readily refuse, referring to the fact that it is too late for signing up. As opposed to the positive resource found in the officer's personal approach above, the individual differences between officers within the range of hardliner and laissez-faire might create considerable tension: between hardliners and inmates, but more importantly between officers. Too many individual differences in dealing with inmates represent an Achilles' heel in everyday work, stirring up conflict and thus jeopardizing security. As demonstrated below, in the second theme of the analysis, the resource of belonging to the group is an important piece in the puzzle to understand this ambiguity.

Belonging to the Officer Group

Figure 16.2 shows two male officers standing arm in arm in a doorway, posing and smiling for the camera. Given the close-up, it could be a selfie. As such, it is a photograph with a clear message to the viewer: look how happy and friendly we are with each other. The text supports this impression by simply saying: 'two happy colleagues'. When putting this photograph on the table, one of the officers explains quite straight forwardly how these happy colleagues are related to resilience. They imply a sense of safety:

> It is two happy colleagues that I have never experienced to be grumpy. They are always happy when they are at work. In addition, this produces safety, when you know, as Peter has also explained earlier, that 'yes, when they are here, then they are happy'.

In this sense, this picture is a good starting point to begin understanding another cornerstone and source of resilience in prison work: the relationship with colleagues. As reported below, the strong affiliation between prison officers is however

Figure 16.2 Two happy colleagues

also ambiguous. While group affiliation affords the safety of a single officer, it also carries the potential of exposure and exclusion of the single officer given very strong group norms. When we followed officers around and talked to them about their job and in particular their relation to fellow officers, peer solidarity and trust appeared as deeply ingrained occupational norms of prison officers. To maintain order and security in prisons, they rely strongly on backing from their peers, particularly in situations of crisis. The outside risk posed by aggressive inmates readily turns the officers into a well-oiled machine of solidarity and joint effort, making sure that they stand strong and act as a coherent whole against any kind of trouble. In line with the ethos of the photograph above, there is an esprit de corps among prison officers that is always presented with great pride. Good colleagues are there for each other, especially in situations of crisis.

Although we did not observe any situations of crisis, we did observe how prison officers enact team solidarity in everyday work. When a conversation between an inmate and an officer would suddenly escalate, the simple act by a fellow officer of becoming visible to the inmate represents one form of group solidarity. Taking care of paperwork during your own shift to 'clear the desk' for colleagues in the following shift is another example. Sharing details about a specific situation, letting a colleague know how it was tackled and getting his or her approval represent a third example. On a day-to-day basis and in the smallest of gestures, prison officers seek to confirm and build their group affiliation and mutual trust through a variety of ways. Returning to Figure 16.2, the 'safety', which is related to the happy smiles, is specifically associated with this third aspect. Happy colleagues are accessible colleagues, acting as resources in the daily handling of inmates. The officer explains this notion by referring to the two specific colleagues in the picture:

> When Hans and Peter are at work, well, then you will go into whatever situation, and maybe even get into trouble, because you know that they have your back. You can always get help. It is never a bother when you ask.

Having happy colleagues equals safety because it represents an important support and resource in the relational work with prisoners.

Belonging to the Group?

Being affiliated with the officer group also made us feel that it was safe to conduct fieldwork in the prisons. We were always either hanging out in the guardroom with officers or following one or two officers around to observe them doing their daily work. This physical proximity to the officers on duty prompted many officers to share their personal reactions and reflections about work with us, helping us to become immersed in and increasingly knowledgeable of the prison setting as well as allowing us to engage more deeply in our exploration of the resilience phenomenon in situ. Being offered alarms was a particular ritual that served to stress an immediate sense of belonging, as illustrated in this observational note:

> The first thing that the officers do when arriving in the morning, besides greeting colleagues and getting rid of their private stuff in separate cupboards, is to get properly equipped: adding keys and an alarm to their uniform. When I arrived on my first day in the field, I was also prompted to follow the same routine as the officers: I was handed an alarm, and in the detention, I was also given a set of keys. The alarm was for safety reasons, and I had the keys so that I was able to use the officer's bathroom in the detention. Instructions were given as to how to use the alarm in case I experienced any trouble. If something happened, they would come to my rescue, just like they would with any fellow officer. I was part of the group.

Wearing the alarm was also a very obvious, physical sign of group membership and a guarantee that we could count on the group of officers for our personal safety despite our role as researchers.

However, many episodes equally revealed that we did not truly belong to this group, causing questions of risk and safety to reappear although in less explicit ways. One aspect of this was evident as our norms seemed to clash with the norms prevalent within the officer group, thus threatening our group membership from within. The following note is from the detention facility; the first author was allowed to listen in on an action-plan conversation with an inmate:

> We are sitting in the glass 'cage', located between the guardroom and the detention hallway. Officers are passing through from both sides during

the conversation. All of a sudden loud music comes from the guardroom through the open door. There is no space to build a trustful relationship. We are all surrounded by noise, gazes and other people's presence, as officers continuously show up and disappear in the doorway. Meanwhile, the inmate politely replies to all the questions in the online template: Family status? Previous occupation? Hopes for future education or job? I cannot help but wonder why the other colleagues do not seem to pay more respect towards what is going on. At some point, I try to lean to one side and close the door, but I give up. I'd better not interfere.

In this note, the researcher is literally caught in the middle between the world of the inmates and the world of officers. The researcher is appalled by the insensitivity with which the group chose to deal with this situation, yet she felt unable to act accordingly. The simple act of closing the door would reveal her illegitimate norms and emotions to the group that she was officially part of. Therefore, she left it open.

In other instances, it was equally made clear; no matter how subtle, we were outsiders and therefore treated with caution and suspiciousness. In one unit, this was particularly noticeable. The officers for instance tended to 'forget us' when they did their rounds on the wing, although we repeatedly explained that we were there to follow them around and observe the work that prison officers do. In addition to forgetfulness, they excused themselves by insisting that it was boring work not worth us spending time on. However, to both of us, the message was quite clear: we were not truly welcome. Some officers also avoided formal interviews by either downright refusing to participate or simply by not showing up on the day of the interview. These subtle acts of resistance made us feel unwelcome and sometimes even rejected by the officers. Once again, this served to stress the fragility of our group membership. This sense of fragility was not exclusive to our position as outsiders, since the potential of not belonging to the group was a risk to be carefully managed also by the officers themselves.

A Suspicious Mind

As we got on closer terms with some of the prison officers, we learned that the characteristic suspicious mindset, which serves an important role to maintain security, had a number of adverse effects on officers' relationships with each other. Suspicion and mistrust would quickly rise in the officer group if an officer somehow violated the thin line between 'them and us', i.e., by expressing too much sympathy with prisoners. Expressing sympathy for prisoners could result in exclusion from the officer group.

This exclusion was evident in an officer group when one night, a prisoner developed severe heart failure, was rushed to hospital and died. The officer who was on watch that evening tried to resuscitate the prisoner and was deeply affected by the incidence. Her emotional distress and despair was so overwhelming that it clashed with the officer group's norms of emotional detachment from prisoners. While the officer saw the death of the prisoner as a tragic loss of a father and a husband, her colleagues reacted by only noticing the insignificant death of a prisoner. As the officer realized that her expression of sympathy with the prisoner was regarded as inappropriate by her colleagues, she was already excluded from the officer group:

> I got no backing whatsoever. No one asked how I felt or tried to under-stand why I had all these emotions. It took six months, where I went to work every day in a truly bad state; my body was shaking when I entered the prison gate and I felt terrible. I completely isolated myself. However, they were the ones who let me down, even people whom I'd been friends with and whom I'd never expected to be like this.

The officer ultimately realized that it was not the actual death of the prisoner that brought her to the edge but the lack of support from colleagues. Given that she did not conform to the norms of emotional detachment from prisoners, she was not supported by her colleagues and became excluded from the officer group. Her norms and attitudes were viewed as a threat from within and were therefore silenced to death.

These observations allude to another important insight about resilience among prison officers. While belonging to the team serves a positive and highly pronounced resource in prison work, it also carries an inbuilt fragility, an ambiguity, which we as researchers also experienced. Since the group appeared unable to contain diversity among officers, being part of the group notoriously presents a risk of potential exclusion to the individual.

Conclusion

In the resilience literature, primary attention has been directed towards identifying the resources and factors that may positively aid individuals or organizations to counter adversity and risk. Efforts have been made to develop common scales to measure and compare across individuals, groups and organizations and to specify the dos and don'ts of resilient organizing. In a prison setting, which is generally charac-terized as a risky and stressful work environment, resilience may thus seem an apt focus. From our experiences, however, as we have explored and felt the risks as well as the resources in prison work, this factor-oriented and one-dimensional version of resilience calls for far greater nuance and methodological sensitivity.

Using ethnography, and in particular the approaches available in sensory ethnog-raphy, we have taken a deeper dive into the specific setting of prison work observ-ing as well as experiencing in our own bodies the multifaceted and ambiguous character of resilience. Using visual methods, we have tried to invoke and involve more closely the informants in our knowledge acquisition. Furthermore, we have deliberately included our own emotional experiences and responses as vital data to understand the emotion rules guiding the world of prison officers.

From this ethnographic approach, a different picture of resilience unfolds. Based on our analysis, we can conclude that positive resources in prison work simultaneously carry with them certain risks. *Relating to inmates* builds resilience as it supports a strong relationship to prisoners, strengthening the primary task of producing security and thus representing an important resource in work. It gives prison officers the opportunity to become someone more human than the strict 'keeper of the keys'. However, this inmate-relationship also produces risk. When prison officers relate individually to inmates, placing themselves on a continuum of 'hardliners or laissez-faire' officers, this may position colleagues against each other, thus turning the individualized relationship to inmates into a potential risk. Similarly, *belonging to the officer group*, which is characterized by the proud esprit de corps and the strong group norms, serves as a highly important and appreciated resource among prison officers, especially when confronting aggressive or difficult inmates. However, strong group cohesiveness may suddenly represent drawbacks to the very same officers. If an officer violates group norms, they are quickly and mercilessly excluded as they are considered a potential breach of safety. In this sense, the positive resource of belonging to the group becomes a two-edged sword as it poses the risk of potential exclusion.

Given the inter-relational work distinct to prison work, risk and resilience thus becomes part and parcel of the same processes. Risk is not just an external factor to be mindfully managed by a resilient subject, group or organization. Risk and resilience are inevitably embedded in the very fabric of the work processes, the social inter-relations, and even in the prison officers themselves. Managing risk and becoming resilient are a highly demanding and to a large extent also individualized balancing act of the single officer.

Engaging ourselves in the field, we experienced this balancing act as we found ourselves part of as well as caught up in similar dilemmas and ambiguities as those of prison officers. We felt safe in the immediate affiliation with the group of officers, but we soon learned that belonging to the group could be a precarious affair. This became obvious as prison officers treated us with suspicion, ignoring our attempts to follow them around or deliberately avoiding our presence. More subtly, this also appeared as an emotional dilemma of ours. We felt torn between our moral and emotional inclination to sympathize with inmates on one hand but felt obliged to stay loyal to the emotion rules governing the group of prison officers on the other.

In terms of methodological takeaways, using sensory ethnography was highly valuable to our research. However, consistent with our findings on resilience, this claim also calls for more nuance. To use sensory ethnography also presents as a rather ambiguous affair in itself. Even if we engaged our informants in knowledge production by making it possible for them to use not only words but also express themselves by visual and more aesthetic means, the autophotographs did not succeed in truly engaging the prison officers. In many cases the camera was considered an alien in the prison setting, producing resistance rather than engagement. Furthermore, although we deliberately immersed ourselves in the field, using our bodies as well as our emotions actively in producing knowledge, we did not manage to become part of the field.

Certainly, one could argue that this was but a matter of time, because spending more time with the prison officers would have made it easier for them to accept us and vice versa. However, the point made by Czarniawska-Joerges seems more to the point: that doing fieldwork is not about becoming an insider but rather about cultivating the fact that the observer and the observed are inherently 'different' (2007: 21). While this may be far from the idealized version of 'going native', embracing the fact of difference and producing knowledge from this outside position invites researchers to engage in a respectful and mutual learning process rather than to be looking for sameness. As we were shadowing prison officers, we certainly did not manage to develop a competent and sensory 'know how' of risk and resilience, matching the one enacted by the prison officers. However, putting our bodies and emotions on the line and engaging ourselves in sensory ethnography, drawing on a wider spectrum of data than mere observations and words, we did develop a unique feel of the place. Despite the fact that this feeling may not have been the same as those of the officers and that this feeling was occasionally both unwelcome and unpleasant, it served as an eye-opening gateway to the emotional tensions equally at play among the officers.

Following Morgan and Pink (2018) who assessed the related field of organizational health and safety (OHS), the ability to produce safety or resilience for that matter does not involve factors to be known and audited and thus properly anticipated. Similar to resilience, safety is a situated and mundane accomplishment inherent to the social, physical and emotional 'orders' of the specific work environment. Resilience, safety, stress and similar complex organizational phenomena invite research approaches that are not merely attentive towards factors and formal rules. They call for researchers and methods that are able to engage in the creation of the phenomenon in situ as 'a multisensory, bodily and affective experience' (Morgan & Pink, 2018: 404). The ability to act as researchers who not only observe but equally 'feel' the resources as well as their inherent risks in prison work has certainly given us a unique insight into the fine-grained balancing acts between risk and resilience that prison officers are continuously negotiating and finding in their everyday work, even if it was from an outside position of incompetence, difference and sometimes even moral disdain.

References

Andersen, D. R., Andersen, L. P., Gadegaard, C. A., Høgh, A., Prieur, A., & Lund, T. (2017). Burnout among Danish prison personnel: A question of quantitative and emotional demands. *Scandinavian Journal of Public Health*, 45(8), 824–830.

Anderson, B. (2015). What kind of thing is resilience? *Politics*, 35(1), 60–66.

Bardoel, E. A., Pettit, T. M., De Cieri, H., & McMillan, L. (2014). Employee resilience: An emerging challenge for HRM. *Asia Pacific Journal of Human Resources*, 52(3), 279–297.

Bhamra, R., Dani, S., & Burnard, K. (2011). Resilience: The concept, a literature review and future directions. *International Journal of Production Research*, 49(18), 5375–5393.

Bourrier, M. (1996). Organizing maintenance work at two nuclear power plants. *Journal of Contingencies and Crisis Management*, 4, 104–112.

Cameron, K. S., & Spreitzer, G. M. (Eds.). (2011). *The Oxford handbook of positive organizational scholarship*. Oxford: Oxford University Press.

Cheek, F., & Miller, M. D. S. (1983). The experience of stress for prison officers: A double-bind theory of correctional stress. *Journal of Criminal Justice*, 11, 105–120.

Cullen, F. T., Link, B. G., Cullen, J. B., & Wolfe, N. T. (1990). How satisfying is prison work? A comparative occupational approach. *Journal of Offender Counseling Services Rehabilitation*, 14(2), 89–108.

Czarniawska-Joerges, B. (2007). *Shadowing: And other techniques for doing fieldwork in modern societies*. Denmark: Liber, Copenhagen Business School Press.

Dowden, C., & Tellier, C. (2004). Predicting work-related stress in correctional officers: A meta-analysis. *Journal of Criminal Justice*, 32(1), 31–47.

Dutton, J. E., Glynn, M. A., & Spreitzer, G. (2008). Positive organizational scholarship. *The SAGE Handbook of Organizational Behavior*, 1, 693–712.

Farkas, M. A. (1999). Correctional officer attitudes toward inmates and working with inmates in a "get tough" era. *Journal of Criminal Justice*, 27(6), 495–506.

Garmezy, N. (1993). Children in poverty: Resilience despite risk. *Psychiatry*, 56(1), 127–136.

Hepburn, J. R., & Knepper, P. E. (1993). Correctional officers as human services workers: The effect on job satisfaction. *Justice Quarterly*, 10(2), 315–337.

Hochschild, A. R. (1990). Ideology and emotion management: A perspective and path for future research. *Research Agendas in the Sociology of Emotions*, 117, 117–142.

Hollnagel, E. (2011). Prologue: The scope of resilience engineering. *Resilience engineering in practice: A guidebook*. Farnham: Ashgate Publishing.

Jackson, D., Firtko, A., & Edenborough, M. (2007). Personal resilience as a strategy for surviving and thriving in the face of workplace adversity: A literature review. *Journal of Advanced Nursing*, 60(1), 1–9.

Johnson, R., & Price, S. (1981). The complete correctional officer: Human service and the human environment of prison. *Criminal Justice and Behavior*, 8(3), 343–373.

King, D. D., Newman, A., & Luthans, F. (2016). Not if, but when we need resilience in the workplace. *Journal of Organizational Behavior*, 37(5), 782–786.

Kossek, E. E., & Perrigino, M. B. (2016). Resilience: A review using a grounded integrated occupational approach. *The Academy of Management Annals*, 10(1), 729–797.

La Porte, T. R. (1996). High reliability organizations: Unlikely, demanding and at risk. *Journal of Contingencies and Crisis Management*, 4(2), 60–71.

Lambert, E. G., Hogan, N. L., & Barton, S. M. (2002). Satisfied correctional staff: A review of the literature on the correlates of correctional staff job satisfaction. *Criminal Justice and Behavior*, 29(2), 115–143.

Lee, R. M. (1995). *Dangerous fieldwork* (vol. 34). Thousand Oaks, CA: Sage.

Lee-Treweek, G. (2000). The insight of emotional danger. In Lee-Treweek, G. & Linkogle, S.. (Eds.). *Danger in the field: Risk and ethics in social research*, (pp. 114–131). London: Routledge.

Lee-Treweek, G., & Linkogle, S. (Eds.). (2000). *Danger in the field: Risk and ethics in social research*. London: Routledge.

Leip, L. A., & Stinchcomb, J. B. (2013). Should I stay or should I go? Job satisfaction and turnover intent of jail staff throughout the United States. *Criminal Justice Review*, 38(2), 226–241.

Lengnick-Hall, C. A., Beck, T. E., & Lengnick-Hall, M. L. (2011). Developing a capacity for organizational resilience through strategic human resource management. *Human Resource Management Review*, 21(3), 243–255.

Luthans, F., Avey, J. B., Avolio, B. J., & Peterson, S. J. (2010). The development and resulting performance impact of positive psychological capital. *Human Resource Development Quarterly*, 21(1), 41–67.

Luthar, S. S., & Cicchetti, D. (2000). The construct of resilience: Implications for interventions and social policies. *Development and Psychopathology*, 12(4), 857–885.

Masten, A. S. (2001). Ordinary magic: Resilience processes in development. *American Psychologist*, 56(3), 227.

Masten, A. S., Best, K. M., & Garmezy, N. (1990). Resilience and development: Contributions from the study of children who overcome adversity. *Development and Psychopathology*, 2(4), 425–444.

Mikkelsen, E. N., & Wåhlin, R. (2020). Dominant, hidden and forbidden sensemaking: The politics of ideology and emotions in diversity management. *Organization*, 1350508419830620.

Mogensen, M. (2012). *The Organization (s) of Well-being and Productivity:(Re) assembling work in the Danish Post.* PhD Dissertation, Copenhagen Business School.

Morgan, J., & Pink, S. (2018). Researcher safety? Ethnography in the interdisciplinary world of audit cultures. *Cultural Studies ↔ Critical Methodologies*, 18(6), 400–409.

Morgan, R. D., Van Haveren, R. A., & Pearson, C. A. (2002). Correctional officer burnout: Further analyses. *Criminal Justice and Behavior*, 29(2), 144–160.

Pink, S. (2011). Multimodality, multisensoriality and ethnographic knowing: Social semiotics and the phenomenology of perception. *Qualitative Research*, 11(3), 261–276.

Pink, S. (2015). *Doing sensory ethnography.* London: Sage.

Putnam, L. L., & Mumby, D. K. (1993). Organizations, emotion and the myth of rationality. *Emotion in Organizations*, 1, 36–57.

Rochlin, G., LaPorte, T., & Roberts, K. (1987). The self-designing high reliability organization: Aircraft carrier flight operation at sea. *Naval War College Review*, 40, 76–90.

Rutter, M. (1985). Resilience in the face of adversity: Protective factors and resistance to psychiatric disorder. *The British Journal of Psychiatry*, 147(6), 598–611.

Schaufeli, W. B., & Peeters, M. C. (2000). Job stress and burnout among correctional officers: A literature review. *International Journal of Stress Management*, 7(1), 19–48.

Schwartz, D. (1989). Visual ethnography: Using photography in qualitative research. *Qualitative Sociology*, 12(2), 119–154.

Sluka, J. (1990). Participant observation in violent social contexts. *Human Organization*, 49(2), 114–126.

Tusaie, K., & Dyer, J. (2004). Resilience: A historical review of the construct. *Holistic Nursing Practice*, 18(1), 3–10.

Vogus, T. J., & Sutcliffe, K. M. (2007). Organizational resilience: Towards a theory and research agenda. In *2007 IEEE International Conference on Systems, Man and Cybernetics* (pp. 3418–3422). IEEE.

Walsh-Dilley, M., & Wolford, W. (2015). (Un) Defining resilience: Subjective understandings of 'resilience' from the field. *Resilience*, 3(3), 173–182.

Warren, S. (2002). Show me how it feels to work here: Using photography to research organizational aesthetics. *ephemera*, 2(3), 224–245.

Warren, S. (2005). Photography and voice in critical qualitative management research. *Accounting, Auditing & Accountability Journal*, 18(6), 861–882.

Weick, K. E. (1990). The vulnerable system: An analysis of the Tenerife air disaster. *Journal of Management*, 16(3), 571–593.

Weick, K. E., & Sutcliffe, K. M. (2007). *Managing the unexpected: Resilient performance in an age of uncertainty* (vol. 8). San Francisco, CA: John Wiley & Sons.

Weick, K. E., Sutcliffe, K. M., & Obstfeld, D. (2008). Organizing for high reliability: Processes of collective mindfulness. *Crisis Management*, 3(1), 31–66.

Werner, E. (2005). Resilience and recovery: Findings from the Kauai longitudinal study. *Research, Policy, and Practice in Children's Mental Health*, 19(1), 11–14.

PART III

Beyond Organizations

17

ORGANISATIONAL DILEMMAS, GENDER AND ETHNICITY

A Video Ethnographic Approach to Talk and Gestures in Homeless Shelter Consultations

Nanna Mik-Meyer

Introduction

Most qualitative research in organisations is based on interviews (Silverman, 2014). Interview studies can illuminate the 'experience' of the people studied. However, interviewees retelling and restructuring their narratives in accordance with the agenda of the researcher (Gubrium & Holstein, 2009) may not be the most appropriate means of understanding *why and how* people act the way they do. This chapter will demonstrate how an ethnographic approach that primarily uses video recordings of real-time interactions between homeless individuals and service providers can illuminate aspects of the organisational life of homeless people that cannot be captured in interviews or observation notes of the researcher.

Video Ethnography in Organisational Research

Decades ago, Howard Becker warned against methodological purism when researching social life (Becker, 1995). According to him, visual methodologies such as photography, photojournalism, etc., qualify analyses of the social sites sociologists investigate (Becker, 1995). Similarly, organisational scholars emphasised long ago that investigating social life in organisations necessitates the inclusion of various kinds of visual representations (e.g., Meyer, 1991). Video recording is one useful data-acquisition tool as it enables the researcher to acquire informal and detailed knowledge about the object of the study (Cassell, 2017; Heath et al., 2010; Heath & Luff, 2012; Myers, 2009).Video recordings provide information about what organisational theory calls tacit and silent knowledge (Polanyi, 1966).Thus, researchers are enabled to spot actions and perceptions that are taken for granted in the organisation to such an extent that organisational members do not consider them in their everyday work life. Such actions and perceptions will therefore not be revealed in an interview setting. Knoblauch (2012: 253) suggests the term 'videography' to pinpoint that video analysis is an interpretive approach and that the researcher must go to 'where the action is' (Knoblauch, 2012: 252).

Hence, video recordings are a reflexive, self-conscious approach to the data and it is the responsibility of the researcher to 'reveal the constructedness of her or his text' (Pink, 2001: 589). For instance, the angle of the video recorder may have different effects. A 'mid-shot' angle (as with my video recordings in this chapter) fixates on one perspective on the situation recorded, whereas multiple shots provide more perspectives on the situation recorded (Luff & Heath, 2012: 268). Luff and Heath (2012) argue for the benefits of pointing a camera towards the action. For instance, aiming the camera, in a sit-down meeting, towards the table-activity such as pouring coffee, adding sugar, taking notes, etc., as these activities can be ways for participants to abstract from awkward situations, etc. In addition, the camera can 'zoom in' (to record the participants' micro behaviour) or 'zoom out' (to record the context of the interaction) (Jarrett & Liu, 2016: 371–3). The point is that whichever choice the researcher takes (angle of the camera, zooming in or out, etc.) will bear an effect on the analysis. However, scholars must not only tend to technical matters when recording real-life encounters. The participants' actions will also be affected by the recording (Hazel, 2016). They may act in a 'recording-appropriate or -inappropriate conduct' (Hazel, 2016: 446) or they may even talk about the recording while the camera is filming (Aarsand & Forsberg, 2010: 256) – which happened in my recordings as well. Hence, video recordings are not representations of a pure or true insight in the social worlds being recorded as participants are always aware of the camera (Aarsand & Forsberg, 2010). Hazel (2016) describes this participant awareness as 'the observers paradox', that is, the way 'the object of investigation is transformed in the process of being observed' (Hazel, 2016: 447). When, for instance, participants perform for the video camera they become a proxy for the observer (Hazel, 2016: 459). For this reason Jarrett and Liu (2016: 374 – my emphasis) suggest 'zooming *with*' the participants. 'Zooming with' describes a reflexive process where the participants afterwards see the video clips and interpret the recordings together with the researcher (Jarrett & Liu, 2016: 374).

However, including participants' opinions in the analysis of data does not solve the key problem with this methodology (or any other methodology).Video recordings will never be a true representations of real-life encounters.Video recordings of real-life encounters are *recordings* of real-life encounters. Nevertheless, video recordings represent a different kind of data; an 'elusive knowledge' (Toraldo et al., 2018), as the recordings show the tacit, non-verbal and embodied aspects of organisational life. This kind of tacit, non-verbal knowledge may be challenging to grasp and communicate through traditional methodological tools such as, for instance, interviewing (Becker, 1995; Meyer, 1991; Soulaimani, 2018; Toraldo et al., 2018). Video recordings reveal the non-verbal knowledge of organisational life; the 'habitualised knowledge implicit in social action'(Toraldo et al., 2018: 439). Hence, although participants will be well aware of the fact that a recording is taking place, the recording can still disclose the participants' social worlds that are shaped in mundane actions and visible through their verbal and body language (Soulaimani, 2018; Toraldo et al., 2018: 446). Smiles, bodily orientation and silence are all key expressions for analysing the intersubjective communication among participants (Soulaimani, 2018). Thus, body language such as expressions of anger, leaning towards a person, being silent, etc., are actions of participants that supplement what they are saying verbally and that makes the interaction meaningful and coherent.

In one study of job interviews, the video recordings of the interview situation revealed that successful applicants internalised the organisational discourse of teamwork, flexibility and the productivity of time management (Campbell & Roberts, 2010: 248) – key organisational norms. However, these skills were irrelevant to the job in question, leading to the concluding analysis that the job interview is as much a ritual about the norms of the organisation as it is about hiring the right candidate (Campbell & Roberts, 2010: 267). Similarly, video recording of palliative care consultations demonstrated how doctors' verbal and bodily display of empathy towards the dying patient reflected an organisational narrative about accommodating patients' subjective experiences – and did not relate to the key goal of doctors to deliver a biomedical, task-driven, correct treatment to patients (Ford et al., 2019). In this study, the organisational norm of empathy was displayed in the video-recorded sessions both verbally and non-verbally. In a third study of real-life encounters, Pino's (2016) video analysis showed how professionals' disciplinary treatment of clients was accepted by the clients. In this case, the video recordings exposed how professionals' use of anecdotes was an indirect way for them to correct or modify clients' behaviour – and hence an interactional tool that secured the cooperation of clients. The video recording of a fourth study highlighted how the routine-based question-response sequences in a dementia consultation foregrounded co-remembering of patients and professionals: 'questions are a powerful tool to control interaction [in organisational encounters]: they pressure recipients for response, compose presuppositions, agendas and preferences' (Williams et al., 2019: 395). In this case, the analysis revealed that the interaction between professionals and persons with dementia resembled witness questioning in a courtroom. Just as in courtrooms, yes/no questions in a dementia setting were a powerful tool for establishing facts. William and colleagues' video analysis emphasised the 'face work' of the two parties in the intersubjective process of remembering. The choice of video recording of another study resulted in an analysis that displayed how participants drew on gender stereotypes when supporting their own arguments (Robles & Kurylo, 2017; Stokoe, 1998). In this case, the participants were students in tutorial sessions who talked about themselves as non-sexist individuals whilst actively reproducing gender generalisations and stereotypes (Stokoe, 1998).

All of these studies demonstrate how working with video-recorded real-life encounters often results in discovering new, surprising relations and perceptions in a field (Patton, 1990). The focus of this chapter on gender in encounters with the homeless is similarly a result of my scrutiny of video-recorded placement meetings that revealed that these encounters were indeed about gender (as well). Thus, the focus of the chapter on gender is not a result of a pre-conceived idea of gender being a central theme in homeless placement meetings. However, the data used for analysis is not only video recordings; I have supplemented with interview data. Inspired by Meyer's (1991: 232) observation that a weakness of one method can be the strength of another made my choice of combining video recordings with interview an obvious choice (Meyer, 1991: 232).

Dilemmas in Public Organisations

Public organisations, including shelters for homeless people, can be described as hybrid organisations that operate with divergent goals, resulting in a range of dilemmas (Hoggett, 2006; Mik-Meyer, 2017; Noordegraaf, 2015; Sturdy et al., 2014). A central dilemma at Danish shelters is that a stay should not be so homely and pleasant that the clients do not want to leave the place. On the other hand, most staff members do not believe it would be morally justifiable to work in a shelter that clients dislike. This dilemma is related to a central question for the staff: Are the clients capable of living on their own and taking care of themselves, or are they so heavily burdened with problems that living independently becomes an unrealistic goal? The video recordings show this dilemma. Often, the social workers address the clients' will to engage in daily activities and the requirements of the shelter. They focus on the will of the clients to change their life, take responsibility and engage in a process of change. However, the clients' everyday actions indicate that they often cannot live up to the organisational sanctioned demands and requests of staff. Thus, staff *wish* that the clients had all these positive qualities that the activities in the facilities demand of clients. Moreover, clients prefer to focus on the structural problems related to their situation: lack of housing, money, and so on.

Another dilemma relates to housing shortage. In homeless shelters, staff must find affordable housing for the homeless individuals, but the task is challenging. Just like other larger cities in Europe, apartments and rooms in most Danish cities are too expensive for clients living off social welfare. In addition, there is typically a year-long waiting list for the few available apartments/rooms that clients can afford. Housing on the so-called short-lists for vulnerable clients costs approximately £460 a month. However, if you are a refugee or an immigrant, or under the age of 30 and receive the so-called 'integration benefit' or 'youth benefit' (amounting to £680 monthly), then your disposable income does not cover the cost of food and clothes after the rent is paid – even when including subsidy for the rent. In the city of Copenhagen, a rule states that clients should have at least £460 *after* every fixed cost is paid. Therefore, a bed in a shelter that costs around £4,100 may be the only solution for this group of clients (Mik-Meyer, 2018).

Recent international studies similarly report that the field of homelessness has scarce financial resources (Kadi & Ronald, 2016) and that homeless people have difficult access to housing and aid (Perez, 2014; Sznajder-Murray & Slesnick, 2011). However, it is not only structural factors that create dilemmas in the field of homelessness. Social workers who try to solve the problem of homelessness often work with highly ambiguous goals (Ravenhill, 2008; Smith-Carrier & Lawlor, 2016; Stonehouse et al., 2015). Social workers must sort out the complex troubles of the situations among homeless people (drugs, psychiatric issues and family troubles), as well as discuss with them what a better life might entail (Dwyer et al., 2015; Mik-Meyer, 2018).

In order to investigate the organisational dilemmas related to homelessness, an ethnographic approach that centres on the context and the actual encounters between professionals and clients is pivotal (Carr, 2011; Marvasti, 2002; Smith & Hall, 2018). An ethnographic approach can shed light on how policy, power and everyday perceptions of clients and staff play out in real-life situations. This chapter will analyse homeless consultations among shelter residents and social workers in three Danish shelters. During these consultations, social workers try to fit the complex situations of the homeless with the activities and goals of the shelters. I will focus on gender and ethnicity issues since a key dilemma has to do with the fact that shelter residents (predominantly men) have to learn to 'open up', cook, tidy up the kitchen, and take on other tasks stereotypically associated with women. There are two 'idealised' perceptions (Mumby & Ashcraft, 2004: 132) of clients, either as weak individuals (Gubrium & Järvinen, 2014a) or too 'masculine' and strong (usually applicable to men) (Edley & Wetherell, 1995). These perceptions clash in the everyday organisational lives of the homeless.

Taking a Goffmanian Approach

The chapter is inspired by Goffman's work on interaction, face work, and front/back stage behaviour. 'Interaction (that is face-to-face-interaction) may be roughly defined as the reciprocal influence of individuals upon one another's action when in one another's immediate physical presence' (Erving Goffman, 1990: 26). The concepts of 'interaction' and 'face work' direct attention to the social situation in which the interaction takes place. When analysing homeless consultations, the focus is placed on the roles of the participants and how these roles relate to situation or 'framework' (Goffman, 1974b; 1990) in which the interaction occurs. Participants can be 'in face' (acting in accordance with the situational roles) or in 'wrong face' (contradicting the situational roles) (Goffman, 1990). Additionally, his concepts of 'front stage' and 'back stage' direct attention to levels of formality. Consultations are front stage meetings where a number of predefined issues must be discussed (e.g., the so-called Action Plan for the client). However, the video recordings display back stage behaviour as well. For instance, social workers may kindly touch or pat the clients, laugh and sit in open postures to create a cosy and informal environment. The participants – social workers and clients alike – switch between front stage and back stage constantly, as a formal front stage approach of social workers gets in the way of solving the complex problems of the clients. In many cases, tensions occur and the participants, especially the social workers, react by giggling (Douglas, 1999; Mik-Meyer, 2007). Laughter plays diverse roles; social workers use laughter to direct attention away from the situational tensions/ambiguity in the work. They try to overcome the organisational contradictions that occur when the goal of the work is to solve the (unsolvable) complex problems of homeless individuals.

The Danish Context and Key Dilemmas

Every year, 6,400 people use 85 homeless shelters that are available in Denmark (Benjaminsen, 2019). These shelters fall under the Danish Social Service Law §110, which states that municipalities are obliged to provide temporary housing for persons, who, due to not having a place to stay, or not being able to live by themselves, need housing and care. The standard price for the Danish welfare state for a bed in a shelter is roughly £4,000 a month. Approximately, 77% of those living in the 85 Danish shelters are men and 24% are women. A third of the homeless population stay at a shelter, which makes it the most common solution during homelessness. The second most common place to stay during homelessness is with family and friends (25%), and only 11% sleep on the streets (Benjaminsen, 2019: 25). Because Danish residents have a right to a shelter bed, it is the most vulnerable homeless people that end up as 'rough sleepers' sleeping on the streets (Benjaminsen, 2019: 31). In this study, the participants are on average around 45 years old. They were all unemployed, and most of them collected unemployment benefits (45%) or social pensions (27%). The participants had comparable issues: they needed a place to stay/sleep; they usually had a high intake of different drugs; and they usually had several physical and psychological challenges according to themselves and staff reporting. In addition to social activities, such as participating in morning gatherings and in workshop activities, shelter residents were offered support to sort out their financial situations, find a place to live, contact partners and children, and if necessary, sign up for treatment for their drug abuse.

Methodological Approach

The chapter is based on video-recorded consultations between homeless individuals and social workers, as well as interviews with the participants after the consultations. We chose to focus on the routine consultations because these meetings involved making decisions on how to solve the homeless individuals' problems. The themes discussed at the consultations were highly complex, making naturalistic data very suitable (Heath & Luff, 2012: 35). The data consists of 23 recorded consultations with 19 homeless men and 4 homeless women, and 77 individual interviews with the participants conducted after the consultations. The recordings took place by the year-end between 2017 and 2018. The meeting participants included a shelter resident, a shelter social worker, a municipality social worker, and in some instances also client relatives, mentors, or other staff such as drug counsellors. On average, four persons participated and each consultation lasted approximately one hour.

The participants of the study were recruited through the managers of the three shelters. By contacting the managers, the shelters' acceptance of participation in the study was ensured, and further contact with shelter social workers with current cases was established. Once an arrangement with one shelter social worker was agreed upon, it often generated more meetings with other shelter residents and municipal social workers. As an ethical standard, the contacted shelter social worker was always asked to make sure that all participants fully agreed to partake in the study and that all participants knew that they could withdraw from the study at any point in time. At the start of the consultation participants met with me or my student to ensure that everyone participated voluntarily and we explained to the shelter residents that their participation would not affect the administrative handling of their 'case'. We explained (yet again) that they were given anonymity and we re-asked all participants for permission for the video recording. It was explained to them that the video recordings would only be viewed by the research team and that data (footage and interviews) would be stored in a safe space where only the research team had access. After the consultations most participants were interviewed individually about how they experienced the consultation and the decisions made. In the study, all participants have been given anonymity and all mentioned names and places in the analysis are fictionalised.

I started my analytical process by reviewing all 23 recordings to get a sense of the material at large (and to develop ideas for the following coding process). Hereafter, all video recordings and interviews were transcribed in full, including notations of long pauses, interruptions, and laughter. For analytical purposes, body movements and gazes are indicated in the selected passages of the video recordings presented in this chapter. The video recordings and interviews were coded using the software program NVivo 11. In line with a constructionist grounded approach (Charmaz, 2006), an open reading of the dataset was sought. That means that specific hypotheses on gender and ethnicity issues (the focus of this chapter) were not developed prior to the coding process. However, the first initial coding process of the consultations and interviews revealed that gender and ethnicity were the sociological factors that both groups engaged in and hence served as a central theme in the dataset. In most recordings (video and audio), the participants negotiated what could be broadly described as 'gender and ethnicity issues'. For instance, 'gender issues' cover gender stereotypes of social workers and clients and include 'gendered stories' of what it takes to be a man/woman and pronounced gendered negotiations. These stories were intersected with the ethnicity of the clients in surprising ways. Consequently, since gender issues, weaved together with questions of ethnicity, occurred so frequently in the dataset, we conducted a more 'focused coding' (Charmaz, 2006: 57–60) of the entire dataset for quotes/discussions on these topics.

Analysis: Ethnic Danish Men Negotiating Masculinity and Clienthood

Consultations typically start with small-talk and the offering of coffee. The goal of the first part of the meeting is to establish a friendly atmosphere of equality and mutual empathy. It is a guiding norm at these consultations that social workers act as facilitators, who enable clients to help themselves. An obligatory passage point (Clegg, 1989: 205) that guides all consultations is the Action Plan. For instance, all clients are asked about money issues, their network/social life, drug problems, mobility issues, economy, and ability to take care of housework (cooking, cleaning, and so forth). It is a trick list that ensures that the social workers can decide on the amount of help and assistance needed.

Hank – Accepting Psychological Problems

Gender aspects are very visible during the consultation with Hank, a man in his fifties who has been evicted from his apartment because he failed to pay the rent. He sits with his outdoor jacket on to signal that he may be leaving at any moment. He is not very talkative and clearly uncomfortable with the personal questions asked by the young female social worker in her 20s (still a student). It is quickly apparent that his perception of his situation does not align with that of the social workers (Pauline, Brenda and Linda). What they think Hank *needs* is not the same as what Hank *wants*. A consultation with him reveals this dilemma:

> Pauline: The two of us [looking at Hank], when we talked earlier, we talked about needing a longer perspective on your situation. We discussed that we should assist you with getting your own residence, and stuff like that, and you said 'maintaining some contact with us could be ok' [indicating with her tone of voice that this is speculative]. I'm thinking [points to Becky] that you need us to help you check your *e-boks* [a Danish mail system for official mails].
>
> Hank: Yes, yes. [Sitting in a lofty pose, leaning back, gesturing with his body language that he is bored/annoyed] But, I mean, I can easily check my own *e-boks*. That's not my problem [looks down and speaks in a low voice].
>
> Pauline: [Puts her hand on Hank's arm] I don't doubt that you can do that at all.
>
> Hank: But it's just … I can't pay the bills I get [shakes his head in a humble way and makes eye contact with his head down].
>
> Pauline: No, no.

He continues to talk about his need of a place to stay and lack of financial resources (two structural problems, lack of housing and little money, which are a real challenge to solve for the social workers as well). According to him, these are his main problems. However, Pauline wants to help him with his *e-boks*. By touching his arm, Pauline steps backstage and tries to calm him down. She momentarily takes back her statement indicating that she never doubted his abilities. Her comforting touch on his arm comes off as a mother caring for a child in need of comfort. However, seen from Hank's perspective this should be neither a technical issue (*e-boks*) nor an emotional, caring issue that demands touches or pats, but a financial issue. His body language clearly indicates that he does not appreciate Pauline's caring, backstage approach. This idea that male clients may have other problems than the ones they think they have is shared by most social workers. After the consultation one of the other participating social workers shares her perception of men such as Hank, that is, male clients in their fifties:

> It is really good to have a shelter, where there is someone to talk to, and where a guy like Hank can learn to talk about all the problems he has. He is a man too, you know, and they are not that talkative. That goes for his entire generation, right?

Similarly to her colleagues, she has gender- and age-specific expectations, including the idea that Hank and other men of his generation need to learn how to talk about their problems. When talking to Hank after the consultation, he touches upon this emotional interaction with the female social workers and states that he finds it annoying. He associates this kind of interaction with a loss of status. He explains:

> It's a bit difficult for me to stay here. Because I haven't done that before. I've never opened myself up to four women that way. That way it's difficult but, well, now I'm at rock bottom, so it actually doesn't hurt that much. It'd probably be worse if you'd been all the way up there [indicates with his hands] and then had to sit and listen to that kind of talk, right?

Thus, being at 'at rock bottom' implies that his masculinity is lost and that he is unable to fight off the social workers' emotional and caring relations. This loss of masculinity may explain his infelicitous act (Austin, 1975) when at the end of the meeting, he asks out the young social worker-student (Brenda). After summing up the discussion of the consultation, Brenda asks if there is anything they have not touched upon. She continues:

Brenda: Is there anything you want to ask about?

Hank: Yes. Do you want to go out on a date? [Everybody laughs]

Brenda: No. We are not going out on a date.

Hank: Aha. So you don't think so?

Brenda: We can schedule a consultation on January 5?

Hank: Yes. Okay. And then we take it from there.

Before asking her out, he compliments her looks. For an observer, it is clear that Hank has overstepped a line, making everyone uncomfortable. The function of the joint laughter of social workers is to 'solve' the tension his infelicitous question has created (Douglas, 1999; Mik-Meyer, 2007; Potter & Hepburn, 2010). His position as a homeless man with the accompanying associations of failure and loss does not align well with the rules of a dating game of mutually interested parties.

Rick – Accepting Parental Caring

The social workers' caring approach to clients often creates an imbalanced relationship between clients and social workers. In these situations, the social worker will repeat the name of the client several times, just as parents do when addressing (and correcting) their children. Rick, who is currently in his forties, started drinking when his wife left, 'forgot' to pay rent and ended up on the street. In the following dialogue, Beth (a social worker) compliments Rick for his honesty:

> Beth: [leans towards Rick and looks him in the eye with her head tilted] I think that you're just deeply honest, calling things out, and you know what – that's actually what's really nice about you. Also, that when I ask you something, I actually get an answer from you.
>
> Rick: Yeah [very low voice].
>
> Beth: I mean, it's never like I sit around and think 'oh now he might be saying something that's not true', because no, you wouldn't [raises her voice encouragingly and shakes her head].
>
> Rick: Mmm [shakes his head]
>
> Beth: You say what you mean and then you actually don't care how we perceive it. And that's really nice because it provides us with a fitting image of you.

Beth applauds Rick for being honest. The logic must be that she cannot expect him as a client to tell the truth, which in other conversations among adults is a surprising logic. She continues to compliment him for his 'fine development':

> Beth: When we last met, we also had a good talk [nods while talking, looks at Rick and then at the other participating social workers].
>
> Linda: Yes, I completely agree.
>
> Beth: Definitely, but it really was a completely different conversation.
>
> Rick: Yes [nods solemnly while he touches his face with one hand, somewhat shyly/embarrassed].

Beth: But that was a long time ago.

Linda [second social worker]: Yes, that was a long time ago now.

George [third social worker]: [looks down and talks calmly while nodding] Yes, you've come far, you've come far – that's for sure, in terms of your behaviour.

Their appraisal is obviously well-intentioned and caring, but it speaks to the idea of an imbalance in the client-staff relationship as it is disproportionate – why should Rick not be someone that could be trusted? From the way they interact, it appears the social workers are taking a much more active role in Rick's behavioural change than Rick himself. They are encouraging and praising Rick, but he is responding with silence (Dupret, 2018), and he appears to find the situation somewhat awkward and embarrassing.

The three social workers try to deal with the basic dilemma pertaining to the awkwardness of their roles. They have to impose certain plans and values on Rick, hoping that he will adopt them. However, they are undertaking such an active role compared to him that his personal development almost comes off as their achievement, rather than his, and he goes along with it *because* he is the client (and not because he has changed dramatically). What is key in this and other consultations is that the client's loss of status and loss of masculinity is avoided. However, since the role of client necessitates indicating problems and weaknesses, which resonate poorly with masculinity, strengths, and control (stereotypical male attributes), male clients in particular may find the praising and caring approach downgrading. It becomes evident in the next part of the analysis that the mix of roles and expectations (client/male) is further strengthened when the male clients have a Greater Middle Eastern (GME) background.

Analysis: Greater Middle Eastern Men Negotiating Masculinity and Clienthood

Observations of Danish male clients' show some familiarity with the role of client (e.g., Hank's explanation of hitting 'rock bottom'), which are not found in consultations with men with a GME background. Their negotiation with social workers takes a somewhat different route. The video recordings indicate that these clients may experience an even stronger perceived loss of masculinity than their ethnic Danish 'colleagues'. Where the ethnic Danish men seem to understand and accept the role of client, the GME men do not always understand this role and therefore have a difficult time navigating within the framework of the system they are now part of. They have a hard time accepting the loss of independence/autonomy that comes with being a client. With this follows that they often appear confused by the role of social workers, especially when social workers try to discipline them into doing domestic chores.

Walid – Stating the Obvious

Walid is in his forties and has been living in the shelter for quite some time. The goal of his consultation (for him and the shelter social workers) is to be reassigned to the short list of cheap housing. He was taken off the list due to heavy drinking, but this behaviour has stopped. The presented sequence displays how an awkward situation (and related distribution of roles) is managed by the client (silence) and social workers (laughing). We enter when Bridget (a social worker from his ward) compliments him:

> Bridget: I think you're a tremendous resource up at the ward. I mean you help out, even if you weren't the assigned responsible one [smiles cunningly at Walid], you still help out … [Pauses] And you cook and keep your room tidy … [Pauses] And it's going pretty damn well.
>
> Walid: Of course [smiles and nods]: [Carol and Samantha laugh in a nervous manner as Walid leans forward with a smile on his face looking down. His shoulders are pulled up, his body made small, and he is rubbing his inner thighs with his hands, almost as if he were freezing]
>
> Carol: Yes.
>
> Samantha: Yes, so we're hoping for the best.
>
> Walid: Yes [Speaks in a low voice and looks at Samantha]

The awkwardness is revealed in Walid's body language and the social workers' awkward pauses and nervous laughs. Walid's lack of verbal response, his silence, and a tense forward leaning position indicate that he does not see these domestic chores as related to anything. His only verbal reaction is 'of course' and 'yes', indicating that they are stating the obvious. For him, this conversation has no point. As opposed to the ethnic Danish men interviewed, he cannot see any reason for discussing this issue in a consultation with his municipality social worker (Jonathan) visiting the shelter. The social workers' nervous laughter, which is partly caused by Walid's body language, makes it clear that the situation is tense. His change of position (leaning forward) emphasises his annoyance with what is being said. It is as if he tries to bring himself into a front-stage character with which he could potentially meet their expectations, but ends up deciding against his involvement. His reaction is similarly documented in other consultations with GME men. In several consultations, this group is quite outspoken about independence and explicitly connotes independence with masculinity. The subject of independence is clearly demonstrated in these consultations, as opposed to the consultation with the Danish men where independence and autonomy are more of an implicit issue. Thus, Walid states explicitly that it is an embarrassment for him to receive financial assistance, as he is a (criminal) man of action:

Walid: No [I don't like receiving social welfare] because that implies that you've sunken to a low level. Because as a man, I've never ever needed social welfare. I'm ... I'm not proud of this. I am a criminal. I am a criminal. I function by selling and being a salesman and using my street abilities to be a good salesman. I could work somewhere else, in a factory or something like that.

Walid refers both to his maleness and his criminal skills as relevant to his lack of reliance on social welfare. He thereby paints a picture of himself as an independent 'man of action', who can handle himself in these respects. The paradox is hard to overlook. He cannot possibly be as independent and self-sustaining as he wants to suggest, as he is currently homeless and enrolled in the social welfare system.

Wasim – Not Going along with the Frame

Wasim is in his twenties and has a strong desire for independence. He explains this to his social worker (Annie) in the consultation several times. However, staying at a shelter challenges this important goal (as in the case of Walid):

Annie: [Leaning in, gesticulating with one hand and shaking her head] It is important to have daily chores and getting them done. It's not as if I'm saying there needs to be personnel watching you all the time, Wasim – not at all – I totally get that it is important to you ...

Wasim: [Interrupts while Annie puts her flat hand out towards him like a stop-sign] I am independent [leans back, stares at Annie with an empty facial expression].

Annie: [Keeps waving her stop-sign hand] To be independent and have your own ... I completely understand. I just get a little bit worried about you if you don't get any help at all.

Wasim: Once in a while [I can accept], but not always.

Annie: No of course [shakes her head], of course [nods].

Wasim reacts reluctantly both verbally and bodily to Annie's worries. It is clearly important to him to be considered independent, which he keeps stating somewhat stubbornly. This repetition indicates that he does not think Annie understands him 'completely' as she says. To him, his independence does not match the perception of independence by his social worker, even when she emphasises her empathy towards him by saying that she 'totally gets it'. Her body language indicates that she is desperately trying to convince him of her ability to connect with him, but she fails miserably. She shakes her head and nods which are gestures that are almost symbolic for the entire conversation: Wasim's wishes are unrealistic, but this cannot be stated outright as he also has to be considered active and responsible.

Rashid – Unrealistic Expectations

Rashid has recently emigrated from Lebanon to Denmark. He was educated as a physician and is currently in his fifties. He has limited knowledge of Danish and communicates with an interpreter. He is recently divorced and desperately wants to live close to his two early-teenage children and the local hospital where he hopes to work. His social worker (Samantha) tries to bring his expectations down:

> Samantha: [Leaned in towards Rashid] No, no … So, because it's, you know, there's a very, very long waiting list for apartments where you want to live, so it's really … [Rashid nods, stands up and sits down again]. So I'm thinking that, uhm, you … [draws out her words] you have to consider getting registered in some housing, located a bit, maybe in the surrounding municipalities [draws a circle in the air], or a bit further away where the waiting list is shorter [Rashid takes a sip of his coffee].

> Translator/Rashid: [Rashid makes the 'stop' signal with his hands while talking to the translator and gesticulates while the translator speaks Danish] My entire family is living in this town; they work in there. I also want to work at the hospital situated in this town. And I don't have the money – £300 a month to get back and forth all the time with public transportation. My friends all live there.

> Chad: Yes [nods and takes notes].

> [Rashid breathes out frustrated].

> Samantha: Yes [pauses] I mean … [Leans back so she is sitting further from the table, corrects her glasses and lays down her pen on the table] You could say that, and I totally … [claps her hands so they are folded in the air and looks at Rashid] … I totally understand Rashid that it would be nicest for you to be near your children, and near your friends, and near work if … uhm … you hopefully get it at some point. But [raises her voice and breathes out] you can, I mean, it might be necessary [points her two index fingers into the air] to have a look in other municipalities as well, because you can't stay here forever.

As the passage shows, Rashid's expectations are too high. He imagines that he can get a job as a doctor in a Danish hospital and get an apartment near his children and friends. However, his social worker's focus is at a much more basic level: he needs a roof over his head. She tries to correct his expectations, while at the same time trying (and failing) to not be too discouraging: 'if, uhm, you hopefully get it at some point' ('it' referring to work). In the first part of the sequence, her body language indicates a personal and empathetic (backstage) attitude towards Rashid, but it changes in the last part where she takes on a professional body language, understanding now that she needs to be the voice of reason. The tension lies within the fact that Rashid still sees himself as an independent and capable man in control with a high level of opportunities in life, while Samantha indicates that this is probably not the case. His problem is that he does not understand what it means to be a client, that is, what and how much (or little) a client is entitled to ask of the system, or what is expected of him and why.

Concluding Discussion

In this chapter, I have demonstrated how a 'videography' approach (Knoblauch, 2012) qualifies an analysis of what it means to be a man and a client in Danish homeless shelters. This chapter's analysis has revealed how a caring approach is an important organisational norm of professionals – even though caring may inadvertently work against another important stated goal of giving clients a voice and the responsibility to decide over their lives. Organisational dilemmas are the key in most organisational research (Hoggett, 2006) studying the relationship between professionals and clients (Gubrium & Järvinen, 2014b). However, most of the research does not provide *concrete* displays of how the dilemmas are negotiated in everyday organisational life. A videography approach to the many small everyday practices of organisational life demonstrate the way professionals and clients actually interact – and manage the dilemmas – in specific situations. Hence, video recording organisational encounters is a useful approach if the aim is to conduct a fined-grained analysis that will reveal people's behaviours during meetings.

The chapter's analysis reveals that it is difficult to reconcile the role of clients' weakness with stereotypical perceptions of masculinity and strength. I have exerted attention on caring, parent-child relationships, and other ambivalent relations and positions that create problems for both clients and professionals. These ambivalent relations are particularly visible in the video recording of the participants' body language (including gestures, silent pauses, and laughter). Thus, the video recordings showed many situations where the client responded with silence and the social worker reacted to this pause with giggling. In these cases, the social workers especially try to 'solve' the tense, ambivalent situation by giggling. The word 'solve' is put in quotation marks as the situations remain ambivalent and tense. In the situation, the parties only momentarily maintain their 'faces' by laughing. The analysis of the chapter weighs the bodily dimension of the client-social worker encounters. The reason for emphasising body language is to present the strength of video data when one wants to understand why and how people interact the way they do. As the analysis has demonstrated, body actions are just as important in the analysis as the spoken language. The body reveals how the participants relate to the situation (Soulaimani, 2018), and for this reason it is quite surprising that video data is not used much more than is actually the case.

An ethnographic approach that takes the lead in video footage of real-life interactions can illuminate the ambivalence of much of the work in public organisations. As Hoggett (2006) points out, public organisations are highly affected by dilemmas, and video data can be quite useful data in helping us to better understand these dilemmas.

This chapter's analysis has also examined how gender permeates the work of organisations. Gender and organisations are inseparable entities. Gender, as well as ethnicity and age, must be taken into consideration when we research why people act the way they do. These factors are equally important if we want to better understand why some organisational members' actions are deemed reasonable while others are not. In this context, clients with a background in GME seem to be particularly challenged, as they find it more difficult than their Danish counterparts to accept the passivity, care, and the childish role attached to their position. Even though social workers like to see clients take responsibility and have control over their situation, they often reproduce a practice that takes the clients' lack of responsibility for granted. By using a videography approach that explores how both parties negotiate the stereotypes connected to gender, ethnicity and clients, it becomes possible to analyse the many ambiguities that characterise public organisations such as shelters. This chapter's analysis has thus demonstrated one of the greatest forces of an ethnographic approach, namely why people actively reproduce the practices from which they explicitly distance themselves. In this case, many practices reinforce passivity in clients despite an explicit stated wish of social workers to achieve exactly the opposite: to enable clients to become active and responsible for their own situations.

References

Aarsand, P., & Forsberg, L. (2010). Producing children's corporeal privacy: Ethnographic video recording as material-discursive practice. *Qualitative Research, 10*(2), 249–268.

Austin, J. L. (1975). *How to Do Things with Words.* Oxford: Clarendon Press.

Becker, H. S. (1995). Visual sociology, documentary photography, and photojournalism: It's (almost) all a matter of context. *Visual Sociology, 10*(1–2), 5–14.

Benjaminsen, L. (2019). *Hjemløshed i Danmark 2019: National kortlægning.* Copenhagen: VIVE.

Campbell, S., & Roberts, C. (2010). Synthesizing the institutional and personal: Migration, ethnicity and competing discourses in the job interview. *Discourse & Society, 18*(3), 243–271.

Carr, E. S. (2011). *Scripting Addiction: The Politics of Therapeutic Talk and American Sobriety.* Princeton, NJ: Princeton University Press.

Cassell, C. (2017). Engaging with the visual: Opportunities for qualitative organizational researchers. In R. Mir, & S. Jain (Eds.), *The Routledge Companion to Qualitative Research in Organization Studies* (pp. 393–407). Oxford: Routledge.

Charmaz, K. (2006). *Constructing Grounded Theory: A Practical Guide through Qualitative Analysis.* London: Sage Publications.

Clegg, S. R. (1989). *Frameworks of Power.* London: Sage Publications.

Douglas, M. (1999). *Implicit Meanings: Selected Essays in Anthropology.* New York: Routledge.

Dupret, K. (2018). Performative silences: Potentiality of organizational change. *Organization Studies, 40*(5), 681–703.

Dwyer, P., Bowpitt, G., Sundin, E., & Weinstein, M. (2015). Rights, responsibilities and refusals: Homelessness policy and the exclusion of single homeless people with complex needs. *Critical Social Policy, 35*(1), 3–23.

Edley, N., & Wetherell, M. (1995). *Men in Perspective: Practice, Power, and Identity.* London: Prentice Hall / Harvester Wheatsheaf.

Ford, J., Hepburn, A., & Parry, R. (2019). What do displays of empathy do in palliative care consultations? *Discourse Studies, 21*(1), 22–37.

Goffman, E. (1974a). *Asylums: Essay on the Social Situation of Mental Patients and Other Inmates.* Harmondsworth: Penguin Books.

Goffman, E. (1974b). *Frame Analysis: An Essay on the Organization of Experience.* London: Harper and Row.

Goffman, E. (1990). *The Presentation of Self in Everyday Life.* New York: Doubleday.

Gubrium, J. F., & Holstein, J. A. (2009). *Analyzing Narrative Identity*. Thousand Oaks, CA: Sage Publications.

Gubrium, J. F., & Järvinen, M. (2014a). Troubles, problems, and clientization. In J. F. Gubrium, & M. Järvinen (Eds.), *Turning Troubles into Problems: Clientization in Human Services* (pp. 1–13). London: Routledge.

Gubrium, J. F., & Järvinen, M. (Eds.). (2014b). *Turning Troubles into Problems. Clientization in Human Service*. London: Routledge.

Hazel, S. (2016). The paradox from within: Research participants doing-being-observed. *Qualitative Research, 16*(4), 446–467.

Heath, C., Hindmarsh, J., & Luff, P. (2010). *Video in Qualitative Research. Analysing Social Interaction in Everyday Life*. London: Sage Publications.

Heath, C., & Luff, P. (2012). Video analysis and organisational practice. In H. Knoblauch, B. Schnettler, J. Raab, & H.-G. Soeffner (Eds.), *Video Analysis: Methodology and Methods* (pp. 35–50). Frankfurt am Main: Internationaler Verlag der Wissenschaften.

Hoggett, P. (2006). Conflict, ambivalence, and the contested purpose of public organizations. *Human Relations, 59*(2), 175–194.

Jarrett, M., & Liu, F. (2016). 'Zooming with': A participatory approach to the use of video ethnography in organizational studies. *Organizational Research Methods, 21*(2), 366–385.

Kadi, J., & Ronald, R. (2016). Undermining housing affordability for New York's low-income households: The role of policy reform and rental sector restructuring. *Critical Social Policy, 36*(2), 265–288.

Knoblauch, H. (2012). Introduction to the special issue of Qualitative Research : Video-analysis and videography. *Qualitative Research, 12*(3), 251–254.

Luff, P., & Heath, C. (2012). Some 'technical challenges' of video analysis: Social actions, objects, material realities and the problems of perspective. *Qualitative Research, 12*(3), 255–279.

Marvasti, A. B. (2002). Constructing the service-worthy homeless through narrative editing. *Journal of Contemporary Ethnography, 31*(5), 615–651.

Meyer, A. D. (1991). Visual data in organizational research. *Organization Science, 2*(2), 218–236.

Mik-Meyer, N. (2007). Interpersonal relations or jokes of social structure? Laughter in social work. *Qualitative Social Work, 6*(1), 9–26.

Mik-Meyer, N. (2017). *The Power of Citizens and Professionals in Welfare Encounters: The Influence of Bureaucracy, Market and Psychology*. Manchester: Manchester University Press.

Mik-Meyer, N. (2018). *Fagprofessionelles møde med udsatte klienter: Dilemmaer i den organisatoriske kontekst*. Copenhagen: Hans Reitzels Publishers.

Mumby, D. K., & Ashcraft, K. L. (2004). *Reworking Gender: A Feminist Communicology of Organization*. Thousand Oaks, CA: Sage Publications.

Myers, M. D. (2009). *Qualitative Research in Business and Management*. Los Angeles, CA: Sage Publications.

Noordegraaf, M. (2015). Hybrid professionalism and beyond: (New) Forms of public professionalism in changing organizational and societal contexts. *Journal of Professions and Organization, 2*(2), 187–206.

Patton, M. Q. (1990). *Qualitative Evaluation and Research Methods*. Newbury Park, CA: Sage Publications.

Perez, J. L. (2014). The cost of seeking shelter: How inaccessibility leads to women's underutilization of emergency shelter. *Journal of Poverty, 18*(3), 254–274.

Pink, S. (2001). More visualising, more methodologies: On video, reflexivity and qualitative research. *The Sociological Review, 48*(4), 503–522.

Pino, M. (2016). Delivering criticism through anecdotes in interaction. *Discourse Studies, 18*(6), 695–715.

Polanyi, M. (1966). *The Tacit Dimension*. Garden City, NY: Doubleday.

Potter, J., & Hepburn, A. (2010). Putting aspiration into words: 'Laugh particles', managing descriptive trouble and modulating action. *Journal of Pragmatics, 42*(6), 1543–1555.

Ravenhill, M. (2008). *The Culture of Homelessness*. Aldershot, UK: Ashgate Publishing Limited.

Robles, J. S., & Kurylo, A. (2017). 'Let's have the men clean up': Interpersonally communicated stereotypes as a resource for resisting gender-role prescribed activities. *Discourse Studies, 19*(6), 673–693.

Silverman, D. (2014). *A Very Short, Fairly Interesting, Quite Cheap Book about Qualitative Research*. London: Sage Publications.

Smith, R. J., & Hall, T. (2018). Everyday territories: Homelessness, outreach work and city space. *British Journal of Sociology, 69*(2), 372–390.

Smith-Carrier, T., & Lawlor, A. (2016). Realising our (neoliberal) potential? A critical discourse analysis of the poverty reduction strategy in Ontario, Canada. *Critical Social Policy, 37*(1), 1–23.

Soulaimani, D. (2018). Talk, voice and gestures in reported speech: Toward an integrated approach. *Discourse Studies, 20*(3), 361–376.

Stokoe, E. H. (1998). Talking about gender: The conversational construction of gender categories in academic discourse. *Discourse & Society, 9*(2), 217–240.

Stonehouse, D., Threlkeld, G., & Farmer, J. (2015). 'Housing risk' and the neoliberal discourse of responsibilisation in Victoria. *Critical Social Policy, 35*(3), 393–413.

Sturdy, A., Wright, C., & Wylie, N. (2014). Managers as consultants: The hybridity and tensions of neo-bureaucratic management. *Organization, 23*(2), 184–205.

Sznajder-Murray, B., & Slesnick, N. (2011). 'Don't leave me hanging': Homeless mothers' perceptions of service providers. *Journal of Social Service Research, 37*(5), 457–468.

Toraldo, M. L., Islam, G., & Mangia, G. (2018). Modes of knowing: Video research and the problem of elusive knowledges. *Organizational Research Methods, 21*(2), 438–465.

Williams, V., Webb, J., Dowling, S., & Gall, M. (2019). Direct and indirect ways of managing epistemic asymmetries when eliciting memories. *Discourse Studies, 21*(2), 199–215.

18

CAPTURING THE MICROFOUNDATIONS OF INSTITUTIONS

A Confessional Tale of the Glorified Field

Hendra Raharja Wijaya

Ontological and Epistemological Reflections

Neo-institutional theory has recently been criticized for its inability to make a practical contribution to the society at large (Greenwood, Oliver, Lawrence, & Meyer, 2017). This is largely driven by the theory's primary focus on macro-level environmental pressures in the early days (DiMaggio & Powell, 1983; Meyer & Rowan, 1977; Zucker, 1977) and its serious neglect of the microfoundations of institutions, preventing institutional theorists from developing a more comprehensive theory and establishing wide-ranging relevance (Gehman, Lounsbury, & Greenwood, 2016; Thornton & Ocasio, 2008; Zilber, 2016). Despite its leading and perhaps dominant status within organization studies, neo-institutional theory has been very slow in weaving actors' normative/cognitive/affective components and their behavioral implications into institutional analyses (Greenwood, Hinings, & Whetten, 2014; Lawrence, Suddaby, & Leca, 2009; Powell & Colyvas, 2008). In other words, what has been consistently called for to better understand the complexities of institutional processes is actors' rich experiences that *micro-shape* the institutions they inhabit (Hallett & Ventresca, 2006; Lawrence et al., 2009; Thornton, Ocasio, & Lounsbury, 2012; Voronov & Vince, 2012). Only by rigorously examining the microfoundations of institutions, alongside the more established structural explanations of macro-level isomorphic forces (Heugens & Lander, 2009; Scott, 2014), can neo-institutional theory start to open the black box of institutions. By treating individuals and institutions equally, institutional scholars will be able to offer a much-needed multilevel paradigm, whose significance could be profoundly useful for academics, professionals, and policy makers (Ferraro, Etzion, & Gehman, 2015; Schilke, 2018; Zucker, 1983, 1991).

Attending to the microfoundations of institutions directs our efforts to examining actors' engagement with their historical baggage, sense of morality, cognitive reasoning, emotional investment and competence (Creed, Hudson, Okhuysen, & Smith-Crowe, 2014; Foster, Suddaby, Minkus, & Wiebe, 2011; Kraatz & Flores, 2015; Thornton et al., 2012; Voronov & Weber, 2016), their dynamic social interactions and interpretations of the contexts in which they are situationally embedded (Collins, 2004; de Rond & Lok, 2016; Lawrence & Dover, 2015), and their mundane yet deliberate practices aimed to create, maintain, disrupt, or change institutional arrangements (Lawrence et al., 2009; Schatzki, 2001; Smets, Jarzabkowski, Burke, & Spee, 2015). For instance, Fan and Zietsma (2017) found that different stakeholders – despite residing in different institutional fields, holding different backgrounds, and ascribing to different institutional logics – came together and interacted cognitively and emotionally to create a new, shared logic that governed the water usage in the Okanagan, Canada. Moreover, Lok and de Rond (2013) immersed themselves at the Cambridge University Boat Club and observed that the institutional arrangement of training/selection system was reproduced through actors' containing and restoring practice breakdowns. They further contended that institutional reproduction entailed a degree of plasticity whereby institutional scripts could be stretched to accommodate these breakdowns without necessarily effecting structural changes. Another example comes from a study of a rape crisis center in Israel by Zilber (2002) who argued that a single predominant meaning system promoted institutional maintenance, while multiple ones enabled institutional change because these meaning systems, which were advocated by different actors and instantiated into their everyday practices, were competing for dominance as to how best to handle the rape victims.

While objectivism was the predominant ontology in much of the early development of neo-institutional theory, recent advances in the microfoundations of institutions require a novel way of perceiving what constitutes a social reality: one that is not only existing independently waiting to be discovered by actors, but also socially constructed and continuously accomplished on the ground. Accordingly, this ontological perspective reflects a more balanced view of the relationship between individuals and institutions (Zilber, 2016). This way, both the macro and the micro interact recursively and shape each other (Smets, Morris, & Greenwood, 2012; Tracey, Phillips, & Jarvis, 2011). The structures (e.g., institutional arrangements, institutional logics, or meaning systems) are interpreted, internalized, and taken for granted by actors (i.e., the *pulled-down* or *top-down* approach), who create new structures or reproduce, disrupt, or change existing ones through their day-to-day activities (i.e., the *built-up* or *bottom-up* approach). Recent studies on the micro-lines of institutional analysis provide greater depth to the breadth of macro-level accounts, thereby presenting a more complete picture of the complex institutional processes and enabling various audiences to apprehend and appreciate their potential impact (Greenwood et al., 2017; Powell & Colyvas, 2008; Thornton et al., 2012; Zucker, 1991). Nonetheless, while institutional theorists have now realized the ontological importance of unearthing, understanding, and utilizing the microfoundations to answer the questions of why and how they matter for institutions, little is known about how to empirically capture the concept to foster rigorous theorization (Cornelissen, 2017; Reay & Jones, 2016; Zilber, 2016).

Microfoundations of institutions are concerned with *how* individual actors value, think, feel, and behave, *how* groups interact and operate, and *how* organizations purposefully shape institutions. Therefore, in order to tackle the *how* research questions, institutional scholars are urged to delve into an epistemological approach that can properly address such questions (Eisenhardt, Graebner, & Sonenshein, 2016; Langley, 1999). Inductive methods (i.e., approaches to build theory) have been argued to convincingly eclipse their deductive counterparts (i.e., approaches to test theory) in elucidating the processes by which embedded actors, groups, and organizations influence the higher-level institutions. Such methods allow researchers to focus on the depth of institutional phenomena through total immersion in a single or a few theoretically sampled case(s) in order to generate theory from data (Geertz, 1973; Glaser, 1978; Strauss & Corbin, 2008; Van Maanen, 1988). When inductive methods are opted for, institutional researchers mostly collect a form of data that is more qualitative in nature. In most instances, primary qualitative data is gathered through first-hand interviews (formal, informal, structured, semi-structured, or unstructured), while secondary qualitative data consists of textual or audio-visual material produced by other parties (e.g., books, print media, brochures, catalogs, booklets, (annual) reports, meeting minutes, archives, emails, recorded interviews, or video footages). However, in order to truthfully grasp the microfoundations of institutions, researchers need to employ an inductive method that is not only suitable for, but also capable of identifying, describing, translating, measuring, and recording the mundane intricacies of organizational life, the meanings attached to them, and the rich experiences of organizational members (Cunliffe, 2010; Reay & Jones, 2016): that method is ethnography (Denzin, 1997; Hammersley & Atkinson, 2007).

Ethnography, which has its roots in anthropology and sociology, is a style of social science writing that seeks to understand the overall cultural framework within which actors' lived experiences and contextualized meaning-making occur (Cunliffe, 2010; Watson, 2011). For organizational ethnographers in particular, there is an added emphasis on the in-situ organizational practices, processes, and patterns (Watson, 2012). Immersing themselves in actors' naturally occurring environment, ethnographers typically spend an extended period of time to be able to *go native* by passively observing and actively interacting/participating with the subjects under study (Malinowski, 1922). Yet it is necessary for ethnographers to be reflexive so that they do not risk compromising their objectivity and can develop a relatively value-free, insider viewpoint that zooms in on how actors experience and make sense of the complexity and mundanity of their activities (Cunliffe, 2003). In order to generate such an unprejudiced, from-within standpoint, ethnographers must also engage in the production of *thick descriptions* (Geertz, 1973) that offer rich, detailed accounts of how actors live their (organizational) lives and construct meanings intersubjectively, captured through a blend of systematic writing and documentation of primary and secondary data (Czarniawska, 2007; Van Maanen, 1988). Illuminating the situatedness and the sociality of interactions, values, cognitions, emotions, behaviors, events, rituals, artifacts, language, and space, ethnography reveals what actors cannot or will not share in a standard interview setting (Bechky, 2011), and is therefore a powerful inductive method "to uncover and explicate the ways in which people in particular work settings come to understand, account for, take action, and otherwise manage their day-to-day situation" (Van Maanen, 1979: 540).

When conducted appropriately, ethnography has the potential to address the question of how things work from the lens of organizational actors (Watson, 2011) and is thereby epistemologically compatible with the constructivist ontology of the microfoundations of institutions (Zilber, 2016). An example of institutional study that benefits from ethnography is one carried out by Siebert, Wilson, and Hamilton (2017) who studied how Scottish legal advocates used organizational space in institutional processes. For 110 days, the authors followed the actors during multiple events such as training sessions, lectures, ceremonies, and court hearings, to understand how these actors made sense of and maneuvered through the space around them to maintain the professional boundary and status order. Moreover, McPherson and Sauder (2013) studied the decision-making processes at an American drug court by attending court proceedings and team meetings over the period of fifteen months. They observed first-hand and on the ground how actors exercised a great deal of agency in their pragmatic, strategic, and creative use of home or non-home logics. Finally, in their study of Pentecostal churches in Indonesia, Wijaya and Heugens (2018) attempted to understand how actors' emotions functioned in institutional processes characterized by a high degree of moral perturbation. Through a 212-day ethnographic journey they gleaned a great deal of highly sensitive information pertaining to actors' strong values and negative emotions, which were extremely difficult to extract because they were deeply rooted and could only be unveiled discreetly to protect actors' employment status.

What is common in these studies is how ethnography enabled researchers to witness and register the subtleties and non-verbal cues (e.g., how organizational space, actors' everyday activities, or their values and emotions mattered for the institutions in which actors were embedded) that would otherwise go unnoticed and uncharted by conventional interviews. Or as Watson (2011: 204), who called for a greater adoption of ethnography in management over and beyond the usage of interviews alone, put it, "we cannot really learn a lot about what *actually happens* or about *how things work* in organizations without doing the intensive type of close-observational or participative research that is central to ethnographic endeavor." However, academic articles have been particularly silent about the actual ethnographic processes of capturing the microfoundations of institutions. Researchers normally compress their long, arduous journey of data collection into only a single impersonal paragraph or two, leaving institutional theorists methodologically uninformed and muddled. Therefore, the purpose of this chapter is not only to promote ethnography as one of the most powerful inductive methods in organization studies, but also to offer institutional fieldworkers facing time and budget constraints some hands-on recommendations on entering the field, documenting how things actually work on the ground, and, perhaps more importantly, managing the cognitive struggles and emotional turbulences inherent in all forms of ethnography. Finally, in order to accomplish that purpose, in the next section I will adopt a confessional style of writing (Van Maanen, 1988). This style was chosen over the others (i.e., realist or impressionist) because I believed it would help narrate my journey more honestly, sincerely, and reflexively, without exaggerating the successes or trivializing the low moments.

A Confessional Tale of Tasting and Transcribing Cultures

It was in the second week of October when my then-advisor and I decided to delve into the empirical context of Pentecostalism in Indonesia. Specifically, a deeper examination of the internal operations of Pentecostal churches and the dynamic relationship with their wider environment. At first, I was hesitant to go back to my motherland due to some disheartening images. First, Indonesians, at least compared to the Dutch, had a strikingly different perception of time. Time was more fluid and unbinding. The act of making an appointment was not customary and could even be seen as a sign of Western pretentiousness, and everything moved slowly under the Indonesian sun. How quickly could I adjust to this part of the culture to which I strongly objected? Second, Indonesia was ostensibly a very religious country where all citizens were *obliged* to adhere to one of the six recognized religions that would be displayed on their ID card. Growing up, I was raised by a mother who would label herself a Protestant and by a father who did not believe in the notion of theism. Further, living in the mainly secular culture of the Netherlands steadily *enlightened* me and drained away any remnants of faith. How would this affect my perspectives on religions and would these churches let in and confide in an atheist scholar? Third, as a PhD student I had limited time and budget to collect data on the topic with which I was not familiar. I knew very little about the history or current movement of Pentecostalism, the distinctive features of this denomination, the characteristics of its people, and most importantly, how to gain access. Would six months and €6,000 be adequate to fully understand the field and collect high-quality data? In short, nothing but the topic of my dissertation was assured.

On Pre-fieldwork Planning

Compared to ethnographies in the anthropological tradition, a six-month duration was considerably brief. Anthropologists generally required a much longer time to *go native*, as it was necessary to learn the local language(s) of the people they study, which was/were most often foreign. But in my case, I was fluent in speaking *Bahasa Indonesia* (i.e., Indonesia's national language) and low Javanese (i.e., a regional language spoken in most parts of East Java province). To counter the lack of time and budget, I studied the topic intensively prior to entering the field, so that when I arrived in Indonesia I could devote myself to the sampling and data collection. The following were the activities carried out in preparation for the actual fieldwork.

Conducting Systematic Desk Research

Some ethnographers entered the field with a relatively blank slate, but with the time and budget constraints ahead, I filled my tabula rasa with relevant information to optimize my six-month low-budget stay in the Emerald of the Equator. For instance, textual materials (e.g., books, academic articles, print media, reports, etc.) on the historical and current development of both global and Indonesian Pentecostalism helped me contextualize the world's fastest growing Protestant denomination and its relations with other religions (especially Islam, as Indonesia has the largest Muslim population in the world). Moreover, I also watched publicly accessible documentaries and videos on Pentecostal movements, Sunday services, revival meetings, and interviews with senior pastors (i.e., the highest leader of a Pentecostal church). I learned that Pentecostalism was a relatively young denomination conceived in Los Angeles in 1906 that has since spread throughout the world and gained dominance in the Global South (i.e., Latin America, Africa, Asia, and Oceania). One of the factors that contributed to this rapid growth was its expressive and supernatural allure. During services and (usually large-scale) revival meetings, members enthusiastically and rhythmically clapped their hands and jumped to the songs, regularly shouted "amen" or "hallelujah" throughout the sermon, and sobbed uncontrollably because they felt they were being divinely touched or miraculously healed by the Holy Spirit. Although conducting systematic desk research enabled me to visualize what the real field *may* look like, it did not provide me with any *actual* information on the daily operations of these churches, the distinctive traits of their leaders and members, the relationship with their wider environment, or any feasible tactics to gain access as an academic and an outsider. This lack of knowledge led me to perform the following.

Conducting Pilot Ethnographic Exercises

After seven weeks conducting systematic desk research, I came to believe that I had obtained sufficient background on (Indonesian) Pentecostalism. But since I was motivated to find some sort of clarity to the remaining unresolved issues, I reconnected with some of my relatives, friends, and acquaintances in the Netherlands and Indonesia. With those in the Low Land we had casual visits, while with those in Indonesia we communicated via Skype or email. All were made aware of my research agenda and were chosen because of their familiarity with either (Indonesian) Pentecostal history and movement, (Indonesian) Pentecostal leaders and members, (Indonesian) Pentecostal churches and their relationship with the wider environment, or Indonesia's religious landscape in general. Whereas informal talks and calls were not audio recorded in order to avoid overanalysis and to keep an open mind while in the field, notes were meticulously taken and email correspondence was electronically stored. From these activities I was connected to other relevant informants residing in both countries. In the Netherlands I was invited to join a couple of Indonesian-style Pentecostal services, where I could *taste* the movement and practice being a fieldworker. My respondents in Indonesia not only gave me valuable insights into actual happenings, but also helped me gain access to a Pentecostal church in Surabaya, Indonesia's second largest city. I discovered that Pentecostalists were real fanatics who took the Bible quite literally; that they were friendly but would relentlessly *chase* and compete for new members; that getting access would be an uphill battle due to an innate wall of exclusivity and confidentiality; that Islam was multi-faceted in that different tribes had different interpretations of Islam; and that Islam influenced the Pentecostal movement in several different ways and to different degrees.

The pre-fieldwork activities of systematic desk research and pilot ethnographic exercises worked hand-in-hand instead of sequentially, with the former concluded only on the very last day of my fieldwork. These activities helped me develop a better understanding of the topic and catch a glimpse into the organizations, the people, and the micro-level activities, enabling me to narrow down the geographical focus of my sample to Java, one of Indonesia's 17,500 islands. Considered to be the heart of Indonesia's politics, economy, and culture, Java was the epicenter of Pentecostalism with the most sophisticated church development in terms of size, structure, and management system. The next sampling issue to address was determining which cities and synods (i.e., the governing body of a particular church) would constitute my final sample. But in order to resolve this, I had to be in the field to experience the phenomena myself, evaluate my odds of gaining access, and make final decisions. Finally, 20 weeks after the empirical context was determined, I was ready, cognitively and emotionally, to embark on my ethnographic journey. Upon arrival in Indonesia, with a somewhat filled tabula rasa, I could immediately focus on finalizing the sample and gathering the data.

In summary, when research time and budget are restricted, *doing homework* as much as possible to get comprehensive knowledge about the field and its dynamics beforehand can effectively help optimize the usage of those resources.

On Fieldwork Execution: Handling Data

After a 16-hour flight from Amsterdam to Surabaya, I went straight to my hometown of Kediri. I spent the first three days having family visits, settling phone and internet subscriptions, fighting the jetlag, and getting used to the über-relaxed *santai* culture. I then began my ethnographic expedition covering the most prominent cities on Java. I started off in the east and moved westward, ending the orientation in the capital city of Jakarta on day 32. From day one, I was constantly observing the field and talking to as many demographically diverse people as possible. While some of their accounts verified/contradicted what I had been reading and hearing, some were completely new: Islamic cultures on Java had differing degrees of devoutness and radicalism, influencing the relationship between Pentecostalists and Muslims; the categorization of Pentecostal churches found in the Western literature was not perfectly applicable to the Indonesian circumstances; due to its extreme nature, Pentecostalism was loved by their fanatic followers and hated by the disgruntled dissidents; Pentecostalism as a denomination consisted of multiple synods or church *brands* in the Indonesian context, and under one synod there were multiple independent senior pastors, each of whom founded, led, and claimed outright *ownership* of multiple churches (i.e., a mother church and several satellite ones); Pentecostal churches were prone to organizational misconducts due to the entanglement of big money and ego-charged politics; and unlike a typical church with only a couple of activities per week, Pentecostal churches could have up to ten, ranging from Sunday services (and schools), teen/youth/golden age services, women/professional/entrepreneur services, cell groups, bible classes, morning/night/fasting/restoration prayers, worship nights, to deliverance services. Access to these activities proved both beneficial and laborious, due to the abundance of rich data to be managed.

Utilizing Multiple Tools

Throughout my 32-day orientation across Java I gleaned a great deal of primary data from talks and observations. When about neutral issues or appropriate to do so, I would freely take notes. When driving, occupied, or unable to immediately record the data, I relied on memory until I had the chance to jot down key points or audio record them with my phone. To assure confidence when informants shared sensitive issues, I would conceal my notebook and listen attentively to what was often controversial information. For example, multiple people residing in different cities narrated a similar story, with varying degrees of dramatization, about a financial scandal that was hitting one of the biggest Pentecostal churches. Some also shared what they saw as organizational *flaws*, such as the unhealthy competition for members (e.g., poaching other church's members by surreptitiously scheduling free pick-ups just minutes before other church' buses were to arrive) or the discriminatory nature of evangelization (e.g., primarily targeting Chinese ethnics as they were the biggest donators). When relevant details worth recording came to light in the middle of a conversation, I would excuse myself to go to the restroom to access my notebook or phone. Yet when I sensed that putting the conversation off would break the momentum, which was mostly the case, I would quickly write down key words in my notebook and immediately return it to my bag. Collecting rich data was not only about encouraging people to share thick information, but also about recording it accurately by utilizing the most effective tools.

Recapitulating Data Daily and Reviewing Data Weekly

In order to decide on my final sample, in addition to assembling secondary data, I talked to 100 respondents and joined 19 church services and activities during the 32-day expedition. As the primary data recorded in my notebook and phone was mostly disjointed, jumbled, and unstructured, I developed a daily habit of data recapitulation. Every night before going to bed, depending on the workload and type of work involved, I spent 30–90 minutes transferring, organizing, and synthesizing the data collected during the day into an orderly textual chunk. When what occurred during the day was too overwhelming or too fast to process, particularly in the early stages when everything was so new, I also documented my candid thoughts and feelings. This nocturnal exercise helped me tremendously make sense of not only the abundance and messiness of the data, but also my cognitive and emotional state. Moreover, on Mondays (i.e., the churches' least busy day, hence the least amount of workload) I reviewed what I had collected and written over the previous week so that I could contextualize the phenomenon and keep track of the data that was most interesting and worthy of further scrutiny. The benefit of these daily and weekly activities was apparent when on the fifth week I had more clarity on the typology of Indonesian Pentecostalism that did not perfectly align with Western literature. In Indonesia, the movement was categorized into two, rather than three, types: those that performed the manifestation of the Holy Spirit and those that did not. I used the former as a criterion to select the final synods since one of the key theological tenets of Pentecostalism was the visible work of the Holy Spirit. Another benefit was reaped when on week seven I chose Surabaya, Surakarta (locally known as Solo), and Bandung for my final sample. In the beginning I had six cities on my shortlist, but upon daily and weekly reflections, I realized that it was imperative to allow consistent comparison across cases and so I focused on cities in which all sizes of Pentecostal churches (i.e., from small to mega-church) were to be found.

In summary, modern-day ethnographers can, and perhaps should, rely on the utilization of multiple tools to accurately record the data observed in the field. But more often than not, fieldworkers are overwhelmed by the abundance, richness, and messiness of their own data, and are confused by or uninformed of their own cognitive and affective state. Therefore, daily data recapitulation and weekly data review will provide not only a greater understanding of the field, but also a sense of reflexivity that is much needed in any ethnographic endeavor.

On Fieldwork Execution: Winning Trust and Creating Comfort

As a result of the pre-fieldwork planning in the Netherlands and the 32-day expedition across Java, I came to realize that gaining organizational access would be grueling for two primary reasons: exclusivity and confidentiality.

First, Pentecostal churches were famous for their exclusive status achieved through their tight-knit communities that were highly uniform and extremely resistant to external ideas. In their daily interactions, actors would espouse, defend, and spread Pentecostal values that in turn served as institutional glue strengthening their bond. For example, all of the weekly church activities were designed not only to socialize (*indoctrinate*) members with fundamental teachings, but also to offer them an opportunity to express and reinforce their faith on a daily basis through worship, prayers, services, or evangelical efforts. As a result, towards existing and potential members, Pentecostalists urged homogeneous thinking and blocked any types of deviation from the original theological principles. As a researcher who always questioned things and tried to discover the *truth*, this was not an ideal situation. But unless I thought and behaved like a native, they would always consider me an outsider, preventing me from gaining access and gathering data.

Second, confidentiality was a distinctive attribute of Pentecostal churches. Unlike their mainline Protestant counterparts whose main focus was to disciple their existing congregation, Pentecostal churches competed harshly against each other for new members, breeding a phenomenon known as *pencurian domba* (sheep stealing), in which a church was accused of stealing or attracting members of other Pentecostal, Protestant, or Catholic churches. In its defense, an accused church would argue that the accusing churches did not provide their own *sheep* (i.e., congregation) with enough quality *grass* (i.e., spiritual nourishment such as sermons or church activities) so their members felt spiritually neglected and migrated to another church with richer pastures, begetting another term *pencurian rumput* (grass stealing). Such accusations were usually made against bigger churches because of their extensive resources and capabilities. Urged to protect their *methods* from being copied or surpassed by their rivals, they were extremely cautious of an unfamiliar, external audience attempting to study their internal operations. As a researcher I had to assure these churches through words and actions that I was grounded in scientific integrity and would safeguard any divulged information for strictly academic purposes. But in practice, things were much easier said than done.

This discouraging nature of the field with its protective actors, combined with the worry that my research time and budget would not be enough, initially blinded me from seeing the big picture. Ethnography was not merely about gaining organizational access – clearly without access there would not be data – but about something more essential: building a genuine relationship with the organizational actors that was based on winning trust and creating comfort. Growing up I was exposed to the Indonesian proverb *tak kenal maka tak sayang* (literally, do not know thus do not love, or figuratively, one cannot love someone s/he does not know). But it was only at the beginning of the third month that I was reminded of this proverb. I then realized that unless a high level of trust and comfort was present, a strong relationship would not be developed and access to rich data would not be granted. The results of the first two months in the field supported this notion as I had only secured access to three churches (in three cities from two different synods) and formally interviewed only five actors.

Being a Natural Native

From my experience of being in the field for 212 days, it was impossible for me to be 100% native. I could not speak the local languages with authentic accents like the natives in Solo and Bandung did, and neither could I value, think, feel, or act exactly like Pentecostal members. However, I did push my limits to appear native, while trying to not be obvious. Although Java was the smallest of the five major islands, it was home to numerous languages and countless accents in just the three cities I was studying. Because I grew up in East Java province, it was natural for me to speak my mother tongue of low Javanese when I was in Surabaya. Located in Central

Java, Solo, where high Javanese was spoken with a slightly heavier accent, was more of a challenge. Bandung, however, posed the most difficult circumstances as West Javanese people spoke Sundanese, a completely different language with a much softer accent. So, in Bandung I had to learn some basic Sundanese (e.g., greetings, numbers, simple daily phrases, etc.) and speak the national language and my second tongue of *Bahasa Indonesia* with a West Javanese accent. In both Solo and Bandung respondents noticed that I was not a native, but they were appreciative that I did my best to respect their culture by attempting to assimilate linguistically.

While becoming a true Pentecostalist was a rather far-fetched aspiration, I did aim realistically at becoming a trustworthy and comforting academic who knew a great deal about the Pentecostal movement and wanted to genuinely learn how the members lived their lives. During the course of seven months in the field, I became more *Pentecostal* than I had ever been. Not only was I versed in the history and current development of the movement, but I also learned some Pentecostal jargon and mastered Pentecostal discourse (e.g., their main values, theological teachings, cognitive framings, emotional attachments, and general attitudes) to make my interactions with the organizational members more natural or less awkward. For example, Pentecostalists used the phrase *full-timer* (in English) when referring to *karyawan/pegawai gereja* (church employees). While in a general context the word *berkat* (blessing) represented many types of blessings (e.g., from health, happiness, to wealth), in the Pentecostal context it was used mainly in reference to financial favor. That was the reason that *teologi kemakmuran* (prosperity gospel) became one of Pentecostal churches' most effective *differentiators*. This theological teaching was considered controversial as Pentecostal churches used parts of the Bible to justify the promise of a financially prosperous life to its followers. However, I learned that these churches by no means wanted to be accused of being commercial or *selling Jesus* to their prospective or existing members. In other words, this was a taboo term within Pentecostal churches, and therefore I had to be cautious as to when (not) to use it.

Furthermore, Pentecostalists believed in the notion of fighting against the work of evil forces interfering with daily human affairs. One Pentecostal church in Bandung planned to attract a new batch of students by handing out brochures on the first day of college. But because they believed that the demons had all kinds of tricks to close the hearts of these students from accepting the gospel, they had to *fight* against these bad spirits. One day before the orientation day commenced, they organized two groups of people to do a *doa keliling* (encircling prayer). One group encircled the whole campus by walking, praying, spreading salt and anointing oil on the ground, and another group encircled the city periphery with cars while praying, singing, and worshiping. They believed that doing this ritual would open up the new students' hearts to accept Jesus Christ more easily. Knowing what spiritual warfare was and how it actually worked on the ground (i.e., the microfoundations), I signaled them that I was open to socialization (*indoctrination*) and that I assimilated their values. As a result, they did not consider me as a total outsider, but as an academic observer who was not afraid to be *one of them*.

Being a Diplomatic (Undercover) Agent

Considering the intensity of rivalry among Pentecostal churches, I had to present my image smartly by eliminating any signs that I was a potential spy from another church and by creating the impression that I was someone they could trust and with whom they could feel comfortable being open. Since these churches were so concerned about their *secret recipes* getting leaked to others, they were not keen on having unfamiliar people looking into their internal processes. They had accordingly turned down many research-related requests and had previously granted access to only very few scholars, if at all. But when they did, as in my case, outsiders were required to pass several hurdles before being given the chance to meet and interview the highest leader. In all cases, lower-ranking full-timers acted as the initial and most critical gatekeeper; they asked the highest number of questions with the highest degree of scrutiny. So, when an initial formal interview was finally granted, it was always with someone from this lower-ranking position first. At introduction, I always handed them my business card and a signed letter from the university with a short research proposal enclosed, while summarizing the objectives of my study. By adopting the university's code of ethics and scientific integrity, I sought to authenticate my role as an academic who truly wanted to know more about the day-to-day operations of Pentecostal churches and the relationship with their wider environment (i.e., the link between the microfoundations and the macro-level institutions).

In every church, except for one whose access I gained conveniently, I was always asked by the first one to three interviewee(s) whether I was also studying other churches in the city. I always diplomatically replied with a question:

> I would love to! The more data I get, the better it is for my research project. But I heard the senior pastor of (name of another church) is an extremely busy figure and I really don't know how to get to interview him (all senior pastors were men). Is there any way that you could help me connect with him? I would really appreciate it.

My answer was honest yet confusing, for a reason. Honest, because I would love to gather as much rich data as possible from people of all organizational levels yet I did not know anybody in the other, possibly rival, churches who could refer me to their highest leader. Confusing, in that one might wonder why I asked such a question of a lower-ranking full-timer who most likely had no connection to the highest leaders of the other churches. But that was exactly the point. By being honest and confusing at the same time, I diplomatically projected an image of a genuinely naïve researcher with no other agenda than to collect data for academic purposes, which was my true and sole intention. As trust and comfort were steadily built, these people asked fewer and less critical questions, and even referred me to other full-timers in higher positions.

However, being diplomatic was not only about tackling tricky questions and situations, but also about asking the right questions in order to not compromise an already established level of trust and comfort. For example, geographical proximity mattered and, when not managed, could pose a problem, especially in the initial phase when developing trust and comfort was vital. Solo was a much smaller city than Surabaya and Bandung, and the three churches I studied simultaneously were located very close to each other (i.e., less than five minutes by car), making awkward public encounters with people from different churches inevitable. If I was to be spotted with people of a particular church (e.g., when having dinner or hanging out together) by people from a rival church, I risked being viewed as an *enemy spy* and having my true motives brought into question. In Bandung the situation was even more challenging because two (out of four) churches I studied were located in the same part of a mall but on different floors. This was because building a physical church in this city was almost unheard of due to a high level of Islamic threats. To protect my image and avoid unnecessary investigative questions or gnawing doubts in informants' mind, which could actually compromise the relationships being generated, I always asked where they usually hung out. So, when a possible overlap occurred, I could ask for an alternative. It was only in the first weeks that I activated this exceptionally high level of cautiousness. After a few weeks when my relationships with them were strong enough, I did not have to hide the fact that I was also studying other churches and building relationships with their actors.

Being an Empathetic Listener

As an ethnographer I collected data from seeing, feeling, talking, and listening. The latter, however, was a vital skill that could *make or break* the richness of data. People generally loved to tell stories, as this was one of the ways they could make sense of the world surrounding them. But oftentimes when asked a particular question, instead of focusing on answering the original question, they took me through an unorganized temporal labyrinth. On the one hand, they gave me a more detailed glimpse of their life, but on the other hand, I had to be able to instantaneously weave these chunks floating around the spectrum of time. In this case, listening was not only about looking someone in the eye, staying awake without yawning, or being enthusiastically engaged throughout the conversation, but also about being absorbed in the story and linking random bits of information together. Once I was able to place myself in their shoes and retell their unstructured and messy accounts, I gave them the impression that they were genuinely heard, hence creating a stronger bond of trust and comfort. For example, one respondent told me about his dark past, current struggles at the church, and future goals in an unchronological order. Because I had never met him before, the story was scattered and hard to follow. But when I began to empathize with his life, it was relatively easy to connect the dots. Once the trust and comfort were established, even more information was shared.

Furthermore, some actors trusted me so extensively and felt so comfortable during the interview that they disclosed not only sensitive information, but also their deepest heartfelt emotions. When respondents narrated their first callings to serve God, as either a full-timer or a volunteer of the church, some trembled while others actually wept. Such a response was triggered by their own thought that as sinners they did not deserve to be loved, yet God accepted them for who they were and loved them unconditionally. When I first experienced an emotional interviewee like this, I felt very awkward and did not know what to do. So, my first reaction was to move on to the next neutral question with the intention of settling their emotions. But doing so actually broke the momentum and significantly reduced their openness. I soon learned that interviewees wanted their emotions, however embarrassing they might be, to be acknowledged and respected. Later when I encountered other emotionally charged interviewees, I activated my empathy, validated their emotions by saying I could understand how powerful it must be for anyone to experience the divine, and then continued with follow-up questions. Using this strategy, I was able to show appreciation for their disclosed vulnerability by creating space where they could be themselves. This resulted in greater levels of trust and comfort, reinforcing the positive cycle required to gather rich data.

Finally, both empathy and listening skills were crucial in a field that was filled with multiple ideologies, because organizational actors could have a strong sense or conflicting interpretations of what they considered good or evil. During my time in the field I observed several organizational practices that stirred moral discussions, even among members of the same organization. For example, the extravagant lifestyles of senior pastors and their family members angered some church full-timers and volunteers because these actors espoused the value of modesty that was also aligned with the teachings of Jesus Christ. But for the proponents, this practice was perfectly justifiable because being the followers of a mighty God made them deserve mighty (financial) blessings too. Some even quoted biblical verses to enhance the legitimacy of their arguments. When talking with or interviewing these respondents, I could never escape from my own judgment of, and disagreement with, their upheld moral values. But I realized that my role as an ethnographer was not to preach about what was right or wrong, but to gather information solely from their perspectives. Therefore, in a field with highly charged morality, I had to activate my empathy when interacting with all respondents and be patient when listening to their narratives, regardless of whether or not they violated my worldview. It was impossible for me to be value-free, but if I could at least empathize with them, enough trust and comfort could be built for them to be freely open in disclosing how they viewed the world around them.

By the end of my fieldwork, owing to my ability to win trust and create comfort among organizational actors, I was able to gain access to eleven churches in total from five different synods and collect rich data from the observations of 110 church activities and formal interviews with 100 church leaders, employees, and volunteers.

In summary, when ethnographers face an exclusive and/or confidential wall that separates them from the organizations they wish to study, gaining access and collecting data from the inside might seem to be intimidating or even implausible. This seemingly impenetrable wall, however, should not be considered a dead end. Establishing and maintaining a genuine relationship with organizational actors can actually open doors, smooth entry, and facilitate observations of the organizations. Becoming a natural native, a diplomatic (undercover) agent, and an empathetic listener is an effective strategy to foster trust and comfort in order for any form of relationship to work. It should be noted, however, that building such a relationship should be consistent throughout the ethnographic process.

On Fieldwork Execution: Managing Cognitive and Emotional Battles

Reflecting on my 212-day ethnographic study, while I managed to gather rich data both quantitatively (i.e., hundreds of hours of informal talks, observations, and formal interviews; hundreds of photos; and tens of pounds of secondary data) and qualitatively (i.e., respondents from all walks of life and all organizational levels sharing their thick, morally charged, heartfelt accounts), what lay beneath was the foundation of those remarkable results: my ability to deal with the cognitive struggles and emotional turbulences inherent in all types of ethnography.

Building a Support System

Before going back to Indonesia, I talked with a Canadian ethnographer whose work and passion for qualitative research I deeply admired. Although she knew I was Indonesian she said candidly before departing from the university pantry, "You will be lost there, but that's part of the fun!" I shrugged it off and said to myself, "I'm *not* going to be lost! It's my hometown, I grew up there, I know the culture, and I can speak the language!" But in the end, she was right. I was indeed lost in the wilderness of ethnography. Knowing the local cultures and learning the local languages was the easiest part. The biggest challenge was building genuine relationships. At the beginning, the limited time and budget blinded me from seeing the big picture and slowly altered my ultimate focus, from gathering thick data to gaining access as quickly as possible. As a result, I conducted as few as five formal interviews in the first two months, making me second-guess my abilities as an ethnographer. At the time my mind wandered to dark places and my emotions were filled with immense angst and inadequacy, leading me to reconsider my PhD trajectory. But instead, I faced my negative thoughts and feelings, and more importantly I found support from people close to me (e.g., my family, advisor, and best friends in the Netherlands and Indonesia). During the most difficult days I would call or Skype with them to share the progress of my research and the cognitive/emotional battles that I faced. This ritual helped me not only make sense of the phenomenon being studied, but also come to terms with the state of my mind and heart. It should be noted, however, that the members of my support system were not part of my respondents because data objectivity needed to be maintained and shielded from the compromising effect of the diminishing boundary of the professional and the personal. It became clear to me that ethnography was not for the faint-hearted. The intimidation from the field (and its members) combined with the overwhelming amount of information that had to be grasped could easily shake my sanity. Yet my support system offered me warm consolation and their encouragement helped me continue to build genuine relationships with my informants by winning their trust and creating comfort in order to access richer data.

Taking Short Breaks

Because of my Dutch nationality, after my first two-month visa, subsequent visits of only 30 days were permitted. To extend my stay, I would leave Indonesia and return after three or four days to not break the momentum. Albeit short, the breaks allowed enough time to relax and gain some perspective on the previous 30 days of stressful ethnographic activities in a highly exclusive and confidential environment. Seeing new cultures in a more relaxed environment was a constructive way for me to unwind while still providing the perfect amount of time to reflect on my research project and life in general. Experiencing different contexts and interacting with people with different backgrounds helped me not only to understand the (Indonesian) Pentecostal field better (i.e., how and why the actors valued, thought, felt, behaved the way they did), but also to consider some bigger *life* questions.

When I was in the Philippines, I learned that, unlike Pentecostalism in Indonesia that was rigid and restricting, Catholicism was comparatively progressive and liberating. I found an almost tolerant vibe in the capital city that would take decades, if at all, to develop in Jakarta or Indonesia's other big cities. Although both Christian religions worshiped the same God, their followers experienced and interpreted the religions differently. It could also be the case that in Indonesia both Islam and Pentecostalism were reinforcing each other's conservative values. Moreover, while in East Timor I was struck by the notion of happiness from observing kids playing football (soccer) on the beach and from listening to their stories. I learned at that moment that attaining happiness was as simple as activating the habit of being grateful and living in the present. In contrast to my first three months in the field when my fear of failure to gain access and collect rich data was manifested in constant angst and incompetence, after that short trip I felt determined to develop healthier habits, however difficult it would be. These experiences tangibly resulted in both an increased comprehension of the research topic and a growing level of peace of mind. Relationships were built more organically and genuinely on a foundation that was about more than just data gathering. With the trust and comfort strengthened, the odds of gathering richer data immediately improved.

In summary, ethnography is hard work that can be physically and emotionally draining. Therefore, the success of an ethnographic endeavor is dependent not only on fieldworkers' passion and ability to understand a particular culture and how it works on the ground, but also on their healthy state of mind and heart. To achieve the latter, fieldworkers can build and activate a support system of family, friends, and mentors, and take short breaks to relax and reflect.

Epilogue

Before neo-institutional theory can make a significant and relevant impact on management, organizations, and society at large (Ferraro et al., 2015; Schilke, 2018; Zucker, 1983, 1991), scholars ought to truly appreciate and incorporate the microfoundations of institutions in their analyses (Greenwood et al., 2014; Lawrence et al., 2009; Powell & Colyvas, 2008; Thornton et al., 2012). By attempting to open the black box, the literature as a whole will benefit from a much-needed multi-level paradigm that seamlessly connects the macro- and micro-level components of institutions, hence offering a more comprehensive understanding of the complex institutional processes (Schilke, 2018). Despite being equipped with an ontology that reflects a more balanced view on the relationship between individuals and institutions (Zilber, 2016), institutional theorists examining the microfoundations of institutions are still epistemologically uninformed about how to empirically capture the concept beyond the usage of interviews alone (Cornelissen, 2017; Reay & Jones, 2016).

This is especially true for those (interested in) using ethnography as an inductive method, which is ideally suited for identifying, describing, translating, measuring, and recording the mundane intricacies of organizational life and the rich experiences of organizational members (Denzin, 1997; Hammersley & Atkinson, 2007). In this chapter, supporting Watson (2011), I argue that ethnography is among the most appropriate and powerful qualitative methods to capture the microfoundations of institutions and how they were meaningfully experienced by the actors. Providing thick descriptions of the phenomenology of institutions (Cunliffe, 2010; Geertz, 1973), ethnography, when carried out properly, can reveal what actors cannot or will not share in a standard interview setting (Bechky, 2011). It is clear that had I relied on interviews only, I would not have built quality relationships with the organizational actors that enabled me to gather rich data on their biographies, values, cognitive framing, emotional attachments, social interactions and interpretations, and bottom-up purposeful activities that *micro-shape* their organizations and the wider institutions.

Immersing myself in the actors' naturally occurring environment, I divided my time into two phases: planning (in the Netherlands) and execution (in Indonesia). In the planning phase, conducting systematic desk research and pilot ethnographic exercises helped me keep track of the limited time and budget. However, in the end, an extra month was needed as many appointments were rescheduled and I was able to get some extra funding to recompense some of the research costs incurred beyond the original budget. In the execution phase, I utilized multiple tools to glean data in the field, and in order to handle the abundance, richness, and messiness of the data collected, I engaged in daily data recapitulation and weekly data review. More-over, as the field was walled off by a high degree of exclusivity and confidentiality, I learned that the essence of ethnography was about building genuine relationships with the actors. By becoming a natural native, a diplomatic (undercover) agent, and an empathetic listener, I could win actors' trust and create comfort with them, both of which were key to gaining access and rich data. But in the end, I owed any success to my support system and the short breaks I took, because without them, I would not have overcome the cognitive and emotional battles inherent in all forms of ethnography.

To summarize my ethnographic journey in Indonesia, I reflect on moments of feeling lost, stumbling, and many tears, yet in the end I succeeded, handsomely.

I realize that I have accomplished what I never thought I could, converting what I saw initially as a troubling endeavor into a profoundly self-transformative experience of courage and tenacity. Finally, I hope that some of the reflexive and hands-on recommendations offered in this chapter are useful for institutional scholars aiming to empirically and qualitatively capture the microfoundations of institutions.

References

Bechky, B. A. 2011. Making organizational theory work: Institutions, occupations, and negotiated orders. *Organization Science*, 22: 1157–1167.

Collins, R. 2004. *Interaction ritual chains*. Princeton, NJ: Princeton University Press.

Cornelissen, J. P. 2017. Preserving theoretical divergence in management research: Why the explanatory potential of qualitative research should be harnessed rather than suppressed. *Journal of Management Studies*, 54: 368–383.

Creed, W. E. D., Hudson, B. A., Okhuysen, G. A., & Smith-Crowe, K. 2014. Swimming in a sea of shame: Incorporating emotion into explanations of institutional reproduction and change. *Academy of Management Review*, 39: 275–301.

Cunliffe, A. L. 2003. Reflexive inquiry in organization research: Questions and possibilities. *Human Relations*, 56: 983–1003.

Cunliffe, A. L. 2010. Retelling tales of the field: In search of organizational ethnography 20 years on. *Organizational Research Methods*, 13: 224–239.

Czarniawska, B. 2007. *Shadowing, and other techniques for doing fieldwork in modern societies*. Frederiksberg: Liber/CBS Press.

de Rond, M., & Lok, J. 2016. Some things can never be unseen: The role of context in the psychological injury at war. *Academy of Management Journal*, 59: 1965–1993.

Denzin, N. K. 1997. *Interpretive ethnography: Ethnographic practices for the 21st century*. London: Sage.

DiMaggio, P., & Powell, W. W. 1983. The iron cage revisited: Institutional isomorphism and collective rationality in organizational fields. *American Sociological Review*, 48. 147–160.

Eisenhardt, K. M., Graebner, M. E., & Sonenshein, S. 2016. Grand challenges and inductive methods: Rigor without rigor mortis. *Academy of Management Journal*, 59: 1113–1123.

Fan, G. H., & Zietsma, C. 2017. Constructing a shared governance logic: The role of emotions in enabling dually embedded agency. *Academy of Management Journal*, 60: 2321–2351.

Ferraro, F., Etzion, D., & Gehman, J. 2015. Tackling grand challenges pragmatically: Robust action revisited. *Organization Studies*, 36: 363–390.

Foster, W. M., Suddaby, R., Minkus, A., & Wiebe, E. 2011. History as social memory assets: The example of Tim Hortons. *Management & Organizational History*, 6: 101–120.

Geertz, C. 1973. *The interpretation of cultures: Selected essays*. New York, NY: Basic Books.

Gehman, J., Lounsbury, M., & Greenwood, R. 2016. How institutions matter: From the micro foundations of institutional impacts to the macro consequences of institutional arrangements. In J. Gehman, M. Lounsbury, & R. Greenwood (Eds.), *Research in the sociology of organization, volume 48A: How institutions matter!*: 1–34. Bingley: Emerald Publishing Limited.

Glaser, B. G. 1978. *Theoretical sensitivity: Advances in the methodology of grounded theory*. Mill Valley, CA: Sociology Press.

Greenwood, R., Hinings, C. R., & Whetten, D. 2014. Rethinking institutions and organizations. *Journal of Management Studies*, 51: 1206–1220.

Greenwood, R., Oliver, C., Lawrence, T. B., & Meyer, R. E. 2017. *The Sage handbook of organizational institutionalism*. Los Angeles, CA: Sage.

Hallett, T., & Ventresca, M. J. 2006. Inhabited institutions: Social interaction and organizational forms in Gouldner's patterns of industrial bureaucracy. *Theory and Society*, 35: 213–236.

Hammersley, M., & Atkinson, P. 2007. *Ethnography: Principles in practice*, 3rd edition. New York, NY: Routledge.

Heugens, P. P. M. A. R., & Lander, M. W. 2009. Structure! Agency! (And other quarrels): A meta-analysis of institutional theories of organization. *Academy of Management Journal*, 52: 61–85.

Kraatz, M. S., & Flores, R. G. 2015. Reinfusing values. In M. S. Kraatz (Ed.), *Research in the sociology of organizations, volume 44: Institutions and ideals: Philip Selznick's legacy for organizational studies*: 353–381. Bingley: Emerald Publishing Limited.

Langley, A. 1999. Strategies for theorizing from process data. *Academy of Management Review*, 24: 691–710.

Lawrence, T. B., & Dover, G. 2015. Place and institutional work: Creating housing for the hard-to-house. *Administrative Science Quarterly*, 60: 371–410.

Lawrence, T. B., Suddaby, R., & Leca, B. 2009. *Institutional work: Actors and agency in institutional studies of organizations*. Cambridge: Cambridge University Press.

Lok, J., & de Rond, M. 2013. On the plasticity of institutions: Containing and restoring practice breakdowns at the Cambridge University Boat Club. *Academy of Management Journal*, 56: 185–207.

Malinowski, B. 1922. *Argonauts of the Pacific*. New York, NY: Holt, Rinehart & Winston.

McPherson, C. M., & Sauder, M. 2013. Logics in action: Managing institutional complexity in a drug court. *Administrative Science Quarterly*, 58: 165–196.

Meyer, J. W., & Rowan, B. 1977. Institutionalized organizations: Formal structure as myth and ceremony. *American Journal of Sociology*, 83: 340–363.

Powell, W. W., & Colyvas, J. A. 2008. Microfoundations of institutional theory. Institutional logics. In R. Greenwood, C. Oliver, K. Sahlin, & R. Suddaby (Eds.), *The Sage handbook of organizational institutionalism*: 276–298. Los Angeles, CA: Sage.

Reay, T., & Jones, C. 2016. Qualitatively capturing institutional logics. *Strategic Organization*, 14: 441–454.

Schatzki, T. R. 2001. Introduction: Practice theory. In T. R. Schatzki, K. Knorr-Cetina, & E. V. Savigny (Eds.), *The practice turn in contemporary theory*: 1–14. London: Routledge.

Schilke, O. 2018. A micro-institutional inquiry into resistance to environmental pressures. *Academy of Management Journal*, 61: 1431–1466.

Scott, W. R. 2014. *Institutions and organizations: Ideas, interests, and identities*, 4th edition. Los Angeles, CA: Sage.

Siebert, S., Wilson, F., & Hamilton, J. R. A. 2017. "Devil may sit here:" The role of enchantment in institutional maintenance. *Academy of Management Journal*, 60: 1607–1632.

Smets, M., Jarzabkowski, P., Burke, G. T., & Spee, P. 2015. Reinsurance trading in Lloyd's of London: Balancing conflicting-yet-complementary logics in practice. *Academy of Management Journal*, 58: 932–970.

Smets, M., Morris, T., & Greenwood, R. 2012. From practice to field: A multilevel model of practice-driven institutional change. *Academy of Management Journal*, 55: 877–904.

Strauss, A. L., & Corbin, J. 2008. *Basics of qualitative research: Techniques and procedures for developing grounded theory*, 3rd edition. Newbury Park, CA: Sage.

Thornton, P. H., & Ocasio, W. 2008. Institutional logics. In R. Greenwood, C. Oliver, K. Sahlin, & R. Suddaby (Eds.), *The SAGE handbook of organizational institutionalism*: 99–129. London: Sage.

Thornton, P. H., Ocasio, W., & Lounsbury, M. 2012. *The institutional logics perspective*. London: Oxford University Press.

Tracey, P., Phillips, N., & Jarvis, O. 2011. Bridging institutional entrepreneurship and the creation of new organizational forms: A multilevel model. *Organization Science*, 22: 60–80.

Van Maanen, J. 1979. The fact of fiction in organizational ethnography. *Administrative Science Quarterly*, 24: 539–550.

Van Maanen, J. 1988. *Tales of the field: On writing ethnography*. Chicago, IL: University of Chicago Press.

Voronov, M., & Vince, R. 2012. Integrating emotions into the analysis of institutional work. *Academy of Management Review*, 37: 58–81.

Voronov, M., & Weber, K. 2016. The heart of institutions: Emotional competence and institutional actorhood. *Academy of Management Review*, 41: 456–478.

Watson, T. J. 2011. Ethnography, reality, and truth: The vital need for studies of 'how things work' in organizations and management. *Journal of Management Studies*, 48: 202–217.

Watson, T. J. 2012. Making organisational ethnography. *Journal of Organizational Ethnography*, 1: 15–22.

Wijaya, H. R., & Heugens, P. P. M. A. R. 2018. Give me a hallelujah! Amen! Institutional reproduction in the presence of moral perturbation and the dynamics of emotional investment. *Organization Studies*, 39: 491–514.

Zilber, T. B. 2002. Institutionalization as an interplay between actions, meanings, and actors: The case of a rape crisis center in Israel. *Academy of Management Journal*, 45: 234–254.

Zilber, T. B. 2016. How institutional logics matter: A bottom-up exploration. In J. Gehman, M. Lounsbury, & R. Greenwood (Eds.), *Research in the sociology of organization, volume 48A: How institutions matter!*: 137–155. Bingley: Emerald Publishing Limited.

Zucker, L. G. 1977. The role of institutionalization in cultural persistence. *American Sociological Review*, 42: 726–743.

Zucker, L. G. 1983. Organizations as institutions. *Research in the Sociology of Organizations*, 2: 1–47.

Zucker, L. G. 1991. Postscript: Microfoundations of institutional thought. In W. W. Powell, & P. J. DiMaggio (Eds.), *The new institutionalism in organizational analysis*: 103–106. Chicago, IL: University of Chicago Press.

19

FIVE WAYS OF SEEING EVENTS (IN ANTHROPOLOGY AND ORGANIZATION STUDIES)

Stefanie Mauksch

What do ethnographers see when they study events? Which assumptions drive their engagements? How do they set apart the event from more mundane aspects of social life? In this chapter, I set out to list typical forms of ethnographic interpretation of events in the two disciplines of Anthropology and (Management and) Organization Studies. I here focus on events as planned occasions, thus bracketing other notions of the term such as "surprising rupture" (e.g. Wagner-Pacifici, 2017) and the process philosophical conceptualization of events as "things that happen" (e.g. Hussenot and Missonier, 2016). I engage in a review that moves back and forth between the study of culture and the study of organization to show that events may be viewed as (1) windows into society, (2) agentic tools, (3) global forms, (4) spaces of practice, (5) processes. These divergent ways of "seeing" events are, for the sake of idealization, disentangled from the complex, collectively evolving lines of thoughts they evolved from. And yet they are, as I hope to show, clearly marked by assumptions about the significance of events in producing social practice that remain rather unacknowledged and undertheorized (Handelman, 1998). It is my aim in this chapter to carve out these epistemological premises in order to render them more explicit and, hence, open to comparison, critique and reflection.

By way of organizing this chapter, I deliberately move from my disciplinary home of Anthropology into Organization Studies, rather than the other way around, and this is how the sections are arranged. While Anthropology has traditionally viewed events in terms of stability rather than change, Organization Studies' engagement with events has been "processual" and often "agentic" since its (comparatively late) inception. This seems related to the diversity of geographical locations into which anthropologists and organizational scholars embedded their ethnographic agencies, the study of which is still fed by a postmodern tendency of emphasizing change here (in "Western" managerial meetings) and stagnation there (in "non-Western" ceremonies) (Said, 1978). And yet, for the sake of theorizing events, Organization Studies occasionally "poached" Anthropology's terrain (Czarniawska, 2012). Organizational studies of events have revitalized Bourdieu's field and capital theory (e.g. Anand and Jones, 2008; McInerney, 2008), Victor Turner's ritual symbolism, drama and liminality (e.g. Johnson et al., 2010; Toraldo and Islam, 2017), Arjun Appadurai's tournaments of value (e.g. Anand and Watson, 2004) and frequently privilege ethnography as a distinct mode of studying events (e.g. Garud, 2008; Zilber, 2011). The two disciplines also share common ground in what has been coined as "ontological turn" or "(re)turn to process" (Hernes and Maitlis, 2010; Vigh and Sausdal, 2014). I will end this chapter with contemporary contributions from Anthropology and Organization Studies that co-create a perception of events as shaped by flux, potentiality and intensity. It is here where the disciplines move closest.

Anthropology was once described as the discipline of "non- events," given its long-lasting focus on structural continuities and their social reproduction (Hoffman and Lubkemann, 2005). Much of the work on events grew wings under the key word "ritual," itself a "fuzzy concept" with Eurocentric notions (it commonly brings to mind exotic imagery of primitive others engaged in mystical activities) that was later replaced by "public event" or "cultural performance" (Handelman, 1998). As Rosaldo (1993 [1989]) remarks, "[r]itual itself is defined by its formality and routine; under such descriptions, it more nearly resembles a recipe, a fixed program, or a book of etiquette than an open-ended human process" (p. 12). Anthropologists, more often than not, assumed that the typical worlds they encountered – non-industrialized, village-like settings – were embedded in a cyclical mode of temporality (Wagner-Pacifici, 2017). But if there is anything like an Anthropology of Events, the description of historical traces would most probably start with Max Gluckman. Diverting from a (Malinowskian) fashion of using events as "apt illustrations," whereby cases were made relevant only to depict larger systems, Gluckman selected events that were atypical and crisis-ridden (Gluckman, 1961; Kapferer, 1987). He laid the groundwork for a form of analysis that essentially draws from events long before process ontologies started to impact the discipline (Kapferer, 2015). In Gluckman's pioneering texts, we find both a tendency to reduce events to mere representations of social systems, but also glimpses at how we may study events once we accept their disruptive potential. Beyond Gluckman, other famous anthropologists like F.G. Bailey, Clifford Geertz, Victor Turner and Michael Jackson delved into events and demanded paradigmatic shifts in Anthropology – towards agency, towards thick description, towards symbolism, towards the body – but circumvented the question of what events are and what it is that marks their specificity. Against this general neglect, a handful of scholars made events their explicit subject of inquiry, carving out the different philosophical underpinnings that had guided previous anthropological gazes on events (Schwartzman, 1989; Handelman, 1998; Kapferer, 2015).

In Organization Studies, scholarship clusters, more narrowly, around particular types of events, such as meetings, conferences, or trade fairs. However, with growing popularity of field configuration as an approach studying the ways in which occupational, industrial, or professional fields emerge and change, scholars developed a more consistent strand of analysis (Lampel and Meyer, 2008). In cross-fertilization with, but also beyond this strand, events provoked attention as contexts for and forms of strategy-as-practice (e.g. Johnson et al., 2010), as agentic tools or collective rituals producing industries and professions (e.g. Lampel and Meyer, 2008), as practical accomplishments (Schwartzman, 1989), as enactments (e.g. Garud, 2008), as performative spaces (e.g. Mauksch, 2018), as processes of domination and self-subordination (e.g. Ford and Harding, 2008), or as forums for sensemaking (e.g. Anand and Peterson, 2000). These contributions differ in spotlighting either radical rupture (e.g. Islam, 2015) or failure and stagnation (e.g. Schüssler and Wittneben, 2014), but are generally sensitive to change, asking how an event's "outcome" was processually achieved. Similar to anthropologists, organization studies scholars show strong commitment to cases, but rarely openly formulate the heuristic premises guiding their orientation to events (for exceptions, see Schwartzman's (1989) account of meetings, or Toraldo and Islam (2017) on festivals). This review is thus focused not so much on empirical contents, but seeks to unravel what scholars of both disciplines take for granted as the ontological and epistemological basis of their diverse analytical engagements with events.

Events as Representations

Anthropology, for a large part, has viewed events as micro representations of societies (Hoffman and Lubkemann, 2005; Kapferer, 2015). The central idea is that events bring to the surface a social system that lies underneath, thus embodying or dramatizing the essence of a culture and its visions of reality. As Handelman (1998) describes this view:

> it is in various public occasions that cultural codes – usually diffused, attenuated, and submerged in the mundane order of things – lie closest to the behavioral surface. Here they are most graspable in various sensory and cognitive modalities, not only by natives but also by ethnographers. ... The analyst mines these rich veins of cultural intricacy for insights into the very premises of a people – of their cosmologies, world views, and values. For the ethnographer, public events are privileged points of penetration into other social and cultural universes.
>
> *(p. 9)*

A particularity of such a society-writ-small approach is that answers to what an event is and does are not located in the event itself, but in the wider social order (Handelman, 1998: xii). Gluckman's (1940) seminal essay "An Analysis of a Social Situation in Modern Zululand" – shortly referred to as "The Bridge" – despite laying groundwork for the study of social change, is larded with comments on the representational role of events. Studies of events would reveal, in Gluckman's (1940) words, "the underlying system of relationships between the social structure of the community, the parts of the social structure, the physical environment, and the physiological life of the community's members" (p. 10). Gluckman intellectually inherited from structural functionalist Radcliffe-Brown a procedure by which each single ethnographic account sought for the general principles that appeared in the study of a society (Turner, 1980), thus categorizing the event as conformational rather than creational. In "The Bridge," Gluckman analyzes happenings against the background of his knowledge of the social system and the way it is being arranged by and reflected in smaller units' relations towards each other. He describes practical action and material arrangements, such as the collective singing of a hymn or the separate eating practices of Zulu and European group members, in order to induct from these more abstract principles of organization. Nevertheless, Gluckman is an early advocate of introducing process ontology to the study of events. Later (more explicitly processual) readings of events, such as Victor Turner's, owe their process sensitivity to Gluckman's advocacy of "situation," "crisis" and "social change." I will, later in this chapter, get back to this alternative reading of Gluckman's intervention.

Clifford Geertz (1973a), in his famous essay "Deep Play: Notes on the Balinese Cockfight," revitalizes a tradition of drawing from detailed description of an event in order to produce an analysis of society. Gluckman's and Geertz's framings share in common a layered understanding of the relation between event and society, whereby an analysis of the former reveals the deeper workings of the latter. In Geertz's vision, the Balinese power arrangement "migrates" into "the body of the cockfight" (Geertz, 1973a: 436) so that the informed ethnographer can "read" this hierarchy from event-based happenings (Geertz, 1973a). The cockfight emerges as a form of status gambling that renders obvious hierarchies and recreates power. Geertz (1973a) notes that "no one's status is actually altered by the outcome of the cockfight; it is only momentarily affirmed or insulted" (p. 433) and that "men [...] generally dominate and define the sport as they dominate and define the society" (p. 435). For the ethnographer, the event operates as a text which elucidates the structural workings of a society that is basically bounded, discrete and integrated rather than fluid, expansive and permeable.

It is important to note that Geertz diverts from Gluckman's positivism by viewing culture as a text that the ethnographer "reads" and interprets (Geertz, 1973c). Geertz stresses the "observer-dependency" of the "event-that-models" so that the relationship between analyst and event should be one of critical self-awareness (Handelman, 1998). He argues that a description is always already of a second or third order, and inevitably produces a fiction or imagination rather than directly accessing "reality" (Geertz, 1973c). By the same token, Geertz creates space for the interpretative acts of "native" participants and organizers, who – by means of events – tell a story about themselves to themselves (Geertz, 1973a). Events thus serve not just as models *of*, but also models *for* the structural workings of society:

Where for "visitors" religious performances can, in the nature of the case, only be presentations of a particular religious perspective, and thus aesthetically appreciated or scientifically dissected, for participants they are in addition enactments, materializations, realizations of it – not only models *of* what they believe, but also models *for* the believing of it. In these plastic dramas men attain their faith as they portray it.

(Geertz, 1973b: 113–114; original emphasis)

Some of Geertz's remarks are indicative of later practice and performance theories. He notes that cultural preoccupations are "brought into being" by the social situation (Geertz, 1973a) and elsewhere insists that "it is through the flow of behavior – or, more precisely, social action – that cultural forms find articulation" (Geertz, 1973c: 17). Sherry Ortner (1984) remarks that Geertz acknowledged one dimension of practice – the production of subjects through (structured) practice in the world – but not the second, more agentic dimension of practice: the production of the world through subjects. Thus, the emphasis in Geertz's event analysis lies on how actors "substantialize" (and not so much on how they performatively create) the abstract organizational principles of society they adhere to (Kapferer, 2015). It is Geertz's metaphor of a more or less coherent narrative ("a story that the Balinese tell themselves about themselves" Geertz (1973a)) that critics problematize, because

[a]rguing explicitly or implicitly that ritual (in general) is organized as narrative again drives ritual towards becoming a medium of representation. … There is only representation without transformation. The relationship of persons to their horizon-of-being is fixed, in-place. Then there is little curiosity, imagination, or shock in ritual, but only a recycling of cultural lessons learned and yet to be learnt.

(Handelman, 1998: xvi)

The idea of studying (small) events in order to study (big) structure of society/ organization also emerges, although in a more sidelined way, from Organization Studies' engagement with events. Early literature on organizational culture promoted viewing organizations as societies-writ-small – an analogy that legitimizes scholarly occupation with the "cultural traits" of organizations, their ethos, symbols, myths, stories and the like (Allaire and Firsirotu, 1984). In this context, organizational events gained relevance as superficial manifestations that reveal cultural patterns located at the depth of the organization (Schein, 1996; Schultz, 2012). More recent literature echoes this notion by describing the event as "a unique *window* on participants' social, occupational, and organizational worlds" (Lampel and Meyer, 2008: 1026; my emphasis). An in-depth account of the London Fashion Week, for instance, seizes the notion that the event "renders visible, through its orchestration, wider field characteristics, such as field boundaries, positions, position taking and habitus" (Entwistle and Rocamora, 2011: 250). Following Bourdieu, the authors harvest from the example of an air kiss to show how gestures and other forms of body symbolism bring to surface and performatively reinforce abstract field relations. Similarly, large-scale events are sometimes viewed as tournament rituals that dramatize existing structures, such as (vertical) power relationships or (horizontal) networks (Anand and Watson, 2004; Anand and Jones, 2008; Moeran and Pedersen, 2011). There are parallels in thinking between Geertz's model *of* / model *for* and event scholars' underlining of the "dual character" of events that impact on, and are being impacted by a larger unit – the field (Lampel and Meyer, 2008). Such concept of field structuration allows for a more flexible and processual vision of social arrangements. But one of the undergirding thoughts, similar to the above examples from Anthropology, is that events represent cultural order.

Events as Agentic

Instead of highlighting the ways in which events symbolize social systems or a cultural ethos, a second view focuses on individuals who exercise power through events. Handelman (1998) rightly argues that a "functional" argument is intrinsic to all analytical engagements with events – the event always "does" something for somebody. And yet, scholars fundamentally differ with respect to the weight they put on agency and intentionality. Political anthropologists of the late 1960s began to put priority on "locating the individual in … social organization" (Vincent, 1978: 175). They provoked a shift from a concept of stable society towards the interpersonal occasions in which "society" is being realized (Schwartzman, 1989). Anthropology, by then still dominated by equilibrium theories (Gluckman's among them), developed new methodological angles sensitive to political behavior such as decision-making, strategizing, manipulating and career-building (Vincent, 1978). It portrayed the antagonistic games of leaders, their strategies of alignment and rhetorical tricks, stressing issues of power, domination, and subordination as they evolved from "clearly occurring events, that is, people speaking to each other" (Bloch, 1975; cited in Schwartzman, 1989: 6). The title of Bailey's book "Stratagems and Spoils" (2018 [1969]) already connotes a move from the consensual maintenance of social order towards conflict, self-interest and a view of politics as a competitive game. Bailey (1965) advocated taming symbolic interpretation to create space for portrayals of rational decision-making:

> If (a) is symbolic action, what does it symbolize? Specifically, what does avoidance of open disputation, in the Pentrediwaith fashion, symbolize? […] we might be tempted to say that it symbolizes the collectivity, village unity, or something of that kind. But I do not think we need go so far. The man who avoids putting a controversial motion and manœuvres an Englishman into doing so, is symbolizing his own reasonableness.
>
> *(p. 7)*

Such enhanced attention to culture-specific forms of argument and reason produced, almost as a side effect, a wave of interest in microcosmic settings such as council meetings and committees (Howe, 1986; Myers, 1986; Richards and Kuper, 1971). Some of these depictions of politically speaking subjects overlapped with the symbolic, representational analysis of events just outlined. Howe (1986), for example, described how Panamanian Kuna assembled in both "sacred" singing gatherings providing a social and symbolic foundation and "secular" talking gatherings that realize and affirm Kuna politics in quite practical ways. In any case, focal points of this strand of political anthropology again sidelined the event as mere context in which choice-making, role-playing "rational men" who hold office and possess wealth (this literature revived both Weber and Marx) control the actions of others (Firth, 1954; Schwartzman, 1989). Individuals here seemed to have "great latitude to strategize and negotiate in their attempts to realize intentions" (Schwartzman, 1989: 28), which again diverted attention from the inherent contingency of events. Nevertheless, ethnographies of political language provoked attention to the simultaneous workings of structure and interaction, thus preparing ground for the new guiding theme of "practice" (Ortner, 2006).

In Organization Studies, the agentic approach evolves less from analyses of political speech than from an instrumental or managerial perspective on social gatherings. Events, so the commonplace assumption shared by theorists and practitioners of management alike, serve as a cure for organizational problems and enable decision-making. Workshops are valued as instruments in developing and implementing strategy, meetings are viewed to help reaching decisions, and so on (for review and critique, see Hodgkinson et al., 2006; Jarzabkowski and Seidl, 2008). A more complex, but still instrumental view evolves from some fractions of the field-configuring events literature, where scholars highlight actors' conscious, collective desire to shape an organizational field and illustrate how strategic action of entrepreneurs impacts on creational field processes (e.g. McInerney, 2008; Zilber, 2011). Anand and Jones (2008), for example, track how "micro-level actions [...] resulted in the meso-level effect of establishing the Booker Prize as a recognizable and robust symbolic system" (p. 1052). Scholars adopt agentic interpretations of Bourdieu's capital theory, tracing how individuals maneuver to exploit (symbolic, social and economic) resources to improve their field position, thereby conversing values into others (Lampel, 2011; Thompson, 2011). Quite a few contributions delineate the cumulated actions of (groups of) institutional entrepreneurs (e.g. Montgomery and Oliver, 2007; McInerney, 2008)

The language of a game-like competitive interaction in events recalls the strategic politics perspective anthropologists adopted in their analyses of councils. But the "system" (e.g. industry branch, profession or business movement) emerges from these accounts not as a pre-given ground, but as an outcome of the activities of powerful agents who "marshal social and political process to edit the categorical constitution of a field" (Anand, 2011: 325). Schwartzman (1989) criticizes such perspectives that, in her view, stress the agentic over and above the structural. While events are here appreciated as technical tools to achieve pre-defined objectives, she argues, the tool itself is not attributed a potential to affect organizations, communities, or societies. Depictions of entrepreneurial maneuvering contain the risk "of the pendulum swinging too far in the other direction" (Hardy and Maguire, 2017: 276). They may glorify single actors, overemphasize rational decision-making, and ignore the contingent nature and coercive potentials of events (Hardy and Maguire, 2017).

Another agentic take on events turns the gaze towards such "concealing" aspects and subtle instantiations of power. Organizers evolve from these accounts as "orchestrators," "dramatic engineers" and "puppeteers" who manipulate audiences via "enchantment." In Anthropology, covert strategies of leaders are a well-explored theme. Raymond Firth (1973) already highlighted the "manipulability" of social symbols and sought to reconcile studies of pragmatic action with studies of symbolic action. Bailey (1986), in a short essay on "The Tactical Uses of Passion," too, examined the "emotional strain" of events such as town meetings, constitutional debates, or academic committee meetings. He observed a contradiction between an overt tribute to "rationality" and a covert dominance of passion, which enables rulers to subtly manipulate their audiences and political competitors through sophisticated rhetorics (Bailey, 1986). Shifting such accent on manipulative strategies to organizational contexts, Anand (2011) contends that planners may modify iterations of ritualistic events in opportunistic ways, while "encoding" their own intentions. Agency here seems limited to organizers, with little interest in the ways in which participants or customers circumvent, ignore or rebel against "enchantment." And yet this literature evidences how experiences of joy and extraordinariness may become targets of soft-power strategic manipulation.

This line of thinking – loosely organized around the production of conviction – has also been adopted by ethnographies that focus on background organizing and material realization. Land and Taylor (2014) and Mauksch (2017), for instance, studied the highly ambivalent, artistic tactics event organizers develop to "sell" participants a particular vision of the world's future. This literature reveals dilemmatic practices of navigating between retrospective and progressive temporalities (Land and Taylor, 2014), between enchantment and disenchantment (Mauksch, 2017), between underorganizing and overorganizing (Chen, 2009), in order to grant both joyful flow and practical control (Toraldo and Islam, 2017). A related set of studies investigates techniques of narrative persuasion. Hardy and Maguire (2010), for instance, study – within the context of a United Nations conference on pollution – the crafting of powerful stories by speaking or writing individuals. Depending on the context in which they are being produced, distributed and consumed, they argue, such "texts" (Hardy and Maguire, 2010), which are elsewhere called "conventionalizing accounts" (McInerney, 2008), gain power in producing discursive shifts. Ruebottom and Auster (2018), for instance, traced how tropes of injustice contributed to the dis- and re-embedding of audience members of the WeDay festivity from old to new ideological commitments. This kind of inquiry spotlights the strategies of constructing identity through the "weapon" of text (Hardy and Maguire, 2010). Organizational scholars' emphasis on intentional speech is in accord with the anthropological project outlined above, but moves beyond it by attending to collectivity and context of text circulation (McInerney, 2008) and attached emotions (Ruebottom and Auster, 2018) rather than the characteristics of formalized speech.

Events as Forms

"Events as forms" seeks to capture a style of analysis that investigates – by ways of cross-cultural or cross-organizational comparison – the "structuredness" of events themselves. Both anthropologists and Organization Studies scholars were intrigued by variations and similarities in the form and function of events in societies across the world (e.g. Bailey, 2018 [1969]; Howe, 1986; Myers, 1986) or across different organizations (e.g. Hodgkinson et al., 2006; Jarzabkowski and Seidl, 2008). An early example from Anthropology of one such comparison is Bailey's (1965) work on councils that scrutinized consensus procedures in diverse contexts of decision-making (Indian panchayats vs. Western Universities). It was also Bailey (1965) who drew a global distinction between "elite" and "arena" councils, contributing to the idea that there is something like "conciliar behavior" defining a space of formalized human action that is set apart from other behavioral contexts. While such global comparison advocated the unity of mankind (a comparison always assumes a common ground), it also produced the insight that the form itself is "cultural." Schwartzman (1989), for instance, draws from this literature to propose a view on meetings as social validators, because "acceptance of the form requires, at least in part, acceptance of the current social order" (p. 41). Participants submit to a meeting culture in its formal arrangements, rules of order and codes of talk.

For a large part, Turner's early texts on ritual (even though he invented a symbolic tradition independently from him, see Ortner (1984)) equals in style the kind of analysis Geertz pursued in his cockfight essay. In his book on Ndembu ritual, Turner (1966) provides a context-sensitive explanation of ritual symbolism, drawing out binary oppositions and other structural arrangements (triads, for instance). Like Geertz, Turner presents a cumulated, ideal version of particular rituals rather than engaging with the specificity of singular events. But, beyond such interpretive exercise, he intersperses his listing of locally relevant symbols with global structural comparisons in the tradition of the French structuralist Lévi-Strauss:

> The powers that shape the neophytes in liminality for the incumbency of new status are felt, *in rites all over the world*, to be more than human powers, though they are invoked and channeled by the representatives of the community.
>
> *(Turner, 1966: 106; my emphasis)*

In the context of anthropological thought in which Turner was moving, the idea of global unison in ritual evoked a deeply political message. Turner formulated his project against Lewis Henry Morgan's dismissal of "primitive religion" as "grotesque and to some extent unintelligible," instead reinforcing the sentiment that all humans share similar intellectual properties, but are shaped by different cultural experiences (Turner, 1966: 1–2). By adopting Van Gennep's three-partite structure of rituals, he assumed a similar scheme at the core of rituals everywhere in the world. Eventually, it is this global appeal that motivated Organization Studies scholars to adopt Van Gennep/Turner's model of ritual process to a range of events with ceremonial character, such as the Grammy awards (Anand and Watson, 2004) or the Booker Prize (Anand and Jones, 2008), but also less spectacular dining events (Dacin et al., 2010) and meetings (Johnson et al. (2010); see Islam (2015) for an overview).

Don Handelman, in his book *Models and Mirrors* (1998) also embraces a comparative mode of analysis. But instead of discovering similarities in elements, he sets out to categorize events along the degree in which they "make order," their "logics of design." He positions highly formalized events that predominantly represent (mirrors) at one end and unstructured, open events (models) at the other end of a continuum. The latter, more open formats may lead to new structural arrangements. For Handelman, events are thus not unidirectional "expressions" of society, but exhibit variable degrees of potential to change society. He seeks a middle path of embracing contextualism while drawing broader parallels in the ways events are being organized across the world. Even though Handelman is less attentive to processes of transformation in the seemingly most routine occasions (Feldman and Pentland, 2003), or the reproduction of power in seemingly radically new contexts (Land and Taylor, 2014), he brings into dialogue divergent perspectives on events and shows that events may actually do both: reveal and/or disrupt order.

Organization studies scholars, too, explored the form of (subtypes of) events in a comparative mode, partially by embracing Turnerian ritual (see above), partially through other theory lenses. Jarzabkowski and Seidl (2008), for instance, adopt Luhmann's systems theory concept of "episodes" to examine how University meetings either stabilized or proposed new orientations that cumulatively produced change on an institutional level. They show how typical "evolutionary paths" led to particular outcomes of strategic practices, thus privileging form over contents. Schüßler and colleagues (2014) studied the evolution of a series of global climate events, tracing variations in event structures, processes, and outcomes, in order to find out why a major UN conference in Copenhagen, despite waves of positive media attention, failed to achieve legally binding transnational commitments. In a similar manner, Johnson et al. (2010) examined how workshops vary with respect to "degree of removal" from the everyday, the use of liturgy and the role of specialists (facilitators) and how these parameters influence their success. This literature connects the study of form (or event characteristics) with the study of performance-related outcomes.

Comparative analyses in both disciplines, although allowing for inspection of the formal and formative qualities of events, create two problems related to their universalizing ambitions. One is the positioning of an omnipresent authoritative observer who – similar to the symbolic analyst – remains outside or above the happenings (Handelman, 1998). The second, related issue is that comparisons may produce normative, homogeneous interpretations that create barely any room for multiplicity and contingency, i.e. differential interpretations of the significance, direction, or "outcome" of events (Moore, 1995).

Events as Practice

Practice theory arrived at Anthropology in the late 1970s, roughly about a decade before it started to impact Organization Studies in the 1990s (for reviews, see Ortner, 2006; Nicolini, 2012). The rubric of practice brought together a few now well-known anthropologists who began to innovate the analysis of events. Its advocates diverted from both the terminologies of "structure," "system," "meaning" on the one hand, and from "agency" and "interaction" on the other, instead tracing how the practical doings of people remake the social worlds they encounter. Drawing mainly from the analytical repertoires of Bourdieu and Giddens, scholars conceived of identity, power, or knowledge not as pre-given substrates, but as practical accomplishments (Ortner, 2006; Sahlins, 1981). Michael Jackson (1983), for instance, in an article on girls' initiation rites in Sierra Leone, abandoned the typical project of "decoding" ritual activities as if they were symbolic representations of a "superorganic" (a reference to Durkheim), "something separable from the quotidian world of bodily movements and practical tasks" (p. 332). Instead of seeking cultural scripts, Jackson argued, scholars should study rituals as bodily enactments of a social order that comes into being and is being reproduced and adapted in the very moment of performance. For Handelman (1998), too, (along with his interest in form) social order is not grounded in macro-structures, but accomplished in events where members communicate to themselves in concert about the characters of their collectivities, thereby accepting constitutive entities of society as "real." Events, to some degree at least, are "operators of social order [...] Their mandate is to engage in the ordering of ideas, people, and things" (Handelman, 1998: 15–16). Events are thus constituted by both structure and practice, by text and enactment (Handelman, 1998). This vision of events reconciles and ropes into a common picture previous visions of events-as-representations and events-as-agency. Events are structured to the degree that actions are inevitably pre-shaped by power formations, habits and modes of experience, but yet not foreclosed, because people make choices within these set parameters.

If social order is achieved through continuous, recursive practice, it follows that the spectacular-mundane distinction that shapes symbolic inquiry and also some of the agentic depictions above become inadequate, or at least more porous. Ethnomethodologists provoked a shift from the spectacular (from ritual) to the mundane, critically estranging instead routine aspects of local life. The basic contention was that the study of society refers not to abstract forms but to interaction among individuals – a conviction that life takes place in the here and now (Simmel, 1950; Leach, 1982). Even global events of high impact are thus just "nodes in complex entanglements of social relations stretching out in different directions" or "particular, local sites of temporary character," like "a village of professionals" (Nyqvist et al., 2017: 3–4).

Other practice-oriented anthropologists equally divert from Geertzian symbolic structuralism, but find value in his contention that events reveal to participants the structural workings they adhere to. But different from Geertz's view, it is here assumed that such revelation inherently changes structural arrangements during and through the very act of utterance. Fred Myers (1986) notes on his study of meetings by Aborigines of Australia's Western Desert that these generate and display/visualize social relationships for participants. The polity (the political space) is here not an outside referent to his interlocutors, but "the social form of language [...] facilitates the process of mediation through which the polity is continually renegotiated" (Myers, 1986: 432). A contribution on the Ashura Shiite ritual celebrations in Bah- rain feeds into this theme by showing how participants, within the emotional peaks of these events, analyze their present-day social situation in relation to past events and the moral order of Islam (Fibiger, 2015). Similarly, Harvey (2013 [1996]), in her ethnography of the Expo 92 in Switzerland, fleshes out how the event initiated "a politics of reflexivity which invites visitors to question what they see while simul- taneously ordering their responses" (p. 135) – "a spectacle offered for interpretation and massively interpreted" (p. 48). Such stress on reflexive practice assumes partic- ipants as active and critical co-producers, rather than as passive observers who are "intoxinated" (see Toraldo and Islam, 2017: 7), overwhelmed or blindly governed (Bloch, 1975) by public spectacles.

The study of events in Organization Studies widely adopts a practice approach, with typical demands to find a "middle ground" between agency and structure (Lampel and Meyer, 2008; Moeran and Pedersen, 2011). Schwartzman (1989), in her late 1970s' study of meetings in a healthcare center, was a pioneer in trans- lating the notion of practice into studies of managerial events, arguing that the meeting *is* the organization. In parts, her study maintains the idea of a society-like unit (the organization) and an emphasis on symbolic interpretation. But she also exemplifies a methodology of ethnographic immersion into events for the sake of studying the collective remaking of organization, rather than viewing events as "lenses into" an organization that lies underneath. Schwartzman shows how the meeting

> provided everyone with a forum (it often seemed like a stage) for very emotional and frequently conflictual commentary on their relationships to each other – legitimate what otherwise might seem to be disparate talk and action, whereas they also enable individuals to negotiate and validate their relationships to each other.
>
> *(Schwartzman, 1989: 10)*

It follows from the latter perspective that we cannot disentangle the meeting from the social organization in which it is seemingly embedded.

More recent studies of events refer to organization theorist Karl Weick (1979) in order to approach the verb-like activities within rather than the noun-like entities behind events, i.e. the organizing processes and forms that "enact" an organization, network, or organizational field (Moeran, 2011). They advocate not just to study networks, but also "networking": the making of connections (Moeran, 2011) and "boundary-making," i.e. the complex negotiations around who is allowed access to particular subspaces – practices that "consecrate" the event (Thompson, 2011). The general approach to field-configuring events is one that shows how happenings conform to dominant field logics but at the same time leave room for individual initiative and creativity (Lampel and Meyer, 2008). Scholars of organization also embrace practice when highlighting the specific character of "interactions at events, for actors that usually do not meet in a common arena can initiate relationships and acquire knowledge that otherwise would have been impossible or at least unlikely to gain" (Schüßler et al., 2015: 166). These authors shift emphasis from the extraordinariness or "sacredness" of events towards the importance of bodily immediacy in producing social collectives (Entwistle and Rocamora, 2011).

Similar to Anthropology, organizational literature revitalizes (without however making explicit reference to) Geertz's (1973a) perception of events as reflective sites, producing metasocial commentary. Events such as conferences and trade fairs figure as occasions for reflection processes that lay bare the "invisible arrangements" (Ruebottom and Auster, 2018) and "shared cognitions" (Oliver and Montgomery, 2008) that organize the social. Scholars study, for instance, how events reveal competing visions for the future of an industry (Oliver and Montgomery, 2008), allow participants to create mutual awareness of a common enterprise (Anand and Watson, 2004), to resolve conflicts among them (Moeran, 2011) and to cope within fast-changing markets (Aspers and Darr, 2011). Scholars also engage with the performative outcomes of events. Markets, for instance, are perceived as a secondary achievement of sensemaking, and not as an original arrangement (Anand and Peterson, 2000; Aspers and Darr, 2011), so that events take a role in co-creating what is later perceived as a "real" market.

The trope of practice smoothly leads over to "process." There are no sharp distinctions since the practice agenda already entails a processual vision of society. But contributions listed in the next section more explicitly demarcate a "radically processual" or "flat ontology" view, questioning the stabilities of time, space, subjects and objects that seem to be taken for granted in most other event analyses.

Events as Processes

Starting from the 1940s, Gluckman (following Radcliffe-Brown's contention of life as a social process, see Ingold (2008)) provoked attention to the contingency and rupture contained in events. He advocated an Anthropology capable of responding to the crisis-ridden moments anthropologists encountered after World War II: the decline of the post-colonial nation-state and drastic effects of emerging globalization and neo-imperialism (Kuper, 1983). "The Bridge" is indicative of this new processual sensitivity and attention to the complexities of the contemporary. Gluckman envisioned a conflictual potential (here: between two color-groups) that occasionally "breaks out" in and through events, eventually overturning the system. It is in these methodological priorities that Gluckman moves beyond a pure representational approach, showing that the relative positioning of social segments is subject to change.

Such emphasis on processuality continued with Turner. The "late" Turner, in particular in his analysis of the social drama, more explicitly than others, suggested that it is through a focus on events that anthropologists can come to grips with social processes in their creative and generative moments (Kapferer, 2015). While Geertz appreciated events as analytic windows onto culture, Turner saw them as "operators" in the social process (Ortner, 1984). In a 1979 book (Turner died in 1983), he uttered his "disillusion" with the (by then) "fashionable stress on fit and congruence" (Turner, 1979: 62). While the "early" Turner had stressed rituals' potential to reaffirm social order through the concept of "communitas," the "late" Turner was intrigued by the ways in which the transformative quality of rituals "can generate and store a plurality of alternative models for living, from utopias to programs" (Turner, 1982; cited in Krøijer, 2015: 140). The "mounting crisis" encompassed in social drama, he argued, may create "momentous junctures" or "turning points" in the relations between components of a social field (Turner, 1980). Turner attributed to "reflexive narratives" that are being told in the course of a social drama a "potentiality, the possibility of becoming" (Turner, 1980: 158). However, even though developing the aspirations of Gluckman into more radical directions, the Turnerian view still upheld a notion of relatively constant and stable social relations. It promoted a gradual, teleological rather than disruptive course of history (Krøijer, 2015). In their edited book *In the Event: Towards an Anthropology of Generic Moments*, Lotte Meinert and Bruce Kapferer (2015) revisit the Manchester School's hints at potentiality and becoming and bring them into dialogue with newly evolving process philosophical orientations, such as that of Gilles Deleuze. The chapters collected exemplify a shift towards changing the ontological (rather than merely epistemological) view on events. Events in general, and not just particular types of events, are here perceived as "thoroughly tensional," manifesting a "multiplicity" and "opening towards new horizons of potential" (Kapferer, 2015: 16).

The anthropologist-historian Marshall Sahlins, independently from the Manchester School, sought to lay bare an event-based dynamic that is irreducible to social order. Like other practice theorists, Sahlins' studies of critical historical moments in Hawaii and Fiji revealed how "structures interact in the medium of people's projects" (Sahlins, 1991: 83), but moved beyond them theorizing on the discontinuity and contingency of events. Starting with a critique of the "exaggerated opposition between event and structure" (Sahlins, 1991: 37), he sketches a model of change comprising three moments in a dialectic between event and system. The first is what Sahlins calls "instantiation," which is a variant of the society-writ-small approach: larger cultural forces substantialize into particular doings (he names the example of Fijian rulers, whose actions are perceived as actions of the whole kingdom). Within the pragmatic actions of thinking and feeling subjects, different structures intersect, producing a "conjunction" of structural planes. The second moment is "denouement" – the actual incidents, what "historical agents actually do and suffer" (Sahlins, 1991: 82). The third one is "totalization," by which local actions expand to global significance: the act returns to the system. Each of these moments contains structural discontinuities, so that local structures may "restrain, intensify, orient, and otherwise direct the development of larger historical forces" (Sahlins, 1991: 83). By ways of such productive "moments of conjuncture," Sahlins' event is thus not simply a representation of the system, but a site of emergence out of which novel articulations of practiced reality arise (for an extended comment on Sahlins' contribution, see Kapferer, 2015: 15).

Organization Studies accounts have steadily viewed events as processes that reorganize systems, thus upholding a dichotomy between "event" and "structure," but tend to think in a direction opposite to anthropological traditions. Events do not simply represent, but create systems. This idea is at the core of field-configuring events literature that – with varying degrees in emphasis on agency (see above) – assumes that events co-create new organizational fields, i.e. recognized realms of institutional life. One may view such constructions as "weakly" processual: they provide "the arrows that connect pre-existing, relatively stable boxes […], i.e. to understand the temporal evolution of things or substances that nevertheless retain their identity over time" (Langley and Tsoukas, 2016: 3). The "boxes," as predominantly viewed by this literature, are field-configuring, goal-directed agents and organizations who engage in time and space bounded events in order to jointly configure/produce/shape a "field" (Lampel and Meyer, 2008; Moeran and Pedersen, 2011; Schüßler and Sydow, 2015).

Other more "radical" views on process in/of events avoid and problematize dichotomies of spectacular-mundane and event-structure (or, generally, are set against dualisms and conceptualism) and seek to deconstruct the idea of units that impact on each other (actors on fields, structures on other structures etc.). Instead, they propose a diachronic, relational view on the unfolding of more stable identities, objects and structures as transient outcomes of organizing in the realization of events. This is how a "strong" process view radically differs from other visions of events examined so far, which equals the "ontological" turn that Meinert and Kapferer (2015) suggested for the anthropological treatment of events. The world is perceived not as a pre-given state, but as in continuous flux, with stability being the mere result of our "conceptual intervention of the intellect onto what is essentially a 'mobile' reality" (Chia, 1997: 696).

This committed attitude towards process motivates a handful of ethnographic projects in both disciplines. Pipan and Porsander (2000) adopt Latour's actor-network-theory (ANT) to the study of city events to show how actors' identities (including the researcher's) emerge as secondary achievements of action nets. Similarly, Garud (2008) draws from what he calls a "sociology of associations," (based on ANT and praxeology), studying how particular forms of in/human encounter and connections produced more stable entities. His terminology of "pre-formation processes" and "proto-institutions" highlights the transient character of elements-in-the-making, reflecting commitment not to a world of discrete entities with stable characteristics, but to a "web ontology" (Orlikowski and Scott, 2008). In a very different approach to "event power," Ford and Harding's (2008) reflexive ethnography of a conference draws from Henri Lefebvre's (1991) claim that places and selves come into being simultaneously and dialectically. The authors studied how their embodied encounter or "being at the conference" performatively produced space/place and themselves as objects/subjects. In a similar vein, Mauksch (2018) scrutinized the performative making of social entrepreneurs in and through events. Drawing from Judith Butler's contention that there is no subject prior to discourse (and no discourse prior to subjectification), she engages with the event-anchored configurations that powerfully set in place and "call for" identification with a social business mindset.

Events may here produce (plateaus of) "intensity." "Intensity" is one of the complex terms put forward by Deleuze that envisions a dynamic flow of differential processes chiefly tied to both sensations and concepts. The term probably catches some of the "historically shaped material and spatial qualities" of events, the ways in which they produce "elements of festivity" (Aspers and Darr, 2011), "spectacle," and "carnival time" (Moeran and Pedersen, 2011). Following this notion, Krøijer (2015) reveals how a protest performance during a NATO anniversary summit momentarily (re)organized time and space. She carves out what she calls "multiple ontologies of time," i.e. bodily felt temporalities like a "dead time" vs. a positive, synchronic collective "pulse," that evolve from and through the compression and density created by a particular protest situation. Harvey (2013 [1996]) instead prefers to depict the Expo as an assemblage, by showing how the event carries traces of original ethos and forms that sit "unproblematically alongside what might appear to be paradoxical and opposing narratives" (p. 109). The Expo thus produces a space whose participating entities are rendered equivalent, so that they generate and display "commensurable difference" (p. 129). These are just a few examples of how "ontologically flat" engagements with events study not essences, but moments of intensification and different confrontations. Such processual reading of events focuses on processes of objectification, transgression, or assemblage that produce subjectivity, objects, technology or representations as an outcome, while also reflecting, to the degree possible, on the researcher's own efforts to conceptualize, which "freeze" what is actually to be conceived of as flux and flow.

Conclusion

So, what is it that marks events as distinct? As representations, events bring to surface invisible principles of social ordering. In agentic depictions, events evolve as a space-time-bound context in which powerful change-makers meet, compete and shape their cultural worlds. For scholars of form, events reveal similarities in organizing between diverse social contexts. For practice theorists, it is the bodily immediacy, enhanced reflexivity and practical accomplishment of social order that render events as distinct from everyday routines. And from the perspective of process theory, events produce moments of density that enable new connections between indeterminate things. My aim here was not to argue for the superiority of one approach over others, but to bring into dialogue divergent perspectives to again ask "what is an event?" beyond being the mere context of our research.

Such cross-disciplinary overview of typical understandings of events furthers the encounter between Anthropology and Organization Studies in at least three ways. First, the chapter shows that scholars from both fields share certain perceptions of what the study of events allows them to see, but rarely defend their heuristic premises against other potential views. Such reflexivity on a particular stance towards events is crucial for attending to the worldview that it carries within itself and for gaining a sense of its analytical strengths and weaknesses. The focus on sensemaking, for instance, positively embraces reflection, but less so the ways in which reflective practice and modes of self-reassurance may themselves be acts of subversion to a particular discourse of power. Or, an embracement of ritual as a central metaphor for understanding events may lead scholars towards emphasizing repetition and continuity over rupture and contingency, with a latent danger to recreate the idea of a superficial layer of "symbols" behind which social structure hides.

Second, critics from Anthropology and Organization Studies bemoan the flawed translation of anthropological methodology (often reduced to "quasi"-ethnography) and "culture" into Organization Studies (Bate, 1997; Wright, 2000). My reading on events confirms the impression that anthropological ideas are sometimes adopted in a rather eclectic, simplified way, stripping concepts off from their original complexity. Victor Turner's theorizing on events, for example, has been embraced by scholars of organization for the Durkheimian contention that rituals articulate central social categories (Anand and Jones, 2008), but less so for his account of performance in a world of continual becoming that marks him as distinct from other anthropologists of ritual (for a similar critique, see Islam, 2015). I hope this review helps to popularize not only the complexity of anthropological thinking, but also a few less-known takes on events such as Handelman's (1998) "logics of design," Sahlins' (1981) "structure of the conjuncture" or Meinert and Kapferer's (2015) "Anthropology of generic moments." All of these focus on questions of organizing very similar to that of Organization Studies (how do events create change?), so that Organization Studies scholars may see potential in following these threads.

Third, as the last sections have shown, there is a chance for cross-fertilization between Anthropology and Organization Studies, especially at a moment when both disciplines embrace process as a guiding metaphor for the study of events (Garud, 2008, Meinert and Kapferer, 2015). Both disciplines move towards studying the kind of organizing that is realized in events, engaging with how people alter their life worlds through encounters (occasions, events) they deem important and distinct from other routines of organizing, creating new orders in and through them. These orders are co-shaped by contingency, emergence and rupture set in place through diverse forms of in/human encounter, connection and differentiation.

References

Allaire, Y., and Firsirotu, M. E. (1984) Theories of organizational culture. *Organization Studies* 5(3): 193–226.

Anand, N. (2011) The retrospective use of tournament rituals in field configuration: The 1976 'Judgement of Paris' wine tasting. In: Moeran, B., and Pedersen, J.S. (eds) *Negotiating values in the creative industries: Fairs, festivals and competitive events*. Cambridge: Cambridge University Press, 321–333.

Anand, N., and Jones, B. C. (2008) Tournament rituals, category dynamics, and field configuration: The case of the Booker Prize. *Journal of Management Studies* 45(6): 1036–1060.

Anand, N., and Peterson, R. A. (2000) When market information constitutes fields: Sensemaking of markets in the commercial music industry. *Organization Science* 11(3): 270–284.

Anand, N., and Watson, M. R. (2004) Tournament rituals in the evolution of fields: The case of the Grammy awards. *Academy of Management Journal* 47(1): 59–80.

Aspers, P., and Darr, A. (2011) Trade shows and the creation of market and industry. *The Sociological Review* 59(4): 758–778.

Bailey, F. G. (1965) Decisions by consensus in councils and committees: With special reference to village and local government in India. In: Banton, M. (ed) *Political systems and the distribution of power*. London and New York: Routledge, 1–20.

Bailey, F. G. (1986) The tactical uses of passion: An essay on power, reason, and reality. *Philosophy and Rhetoric* 19(1): 73–76.

Bailey, F. G. (2018 [1969]) *Stratagems and spoils: A social anthropology of politics*. London: Routledge.

Bate, S. P. (1997) Whatever happened to organizational anthropology? A review of the field of organizational ethnography and anthropological studies. *Human Relations* 50(9): 1147–1175.

Bloch, M. (1975) *Political language and oratory in traditional society*. London: Academic Press.

Chen, K. K. (2009) *Enabling creative chaos: The organization behind the Burning Man event*. Chicago: University of Chicago Press.

Chia, R. (1997) Essai: Thirty years on: From organizational structures to the organization of thought. *Organization Studies* 18(4): 685–707.

Czarniawska, B. (2012) Organization theory meets anthropology: A story of an encounter. *Journal of Business Anthropology* 1(1): 118–140.

Dacin, M. T., Munir, K., and Tracey, P. (2010) Formal dining at Cambridge colleges: Linking ritual performance and institutional maintenance. *Academy of Management Journal* 53(6): 1393–1418.

Entwistle, J., and Rocamora, A. (2011) Between art and commerce: London fashion week as trade fair and fashion spectacle. In: Moeran, B., and Pedersen, J. S. (eds) *Negotiating values in the creative industries: Fairs, festivals and competitive events*. Cambridge: Cambridge University Press, 249–269.

Feldman, M. S., and Pentland, B. T. (2003) Reconceptualizing organizational routines as a source of flexibility and change. *Administrative Science Quarterly* 48(1): 94–118.

Fibiger, T. (2015) Ashura in Bahrain – Analyses of an analytical event. In: Meinert, L., and Kapferer, B. (eds) *In the event – Towards an anthropology of generic moments*. New York: Berghahn, 29–46.

Firth, R. (1954) Social organization and social change. *The Journal of the Royal Anthropological Institute of Great Britain and Ireland* 84(1/2): 1–20.

Firth, R. (1973) *Symbols: Public and private*. Ithaca and New York: Cornell University Press.

Ford, J., and Harding, N. (2008) Fear and loathing in Harrogate, or a study of a conference. *Organization* 15(2): 233–250.

Garud, R. (2008) Conferences as venues for the configuration of emerging organizational fields: The case of cochlear implants. *Journal of Management Studies* 45(6): 1061–1088.

Geertz, C. (1973a) Deep play: Notes on the Balinese cockfight. In: Geertz, C. (ed) *The interpretation of cultures*. New York: Basic Books, 412–453.

Geertz, C. (1973b) Religion as a cultural system. In: Geertz, C. (ed) *The interpretation of cultures*. New York: Basic Books, 87–125.

Geertz, C. (1973c) Thick description: Toward an interpretive theory of culture. In: Geertz, C. (ed) *The interpretation of cultures*. New York: Basic Books, 3–30.

Gluckman, M. (1940) Analysis of a social situation in modern Zululand. *Bantu Studies* 14(1): 1–30.

Gluckman, M. (1961) Ethnographic data in British social anthropology. *Sociological Review* 9(1): 5–17.

Handelman, D. (1998) *Models and mirrors: Towards an anthropology of public events*. New York: Berghahn Books.

Hardy, C., and Maguire, S. (2010) Discourse, field-configuring events, and change in organizations and institutional fields: Narratives of DDT and the Stockholm convention. *Academy of Management Journal* 53(6): 1365–1392.

Hardy, C., and Maguire, S. (2017) Institutional entrepreneurship and change in fields. In: Greenwood, R., Oliver, C., Lawrence, T. B., et al. (eds) *The SAGE Handbook of organizational institutionalism*, 2nd ed. London: SAGE, 261–280.

Harvey, P. (2013 [1996]) *Hybrids of modernity: Anthropology, the nation state and the universal exhibition*. New York: Routledge.

Hernes, T., and Maitlis, S. (2010) *Process, sensemaking, and organizing*. Oxford: Oxford University Press.

Hodgkinson, G. P., Whittington, R., Johnson, G., and Schwarz, M. (2006) The role of strategy workshops in strategy development processes: Formality, communication, co-ordination and inclusion. *Long Range Planning* 39(5): 479–496.

Hoffman, D., and Lubkemann, S. (2005) Introduction: West-African warscapes: Warscape ethnography in West Africa and the anthropology of "events". *Anthropological Quarterly* 78(2): 315–327.

Howe, J. (1986) *The Kuna gathering: Contemporary village politics in Panama*. Austin: University of Texas Press.

Hussenot, A., and Missonier, S. (2016) Encompassing stability and novelty in organization studies: An events-based approach. *Organization Studies* 37(4): 523–546.

Ingold, T. (2008) Anthropology is not ethnography. *Proceedings of the British Academy*. 69–92.

Islam, G. (2015) Organizational ritual: Rupture, repetition, and the institutional event. In: Mir, R., Willmott, H., and Greenwood, M. (eds) *The Routledge companion to philosophy in organization studies*. London: Routledge, 542–549.

Jackson, M. (1983) Knowledge of the body. *Man* 18(2): 327–345.

Jarzabkowski, P., and Seidl, D. (2008) The role of meetings in the social practice of strategy. *Organization Studies* 29(11): 1391–1426.

Johnson, G., Prashantham, S., Floyd, S. W., and Bourque, N. (2010) The ritualization of strategy workshops. *Organization Studies* 31(12): 1589–1618.

Kapferer, B. (1987) The anthropology of Max Gluckman. *Social Analysis: The International Journal of Social and Cultural Practice* 22: 3–21.

Kapferer, B. (2015) Introduction: In the event - toward an anthropology of generic moments. In: Meinert, L., and Kapferer, B. (eds) *In the event: Toward an anthropology of generic moments*. New York: Berghahn Books, 1–28.

Krøijer, S. (2015) Figurations of the future: On the form and temporality of protests among left radical activists in Europe. In Meinert L., and Kapferer B. (eds) *In the event: Toward an anthropology of generic moments*. New York: Berghahn Books, 139–152.

Kuper, A. (1983) Leach and Gluckman. In: Kuper, A. (ed) *Anthropology and anthropologists - the modern British school*. London: Routledge & Kegan Paul, 142–166.

Lampel, J. (2011) Afterword: Converting values into other values: Fairs and festivals as resource valuation and trading events. In: Moeran, B., and Pedersen, J. S. (eds) *Negotiating values in the creative industries: Fairs, festivals and competitive events*. Cambridge: Cambridge University Press, 334–347.

Lampel, J., and Meyer, A. D. (2008) Guest editors' introduction: Field-configuring events as structuring mechanisms: How conferences, ceremonies, and trade shows constitute new technologies, industries, and markets. *Journal of Management Studies* 45(6): 1025–1035.

Land, C., and Taylor, S. (2014) The good old days yet to come: Postalgic times for the new spirit of capitalism. *Management & Organizational History* 9(2): 202–219.

Langley, A., and Tsoukas, H. (2016) Introduction: Process thinking, process theorizing and process researching. In Langley, A., and Tsoukas, H. (eds) *The SAGE handbook of process organization studies*. London: SAGE, 1–25.

Leach, E. R. (1982) *Social anthropology*. Oxford: Fontana Paperbacks.

Lefebvre, H. (1991) *The production of space*. Oxford: Basil Blackwell.

Mauksch, S. (2017) Managing the dance of enchantment: An ethnography of social entrepreneurship events. *Organization* 24(2): 133–153.

Mauksch, S. (2018) 'It is exactly what it was in me': The performativity of social entrepreneurship. In: Dey, P., and Steyaert, C. (eds) *Critical perspectives on social entrepreneurship*. Cheltenham: Edward Elgar, 137–158.

McInerney, P. B. (2008) Showdown at Kykuit: Field-configuring events as loci for conventionalizing accounts. *Journal of Management Studies* 45(6): 1089–1116.

Meinert, L., and Kapferer, B. (2015) *In the event: Toward an anthropology of generic moments*. New York: Berghahn Books.

Moeran, B. (2011) The book fair as a tournament of values. In: Moeran, B., and Pedersen, J. S. (eds) *Negotiating values in the creative industries*. Cambridge: Cambridge University Press, 119–144.

Moeran, B., and Pedersen, J. S. (2011) *Negotiating values in the creative industries: Fairs, festivals and competitive events*. New York: Cambridge University Press.

Montgomery, K., and Oliver, A. L. (2007) A fresh look at how professions take shape: Dual-directed networking dynamics and social boundaries. *Organization Studies* 28(5): 661–687.

Moore, D. (1995) Raves and the bohemian search for self and community: A contribution to the anthropology of public events. *Anthropological Forum* 7(2): 193–241.

Myers, F. R. (1986) Reflections on a meeting: Structure, language, and the polity in a small-scale society. *American Ethnologist* 13(3): 430–447.

Nicolini, D. (2012) *Practice theory, work, and organization: An introduction*. Oxford: Oxford University Press.

Nyqvist, A., Leivestad, H. H., and Tunestad. H. (2017) Individuals and industries: Large-scale professional gatherings as ethnographic fields. In: Leivestad, H. H., and Nyqvist, A. (eds) *Ethnographies of conferences and trade fairs: Shaping industries, creating professionals*. Basingstoke: Palgrave Macmillan, 1–21.

Oliver, A. L., and Montgomery, K. (2008) Using field-configuring events for sense-making: A cognitive network approach. *Journal of Management Studies* 45(6): 1147–1167.

Orlikowski, W. J., and Scott, S. V. (2008) Sociomateriality: Challenging the separation of technology, work and organization. *The Academy of Management Annals* 2(1): 433–474.

Ortner, S. B. (1984) Theory in anthropology since the sixties. *Comparative Studies in Society and History* 26(1): 126–166.

Ortner, S. B. (2006) *Anthropology and social theory: Culture, power, and the acting subject*. London: Duke University Press.

Pipan, T., and Porsander, L. (2000) Imitating uniqueness: How big cities organize big events. *Organization Studies* 21(1): 1–27.

Richards, A. and Kuper A. (1971) *Councils in action*. Cambridge: Cambridge University Press.

Rosaldo, R. (1993 [1989]) *Culture & truth: The remaking of social analysis: With a new introduction*. Boston: Beacon Press.

Ruebottom, T., and Auster, E. R. (2018) Reflexive dis/embedding: Personal narratives, empowerment and the emotional dynamics of interstitial events. *Organization Studies* 39(4): 467–490.

Sahlins, M. D. (1981) *Historical metaphors and mythical realities: Structure in the early history of the Sandwich Islands Kingdom.* Ann Arbor: University of Michigan Press.

Sahlins, M. D. (1991) The return of the event, again: With reflections on the beginnings of the great Fijian War of 1843 to 1855 between the Kingdoms of Bau and Rewa. In: Biersack, A. (ed) *Clio in Oceania: Towards a historical anthropology.* Washington and London: Smithsonian Institution Press, 37–99.

Said, E. (1978) *Orientalism: Western representations of the orient.* New York: Pantheon.

Schein, E. H. (1996) Culture: The missing concept in organization studies. *Administrative Science Quarterly 41(2), 40th Anniversary Issue:* 229–240.

Schultz, M. (2012) *On studying organizational cultures: Diagnosis and understanding.* Berlin: Walter de Gruyter.

Schüssler, E., Rüling, C. C., and Wittneben, B. B. (2014) On melting summits: The limitations of field-configuring events as catalysts of change in transnational climate policy. *Academy of Management Journal* 57(1): 140–171.

Schüßler, E., Grabher, G., and Müller-Seitz, G. (2015) Field-configuring events: Arenas for innovation and learning? *Industry and Innovation* 22(3): 165–172.

Schüßler, E., and Sydow, J. (2015) Organizing events for configuring and maintaining creative fields. In: Jones, C., Lorenzen, M., and Sapsed, J. (eds) *Oxford handbook of creative industries.* Oxford: Oxford University Press, 284–300.

Schwartzman, H. B. (1989) *The meeting.* New York: Springer.

Simmel, G. (1950) Sociability. An example of pure, or formal, sociology. In: Wolff, K. H. (ed) *The sociology of Georg Simmel.* New York: The Free Press, 40–57.

Thompson, D. (2011) Art fairs: The market as medium. In: Moeran, B., and Pedersen, J. S. (eds) *Negotiating values in the creative industries: Fairs, festivals and competitive events.* Cambridge: Cambridge University Press, 59–72.

Toraldo, M. L., and Islam, G. (2017) Festival and organization studies. *Organization Studies 40(3): 309–322.*

Turner, V. (1966) *The ritual process: Structure and anti-structure.* Cornell: Cornell University Press.

Turner, V. (1979) *Process, performance, and pilgrimage: A study in comparative symbology.* New Delhi: Concept Publishing Company.

Turner, V. (1980) Social dramas and stories about them. *Critical Inquiry* 7(1): 141–168.

Turner, V. (1982) *From ritual to theatre: The human seriousness of play.* New York: PAJ Publications.

Vigh, H. E., and Sausdal, D. B. (2014) From essence back to existence: Anthropology beyond the ontological turn. *Anthropological Theory* 14(1): 49–73.

Vincent, J. (1978) Political anthropology: Manipulative strategies. *Annual Review of Anthropology* 7(1): 175–194.

Wagner-Pacifici, R. (2017) *What is an event?* Chicago: University of Chicago Press.

Weick, K. E. (1979) *The social psychology of organizing.* Columbus: McGraw-Hill Humanities.

Wright, S. (2000) "Culture" in anthropology and organizational studies. In: Wright, S. (ed) *Anthropology of organizations.* New York: Routledge, 1–31.

Zilber, T. D. (2011) Institutional multiplicity in practice: A tale of two high-tech conferences in Israel. *Organization Science* 22(6): 1539–1559.

20

TWEETING THE MARGINALIZED VOICES

A Netnographic Account

Snehanjali Chrispal and Hari Bapuji

"Three workers die in a manhole in Mumbai suburb. How many deaths will it take till India knows that too many people have been murdered in manhole" – @scribeit

#stop killing us – @*Dalit*Activist1

"Universities are nothing but Brahminical forts and getting a work done there is as equal as fighting against caste system. You literally have to brawl to get treated with respect, try hard to make them understand" – @*Dalit*Respect

Twitter is used by around 126 million users daily as a platform for conversation and microblogging, using tweets (Gil, 2019). These tweets, in turn, provide researchers with a cost-efficient way to examine novel questions and contexts that were previously difficult, if not impossible, for researchers to gain access to (Kantanen & Manninen, 2016). For example, one study examined over 60 million tweets from individuals in the 200 most populous metropolitan areas in the United States to study whether people in racially diverse neighbourhoods were more prosocial (Nai, Narayanan, Hernandez, & Savani, 2018). Other studies examined tweets on customer service experiences in the airline industry to optimize service performance (Misopoulos, Mitic, Kapoulas, & Karapiperis, 2014); how marketers use tweets across B2B and B2C and thus, determine factors that influence the message strategies utilized in each context (Swani, Brown, & Milne, 2014); and also how bots masquerading as activists intensify the magnitude of a protest on Twitter (Salge & Karahanna, 2018). For many of these studies, Twitter is a source of large online data that can be captured in real-time as issues emerge and events evolve.

While Twitter and other online platforms provide large data for quantitative analysis, they also offer the possibility to examine and analyse diverse perspectives and behaviours in realistic or naturalistic contexts that may otherwise be difficult to gain access to. As such, scholars have used this opportunity to conduct research into online communities, particularly by adapting netnography, i.e., use of ethnographic methods to understand online communities and cultures (Kozinets, 2002). For example, one study conducted netnography on intercultural wedding message boards within the wedding planning virtual community, to investigate how cross-cultural ambivalence affects brides-to-be as they plan their cross-cultural weddings (Nelson & Otnes, 2005). Another study investigated wine tourism experiences using TripAdvisor online reviews of tourists to Cognac, France (Thanh & Kirova, 2018).

Studying online communities and cultures is a worthy endeavour but considering how social inequalities manifest in the digital space, such ethnographic studies tend to, perhaps unknowingly, focus on the privileged, exotic, and even the forbidden. The voices of the disadvantaged are far fewer online, but they do exist. Reaching the underprivileged and the marginalized communities in the real world may be difficult for researchers, but Twitter and other social media platforms afford researchers a chance to reach out to them and examine novel questions. Given the sensitivities involved in engaging with the underprivileged and marginalized communities, netnographic techniques are particularly useful for researchers to easily and unobtrusively immerse themselves in these online communities.

We engaged in a netnographic exploration of *Dalits* or the untouchables, who are at the bottom of the Indian caste system. Like many marginalized groups, their voices are often subdued and ignored, but they use Twitter to articulate their experiences and express their views. The tweets we headlined at the beginning of this chapter are just a minute representation of the ways that *Dalits* use Twitter as a platform to shed light on the caste system and its pervasiveness in modern India.

In this chapter, we present netnography as a method and illustrate its use with our study of a marginalized group on Twitter. We take the reader on a journey with characters, stories, obstacles, and revelations. We start with a description of the netnography (as a method) and the caste system (as the context in which we conducted our study). We then present details of our study and provide a snapshot of our data analysis – thematic and narrative analysis, to show how *Dalits* underscored the pervasiveness of caste. We conclude with a reflection on our experience and by assessing the advantages and disadvantages of netnography and how to overcome them.

Method and Context – Background

In this section, we proffer a brief discussion on netnographic method and the caste system to set the stage for an exploratory examination of an entrenched institution like the caste system through the eyes of those disadvantaged by it.

Netnography

A "netnography" is where ethnographic techniques are adapted to research cultures and communities that materialize from online communications (Kozinets, 2002). It surfaced in the 1990s when the internet was still in its infancy, where social media and other computer-mediated communication tools were far less prevalent than now. Netnography is an adaptable and responsive approach that enables researchers to examine and analyse cultures in their local contexts and naturally ensuing behaviours (Kozinets, Dolbec, & Earley, 2014).

Culture, as a post-structural concept, is heterogeneous, paradoxical, arbitrary, and unstable rather than a manifestation of stringent conditions of consistency, fixedness, dependability, enduring, evolved and confined (Kozinets, 2010). Although culture is an attribute of a social collective, ontologically the individuals, along with their diversity, incongruity, and inconstancy, need to be given priority over culture and community. Like real communities, online communities cultivate and evidence cultures, traditions, values and institutions that seek to establish, monitor, and navigate the behaviours of individuals within a particular society (Bowler Jr., 2010; Kozinets, 2010). Nevertheless, online culture and community aligns with a more fluid perspective of "consocial identity and interaction"; where consociality is "'what we share', a contextual fellowship, rather than 'who we are', an ascribed identity boundary such as race, religion or gender" (Kozinets, 2010: 11). Hence, to some extent, netnographers need to dissect the connection to a community or adherence to cultural standards as an individual's election rather than a need or obligation. The adoption of these online cultural and community identities by individuals can occur in varying degrees, from brief adoption to occasional and frequent adoptions (Kozinets, 2010).

By the early 2000s through the work of Kozinets (2002) and De Valck, Van Bruggen, and Wierenga (2009), netnography emerged as a new and innovative qualitative research methodology for the study of communities and cultures online, or through computer-mediated communications. With new forms of online developments like blogging, tweeting, social networking, podcasting and so forth, netnographic methodologies were set apart, according to Kozinets, from other ethnographic online research like cyber-ethnography (Ward, 1999), virtual ethnography (Hine, 2000) and connective ethnography (Dirksen, Huizing, & Smit, 2010). These new forms of netnography offered a "more systematic, step-by-step approach to addressing the ethical, procedural, and methodological issues specific to online research" (Costello, McDermott, & Wallace, 2017: 2).

Netnography is a form of ethnography, but unlike ethnographic immersion that often involves participant observation, netnography does not always involve participant observation. This does not mean that researchers conducting netnography are any less immersed in the community; they just have varying and flexible levels of commitment to observing online social interaction (Kozinets, Dolbec, & Earley, 2014). Like an ethnography, the researcher in netnography is the instrument for data collection and creation. Netnography is also descriptive, in that it seeks to provide rich and vivid descriptions of the lived experience of the online community and culture. As in ethnography, the netnographic researcher adopts the role of a bricoleur, espousing various multimodal techniques to access the fertile cultural experience that individuals share and engage within the online community (Kozinets, 2007).

Four characteristics distinguish online interactions from face-to-face interactions. First, is the adaptation process, whereby participants need to familiarize themselves with the codes, behavioural norms, and technological media online so that they can engage in dialogue and conversations within these online communities (Kozinets, 2010; Serafinelli, 2018). Second, is anonymity, where online community members can conceal their real identities through the use of pseudonyms to freely articulate their perspectives, feelings, creativity and identity (Kozinets, 2010). Third, online interactions are more accessible as the lines between social worlds get blurred online, allowing access and openness to diverse virtual voices and cultures (Kozinets, Dolbec, & Earley, 2014; Serafinelli, 2018). Lastly, archiving is possible due to the opportunities the online platforms provide to revisit archived data. This data is also ephemeral and can be analysed in "real time" or taken down at any moment by the user or platform owners (Kozinets, 2010; Logan, 2015).

While the online arena provides a rich setting for research, the debate around ethical processes to be followed in conducting netnographic research is everincreasing. These debates revolve around participant consent, participant anonymity, and research transparency.

Participant Consent

Some scholars suggest that researchers need to get prior consent from online community members (Kozinets, 2012). Others assert that informed consent may be required for private and restricted online communities but is not needed for public online data or in large communities where the member might not have a reasonable expectation of privacy (Langer & Beckman, 2005; Sugiura, Wiles, & Pope, 2017).

Participant Anonymity

Another ethical dilemma that arises when conducting netnographic studies relates to participant anonymity. Ensuring full anonymity may be impossible due to online search facilities, but the identity of the participants is often protected by omitting all identifying data and removing names before publication. Use of verbatim quotes raises another challenge to anonymity. Some researchers believe that verbatim quotes may directly identify a participant; however, others suggest that these quotes can be used, even without consent from public online sites. However, participants often use pseudonymous identities online, and so researchers need to treat these identities as legal identities. Hence, researchers may use further pseudonyms to protect participants in the study, thus ensuring the safety of the individual (Kozinets, 2014).

Research Transparency

Disclosing a researcher's presence might hinder the benefits of unobtrusiveness and dilute the advantages of netnography. The issue of consent, however, is far from settled and continues to evolve, thus making it necessary for researchers to be mindful of the nuances of privacy in online interactions and respect it.

Our experience suggests that the issues of participant consent and anonymity are too complex to arrive at a single solution; researchers should make a decision based on the context and the sensitivities involved. In our case, we did not seek consent because we followed public accounts that did not need prior approval from the account to follow. We were also comfortable doing so because many of these tweeters were driven to influence the broader discourse on caste, which can also be served by their inclusion in our study. We decided to give verbatim quotes to maintain the authenticity of the experiences, feelings, and thoughts of the participants; although some commonalities exist in the experiences of *Dalits* (e.g., discrimination), these experiences manifest differently from context to context, and person to person. However, to maintain anonymity, we do not give the Twitter handle name unless the handle name is already anonymous or belongs to a collective.

In sum, netnographic methodologies have emerged as an important tool to conduct research online. The ethics of conducting research online are evolving but the issues of consent and anonymity pose a greater challenge relative to traditional research methods. As such, researchers adopting these techniques need to be sensitive to these developments so that the protocols of ethics are maintained.

The Caste System

The caste system is endemic to social stratification in the Indian subcontinent. It divides individuals into four hierarchal divisions known as "*Varnas*". At the top of this order are the *Brahmins*, followed by the *Kshatriyas*, then the *Vaishyas*, and the *Shudras*. Our study is focused on *Dalits*, the "broken" people, or untouchables, who were not part of this *Four-Varna* system, but are considered to be outcastes who are at the bottom of the hierarchy (Deshpande, 2010). The elemental doctrine of this social order is to constrain the structure, so as to safeguard the women, land, and ritual essence within it (Yalman, 1963).

The effects of the caste system on the social lives of people who are within it are tremendous. Caste restricts and prohibits upward mobility; an individual's position in the caste hierarchy is determined by birth (through a patriarchal lineage) and cannot be altered by an individual's actions in their lifetime. Caste governs social interaction between castes through endogamous marriages, segregated housing in villages and towns, and prescription of rules for interaction between higher and lower castes. As a result, those in the *Four-Varna* system lived in the villages within their own blocks, but the *Dalits* lived outside of the villages, mostly on the wastelands, without access to village resources, such as community wells (see Bapuji & Chrispal, 2018 for details).

In addition to influencing the social lives of individuals, the caste system affected their economic lives by determining their occupations, with *Brahmins* occupying knowledge-based roles, such as priests, scholars, or advisors. *Kshatriyas* were kings, administrators, and landowners, while *Vaishyas* were traders and merchants, and the *Shudras* were given occupations that involved skill, like masonry, pottery, blacksmithing and so forth. *Dalits* were restricted to occupations involving sanitation and cleaning: sweeping streets, cremating the dead, and cleaning sewers, human waste and toilets. Because of the restrictions and the confinement of the caste-based assignment of occupations, the upper 30% (consisting of *Brahmins*, *Kshatriyas*, *Vyshyas*, and some dominant *Shudra* castes) had control over resources, and thus, control over economic activities. In contrast, the remaining 70% of the population were forced toward the "lower caste" occupations, like farming, fishing, hunting, etc. (Bapuji & Chrispal, 2018).

The constraints put on lower castes often prevents them from attaining resources like land and capital, as well as knowledge and status. For instance, lower castes, particularly *Dalits*, own very little land, despite land reforms that attempted to spread land ownership (Tagade, Naik, & Thorat, 2018). The caste system has also restricted access to education and healthcare, as well as to judicial and legislative institutions. Similarly, despite affirmative actions that aimed to increase representation of the disadvantaged in education, public service, and politics, the representation of *Dalits* is abysmally low, particularly in middle and upper levels of the government (Aggarwal, Drèze, & Gupta, 2015). The private sector actively resisted the implementation of caste-based affirmative action, and thus likely has an even lower representation of the lower castes. For example, despite India's modernization, poor individuals within the caste system are constrained to adopt occupations of their forefathers, i.e., caste-based occupations. The first tweet at the beginning of this chapter relates to the deaths of sanitation workers, typically *Dalits*, cleaning sewers. These deaths of the breadwinners of the family in a patriarchal society often create risks for the livelihood of the family.

Over the years, *Dalits* have attempted to bring their plight to the notice of the rest of the society. They took to literature and poetry to express their emotions, feelings, and views. Broadly, *Dalit* literature often reproduces the disheartening, lived experience of their oppression (Rani, 1998). With growing digitalization and the emergence of social media platforms like Twitter, *Dalits* and other marginalized communities have found a way to express their opinions and draw attention to the oppression they face under the caste system. It afforded them a tool to speak up against certain issues by breaking traditional barriers and participating in the public sphere. This also helps them increase their social networks, unlike the rest of the marginalized who are unable to access the digital world and use social media.

In sum, the caste system influences the social and economic lives of individuals under it and those who come in contact with it. It disadvantages the lower castes, particularly *Dalits*, whose voices are subdued, but the online world opened up an avenue for them to express their views and engage in the public discourse. Our research used netnography to study this engagement and this chapter is an attempt to bring to light the usefulness of the netnographic methodology to study difficult issues, marginalized communities, and vulnerable populations.

Netnography in Action – Example

In this section, we present details of the method and analysis to help understand how to employ netnography.

Through the Looking Glass: The Data Collection Process

We collected and analysed the data by adapting the methodological techniques of previous netnographic accounts (Kozinets, Dolbec, & Earley, 2014). First, an ideal netnography starts with an "ethnographic siting", which means starting narrow and broadening the site (Kozinets, Dolbec, & Earley, 2014: 269). This means focusing on a few posts (tweets), or a restricted data set to first establish a familiarity with the culture and get a sense of "what is transpiring". In turn, the analysis can either expand or deepen. Second, researchers should use the initial set of posts to develop an understanding of "ethnographic communicating" or communication that is practised, managed, and comprehended the way that community members experience them (Kozinets, Dolbec, & Earley, 2014: 269). The communication needs to be analysed and processed in their naturalized way, in "real-text" by the researcher; software should only be used to aid in the process of deciphering meaning. Finally, we decided to not use archival data for the analysis but used "ethnographic timing" (Kozinets, Dolbec, & Earley, 2014: 270). This means that the tweets were experienced and interpreted, and analysed in "real-time", as they appeared on the site, rather than accumulating all the data and then analysing it. As in ethnographic research, the culture is exemplified and interpreted in netnography through the collection of different types of data – textual data, photos, videos, articles, interview transcripts, and screenshots.

We conducted our data collection over a span of three months, during which we collected and studied over 6,200 tweets, as part of a larger project to study socio-economic inequalities. The process of collecting the data for analysis was intensive and we needed to strike a balance between "how much was too much" and "how much was too little". We started the sampling by identifying a few prominent *Dalit* tweeters and following them. This allowed us to find our bearings while exploring this new research site. Additionally, it helped us learn the norms of engagement, language, topics of interest, and so forth, before we completely immersed ourselves in this setting. However, as we learned later, doing this did not completely prepare us to observe and analyse the complete gamut of tweeters – at times it was like wading through dark waters, where learning occurred as we encountered new trajectories. By following them and their interactions with others, we identified additional tweeters. We also conducted a search on Twitter for usernames that contained the word *Dalit*, and followed them. In all, we followed 35 *Dalit* tweeters. Among these, some were anonymous or used pseudonyms to protect their identity. On the other hand, others provided sufficient personal information in their bios and tweets to get a sense of their background. This helped us create a diverse sample that included those who were anonymous, or we knew little to nothing about, to those who were different genders, employment backgrounds, age groups, and even the countries and cities they lived in.

Along with netnography, we used a thematic analysis to decipher overlying patterns, themes and metaphors that encompass the ideas represented in the tweets and observations. These themes were refined appropriately to maintain consistency and intuitive interpretation (Fereday & Muir-Cochrane, 2006).

Looking In – The Observations

We noted several broader observations during our study. First, *Dalit* tweeters tended to post tweets about the caste system, its various manifestations in social and economic life, effects of the caste system, denial of the caste system by the upper castes, and the marginalization of lower castes in general. Second, they tweeted about the occupational discrimination faced by *Dalits* and their restriction to sanitation jobs, and posted numerous news articles about the deaths of *Dalits* due to unhealthy practices forced on them. Third, *Dalit* tweeters provided solidarity and support for each other on Twitter. Fourth, they traversed between traditional writing (i.e., media articles they authored) and the language of the social media, as well as between writing in their native language and English. Fifth, a few *Dalit* tweeters delve into the history of the caste system and its religious foundations. Finally, compared to men, women were more active and vocal on Twitter, raising many issues and offering their viewpoints on issues surrounding the intersections between gender and caste. The *Dalit* women are seen to be doubly oppressed because of caste and gender, by the upper caste men and women, and then by their "own" men.

In the backdrop of above general observations, we now present one specific example to present the method of analysis. This example pertains to the engagement of *Dalit* women with a campaign of Lean In India, which is part of the Lean In movement that sprang out of the hugely popular book authored by Sheryl Sanderg, the COO of Facebook. With the mission to "help women achieve their ambitions and work to create an equal world", the Lean In movement now has over 43,000 Lean In circles in 170 countries (Lean In, 2019). The circles are groups of women helping each other develop skills and get ahead in their lives and careers. The Lean In movement aims to influence public policy and affect institutional change through a number of initiatives. It should also be noted that the Lean In movement has been criticized for making women responsible for their advancement rather than highlight and address the structural barriers that women face in their advancement (Kim, Fitzsimons, & Kay, 2018).

Lean In India is an official chapter of the Lean In organization. The India chapter has over 3,000 members and runs 86 circles around the country (Lean In India, 2019). On December 7, 2018, Lean In India launched "Lean In Women of Color India" and asked brown women to share the discrimination they faced because of their skin colour. Under the tagline of "Women of Color India" they presented messages that said, "Celebrate every shade of beautiful" and "For over centuries, brown skinned women in India are frowned upon and discriminated against, in all the spheres of life. It's time we break those stereotypes and bring back your confidence, because, #darkisbeautiful."

The tweets by Lean In India triggered a frenzy of chatter. Many *Dalits* responded to the tweet with criticism and accused the tweeter of importing Western frames of discrimination into the Indian context and not paying attention to caste, which is a primary cause of discrimination in India. Although some dark-skinned people can be found among the upper castes, a vast majority of them tend to be light-skinned. Likewise, light-skinned individuals can be found among lower castes, including *Dalits* but the majority of them tend to be dark-skinned. Also, people from the northern parts of India tend to be light-skinned compared to those from the southern parts of the country.

One *Dalit* handle asked who people of colour in India would be and pointed out that "colour" is actually used to refer to those who are light-skinned in Tamil. Another comment was made alluding to how some concepts are imported without knowing the market. However, in response to that comment another handle asserted that Lean In India knew its market well and that they were selling victimhood to upper caste women, who tend to be light-skinned. Some suggested that even light-skinned women of the lower caste face discrimination because of the caste system. Furthermore, many associated with lower castes were often associated with dark skin, but the oppression against them was based on caste more than their skin colour. In response to these tweets, Lean In India blocked some tweeters. It resulted in further chatter about the organization not being open to criticism and discourse on problems faced by women in India due to caste, but was trying to impose an alien "women of color" campaign in India. This resulted in Lean In India unblocking those it previously blocked.

Detangling the Knots – The Analytical Process

The incident involving Lean In India and its "Women of Color" campaign is just one example of how *Dalits* use Twitter to draw attention to caste and voice their opinions about various issues and situations. To better understand this example, we analysed the tweets to identify the themes and also to develop a narrative.

Thematic Analysis

We conducted a thematic analysis of the netnography to establish significant themes that emerged from the online interactions of the *Dalits*. The thematic analysis process requires the identification of themes through the repetitive review of data (Rice & Ezzy, 1999), and a recognition of patterns that accentuate these themes (Fereday & Muir-Cochrane, 2006). In this study, we particularly focused on events or situations that the *Dalits* tweeted substantially about. These events are associated with the oppression and problems *Dalits* face within the caste system. We individually followed the tweeters, maintained fieldnotes and identified examples that reveal the lived experience of the marginalized group. For example, we observed the "women of color" post and the responses that the *Dalits* had given. In one instance, a *Dalit* wrote "I am confused. Who are the 'Women of Color' in India?" criticizing the ignorance of those who try to implant Western campaigns into the Indian context.

We accumulated and linked various tweets and their messages into three emerging themes (see Table 20.1 for an illustration): *misframing* (pointing out the transplanting of Western framing to Indian contexts and the issues that stem from it); *nuancing* (highlighting the nuances of colour and caste in India); and *confronting* (questioning the blocking of *Dalits* who voiced opposition).

The themes we presented in Table 20.1 are an example of the coding scheme, but these themes will undergo revisions as analysis continues and gets refined as part of our broader project. However, reflecting on the above themes helps to develop a narrative.

Narrative

A narrator knits "the nexus of power relations, the historical and cultural conditions and the practices under scrutiny" while continuously forming novel surmises and connections among these points (Gergen, 2009; Tamboukou, 2013: 112).

Table 20.1 Thematic analysis of tweets on Lean in India campaign.

Tweets or Observations	Themes
"Now why are these @LeanInIndia peeps lazily importing such stuff into our context?"	Misframing
"Gender is a sensitive and nuanced issue. Western solutions and campaigns can't blindly be applied in India"	
"… but at my place, those that are lighter-skinned are typically referred to as 'colouru' … they are very light-skinned"	Nuancing
"Good example of importing without knowing the market"	
"They know their market perfectly. They're selling victimization to UC's" (Note: UC's refers to upper castes)	
"Too bad that you have blocked someone 'coz you didn't like their reply to the survey. Sometimes you gotta chill"	Confronting
Many of the *Dalit* tweeters retweeted the messages sent by @ LeanInIndia saying they were blocked by the user	

We needed to create an amalgam, accommodating aspects of a multimodal approach and Gergen's (2009) narrative conventions, to delineate the story. To uncover narratives within the tweets, we subscribe to Riessman (2005) narrative analysis in which the first step is the thematic analysis through the content of the text. Deciphering "what" is said is crucial to delineating typologies of narratives organized by theme. Second, a structural analysis will assay the "way" a story is being told (Riessman, 2005). Within the structure of the narrative, there exists the "abstract" or the summary of the story; the "orientation" which includes the time, setting, characters and context; "complicating action" or the sequence of events that contains a crisis or catharsis; the "evaluation" where the narrator adopts the role of the observer to reflect on the meaning and to understand the emotion; the "resolution" or the consequence of the story; and "coda" which is the culmination of the plot (Riessman, 2005). These elements of the structure do not necessarily all have to be part of a given narrative.

Narratives are also co-constructed in that the reader and the story-teller together construct meaning in an interactional analysis. As researchers, we position ourselves as outsiders, but extract meaning from the tweets as they exemplify the *Dalit* struggle and the voices subdued by the dominant beliefs and structures. The narratives that form from the tweets can find similitude and breed collectivity. These collective stories are persuasive and become agentic to the way that the marginalized use the online platform for their agenda.

In the following, a narrative is woven through the "women of color" tweet and the dialogue it spurred. The abstract of narrative is that there were conflicting viewpoints between different characters around a particular social issue. The narrative is situated in a context where a marginalized group already faces discrimination based on their caste and use Twitter to draw attention to this problem. In addition, this group also faces colour discrimination as their caste is associated with a darker skin colour. The characters involved include the *Dalits*, the Twitter handle that started the "women of color" campaign, and other Twitter users who commented on the tweet. The tweeting of the "women of color" tweets act as the complicating action in this narrative. They elicit various reactions from the other characters. *Dalits* see this as a way for upper caste women to feel victimized through the discrimination of their brown skin in the US and outside India broadly, whereas in the context of India those facing discrimination are the dark-skinned *Dalits* and lower caste women. Further, they feel the "women of color" campaign just transplants Western frames of discrimination into an Indian context, reflecting that upper caste women are more in touch with their counterparts in the West rather than the fellow women in their own country. Lean In India blocking the tweeters served as yet another complicating action, while the culmination of the narrative is the unblocking of those who were earlier blocked.

In sum, netnography involves the researcher embedding in an online community to collect various types of data and understand the discourse as it evolves by maintaining a reflective journal, which includes observations and screenshots. The journal forms the main source of data for analysing the themes and developing narratives, using traditional techniques for qualitative analysis.

Experience of Netnography – Reflections

An important part of netnography, as in ethnography, is the positionality of the researcher, which must be considered for its impact on the analysis. Further, while leveraging the advantages of netnography, it is also necessary to address its disadvantages. We discuss each in this section and present some concluding thoughts.

Where Do I Stand? – Researcher Positionality

Both researchers are of Indian descent and have spent considerable time in India. The caste system affects everyone in the hierarchy, oppressing many and privileging a few. No matter the experience and awareness, it is fair to say that caste affects everyone under it and/or who comes in close contact with it. As such, our exposure to and experiences with the caste system are varied. Given our own cultural background and experiences, but being exposed to the Western world for a long period and being away from the Indian subcontinent, we come to the research setting somewhat as outsiders. Nevertheless, we approach this study with the intention of gaining insights into the way *Dalits* use Twitter to bring light to caste issues and voice their opinions. So, we come from a place of openness and credulity, yet privileging the voices of the *Dalits*, "the broken" people.

The data collection process was a profound, yet an emotional one. As researchers, we spent significant time looking at tweets and making note of our observations; however, at times we were so engrossed in the tweets for hours at a time that we felt a need to disconnect. So, we forced ourselves to stop and step away from the research setting. Being able to dictate a time to stop is critical in netnographic research because it is taxing and stressful. Yet, this disconnecting is nearly impossible to achieve given the extent to which our social lives are intertwined with the virtual world, particularly with the social media.

Being reflexive is an integral part of netnographic research. Reflexive research

> turns back upon and takes account of itself, to explore the situated nature of knowledge; the institutional, social and political processes whereby research is conducted, and knowledge is produced; the dubious position of the researcher, and the constructive effects of language.
>
> *(Alvesson, Hardy, & Harley, 2008: 480)*

It was difficult to be reflexive and not let preconceived notions cloud our judgment during the data collection and analysis phases. This is because we had to remain impartial towards the actors within the netnography and look at the data objectively. For instance, there was post by a *Dalit* tweeter about the differences of opinion of upper caste women and *Dalit* women. In response to this tweet, another Twitter handle used obscene language and attempted character assassination of the *Dalit* tweeter. It was hard to remain reflexive in this moment and our anger inhibited our observations – thinking how individuals can use abusive, demeaning and hurtful language on a public platform. This is where reflexivity is pivotal to the process, where the researcher is a significant instrument through which the story is told, rather than separating his/her own contexts and frameworks from the artefacts of study (Finlay, 2002). Memoing or journaling helped us in remaining reflexive, as we could document our own reflections, experiences, and tensions. In addition, to maintain reflexivity, we often shared our insights and interpretations of the data with each other and discussed the cogency of the observations. This is essential for obtaining "critical distance" in order to manoeuvre between data and theory (Alvesson, Hardy, & Harley, 2008; Cunliffe, 2010; De Rond & Lok, 2016).

Netnography – A Balancing Act

There are numerous methodological advantages of conducting a netnography. First, netnography is an unobtrusive method, which implies that the researcher's observation of the interactions and communication between participants within the community is non-manipulative (Pollok, Lüttgens, & Piller, 2014). Netnography avoids the constraints of quantitative survey research that is solely based on the memory of the participant, and therefore, broadens the credibility of the data (Gupta, 2009). Second, netnography can be considered "voyeuristic" because situations and interactions that are atypical, and even stigmatic can be observed (Kozinets, 2015). Netnography is particularly relevant when researching personally or politically sensitive topics where anonymity may be necessary for a free expression of views, and participants can conceal their identities (Costello, McDermott, & Wallace, 2017). Netnography is also beneficial in studies of the marginalized and vulnerable groups who want to maintain anonymity. Furthermore, netnography still finds roots in ethnographic research where the researcher is expected to be fully immersed in the setting to provide a "thick description" (Kozinets, 2010). Netnography realizes that online communities have cultures that are co-created by members who are dedicated to their development. Therefore, the revelations and descriptions of these communities and the theory that is postulated from it are contingent on these members (Costello, Witney, Green, & Bradshaw, 2012).

During the process of collecting data, we also noted some disadvantages of netnographic research. First, dialogic conversation is often not possible within netnographic research, especially when trying to be unobtrusive; occasionally, there were instances where a participant writes something, and we wanted to delve deeper into the thought behind it or extrapolate the experience but were unable to do so. In addition, netnographic research can leave room for misinterpretation of what is said by members in the online community. The researcher is the instrument through which the data is processed and interpreted. Researchers have to often navigate a delicate balance between the participants' viewpoints and the researcher bias. This is where reflexivity is critical to analysing data and maintaining objectivity.

In order to overcome the disadvantages of a netnography – lack of dialogic conversation and misinterpretation – we conducted interviews with selected members of the *Dalit* tweeting community. An interview is a passage to revealing that which is blind to us, but is observed by others (Stake, 1995). Interviews give us access to recognizing different realities where the "interviewer is the repository". Interviews are enmeshed within a dialogic conversation, of "mutuality and egalitarianism" (Kvale, 2006: 481) that ties individuals to a broader moralistic context, converting information to a "shared experience" (Denzin, 2001: 24). Kvale (2006: 481) asserts that interviews "attempt to understand the world from the subjects' points of view and to unfold the meaning of their lived world. The interviews give voice to common people, allowing them to freely present their life situations in their own words." These interviews supplement the netnographic research, either reinforcing observations and analysis, or contradicting researcher interpretations. This is a dialogical approach to data collection and analysis so that the voices and stories of the participants are respected and are not unintentionally misrepresented.

Discussion

This netnographic journey, unveiling the experiences of *Dalits* on Twitter, has not only provided insights into the voices and issues that are brought to the forefront, but also the methodology used to capture them. Management research has sparsely utilized netnographic methods, particularly to study the way online platforms are used by marginalized communities.

Through this study, we seek to make two contributions. First, we try to add to the literature showing how the use of netnography can help researchers to access and study communities and individuals that may not always be possible through other forms of research. Second, we seek to draw attention to the caste system as a system of inequality and how those marginalized and oppressed by it raise awareness about it to shape a more equal world.

In conclusion, online communities are a versatile and rich setting for conducting research on diverse topics because digitization is dissolving the traditional geographic and socioeconomic boundaries. Specifically, online platforms allow for those groups who are marginalized by the elites to engage in discussions and point out important issues that are otherwise hidden. Voices of the marginalized that are often repressed and muted in the real world can be projected and amplified online, thus providing a great opportunity for researchers to study the grand challenges of inequality facing organizations and societies. We hope that this chapter serves as an inspiration to scholars to conduct netnography as well as study pervasive inequalities.

References

Aggarwal, A., Drèze, J., & Gupta, A. (2015). Caste and the power elite in Allahabad. *Economic and Political Weekly*, *50*(6), 45–51.

Alvesson, M., Hardy, C., & Harley, B. (2008). Reflecting on reflexivity: Reflexive textual practices in organization and management theory. *Journal of Management Studies*, *45*(3), 480–501.

Bapuji, H., & Chrispal, S. (2018). Understanding economic inequality through the lens of caste. *Journal of Business Ethics, 162*(3), 1–19.

Bowler Jr, G. M. (2010). Netnography: A method specifically designed to study cultures and communities online. *The Qualitative Report, 15*(5), 1270.

Chakravarti, U. (1993). Conceptualising Brahmanical patriarchy in early India: Gender, caste, class and state. *Economic and Political Weekly, 28*(14), 579–585.

Costello, L., McDermott, M. L., & Wallace, R. (2017). Netnography: Range of practices, misperceptions, and missed opportunities. *International Journal of Qualitative Methods, 16*(1), 1–16.

Costello, L., Witney, C., Green, L., & Bradshaw, V. (2012). Self-revelation in an online health community: Exploring issues around co-presence for vulnerable members. ANZCA Conference 2012, Melbourne, Australia.

Cunliffe, A.L. (2010). Retelling tales of the field: In search of organizational ethnography 20 years on. *Organizational Research Methods, 13*(2), 224–239. DOI: 10.1177/1094428109340041.

De Rond, M., & Lok, J. (2016). Some things can never be unseen: The role of context in psychological injury at war. *Academy of Management Journal, 59*(6), 1965–1993.

De Valck, K., Van Bruggen, G. H., & Wierenga, B. (2009). Virtual communities: A marketing perspective. *Decision Support Systems, 47*(3), 185–203.

Denzin, N. K. (2001). The reflexive interview and a performative social science. *Qualitative Research, 1*(1), 23–46.

Deshpande, M. S. (2010). History of the Indian caste system and its impact on India today. San Luis Obispo: Senior Project Social Sciences Department, College of Liberal Arts, California Polytechnic State University.

Dirksen, V., Huizing, A., & Smit, B. (2010). "Piling on layers of understanding": The use of connective ethnography for the study of (online) work practices. *New Media & Society, 12*(7), 1045–1063.

Fereday, J., & Muir-Cochrane, E. (2006). Demonstrating rigor using thematic analysis: A hybrid approach of inductive and deductive coding and theme development. *International Journal of Qualitative Methods, 5*(1), 80–92.

Finlay, L. (2002). Negotiating the swamp: The opportunity and challenge of reflexivity in research practice. *Qualitative Research, 2*(2), 209–230.

Gergen, K. J. (2009). *Relational being: Beyond self and community.* Oxford University Press.

Gil, P. (2019). What is Twitter & how does it work? Retrieved from www.lifewire.com/what-exactly-is-twitter-2483331

Gupta, S. (2009). How do consumers judge celebrities' irresponsible behavior? An attribution theory perspective. *Journal of Applied Business and Economics, 10*(3), 1.

Hine, C. (2000). *Virtual ethnography.* Sage.

Kantanen, H., & Manninen, J. (2016). Hazy boundaries: Virtual communities and research ethics. *Media and Communication, 4*(4), 86–96.

Kim, J. Y., Fitzsimons, G. M., & Kay, A. C. (2018). Lean In messages increase attributions of women's responsibility for gender inequality. *Journal of Personality and Social Psychology, 115*(6), 974.

Kozinets, R.V. (2002). The field behind the screen: Using netnography for marketing research in online communities. *Journal of Marketing Research, 39*(1), 61–72.

Kozinets, R.V. (2007). Netnography 2.0. In Belk, R. W. (Ed.), *Handbook of qualitative research methods in marketing.* Edward Elgar Publishing, 129–142.

Kozinets, R.V. (2010). *Netnography: Doing ethnographic research online.* Sage.

Kozinets, R.V. (2012). Marketing netnography: Prom/ot (ulgat) ing a new research method. *Methodological Innovations Online, 7*(1), 37–45.

Kozinets, R.V. (2014). Social brand engagement: A new idea. *GfK Marketing Intelligence Review, 6*(2), 8–15.

Kozinets, R.V. (2015). *Netnography Redefined.* London: Sage.

Kozinets, R. V., Dolbec, P. Y., & Earley, A. (2014). Netnographic analysis: Understanding culture through social media data. In Flick, Uwe. (Ed.), *The SAGE Handbook of Qualitative Data Analysis*. London: Sage, 262–276.

Kvale, S. (2006). Dominance through interviews and dialogues. *Qualitative Inquiry, 12*(3), 480–500.

Langer, R., & Beckman, S. C. (2005). Sensitive research topics: Netnography revisited. *Qualitative Market Research: An International Journal, 8*(2), 189–203.

Lean In. (2019, February 11). Retrieved from https://leanin.org/

Lean In India – A Lean In Network. (2019, February 11). Retrieved from https://leanin.org/circles-network/lean-in-india

Logan, A. (2015). Netnography: Observing and interacting with celebrity in the digital world. *Celebrity Studies, 6*(3), 378–381.

Misopoulos, F., Mitic, M., Kapoulas, A., & Karapiperis, C. (2014). Uncovering customer service experiences with Twitter: The case of airline industry. *Management Decision, 52*(4), 705–723.

Nai, J., Narayanan, J., Hernandez, I., & Savani, K. (2018). People in more racially diverse neighborhoods are more prosocial. *Journal of Personality and Social Psychology, 114*(4), 497.

Nelson, M. R., & Otnes, C. C. (2005). Exploring cross-cultural ambivalence: A netnography of intercultural wedding message boards. *Journal of Business Research, 58*(1), 89–95.

Pollok, P., Lüttgens, D., & Piller, F. T. (2014). Leading edge users and latent consumer needs in electromobility: Findings from a netnographic study of user innovation in high-tech online communities. *RWTH-TIM Working Paper, February*.

Rani, C. S. (1998). *Dalit* Women's writing in Telugu. *Economic and Political Weekly, WS21–WS24, 33*(17).

Rice, P. L., & Ezzy, D. (1999). Qualitative research methods: A health focus (vol. 720). *Victoria, Australia: Oxford University Press.*

Riessman, C. K. (2005). Exporting ethics: A narrative about narrative research in South India. *Health, 9*(4), 473–490.

Salge, C. A. D. L., & Karahanna, E. (2018). Protesting corruption on Twitter: Is it a bot or is it a person? *Academy of Management Discoveries, 4*(1), 32–49.

Serafinelli, E. (2018). *Digital life on Instagram: New social communication of photography.* Emerald Publishing Limited.

Stake, R. E. (1995). *The art of case study research.* Sage.

Sugiura, L., Wiles, R., & Pope, C. (2017). Ethical challenges in online research: Public/private perceptions. *Research Ethics, 13*(3–4), 184–199.

Swani, K., Brown, B. P., & Milne, G. R. (2014). Should tweets differ for B2B and B2C? An analysis of Fortune 500 companies' Twitter communications. *Industrial Marketing Management, 43*(5), 873–881.

Tagade, N., Naik, A. K., & Thorat, S. (2018). Wealth ownership and inequality in India: A socio-religious analysis. *Journal of Social Inclusion Studies, 4*(2), 196–213.

Tamboukou, M. (2013). A Foucauldian approach to narratives. In Andrews, M., Squire, C. & Tamboukou, M. (Eds.), *Doing Narrative Research*, 2nd ed., London: Sage, 88–107.

Thanh, T. V., & Kirova, V. (2018). Wine tourism experience: A netnography study. *Journal of Business Research, 83*, 30–37.

Ward, K. J. (1999). Cyber-ethnography and the emergence of the virtually new community. *Journal of Information Technology, 14*(1), 95–105.

Yalman, N. (1963). On the purity of women in the castes of Ceylon and Malabar. *Journal of the Royal Anthropological Institute of Great Britain and Ireland, 93*(1), 25–58.

21

WHAT ARE WE MISSING?

Exploring Ethnographic Possibilities beyond MOS Conventions

Patrizia Zanoni and Tammar B. Zilber

In this chapter, we draw on four ethnographic monographs published in other social sciences over the last two decades to showcase ways of crafting ethnography that are fundamentally different from ethnographies published in management and organization studies (MOS) journals. Our analysis:

- unveils the multifarious possibilities for crafting powerful ethnographic texts, raising awareness about how MOS conventions impoverish ethnographies in our discipline;
- specifically illustrates and discusses: 1) ways of relating ethnographic research to 'Big Questions' in social theory; 2) alternative understanding of the research field; 3) enacting post-positivistic understandings of social science in terms of truth claims and reflexivity; 4) ways of embodying and materializing ethnographic research; 5) various possibilities to reconnect micro- and macro-dynamics of power;
- calls for loosening current conventions in MOS and drawing from other disciplines to enact and craft ethnographies that redress the relation between scientific theory and ethnographic case as a powerful entry into social realities;
- identifies aspects PhD students and early scholars might consider to deal with the current conventions of crafting ethnography in MOS.

Our conversation about ethnography started a decade and a half ago, at the Standing Conference on Organizational Symbolism (SCOS) that took place in Budapest, Hungary, in 2002. At the time Patrizia was in the first half of her PhD, still being socialized into MOS and trying to figure out what her research would end up focusing on. Tammar was fresh out of her PhD, recently appointed lecturer in a Business School, also looking for a direction for her research. We started to talk on a boat trip on the Danube, and realized we had a common passion: ethnography. Patrizia had studied international sciences, social and cultural anthropology, had lived in North Africa and worked in development co-operation before starting her PhD on diversity. Tammar traveled intellectual domains, moving from social psychology to anthropology, falling in love – like Patrizia – with ethnography as a research method and a way to navigate the world. Tammar's first paper based on her PhD thesis, an ethnographic study of an Israeli rape crisis center, had just been published (Zilber, 2002). While Tammar was elated it had been published in the *Academy of Management Journal*, she was still somewhat perplexed at the review process and the changes she was asked to do in order to fit the story into a legitimate and acceptable format. Tammar was lamenting all those parts of the story she had had to leave outside, and in our talks we were debating the fine line between staying faithful to the research approach and our identities as ethnographers, and the compromise that needed to be made in order to share our ideas with our research community.

SCOS was the right type of academic context to share our dismay at the impoverished way ethnography had been used in MOS. In particular, we both felt that management journals straightjacket ethnography into a method to produce and present massive amounts of data, and semi-positivistic causal arguments largely miss out on its potential to tell compelling stories that capture the nuances and idiosyncrasies of the social world, at work and in organizations, and the people inhabiting it. As is often the case in the liminal space of conferences, we embarked on an ambitious project that would last until the present day: a systematic review of ethnographic studies published in leading MOS journals since the early days of the discipline.[1]

This comprehensive analysis confirmed and qualified our initial hunch. We found that, since its origins in the 1950s, ethnographic studies remain numerically negligible in our discipline. For instance, only 4% of the articles published in the *Academy of Management Journal* were based on ethnographic methods, 9% of the articles in *Administrative Science Quarterly*, and about 11% of the empirical articles in the *Journal of Management Studies*. What is perhaps even worse, and relevant to our argument, is that the ethnographic articles that were published largely and increasingly mimic non-ethnographic ones in terms of quantity of data, the preference for seemingly 'universal' generalizations over context-sensitive findings, and 'objective', detached representations of social reality. In *ASQ*, for example, we found a clear temporal trend away from rich ethnographic narratives. With the years, ethnographic papers have become heavier on methodological details, as if replication is desirable or even possible. Methodological sections also celebrate quantities of data, presented with the help of 'data structure' and 'supporting data' tables that seemingly offer analytical bits rather than context-sensitive interpretations.

In other words, ethnography has been incorporated into MOS scholarship at the cost of harsh 'domestication', to use an anthropological trope. Overall, leading MOS journals appear to have skipped the crisis of representation that has traversed the social sciences since the 1980s altogether, publishing ethnographic papers that perform themselves as positivistic and promote naturalistic understandings of organizations and organizing. What is worse, even (European-based) journals that have historically been somewhat more hospitable to multiple forms of research, including research not relying on a positivistic epistemology and transgressing MOS writing conventions, seem to increasingly abide by them. This suggests that the domestication of ethnography in our discipline is highly unlikely to be reversed any time soon.

We would like to use the forum created through this edited volume to lay out a vision, inspired by four powerful ethnographies published since the turn of the century, pushing our imagination on how ethnography – as an epistemology, a method and a genre (Clifford and Marcus, 1986; Marcus and Fischer, 1986; Van Maanen, 2011) – could be practiced and told differently in MOS (see Rouleau, de Rond and Musca, 2014). We do this by discussing how four books in anthropology, empirical philosophy, feminist sociology, and migration studies use ethnography to craft powerful and inspiring social science.

Powerful Ethnographies that Remain with You

The first and oldest book is Gelya Frank's (2000) *Venus on Wheels: Two Decades of Dialogue on Disability, Biography, and Being Female in America* (hereafter *Venus on Wheels*), which combines ethnography and life history to read changes in mainstream American culture in the second half of the twentieth century through 20 years in the life of Diane DeVries, 'a woman born with all the physical and mental equipment she would need to live in our society – except arms and legs' (p. 1). Frank narrates how her relation to Diane led her to deconstruct cultural representations of disabled women as victims, which were dominant at the time, and, conversely, to come to see Diane as a perfect example of an American woman coming of age in the second half of the twentieth century. It further forces her to come to terms with her own 'invisible disabilities', which unconsciously motivated the study.

The second book is Lori Kendall's (2002) *Hanging Out in the Virtual Pub: Masculinities and Relationships Online* (hereafter *Hanging Out in the Virtual Pub*), an ethnography of the performance of gender, class, and race identities in an online community, which she gives the pseudonym BlueSky. Written in the early days of Internet-mediated communication, this ethnography investigates what such type of communication does to participants' identities. Against expectations, Kendall discovers that the inhabitants of this virtual community craft virtual identities that remain close to who they are in their non-virtual lives.

Third, we draw on Annemarie Mol's (2003) *The Body Multiple: Ontology in Medical Practice* (hereafter *The Body Multiple*), an ethnography of a Dutch hospital investigating how the body is enacted in multiple ways in the day-to-day medical practice of diagnosing and treating atherosclerosis. Mol narrates how multiple medical practices, in different moments, places, apparatuses, specialties, or treatments, perform atherosclerosis in multiple, slightly different ways. The disease however ultimately coheres through a range of daily practices including sharing documents, such as forms and files, and images across spaces, and holding case conferences and doctor-patient conversations, through which some performances of atherosclerosis come to prevail over other ones.

Finally, the last book is Ruben Andersson's (2014) *Illegality, Inc.: Clandestine Migration and the Business of Bordering Europe* (hereafter *Illegality, Inc.*), an ethnography of the industry organizing migration flows from Senegal to the European enclaves of Ceuta and Melilla on the coast of North Africa. The focus is on how this industry – its institutional actors, settings, conflicting rationales and interests, competition, and incoherence – itself produces 'illegal immigrants', and how this category is in turn variously mobilized to capture part of the economic value of the industry of 'illegality'.

We originally read these books because we are personally and professionally interested in what they research. While outside MOS, they do address empirical issues that are of relevance to our discipline, including disability, rehabilitation and access to paid work, professional practices, meaning and power, technology, social identities and power relations, and the relation between capitalist institutions and migration. We chose to reflect on them here because they stayed with us a long time after we read them, making us reflect not only about the objects and subjects they study, but also, above all, about the freedom of these scholars in crafting these ethnographies, a freedom we do not see within MOS.

Our reflection is structured around five key dimensions of doing ethnography differently: the relation between research and social theory; the relation between the field and social worlds on various levels; how they construct and understand the truth value of their insights, superimposing subjects and reflexivity; how they treat the body and materiality; and how they express a deeper sensitivity to power relations.

Redefining the Relation between Ethnography and Social Theory

A first intriguing feature of these four books is how they relate ethnography differently to social theory than most ethnographic studies in MOS. These latter generally cast ethnography as a particularly suitable methodology to close a specific 'theoretical gap' or, more rarely, to solve a (theoretical) 'mystery' on a specific empirical phenomenon. The use of ethnography is accordingly invariably justified in terms of enabling the researcher to (build a claim to) deliver a novel theoretical contribution to the existing scholarly debate. Ethnographic studies published within MOS seem to reflect a hidden assumption that an empirical study is only worth conducting if it fills or solves something that is narratively constructed as a theoretical problem. While this stimulates MOS scholars to engage with data analytically and not just descriptively (Yanow, 2009), the emphasis on the primacy of theory building over 'empirics' within our discipline also fundamentally constrains how we understand ethnography, how we construct it textually, and, as a result, limits the kinds of insights we can learn from it.

The required emphasis on theory – and a specific, factor-analytic kind of theory (Cornelissen, 2017) – forces us to position ethnography in explicitly instrumental terms, as a methodological tool suitable to solve the specific theoretical puzzle or to fill the gap we have ourselves staged, and to gloss over the epistemological and theoretical assumptions ethnography itself comes with. Once cast as a tool to achieve the end of theory building, ethnography is implicitly systematically devalued as a specific modality of 'data collection', a necessary step to gather a lower form of practical knowledge in the 'real world' from which a higher form of abstract knowledge – theory – should be generated. This hierarchical relationship is enforced through the highly standardized structure of journal articles in MOS, whereby the relevance of both the need to conduct an ethnographic study and the insights generated through it need to be argued in dialogue with theory, in the front and back end of the text respectively.

Scholars who only get in touch with ethnography published in MOS might come to believe that this type of relation between ethnography and theory is inherent in ethnography. The books discussed here however reveal that this is not the case, and that such relation is rather produced by our own discipline's journal conventions. Using various narrative strategies, the authors of these four ethnographies achieve a more balanced, 'fairer' relation between what they have observed and narrate ethnographically and more or less Grand Theories than most ethnographic studies in MOS. Arguably, the most radical alternative is offered by Annemie Mol, who gently navigates multiple social realities enacted by various professionals in their medical practice. She shows – through narrative snapshots of how diagnoses of atherosclerosis are made – how different professionals deploy multiple technologies to construct multiple and even competing bodies of the same patient with atherosclerosis, and how these bodies then need to be reconciled within one medical file in order to decide which treatment should be given. Adopting a praxiographic approach, she moves away from epistemology, which leads to understand medicine as 'socially constructed' – and thus ontologically separate from materiality – to argue for a form of being that does not pass through representation, but rather is fundamentally, ontologically anchored in a specific locale. So, she argues, atherosclerosis *is* one thing in the department of pathology (that is, a specific observed condition of a vessel in the body) and *is* another thing in the patients' clinic (felt pain and a poor nourished skin). The specific being cannot be severed from a place, as ontologies are only brought into existence, sustained and eventually erased through specific everyday sociomaterial practices (*The Body Multiple*, p. 6, upper text). The use of praxiography allows her to question the classical boundaries between 'disease' as a matter of medical science as opposed to 'illness' as a matter of social sciences.

Mol's book also differs the most from our scholarly mores due to the surprising way it spatially organizes the relation between ethnography and theory. Basically, she writes two books in one. A main narrative embroidering snapshots of the enactment of atherosclerosis in the hospital and her theoretical reflections on the local practices she observed is located in the upper part of the page. A broader, theoretical conversation with social science on medicine and beyond is located in the lower part of the page. Tellingly, this latter is written in a different, smaller font, and occupies less space on each page, at first glance conveying a lower status than the former. However, it cannot be mistaken for a footnote, as it lacks referencing numbers, has own sub-titles and is laid out in two columns. This double structure allows Mol to do 'empirical philosophy' (p. 1, upper text), moving swiftly between 'locally inscribed praxis' and 'big ideas', while also leaving the relation between the two much more ambiguous (pp. 2–6, lower text) than common notions of generalizability would allow in MOS.

Although *The Body Multiple* goes the farthest in challenging scholarly conventions on the relation between theory and ethnographic empirics, all four books integrate extensive narrative fragments reporting their observations, using them as a thread through the text. They do not do so to substantiate their theoretical claims. Rather, they put the field at center stage so that their theoretical arguments can emerge out of it. Whereas Kendall and Frank largely interweave field observations and analysis, Andersson inserts scenes occurring in different locations along the migration route he reconstructs, such as villages in black Africa and detention centers on Spanish islands, to vividly picture actors' distinct roles, interests, and perspectives in this human flow. Kept separated from the main text and printed in italics, these scenes gradually build a sense of incoherence and contradiction from which migration can be theorized as an industry, that is, as something (institutionally) organized and involving a massive flow of resources, competition, waste and other externalities, and above all, not helping individuals or communities build better lives.

Not only do the four authors clearly see their empirical case(s) as central, their approach to both the empirical case and theory is way more humble, and at the same time way more ambitious, than the common approach of ethnographies published in MOS. They tackle 'Big Questions', and they so by building on 'Grand Theories'. Whereas in our discipline we are pushed to narrow down the theoretical scope of our studies, these ethnographers seem to be at ease positioning themselves at the midst of wide and far-reaching theoretical conversations. To do so, they do not reduce the cases to those aspects that are similar across cases (or assumed to be), or can be convincingly measured and placed within clear-cut process models. As Mol puts it:

> In the ethnographic stories I tell throughout this book, I do not try to sum things up. I do not describe western medicine, but particular events in a single Dutch university hospital. And I assume that events in the next hospital, thirteen kilometers away, or over the border in Germany, or across the Atlantic have a complex relation with those that I have witnessed. A comparative analysis would show that there are similar patterns. Similar gestures. Similar machines. But also different self-evidences. Different needles and different norms. Different jokes. But which different exactly? And what are their interferences and their diffractions? I haven't studied this.
>
> *(2003, p. 2)*

These ethnographic studies, unlike ethnographic studies in MOS, avoid a comparative approach (e.g. the Eisenhardt method, Eisenhardt, 1989) or a focus on patterned similarities and differences (e.g. the Gioia method, Gioia, Corley and Hamilton,

2012), as ways to allow for generalizations (and see Langley and Abdallah, 2011). Rather, they move even further away from statistical, analytic or heuristic generalization (Schwandt, 2015, pp. 128–130; Tsoukas, 2009) to theoretical pondering and deliberations, verging on the philosophical.

Adopting such a new balance between theory and case in MOS studies may not only free organizational ethnographers, but may also help us as a discipline better reconnect our theoretical discussions and the everyday experience of people at work (Delbridge and Sallaz, 2015; Zanoni, 2011; Zanoni and Janssens, 2015). While ethnographers come in direct contact with people in organizations, the norms in our discipline and the review process too often drives them away from the data, 'resulting in abstract theories that privilege structure and contradict people's experience' (Barley and Kunda, 2001; Bechky, 2011, p. 1157). A new balance between theory and case may open a space for more relevant theories (Keiser, Nicolai, and Seidl, 2015), and redraw the lines between rigor and relevance (e.g. Gulati, 2007; Keiser and Leiner, 2009).

Redefining the 'Field' and Interweaving Levels of Analysis

These four ethnographies further triggered us to reflect on what has traditionally been seen as a legitimate 'field' in MOS. Despite the ubiquitous parlance of the spatiotemporal fragmentation of organization and employment in post-Fordist, globalized service economies, as a whole, we have remained as a discipline remarkably attached to classically defined firms and workplaces as settings for our ethnographic inquiries (for exceptions, see also Zilber, 2014, 2016; Jarzabkowski, Bednarek and Cabantous, 2015). Taken together, these four ethnographies show that the meaning of field and the practice of fieldwork can be considerably stretched beyond MOS norms. In this respect, Gelya Frank's fieldwork on two decades in the life of one individual, on which *Venus on Wheels* is based, is unique and illuminating. Tellingly, she observes that this choice 'obliged [her] to account for [her] choices not only to remain in the United States but also to study only one individual' (pp. 7–8), at a time, the mid-1970s, when they were exceptional in anthropology! Frank combines elements of ethnography – a first-hand description of people's way of life – and life history – a genre tracing how a culture influences the experiences of a specific individual – into a cultural biography 'enhancing [her] understanding of both Diane DeVries and the culture to which she belongs' (p. 3). Prolonged empirical observation at the micro level of analysis represents a window into culture at the macro level.

Specifically, Frank reconstructs through the life of Diane the evolution of American culture surrounding disability, between the historical peak of medical authority in the definition of normalcy and deviance in the 1950s and the antiauthoritarian disability rights movement which emerged in the 1970s. At the same time, her analysis is highly informative of gender roles in American society at the time. Interestingly, Frank explicitly claims sole authorship, as a scholar, of Diane's cultural biography (despite the inclusion, throughout the ethnography, of a highly self-reflective, in-depth analysis of her relation to Diane).This allows her to take full responsibility for moving back and forth between her representation of one subject – Diane – and her interpretation of how US society – e.g. the health system, the institutionalized (gendered) norms about parenthood and marriage, rising individualism and consumerism, the welfare state, the educational system and employer – co-shape her life and her sense of who she is, through inscription in collective norms of ablebodiedness, gender, and class.

MOS research, and MOS research on historically subordinated groups in particular, can draw great inspiration from an approach, such as Frank's, which centers on the subject(s), rather than a specific context, to understand how she is constituted in sociality, through multiple and dynamic relations of power, and how oppression occurs.This reduces the very real risk of reifying the workplace and simply assuming its primacy in the dynamics of identity and power, and enables reconnecting it to the (broader) context which co-shapes it (e.g. Siebers, 2010; Zanoni and Janssens, 2007).

Ruben Andersson's conceptualization of the field is quite distinct from Frank's. He devotes a whole appendix in *Illegality, Inc.* to discussing this notion in studies of migration and illegality and his own positioning within it. He poses the question of the (im)possibility of studying migration ethnographically as a system, given its dispersed geography and, conversely, following Latour, about whether anthropology is condemned to territoriality (*Illegality, Inc.*, p. 284; Latour, 1993; see also Glick-Schiller and Wimmer, 2003). Andersson argues that, while based on participant observation in multiple places, his work should not be seen as a multi-sited ethnography (Marcus, 1995).The many locales should rather be understood as constituting *one* site and allowing the 'tracking, tracing and mapping of the *system* of the transnational illegality industry and the modalities of migranthood it produces' (*Illegality, Inc.*, p. 284, emphasis in original).

This type of understanding of ethnography foregrounds macro-structures which are illustrated through the empirically observed enactments of different actors, who each have a distinct, if related, stake, negotiation power, and who obviously bear very different consequences.This conceptualization and methodological operationalization is particularly relevant to MOS as it helps envisioning ethnographic research designs better suited to deal with globally dispersed production networks and foregrounding the complex power dynamics informing them (see Jarzabkowski, Bednarek and Cabantous, 2015). Further, it may help us expand the common method we now use to study process – as we usually limit the spatiotemporal window we use to follow 'process', and hence what we consider as 'process data' (Langley, 1999). If, instead of attempting to capture the totality of a process by limiting its scope, we allow the following of people, events, practices, or materials across boundaries, new insights about diffusion (e.g. Boxenbaum and Jonsson, 2017), translation (e.g.Wedlin and Sahlin, 2017) and process more generally may be gained, including the very understanding of how and why a 'process' is constructed as such (see, for example, Munir, 2005 on the construction of 'crisis').

Subjects, Truth and Reflexivity

The reflexive turn taken by anthropology in the mid-1980s to address the 'crisis of representation' (Clifford and Marcus, 1986; Marcus and Fischer, 1986) resonated in all social sciences, yet failed, as a whole, to question ethnography in MOS (Neyland, 2008; Yanow, 2009). Grounded in a positivistic epistemology, many studies in our discipline retain a strikingly 'realist' understanding of ethnography, in which researcher and subjects are ontologically distinct, pre-exist interaction in the field, and stand in a fundamentally different relation to the knowledge that is generated through the research process (Ybema, Yanow, Wels and Kamsteeg, 2009). Endowed with theoretical knowledge and 'interpretative omnipotence' (Van Maanen, 2011), the researcher is invested with producing 'objective' scientific knowledge by capturing the structures of social reality underpinning subjects' (organizational) life-world. Insights need to go beyond the representation of a specific life-world and tell something 'universal' about social life, indeed a theoretical contribution which can subsequently be used to interpret other fields, and that can, ideally, be modeled for final verification through the quantitative testing of hypotheses.

MOS ethnographies achieve authority through strict adherence to the disciplinary norms on methodological rigor and a writing style in accordance with the scientific ideal of objectivity (Czarniawska, 2016; Yanow, 2009). This is conveyed by presenting the natives' point of view as 'facts' in a third, godlike voice, with no reflection on the researcher's role in interpreting the collected data (Cunliffe and Karunanayake, 2013; Van Maanen, 1996; Zickar and Carter, 2010). This understanding of ethnography as producing 'true' and 'objective' accounts and of the researcher as the sole knowledge-producer fundamentally marks MOS ethnographies.

Three of the four ethnographies discussed in this chapter – *Venus on Wheels, Hanging Out in the Virtual Pub* and *Illegality, Inc.* – devote substantial space to discussing the relation between the researcher and the subjects, albeit in different ways (Driver, 2016). The fourth, *The Body Multiple*, on the contrary, completely evades this question. While medical staff's production of the patient's multiple bodies is at the core of the analysis, the role of the researcher herself in producing 'truth' about medical practice is completely obscured. This neglect is coherent with a casting of the study as one in 'empirical philosophy' – rather than medical anthropology – and with a praxiographic approach that refuses to give primacy to meaning over matter, and which accordingly shifts the scientific gaze from subjects themselves (or the researcher, as a matter of fact) to their doings and the realities that these doings produce.

Perhaps because of the extremely vulnerable position of his many informants compared to himself, the transitory nature of his fieldwork dispersed across multiple locales, and its journalistic style, Andersson's account also largely lacks the reflexivity that the reader would expect to feature in contemporary ethnography. While extensively reporting the 'natives' point of view', these perspectives function to reconstruct, from multiple perspectives and voices, the structure of the migration industry as *he* sees it. He poses the ethical dilemmas largely in terms of be(com)ing himself part of such an industry. Specifically, Andersson reflects on how the relation he was able to establish with subjects in the field was shaped by his own need for accounts and information. Such need associated him, in the eyes of his informants, with the many journalists and researchers who had previously passed by to gather stories of illegal migration, but had seldom given something back to respondents and their communities (*Illegality, Inc.*, pp. 60–61). While he reports how he tried to deal with this, he does not dwell on the ethical dilemmas he himself faces as a researcher in the field deriving from the powerlessness of his respondents vis-à-vis the macro-structures he describes.

Kendall also retains clear authorship over the narrative – 'The stories I tell here are not the stories that people of BlueSky would tell' (*Hanging Out in the Virtual Pub*, p. 246), she states; however, she does extensively reflect on her role as an ethnographer in an appendix to the main text, with the telling title '"Mudders in the Mist": Ethnography in a "partly compatible" setting'. She reports conversations negotiating her presence in the community, being compared to Dian Fossey studying gorillas in the jungle or to a 'sociologist that is studying us like bugs in ether bottles' (p. 238). She also shares her sense of vulnerability by acknowledging the key role of one influential member in helping her get accepted in the community, as well as the ethical dilemmas she encountered, as a feminist scholar of a virtual community largely inhabited by men, when witnessing enactments of hegemonic masculinity and sexism. Entering in dialogue with prior literature on the ethics of ethnographic fieldwork, she argues that most research sites are only 'partly compatible' with a researcher's own convictions, avowing that, while she sometimes openly challenged the sexism she experienced, 'caught between [her] own cultural allegiances to feminism and [her] attempts to join and respect the culture of BlueSky' (p. 245) many times she 'went along to get along'. Reflecting the ambiguous and multiple dynamics of the relationship between researcher and respondents (Cunliffe and Karunanayake, 2013), she esteems having been changed more by BlueSky than she could change it.

Frank's ethnography stands out because it provides a highly introspective account of how trying to understand Diane led the ethnographer to better understand herself (also with the aid of psychoanalytic therapy). The text is written in a strongly dialogical way, whereby Frank enters into conversation with the anthropological tradition, the societal institutions shaping the life of Diane, but also, importantly, Diane herself and a few key people in her life. This latter engagement produces extensive parts in the text in which her voice and the voice of Diane are related in dialogues or juxtaposed through documentary sources, despite Frank's insisting that the book is hers and hers only (as agreed with Diane). The 'thick', highly reflexive descriptions of their interactions within a prolonged relationship convey a seldom seen sense of inter-personal openness and generosity (Rhodes and Carlsen, 2018), which however also acknowledges the tensions that come with it, concrete situations of conflict, and strategies to make things work for oneself (*Venus on Wheels*, pp. 127–128).

While we can use these different approaches to reflexivity to enrich the repertoire of reflexive writing within MOS (see Alvesson, Hardy and Harley, 2008), what we have to gain is even more important. Current norms in our field are largely preoccupied with the preservation of objectivity, rigor, and validity. Judging qualitative research through normative concepts that were developed under very different paradigmatic assumptions however sterilizes ethnographic studies and strips them from their ability to make the contribution they are supposedly better positioned to make. This is especially so when it comes to reflexivity, that in too many ethnographic studies within MOS is only ceremonially used (Gilmore and Kenny, 2015; Mahadevan, 2012; Zanoni and Van Laer, 2016). Ethnographic authors find themselves in a trap, as being fully reflexive and admitting the constructivist nature of their research endeavor – from posing a question to choosing a field, through data collection and analysis, to the writing of the final text – will pull the rug from under their feet, as they are expected to offer an objective report on an existing reality. Thus, most of us offer a shallow reflection of where we came from or how we felt in the field (Dallyn, 2014). Rarely do we see reflections that are used to refine the analytic approach or enrich the interpretation. Redefining criteria of quality from a constructivist and interpretative stand (e.g. Tracy, 2010) will allow qualitative scholars to better reconnect reflexivity to the study (and not only as an afterthought). Acknowledging the role of the self-in-relation in the process of knowledge generation will help produce qualitatively stronger and deeper insights into the social reality under study than is today the case.

Ethnography, Materiality and the Body

Ethnography appears also particularly relevant to us in light of the current debates in MOS about the need to find better ways to account for embodiment and materiality in the way we understand work, organizations and organizing, institutions and power relations (e.g. Dale, 2001; Fotaki and Pullen, 2019; Gherardi, Meriläinen, Strati and Valtonen, 2013; Hassard, Holliday and Willmott, 2000; Hindmarsh and Pilnick, 2007; Putnam, 2015). Of course there have long been rich, long-lasting traditions of MOS scholarship specifically dealing with the body and material objects as phenomena within organizing. However, the increasingly omnipresent role of technology, spatiotemporal-legally fragmented organizations, embodied (emotional) service work, workers' socio-demographic heterogeneity, and control through biopower are reconfiguring embodiment and materiality as essential *dimensions* of organizing. These dimensions necessitate adequate theorization and empirical investigation, as they can help us reach beyond the symbolic, that is, text, language, narrative, discourse, frames, and sense-making.

While none of these four ethnographies is positioned in this debate or, as a matter of fact, focuses specifically on embodiment and materiality, they all speak in important ways to these dimensions. Through medical practice, both Frank and Mol put the body and its relations to technology at center stage, yet do so in very different ways. Frank narrates Diane as an embodied subject engaged and struggling not only with bodily norms but also, more specifically, with an institutionally shaped materiality that disables her. Such a materiality is epitomized in prosthetic limbs that primarily meet the able-bodied medical staff's own need to fill in for Diane's missing body parts, to make her fit an able-bodied ideal and ensure that the vision of her limbless body is not 'offensive' to others (*Venus on Wheels*, p. 53). Diane actively resisted this oppressive materiality as unaesthetic and useless to her. Not only is it in contradiction with her own sense of femininity and beauty – 'Diane felt that the artificial arms were disfiguring and made her look like a "little Frankie" (a Frankenstein monster)' (p. 53) – but it also does not help her live more independently. These medical artifacts are contrasted to the inventive tools her father made for her so that she could join her peers' playing during her childhood, and her own embodied skills to do things despite lacking arms or legs. Frank also extensively narrates her own embodied experience of Diane and her relation with her, ranging from her initial (wrong) assumptions about her sexual life to her gagging while helping her on the toilet due to her own pregnancy. This ethnography impressed us for its skillful blurring of the common boundaries between (bodily) life and social science, which are remarkably well policed in MOS ethnographies (yet for exceptions, see Katila, 2019; Pullen, 2018), while at once avoiding to fall into simple mundane description or worse, voyeurism.

In Mol's work, the body is located at the other opposite of the subject–object spectrum. No longer the place of a subjects' embodied experience, it is the temporary, context-bound product of specific professionals' skillful practice. For instance, her detailed description of surgical practice is as detached, 'cold', and sanitized as we imagine an operation room to be. The mere listing of the implications of a diagnosis and the decision of invasive treatment – admission to the hospital, fasting, sedation, rolled into the operation theater, anesthesia and opening up (*The Body Multiple*, p. 90) – instantaneously dehumanizes the patient, reducing him or her to a medical body to be corrected and brought back to scientifically defined health norms through a standardized procedure. In these descriptions, materiality – e.g. medical tools, protocols, and spaces – always occupy a central place, and the body is reduced into an object. This type of writing makes the reader feel the social space, the scene, and the action through her own body.

Andersson's perspective shares with Mol an understanding of bodies as an object of institutional control through specific tools, procedures, and spaces, but in his ethnography it is about the political, legal, and economic control of bodies – a collective – moving globally along shared migration routes. To unveil the macrostructures of the illegality industry, Andersson represents bodies as a human flow shaped and regulated by various actors in nodal places, each enacting their own institutional logic. Bodies are thus hidden, transported, smuggled, trafficked, rescued, deported, incarcerated, and left behind. In many of these treatments, advanced technology plays a key role, foregrounding the materiality of policing above and beyond any discursive justification of institutional control of clandestine migration.

In Kendall's work, as well, technology – the computer screen – is inherently connected to a border, the border between virtual and non-virtual reality. The computer screen is both the place that unites and disconnects subjects in BlueSky – as they share texts through which they represent themselves, yet their bodies and practices remain hidden behind it. Although much of this ethnography is about interactions happening in virtual space, Kendall's description points to how much effort is invested in mimicking and filling in for the lack of embodiment, to compensate for it for human interaction to take place and for subjects to become intelligible to each other. In a disembodied, technology-mediated space like this one, tacit knowledge of the community and its inhabitants is even more important than elsewhere to navigate it competently. Indeed, despite the contemporary fascination with the fluidity of identity, and the expectation that such fluidity might expand thanks to virtual spaces, Kendall observes that virtual subjectivities remain quite faithful not only to the individual (embodied) subjects producing them but also, importantly, to the social norms that regulate their performance in face-to-face social interactions.

MOS has much to gain by directing our attention to bodies and materiality at work (see for example in regard to institutional theory, Zilber, 2017). While the landscape of organizational behavior and organizational theory changed dramatically with the discursive turn focusing on what people say (Alvesson and Karreman, 2011; Phillips and Oswick, 2012; Reed, 2000; Thompson and Harley, 2012) and then the practice turn, illuminating what people actually do (Feldman and Orlikowski, 2011), these two waves of extension, which opened a rich array of new research questions, also came with a price – an overly linguistic and behavioral emphasis respectively. People in organizations, as reflected from our studies in the past 30 years, are behaving and thinking. They produce texts through language and do things in the world, mostly conscious and strategic. They hardly lust, hate, smell, or even sneeze. Their bodies are harnessed for the pursuit of goals, motivations, responsibilities. Rarely do we meet in our studies experiences 'more immediate than words' (Pickering, 2017, p. 7) – the same kinds of physical discomfort, exhaustion or pleasure that we know from our own lives.

In this, our research adheres to the same norms that regulate bodies at work. The primacy of interviews over observations may be partially responsible, as the talk about bodies is very different than looking at bodies or experiencing work through bodies – possibilities opened by ethnographic studies. This may require much longer studies and new ways to document and analyze data (e.g. Michel, 2011). In addition, if we let bodies into our data, reflections, and theorization, we will be better equipped to explore their intersection with technology and other aspects of the material environment as well. Following sociological and feminist theorizing, previous studies have already started to look at the body as a site of culture and society, and especially as a site of domination. The great promise yet to materialize is the study of bodies as one dimension of that which is not cognitively processed or readily available for observation and control. That is, the study of the irrational aspects of organizing, the only seemingly most rational pursuit of all.

Reclaiming the Politics of Ethnography

Although ethnography does not come with an explicit mission to do politics, it is never far away from it. Because of anthropology's historical origins in colonial practice (Alcadipani, Westwood and Rosa, 2015; Yanow, 2009), the relation between ethnography and power has been widely debated. A rich strand focused on how scholars' historical and geographical – and institutional – location affects their choice of the object of study, the power and ethics involved in fieldwork (Marcus and Fischer, 1986), as well as the politics of representation (Clifford and Marcus, 1986). This rich debate keeps us alert that, no matter how close (we claim) we come to a social phenomenon and the subjects who inhabit and constitute it, ethnography never occurs in a social vacuum. Our scholarly practice is always embedded in fields that are structured by power. This awareness appears to us of particular relevance to MOS, at a historical time when the suitability of businesses, markets, and capitalism as a mode of organizing the economy and society is increasingly called into question, due to its significant externalities not only on human beings but also the planet (Fotaki and Prasad, 2015; Seray, Calás and Smircich, 2018).

Whereas the four monographs we discuss here do not brand themselves as critical scholarship, they certainly do not eschew addressing power as a constitutive dimension of social reality. First of all, by bringing human beings and their everyday, mundane realities to the forefront of social science, they make a political statement about them, saying that they are worth our time and expertise as scholars. This is quite different from a tendency, widespread in MOS, to represent individuals as 'actors', and to largely concentrate empirical investigations on social groups that are more accessible because they resemble us in key ways (for instance in terms of types of workplaces, rank, education, language, etc.) (Zanoni and Van Laer, 2016). Second, these ethnographies all denaturalize taken-for-granted representations of the social phenomena they study, and by so doing gently but firmly educate the reader to self-reflect and revise her own assumptions. Third, and most importantly, they empirically unveil and variously theorize the mechanisms through which certain meanings become dominant and institutionalized, shaping social reality in a certain way, unequally affecting subjects. They also discuss, in one way or another, how subjects-so-constituted, from their own positioning, might (or might not) in turn be able to challenge such meanings and their effects.

As we highlighted above, Kendall's analysis addresses power in terms of the heterosexual, classed matrix through which subjects conceive of themselves and others. She shows how, contrary to optimistic expectations, subjects struggle to conceive of themselves and others outside social norms, such as the heterosexual matrix (*Hanging Out in the Virtual Pub*, p. 107), as radically other, despite the arguably broader possibilities offered to them by virtual spaces. In this book, power is thus in first place the power of social norms to produce and reproduce the self and sociality independent of strong exogenous forms of policing outside sociality itself.

Both Mol's and Frank's ethnographies highlight the role of institutions – such as the medical profession and the health system – in enforcing meanings about oneself and one's social practice through norms, rules, and access to services and income. While Mol's descriptive narrative leaves the reader to autonomously draw the political lesson from between the lines, Frank's more explicitly points to the disempowering and unjust workings of institutions, which are in principle expected to support those in need, yet often precisely fail in this, leaving them to struggle with institutional rules on top of the barriers they encounter.

Unsurprisingly perhaps, *Illegality, Inc.* is the most explicitly political ethnography of the four. On the one hand, it deals with how political institutions directly shape border controls that are constitutive of the migration industry and its underlying (ir)rationales. On the other hand, it zooms in on what Andersson calls the 'policy-practice nexus', highlighting the role of practice in constituting the system:

> materialities, geographies, and social configurations 'on the ground' are not simply temporary manifestations of a predefined system but rather function as key constitutive arenas. By moving away from the nebulous world of the policy apparatus and focusing on the interfaces where the border machinery rubs against specific places, people, and structures – what Anna Tsing terms 'friction' – we can hopefully produce an ethnographic account that spans the overarching logics of Europe's response to clandestine migration and those crucial 'grains of dust that jam the machinery'.
>
> *(p. 285)*

Andersson further reflects on the opportunities and limitations of Actor Network Theory (ANT) as a theoretical scaffold to understand this industry. While ANT helps bridge policy (at the macro level of analysis) and subjects' experiences (at the micro level), the emphasis of this lens on the interactions between materiality, machines ('fences, patrol boats, radars, TV cameras, and rescue equipment', p. 286), and people is less conducive to foregrounding the complicity of subjects – including himself – with such a system (pp. 285–287). Yet it is precisely this complicity that is key to exposing its micro-politics.

Taken together, then, the ethnographies we discuss here may show MOS distinct and novel ways to articulate macro-level 'politics' and micro-level 'power relations' in more sophisticated ways. Much ethnographic research in MOS remains overly focused on the level of meaning at the organizational level, for instance through concepts such as sense-making and identity, only tangentially dealing with power relations – conceptualized as domination, oppression privilege and structural (dis)advantage – or the institutionalized structures and processes that enforce them.

Concluding Thoughts

We believe that the five key dimensions we discussed above – the relation between research and social theory; the relation between the field and social worlds on various levels; how they construct and understand the truth value of their insights, superimposing subjects and reflexivity; how they treat the body and materiality; and how they express a deeper sensitivity to power relations – are most productive to spur a debate on ethnography of organizations and organizing. Our goal is to call for MOS to renegotiate its affordances to ethnographic studies by drawing from beyond its own disciplinary borders, in order to revise its research conventions while also building on its own intellectual traditions (see, for instance, Rouleau, de Rond and Musca, 2014).

We are of course aware that, written as monographs, these modalities of crafting ethnography cannot simply be replicated in MOS, where scholarship is largely written out in article form – precisely the article form, and the (hierarchically ranked), international, peer-reviewed journals in which articles appear to play a key role in pressuring MOS scholars to conform to strictly defined methodological practice (Zanoni and Van Laer, 2016) at the cost of freedom and innovation, domesticating ethnography (Locke, 2011). Nonetheless, we believe that these books can help realize what we are missing out on by abiding by these conventions and help further the horizon of the possible than where it stands today. We hope to stir up conversation that will result in opening up the terrain, to widen the conditions of possibility in terms of what is considered a legitimate field of study, worthy research questions, 'data', 'trail of evidence' interpretation, and modes of representation (Reay, Zafar, Monteiro and Glaser, 2019) and, more fundamentally, the very role of the ethnographer in producing scientific knowledge (Clifford and Marcus, 1986; Marcus and Fischer, 1986; Van Maanen, 2011). The four ethnographies we discussed in this chapter each direct us in a different way, privileging certain sensibilities and goals over others. Together, they offer a vision that can broaden our thinking and our practice as ethnographers of organizations and organizing.

As the domestication occurs systemically, it is hard for each one of us to avoid the pressures to conform. This is particularly true for PhD students and early career scholars who still need to establish themselves and claim a voice in MOS. Still, we believe that it is important to be aware of the methodological disciplining occurring in our discipline, and the cost involved in limiting the array of legitimate ethnographic practices we can use. One way to try to avoid this channeling is to actively look for conversations around ethnography in other disciplines, to keep seeing how it is done and can be done differently. Reading ethnographic work grounded in other disciplines, attending courses about ethnography and entering conversations on ethnography occurring in other disciplines are a first step, one that can help then to connect with more liberal strands of ethnography within our own discipline.

This reconnection can be for instance through streams in conferences like the European Group of Organization Studies (EGOS), International Critical Management Studies (ICMS), and SCOS, but also specialized conferences and workshops on ethnography and professional development workshops at the Academy of Management annual meetings. Next to individual choices to diversify one's publication genres and formats to enhance the possibilities of publishing diverse forms of ethnography (e.g. monographs, book chapters, videos and other kinds of formats), which to some extent depend on the context and the career phase one is embedded in, it is particularly important to create and sustain conversations within MOS about the need to broaden ethnography. This type of engagement both facilitates the sharing of knowledge and strengthens the network with peers engaged with ethnography (Easterby-Smith, Golden-Biddle and Locke, 2008). From the very first phase of their academic trajectory, PhD students in MOS with a passion for ethnography should consider joining and actively contributing to the communities engaged with this type of scholarship, to collectively open up spaces in quality journals for less domesticated, more 'wild' versions of organizational ethnography.

Note

1 This is still an ongoing project, which has relied over the years not only on our own work but also on that of research assistants and junior researchers. Parts of this analysis were developed in a paper we presented at the Harvard-MIT seminar on economic sociology (Boston) and The Centre for Strategy Studies in Organizations and Strategy & Organization Area Seminar, Desautels Faculty of Management, McGill University (Montreal) in 2012, 'A Story Never Ending: The Emergence of "Ethnography" in Organization Studies'; and another paper we presented in EGOS 2017 in Copenhagen 'Co-opted ethnography: A Review of 40 years ethnography in OS top journals (1974–2013)' in Sub-theme 04: Long shots and close-ups: Organizational ethnography, process and history (De Coster, Zanoni and Zilber, 2017).

References

Alcadipani, R., Westwood, R., and Rosa, A. (2015). The politics of identity in organizational ethnographic research: Ethnicity and tropicalist intrusions. *Human Relations* 68(1): 79–106.

Alvesson, M., Hardy, C., and Harley, B. (2008). Reflecting on reflexivity: Reflexive textual practices in organization and management theory. *Journal of Management Studies* 45(3): 480–501.

Alvesson, M., and Karreman, D. (2011). Decolonializing discourse: Critical reflections on organizational discourse analysis. *Human Relations* 64(9): 1121–1146.

Andersson, R. (2014). *Illegality, Inc.: Clandestine Migration and the Business of Bordering Europe.* Oakland: University of California Press.

Barley, S.R., and Kunda, G. (2001). Bringing work back in. *Organization Science* 12(1): 76–95.

Bechky, B.A. (2011). Making organizational theory work: Institutions, occupations, and negotiated orders. *Organization Science* 22(5): 1157–1167.

Boxenbaum, E., and Jonsson, S. (2017). Isomorphism, diffusion and decoupling: Concept evolution and theoretical challenges. In R. Greenwood and T. Lawrence (Eds.), *Handbook of Organizational Institutionalism* (revised 2nd edition, pp. 77–101). Los Angeles: Sage.

Clifford, J., and Marcus, G. (1986). *Writing Culture: The Poetics and Politics of Ethnography.* Berkeley: University of California Press.

Cornelissen, J.P. (2017). Preserving theoretical divergence in management research: Why the explanatory potential of qualitative research should be harnessed rather than suppressed. *Journal of Management Studies* 54(3): 368–383.

Cunliffe, A.L., and Karunanayake, G. (2013). Working within hyphen-spaces in ethnographic research: Implications for research identities and practice. *Organizational Research Methods* 16(3): 364–392.

Czarniawska, B. (2016). Reflexivity versus rigor. *Management Learning* 47(5): 615–619.

Dale, K. (2001). *Anatomising Embodiment and Organisation Theory.* Houndmills: Palgrave Macmillan.

Dallyn, S. (2014). Naming the ideological reflexively: Contesting organizational norms and practices. *Organization* 21(2): 244–265.

Delbridge, R., and Sallaz, J.J. (2015). Work: Four worlds and ways of seeing. *Organization Studies* 36(11): 1449–1462.

De Coster, M., Zanoni, P., and Zilber, T. (2017). Co-opted ethnography: A Review of 40 years ethnography in OS top journals (1974–2013), EGOS Conference, Copenhagen, July, 5–7.

Driver, M. (2016). Making the absent subject present in organizational research. *Human Relations* 69(3): 731–752.

Easterby-Smith, M., Golden-Biddle, K., and Locke, K. (2008). Working with pluralism. Determining quality in qualitative research. *Organizational Research Methods* 11(3): 419–429.

Eisenhardt, K.M. (1989). Building theory from case study research. *Academy of Management Review* 14: 532–550.

Feldman, M.S., and Orlikowski, W.J. (2011). Theorizing practice and practicing theory. *Organization Science* 22(5): 1240–1253.

Fotaki, M., and Prasad, A. (2015). Questioning the neoliberal capitalism and economic inequality in business schools. *Academy of Management Learning & Education* 14(4): 556–575.

Fotaki, M., and Pullen, A. (Eds.). (2019). *Diversity, Affect and Embodiment in Organizing*. Cham, Switzerland: Palgrave Macmillan.

Frank, G. (2000). *Venus on Wheels: Two Decades of Dialogue on Disability, Biography, and Being Female in America*. Berkeley: University of California Press.

Gherardi, S., Meriläinen, S., Strati, A., and Valtonen, A. (2013). Editors' introduction: A practice-based view on the body, senses and knowing in organization. *Scandinavian Journal of Management* 29(4): 333–337.

Gilmore, S., and Kenny, K. (2015). Work-worlds colliding: Self-reflexivity, power and emotion in organizational ethnography. *Human Relations* 68(1): 55–78.

Gioia, D.A., Corley, K.G., and Hamilton, A.L. (2012). Seeking qualitative rigor in inductive research: Notes on the Gioia methodology. *Organizational Research Methods* 16(1): 15–31.

Glick-Schiller, N. and Wimmer, A. (2003). Methodological nationalism, the social sciences and the study of migration. *International Migration Review*, 37(3): 576–610.

Gulati, R. (2007). Tent poles, tribalism, and boundary spanning: The rigor-relevance debate in management research. *Academy of Management Journal* 50(4): 775–782.

Hassard, J., Holliday, R., and Willmott, H. (Eds.). (2000). *Body and Organization*. London: Sage.

Hindmarsh, J., and Pilnick, A. (2007). Knowing bodies at work: Embodiment and ephemeral teamwork in anaesthesia. *Organization Studies* 28(9): 1395–1416.

Jarzabkowski, P., Bednarek, R., and Cabantous, L. (2015). Conducting global team-based ethnography: Methodological challenges and practical methods. *Human Relations* 68(1): 3–33.

Katila, S. (2019). The mothers in me. *Management Learning* 50(1): 129–140.

Keiser, A., and Leiner, L. (2009). Why the rigour-relevance gap in management research is unbridgeable. *Journal of Management Studies* 46(3): 516–533.

Keiser, A., Nicolai, A., and Seidl, D. (2015). The practical relevance of management research: Turning the debate on relevance into a rigorous scientific research program. *Academy of Management Annals* 9(1): 143–233.

Kendall, L. (2002). *Hanging Out in the Virtual Pub: Masculinities and Relationships Online*. Berkeley: University of California Press.

Langley, A. (1999). Strategies of theorizing from process data. *Academy of Management Review* 24(4): 691–710.

Langley, A., and Abdallah, C. (2011). Templates and turns in qualitative studies of strategy and management. In D. Bergh and D. Ketchen (Eds.), *Building Methodological Bridges: Research Methodology in Strategy and Management* (Vol. 6, pp. 201–235). Bingley: Emerald Group.

Latour, B. (1993). *We Have Never Been Modern*. Hemel Hempstead, UK: Harvester Wheatsheaf.

Locke, K. (2011). Field research practice in management and organization studies: Reclaiming its tradition of discovery. *The Academy of Management Annals* 5(1): 613–652.

Mahadevan, J. (2012). Translating nodes of power through reflexive ethnographic writing. *Journal of Organizational Ethnography* 1(1): 119–131.

Marcus, G.E. (1995). Ethnography in/of the world system: The emergence of multi-sited ethnography. *Annual Review of Anthropology* 24: 95–117.

Marcus, G.E., and Fischer, M. (1986). *Anthropology as Cultural Critique*. Chicago: University of Chicago Press.

Michel, A. (2011). Transcending socialization: A nine-year ethnography of the body's role in organizational control and knowledge workers' transformation. *Administrative Science Quarterly* 56(3): 325–368.

Mol, A. (2003). *The Body Multiple: Ontology in Medical Practice*. Durham and London: Duke University Press.

Munir, K.A. (2005). The social construction of events: A study of institutional change in the photographic field. *Organization Studies* 26(1): 93–112.

Neyland, D. (2008). *Organizational Ethnography*. London: Sage.

Phillips, N., and Oswick, C. (2012). Organizational discourse: Domains, debates, and directions. *Academy of Management Annals* 6: 435–481.

Pickering, A. (2017). The ontological turn: Taking different worlds seriously. *Social Analysis* 61(2): 134–150.

Pullen, A. (2018). Writing as labiaplasty. *Organization* 25(1): 123–130.

Putnam, L. (2015), Unpacking the dialectic: Alternative views on the discourse–materiality relationship. *Journal of Management Studies*, 52(5), 706–716.

Reay, T., Zafar, A., Monteiro, P., and Glaser, V. (2019). Presenting findings from qualitative research: One size does not fit all. *Research in the Sociology of Organizations* 59: 201–216.

Reed, M. (2000). The limits of discourse analysis in organizational analysis. *Organization* 7(3): 524–530.

Rhodes, C., and Carlsen, A. (2018). The teaching of the other: Ethical vulnerability and generous reciprocity in the research process. *Human Relations* 71(10): 1295–1318.

Rouleau, L., de Rond, M., and Musca, G. (2014). From the ethnographic turn to new forms of organizational ethnography. *Journal of Organizational Ethnography* 3(1): 2–9.

Schwandt, T.A. (2015). *The Sage Dictionary of Qualitative Inquiry* (4th ed.). Los Angeles: Sage.

Seray, E., Calás, M.B., and Smircich, L. (2018). Ecologies of sustainable concerns: Organization theorizing for the anthropocene. *Gender, Work & Organization* 25(3): 222–245.

Siebers, H. (2010). The impact of migrant-hostile discourse in the media on racioethnic closure in career development in the Netherlands. *International Sociology* 25: 475–500.

Thompson, P., and Harley, B. (2012). Beneath the radar? A critical realist analysis of 'the knowledge economy' and 'shareholder value' as competing discourses. *Organization Studies* 33(10): 1363–1381.

Tracy, S.J. (2010). Qualitative quality: Eight 'big-tent' criteria for excellent qualitative research. *Qualitative Inquiry* 16(10): 837–851.

Tsoukas, H. (2009). Craving for generality and small-n studies: A Wittgensteinian approach towards the epistemology of the particular in organization and management studies. In D.A. Buchanan and A. Bryman (Eds.), *The Sage Handbook of Organizational Research Methods* (pp. 285–301). Los Angeles: Sage.

Van Maanen, J. (1996). Commentary: On the matter of voice. *Journal of Management Inquiry* 5(4): 375–381.

Van Maanen, J. (2011). *Tales of the Field: On Writing Ethnography* (2nd ed.). Chicago: University of Chicago Press.

Wedlin, L., and Sahlin, K. (2017). The imitation and translation of management ideas. In R. Greenwood and T. Lawrence (Eds.), *Handbook of Organizational Institutionalism* (revised 2nd ed., pp. 102–127). Los Angeles: Sage.

Yanow, D. (2009). Organizational ethnography and methodological angst: Myths and challenges in the field. *Qualitative Research in Organizations and Management: An International Journal* 4(2): 186–199.

Ybema, S., Yanow, D., Wels, H., and Kamsteeg, F. (Eds.). (2009). *Organizational Ethnography: Studying the Complexities of Everyday Life*. London: Sage.

Zanoni, P. (2011). Diversity in the lean automobile factory: Doing class through gender, disability and age. *Organization* 18(1): 105–127.

Zanoni, P., and Janssens, M. (2007). Minority employees engaging with (diversity) management: An analysis of control, agency, and micro-emancipation. *Journal of Management Studies*, 44(8): 1371–1397.

Zanoni, P., and Janssens, M. (2015). The power of diversity discourses at work: On the interlocking nature of diversities and occupations. *Organization Studies, Special Issue on Worlds of Work* 36(11): 1463–1483.

Zanoni, P., and Van Laer, K. (2016). Collecting narratives and writing stories of diversity: Reflecting on power and identity in our professional practice. In R. Bendl, I. Bleijenbergh, E. Henttonen and A.J. Mills (Eds.), *Oxford Handbook of Diversity* (pp. 337–354). Oxford: Oxford University Press.

Zickar, M., and Carter, T. (2010). Reconnecting with the spirit of workplace ethnography: A historical review. *Organization Research Methods* 13(2): 304–319.

Zilber, T.B. (2002). Institutionalization as an interplay between actions, meanings and actors: The case of a rape crisis center in Israel. *Academy of Management Journal* 45: 234–254.

Zilber, T.B. (2014). Beyond a single organization: Challenges and opportunities in doing field level ethnography. *Journal of Organizational Ethnography* 3(1): 96–113.

Zilber, T.B. (2016). Studying organizational fields through ethnography. In K. Elsbach and R. Kramer (Eds.), *The Handbook of Qualitative Organizational Research* (pp. 86–95). New York: Taylor & Francis/ Routledge.

Zilber, T.B. (2017). A call for a strong multimodal research in institutional theory. *Research in the Sociology of Organizations* 54A: 63–84. (special issue on Multimodality, Meaning, and Institutions, edited by Jancsary, D., Daudigeos, T., and Höllerer, M.).

22

WHY DOES THE STUDY OF ALTERNATIVE ORGANIZATIONS (SO BADLY) NEED ANTHROPOLOGY?

Stéphane Jaumier

What to do? First of all, generate alternative descriptions.

B. Latour (2018)

Introduction

Management studies have witnessed a surge of interest in alternative organizations and organizing in recent years (Parker *et al.* 2014). Such intensifying interest is of course not unrelated to the global crisis of capitalism, whereby the combination of irreversible damage inflicted on the planet, instability of the financial system, and explosion of wealth inequality have provided an increasingly acute sense of urgency towards documenting and promoting alternatives to dominant capitalist modes of organization (Gibson-Graham 1996). In the present chapter, I contend that anthropology has a major role to play in the further development of this growing endeavour that seeks to better understand and promote existing alternatives, as well as imagine new ones. In particular, I wish to focus on two important features of anthropology that are particularly suited to address these tasks, that is, some form of openness to the unknown and also the ethnographic method. Before I substantiate these claims, I provide a summary of certain relevant elements in order, first, to allow a better grasp of the field of study of alternative organizations and of some of its main challenges; and, second, to put into perspective the contribution of anthropology to the broader field of management studies.

There is no clear-cut definition for an "alternative organization" nor of what is meant by "alternative organizing". In fact, what does or should count as alternative is itself an object of contention for scholars interested in the field. Perhaps one of the first challenges associated with the study of alternative organizations is therefore one of scope of delimitation. Critical management studies,[1] which have to date been the main promoters of this field of study, tend to conceive of alternative organizations and organizing in terms of a marked contrast to capitalism; they are deemed alternative forms of organizing that position themselves either outside or against capitalism. The former may exist alongside capitalism, without mounting a direct challenge to its basic structures. The latter may adopt a more confrontational stance towards capitalism, with an explicit aim of undermining its dominance (Parker *et al.* 2014). The study of alternative organizations is thus concerned with both relatively new forms of organizing such as open source communities (Pearce 2014) and recent developments around the gift economy (Acquier *et al.* 2017), and with ancient but enduring models including intentional communities (Farias 2017) and co-operatives (Cheney *et al.* 2014). As well as these examples, organizations for which economic activities are not a main purpose may also receive some attention, since the focus is on alternative forms of both social and economic organizing. For instance, social movement organizations constitute an important object of study, insofar as they display novel ways of organizing, notably in terms of egalitarian decision-making and, more broadly, of avoidance of relationships of domination (Sutherland *et al.* 2014).

In contrast to critical management studies, a second perspective on alternative organizations and organizing exists, which is more inclusive in its scope. Under this alternative umbrella will fall various forms of organizing that differ from the dominant for-profit model of corporations but without departing from capitalist principles (Barin Cruz *et al.* 2017). Social enterprises are a case in point, which pursue a social mission but still accommodate the basic structures of ownership and accumulation that are the defining features of capitalism. The risk associated with such an extended perspective on alternative organizing is, first, that of including research objects that may in the end be conflated with mere corporate social responsibility initiatives and governance best practices. Another risk is that of framing alternatives in capitalism's own terms, thus limiting from the outset the possibilities for emergence and recognition of more radical pathways. For these reasons, I confine myself in this chapter to the most restrictive perspective on alternative organizations, that is, critical management studies. Therefore, I focus in my examples and illustrations on organizations that meet a broad consensus as to their being alternative. Nevertheless it is important to keep in mind that almost any form of alternative organizing may carry real emancipatory potential while at the same time being exposed to continuous threats of neo-liberalization and capitalist co-optation (see Acquier *et al.* 2017; Vidaillet and Bousalham 2020). The assessment of such potentialities and threats is therefore integral to the study of alternative organizations, as will clearly be demonstrated in the later discussion of Sharryn Kasmir's study of Mondragon.

Having conveyed some sense of the nature of the field of alternative organizations, I will now set the context for the relationship existing between anthropology and management studies and, more specifically, organization studies. This context is necessary if the relationship between anthropology and alternative organizations is to be conceived of as one of a prolongation of that already existing between them. Wright (1994) distinguishes three important points in time in terms of the contribution of anthropology to the study of organizations. The first point occurred in the early 30s with the involvement of anthropologist W. Lloyd Warner in the Hawthorne studies (Morey and Luthans 2013[1987]). Warner envisaged the shop-floor "as a small society in which every aspect of life [is] interconnected in a social system" (Wright 1994, p. 6). This allowed him to reveal the importance of the informal system of an organization and to assert, against Mayo's own conclusions, the rationality of a lack of positive response from workers to management incentives. The North-American legacy of Warner is, for example, apparent in the works of William Foot Whyte, Donald Roy and Melville Dalton, in that they rely on anthropological fieldwork methods and focus on informal relations (Morey and Luthans 2013[1987]). The second point singled out by Wright is a British one, that of the shop-floor studies carried out by Manchester University in the 50s and 60s. Observation was extended to full participation methods, with every researcher spending a minimum of six months as a full factory worker. Another important anthropological bent lay in the fact that the organization was no longer understood as a closed system, but instead resituated within the wider social structures within which it operated (Wright 1994). Finally, the third important point corresponded to the adoption by management from the 80s onwards of the concept of culture. An important idea drawn from anthropology is that according to which an organization can be understood metaphorically as a culture, with a corresponding focus on meanings and the symbolic aspects involved in organizing (Smircich 1983; Chapman 2001).

Despite these high points, it is fair to say that the link between anthropology and organization studies has always remained somewhat loose (Czarniawska 2012). In contrast to that of other disciplines, such as economics, psychology and sociology, the influence of anthropology on management studies has never fully reached potency. Not only has there never been any sustained presence of anthropology in the field of management studies, but on those occasions when anthropology has emerged, it has been in such a way that professional anthropologists regard it as either outdated or sanitized. For instance, a majority of anthropologists see in the notion of "corporate culture" – which became the mainstream understanding of the concept of culture within management studies during the 80s–90s – a misappropriation of anthropological thinking (Smircich 1983; Wright 1994). To summarize, one may agree with Czarniawska (2012, p. 199) that, to date, "organization scholars have poached within anthropology's terrain" rather than fully engage with it. This lacking situation explains why management studies witness regular calls for better acknowledgment of the potentialities of anthropology and invitations to engage in the various research programmes that this may inspire (*e.g.* Bate 1997; Linstead 1997; Czarniawska 2012). Proponents of further extending the reach of anthropology insist of course on the richness of the concept of culture, together with that of other key notions (myths, rituals, taboos, artefacts, etc.) that permit grasp of organizations in their symbolic dimensions. Such supporters also praise anthropology for its holistic spirit, which aims to resituate the object of study within its broader context (Hirsch and Gellner 2001). They value the fact that anthropological research questions and problems emerge from the fieldwork process itself, rather than stemming from some *ex ante* abstract theorization (Luthans *et al.* 2013; Yanow 2013). And finally, they emphasize that these epistemological orientations are reflected in the ethnographic method, which without doubt remains the contribution of anthropology to management studies that comes most naturally to mind (van Maanen 2001).

The study of alternative organizations has already benefited from some of these anthropological insights. Indeed, there currently exist many important works that apply an anthropological perspective to alternative forms of organizing; examples would include the works of William Foote Whyte and Sharryn Kasmir on the Mondragon complex of Basque co-operatives or those of David Graeber and Marianne Maeckelbergh on anti-globalization social movement organizations. To my knowledge, however, there has not yet been any systematic reflection by the community of management scholars dedicated to the study of alternative organizations on the possible contributions of anthropology. The present chapter represents a modest attempt in this direction. The aim is to demonstrate that the advantages presented by anthropology for the study of organizations are all the more valid when applied more specifically to the study of alternative organizations.

In order to structure my argument, I will draw on the distinction proposed by Bate (1997), who successively envisages anthropology "as a paradigm", "as a method" and "as a way of writing". My primary focus in this chapter will be on the first two dimensions of anthropology, that is, the paradigmatic and methodological. It is of course difficult to strictly separate these two dimensions since the former is quite faithfully reflected in the latter, which explains why many management scholars regularly conflate anthropology with ethnography. The use of this distinction, such as will be apparent in the following pages, is therefore best understood as a practical and flexible analytical device rather than as a neat categorization. In line with this, I will first discuss the potential benefits of anthropology for the study of organizations when it is envisaged as a "frame of mind" or a "kind of intellectual effort" (Bate 1997, p. 1151). In a second stage, I will then discuss the potential benefits of anthropology for the study of alternative organizations when it is envisaged in terms of fieldwork activities. Finally, I will illustrate these sets of arguments by discussing model studies of alternative organizations and organizing by anthropologists, that is, Sharryn Kasmir's *The Myth of Mondragon* (1996) and, subsequently, David Graeber's *Direct Action* (2009).

Anthropology as a Paradigm: With "As Few Prejudices as Possible"

Openness to the strange and the surprising is, from a paradigmatic perspective, no doubt one of the features of anthropology that is of most value to the study of alternative organizations. Indeed, the spirit of the former directly echoes the intent of the latter, which lies in the discovery and analysis of unforeseen ways of doing things. James C. Scott once said: "An anthropologist goes in and tries to have as few prejudices as possible and be as open as possible to where the world leads you" (The New York Times 2012). Like many other human sciences, organization theory is indeed burdened by the overwhelming weight of its dominant theories. Because they tend to drastically narrow down the number of ways research problems can be framed, these theories appear in the end sorely ill-adapted to deal with difference and empirical idiosyncrasy. Patrick Reedy (2014) provides a compelling illustration of this problem in his critical reading of Ahrne and Brunsson's works on so-called "partial" organizations. As shown by Reedy, in their attempt at extending the scope of organization theory to novel ways of organizing, the two authors simply force the application of theories of conventional organizations into non-conventional organizations. In this way, managerial categories of analysis are applied to alternative organizations, which find themselves defined by what they are not, rather than by what they are. The paradoxical outcome of this is that:

> We have entities that manifestly organise ... but that we may not call organisations. They are then definitionally *impossible organisations* and relegated to the margins of organisational studies.
>
> *(Reedy 2014, p. 643)*

One of the precise strengths of the anthropological perspective is a candid re-examination of the most ingrained and taken-for-granted beliefs (Bate 1997; Linstead 1997). This is of course particularly suited to the study of alternative organizations, whose profession of faith can be summarized as follows:

> The key issue ... is an awareness of the consequences of particular forms, and to always understand that there are other ways of doing things. We have choices, individually and collectively, and we must never assume that "there is no alternative" because of certain immutable laws of markets or organizing.
>
> *(Parker et al. 2014, pp. 31–32)*

In order to further illustrate this spirit of openness and demonstrate the way that anthropology can contribute to a broader understanding of alternative organizing, I will first take as an example my own ethnographic study of Scopix. I will then elaborate on the potential benefits for organization studies of an anthropologically informed approach to the concept of democracy.

Scopix is a French worker co-operative of 25 worker-owners, which is active in sheet-metal work (see Jaumier 2015, 2017). A striking feature of Scopix is that its bosses have almost no power nor authority although the co-operative is seemingly organized in a classic hierarchical manner. The individuals who, in theory, are subordinate to the bosses spend a lot of their time overtly deprecating those they have democratically elected, with the results that these people cannot in the end behave as real bosses. In addition to being mean to their bosses, members of Scopix do many other things that they are normally supposed not to – they "misbehave", as Ackroyd and Thompson (1999) describe it. For instance, the members smoke on the shop-floor, have repeated coffee breaks, continue to chat whenever they are back at their work station, and reject from the outset any kind of managerial expertise. For most observers, the absence of power and authority in the hands of Scopix's "bosses" and the rather lax attitude of the members would be deemed highly problematic. At a similar time to my fieldwork, a team of researchers from another institution conducted a broader study of workers' co-operatives located in the same geographic area as Scopix (Charmettant *et al.* 2013). Their sample was composed of several tens of organizations, among which they had included Scopix. Unsurprisingly, these researchers characterized Scopix as a largely dysfunctional co-operative. In the multi-dimensional model that they eventually proposed, Scopix is portrayed as a typical instance of a co-operative that is unable to balance the socio-political and economic dimensions of co-operation; the former is said to have taken precedence over the latter, meaning that members behave rather too much as owners but not enough as workers.

In the frame of my fieldwork, I acted as a factory worker at Scopix for 12 months. And my first reflections on the co-operative were, in fact, not too different from those of the other researchers. Some of my early field notes testify to my initial negative impressions of the way in which Scopix was functioning. Having been trained as an engineer and then as a management scholar, I have always been concerned with efficiency. On this basis, many of the features of Scopix made little sense to me. To start with, it was difficult to understand that the members officially characterized their organization as a classic vertical hierarchy while it was actually horizontality, even reverse verticality – that is, the domination of the rank-and-file over their bosses – that was so obviously directing informal relations within the co-operative. Similarly, I could not understand why soldiering – that is, workers' purposive restriction of their output – operated to such an extent on the shop-floor, particularly as Scopix's by-laws guaranteed the equal sharing of economic benefits between members, rather than disproportionately accruing to managers and investors. In sum, the behaviours of the members seemed to me to be largely irrational from the outset. But the disqualification of natives' deeds on normative grounds is rarely satisfying from an anthropological perspective. The members were perhaps not supposed to act in this way, and yet they did. To follow Morey and Luthans (2013[1987], p. 87), the anthropological gaze implies a radical departure, "from looking at organizations in the normative sense of what they 'ought' to be like and how members 'ought' to behave, to a concentration of what they actually [do] and [are] like".

This is no easy departure. In the case of Scopix, a compounding issue was that members had integrated the idea that they were not offering the ideal image of co-operation that would normally be expected by an external observer. This was made especially visible during the first weeks of my fieldwork, when I would introduce myself to co-operators and explain my wish to gain a better understanding of their ways of organizing:

> I am meeting Roger, Scopix's delivery-driver, for the first time … When I tell him that I am here to study co-operatives, he says exactly the same as the other members, *i.e.* that Scopix is not a normal co-operative and that it is therefore probably not the right object for me to study.
>
> *(Field diary, 9 September 2013)*

Members' awareness that their practices were not legitimate required that even more attention be paid to possible gaps between their discourses and practices. In this context, adopting an anthropological frame of mind meant above all a refusal to reject as anomalies the seemingly incomprehensible or obviously deviant practices that were clear from my observations, and sometimes even required complicity on my part. Compelling myself to explain why the co-operators acted as they did led me eventually to rationalize their practices, but most often in a form that was totally foreign to managerial rationality. Over time, it became clear to me that Scopix's formally hierarchical organization, within which the bosses played a purely symbolic role, was instrumental in guaranteeing egalitarian functioning of the co-operative. Similarly, when associated with an activity that is as physically draining as sheet-metal work, the co-operators' frequent soldiering could be seen as a key way for them to reclaim control over their jobs and lives. And the rejection of any kind of managerial expertise could best be envisaged as a way for the sheet-metal workers to reaffirm the craft-like rather than industrial nature of their tasks and professional identities.

Comparing again my own interpretation of the functioning of Scopix with that of my fellow research colleagues does not lead to an opposition between quantitative and qualitative research or a shift from positivist to interpretative stances, as is often the case when anthropology is invoked (*e.g.* Chapman 2001). The other researchers' understanding of Scopix as a dysfunctional organization was also the outcome of a qualitative inquiry, most of the relevant data being gained from interviews. Rather, the difference lies in the degree of openness that is granted towards practices that so conspicuously depart from best management practices. It is about some willingness to distance oneself from management-centric perspectives on organizing and to remain open to alternative ways of conducting economic activities that are not clogged by dominant managerial imaginaries from the outset (Bate 1997; Reedy 2014). This approach echoes that advocated by Talal Asad (1986) who proposes that a "relativistic functionalism" be applied in the field, that is to say, careful attention be paid to the social context so allowing a coherence to be restored to the observed facts. In doing so, Asad fully takes on the risk of "excessive charity" vis-à-vis natives against which David Gellner had earlier warned. In the case of Scopix, this frame of mind allowed consideration of the shared practices of the members as logical, although they rested on premises that were at odds with those of classic for-profit organizations. It then became possible to view the co-operative no longer as an organization that lacked management or was poorly managed, but instead as an organization that was purposefully set against management. Obviously, this was not to exclude the possibility that members of Scopix might from time to time act inconsistently, but to assert that such inconsistencies – in order to be interpreted as inconsistencies – needed to be linked to a set of coherent practices to which the researcher's interpretative work would previously have provided the key. Such open-mindedness, or "excessive charity" to reverse Gellner's stigma, is certainly important for the identification of alternative ways of organizing, making sure that these are not overlooked or simply classified as abnormal or deviant as a result of an excessively management-centric research lens. But it is likely to be similarly important with respect to the invention of alternatives that do not yet exist, this being another objective claimed by the research community focused on alternative organizations. Here again, engaged scholars and practitioners alike need to put preconceived ideas aside and remain open to the unforeseen.

The second example I want to draw on in order to emphasize the relevance of anthropology as a paradigm for our understanding of alternative organizing relates to the concept of democracy. A concept such as this is of the utmost importance for participants in alternative organizations, most of whom endeavour to live according to forms of organizing that are as egalitarian and devoid of domination as possible. Unfortunately, organization studies are heavily biased towards an understanding of democracy that stems from a model of Western liberal democracy. Researchers of organizational democracy tend therefore to treat governance as their key concept, which implies a narrow focus on representative processes and institutions, leaving aside the existence of competing conceptualizations of democracy (Barros and Michaud in press). Faced with this problem, students of alternative organizations could again rely on anthropology in order to open up the field of democratic possibilities and to propose novel imaginaries of egalitarian social relationships. Indeed, anthropologists have long been aware that, as understood in the broad sense of ordinary people taking responsibility for their own affairs within the framework of a relatively open and egalitarian process of public discussion, democracy had been practised long before the term "democracy" was coined (Graeber 2013). During all periods and on all continents, various communities have indeed lived in a fairly egalitarian manner, allowing their members to have an equal say in decisions; the diverse experiences of these communities can represent a valuable resource for alternative organizations. Whilst not focussing specifically on organizational democracy, Paley's (2002) proposed move "toward an anthropology of democracy" helps provide a sense of what a more open conceptualization of democracy may mean for the study of alternative organizations. In speaking of "alternative democracies", Paley calls for a shift in focus from hegemonic definitions of liberal democracy towards local struggles over the contested meanings of democracy. This allows for a consideration of practices and discourses that diverge from the dominant normative conceptions of democracy. Paraphrasing Paley (2002, p. 471), I want eventually to suggest that eschewing "an a priori definition of democracy [may be] one of the central contributions of an anthropological approach" to the study of alternative organizations.

Anthropology as a Method: In Search of "Mundaneity and Everydayness"

The second dimension of anthropology with some relevance for the study of alternative organizations and organizing lies in its method, namely, ethnography. Again, the advantages of ethnography for the conduct of organizational analysis have frequently been stressed (*e.g.* Kunda 2013), and ethnographic methods have naturally found their place in the study of alternative organizations and organizing (see, *e.g.* Farias 2017; King and Land 2018; Ouahab 2018 for recent examples). Nonetheless, my aim in the following paragraphs is to make the advantages of anthropology as a method more explicit, further demonstrating that ethnography is all the more useful in the case of alternative organizations. To that purpose, I will reflect on three important features of an ethnographic approach – methodological holism, field-based problematization and field access.

A simple way to explain what is meant by methodological holism lies in saying that anthropologists tend to consider "everything is related to everything else" (Chapman 2001, p. 24) and consequently anything is potentially relevant to the research effort (see also Hirsch and Gellner 2001). While anthropology's rhetorical turn of the 80s has to some extent tempered this holistic orientation by insisting on the contested and fragmented nature of cultural elements, it nonetheless remains a distinctive feature of ethnography (Bate 1997; van Maanen 2001). This inclusive endeavour must be understood from at least two points of view: on the one side, attention is paid to the wider context in which organizing takes place and, on the other, it is paid to the mundane and a priori most insignificant aspects of organizing in an attempt to connect the micro and the macro (Linstead 1997). As mentioned earlier, putting organizations back into their broader context and environment became a point of attention for organizational anthropology as early as the Manchester shop-floor studies, which sought to understand how the British dominant capitalist regime and social relationships at the time were affecting the dynamics observed within the factory (Wright 1994). Later in my text, Sharryn Kasmir's works on Mondragon provide a good illustration of how illuminating this can prove in overcoming the analytic boundaries that are often artificially erected in order to separate an alternative organization from its environment. There is no further development of this dimension here since, in my view, it is already fairly well taken into account in the literature, as exemplified by Barin Cruz *et al.*'s (2017) recent call for a relational approach to the study of alternative organizations. Instead, I will concentrate here on the other end of the spectrum, that is, the concern of ethnography for everyday practices.

As a means of rendering organizational life in all its complexity and nuances, ethnography has for its main approach paid close attention to the actual practices of organizational members, such as is possible only by direct observation and, sometimes, participation (Linstead 1997; Luthans *et al.* 2013). "Mundaneity and everydayness" are, to quote Bate (1997, p. 1164), the order of the day. This same Bate reminds us that, thanks to its attention to actual practices and mundane facets of organizing, through Warner's participation in the Hawthorne studies, anthropology in fact invented the concept of the informal organization. Later representatives of the anthropological tradition of organizations studies, such as Donald Roy (1959) and Melville Dalton (2017[1959]), then proceeded to illustrate the centrality of informal practices for proper organizational analysis (Jordan and Caulkins 2013; Morey and Luthans 2013[1987]). Alternative organizations occupy an extreme position with respect to informality in that many of them – intentional communities and social movements in particular – do not even display any formal system. Consequently, limiting one's attention to the formal system would condemn these numerous alternative settings to the dark holes of organizational theory (Reedy 2014); the benefit of using ethnography in these cases is straightforward. But even where alternative organizations do display a somewhat developed formal system, it is important to rebalance the focus so as to facilitate understanding of the effects of informal relationships. The study of co-operatives is a good case in point with its overwhelmingly dominant focus on governance issues (*e.g.* Cheney *et al.* 2014; Joannidès and Cortese 2016). Ethnographic works such as those of Katherine Sobering (2019) about the Hotel Bauen, an *empresa recuperada*,[2] demonstrate that decision-making does not happen so much in general assemblies and board rooms, but rather through the tight networks of informal relationships associated with the daily activities of the co-operative (see also Jaumier 2017). In line with Paley's anthropology of democracy, these works invite a radical rethinking of the ways such organizations are empirically apprehended, so allowing the research gaze to shift away from governance bodies to the everyday practices of members, through which equality and co-operation are actually experienced.

The second benefit of anthropology as a method lies in its marked preference for field-based problematization. By this, I mean that, although they may have generic issues in mind, anthropologists do not usually enter the field with preconceived research problems and questions but instead let these emerge from the fieldwork (Luthans *et al.* 2013). As Bate (1997, p. 1152) notes, "the place to find the 'right question' is not in a textbook but out in the field, by following your nose". This implies that anthropologists treat their research object with some heightened reflexivity and keep their methods adaptive and multidisciplinary all along the way (Linstead 1997). According to Yanow (2013), this is where organizational ethnographers have generally been prone to depart from organizational anthropologists; she notices that, unlike the latter, the former have remained more literature- than site-driven. Differences in publishing processes probably account for a significant proportion of this gap, as management journals tend to put a strong emphasis on theoretical problems and contributions. There are however unfortunate consequences of this, especially for the study of alternative organizations. To start with, there exists the risk that what makes a given organization special will be missed. For instance, management studies often frame co-operatives as organizations dealing with two contradictory logics, one economic and the other socio-political, and so having to manage paradoxes (*e.g.* Audebrand 2017; Jaumier *et al.* 2017). While this may no doubt be an illuminating framework, it may also easily impose upon the co-operators under study representations that they do not actually share and distract researchers from the specifics that make the co-operative truly alternative and, hence, are particularly instructive. For instance, in the above-mentioned case of Scopix, it rapidly became apparent to me that to formulate members' experience in terms of their having to deal with contradictory logics and paradoxes would be to miss the point. Further, there exists the risk that a strong theoretical focus will come at the expense of a richness of description. Sadly, the resulting ethnographies are likely to be of far more interest to fellow researchers than to members of the organization being studied and people simply interested in becoming more knowledgeable about it. Given that alternative ways of organizing suffer primarily from ignorance and misinformation, surely this descriptive task is essential to their better appreciation. Unless there happens to be a relaxation of expectations on the part of the main journals within the field of management, the community studying alternative organizations will need to ensure that some room continues to be left for rich description, either through books or dedicated outlets. In this respect, anthropological insights can prove particularly useful as I will demonstrate when commenting on Graeber's *Direct Action*.

To conclude this section, I will discuss the question of access to the field. Another reason why ethnography is all the more suited to the study of alternative organizations is that access to them is generally easier than to classic for-profit organizations. The latter do not readily open their doors to ethnographers and, when they do, may impose demands that are not necessarily congruent with research plans (Fayard and van Maanen 2015). Working for the company under study, as suggested by Chapman (2001), may be a way to address these constraints but this, of course, is often far from being a feasible option. In contrast, alternative organizations often prove more accessible. There may be no restriction to their membership as is the case with consumer co-operatives and most social movement organizations. Also, because alternative organizations generally strive to operate in accordance with and sometimes even actively promote their values, often they may prove more hospitable and transparent than their for-profit counterparts (see, for instance Whyte and Whyte 1991[1988], p. 311; Farias 2019). Demonstrating a sympathy with the core values of an organization and privileging participation over mere observation often proves a sufficient *laissez-passer* for gaining access (Jaumier and Picard 2019). Taking advantage of this feature ought to result in a much greater engagement of students of alternative organizations with ethnography.

Some Inspiring Illustrations

In this section, I further illustrate the benefits of anthropology, both as a paradigm and a method, for the study of alternative organizations. To this end, I draw on two model studies by anthropologists, that of Sharryn Kasmir on Mondragon and David Graeber on anti-globalization social movement organizations.

Kasmir's *The Myth of Mondragon* (1996)

Mondragon is the name of a Basque town as well as that of a vast complex of co-operatives founded there in 1956. Because it was proposing an alternative model of regional development, Mondragon began to receive the attention of international researchers during the 70s. Among them was William Foote Whyte, whose contribution to the tradition of organizational anthropology was at the time already well recognized. Although he had not been directly trained as an anthropologist, Whyte's works were illustrative of his propensity for "full scale anthropological studies" (Morey and Luthans 2013[1987]). *Making Mondragon*, the book co-authored with Kathleen King Whyte, provides a thoroughly documented analysis of Mondragon's impressive development from the 50s to the 70s and the initial steps taken towards adapting to the economic crisis in the 80s (Whyte and Whyte 1991[1988]). In the review she wrote for the journal *Organization Studies*, Gillian Ursell was particularly enthusiastic at the time, praising the Whytes for opening a path towards no less than a new academic discipline, namely, a "social anthropology of advanced organizations" (Ursell 1989, p. 597). In hindsight, this seems a bit exaggerated. Certainly, Whyte and Whyte display an extensive knowledge of the Mondragon co-operative complex, their own inquiry benefiting from the fieldwork of a whole team of researchers from Cornell University. They also engage with the concept of culture so as to characterize their research object and strive to connect this to the Basque context. However, their vision of organizational culture too often remains narrowly limited to a corporate culture perspective, with the (seductive but probably misleading) idea that Mondragon's leaders were able to design the culture of the group and have members adhere to this. A related and disturbing feature of the Whytes' study is their quasi-exclusive reliance on the voice of Mondragon's founders and top managers. Lay workers' positions are seldom acknowledged, and only indirectly so when they are, *i.e.* through their representation on Mondragon's social councils.[3] A revealing sentence reads as follows:

> How did the members view the basic decisions and the process of arriving at them? We have no idea about rank-and-file members, but managers we talked to believed that …
>
> *(Whyte and Whyte 1991[1988], p. 148)*

Despite the limitations apparent in Whyte and Whyte's book, it seems that the promise identified by Ursell was soon to be realized. And interestingly, this happened thanks to a study that had chosen the very same research object as that of the Whytes. In *The Myth of Mondragon* (1996), Sharryn Kasmir indeed goes several steps further in her mobilizing of some of anthropology's defining features, namely, methodological holism, field-based problematization and attitude of openness.

Methodological holism is made salient by Kasmir's resituating of the historical, political, social and economic context in which the development of the Mondragon complex took place. Lengthy pages are dedicated to explaining the history of the

Basque region together with its complex system of political parties and unions, how this evolved under the Franco regime and subsequently, as well as specific details about the town of Mondragon in terms of class structure and working-class activism. Such in-depth analysis will later prove decisive for Kasmir to ground her appreciation of the significance of the Mondragon experience and that in hindsight appears only to be touched upon by Whyte and Whyte. These differing approaches probably explain why the context provides no more than a detached background in the Whytes' account (they claim in the end that the influence of the broader Basque context on the story of Mondragon is minimal), whereas it is firmly connected to Kasmir's analysis of the very same episodes. For instance, the 1974 strike at Ulgor – the first co-operative of the Mondragon complex to be established and the largest at the time – takes on a different flavour once its narration integrates the intricacies of the Basque political milieu and the distinct positions of the different actors towards Basque nationalism.

Another advantage of the ethnographic perspective adopted by Kasmir is her provision of greater space for research problems to emerge from the field. Kasmir's immersion in the life of the town and focus on lay workers' feelings and experiences allows, for instance, for workers' resentment towards perceived inequality within the co-operative and their limited sense of ownership to surface; this is in sharp contradiction to the consensual and overly positive accounts drawn from the interviews held by Whyte's team with the prominent figures of Mondragon. As a result of such distinct methodological choices, Kasmir's overall interpretation of the significance of the co-operative complex ultimately stands at odds with that of Whyte and Whyte. Mondragon is no longer envisaged as a pragmatic and apolitical project, but instead as one that espouses the conservative stance of Basque nationalism. In this frame, the ideology of co-operativism serves above all to facilitate the overcoming of class conflict through the taming of working-class activism. Ultimately, an important contribution made by the book to our understanding of alternative organizations lies in the idea that a healthy organizational democracy depends much more on the maintenance of a certain quality of lay activism, rather than on the theoretical rights bestowed upon workers by the co-operative model.

Kasmir's diverging interpretation of the significance of Mondragon illustrates the importance of anthropology as a method. As she aptly reflects, "it is this ethnographic vantage point that most distinguishes my work" (Kasmir 1996, p. 17). But anthropology as a paradigm, *i.e.* the adoption of an open attitude towards one's research object, also plays an important role here. As she explains in the introduction to her book, Kasmir's opinion of Mondragon before entering the field is a very positive one. This stems from the fact that the Basque complex is at the time widely celebrated within alternative scholarly circles as a consensual model of egalitarian organization. Unravelling the "myth" of Mondragon therefore implies for Kasmir a painful re-examination and renunciation of some of her most cherished beliefs and hopes. It is in such an undertaking that the attitude of openness deemed earlier the marker of anthropology as a paradigm is the most salient. Kasmir's severe diagnosis of course remains open to debate. Even if some of Mondragon's flaws as identified in Kasmir's study have since been rendered increasingly acute due to the subsequent accentuation by the Basque co-operative of its internationalization process, it is indeed still possible to see the glass as half-full rather than half-empty (*e.g.* Gibson-Graham 2003). But my point here concerned not so much the normative judgment that should eventually be expressed about Mondragon, rather the various advances permitted by Kasmir's approach, whereby anthropology is successfully embraced as both a method and a paradigm.

Graeber's *Direct Action* (2009)

The second model study that I highlight here is David Graeber's *Direct Action* (2009), his ethnography of anti-globalization movements. In this work, the reader is immersed in the daily activities of anti-globalization activism through Graeber's participation in the Direct Action Network (DAN), a federation of anti-capitalist and anarchist groups. While such a topic may at first glance appear quite remote from the concerns of management scholars, it rapidly becomes clear that it has implications of utmost relevance for organization studies. Indeed, Graeber (2009, pp. 211–212) insists that "the basic principles of anarchism – self-organization, voluntary association, mutual aid, the opposition to all forms of coercive authority – are essentially moral and organizational." This is demonstrated persuasively through a very detailed account of the various meetings, starting many months prior to the event, that ultimately led to the mass protest actions held in Quebec City during the 2001 Summit of the Americas. *Direct Action* is another great illustration of the methodological holism promoted by anthropology, but in a manner that is complementary to Kasmir's study of Mondragon. The strength of the latter stemmed from Kasmir's engagement with the macro, that is, with the environment from which the Mondragon experience derived its meaning. In contrast, the distinctiveness of Graeber's effort lies on the side of the micro. In his view, anthropology as a method is about "teas[ing] out the implicit logic in a way of life, along with its related myths and rituals, to grasp the sense of a set of practices" (Graeber 2009, p. 222). This programmatic vision comes to the fore when showing, for instance, how anarchist egalitarian attitudes come to nourish and be nourished by activists' preference for decision-making processes based on consensus rather than on majority voting. Thanks to some meticulous yet vivid reconstituting of exchanges between activists, as well as a training session aimed at introducing consensus-based democracy to aspiring activists, the reader gains some deep insight into how anarchists constantly reflect upon and refine their decision-making processes such that they better embody their egalitarian stance, including instances when faced with ingrained forms of racism and homophobia. Graeber's vision of ethnography is also well illustrated through the ample descriptions he provides of five exemplar styles of action undertaken by activists – protest marches and rallies, picket line, street party, civil disobedience and black bloc action. Again, the entanglement of activists' practices with anarchist logics becomes clear, illuminating for example how the role of violence can be conceived within the framework of the movement.

In both of these examples, whether concerning decision-making processes or exemplar styles of action, Graeber maintains for his main compass the richness of the description, which brings us to another strength of Graeber's anthropological approach. As I noted earlier, a feature of anthropology as a method lies in its site-rather than theory-driven nature. In *Direct Action*, Graeber is not content with solely exemplifying this feature but feels also the urge to make it a manifesto. From the outset of the book, he insists that his contribution will lie in the detailed description of activists' way of life and practices (Graeber 2009, pp. vii–viii). If theory does at times feature within the book, this is not to espouse the form of theory-building, but instead is simply recourse to existing theory where this can act as aid to reinforce the narrative:

> The purpose of ethnography is essentially descriptive. A good description, certainly, requires appeal to theory, but in ethnography, theory is properly deployed in the service of description rather than the other way around.
>
> *(Graeber 2009, p. 509)*

This statement of faith makes all the more sense when it comes to the study of anarchist-based anti-globalization movements. Indeed, most anarchists would contend that anarchism is better understood as an ethical practice rather than a set of theories, which makes ethnography a particularly suitable candidate for studying anarchism. But Graeber then goes one step even further when working through his argument, proceeding to supplement the epistemological justification with a moral one:

> If the aim of an ethnographic description is to try to give the reader the means to imaginatively pass inside a moral and social universe, then it seems exploitative, insulting almost, to suggest that other people live their lives or pursue their projects in order to allow some scholar to score a point in some arcane theoretical debate.
>
> *(Graeber 2009, p. 509)*

Even if one does not adhere to Graeber's normative stance, a possible lesson to be drawn for the study of alternative organizations is the recognition that its current lack of theoretical foundations is probably more of an asset than a problem in need of a solution (see also Parker *et al.* 2014). Indeed, limited extant knowledge about alternative forms of organizing is likely to lead to the acknowledgement that first-hand description should be the priority and that theory-driven problems are at risk of remaining totally moot.

Finally, *Direct Action* also illustrates some benefits of anthropology as a paradigm. An important feature of the book is that it is as much that of an activist as that of a scholar. Graeber's perspective is that of an insider who fully takes on his subjectivity, and his study can thus be considered a reflection of anthropology's growing propensity for the emic perspective. Accordingly, the spirit of open-mindedness, which we have defined earlier as the main characteristic of anthropology as a paradigm, falls above all to the reader in the case of *Direct Action*, rather than to the ethnographer. Graeber's accounts of anarchist practices are so much at odds with those conveyed by the mainstream media (which are usually content with relaying the statements of state officials) that they indeed require his audience to put aside their most ingrained beliefs about activism. This is especially the case with black bloc action, where Graeber's first-hand experience helps one understand that the term "violence" applies more aptly in the end to the behaviour of police forces than to that of the activists.

Conclusion

The works of Kasmir and Graeber provide compelling illustrations of how anthropology, as both a paradigm and a method, can serve the study of alternative organizations. To conclude, I will refer to two additional areas that I anticipate may also provide a contribution. The first of these areas is that of writing and representation. Besides anthropology "as a paradigm" and anthropology "as a method", Bate (1997) in fact has a third category in his framework (not touched upon in this chapter) – that of anthropology "as a way of writing". Anthropology undertook a rhetorical turn in the 80s, reflecting upon the centrality of texts for the discipline and the claims of such texts to be truthful representations (Clifford and Marcus 1986). Although these reflections have only sporadically made their way into management literature, scholars of alternative organizations may for instance draw on them in order to find ways to better include the voices of organizational members in their texts, an endeavour that is generally referred to by the term "polyvocality". Scholars may also draw inspiration from such reflections, allowing them to produce narratives that better reflect the inductive and site-driven nature of their inquiries.

The second of these areas would derive from harnessing more of the concepts and theories offered by anthropology. I noted at the beginning of this chapter the importance of critical management studies for research on alternative organizations. The import of theories drawn from other disciplines has traditionally been one of the trademarks of critical management studies. However, anthropology has remained a rather marginal provider in comparison with, say, philosophy and sociology. The study of alternative organizations could be the right place to begin filling this gap since "anthropologists have a long history of thinking about individuals and social relationships in ways that critique notions of economic rationality and profit maximization" (Kasmir 2012, p. 59). Economic anthropology is indeed replete with examples which show how alternative forms of economic organization may look. The works of Marshall Sahlins and like-minded scholars – *i.e.* those who pertain to the so-called "substantivist" school of economic anthropology – may in some cases facilitate the interpretation of existing alternatives and the devising of new ones. Also, theories on gift are frequently evoked in studies of co-operation and of the sharing economy without such evocations being more than an indication that the authors are distancing themselves from the homo economicus fiction. Teasing out the actual implications of Marcel Mauss' insights and ensuing debates on the meaning of gift and counter-gift for such alternative forms of organizing remains a task largely yet to be done (Caillé 2019). Alternative leadership is another domain that could benefit from anthropological insights, as I have attempted to demonstrate by applying Pierre Clastres' conceptualization of powerless chiefs to the case of a worker co-operative (Jaumier 2017). I anticipate that further engagement with the anthropological literature would lead to the identification of many more opportunities to demonstrate that the study of alternative organizations is in sore need of anthropology.

Acknowledgements

I am very thankful to Raza Mir, Hélène Picard and Genevieve Shanahan for their comments on earlier versions of this text. The responsibility for all remaining errors is of course mine.

Notes

1 Critical management studies (CMS) draw amongst other things on critical theory, post-structuralism and feminism in order to deconstruct dominant managerial narratives. *Organization* is the journal that best exemplifies the range of theories and topics covered by this research community.
2 The name given to companies that were occupied and then taken over by their employees following the Argentinian crisis of 2001–2.
3 Social councils are composed of elected members who ensure representation of lay workers vis-à-vis the management of a co-operative.

References

Ackroyd, S., and Thompson, P., 1999. *Organizational misbehaviour*. London and Thousand Oaks: Sage Publications.
Acquier, A., Daudigeos, T., and Pinkse, J., 2017. Promises and paradoxes of the sharing economy. An organizing framework. *Technological Forecasting and Social Change*, 125, 1–10.
Asad, T., 1986. The concept of cultural translation in British social anthropology. *In*: J. Clifford and G.E. Marcus, eds. *Writing culture. The poetics and politics of ethnography*. Berkeley: University of California Press, 141–164.
Audebrand, L.K., 2017. Expanding the scope of paradox scholarship on social enterprise. The case for (re)introducing worker cooperatives. *M@n@gement*, 20 (4), 368–393.
Barin Cruz, L., Aquino Alves, M., and Delbridge, R., 2017. Next steps in organizing alternatives to capitalism. Toward a relational research agenda. *M@n@gement*, 20 (4), 322–335.
Barros, M., and Michaud, V., in press. Worlds, words, and spaces of resistance. Democracy and social media in consumer co-ops. *Organization*.
Bate, S.P., 1997. Whatever happened to organizational anthropology? A review of the field of organizational ethnography and anthropological studies. *Human Relations*, 50 (9), 1147–1175.
Caillé, A., 2019. *Extensions du domaine du don. Demander, donner, recevoir, rendre*. Arles: Actes sud.
Chapman, M., 2001. Social anthropology and business studies. Some considerations of method. *In*: D.N. Gellner and E. Hirsch, eds. *Inside organizations. Anthropologists at work*. Oxford: Berg, 19–33.

Charmettant, H., Juban, J.-Y., Magne, N., Renou, Y., and Vallet, G., 2013. *La qualité des relations sociales au sein des SCOP. Premiers enseignements d'une enquête en Rhône-Alpes.* Grenoble: Université Pierre-Mendès-France.

Cheney, G., Santa Cruz, I., Peredo, A.M., and Nazareno, E., 2014. Worker cooperatives as an organizational alternative: Challenges, achievements and promise in business governance and ownership. *Organization*, 21 (5), 591–603.

Clifford, J., and Marcus, G.E., eds., 1986. *Writing culture. The poetics and politics of ethnography.* Berkeley: University of California Press.

Czarniawska, B., 2012. Organization theory meets anthropology. A story of an encounter. *Journal of Business Anthropology*, 1 (1), 118–140.

Dalton, M., 2017[1959]. *Men who manage. Fusions of feeling and theory in administration.* Abingdon: Routledge.

Farias, C., 2017. That's what friends are for. Hospitality and affective bonds fostering collective empowerment in an intentional community. *Organization Studies*, 38 (5), 577–595.

Farias, C., 2019. The ethnographer as an intruder. Negotiating the boundaries of intimacy in an intentional community. *M@n@gement*, 22 (1), 115–118.

Fayard, A.-L., and van Maanen, J., 2015. Making culture visible: Reflections on corporate ethnography. *Journal of Organizational Ethnography*, 4 (1), 4–27.

Gibson-Graham, J.K., 1996. *The end of capitalism (as we knew it). A feminist critique of political economy.* 1st ed. Minneapolis and London: University of Minnesota Press.

Gibson-Graham, J.K., 2003. Enabling ethical economies: Cooperativism and class. *Critical Sociology*, 29 (2), 123–161.

Graeber, D., 2009. *Direct action. An ethnography.* Oakland and Edinburgh: AK Press.

Graeber, D., 2013. *The democracy project. A history, a crisis, a movement.* New York: Spiegel & Grau.

Hirsch, E., and Gellner, D.N., 2001. Introduction. Ethnography of organizations and organizations of ethnography. *In*: D.N. Gellner and E. Hirsch, eds. *Inside organizations. Anthropologists at work.* Oxford: Berg, 1–15.

Jaumier, S., 2015. *Pouvoir, contrôle et résistance dans les coopératives de salariés. Une ethnographie d'une coopérative ouvrière.* Paris: Paris IX.

Jaumier, S., 2017. Preventing chiefs from being chiefs: An ethnography of a co-operative sheet-metal factory. *Organization*, 24 (2), 218–239.

Jaumier, S., Daudigeos, T., and Joannidès de Lautour, V., 2017. Co-operatives, compromises and critiques: What do French co-operators tell us about individual responses to pluralism? *In*: C. Cloutier, J.-P. Gond and B. Leca, eds. *Justification, evaluation and critique in the study of organizations. Contributions from French pragmatist sociology.* Bingley: Emerald Group Publishing, 73–106.

Jaumier, S., and Picard, H., 2019. In the field. Conditions, value(s) and stakes of empirical inquiry in critical research. *M@n@gement*, 22 (1), 92–97.

Joannidès, V., and Cortese, C., 2016. Cooperatives: Governance and accountability systems for a better world? *Journal of Accounting & Organizational Change*, 12 (1), 1–7.

Jordan, A.T., and Caulkins, D.D., 2013. Expanding the field of organizational anthropology for the twenty-first century. *In*: D.D. Caulkins and A.T. Jordan, eds. *A companion to organizational anthropology.* Chicester: Wiley-Blackwell, 1–23.

Kasmir, S., 1996. *The myth of Mondragón. Cooperatives, politics, and working-class life in a Basque town.* Albany: State University of New York Press.

Kasmir, S., 2012. Alternatives to capitalism and working-class struggle. A comment on Alice Bryer's "the politics of the social economy". *Dialectical Anthropology*, 36 (1–2), 59–61.

King, D., and Land, C., 2018. The democratic rejection of democracy. Performative failure and the limits of critical performativity in an organizational change project. *Human Relations*, 71 (11), 1535–1557.

Kunda, G., 2013. Reflections on becoming an ethnographer. *Journal of Organizational Ethnography*, 2 (1), 4–22.

Latour, B., 2018. *Down to earth. Politics in the new climatic regime.* Cambridge UK, Medford MA: Polity Press.

Linstead, S., 1997. The social anthropology of management. *British Journal of Management*, 8 (1), 85–98.

Luthans, F., Milosevic, I., Bechky, B.A., Schein, E.H., Wright, S., van Maanen, J., and Greenwood, D.J., 2013. Reclaiming "Anthropology. The forgotten behavioral science in management history" – Commentaries. *Journal of Organizational Ethnography*, 2 (1), 92–116.

Morey, N.C., and Luthans, F., 2013[1987]. Anthropology. The forgotten behavioral science in management history. *Journal of Organizational Ethnography*, 2 (1), 82–91.

Ouahab, A., 2018. *Shopping consent. Controlling the labour process in a new wave food coop.* Tallin: 34th EGOS Colloquium.

Paley, J., 2002. Toward an anthropology of democracy. *Annual Review of Anthropology*, 31 (1), 469–496.

Parker, M., Cheney, G., Fournier, V., and Land, C., eds., 2014. *The Routledge companion to alternative organization.* Oxon and New York: Routledge.

Pearce, J.M., 2014. Free and open source appropriate technology. *In*: M. Parker, Cheney, G., Fournier, V., and Land, C.., ed. *The Routledge companion to alternative organization.* Oxon and New York: Routledge, 308–328.

Reedy, P., 2014. Impossible organisations: Anarchism and organisational praxis. *ephemera*, 14 (4), 639–658.

Roy, D.F., 1959. "Banana time". Job satisfaction and informal interaction. *Human Organization*, 18 (4), 158–168.

Smircich, L., 1983. Concepts of culture and organizational analysis. *Administrative Science Quarterly*, 28 (3), 339–358.

Sobering, K., 2019. Watercooler democracy. Rumors and transparency in a cooperative workplace. *Work and Occupations*, 46 (4), 411–440.

Sutherland, N., Land, C., and Bohm, S., 2014. Anti-leaders(hip) in social movement organizations: The case of autonomous grassroots groups. *Organization*, 21 (6), 759–781.

The New York Times, 2012. *Professor who learns from peasants* [online]. Available from: www.nytimes.com/2012/12/05/books/james-c-scott-farmer-and-scholar-of-anarchism.html.

Ursell, G.D., 1989. Book reviews: William Foote Whyte and Kathleen King Whyte: Making Mondragon: The growth and dynamics of the worker co-operative complex. *Organization Studies*, 10 (4), 594–597.

van Maanen, J., 2001. Afterword. Natives 'R' us: Some notes on the ethnography of organizations. *In*: D.N. Gellner and E. Hirsch, eds. *Inside organizations. Anthropologists at work.* Oxford: Berg, 233–261.

Vidaillet, B., and Bousalham, Y., 2020. Coworking spaces as places where economic diversity can be articulated. Towards a theory of syntopia. *Organization*, 27 (1), 60–87.

Whyte, W.F., and Whyte, K.K., 1991[1988]. *Making Mondragon. The growth and dynamics of the worker cooperative complex.* 2nd ed. Ithaca and London: ILR Press.

Wright, S., ed., 1994. *Anthropology of organizations.* London: Routledge.

Yanow, D., 2013. Editorial. On disciplinary histories – Borrowing anthropology into organisational studies? *Journal of Organizational Ethnography*, 2 (1).

23

CRISIS ETHNOGRAPHY

Emotions and Identity in Fieldwork during the Tunisian Revolution

Héla Yousfi and Chahrazad Abdallah

This chapter is an exploration of the methodological and theoretical challenges facing ethnographers when they study social movements in a crisis context. In this chapter, we aim to open up the reflection on these questions by pointing at two main themes that shaped and transformed our thinking on the "doing" of ethnography in a context of crisis: the role of individual and collective emotions in shaping the process of research and the unexpected identity work that accompanies it. The purpose here is to explore the impact of these emotions both on conducting the field study and on knowledge production. The chapter is less "ethnographic" than reflexive in the sense that we use our ethnographic data as a starting point to engage in a reflection around these various methodological and theoretical challenges that emerged from the study of a social movement in a time of generalized upheaval. We will then focus on what is the anthropologist/ethnographer to do – in a continuing dialectic between the personal, the social and the political – if he/she is to juggle emotions, personal history and political commitment with the need to reflect on the institutional, the social and the historical in the making?

The subject of the intricate relationship between emotions and methods is not new in anthropology (Lutz & White, 1986; Harris, 1997; Boellstorff & Lindquist, 2004; Beatty, 2005; Hage, 2009; Beatty, 2010; Henry, 2012). The role and the place of emotions in the ethnographic research process both in the field and off it was discussed extensively in a variety of disciplines such as sociology (Watts, 2008; Stodulka, 2015), psychology (Zarowsky, 2004), education (Zembylas, 2005), nursing (Allan, 2006), queer studies (Rooke, 2010) and law (Pasquetti, 2013). In organization studies however, this topic needs to be further developed despite the few papers that have directly addressed it (Down et al., 2006; Kisfalvi, 2006; Kenny, 2008; Watson, 2011; Koning & Ooi, 2013; Warden, 2013; Gilmore & Kenny, 2015). Our aim with this chapter is to further the exploration around the role of emotions in fieldwork, headwork, and textwork (Van Maanen, 2011) and to outline the ways in which emotions can act as an enabler of insights and a vector of the researcher's identity work in crisis contexts. Our purpose is to show that in those highly unsettling contexts specifically, emotions actually play a critical role in enabling insights during fieldwork and fuelling reflexive movements during and after ethnographic work.

In this chapter, we build upon our reflexion on doing ethnographic work in crisis contexts by addressing the subject of emotions from two different methodological angles: first as a *resource*, and second, as a critical *tool* in identity work for the ethnographer. By addressing the role of emotions in the conduct of ethnography in crisis contexts, we wish to contribute to both the ongoing conversation on emotions in organizational ethnography (Warden, 2013; Gilmore & Kenny, 2015) and the burgeoning literature on doing ethnography in "extreme" contexts (Rouleau et al., 2014; Hällgren et al., 2018).

Our research project started broadly as an ethnographic exploration of social movements in action. In light of recent events such as the global financial crisis or what was termed the "Arab Spring", social movement theory is as relevant as ever to understand the complexity of our times. Social movement theory has gained an increasing interest from organization scholars in recent years (see, for example, *Administrative Science Quarterly*'s Special Issue, 2008; Hensmans, 2003; Zald, 2017). From a methodological point of view, calls were made for an expansion of levels of analysis and for the reliance on more ethnographic data (Davis et al., 2008). The concepts of multi-sited ethnography (Marcus, 1995) and "mobile ethnology" (Czarniawska, 2004) represent new fruitful developments to capture the complexities of the crossovers between organizations and social movements. Our work tries therefore to respond to these calls by exploring how social movements as multi-dimensional, multi-sited phenomena, take shape and unfold during times of crisis. As we got involved more deeply with the field, new and unsuspected emotional entanglements emerged and called for our attention. We decided to focus more specifically on better understanding these emotions and their role in our ethnographic research process.

The fieldwork for this research took place in Tunisia. In this research, we explore the challenges of studying social movements ethnographically by studying the role of UGTT *Union Générale Tunisienne du Travail* (Tunisian General Labour Union) – the most important trade union in the country – during the Tunisian revolutionary process in the wake of the 2010–2011 popular uprisings that led to the overthrow of the Ben Ali Regime and ultimately sparked the "Arab Spring" in the region.

In what follows, we start by giving a brief overview of our broad research context, which is characterized by an acute national crisis context in which Tunisia experienced the end of a political regime and the fall of its former establishment. We continue with a description of the organizational context of our study by describing the ethnographic setting at the heart of our research (UGTT) and the events themselves. We follow by addressing the two dimensions that emerged from our critical reflection on the role of emotions in our research process and we conclude by a call for a closer examination and more engaged debate on the importance of ethnography in the study of political crises.

Our Research Context: Tunisia in Times of Crisis

The end of the Ben Ali regime in Tunisia officially dates back to 14 January 2011. On that day, Ben Ali and members of his close family fled the country in a privately hired plane from which the rage and indignation of the street – on general strike – could certainly be heard after many days of unprecedented protests and violent police repression in every corner of the country. A strong popular upheaval under the banner of "Justice, Freedom and National Dignity" built strength and swept over the most important cities in the days following the immolation of a street vendor, Mohamed Bouazizi, on 17 December 2010. Social demands for decent jobs and better life conditions for a population subjected to increasing inequalities and unrestrained political and financial greed from a disconnected elite, dated back to years before that particular event but a well-crafted – mainly Western – media-driven storytelling exercise used that spectacular mediatized image of Bouazizi to build the legend of a "Facebook revolution".

Our initial research project aimed to shed light more generally on the transformations of the Tunisian political sphere during an acute political national crisis. We decided to examine the complex role played by an organization, UGTT, as a space for collective organized action and we chose to do so through a three-year personal ethnographic journey that led us to reflect more specifically on the challenges we were faced with while doing the ethnographic work itself. Whilst UGTT was for us not only an organization but also a social movement in and of itself, it was also as an ethnographic field the most relevant in developing a reflection on the ways in which we could capture the multi-layered reality behind the events that unfolded during that time in Tunisia.

Our understanding of a context in crisis is processual. Unlike approaches that study revolutionary episodes only as moments of rupture, focusing solely on the event or episode of mobilization, our aim was to uncover and understand the dynamic of a union organization as an organized space of collective action and as a physical and symbolic shelter for social and political struggles during the revolutionary moment as well as its interaction with other variously structured networks. We saw it as the site of an unfolding revolutionary process that we could only understand by alternating between a total immersion in it for short periods of time and removal from it for longer reflexive periods. For us, ethnography was particularly relevant to avoid any teleological pitfalls that tend to attribute a "beginning", "middle" and "end" to a revolutionary process. We sought to render the fluidity and the contradictions that shape a crisis episode characterized by uncertainty and a continuous re-evaluation of strategies against a particular order of constraints and a rapidly evolving context (Dobry, 1986). It was a need for iterative sense-making and sense-giving that drove our initial interactions with the field but it was soon our multiple emerging interrogations that inhabited our research "space" and that made us very aware of the ambiguities of our situation within it.

In this chapter, we choose to explore the entanglements of emotional, personal and political elements in that particular crisis context through the analysis of three specific episodes (December 2010, February 2011 and December 2011) in which we study the interactions within UGTT as well as its interactions with multiple sets of actors (government, political parties, digital activists, etc.) at the time. To do so, we rely on a set of ethnographic data that range from personal observations (personal notes, field diaries and recordings) to official documentation, press releases, memos, and a total of 50 semi-structured interviews with a wide range of actors (inside and outside UGTT). The ethnographic process was challenging and raised a number of issues for us and, at times, even made us question its whole purpose. The nature of the context, the role of the ethnographer and her status, the nature of the emotions involved in the study of an unfolding life-altering event, were all at the heart of our interrogations. How can an ethnographic approach be true to the events it is purposed to describe in the context of a popular upheaval when senses are heightened and emotional reactions exacerbated? How can ethnographic work render the complexity of a transformational event on the personal as well as the political and social levels? What can the ethnographer do with the emotional entanglements in which she is unexpectedly and unavoidably caught?

UGTT: A Space for Collective Organized Action

Union Générale Tunisienne du Travail (henceforth, UGTT) is the central ethnographic setting of our study. This organization has historically been an area of convergence for militant trade unionism and the struggle against autocratic regimes in Tunisia. UGTT has historically played an important political role in various popular revolts in the country and has been crucial to the unfolding of what is now known as the "Tunisian revolution" (Yousfi, 2017). UGTT is Tunisia's largest (with 517,000 members) and for many years its only union organization. Centred on the public sector, this union is made up of 24 regional unions, 19 sector-based unions and 21 grass roots unions. It brings together a wide range of political persuasions and has members in every part of the country and from many different social groups, including factory workers, civil servants and doctors.

More than a labour union, UGTT is a political organization in which social claims have historically been closely linked to political and national claims (Hamzaoui, 1999). Founded in 1946 by Farhat Hached, UGTT was born from the meeting of social struggles with the national liberation movement. Following its establishment, it served as a cornerstone of the Tunisian national liberation movement during French colonization, and has since played a central role in Tunisian political life. Over the years, UGTT leaders joined the nationalist movement headed by Habib Bourguiba, and also actively participated in the struggle for independence. Once in power, Bourguiba attempted to mobilize UGTT's prestige to establish his own domination, leading to a complex relationship between UGTT and the Tunisian ruling party. However, unlike other Arab unions which were entirely integrated into the machinery of state authority, UGTT was more complex: it had always contained a wing represented by the union bureaucracy that favoured submission to the government and even the near-integration into the state machinery but it was also made up of left-wing political movements and Arab nationalist groups – completely stripped of political expression – which sought to resist the regime and which subsequently took the upper hand when the crisis struck in 2010, bolstered by their control over certain federations in education, the postal service and telecommunications, as well as some local and regional unions.

This dual configuration enabled UGTT to provide structural and political support to social movements in spite of the union bureaucracy's close relationship with the regime. UGTT's centralized structure and its organizational culture combining dependence and autonomy saved the union sections from being co-opted by the regime during the various crises within the organization. Thus and despite a certain degree of ambivalence that UGTT has maintained with the single ruling party over the years, the vast majority of Tunisian social movements have always been structurally and politically supported by UGTT.

Yet, to understand the functioning of UGTT, its complex history must lead us to break away from the binary representations that positions this organization either as "a powerful arm of the ruling regime" or a as a simple labour union. UGTT is neither one nor the other. Rather, it is a political organization that has always played an important political role, sometimes as a partner of the political regime charged with negotiating that regime's economic and social policy with workers, and at other times as a countervailing force, resisting the regime's authoritarian rule.

One of the characteristics of the Tunisian revolution is that the events that have led to the fall of the Ben Ali regime, in all Tunisian cities, have originated from the offices of UGTT. Involved from the start of the uprisings of Sidi Bouzid on 17 December 2010, UGTT organized rallies, marches and general strikes in various regions. Labour union leaders, mobilized since the beginning of the uprisings in December 2010, gave protesters open access to the Union offices and helped them carry their voice to the international media. The pressure they exercised led the executive board of the Union to call for a national strike on 14 January 2011 leading to Ben Ali's departure. It is worth noting that UGTT is the only "intermediate" structure in the country and despite several shortcomings, such as the centralization of decision-making power or the low representation of women in some sectors or regions, UGTT played a decisive role in the protests that have led to the regime change and the subsequent election of the National Constituent Assembly in early 2011.

Our aim in this chapter is to address the destabilizing emotional reactions that emerged during our fieldwork within and around UGTT as our critical ethnographic focal entity and to make sense of their multiple challenges for our research. We build our reflection around the two main methodological takeaways that we identified during and after the completion of the fieldwork. First, we seek to explore the influence of the embodied, emotional, sensory dimensions of fieldwork and the importance of emotions as a resource for the ethnographer when doing ethnographic work. Then, we reflect on the role of emotions as tools of identity work for the ethnographer by discussing the impact of a transformational event (both on the macro and micro levels) on the personal as well as the political and social levels for the researcher.

Emotions as a Resource for Ethnographic Research in a Crisis Context

The critical issue of reflexivity in research emerged in the 1980s and 1990s and was soon strongly encouraged by critical, feminist, and postcolonial approaches (Kanafani & Sawaf, 2017; Mir & Jain, 2018). The researcher's positioning, in particular his/her gender and cultural origin, is increasingly considered critical for analysing and theorizing social experience. The reflexive turn is an invitation for researchers to acknowledge the various social filters that shape both their perception of the world and themselves and the ways others perceive them. Methodological reflexivity is thus a fundamental condition to build an understanding that questions the dominant regimes of knowledge, which reproduce patriarchal and imperialist structures that influence representations of contemporary social realities (Behar & Gordon, 1995). Paradoxically, proponents of reflexivity, despite their insistence on the criticality of the researcher's position, point of view, and identity have often over-sought the embodied, emotional, sensory dimensions of fieldwork that do contribute to a different type of knowledge creation (Davies & Spencer, 2010; De Rond, 2012; Kanafani & Sawaf, 2017). Reflexivity remained somewhat removed from the materiality of senses in methodological accounts.

Social movements and more particularly, revolutionary ones are crisis contexts *par excellence*. The "critical" role of context in this ethnography was twofold: it was a "crisis" context since fieldwork entailed the participation in a series of protests, sit-ins and political meetings, with interviews often held in particular circumstances, which meant that they were frequently interrupted, delayed, and very unpredictable; but it was also a "crisis" due to the nature of the emotions that were at play during fieldwork. Anger, euphoria, disappointment, disillusionment were often felt; difficult interviews with former detainees were very intense but cathartic as they "liberated" unionists from their formatted speech patterns and made them more spontaneous. These "extreme" emotional situations were very frequent during fieldwork and made this ethnography resemble an emotional battlefield. The challenge of conveying this emotional landscape through "conventional" ethnographic work was therefore evident. How were we to do justice to the context if not by choosing to be deeply reflexive about it and accept our own emotional shortcomings in trying to convey it? How could we vividly convey the profound emotional struggles that were at play?

Emotions in Fieldwork

First, it is important to note that most of our ethnographic work and interviews were done at various times during 2011 and 2012 in particularly "passionate" contexts, such as the debates on the legitimacy of the transition-period leadership or the emergence of struggles with the newly established political power. Interview guides were rarely relevant in these situations and interviewees often dismissed them and re-oriented discussions around themes that seemed to have priority for them on that specific day or period. The early days of 2011 were a time when the act of talking was suddenly freed and people found it difficult to participate in conversations that were based on a two-way exchange. The sudden freedom of speech made talking more necessary and not easily interruptible particularly in a charged emotional context. Some interviews resembled monologues rather than traditional discussions. The flow of speech was sometimes unstoppable and we did not try to stop it.

Yet, the emotions expressed by respondents were generative of some discomfort for us: they were contagious and insidious and they got hold of the situation and trapped us, which led us sometimes to losing the control of the ethnographic interview or to "lose it" in the field. However, these were also critical moments of embodied reflection for us that may have been difficult to achieve alternatively and which led to critical insights on the role of unionists in the ongoing revolutionary process. Many of the unexpected challenges raised in this chapter were born of the emotional context at the time of the interviews and during fieldwork more generally. Strong emotions like pain, fear, elation or anger led to the uncovering of a wide range of issues as we attempt to show in what follows.

Pain: Suffering under the Ben Ali Regime

Adel, a unionist primary school teacher, one of the leaders of the 2008 revolt, was arrested and tortured in Redeyef. The 2008 revolt in the mining area of Redeyef, a part of Gafsa Governorate, was the largest social movement in Tunisia since the "bread riots" of January 1984 and the first to deal a significant blow to the Ben Ali regime. When asked about the way he would evaluate the role played by UGTT during the revolutionary episodes, Adel replied:

> First of all, I must tell you how I was arrested and tortured in 2008 …
> I was arrested on April 7th, I was with Adnene Hajji (leader of the movement), dozens of cops and riot police came to take us, they surrounded us and started to hit us, they put handcuffs on us and as they were taking us away to the police station, they continued to hit us, to insult us. It was humiliating, it was terrible … still, it's nothing compared to what I have endured in prison …

He stopped, tears filled his eyes, and silence fell on us.[1] After a long pause, he went on, reading the names of those who were tortured, wounded or killed by police bullets and concluded:

> So you see, Redeyef in 2008 is the heart, the core of the revolution, we must not forget it.

Samir, a unionist doctor described his pain with these words:

> Ben Ali did not let us breathe, I was fired from my job, I was imprisoned but what hurt me the most is knowing that my family members were going to suffer violence because of my political commitment.

Pain as an emotion is difficult to verbalize but it is phenomenologically transmittable to another person from different cues of the body such as tears, a change in voice level or a palpable tension through the body. Pain, when it comes from the deep recesses of the soul is an all-encompassing phenomenon; it not only inhabits the person who feels it but swallows the whole world around him/her. The pain and suffering endured by unionists, who were political prisoners at the time, is still raw and inscribed in their bodies. It is a physical emotion that annihilates any attempt at rationalization while it is experienced and in this case, transmitted. What are we as researchers to do with this type of pain? How can we possibly imagine the horror that was experienced? How can we process it let alone convey it?

One of the biggest challenges for ethnographers faced with these situations is to accept the overwhelming nature of the emotion and to embrace it as part of an embodied connection to fieldwork. The incommensurability of the experience of torture is to be recognized and acknowledged by the ethnographer as an insurmountable limit to the sense that can be built from his/her implication in that intense emotional experience. That moment constitutes a critical research ambivalence: it is "shared" by the interviewee/participant and experienced in the researcher's body but it is by definition, un-sharable.

The question therefore is less what to make of the experience but how to welcome it as part of an inherent interpretive process in our research. Experiencing the emotional turmoil of an intense ethnographic "moment" forces researchers to face an unsolvable dilemma: an emotion as intense as pain experienced by the research participants (especially when it is born of the traumatic experience of being tortured) needs to be conveyed in the most precise and respectful way yet it is inherently impossible to experience it for the researcher. The only way out is to use the researcher's own emotions as vehicles for sense-making and as phenomenological points of reference in the analytical process. The cognitive paralysis that can be induced by those intense emotional moments is a potential source of embodied sense-making during and after fieldwork.

Anger and Resentment: Against the Political Hijacking of the Revolution

Despite the important role played by UGTT in the revolutionary process, numerous critiques (ranging from mild disapproval to direct attacks) were addressed to the union in the following months. A woman unionist interviewed as part of this research reacted very strongly to the campaign led by government against UGTT's leadership which took place in the aftermath of the revolution.

> Everybody knows that UGTT and unionists have played an important role in the fall of Ben Ali and of the first transition government. The rumour according to which Jrad – the then leader of UGTT – could be linked to corruption issues is unbearable and even if proven true, does not justify an attack against UGTT. People don't understand that by insulting Jrad, they insult UGTT. I haven't been at UGTT for long but I love it,

I cannot bear to hear this great organization be insulted. It's the only place where I feel safe. Enemies of UGTT are many but we unionists won't let them do it, we will defend our organization to the end.

Adnene Haji, a militant from the mining uprisings was also adamant:

I am angry with the political class. The people offered them a revolution on a golden plate and instead of guaranteeing the political, economic, and social rupture asked for by the people, political parties and politicians have led a fierce battle to "share the cake", ignoring the demands of the revolution … ironically, these people [former political opponents, now political leaders] attack UGTT that sheltered them for decades of dictatorship. They know the weight of UGTT and they want to destroy it.

A strong sense of injustice is often at the root of the anger felt by participants in this research. The feeling of the organization having been robbed of its own achievements during the revolution period is at the core of the frustration and sometimes rage that was felt by some of our interviewees. Contrary to pain and suffering, anger is externalized more easily during the interviews and is verbalized more thoroughly by interviewees. It can constitute a great resource for researchers because it is always the vehicle or the proxy for underlying silenced considerations. Paying attention to anger and resentment is key in these extreme settings to locate analytical triggers for the researcher.

Elation: Euphoria of the Revolutionary "Moment"

Fethi Dbak, a unionist worker from Tunis described his joy about the revolutionary "moment" of 14 January 2011 in very moving terms:

There was a big gathering on 27th December 2010 here, on the square Mohamed Ali Hammi. It was violently repressed by police; I was violently beaten and hospitalized later on. I can show you a picture if you want [shows a picture of himself on the front page of the newspaper *Echaab* on 28th December 2010]. On 14th January 2011, I couldn't be on the Avenue Habib Bourguiba. I have dreamt of this moment all my life and I could not be there. I was in the hospital and I have never cried so much in my life. But what a joy to later go back to a free country.

Lazhar Gharbi, another unionist, who was headmaster of a school in Sidi Bouzid, the city where Bouazizi's immolation took place on 17 December 2010, also conveyed this feeling of elation and pride. These moments are precious for the researcher since joy is usually a much more pleasant way to "share" an experience. Moments of joy are key "release points" in which a transcending understanding can happen. In a way, doing ethnographic fieldwork research in a crisis context should always be to strive to get that "phenomenology of joy", that moment of "revolutionary love".

For me, one of the most extraordinary moments in Sidi Bouzid, was 11th January when protesters chanted "ya chaab ya majid la la littajdid [O Great People, no to the renewal of Ben Ali's candidacy to the presidential elections]". Police violently reacted on that day, but I felt that something extraordinary was going to happen. We went beyond fear. What we have accomplished is nothing short of spectacular.

Fear: For the Revolution to Be Confiscated

Ahmed Kahlaoui, a militant unionist close to the Arab nationalists was 67 years old when we met him and had been previously imprisoned under both Bourguiba's and Ben Ali's regimes. In his evaluation of the role of UGTT during the revolutionary episode, he declared:

Our country was a country from which wealth was systematically stolen, pillaged and memory confiscated. Memory of colonization, memory of the battle between Bourguiba and Ben Youssef [important figure of the national liberation movement, assassinated in 1961] supporters, memory of who assassinated Farhat Hached [important unionist leader and founder of UGTT]. Ben Ali also tried to bury the memory of Bourguiba. We can't talk of the role of UGTT in the revolution without mentioning its past, its history.

He then went on for 45 minutes to tell the story of the unionist movement and notably the battles between supporters of Bourguiba and those of Ben Youssef. It was impossible to stop him. Suddenly he stopped, seeing a protest against police repression happening in that moment close by, on the neighbouring Avenue Bourguiba. He excused himself and said he needed to go see what was going on.

It is worth noting that this emotional landscape was also a way to creatively and often spontaneously enact various "positions" for the researcher such as manoeuvring, playing ignorant, or being suspicious as a means to navigate the conditions of the field and manage the tensions that resulted from them. For the sake of illustration, written documents or audio archives constituted valuable support during the interviews, allowing, as the case may be, to manage or provoke a strong emotion in respondents. The objective was to stimulate their memory and bring them to constantly rephrase the meaning given to their recollections of their commitments and political strategies.

Emotions and Knowledge Production

The emotional reactions and experiences that constitute the ethnographer's "states of being" are not only essential for learning from the field but are also likely to yield much richer ethnographic knowledge (Devereux, 1980, Enriquez, 2003; Nassif, 2017). If the interviewed unionists used a specific jargon anchored in a very strong organizational culture to evoke the representation of their role in the revolutionary process, emotions such as fear and anger that emerged as the process unfolded would interrupt the formatted discourse and shed a different light on the challenges facing the organization and more generally the revolutionary movement.

The physical space in which interviews took place was also critical. They were held at UGTT offices or in cafes close to highly symbolic locations (Habib Bourguiba Avenue, the Kasbah in Tunis, Sfax city centre, etc.). The proximity of these places with the accounts of participants situated their words in an emotional and symbolic context. To be able to catch the meaning invested in this popular upheaval as well as its individual and collective emotional dimensions is also to address the performativity of protest and the motivations behind mobilization. UGTT is the place where memories of unionist and nationalist struggles are transmitted. The physicality of the emotions and their echoing of multiple temporalities of struggle were key to a better understanding of the revolutionary process itself. Indeed, emotions have revived memories of struggle by building bridges between past experiences, the present moment and the desired future. Unionists were then able to record and imprint the revolutionary episode in Tunisian History.

The circumstances and experiences of our ethnographic journey have provoked different emotions and subjective reactions shared with our interlocutors, such as fear, guilt, anxiety, paranoia and doubt, constituting ever changing "emotional states". During ethnographic fieldwork, emotions often found an expression in the personal memories, sensations and daydreams that have certainly left their imprints on the fieldwork, headwork and textwork (Van Maanen, 2011; Abdallah, 2018).

Emotion and the Ethnographer's Identity: Between the Personal and the Political

A number of personal parameters have impacted the first author and principal ethnographer's interaction with fieldwork. Having lived in a social milieu of political opponents and unionists all her life and having also been a witness to the treatment of political opponents by the former authoritarian regime shaped her understanding of the context and undeniably added richness to her interactions with participants. As shown in Al-Masri's (2017) work, shared experience of crisis meant repeated encounters with the unfolding violence and a constant reminder of lived experience under the former dictatorship. Each encounter with the narrative of the dictatorship enabled the researcher to build bridges between different temporalities (the present moment, the memories of past violence and the shared fears about the future) and created an intimacy of shared experience. The experience of dictatorship is cumulative: it imprints its marks on the bodies and souls of its subjects but its effects vary for each individual at different moments in life. This experience is also intergenerational; the trauma is not only carried for oneself but for former generations while conditioning the expectations of future generations of what a "legitimate and acceptable political regime" should be.

As the daughter of a well-known and respected unionist (who also wrote about the history of the labour movement in Tunisia), the first author and principal ethnographer was confronted with this intergenerational carrying of "memory" and with the inescapable blurring of the personal and the political throughout the course of the research. The doors of this famously secretive organization were opened for her and she was perceived more as a member of the family rather than as a researcher. She started fieldwork by talking to family friends within the organization and moved on to a larger circle of unionists for whom she was "the best person to restore the image of the organization in a difficult political context". Giving attention to the cumulative experience of life under dictatorship has implied a deeper ability to see the authoritarian context and the revolutionary process as conditions of life and intellectual production rather than just as research questions. This was also an instance of "ethnographic vacillation " (Hage, 2010). A particularly intense illustration was when she went back to the offices of UGTT in Sfax, a city where she had spent most of her childhood. The memories and emotions that have emerged from that specific fieldwork configuration have opened unexpected analytical perspectives and have led to a questioning and ultimate refinement of the initial research questions. The personal and the political were constantly entangled during fieldwork and the challenge of making these entanglements visible without stripping them of their strong emotional context constitutes another theme that this research explores.

Being immersed in known and interconnected networks placed the ethnographer in a complex relationship with the ethnographic field and with the people she spoke to. Despite having access to a notoriously "opaque" organization, a role was however assigned to her from the start: the role of a transmitter, the person who would render the "true" image of UGTT and would transmit memories and representations of the revolutionary episode. Some comments are worth noting:

> You are the daughter of Mohamed Lamine Yousfi, so you are the daughter of UGTT. You know it's thanks to your father that I became a member. I know I can trust you, I know you are one of us, and I am counting on you to explain the role of UGTT to those who are leading a campaign against us.
> UGTT functions as a tribe. Unionists' children are our children and we are all the children of UGTT.

This permanent reminder of genealogy and commitment is as explicit as it is difficult and sometimes oppressing. The identity of the ethnographer is in this case not only assigned by the field but also strongly internalized and used by the ethnographer to get access to some unionists who were not aware of genealogy. The ambiguity of the situation was characterized by the continuous superposition of an emphatic rapport with unionists and a challenging need to push them to explicit their opinions and what was supposed to be obvious to the ethnographer because of her assigned identity. This assigned role is very difficult to transcribe and tackle in the writing process: how is it possible to render the complexity in the functioning of this organization without betraying the trust of the field and without falling into a UGTT propaganda trap?

Moreover, the ethnographer was also politically engaged and implicated in the revolutionary movement. Her interest in UGTT was motivated by a need to deconstruct the myth of a spontaneous revolution and the dominant media and political analyses focusing on the event to the detriment of the collective battles led for years by Tunisians against the dictatorship. Therefore, being assigned a particular identity was not in contradiction with personal principles but imposed a reflexive process, which called for critical examination and avoidance of ethnographic "shortcuts". The crisis within the organization and the multiplicity of perspectives was helping not to fall into the idealization trap towards UGTT and to see it in its complexity and ambivalence.

The role of a crisis context can therefore be suitable for a reflexive ethnographic approach when it opens up the possibilities of interpretation that are born of the internal contradictions or conflicts of the field. Emotions, particularly prevalent in these contexts, can play a dual role: as a catalyst for interpretation and sense-making but also as way to open up the relationship with the ethnographer and to acknowledge her particular identity and assigned role in it.

An interesting point needs to be raised here: If embracing the researcher's and participant's subjectivities is inscribed in a phenomenological tradition within which this research is situated, it is however anchored in a Fanonian conception of phenomenology that turned around the phenomenology of the body previously conceptualized by Merleau-Ponty (1945) for whom "the world is what I see, what unfolds in front of me". For Fanon, as Ajari (2014) explains, the starting point is the singular position of an "I ... caught in the opacity of bodily operations" (p. 347). For Fanon, the body is conceived more as an effect rather than a cause, it is spatially constituted by its limits and its collisions rather by its hold on things. The body in an authoritarian context is always placed in the background of a milieu that precedes it, from which it is projected. Dictatorship installs a control, an entrapment that conditions and shapes any body's relationship with the world. It is this perpetual situation of "disquiet" that characterizes both the former dictatorship context and the experienced crisis research context.

The profoundly personal and embodied experience of fieldwork is therefore for us, an invitation to embrace a wider sensibility towards emotional and sensory dimensions of fieldwork in a crisis context and, more importantly, to acknowledge the multiple temporalities at play within that emotional space. The reflexive/analytical moment that follows these deep emotional entanglements with the field was achieved through confrontation between different narratives (supporters and opponents of UGTT) but was also achieved in this particular case by physical distancing from the field: continuous moves between Tunisia and France during and after the study.

Finally, taking into account the influence of emotional and sensorial experiences in conducting fieldwork was done with the full understanding that the purpose of our analysis was not to reconstruct the truth but rather to restore beliefs, expectations and understandings of the world, which can arguably be recognized as imprecise but not as invalid as long as the justifications of our interlocutors allowed to consider them coherent. From a methodological point of view, this is critical as it strongly positions us in an interpretivist tradition for which "truth" is a contested terrain.

Conclusion

This chapter offers a reflexive starting point on the nature of fieldwork in a crisis context. It is driven by a set of interrogations that led us to consider the multiple challenges attached to an embodied ethnography in which emotional and sensory dimensions were absolutely critical. Daily encounters with fear, suspicion, discomfort, doubt and misanthropy but also with solidarity, friendship, affinity and affection, created a special emotional landscape that was unavoidably superimposed on our fieldwork. It is this superimposition of the material, the emotional and the sensory that drive our reflection in this chapter.

Emotions produce a rich material that becomes a turning point in the ethnographic process and not only links the experience of the ethnographer to others (his/her interlocutors and the social milieu), but also connects different places, spaces and temporalities, in and out of the field. Simultaneously, fieldwork generates a multitude of open and imponderable relationships that involve the ethnographic method itself and the researcher at the centre of this process. These relationships are not limited to the relationship between the ethnographer and other(s) in the field but extend to the relationship between the ethnographer and the methodological practice itself, the ethnographer and the materiality of the environment of his/her study and ultimately, the ethnographer him/herself (Devereux, 1980; De Rond & Tunçalp, 2017). Davies calls them "inter-methodology" and "inter-materiality", which considers emerging emotions during the investigation as having "proven" empirical value and as having the ability to validate anthropological data (Davies & Spencer, 2010, p. 23)

Our reflexive analysis invited us to re-examine and to question the approach taken by us while conducting our field study in a crisis context. It showed that this work has been done from a situation of instability related to the conditions of the field, and that this instability was also due in part to a tense/complex relationship with particular epistemologies – based on either "profane knowledge or academic canon – on which we relied to analyse these conditions". Living an ethnographic journey is an intensely emotional and transformative enterprise (Fabian, 2001) and the following question often arises: where and when is the field really constituted? The boundaries of the field start to move between the conditions and emotional states that ethnographic work triggers and which it attempts to grasp. This particular concern regarding the interlacing of intersubjective emotional, sensory and epistemic landscapes with a doubt and anxiety triggering rhetoric far from being paralysing should help fuel the process of methodological "bricolage", so vital for a richer understanding of the social world.

In fine, this work aims to contribute to the ongoing conversation on the challenges of knowledge production in the Global South and in Arab countries (regularly described as "crisis contexts" (Kanafani & Sawaf, 2017)). Ethnography, as an analytical mode of attention (Abu-Lughod, 1989; Nader, 2011) that draws on particular emotional encounters and builds new forms of embodied knowledge, is for us a practical, descriptive, and theoretical enterprise that can ultimately allow emancipation from the universal methodological and theoretical projections of the dominant knowledge production regime (Yousfi, 2013).

Note

1 The excerpts are drawn from the first author's research memos and observation notes.

References

Abdallah, C. (2018). How creative nonfiction can inspire organizational ethnographers. *The Routledge Companion to Qualitative Research in Organization Studies*, R. Mir & S. Jain (Eds.). New York: Routledge, pp. 170–184.

Abu-Lughod, L. (1989). Zones of theory in the anthropology of the Arab world. *Annual Review of Anthropology, 18*(1), 267–306.

Ajari, N. (2014). Race et violence : Frantz Fanon à l'épreuve du postcolonial. (Thesis, Université Toulouse Le Mirail- Toulouse II, France).

Allan, H. T. (2006). Using participant observation to immerse oneself in the field: The relevance and importance of ethnography for illuminating the role of emotions in nursing practice. *Journal of Research in Nursing, 11*(5), 397–407.

Al-Masri, M. (2017). Sensory reverberations: Rethinking the temporal and experiential boundaries of war ethnography. *Contemporary Levant, 2*(1), 37–48.

Beatty, A. (2005). Emotions in the field: What are we talking about? *Journal of the Royal Anthropological Institute, 11*(1), 17–37.

Beatty, A. (2010). How did it feel for you? Emotion, narrative, and the limits of ethnography. *American Anthropologist, 112*(3), 430–443.

Behar, R., & Gordon, D. A. (Eds.). (1995). *Women Writing Culture*. Berkeley: University of California Press.

Boellstorff, T., & Lindquist, J. (2004). Bodies of emotion: Rethinking culture and emotion through Southeast Asia. *Ethnos, 69*(4), 437–444.

Czarniawska, B. (2004). On time, space and action nets. *Organization, 11*, 773–791.

Davies, J., & Spencer, D. (2010). *Emotions in the Field: The Psychology and Anthropology of Fieldwork Experience*. Stanford: Stanford University Press

Davis, G. F., Morrill, C., Rao, H., & Soule, S. A. (2008). Introduction: Social movements in organizations and markets. *Administrative Science Quarterly, 53*, 389–394.

De Rond, M. (2012). Soldier, surgeon, photographer, fly: Fieldwork beyond the comfort zone. *Strategic Organization, 10*(3), 256–262.

De Rond, M., & Tunçalp, D. (2017). Where the wild things are: How dreams can help identify countertransference in organizational research. *Organizational Research Methods, 20*(3), 413–437.

Devereux, G. (1980). *De l'angoisse à la méthode dans le sciences du comportement*. Paris: Flammarion.

Dobry, M. (1986). *Sociologie des crises politiques, la dynamique des mobilisations multisectorielles*. Paris: Presses des Sciences Po.

Down, S., Garrety, K., & Badham, R. (2006). Fear and loathing in the field: Emotional dissonance and identity work in ethnographic research. *M@N@Gement, 9*(3), 95–115.

Enriquez, E. (2003). *L'organisation en analyse*. Paris: Presses universitaires de France.

Fabian, J. (2001). *Anthropology with an Attitude: Critical Essays*. Stanford: Stanford University Press.

Gilmore, S., & Kenny, K. (2015). Work-worlds colliding: Self-reflexivity, power and emotion in organizational ethnography. *Human Relations, 68*(1), 55–78.

Hage, G. (2009). Hating Israel in the field: On ethnography and political emotions. *Anthropological Theory, 9*(1), 59–79.

Hage, G. (2010). *Hating Israel in the Field. Emotions in the Field: The Psychology and Anthropology of Fieldwork Experience*. J. Davies & D. Spencer (Eds.). Stanford: Stanford University Press, pp. 129–154.

Hällgren, M., Rouleau, L., & De Rond, M. (2018). A matter of life or death: How extreme context research matters for management and organization studies. *Academy of Management Annals, 12*(1), 111–153.

Hamzaoui, S. (1999). Champ politique et syndicalisme en Tunisie. *Annuaire de l'Afrique du Nord*, XXXVIII, Paris: Éditions du CNRS, pp. 370–380.

Harris, J. (1997). Surviving ethnography: Coping with isolation, violence, and anger. *The Qualitative Report, 3*(1), 1–13.

Henry, R. (2012). Gifts of grief: Performative ethnography and the revelatory potential of emotion. *Qualitative Research, 12*(5), 528–539.

Hensmans, M. (2003). Social movement organizations: A metaphor for strategic actors in institutional fields. *Organization Studies, 24*(3), 355–381.

Kanafani, S., & Sawaf, Z. (2017). Being, doing and knowing in the field: Reflections on ethnographic practice in the Arab region. *Contemporary Levant, 2*(1), 3–11.

Kenny, K. (2008). Aesthetics and emotion in an organisational ethnography. *International Journal of Work, Organization and Emotion*, 11, 374–388.

Kisfalvi, V. (2006). Subjectivity and emotions as sources of insight in an ethnographic case study: A tale of the field. *M@N@Gement, 9*(3), 117–135.

Koning, J., & Ooi, C. S. (2013). Awkward encounters and ethnography. *Qualitative Research in Organizations and Management: An International Journal, 8*(1), 16–32.

Lutz, C., & White, G. M. (1986). The anthropology of emotions. *Annual Review of Anthropology, 15*(1), 405–436.

Marcus, G. E. (1995). Ethnography in/of the world system: The emergence of multi-sited ethnography. *Annual Review of Anthropology, 24*, 95–117.

Merleau-Ponty, M. (1945). *1962: Phenomenology of Perception*, trans. C. Smith. London: Routledge.

Mir, R., & Jain, S. (Eds.). (2018). *The Routledge Companion to Qualitative Research in Organization Studies*. New York: Routledge.

Nader, L. (2011). Ethnography as theory. *HAU: Journal of Ethnographic Theory, 1*(1), 211–219.

Nassif, H. (2017). To fear and to defy: Emotions in the field. *Contemporary Levant, 2*(1), 49–54.

Pasquetti, S. (2013). Legal emotions: An ethnography of distrust and fear in the Arab districts of an Israeli City. *Law & Society Review, 47*(3), 461–492.

Rooke, A. (2010). *Queer in the Field: On Emotions, Temporality and Performativity in Ethnography*. Farnham: Ashgate, pp. 25–41.

Rouleau, L., De Rond, M., & Musca, G. (2014). From the ethnographic turn to new forms of organizational ethnography. *Journal of Organizational Ethnography, 3*(1), 2–9.

Stodulka, T. (2015). Emotion work, ethnography, and survival strategies on the streets of Yogyakarta. *Medical Anthropology, 34*(1), 84–97.

Van Maanen, J. (2011). Ethnography as work: Some rules of engagement. *Journal of Management Studies, 48*(1), 218–234.

Warden, T. (2013). Feet of clay: Confronting emotional challenges in ethnographic experience. *Journal of Organizational Ethnography, 2*(2), 150–172.

Watson, T. J. (2011). Ethnography, reality, and truth: The vital need for studies of 'how things work' in organizations and management. *Journal of Management Studies, 48*(1), 202–217.

Watts, J. H. (2008). Emotion, empathy and exit: Reflections on doing ethnographic qualitative research on sensitive topics. *Medical Sociology Online, 3*(2), 3–14.

Yousfi, H. (2013). Rethinking hybridity in postcolonial contexts: What changes and what persists? The Tunisian case of Poulina's managers. *Organization Studies, 35*(3), 393–421.

Yousfi, H. (2017). Trade unions and Arab revolutions: The Tunisian case of UGTT. *The Routledge Research in Employment Relations*, New York & London: Routledge.

Zald, M. N. (2017). *Social Movements in an Organizational Society: Collected Essays.* New York: Routledge.

Zarowsky, C. (2004). Writing trauma: Emotion, ethnography, and the politics of suffering among Somali returnees in Ethiopia. *Culture, Medicine and Psychiatry, 28*(2), 189–209.

Zembylas, M. (2005). Beyond teacher cognition and teacher beliefs: The value of the ethnography of emotions in teaching. *International Journal of Qualitative Studies in Education, 18*(4), 465–487.

PART IV

Reflections

24

IT IS NOT THAT ALL CULTURES HAVE BUSINESS, BUT THAT ALL BUSINESS HAS CULTURE[1]

Heung-wah Wong

Introduction

In a car back to my hotel in central Tokyo a couple of years ago, I asked my Japanese friend who was giving me the ride—a part-time anthropologist of Japanese management and a full-time chief executive officer of a small company in Tokyo—whether he read any journal articles published in management studies journals. His reply was a surprising 'no'. When he saw the puzzled expression on my face, he added that he had consulted those kinds of articles when he first took over his father's company many years ago. I immediately asked him why he had stopped doing so. His reply shocked me even more: 'Because the research results published there are simply not real!' This wasn't a typical kind of reply I have heard from businessmen about their reading habits. I usually got comments like 'they are too theoretical,' or 'they are not practical enough for us (businessmen)'. However, I think that the reply from my Japanese friend is more revealing than others I had heard to date because it points to a crucial question concerning our understanding of human phenomena. What do I mean here?

My idea here is basically very simple: business is culture, or it is nothing. For business (including institutions, management, and so on) is culturally constituted and therefore can *only* be understood culturally, by which I mean culture should be seen fundamentally as an independent variable in the sociological chain of being rather than as a residual factor to be added to the more basic reason—be it sociological, economic, ecological, or what Marshall Sahlins (1976) called practical. The general view among the scholars of different disciplines is that culture is always a factor secondary to a more fundamental reason for, or logic of, human behavior. Economists, for example, tend to argue that culture as a residual factor might change the priority of valuable objects people pursue (Sahlins 2013a). But for them the fundamental logic for human behavior is still the principle of maximization of self-interest.

My position is that culture is the essential condition of human existence. In this regard, I would like to invoke some of Clifford Geertz's insights from his famous book, *Interpretation of Cultures* (1973: 33–86); in which he suggested that archeological discoveries proved that the emergence of culture preceded, and to some extent overlapped with, the evolution of pre-human primates into *Homo sapiens*. To contend that pre-human primates become *Homo sapiens* first, and then created culture, is therefore not correct. Culture is rather a part of the environment that asserts selective pressure on the evolution of *Homo sapiens*, which is also to say that the emergence of *Homo sapiens* is both cultural and biological. It follows from this that culture is an essential condition of human behaviors.

Another of Geertz's insights is that the major difference between *Homo sapiens* and chimpanzees lies in the fact that *Homo sapiens* has a much larger brain than the chimpanzee because the former, Geertz argued, needs a larger brain to facilitate culture as a control mechanism to discipline human behavior, while almost all of a chimpanzee's behaviors are genetically determined (Geertz 1973: 33–54). I have to add hastily here that culture is capable not only of controlling but also facilitating human behavior because it can provide meaning and thus reason for it.

All of this speaks to the idea that culture is a species-specific capacity for *Homo sapiens* rather than an additive factor to something more fundamental for human behavior. Culture is a name for, and a term to distinguish, human behaviors as unique phenomena; it is 'the organization of human experience and action by symbolic means. The persons, relations, and materials of human existence are enacted according to their meaningful values—meanings that cannot be determined from their biological or physical properties' (Sahlins 2000b: 158). Anything human—including business behavior, economic organizations, and social institutions—must be cultural, or it is nothing. Everything 'social', 'commercial', or 'political,' is also cultural, because society, commerce, and politics are meaningfully constituted (Sahlins 2000a: 9–32). It follows from this that different cultures attach different meanings to the same behavior, which is also to say that the same behavior in different cultural contexts cannot be treated as the *same* thing. We therefore cannot adopt what Sahlins quoted Boas as writing about the method of the physical sciences: 'The physicist compares a series of *similar* facts from which he isolates the general phenomenon which is common to all of them. Henceforth the single facts become less important to him, as he lays stress on the general laws alone' (Sahlins 2000a: 20; italics mine). For we cannot assume a certain social behavior (such as gift-giving) or economic institution (such as corporation or family business) that are similar in form to have the same meaning in different cultural contexts. Here I am pointing at the formal quantitative methods of physical sciences which are widely adopted in mainstream management sciences. I suggest that our colleagues in management sciences should not treat the formal quantitative methods as more fundamental and thus better alternatives than the so-called interpretative methods simply because the object of management sciences is human rather than physical phenomena. What management scientists should do is the same as what Sahlins said anthropologists are required to do. As Sahlins (2000a: 21) explained:

> In anthropology, the one move and the other required the submission of the analyst, the knowing scientific subject, to the arrangement of the culture, to its own meaningful construction—as opposed to an analytic dismemberment into classes which loses the culture's specific characteristics.

I will return to this in the conclusion of this chapter, but I have already made my point. What follow are several examples including the import of the idea of joint-stock company in Japan, the family business in China and Japan, and the *guanxi* in Chinese society of Taiwan that exemplify it.

The Joint-Stock Company

The idea of the joint-stock company was originally invented in Europe and spread to the rest of the world. We, however, cannot assume *a priori* that the meaning of the joint-stock company remains the same when the idea goes global. My anthropological study of Yaohan Hong Kong, the subsidiary of a Japanese supermarket in Hong Kong, discovered that while the structure of Japanese companies (*kaisha*) is similar to those of their Western counterparts, the meaning of the former is very different from that of the latter (Wong 1999). Masahiko Aoki identifies two major meanings of firms. The first is that firms are understood by neoclassical economists as an instrument to maximize shareholders' return in the market (Aoki 1988: 7). This view, however, does not explain why firms emerge in the first place because if the market mechanism, as most neoclassical economists argue and agree, is the most efficient way to handle economic transactions, the emergence of firms is unnecessary. Ronald Coase (1937) takes up this question in his seminal article 'The Nature of the Firm', arguing that economic transactions through the market have a cost; and whenever a firm emerges in the market, this *must* mean that the cost of the economic transaction through the firm is less than that through the market. As Coase explained, 'a firm would arise and attempt to extend the range of its control as long as its costs were less than the costs of achieving the same result by market transactions' (Aoki 1988: 7). In other words, for Coase, firms emerge as an effective tool to minimize transaction costs, which is the second meaning of the firm identified by Aoki.

We can see that both the neoclassical economist and Coase share a view that the firm is just a means at the most; the former considers the firm as a tool to maximize shareholders' profits, while the latter understands the firm as an instrument for minimization of transaction costs. As a means, the firm itself has no intrinsic value;

it can be got rid of if the firm is no longer needed. As Joan Fontrodona and Alejo Sison (2006: 34) argued:

> As an institution, the firm is of no value in itself. In fact, in an ideal market situation where transaction costs are reduced to minimum, there would be no need for firms at all.

Coase, however, did not explain how and why firms can reduce transaction cost. This task is taken up by agency theorists fifty years later. To simplify enormously, they argued that firms can reduce transaction costs because the shareholders (the principal) subcontract the management of the firm to professional managers (the agent) on their behalf. As Fontrodona and Sison explained:

> Cost reduction is achieved in firms largely through the establishment of what Jensen and Meckling call *agency relationships*—not necessarily explicit nor formal—in which one party (the principal) engages another (the agent) to perform some service on its behalf, delegating certain decision-making power.
>
> *(Fontrodona and Sison 2006: 34; italic original)*

However, the manager as an individual who always determines to maximize her own interest might not necessarily work to maximize shareholders' interests, especially when the former's interest conflicts with those of the latter. The principal therefore must come up with contracts that can ensure that the agent will always act for the principal's best interests. These contracts, as Fontrodona and Sison (2006: 35) insightfully pointed out, are designed based on the assumptions of individualism, utilitarianism or hedonism, and contractualism. As they explain:

> Methodologically, agency theory subscribes to individualism: its basic unit of analysis is the human being fully constituted as an individual and bereft of any social dimension. In every endeavor individual agents seek above all their own utility (utilitarianism) or pleasure (hedonism), the satisfaction of their own desires. They form groups not to fulfil any requirement of their proper flourishing as human beings but only to further their particular interests (contractualism).
>
> *(Fontrodona and Sison 2006: 35)*

Here I am not interested in these assumptions but their implications for the image of the firm. They, as Fontrodona and Sison (2006: 35) pointed out, include:

1   Shareholders own the firm.
2   Shareholders act in accordance with the criterion of utility maximization.
3   The firm is a nexus of contractual relationships.
4   The purpose of the firm is to maximize shareholder value.

These implications envision an image of the firm as a node of contractual relationships designed by the shareholder to ensure that the professional manager will act to maximize shareholder value, which is also to say that the firm is considered to be owned by the shareholder. This image of the firm has been widely accepted not only by economists but also by the public as 'common sense'.

Japanese kaisha *(company) as an End Rather than a Means*

My research on Yaohan, however, discovered that Japanese people tended to treat the *kaisha* as an end rather than a means in itself. They attached intrinsic values to the continuity and prosperity of the *kaisha* because the *kaisha* was considered as having an eternal and supreme existence. In short, the *kaisha* is known as a social entity which has existed from time immemorial, and all the stakeholders of the *kaisha*—including shareholders, management, and employees—have to sacrifice their own interests for the continuity and prosperity of their *kaisha*.

I have offered a thorough analysis of the notion of the *kaisha* elsewhere (Wong 1999: 31–50) and thus want to be very brief here. Under the Japanese *kaisha* system, the shareholder was not seen as the owner of the *kaisha*; he or she, due to a series of institutional arrangements, generally had no control of his or her *kaisha*, which gives management tremendous freedom in running the *kaisha*. However, management, as the representative of the *kaisha* whose absolute power comes from the *kaisha*, must look to the interests of the *kaisha*. Since the overriding interest of the *kaisha* is its survival and prosperity, management staff whose behavior might threaten the survival of the *kaisha* will be forced to step down. In other words, despite the fact that the management has the absolute power to rule the *kaisha*, it can hardly be considered as its owner. Finally, employees of the *kaisha* are expected to be controlled by, and exist for, the *kaisha*. Employees are transformed into corporate persons (*kaisha ningen*) in the sense that they are not merely hired by their *kaisha* but in many ways are 'owned' by it.

Seen as such, the *kaisha* is a far cry from the meaning of the firm understood by neoclassical or transaction cost economists. In other words, the term '*kaisha*' is not just a translation of the Western 'joint-stock company,' even though the two are similar structurally and organizationally. They therefore cannot be treated as having the same meaning. We need to situate *kaisha* in the historical and cultural order that made it possible.

Japanese Ie *(Household)*

In this section, I will argue that the notion of the *kaisha* can be conceived as a modern re-arrangement of the traditional *ie*. The superiority of the *kaisha* over other stakeholders has been a recursive feature of a history starting from the traditional *ie* via pre-modern business establishments to modern corporations in Japan. Of course, *ie* cannot be compared with modern enterprises in terms of structural differentiation and functional specialization. However, if we investigate the nature of *ie* and its relationship with '*mura*' (villages) and *baku-han taisei* (shogunate-domain political system), we will be surprised by the fact that overriding importance is attached to the continuity and prosperity of both *ie* and the *kaisha*.

There have been two contrasting conceptualizations of *ie* among the scholars of Japanese *ie*. Kitano argued that *ie* should be conceived as a pure kinship organization. Ariga, however, suggested that *ie* could not be conceptualized as such because non-kin persons such as servants could be admitted as formal members of *ie*. *Ie*, for Ariga, should be understood as a corporate group defined by co-residential and economic factors. These two contrasting conceptualizations have been influencing the subsequent research on *ie* both within and without Japan (Hasegawa 1991: 55–66).

Zenkei Hasegawa (1991) has recently provided a third conceptualization of *ie* which I follow closely here. Hasegawa suggested that we should investigate the nature of *ie* in the context of *mura* and *baku-han taisei*. Hasegawa asserted that *ie* should be regarded as a unit of rights and duties. He used the *Ninbetsuchō* (census register) of 1663 kept by a founding family of the old Honma village in Nagano Prefecture to reconstruct the 17th-century structure of the village. *Ninbetsuchō* was used by overlords to control peasants, registering village members by the unit of *ie*. All members of the same *ie* were listed together in *Ninbetsuchō*. The old Honma village was a community of nine *ie* with a total number of 91 villagers. The *ie* was called *ikkenmae no ie* (one independent household) in the *Ninbetsuchō*. *Ikkenmae no ie* was the basic unit of the village. Everyone in the village had to be a member of one of these nine *ikkenmae no ie*, otherwise he or she could not live in the village. Hasegawa thus argued that *ikkenmae no ie* implies some kinds of rights in the village (Hasegawa 1991: 71).

The head of *ikkenmae no ie* should be regarded as the representative of the *ie*, enjoying the status of *honbyakushō* in the peasant status system. The system in 17th-century Japan classified peasants into *honbyakushō* and *nago*. *Honbyakushō* was the registered owner of a *yashikichi* (residence land) in the *Kenchichō* (land register). *Yashikichi* can be understood as a spatial medium whereby overlords established a master–servant relationship with *honbyakushō*. Overlords recognized a *honbyakushō* as the owner of *yashikichi*, the latter, in return, admitted his servant status and his various duties owed to the former. Therefore, the *honbyakushō* was also called *yakunin*, a person who was obliged to provide corvee labor and pay the land tax to overlords. These duties should be considered as parts of the services provided by *honbyakushō* as servants to their masters. In return, *honbyakushō* were entitled to participate in village assemblies, hold village offices, draw shares of the common lands of the village, and address the village headman on official business.

Nago did not own *yashikichi*. He had to become a servant of a *honbyakushō* through borrowing a *yashikichi* from the latter in order to enjoy the rights in the village. That is to say, *yashikichi* also serves a spatial medium through which *nago* established a servant–master relationship with *honbyakushō* (Hasegawa 1991: 47).

As mentioned above, the ownership of *yashikichi* implied a bundle of rights and duties to the overlord. Japanese referred to this bundle of rights and duties as *hyakushō kabu* (peasant share). *Yashikichi* was thus a symbol of *hyakushō kabu*. In fact, *hyakushō kabu* was also called *yashiki kabu*. Therefore, *honbyakushō* can be considered as the owner of *hyakushō kabu* through owning a *yashikichi*. If a *nago* had become rich enough to purchase a *hyakushō kabu*, he could become a *honbyakushō*. By the same token, a *honbyakushō* could lose his status and become a *nago* if he sold his *yashikichi*.

Hasegawa discovered that an *ikkenmae no ie* included not only the family of the *honbyakushō* but also those of *nago* who can be the *honbyakushō*'s relatives or persons not agnatically related. *Nago* lived apart from the *honbyakushō*'s family and each had its own household economy. However, *nago*'s families were not referred to as *ikkenmae no ie*. They were instead members of one of the nine *ikkenmae no ie* (Hasegawa 1991: 71). An *ikkenmae no ie* therefore could include different familial groups that formed different economic entities.

In light of the above discussion, we can outline the model of an *ikkenmae no ie* based on Hasegawa's study. *Ikkenmae no ie* can be defined neither as a kinship group nor an economic household. Instead, it can be conceived as a vehicle of a bundle of rights and duties attached to the *honbyakushō*. It thus had the characteristics of a *kabu* (share). In fact, Japanese referred to the *ikkenmae no ie* as *ie kabu* (Hasegawa 1991: 72). Understood as such, the succession of *ikkenmae no ie* did not necessarily take place among kin. By the same token, *ikkenmae no ie* can include non-kin members, a characteristic widely pointed out by scholars (Hasegawa 1991: 7–82). More interestingly, the *ikkenmae no ie* as a share could be bought and sold in Japan. People could purchase an extinct *ie* or an *ie* in which no successor was produced.

Ie *Ethics and the* kaisha

We can further derive a set of *ie* ethics from the above *ie* model. One of them which is the most important and relevant to current discussion is the overriding importance attached to the continuity and prosperity of *ie*. Several cultural mechanisms were devised to ensure the continuity and prosperity of the *ie*, one of which was that sons of *honbyakushō* might be passed over in favor of someone who was not blood-related but competent enough to succeed the *ie*. This practice was neither rare nor considered improper (Bachnik 1983); it was to ensure that the would-be *ie* representative was competent. Or from the *ie*'s point of view, it 'owned' its representative and his family so that it could alter their blood relationship if necessary.

We can also find the parallel in the context of *kaisha*. If the son of a company's founder is not capable enough to run the *kaisha*, he will also be passed over. In this regard, the story of the succession troubles of Yaohan's major shareholder and chairperson, K. Wada, is very illustrative.[2]

K. Wada had three daughters and one son. According to the family tradition of the Wada family, which was similar to that of most Japanese family-owned businesses, the son, Genichi Wada, should succeed as head of the family business. He, however, reportedly did not maintain a good relationship with his family. Wada seldom mentioned him in public, and therefore not many people knew that he had a son. I was first told about the Wada family in 1992 in an interview with a Japanese employee. She told me that Wada did have a son, but that he did not want to mention him. Another informant who used to work with Genichi in Yaohan Japan told me that all employees of the company knew that Genichi was not a promising successor. I was also told by the company's advisor who is very close to the Wada family that Wada had already realized that Genichi held little promise of capitalist success and were considering other candidates.

As of 1997, Wada had not yet decided who would be his successor. The rumor circulating within Yaohan suggested that Wada's son-in-law was a possible candidate. He had been appointed director of Yaohan International in April 1993 and then promoted to president of Yaohan Hong Kong in 1996. Such promotion, as one of my Japanese informants interpreted it, symbolized that Wada had decided to let him take over the company gradually.[3] Wada's decision showed that the continuity of the *kaisha* was more important than that of agnatic relationships. Even the owner of the company still had to sacrifice their family interests for the sake of the perpetuation of the *kaisha*. We can now see how the *ie* ethics is parallel to the institutional logic of *kaisha*: the overriding importance attached to the prosperity and continuity of *ie* and *kaisha*.

Chinese Kinship[4]

We can also detect a close relationship between family and family business in the context of Chinese societies. I have pointed out in my recent article 'What is Chinese Kinship and What is Not?' (Wong 2017) that the best way to understand how native Chinese understand their family is through three major native concepts: *fang/jia-zu* and *qi*.

According to Shiga Shuzo, '*qi*' (or '*ch'i*') literately means 'breath', which 'signifies the male reproductive function and is counterposed to *p'ao* (placenta), which signifies the female reproductive function' (Shiga 1978: 122–123). *Qi* also 'refers to the formless life itself, which is extended through the male reproductive function to sons and grandsons' (Shiga 1978: 123), which is also to say that a son is the extension of his father's life, while a father is the origin of his son's life (Shiga 1967: 35). Shiga further characterized the father–son relation with a phrase from a Chinese classical text, Nan Shih Chuan: *fu zi zhi qin fenxing tongqi* (Shiga 1967: 35), which Allen Chun translated as 'with respect to the relation of father to son, there is a distinction of (corporeal) form but a commonality of ch'i [*qi*]' (Chun 1985: 97). In other words, father and son share the same life which Shiga called '*fu zi tong qi*' ('share the same vital life essence between father and son'). If a son is the extension of his father's life, it logically follows that brothers born from a single father can also be seen as sharing the same life (*tong qi* or *t'ung ch'i*) (Shiga 1967: 37, 1978: 123).

While *qi* as 'shared substance' characterizes the relationship between father and son and among brothers from a single father, it, however, does not apply to the relationship between father and daughter. In other words, daughter cannot succeed *qi* from her father, which is also to say that daughter is not considered as being the same *kind* of persons with her father and brothers. What a daughter can do is to get married to a man by which she comes to share the *qi* of her husband. Through marriage, women and their husbands become *tong qi*; and they are the same *kind* of persons. That is why when a married woman passes away, she will be buried in the same grave as her husband (Shiga 1967: 37).

Shiga further pointed to the ways *qi* is related to the nature of Chinese kinship. First, the fact that father and son, husband and wife, and all the sons born from a single father are *tong qi* defines the membership of *zhong-zu* (a genus of persons, of which members share the same *qi*). Second, the relationships between father and son, husband and wife and among sons of one single father constitute the basic relation of *zhong-zu* (Shiga 1967: 37). Shiga hastened to add that while brothers are *tong qi* in relation to their father, they differentiate from, and oppose each other through their unique identification with their wives (Shiga 1967: 38).

Another two important native concepts which are directly related to Chinese family are *fang* and *jia-zu*. Literally, *fang* refers to the bedroom of 'a married son and his wife' (Chen 1986: 55–56). One can see that *fang* emphasizes a son's conjugal status, designating the son or the son and his wife as a unit or all his male descendants and their wives as a kin set (Chen 1986: 55–56). Metaphorically, *fang* thus takes on the meaning of the *genealogical* status of a son as a conjugal unit in relation to his father. *Jia-zu* is a blend of *jia* and *zu*. *Jia*, as we will discuss in a moment, refers to a co-resident, commensal group, whereas *zu* is a genealogical notion referring to the set of agnates and their wives regardless of their functional aspects (Chen 1986: 64). Taken together *jia-zu* refers to the genealogical status of father in relation to son.

Taking all these together, we can now see clearly that *fang/jia-zu* refers to a genus of people who are *tong qi*. In more concrete terms, son becomes a member of his father's *jia-zu* through the *qi* he shares with his father; brothers become members of their father's *jia-zu* through the same *qi*; and women who have married into the family become members of their father-in-law's *jia-zu* through obtaining the *qi* from their husbands. Chinese family thus is defined by *qi* as shared substance that characterizes the relationship among father, son, and daughter-in-law. In other words, Chinese kinship refers to the relations characterized by *tong qi*, which is also to say that Chinese kinsmen or kinswomen are the same being (*qi*) in distinct corporeal forms (*fen xing tong qi*); they are 'persons who belong to one another, who are parts of one another, who are co-present in each other, whose lives are joined and interdependent' (Sahlins 2013b: 21). Chinese kinship thus is what Sahlins called 'mutuality of being' which is defined as 'people who are intrinsic to one another's existence—thus "mutual person (s)," "life itself," "intersubjective belonging," "transbodily being," and the like' (Sahlins 2013b: 2).

Chinese Family Ethics

Understanding Chinese kinship as 'mutuality of being' can further help us to understand the Chinese family ethics. Recall that the son is the extension of his father's life because the father–son relationship is characterized by *tong qi*. It follows that if a Chinese man can ensure that at least one son is born to his male descendants of each generation, his life can be extended forever, and his life is then deemed eternal. In other words, the eternal life of Chinese men is secured if their *qi* can be perpetuated by the fact that the male descendants of each generation can produce a son. That is why paramount importance is attached to the continuity of *fang/jia-zu*, which always casts an intensive pressure on Chinese men to bear a son because only a son can carry on the family line by creating a *fang* (Chen 1986: 102).

More importantly, the continuity and prosperity of the *fang/jia-zu* line is more important than those of any functional kin group such as *jia*. *Jia* as a functional kin group is different from *fang/jia-zu* as a genealogical set. The membership of a *jia* is basically underlined by the *fang/jia-zu* membership, that is, the male founder, all his male descendants, and their spouses. However, *jia* could also include unmarried female descendants (including daughters and sisters) who acquire their *jia* membership from their father or even their uxorilocal husbands who are related to the *fang/jia-zu* through their wives, which is also to say that while a daughter is not a *fang* member, she is nonetheless a *jia* member.

The difference between *fang/jia-zu* and *jia* can also be seen in the division of family property. Shiga considered *jia* as a 'joint-account' in which members share a common budget to which all *jia* members are expected to contribute (Shiga 1978: 113). The person—usually the wife of the *jiazhang* (head of the *jia*)—who is in charge of the *jia*'s financial budget is responsible for the allocation of the money to members for daily uses. Underlying the financial management of the *jia* is the core *jia* ethic: just as *jia* members are required to support one another unconditionally, they have to share with others all they have, because the *jia* will offer financial help to any member if necessary. The financial management of the Chinese *jia* can be seen as what David Graeber calls 'everyday communism' that 'operates on the principle of "from each according to their abilities, to each according to their needs"' (Graeber 2014: 67).

While members of the *jia* can draw money from the account for daily expense, not all members have a right to the surpluses left over from the account, which will be accumulated as family property, to be apportioned equally among 'brothers' only (Shiga 1978: 113). Once the surpluses become *fang/jia-zu* property, their sharing and ownership are defined not by *jia* but *fang/jia-zu* membership (Chen 1986: 130). Sons can equally share the *fang/jia-zu* property, especially landed estate, when their father decides to pass the household property to them. The division of *fang/jia-zu* property in many cases occurs concurrently with the division of *jia*. Each son will establish a new *jia* and the original *jia* will be terminated upon the division of *jia*, while each *jia-zu* is *genealogically* divided into *fangs* according to the number of sons, but the original *jia-zu* does *not* vanish. We can now see that the division of *jia* as a functional group is fundamentally different from the division of *jia-zu* as a genealogical set. *Jia* is expected not to last long, while *fang/jia-zu* is supposed to continue forever in Chinese societies.

In fact, Chinese people attach overriding importance to the continuity of *fang/jia-zu*, for the sake of which the interest of *jia* can be sacrificed. Take the *kuo-fang* practice in rural Taiwan as an example. *Kuo-fang* is defined as 'a genealogical re-arrangement of an agnate's fang filiation within the same chia-tsu [*jia-zu*]'

(Chen 1986: 174; underline in the original). In the event, the adopted son does not necessarily change his *jia* membership, which is also to say he could still live with his original parents in their *jia*, but is rearranged genealogically to become the son of the deceased man who is the member of another *fang* of the same *jia-zu* so that the deceased man's *fang* line can be continued. The adopted son is entitled to the deceased men's *fang* property, but he is also required to worship the latter *as his father*. Chen argued that the major purpose of *kuo-fang* was to continue the deceased's *fang* line rather than his *jia* (Chen 1986: 174–191). We can see that *kuo-fang* highlights the primary importance of the continuity of *fang/jia-zu* over that of *jia* (Chen 1986: 174).

Chinese Family Ethics and Chinese Family Business[5]

Chinese tend to run their family business in the organizational form of *jia* as we can see from another native term, *jia-ye* (family business). It follows that the Chinese family ethic—the continuity and prosperity of *fang/jia-zu* is more important than those of *jia*—is also applicable to Chinese family business (*jia*). In my forthcoming co-authored book titled *Tradition and Transformation in a Chinese Family Business*, I present an ethnography of a Hong Kong Chinese jewelry company (hereafter FBL), pointing out that the interest of FBL (*jia*) is always sacrificed for the sake of the interest of the *fang/jia-zu* of the founder, F. To cut a long story short, under the leadership of F, the company actively speculated in real estate market. However, following the outbreak of the Asian financial crisis, the stock market and real estate market in Hong Kong experienced a great crash in late 1997. The unexpected property market crash brought about a financial disaster not only to F but also FBL, because F used the company's financial resources to speculate in the real estate market. Despite the fact that F tried his best to repay the loan, he was eventually ordered bankrupt by the court in 2000. F was forced to step down as the chairman of FBL. He, however, remained involved in the management of FBL as he did before. F's younger son took over the leadership of FBL but the company was in a dire financial situation.

F's son therefore endeavored to solve the debt problem of the company, consolidate the controlling stake of his family in FBL, reform the company, and most importantly revamp FBL's brand image after taking up the chairmanship. In 2004, F's son succeeded in attracting one of the world's largest diamond trading companies to invest in FBL. With the injection of new funds, FBL was able to reduce the total debt of the company.

The fundamental factor contributing to the crisis, we contend, is that F continued to run FBL as his *jia* even after the company was publicly listed on the Hong Kong Stock Exchange. As mentioned above, the financial resource of a *jia* is allocated to members according to their needs by the *jiazhang* or his wife. We can even say that the *jiazhang* has the absolute power over the management of the *jia* and its financial budget. Seen in this way, we can now understand why F repeatedly used FBL's financial resource to speculate in the real estate market because it is very natural for F to get money from his company because he considered FBL as his *jia*; and as the *jiazhang* F has the absolute power to decide how the *jia*'s financial budget is distributed and spent. To F, FBL's financial resource is his *jia*'s money which was under his control.

More importantly, the Chinese family ethic gives priority to the interests of *fang/jia-zu* rather than those of *jia*. That is why F could risk the interests of FBL (his *jia*) for the sake of his *fang/jia-zu* by investing heavily in the property market or levying substantial loans on FBL, not to mention appropriating the company's financial resources for his own use, all of which would jeopardize the interest of FBL as a whole including those of its minority shareholders, its employees and other stakeholders. This is the overriding problem of Chinese family businesses.

We can now conclude that Chinese people tend to emphasize the continuity of their *qi*, while Japanese people stress the continuity of *ie* as a share. This difference is also reflected in the family firms in Chinese and Japanese societies. Chinese people do not hesitate to sacrifice the interests of their companies (*jia*) to ensure the continuity of the *fang/jia-zu* line, as we can see from the fact that Chinese people will still pass their business to a son, even if he is clearly incompetent. This further helps explain why there is a Chinese saying that family wealth in Chinese societies never lasts beyond three generations because an incompetent son can ruin his family business. Japanese people, however, will bypass their incompetent sons and pass their *kaisha* to a capable adopted son, and more often to an adopted son-in-law (*muko yōshi*), to ensure the continuity and prosperity of the *kaisha*.

The most important implication of the above discussion is not that all cultures have family, but that all family has culture. We cannot assume that the family as a social institution is the same cross-culturally and thus treat family as a constant. As far as I know, scholars of management/business studies seldom take seriously the fact that different cultures have different concepts of family and that, as a result, family businesses in different cultures will exhibit very different forms of organizational behavior.

Guanxi

In the past 20 years, there has been a growing cottage industry in the social sciences that renders the Chinese concepts of *guanxi* (relationship), *mianzi* (face), and *renqing* (rapport) the *unique* characteristics of interpersonal relationship in Chinese societies, especially in the post-Mao Chinese society in mainland China. More recently, management science has followed suit, taking *guanxi* as the *unique* feature of the interpersonal relationship in the Chinese business context and *guanxi* therefore is seen as an important independent variable in explaining Chinese business behaviors. But as Allen Chun (2017: 143–162) effectively argues, although *guanxi*, *mianzi*, and *renqing* are *semantically* distinguishable, it is very difficult if not impossible to judge *in practice* which behavior of individual Chinese can be attributed to which of these concepts. For the same behavior can be motivated by any of these concepts.

Take an example from my research on the circulation of Japanese adult videos (AVs) in Taiwan (Wong and Yau 2014).[6] Michael went to a graduate school in Taipei which provided a privileged environment for him to gain access to Japanese pornography. In late 2002, Michael was drafted into the 'substitute soldiers'; he was assigned to a high school serving as a security guard. Michael met Jacky in a two-week training course at a military center. After the training, Jacky served his army time in a government-owned tourist center. Jacky happened to be assigned responsibility for room allocation there. Being aware of Jacky's desire for Japanese AVs and the lack of facility for him to acquire free pornography on the Internet, Michael realized that his technologically privileged situation allowed him to give out AVs in exchange for a possible free stay in the center from Jacky. He told us that he first gave Jacky twelve self-made pornographic VCDs for free (MG1). After several rounds of AV-giving (MG2), Michael thought that his friendship with Jacky was good enough for him to ask for a favor from Jacky. He thus directly asked Jacky if he could stay at the country house *for free*. Jacky did indeed offer Michael the free accommodation, but what was more important was that his counter-gift (JG1) went well beyond this because Jacky took Michael and his girlfriend, Jen, on a tour of the city in his car and arranged various leisure activities for them at the country house. In return, Michael gave more AVs to Jacky (MG3). Throughout the rest of their military term, Michael stayed in Jacky's workplace for free several more times (JG2), and each time he went there, he brought along many more Japanese AVs for Jacky as 'gifts' (MG4). Moreover, the two now met not just for AVs or free accommodation, but to have BBQs and go sightseeing together. In other words, they were seeing each other as *friends* now.

After their military service in late 2004, Michael began to work in a large digital company in Taipei while Jacky worked in a small company in Taichung. Jacky did not like the idea of working in Taichung, because his girlfriend worked in Taipei. In 2005, with Michael's help, he managed to find a better job (MG5) which was located in Taipei. One year later, Michael married Jen and they later had a son. In late 2006, they held a joint banquet to celebrate their wedding and their son's first full moon, and invited Jacky to attend. Surprisingly, Jacky and his girlfriend made a cash gift of an amount that was far higher than average (JG3). Michael told us that the reason Jacky offered such a big gift might be because he had helped Jacky to find a job, but he added that it might also be because Jen had recently lost her own job. Michael was very impressed by Jacky because, on the one hand, Jacky had shown concern for their financial situation, and, on the other, he had intentionally brought along his girlfriend to the banquet to make the big gift seem more natural. In addition, Michael told us that Jacky's girlfriend even brought Jen some baby goods as gifts from time to time (JG4). When Michael expressed his gratitude to Jacky, Jacky, we are told, simply told him that, 'everything between us was understood without being said'. That is why Michael said that Jacky indeed is his good friend.

In the light of the above ethnographic example, we can make an important point: the character and form of gift-giving or service provisions are similar if not the same (MG1, MG2, MG3, MG4, and JG3), but the motivation for each gift-giving or service provision turns out to be very different, which is also to say the same behavior can have different meanings in different contexts of the same culture. The question then becomes: how can we as outside observers tell which gift-giving is for which purpose? How, for example, we can know Jacky's big gift is given for *renqing*, and not for building *guanxi*?

The answer lies in the ethnographic context. Michael wanted to have a free stay in Jacky's hotel with his girlfriend and therefore initiated *guanxi* with Jacky by giving him a bundle of Japanese AVs (MG1, MG2, MG3 and MG4); but in the process of *guanxi* building, Michael and Jacky had gradually become good friends. The fact that Jacky gave Michael a big gift at the latter's wedding banquet can no longer be seen as *guanxi* building but as *renqing* to Michael as a friend (JG3). Jacky was grateful to Michael for his introducing him a job and who knew that Michael had just married, that his wife Jen had given birth to their first child, and that she had also lost her job. All of this makes Jacky's motivation for gift-giving (JG3 and JG4) intelligible and transparent: he wanted to help Michael, his friend.

It follows methodologically that we cannot take gift-giving behaviors out of the ethnographic context and assume that they are all motivated by *guanxi*. For we cannot tell which of these gift-giving behaviors is motivated by *guanxi*, *mianzi*, or *renqing* without locating them in a particular context because they are similar if not identical behaviorally. Instead, we should locate gift-giving behaviors in a specific context and identify the motivation behind them.

Ethnographic Understanding of Human Phenomena

The above three examples speak to the importance of context in understanding human phenomena. The most important methodological implication is that any methodology which ignores context simply does not work. I am pointing to the 'formal quantitative methods—assembling data-bases, plotting graphs, calculating rates and proportions, and performing statistical tests' (Sewell 2005: 347) which is a normative method among the mainstream management scientists. Behind the quantitative methods is what William Sewell called mechanistic explanation which 'specifies not paradigm and performances but cause and effect … In the simplest form of mechanistic explanation, the presence of some phenomenon (a cause) determines the appearance of another phenomenon (an effect)' (Sewell 2005: 347). I have to clarify here that I am not arguing against statistical operation in particular and mechanistic explanation in general but the underlying ideology which 'generally conceive[s] of the social as made up of stable entities with measurable attributes or variables and a set of causal connections between the variables that can be stated in law-like form' (Sewell 2005: 347). For our understanding of human phenomena itself is also a human behavior that is meaningful and takes place in terms of that meaning, which is never the only one possible. To understand a human phenomenon is to understand its meaning and to make sense of the meaning of a human phenomenon is to situate it in a particular context.

This comes to my second point. What is missing here is the context in which the human phenomena at issue take place meaningfully. More importantly, human phenomena can also acquire new meaning in another context as we have seen above, where the joint-stock company is given different meaning in Japanese society and transformed into *kaisha*. Human phenomena take place in a process in which human behaviors mediate with their context. A statistical relationship among various variables is insufficient if not impossible to capture this dynamic process. To make human phenomena more complicated, the actor of human behavior can reflect on his or her behaviors and in the course of doing so, he or she can create new meaning. In a discourse of human science, individuals have their own agency. This comes to my final point concerning the narrative structure of a typical management studies paper: it tends to deny the voice of the individuals involved.

Individual voices or individual cases are denied on the pretense of being 'scientific'. Being 'scientific' in management science is to do what the natural scientists are doing, that is, to search a universal law of human behaviors. Individuals or individual cases are relevant *only if* they serve as an 'example' or a 'counter example' of a general trend. What the voice of an individual or the dynamics of an individual case are does not deserve any academic concerns. Toyota is relevant *only if* it constitutes an example of Japanese vertical business groups; Yaohan, a Japanese supermarket that gains its reputation of going overseas, is relevant *only if* it indicates the trend of Japanese companies going overseas in the 1970s. What Toyota or Yaohan looks like does not matter! Neither do they deserve academic attention.

The Ontological Nature of Human Phenomena

The reason that any context-free methodology simply does not work, I have to reiterate, lies in the ontological nature of human phenomena. Following Ferdinand de Saussure, I consider that human phenomena necessarily involve three elements: physical act, meaningful system (culture), and their relations. Human phenomena are the interpretation of physical act in terms of a meaningful system that is not the only one possible. Interpretation here means inserting a physical act in a classification system that is culturally specific and historical. It follows that a physical object can only become a *human* object in a meaningful system. The same physical object can become different human phenomena in different meaningful systems. Your father's brother's son and you are the members of the same family, while your mother's brother's son belongs to a different family in Chinese societies but in the West, they are addressed by the same term 'cousin'. I am of course not suggesting that English-speaking people cannot recognize the difference; I am just suggesting that the difference has no cultural significance in the English-speaking societies. It follows that the cultural category of 'father's brother's son' has different meaning in different societies and therefore cannot be grouped into one single analytical category. In other words, no cultural category is context-free and more importantly, it cannot be understood without a context. The cultural meaning of 'father's brother's son' is defined by other similar but not identical terms in a kinship system. More importantly, the use of this category in everyday life can sometimes transform the meaning of that category (Sahlins 1981). The understanding of human phenomena is therefore very complex. The challenging task is to know how on the one hand the meaningful system gives meaning to a cultural category and how the practice of that category in everyday life transforms the meaning of the category, a task that cannot be tackled simply by any context-free method.

It follows that any understanding of the Other involves two necessary steps. The first step is to suspend our theoretical imposition if not moral judgment of a certain cultural phenomenon but situate that phenomenon into its own cultural context in order to grasp the cultural logic behind the phenomenon. Father's brother's son in Chinese societies shares the same *qi* with his own father who also shares the same *qi* with his brother (Ego's father). Ego also shares the same *qi* with his father's brother's son because ego inherits the *qi* from his father. According to this logic, ego is symbolically equivalent to his father, his father's brother, and his father's brother's son in Chinese societies. Mother shares the same *qi* with her husband, her husband's brother, her husband's brother's son, and her son. All of them belong to the same family. Mother's brother, however, inherits his father (ego's mother's father) and his son inherits his so mother's brother's son has a different *qi* from ego and therefore mother's brother's son is categorically different from ego's father's brother's son in Chinese societies. This is the logic of Chinese agnatic relations.

But why can non-Chinese anthropologists understand this logic? Sahlins (2000a: 19–22) makes a very interesting claim about this possibility of understanding the Other. He argues that what the anthropologist does in ethnography is to reproduce in his or her mind the cultural logic displayed in the behavior of the Other he or she observed in the field. This competence of reproduction of the cultural logic of the Other can, Sahlins further argues, be attributed to the common species-specific capacity: symbolic ability. In other words, for human science, the method and the object of study are the same, which is the minimal definition of ethnography. As Sherry Ortner pointed out, 'it [ethnography] has always meant the attempt to understand another life world using the self—as much of it as possible—as the instrument of knowing' (Ortner 1995: 173). The researcher and the object of study in human science have the same ontological status, while in natural science, the researcher is a species with symbolic ability and the object of study is not. The basic assumption of the distinction between subject and object may not be applicable to human science.

Any understanding of human phenomena therefore involves human *subjective* reproduction of the cultural logic of the Other by the researcher. Consequently, the general impression we generated from natural science that 'objectivity' is a critical criterion of guaranteeing the 'trueness' of the research result may not be applicable to the study of human phenomena. More importantly, if we agree that by reproducing the cultural logic of the Other, we make the Other familiar and thus understandable, it follows that we should understand the Other subjectively from within. This notion of understanding is very different from that in natural science which tends to do the opposite; that is, understanding natural things objectively from outside. As Sahlins argued:

> Indeed, the more we know about physical objects the less familiar they become, the more remote they stand from any human experience. The molecular structure of the table on which I write is far removed from my sense of it—let alone, to speak of what is humanly communicable, my use of it or my purchase of it. Nor I will ever appreciate tableness, rockiness, or the like in the way I might know cannibalism. On the contrary, by the time one gets to the deeper nature of material things as discovered by quantum physics, it can only be described in the form of mathematical equations, so much does this understanding depart from our ordinary ways of perceiving and thinking objects.
>
> *(Sahlins 2000a: 30)*

Now it has become clear why my Japanese friend mentioned at the beginning of this chapter thinks that the research results published in management science journal appear to him as 'unreal'!

Another major reason that ethnography can help understand human phenomena is its commitment to 'thick description' called by Geertz (1973: 3–30), 'to producing understanding through richness, texture, and detail, rather than parsimony, refinement, and (in the sense used by mathematicians) elegance' (Ortner 1995: 174). As Ortner explained, 'thickness' could mean differently in the history of anthropology but the current dominant meaning of 'thickness' is contextualization. By paying close attention to the context in various domains and in different levels through which the complexity of the human phenomena at issue are to be understood, ethnography tries to reproduce the 'authenticity' of the human phenomena. Following Ortner, authenticity here does not mean cultural purity but reproduction of the human phenomena as they are and thus 'real' to us as human subject.

I have to clarify immediately that I am not saying that comparative studies are not necessary because ethnography is comparative by nature. As Sahlins effectively argued:

> No good ethnography is self-contained. Implicitly or explicitly ethnog raphy is an act of comparison. By virtue of comparison ethnographic description becomes objective. Not in the naive positivist sense of an unmediated perception—just the opposite: it becomes a universal understanding to the extent it brings to bear on the perception of any society the conceptions of all the others.
>
> *(Sahlins 2002: 13)*

This comes to the second step of understanding of the Other that we have to distance ourselves from the Other and compare the cultural logic of the Other with that of another Other (Sahlins 2004: 4). The reason is very simple. If the meaning of a sign is determined by the similar but not identical signs in the structure, the meaning of the cultural logic of the Other has to be produced by contrasting this Other with the similar but not identical other Others. That is to say, it, to paraphrase Sahlins, 'take another culture to know another culture' (Sahlins 2004: 5).

Conclusion

The idea of this chapter is basically very simple. Business is a human phenomenon and must be studied culturally, by which I mean we should situate the phenomenon at issue in its own context in order to grasp the cultural logic behind it and then compare that logic with the logic of another culture. I have also suggested that ethnography is an effective method to capture the meaning of human phenomena because ethnography is a commitment to 'thickness', the contextualization of human phenomena.

I am not sure whether the immediate goal of management science should be set to predict human behaviors without specifying the particular context where the behavior takes place, similar to how natural science determines to predict how non-human things would move. The problem of this prediction-oriented approach lies in the ontological nature of human being as a cultural animal. Human behaviors are meaningful and take place in terms of that meaning that is never the only one possible. However, to say that the behavior of a certain person is culturally meaningful does not necessarily mean that we can predict how this person would act in practice. As Sahlins argued, '[j]ust because what is done is culturally logical does not mean the logic determined that it be done—let alone by whom, when, or why— any more than just because what I say is grammatical, grammar caused me to say it' (Sahlins 1999: 409). The way that individuals choose to behave is heavily determined by both the macro and micro contexts in which they conduct their social life. That is to say, any prediction of human behaviors has to be context-specific.

The possible goals of the study of business are to help practitioners of business to understand what a certain behavior means in a particular context, why a certain person does not conform to the cultural system in a specific context, what would be the cultural consequences or effects of a certain management policy, and how people would behave in a certain context. All of this can be achieved only if we understand and study business culturally.

Notes

1 This is a substantial revision of 'Business is Culture, or It is Nothing!' that I presented at the 117th annual meeting of American Anthropological Association at San Jose, California, USA from 14 to 18 November 2018.

2 This story is taken from my book titled *Japanese Bosses, Chinese Workers: Power and Control in a Hong Kong Megastore*, pp. 41–42, Hawaii: The University of Hawaii Press, originally published in 1999.

3 The son-in-law finally did not succeed his father-in-law because the company went bankrupt in 1997.

4   This section of Chinese kinship is a shortened version of 'What is Chinese Kinship and What is Not?' in *Family, Ethnicity and State in Chinese Culture Under the Impact of Globalization*, edited by Min Han, Hironao Kawai and Heung Wah Wong, pp. 83–104, California: Bridge 21, originally published in 2017.

5   This section is a revised version of a chapter of my book *Tradition and Transformation in a Chinese Family Business* co-authored with Karin Ling-fung Chau (2000).

6   This ethnographic example is used in *Japanese Adult Videos in Taiwan* (2014) in different context and for different purpose. I apologize for the repetition here.

References

Aoki, Masahiko. 1988. *Information, Incentives, and Bargaining in the Japanese Economy*. Cambridge: Cambridge University Press.

Bachnik, Jane M. 1983. "Recruiting Strategies for Household Succession: Rethinking Japanese Household Organization." *Man* 18(1): 160–182.

Chen, Chi-nan. 1986. "Fang and Chia-tsu: The Chinese Kinship System in Rural Taiwan." PhD dissertation, Department of Anthropology, Yale University.

Chun, Allen. 1985. "Land Is to Live: A Study of the Concept of Tsu in a Hakka Chinese Village, New Territories, Hong Kong." PhD dissertation, Department of Anthropology, University of Chicago.

Chun, Allen. 2017. "From the Ashes of Socialist Humanism: The Myth of Guanxi Exceptionalism in the PRC." In *Forget Chineseness: On the Geopolitics of Cultural Identification*, edited by Allen Chun, pp. 143–162, Albany: State University of New York Press.

Coase, Ronald Harry. 1937. "Nature of the Firm." *Economica* 4(16): 386–405.

Fontrodona, Joan, and Alejo José G. Sison. 2006. "The Nature of the Firm, Agency Theory and Shareholder Theory: A Critique from Philosophical Anthropology." *Journal of Business Ethics* 66: 33–42.

Geertz, Clifford. 1973. *The Interpretation of Cultures*. New York: Basic Books.

Graeber, David. 2014. "On the Moral Grounds of Economic Relations: A Maussian Approach." *Journal of Classical Sociology* 14(1): 65–77.

Hasegawa, Zenkei. 1991. *Nippon Shakai no Kiso Kōzō: Ie, Dōzoku, Sonraku no Kenkyū [The Structure of the Base of Japanese Society: The Research of Households, Lineages and Villages]*. Tokyo: Horyutsu Bunka Sha.

Ortner, Sherry. 1995. "Resistance and the Problem of Ethnographic Refusal." *Comparative Studies in Society and History* 37(1): 173–193.

Sahlins, Marshall. 1976. *Culture and Practical Reason*. Chicago and London: The University of Chicago Press.

Sahlins, Marshall. 1981. *Historical Metaphors and Mythical Realities: Structure in the Early History of the Sandwich Islands Kingdom*. Ann Arbor: University of Michigan Press.

Sahlins, Marshall. 1999. "Two or Three Thing that I Know about Culture." *The Journal of the Royal Anthropological Institute* 5(3): 399–421.

Sahlins, Marshall. 2000a. "Introduction." In *Culture in Practice: Selected Essays*, edited by Marshall Sahlins, pp. 9–31, New York: Zone Books.

Sahlins, Marshall. 2000b. "Sentimental Pessimism and Ethnographic Experience, or Why Culture Is Not a Disappearing 'Object'." In *Biographies of Scientific Objects*, edited by L. Daston, pp. 158–202, Chicago: The University of Chicago Press.

Sahlins, Marshall. 2002. *Waiting for Foucault, Still*. Chicago: Prickly Paradigm Press, LLC.

Sahlins, Marshall. 2004. *Apologies to Thucydides: Understanding History as Culture and Vice Versa*. Chicago: The University of Chicago Press.

Sahlins, Marshall. 2013a. "On the Culture of Material Value and the Cosmography of Riches." *HAU: Journal of Ethnographic Theory* 3(2): 161–195.

Sahlins, Marshall. 2013b. *What Kinship Is—And Is Not*. Chicago: The University of Chicago Press.

Sewell, William H. 2005. *Logics of History: Social Theory and Social Transformation*. Chicago and London: The University of Chicago Press.

Shiga, Shuzū. 1967. *Chugoku Kazokuho no Genri [Principles of Chinese Family Law]*. Tokyo: Sobunsha.

Shiga, Shuzū. 1978. "Family Property and the Law of Inheritance in Traditional China." In *Chinese Family Law and Social Change: In Historical and Comparative Perspective*, edited by David C. Buxbaum, pp. 109–150, Seattle: University of Washington Press.

Wong, Heung Wah. 1999. *Japanese Bosses, Chinese Workers: Power and Control in a Hong Kong Megastore*. Honolulu: University of Hawaii Press.

Wong, Heung Wah. 2017. "What Is Chinese Kinship and What Is Not?" In *Family, Ethnicity and State in Chinese Culture under the Impact of Globalization*, edited by Min Han, Hironao Kawai and Heung Wah Wong, pp. 83–104, Los Angles: Bridge 21.

Wong, Heung Wah and Karin Ling-fung Chau. 2000. *Tradition and Transformation in a Chinese Family Business*. Oxford: Routledge.

Wong, Heung Wah and Hoi Hoi Yan Yau. 2014. *Japanese Adult Videos in Taiwan*. Oxford: Routledge.

25

ETHNOGRAPHY AND THE TRAFFIC IN PAIN

Mark de Rond

Whereas it may once have been perfectly respectable to generate knowledge for knowledge's sake, management scholars today appear increasingly concerned with the production of societally relevant research. Thus, the 20th editorial committee of the *Academy of Management Journal* defined its three-year term by a focus on "societal grand challenges" (George et al., 2016), culminating in a Special Issue with articles that tackle such varied but fundamental humanitarian issues as neglected diseases (Vakili and McGahan, 2016), conflict minerals (Kim and Davis, 2016), organizational responses to natural disasters (Williams and Shepherd, 2016) and pricing practices in healthcare (Heese, Krishnan and Moers, 2016). A couple of years earlier, twenty-four senior management scholars created Responsible Research in Business and Management (RRBM), a network designed to encourage meaningful research as "a means to a better world". One of its co-founders, Anne Tsui (2013), noted that a considerable number of Academy of Management presidents expressed concern around the *irrelevance* of our research,[1] and not just for practising managers. A subsequent book by one of these, *Engaged Scholarship*, went on to receive one of the Academy's most important prizes,[2] from which the following quote is tell-tale:

> Any scientist of any age who wants to make important discoveries must study important problems. Dull or piffling problems yield dull or piffling answers. It is not enough that a problem should be interesting—almost any problem is interesting if it is studied in sufficient depth … the problem must be such that it matters what the answer is—whether to science generally or to mankind.
>
> *(P.B. Medawar, Nobel Laureate in Medicine and Physiology, as quoted in Van de Ven, 2007: 71)*

Based on such calls for relevance, several scholars have explicitly realigned their research agenda to focus on "the most important problems in the world today" (McGahan, 2010: 1), while some business schools kickstarted initiatives to foster engagement with grand challenges[3] and higher education funding bodies now often consider impact as a major criterion against which to assess research performance.[4]

Early signs are that a new generation of management scholars is rising to the challenge of tackling pressing societal problems for reasons that are multiple and complex (cf. Bothello and Roulet, 2018).[5] However, in engaging with grand societal challenges, whether through old-fashioned fieldwork or ethnographic interviews, they can quickly find themselves confronting real people with real problems: the elderly, victims of political or religious extremism, refugees (e.g. Kornberger et al., 2018), sex workers (e.g. Eberhard, 2017), victims of rape (e.g. Whiteman and Cooper, 2016; Zilber, 2002), prisoners (e.g. Rogers, Corley and Ashforth, 2016), addicts (e.g. Lawrence, 2017), the socially deprived (e.g. Tracey and Phillips, 2016), the obese (e.g. Amis et al., 2012) or those suffering the consequences of fraud, persecution, civil war, genocide or child sexual exploitation. "Suffering is one of the existential grounds of human experience", write Kleinman and Kleinman (1996: 1), and "a master subject of our mediatized times".

While the organizational ethnographer's forays into these challenges are still relatively recent, they will likely gain momentum as more of us look to making a positive difference. This raises the question as to whether, and to what extent, we are prepared for the moral ambiguities that are an inescapable, yet often subtle, feature of societally engaged research. We already know that prolonged contact with suffering others can mobilize strong emotions on the part of the management scholar (Claus et al., 2019), but what about the footprint we leave on the very people we claim our work intends to benefit?

In contrast to organizational ethnography, photojournalism has long kept company with suffering. And, at face value, the two practices aren't a million miles apart. Both earn their keep by telling stories. These are true stories in that they report on real people in real situations. The best of them are meticulously checked for factual errors and errors of omission. And while their production relies on different tools, occasionally toolkits combine such that photographers make notes and ethnographers pictures. There is a long tradition in ethnography of "taking" pictures, including by such early adopters as Malinowski (in the 1910s Trobriands), Evans-Pritchard (in 1920s Sudan), Mead and Bateson (in 1930s Bali) and Bourdieu (in 1950s Algeria). Yet the two worlds rarely converge in practice as each targets a different audience with distinct expectations of aesthetics, analytical rigour, abstraction and theorizing. Besides, ethnographers enjoy the luxury of time not always afforded by the photojournalist, and with ever-higher quality lenses on mobile phones, photographers face a level of competition from non-specialists that academics rarely experience in quite the same way.

This chapter considers well-known examples from photojournalism to explore a set of subtle moral ambiguities involved in the pursuit of societal grand challenge type fieldwork: exploitation, complicity, voyeurism and aestheticization. Photojournalism's head-start on the experience curve allows us to attend to the sources of such ambiguities and help us explore strategies to mitigate the risk of moral compromise involved in our work, however well intended.

Exploitation

One of the celebrated crises of cynicism about documentary photography relates to Dorothea Lange's "Migrant Mother". It is without question the most famous image of the post-depression era and, as is true for all of the photographs discussed here, can easily be found with a Google search. Lange took six photographs of Florence Owens Thompson, in a pea picker's camp in Nipomo, California, over 10 minutes in February 1936, while on the books of the US government's Farm Security Administration program. Thompson had set up camp temporarily while her husband and sons set out for a nearby town to get their car fixed.[6] As Lange explained:

> I saw and approached the hungry and desperate mother, as if drawn by a magnet. I do not remember how I explained my presence or my camera to her, but I do remember she asked me no questions. I made five exposures, working closer and closer from the same direction. I did not ask her name or her history. She told me her age, that she was thirty-two. She said that they had been living on frozen vegetables from the surrounding fields, and birds that the children killed. She had just sold the tires from her car to buy food. There she sat in that lean-to tent with her children huddled around her and seemed to know that my pictures might help her, and so she helped me. *There was a sort of equality about it.*
>
> *(Meltzer, 2000: 133; italics mine)*

Lange's photograph gained iconic power as a "symbolic representation of America's communal faith in its capacity to confront and overcome despair and devastation" (Hariman and Lucaites, 2007: 60) and has variously been modified to feature Thompson as African American (by Black Panther activists) and a Wal-Mart employee (to adorn a 2005 cover of *Nation*). Whatever satisfaction she may have gained from the impact of this photograph—its publication helped generate relief for struggling farmers such that no farmer is known to have died from starvation during this period—Thompson took issue with Lange's account of events.

When interviewed in the 1970s (once her identity had finally been established), she claimed that Lange had promised not to publish the photos and expressed regret over the encounter. She expressed anger at the commodification of her image, divorcing the woman pictured from the real Thompson and, perhaps ironically, also bitterness for not having received a penny for it. "I didn't get anything out of it. I wish she hadn't of taken my picture … She said she wouldn't sell the pictures. She said she'd send me a copy. She never did" (Hariman and Lucaites, 2007: 62).

It may be that Thompson envied Lange for the fame and financial rewards the image brought her (she even tried exercising her property rights to stop further publication) and with both long since dead we are unlikely to ever have a true and full account of the encounter. Yet the image remains a textbook example of a great photograph, sensitively shot, notwithstanding persistent accusations of exploitation.

The exploitative character of non-fiction storytelling, whether through images or text, is captured poignantly in Janet Malcolm's opening lines to *The Journalist and the Murderer*:

> Every journalist who is not too stupid or full of himself to notice what is going on knows that what he does is morally indefensible. He is a kind of confidence man, preying on people's vanity, ignorance, or loneliness, gaining their trust and betraying them without remorse. Like the credulous widow who wakes up one day to find the charming young man and all her savings gone, so the consenting subject of a piece of nonfiction learns—when the article or book appears—his hard lesson.
>
> *(2011: 1)*

What is true for Malcolm's journalist can easily be true for the organizational ethnographer. After all, the dilemmas we face are not dissimilar. What aspects of the lives of others do we have the right to publicly expose? When is informed consent truly informed, and what rights to privacy do informants retain once they've given consent? Is it any surprise that, in many languages, we speak of "taking" and "shooting" pictures, rather than "making" them? One need only consider Carolyn Brettell's *When They Read What We Write* to find plenty examples of ethnographies that, once published, became a source of agitation and dislike to those who featured in them. In contrast to anthropological studies of natives in faraway lands, most of those we study read what we write and are happy to talk back. As Nancy Scheper-Hugher, one of her contributing authors, notes in reflecting on her fieldwork with islanders:

> Like the people of Ballybran and Springdale, the islanders were most offended by the fact that the private had become public—that the ethnographer had foregrounded what the people studied wish to maintain in the background.
>
> *(Brettell, 1996: 14)*

Scheper-Hughes quotes the village schoolmaster:

> It's not your science I'm questioning, but this: don't we have a right to lead unexamined lives, the right not to be analysed? Don't we have a right to hold on to an image of ourselves as different to be sure, but as innocent and unblemished all the same?
>
> *(Brettell, 1996: 13)*

None of this suggests, of course, that our informants are beyond reproach: they can be axe-grinding, self-interested, towing to the party line or mistaken (Rosaldo, 1986). The difficulty with the criticisms levied above is that they are unspecific: what offends is the account existing. The protagonist of Whyte's *Street Corner Society* was so embarrassed by the account, and concerned that others might react badly to it, that he actively discouraged local reading of the book. "The trouble is, Bill, you caught the people with their hair down. It's a true picture, yes; but people feel it's a little too personal" (Whyte, 1973 [1943]: 347).

The implication is not that ethnographies end badly but that we know they can, whereas those who afford us privileged access to their world do not. Informants will likely worry a great deal about what it is you might say about them, realizing that they have no control over your written work (or shouldn't in any case), and that living among them, even if temporarily, will likely smoke out all manner of flaws and imperfections. This conversation is not limited to "gatekeepers", or those with powers to grant us access to the organization, allowing us to hang around, and nor is it granted only once. Access negotiations are ongoing and contingent on the unfolding relationship between researcher and researched. Moreover, given that we wish to access not just the organization broadly, but the private worlds of those inside it, access can only ever be granted privately. But, of course, our friendliness is weaponized: it conceals data-gathering goals and how can it not? It is unlikely we would extend the same courtesy, pleasantries and patience were it not that they have something that we want. Columbia sociologist Herbert Gans made precisely this point in a slap on the wrist gesture to Carolyn Ellis on the publication of *Fisher Folk*, admonishing her for telling people she was their friend: "I told her, 'Yes, you use friendly methods, but you're always a researcher. You arrange to tell people every so often, I'm not your buddy. I'm a researcher'" (Allen, 1997). But considering how precarious access negotiations are in any event, we may feel that we cannot risk letting "the other" in on the likelihood that this may not end well, preferring instead to exploit this information asymmetry in securing access to the field. Informed consent rarely if ever inoculates informants from violence to their right to privacy (cf. Roulet et al., 2017). Ethnographers remain in the field for long periods of time for a good reason: the hope that familiarity will encourage informants to drop their guard and share ever more private details. We thus incur debts that can never be fully repaid (Coffey, 1999: 161).

While exploitation by betrayal will resonate with those who have been around the block, this challenge of exploitation is all the more acute in contexts where the stakes are high for our informants or where informants are vulnerable. Consider, for example, Laud Humphreys' (1975) fieldwork in "tearooms", or public toilets used for impersonal sex between gay men. To facilitate observation of sexual acts, Humphreys offered to act as a "watchqueen" during acts of fellatio, peering out (and, as is obvious from his accounts, also in) from a small window for the arrival of police or a stranger. His study was controversial for several reasons, not least for Humphreys having deceived some of his informants of his real intentions in a follow-up survey, conducted on behalf of a different body, to which he was allowed to add some questions of his own. Some of the men he subsequently interviewed, often in the presence of their wives, he knew had availed themselves of tearooms. He had taken down their licence plate numbers in his role as lookout and was able to obtain their personal details and include them in the survey. But this isn't the primary reason why Humphreys' ethnography is of interest here; it is because, as Warwick (in Humphreys, 1975: 211) points out, "the men in the tearooms could not fight back". His informants were a relatively powerless group of men, unable or too ashamed to retaliate, and when visited in their own homes were at risk of being exposed to their families. Similar criticisms have been levied against those who document homelessness, social depravation, addiction, sexual violence and war. After all, what gives them (and us) the right to study those with no real recourse to legal and other kinds of retribution? What are our responsibilities to those we study, as different from the ones who granted access to the organization (and who, for the most part, can be "photo-shopped" out of the ethnographic text)? And how might we secure informed consent, yet without surrendering to censorship of the account so as to safeguard our responsibilities to scholarship?

Complicity

"Like sexual voyeurism", Susan Sontag (2004) wrote, "[photography] is a way of at least tacitly, often explicitly, encouraging whatever is going on to keep on happening." And, in doing so, we may become complicit in suffering, even if inadvertently. Two examples from photojournalism may help bear this out. The first concerns Kevin Carter's 1993 photograph of a Sudanese infant who had collapsed on her way to a feeding station. An attentive vulture stands in the background. The image became iconic for mobilizing the world to act against death by starvation and won Carter a Pulitzer Prize. The world wanted to know: what did he do to help the girl? Did he pick her up and carry her to the nearby feeding station? Did he call for help? Did he at least chase off the vulture? It wasn't until the eve of the prize ceremony at Columbia University that he came clean with his editor. As reported by Scott Mac Lead in *Time* magazine:

> He heard a soft, high-pitched whimpering and saw a tiny girl trying to make her way to the feeding center. As he crouched to photograph her, a vulture landed in view. Careful not to disturb the bird, he positioned himself for the best possible image. He would later say he waited about 20 minutes, hoping the vulture would spread its wings. It did not, and after he took his photographs, he chased the bird away and watched as the little girl resumed her struggle. Afterwards he sat under a tree, lit a cigarette, talked to God and cried. He was depressed afterward ... He kept saying he wanted to hug his daughter.
>
> (as cited in Kleinman and Kleinman, 1996: 5)

A second example pertains to Eddie Adams' photograph of a Vietnamese chief of police, Brigadier General Nguyen Ngoc Loan, executing a Vietcong suspect in a Saigon street in February 1968. Sontag describes what happened next:

> [The photograph] was staged—by General Loan, who had led the prisoner, hands tied behind his back, out to the street where journalists had gathered; he would not have carried out the summary execution there had they not been available to witness it. Positioned beside his prisoner so that his profile and the prisoner's face were visible to the cameras behind him, Loan aimed point-blank. Adam's picture shows the moment the bullet has been fired; the dead man, grimacing, has not started to fall.
>
> *(2003: 52)*

Similar critiques of complicity have been levied against other photojournalists documenting civil wars and genocides, where people protesting their innocence are dragged in front of murderous crowds to have their way with them. What one rarely sees are the photographers surrounding them, "whose participation helps determine the direction the event will take" (Kleinman and Kleinman, 1996: 9). Judith Butler's evaluation of the Abu Graib photographs likewise implicate those making the photographs in prolonging, perhaps even causing, the suffering on display, "the cameraman or woman … referenced by the smiles that the torturers offer him or her as if to say, thank you for taking my picture, thank you for memorializing my triumph" (2007: 959).

While it is rare for organizational ethnographers to experience violence first-hand, it isn't unheard of. For example, when John Van Maanen returned to the field five years after having completed his research on policing, he was invited to join several of his former police informants on a routine patrol. After a ride around town, the officers were called in to provide assistance in removing a drunk from a downtown bar. The incident is described in his mischievously named "The Asshole" (Van Maanen, 1978). Instead of removing the drunk and letting him off with a stern warning, his "host" officers beat him unconscious. As he recalls 50 years later:

> They beat the shit out of him on the street. And I'm watching, I'm just watching. And they throw him in the back of what they called the van … And I'm up in the front with the driver. We're driving to the jail and I can hear the beating going on in the back … They were showing off. They were showing off that they didn't take shit on the street. They knew what they were doing … They probably would've ignored this case had it not been for my presence.
>
> *(Claus et al., 2019)*

While John never called for the beating, he couldn't help but feel he caused the beating in that it might never have taken place were it not for John being present, his former informants keen to show their mettle.[7]

The difficulty in situations like this is deciding whether to turn up or turn away, to intervene or not to intervene, and this is where complicity is at its most subtle. How does one decide whether to "stand up" or "stand down" when witnessing expressions of racism and sexism, the threat of physical violence and acts of sexual aggression (all of which have featured repeatedly in our own fieldwork)? Moments like these tend to pass quickly but are rarely one-offs, can be deeply uncomfortable, and leave the researcher to decide whether standing up for her ideals is worth putting her research at risk. It is often all too easy to let things pass under the cover of a non-interventionist observer. Richard Leo's study of police interrogations is instructive in that he "consciously reinvented his persona" to facilitate acceptance in his chosen community. He deceived without telling lies. Instead, he shaved his beard, cut his hair, put on a coat and tie (all of which were out of character) and feigned politically conservative views on the death penalty, abortion and homosexuality while also mimicking the crude language of police officers, and particular in reference to women. As he put it:

> I just didn't try to argue with them when they raised the question of abortion or homosexuality. They'd say, 'You're not against the death penalty, are you?' And I'd just laugh. I know I gave the impression that I agreed with them. I just wanted them to think I was a normal person. From their point of view, a normal person was a conservative.
>
> *(Leo, 1995)*

He had little time in which to conduct his fieldwork (500 hours) as a penniless PhD student at Berkeley and needed to "fit in" quickly and acknowledged that his tactics resembled those of "confidence men who wish to set up their marks" (Leo, 1995, as cited in Allen, 1997). Such examples have generated stinging rebukes. As Yale sociologist Kai Erikson writes:

> We do cost-benefit analyses to justify deception ... But most often it's we who get the benefit and they who pay the cost. There have been sociologists who have gone into religious groups or Alcoholics Anonymous. We don't know how much harm it does to research subjects. There are some people who say, 'I'm doing it for the sake of science.' They're doing it for themselves. One of the things that I've noticed is that people who disguise themselves are always looking at groups less powerful than they are.
>
> *(cited in Allen, 1997)*

Humphreys cited acceptance of his work by the gay community in his defence, and Leo called on sociologists to be given the same evidentiary privilege enjoyed by doctors and lawyers, in that they cannot be forced to testify in court about what they see and hear in the field. But neither got off scot free, and each remains a classroom illustration of complicity through deception and exploitation through power.

Voyeurism

Kevin Carter's powerful image gives rise to yet another related source of moral ambiguity, namely voyeurism. Photojournalism and ethnography alike afford windows into the (private) worlds of others but without any requirement to reciprocate the vulnerability our work implies for them. George Bressai, a Hungarian photographer, left little to the imagination in this respect:

> We … are nothing but a pack of crooks, thieves and voyeurs. We are to be found everywhere we are not wanted; we betray secrets that were never entrusted to us; we spy shamelessly on things that are not our business; and end up the hoarders of a vast quantity of stolen goods.

Bill Jay (in Lester, 2015) puts it rather more humorously in a parody on Kodak's "You press the button, we do the rest":

> *Picturesque landscape,*
> *Babbling brook,*
> *Maid in a hammock*
> *Reading a book;*
> *Man with a Kodak*
> *In secret prepared*
> *To picture the maid,*
> *As she is unawares.*
> *Her two strapping brothers*
> *Were chancing to pass;*
> *Saw the man with the Kodak*
> *And also the lass.*
> *They rolled up their sleeves*
> *Threw off hat, coat and vest*
> *The man pressed the button*
> *And they did the rest.*

Susan Sontag wrote of the "aggression implicit in every use of the camera" (2001 (1977). 7)—a view she maintained in *Regarding the Pain of Others* (2004), written 25 years later—while Edmund Burke (1759: Sect. XIV) went further in suggesting that "we have a degree of delight, and that no small one, in the real misfortunes and pains of others." Whether admission or admonition, Burke's observation touches a nerve: our vantage point as ethnographers is one of privilege for it is unlikely (though not impossible) that we have been behind bars, morbidly obese, reliant on hand-outs or subject to sexual exploitation. This privilege, however, need not come with moral ascendency. That is to say, while it is true that we may sympathize with the plights of those we study, it is also true that our voyeurism can generate a sense of smugness or contempt. While we may genuinely wish for our work to alleviate suffering, it is difficult to simultaneously suspend the belief that we are the result of our choices, and that bad choices lead to bad outcomes. Instead, one forgets that the privileges we enjoy have their origins in precisely the sorts of things none of us control: the circumstances of our birth and upbringing. Kleinman and Kleinman (1996: 8), with reference to Carter's photo, put it thus:

> One message that comes across from viewing suffering from a distance is that for all the havoc in Western society, we are somehow better than this African society. We gain in moral status and some of our organizations gain financially and politically, while those whom we represent, or appropriate, remain where they are, moribund, surrounded by vultures ... The point is that the image of the vulture and the child carries cultural entailments, including the brutal historical genealogy of colonialism.

Thinking back of my own fieldwork in Helmand, Afghanistan, in 2011 (see de Rond, 2017; de Rond and Lok, 2016), I still get sick to the stomach when forcing myself to recall what I felt at the time. It was the bloodiest year of the recent war in Afghanistan due to its signature injury: the high double amputee. Every day, typically after early morning and evening patrols, injured soldiers would be ferried in by helicopter to the field hospital, as the result of ever more powerful IEDs. Civilians were not inoculated from the effects of improvised explosives, though they would variously trickle into our emergency room during the day. My private fascination with the blood-soaked spectacle that is war's consequence turned addictive as I craved for ever more dramatic injuries to arrive, as yet another double amputee no longer satisfied my craving for more extreme, and different, fare. Addiction to war, and the suffering other, is little different from that to drugs or pornography: one requires ever-stronger stuff to keep the tedium at bay. The "opium" quickly wears off and leaves behind it a bar to be met. I was never sure which was ultimately the more repulsive: to witness first-hand, and many times daily, the horrendous suffering inflicted by humans on humans, or the small delights I took in voyeurism. It is small comfort to think that many of the doctors seem to have felt the same way.

Aestheticization

While ethnographers haven't usually kept company with death, photography has (Sontag, 2003: 21). Traffic in pain is

> a crucial element of news reporting, obviously, but it also courses through the art market, tourism, even fashion and advertising. Without injured bodies and devastated landscapes, without scenes of death, destruction, misery, and trauma, the contemporary image environment would be

nearly unrecognizable. These scenes of affliction are often formally striking or beautifully rendered: every day, without much effort, one may come
across exquisite images of other people's suffering.

(Reinhardt, 2007: 7)

That photojournalism relies on aesthetic qualities is no great surprise: photographers will go out of their way to get just the right shot, from the right angle,
with just the right type and amount of light. But the emphasis on aesthetics can
become problematic in the context of suffering. Given recent conflicts—the wars
in Afghanistan and Iraq, the various Arab Spring uprisings, and the ongoing civil
war in Syria—this problematic has come to the fore in recent years, the more so
as beautiful images of suffering are the likely recipients of major international
awards.

Consider, for example, the images of such stalwarts of photojournalism as James
Nachtwey, Tom Stoddart, Don McCullin and Sebastiao Salgado. Their representations of human suffering are aesthetically pleasing because they are so carefully
composed, making best use of the available light, showing just the right amount of
detail, having found just that decisive moment to press the trigger, something they
will have been keenly aware of. Nachtwey and Salgado in particular have been criticized for having allowed the aesthetic qualities of their images to mask the suffering
portrayed. As a reviewer writing for *The New York Times* put it:

> [Salgado's] photographs are so stupendously gorgeous that they make
> you forget everything else while you are looking at them. They bespeak
> uncanny formal intuition, a ready repertory of apt allusions to art history
> and peerless timing (and some luck maybe, too, which all great photo-
> journalists have). This applies whether the image is a panoramic blur of
> jostling commuters at a Bombay railroad station, wherein a visual cliché
> of human overpopulation and modern travel is transformed into a minor
> miracle of geometric and textural subtlety; or the fearful, glassy-eyed glare
> of three refugee babies captured through a slit between rough blankets; or
> the silent labor of people dragging a mastless skiff over glossy sand under
> leaden skies, an image screaming with Christian symbolism like so many
> of Mr. Salgado's pictures.

(Michael Kimmelman, New York Times, 13 July 2001)

Photographs of suffering fail in allowing for passive consumption rather than action
or reflection, or as Reinhardt (2007: 22) writes, fail to provide a "genuine understanding of the situations and suffering of those pictured" in allowing strong aesthetic qualities to misdirect the viewer's attention. The emphasis is on the quality of
images—their composition and lighting—rather than their subjects, the display of
human suffering a source of awesome wonder.

Ethnographies, at least partly, rely on their aesthetic qualities to persuade, and it is no great surprise that ethnographers will typically spend a great deal of time polishing their writing. As Van Maanen (2010: 241) writes:

> It may ... be that our silence rests on the vague but unexamined feeling that if we did start looking closely at the ways our major and minor work are put together, we might not like what we find; a fear that if we looked closely at our use of imagery, phrasing, allusion, analogy, and claims of authority, we might discover some literary chicanery or authorial trickery that would undercut our ability to make claims about the worth (and truth) of our findings and theories. If style were shown to play an important persuasive role in research reports, a corrosive relativism might overcome us and authors of organization studies would become players in a mere game of words, trapped in the same "prisonhouse of language" thought to be occupied by poets, novelists, and not-so-cunning memoirists. From this perspective, it is best to imitate the ostrich and not look.

Good ethnographers are often artful writers—where we cannot play the numbers game, we persuade with prose instead. A genuinely well-crafted work of a mean, grim, hard-luck world can provoke strong aesthetic responses of the same sort as photographs do. Moreover, in crafting our ethnographies, are we at risk of romanticizing the lives of the other? As one critic wrote of Goffman's (2009, 2015) account of a south Philadelphia neighbourhood:

> Spend time in the ghetto and you quickly learn that criminals are not victims. The corner boys in West Baltimore are not heading off to college once drugs are legal. They will find new scams. They like crime and the drug game is their version of the self-actualizing career. Take that away and they find a new way to terrorize their communities. There are good arguments against the drug war, but romanticizing these people is naive.[8]

Similar criticisms have been levelled against ethnographies of the working classes (e.g. Paul Willis' *Learning to Labour*, as critiqued by Walker, 1986), The chief source around romanticization is that of aestheticization, namely the unintended consequence of dehumanizing "the other". That is to say, while our craftsmanship helps "hook" the reader, by making our work readable and accessible, it may do so at the expense of the very people whose suffering prompted our engagement in the first place. Can we be let off the hook on the assumption that the portraits we paint are meant to be understood as partial and incomplete? What safeguards can we put in place to protect informants of the risk of us romanticizing or aestheticizing their fate?

And there are other ways in which aesthetics can ride roughshod over content. For example, to comply with (what we think are) expectations of journal editors and reviewers, we go to great lengths to foreground the mechanisms by which we move from data to findings. While this is an important feature of research reporting, it often means that ethnographic data is relegated to "data structure" tables that, in turn, rely on a coding strategy. The observational data ("here is what I saw, and when") tend to disappear altogether, leaving researchers instead to depend on verbatim quotes from (ethnographic) interviews. Whilst relying on "data tabling" (in lieu of storytelling) generates efficiencies that can be used to foreground methods and theorizing, it does have one unintended consequence: readers come to rely almost entirely on the ethnographer to warrant the contextual accuracy of quotes. And, as any ethnographer worth her salt will tell you, context is (almost) everything.

Moreover, our quest for scholarly publish-ability might trump the desire to make our work matter in more fundamental ways to help address, in fairly practical ways, the everyday concerns of those whose worlds and work were our subject. This isn't designed to be a cheap stab at the publishing game for, other merits aside, it keeps our tools sharp. Yet sharp for what? Might we perhaps be able to give voice to those who haven't the means to make themselves heard by leveraging our research more broadly in broadsheets or such outlets as *The Conversation*, *The Atlantic*, *Harpers*, *The New Yorker* and *The Huffington Post*, or by writing "trade" books? The point is a simple one: we owe something to those who took a risk by allowing us into their worlds, and they never appreciated the extent of the risk they took in inviting us, researchers, "on board".

When Ethnographers Traffic in Pain

Given a growing interest in the pursuit of research that meaningfully engages with "societal grand challenges", it is likely that more scholars will engage more often with people that, in one way or another, suffer. On the one hand, it is right that we should focus some of our firepower on grand challenges. On the other, chances are that in doing so we become traffickers in pain in that our scholarly success is inextricably tied to suffering others. As if that weren't enough, our institutional incentives are heavily stacked against them: our writing up their affairs for our scholarly journals does little or nothing to alleviate or resolve their situation. That is to say, our journals exist for us, not them, and while publishing advances our fortunes, it cold-shoulders theirs.

But the point of this chapter was not to debate nor debase our journals but, instead, to identify a set of moral ambiguities to be reflected, and acted, upon by organizational ethnographers who choose to pursue fieldwork in the context of societal grand challenges. While discomfort around exploitation covers familiar territory for experienced ethnographers, this isn't likely to be the case for those around voyeurism, complicity and aestheticization. And it is here that photography has the upper hand in acknowledging, and in raising awareness around, them. The principles of good practice that it advocates are not dissimilar from those espoused by the American Anthropological Association (on which many IRBs rely): to avoid causing harm, to be honest about the purpose, methods and outcomes of the work, to secure informed consent, to recognize that one will likely face competing ethical obligations when working with multiple informants that will need to be weighed up, to make sure one's results are accessible and that the raw data is protected and preserved, and to avoid exploitation (cf. Spradley, 2016: 34–39). Yet, as we have seen, the implementation of these principles is often not straightforward. To avoid harm includes harm to dignity and yet published accounts can be, and often are, embarrassing in some respects for some informants. Photographic portraits can be considered unflattering by those who feature in it, but so too can "warts and all" accounts of organizational behaviour; yet both are ultimately selected for their technical, conceptual and aesthetic qualities with little or no input from informants. Moreover, while ethnographers and documentary photographers will understand why they chose to undertake a particular project, neither are likely to be able to predict its outcome except in the broadest possible sense (e.g. a publication of sorts). The degree to which consent is informed is contingent on the information we provide to them and yet it remains tempting to not spell out all risks to informants. Moreover, what right to privacy do informants retain beyond a signed consent form? What happens to consent as relations grow in familiarity, informants let their guard down and provide a degree of intimacy not envisioned at the study's inception? The anthropologist Eriksen articulates the dilemma thus:

> The strength of ethnographic field method can also be its weakness: it is demanding, and rewarding, partly because the ethnographer invests not only professional skill in it, but also interpersonal skills. The ethnographer draws on his or her entire personality to a greater extent than any other scientist … this degree of personal involvement has important ethical implications.
>
> *(2001: 27)*

If some element of betrayal is par for the course, what then is our responsibility to the next generation of researchers, or even to contemporaries keen to "replicate" the study, if publication burns bridges and makes future access more difficult to negotiate and secure?

Finally, we already established how ethnography (like its photojournalistic counterpart) is essentially exploitative. But perhaps this is also true of other research methods deployed in the study of human behaviour. As Humphreys explains, even the use of public archives can cause harm to others if these distort rather than contribute to the understanding of social behaviour, leaving us to decide what methods may result in more or less misrepresentation of purposes and identity, more or less betrayal of confidence, and more or less positive or negative consequences for our informants (1975: 169). Besides, might it occasionally be appropriate to write a politically sensitive narrative based on one's field account, particularly when it uncovers unfair practices, dirty secrets or discrimination? As Cerwonka and Malkki (2008) put it, one can well imagine circumstances in which an exposé would be tempting or even ethically or politically important to write. And what if there is a public interest argument for exposing the human cost of endemic poverty, obesity, toxic waste and warfare in no-holds-barred, "lived experience" terms?

One "part-way" solution to this ethical quagmire is to write autoethnographically, that is, to write ourselves into our accounts. Sometimes referred to as confessional tales (Van Maanen, 2011), they allow us to be candid about our insecurities, incompetence, practical struggles and indiscretions in the pursuit of a good story but without privileging the self over the other (Coffey, 1999). These tales are told to help socialize the account but not to prioritize or, worse, glorify the self, and need not threaten the purity or conviction of the ethnographic text (Atkinson, 1990, as cited in Coffey, 1999). In fact, a confessional element in an account of fieldwork might actually help the reader appreciate the vantage point of the researcher (which is left obscured in more traditional styles of writing) and understand why it is she came to emphasize particular features or downplay others. Even if an element of personal biography may perhaps lead ethnographers to emphasize only those parts of social reality that make sense in terms of their earlier experiences (Eriksen, 2001), in the end we all rely heavily on our humanity in our fieldwork. It is our humanity that makes our work possible in the first place, and so why not be upfront about its contours, quirks, doubts and dispositions?

A candid appraisal of the self may also go some way to reciprocate the vulnerability we ask of our informants. That is, we make ourselves vulnerable as "payback" for having made the other vulnerable. The difficulty is, of course, that it is never quite a "like for like"; we are not best placed to accurately judge the impact on others from the publication of our account or anticipate the impact we may have on informants during the conduct of our fieldwork. And nor may the other care about the extent to which we write ourselves into our own texts, not least as editorial control over what is divulged or kept hidden remains with us and is a privilege never extended to the other. Nor are we necessarily good judges of what "making ourselves vulnerable" entails. What may feel risqué to us may be of no interest to anyone, let alone our informants. And, besides, a confessional account can occasionally land ethnographers in deep waters. Such was the case for Alice Goffman when, at the end of her account, she admitted to driving the getaway car in a revenge hunt for the killer of one of her informants. She writes poignantly about her emotions at the time, glad, she said, to "learn what it feels like to want a man to die" (Goffman, 2015: 263). What she may not have realized at the time is that, under Pennsylvania law, she had committed a felony by conspiring to murder.

Another "solution" is that of being transparent about criticisms of our accounts and to treat them as generative. Our informants are less ignorant of their own cultures than we often suppose, and "rather than being ruled out of court, their criticism should be listened to and taken into account, to be accepted, rejected, or modified, as we reformulate our analyses" (Rosaldo, 1986: 50). Where criticisms are specific, rather than responding assertively by emphasizing how right we (and thus how wrong they) are, or by framing our interpretation as "science" in contrast to their "lived experience" and suggest the twain shall never meet, one might consider critiques, however stinging, as additional data that shed yet more light on the worlds of others (Rosaldo, 1986: 6–7). Some ethnographers, including Wrobel (1979), have gone so far as to spell out any objections raised by those about whom they had written, in an appendix to the main text. This also implies that we take seriously our obligations post-publication by making sure that we remain easily available and responsive to those whose lives were central to our work. We ought to be prepared to reap what we sow.

Before any of this, of course, we would do well to ask informants how their involvement might put them at risk and whether a "safe word" might be helpful to, for example, kill off an interrogation that involves others. And what are their expectations, if any, as to any benefits of participating? It is likely that they are better judges of what constitutes harm in their specific social context, and the sort of safeguards they'd like to see in place to minimize, if not completely rule out, the risk of harm occurring (Fujii, 2012). While experience has taught us of ethnography's unintended consequences (they may not like what we write), it'd be naïve to assume that we know more about the participant's world than the participant herself.

While this chapter may have provided few resolutions to the ambiguities it articulated, the highlighting of these may serve as a warning beacon to those of us keen to pursue fieldwork in the context of societal grand challenges of the road ahead, not to discourage the pursuit but to invite reflexivity. As Fujii (2012: 722) writes: "ethical research often involves making difficult trade-offs that do not necessarily leave you, the researcher, feeling better about yourself. Do not try to avoid making these trade-offs but be clear about why you're making them." That is to say, whether and how to proceed with fieldwork and publication will remain, to a significant degree, a personal choice that is also likely to be highly situational. And it is a choice made daily as we enter our fields and write up our notes late into the night. The consequences of these choices may never be entirely clear, and so we beaver away as saints or assholes (and never quite sure which), keen to make our work count for something.

Notes

1 These past presidents include Hambrick (1994), Cummings (2007), Hitt (1998), Rousseau (2006), Van de Ven (2002) and Walsh (2011). All are cited in Tsui's (2013) provocative article.

2 The George R. Terry Book Award.

3 For example, Erasmus University (as spearheaded by its business school, Rotterdam School of Management) has explicitly adopted "grand challenges" to help focus, and streamline, its academic activities. Cambridge Judge Business School has created centres to focus on such specific challenges as social innovation, gender equality and energy policy, while its Organization Theory and Information Systems (OTIS) subject group have realigned their research and teaching around societal grand challenges.

4 For example, the United Kingdom's government funding allocation is decided by a periodic Research Excellence Framework, designed to assess research performance by department. In recent years, the REF has made impact on practice a significant component of this assessment exercise.

5 In our research group alone, recent PhD dissertations have focused on the ongoing refugee crisis (Corinna Frey), mobile medicine in less developed countries (Isaac Holeman), sustainable development (Anna Kim), fair trade practices (Juliane Reinecke) and child marriage (Laura Claus).

6 The photographs discussed in this chapter can be easily located with a Google search. They have not been reproduced in this chapter due to copyright restrictions.

7 Similarly, Alice Goffman (2015) suspected that "excessive" expressions of virility by informants during her fieldwork might have been prompted by her presence, as a young woman, in a hyper masculine environment.

8 https://priorprobability.com/2014/06/10/is-alice-goffman-the-new-margaret-mead/

References

Allen, C., 1997. Spies like us: When sociologists deceive their subjects. *Lingua Franca*, 7(9), pp.30–39.

Amis, J.M., Wright, P.M., Dyson, B., Vardaman, J.M. and Ferry, H., 2012. Implementing childhood obesity policy in a new educational environment: The cases of Mississippi and Tennessee. *American Journal of Public Health*, 102(7), pp.1406–1413.

Bothello, J. and Roulet, T.J., 2018. The imposter syndrome, or the mis-representation of self in academic life. *Journal of Management Studies*, 56(4), pp.854–861.

Brettell, C., 1996. *When they read what we write: The politics of ethnography.* Westport, CT: Praeger.

Burke, E., 1998. *A Philosophical Enquiry into the Sublime and Beautiful.* London: Penguin UK.

Butler, J., 2007. *Torture, Sexual Politics and the Ethics of Photography.* Presentation at the *Thinking Humanity after Abu Ghraib Conference*, Stanford University.

Cerwonka, A. and Malkki, L.H., 2008. *Improvising Theory: Process and Temporality in Ethnographic Fieldwork.* Chicago: University of Chicago Press.

Claus, L., de Rond, M., Howard-Grenville, J. and Lodge, J., 2019. When fieldwork hurts: On the lived experience of conducting research in unsettling contexts. *The Production of Managerial Knowledge and Organizational Theory: New Approaches to Writing, Producing and Consuming Theory*, 59, pp.157–172.

Coffey, A., 1999. *The Ethnographic Self: Fieldwork and the Representation of Identity.* London: Sage.

Cummings, T.G., 2007. 2006 Presidential address – quest for an engaged Academy. *Academy of Management Review*, 32(3), pp.355–360.

de Rond, M., 2017. *Doctors at War: Life and Death in a Field Hospital.* Ithaca: Cornell University Press.

de Rond, M. and Lok, J., 2016. Some things can never be unseen: The role of context in psychological injury at war. *Academy of Management Journal*, 59(6), pp.1965–1993.

Eberhard, J., 2017. *A Study of the River City Police Persons at Risk Program to Help Women Exit Street Level Prostitution.* Working Paper. Department of Sociology University of Western Ontario.

Eriksen, T.H., 2001. *Small Places, Large Issues: An Introduction to Social and Cultural Anthropology.* London: Pluto Press.

Fujii, L.A., 2012. Research ethics 101: Dilemmas and responsibilities. *PS: Political Science & Politics*, 45(4), pp.717–723.

George, G., Howard-Grenville, J., Joshi, A. and Tihanyi, L., 2016. Understanding and tackling societal grand challenges through management research. *Academy of Management Journal*, 59(6), pp.1880–1895.

Goffman, A., 2009. On the run: Wanted men in a Philadelphia ghetto. *American Sociological Review*, 74(3), pp.339–357.

Goffman, A., 2015. *On the Run: Fugitive Life in an American City.* London: Picador.

Hambrick, D.C., 1994. 2003 Presidential address – What if the Academy actually mattered? *Academy of Management Review*, 19(1), pp.11–16.

Hariman, R. and Lucaites, J.L., 2007. *No Caption Needed: Iconic Photographs, Public Culture, and Liberal Democracy.* Chicago: University of Chicago Press.

Heese, J., Krishnan, R. and Moers, F., 2016. Selective regulator decoupling and organizations' strategic responses. *Academy of Management Journal*, 59(6), pp.2178–2204.

Hitt, M.A., 1998. 1997 Presidential address – Twenty-first-century organizations: Business firms, business schools, and the Academy. *Academy of Management Review, 23*(2), pp.218–224.

Humphreys, L., 1975. *Tearoom Trade: Impersonal Sex in Public Places.* Berlin: de Gruyter.

Kim, Y.H. and Davis, G.F., 2016. Challenges for global supply chain sustainability: Evidence from conflict minerals reports. *Academy of Management Journal, 59*(6), pp.1896–1916.

Kleinman, A. and Kleinman, J., 1996. The appeal of experience; the dismay of images: Cultural appropriations of suffering in our times. *Daedalus, 125*(1), pp.1–23.

Kornberger, M., Leixnering, S., Meyer, R.E. and Höllerer, M.A., 2018. Rethinking the sharing economy: The nature and organization of sharing in the 2015 refugee crisis. *Academy of Management Discoveries, 4*(3), pp.314–335.

Lawrence, T.B., 2017. High-stakes institutional translation: Establishing North America's first government-sanctioned supervised injection site. *Academy of Management Journal, 60*(5), pp. 1771–1800.

Leo, R.A., 1995. Inside the interrogation room. *Journal of Criminal Law & Criminology, 86,* p.266.

Lester, P.M., 2015. *Photojournalism: An Ethical Approach.* New York: Routledge.

Malcolm, J., 2011. *The Journalist and the Murderer.* London: Granta Books.

McGahan, A., 2010. Reshaping business schools to focus on the most important management problems of our time. Available via: https://inside.rotman.utoronto.ca/anitamcgahan/files/2012/10/statement.pdf (last accessed: 01 March 2019).

Meltzer, M., 2000. *Dorothea Lange: A photographer's life.* New York: Syracuse University Press.

Reinhardt, M., 2007. Picturing violence: Aesthetics and the anxiety of critique. In M. Reinhardt, H. Edwards and E. Duganne (Eds.) *Beautiful Suffering: Photography and the Traffic in Pain,* Williamstown, MA: Williams College Museum of Art, pp.13–36.

Rogers, K.M., Corley, K.G. and Ashforth, B.E., 2016. Seeing more than orange: Organizational respect and positive identity transformation in a prison context. *Administrative Science Quarterly, 62*(2), pp.219–269.

Rosaldo, R., 1986. From the door of his tent: the fieldworker and the inquisitor. In J. Clifford & G. Marcus (Eds.), *Writing Culture: The Poetics and Politics of Ethnography,* London: University of California Press, pp.77–97.

Roulet, T.J., Gill, M.J., Stenger, S. and Gill, D.J., 2017. Reconsidering the value of covert research: The role of ambiguous consent in participant observation. *Organizational Research Methods, 20*(3), pp.487–517.

Rousseau, D.M., 2006. Is there such a thing as 'evidence-based management?'. *Academy of Management Review, 31*(2), pp.256–269.

Sontag, S., 2001 (1977). *On Photography* (Vol. 48). New York: Macmillan.

Sontag, S., 2003. Regarding the pain of others. *Diogène,* (1), pp.127–139.

Sontag, S., 2004. *Regarding the Pain of Others.* London: Penguin.

Spradley, J.P., 2016. *The Ethnographic Interview.* Long Grove, IL: Waveland Press.

Tracey, P. and Phillips, N., 2016. Managing the consequences of organizational stigmatization: Identity work in a social enterprise. *Academy of Management Journal, 59*(3), pp.740–765.

Tsui, A.S., 2013. The spirit of science and socially responsible scholarship. *Management and Organization Review, 9*(3), pp.375–394.

Vakili, K. and McGahan, A.M., 2016. Health care's grand challenge: Stimulating basic science on diseases that primarily afflict the poor. *Academy of Management Journal, 59*(6), pp.1917–1939.

Van de Ven, A.H., 2002. 2001 Presidential address – Strategic directions for the Academy of Management: This Academy is for you! *Academy of Management Review, 27*(1), pp.171–184.

Van de Ven, A.H., 2007. *Engaged Scholarship: A Guide for Organizational and Social Research.* Oxford University Press on Demand.

Van Maanen, J., 1978. The asshole. In P. Manning, and J. Van Maanen, (Eds.) *Policing: A View from the Streets,* New York: McGraw-Hill. pp.221–238.

Van Maanen, J., 2010. A song for my supper: More tales of the field. *Organizational Research Methods*, *13*(2), pp.240–255.

Van Maanen, J., 2011. *Tales of the Field: On Writing Ethnography*. Chicago: University of Chicago Press.

Walker, J.C., 1986. Romanticising resistance, romanticising culture: Problems in Willis's theory of cultural production. *British Journal of Sociology of Education*, *7*(1), pp.59–80. DOI: 10.1080/0142569860070104.

Walsh, J.P., 2011. 2010 Presidential address – Embracing the sacred in our secular scholarly world. *Academy of Management Review*, *36*(1), pp.215–234.

Whiteman, G. and Cooper, G., 2016. Decoupling rape. *Academy of Management Discoveries*, *2*(2), pp.115–154.

Whyte, W.F., 1973 [1943]. *Street Corner Society*. Chicago: University of Chicago Press.

Williams, T.A. and Shepherd, D.A., 2016. Building resilience or providing sustenance: Different paths of emergent ventures in the aftermath of the Haiti earthquake. *Academy of Management Journal*, *59*(6), pp.2069–2102.

Wrobel, P., 1979. *Our Way: Family, Parish, and Neighborhood in a Polish-American Community*. Notre Dame, IN: University of Notre Dame Press.

Zilber, T.B., 2002. Institutionalization as an interplay between actions, meanings, and actors: The case of a rape crisis center in Israel. *Academy of Management Journal*, *45*(1), pp.234–254.

26

FIELDWORK IN WORK WORLDS

Robert Jackall

As chairman of the joint Department of Anthropology & Sociology at Williams College in the 1980s, I interviewed a candidate from Stanford University for a job in our Anthropology wing. Since she had done her fieldwork in the Pacific, I asked if she knew an anthropological study done on the archipelago of Palau called *The Political Impact of Colonial Administration* by Arthur J. Vidich. It was Art's 1953 doctoral dissertation in the Department of Social Relations at Harvard University. Not only did the young woman know the work, she exclaimed, but it was, she thought, the single best anthropological work on the Pacific that she knew of.

But then she said: "But Vidich never wrote anything else." Art and I laughed about this, not only because of the compliment the young woman paid to his work and his anthropological heritage—it is important here to note that Art's doctoral degree from Harvard's Department of Social Relations was in social anthropology—but also because of the disconcerting comment it made about the provincial specialization of what were once unified disciplines. Anthropology and important segments of sociology once shared a common methodology, namely intensive fieldwork, a noble tradition that still has the potential to link disciplines that today seem far apart.

Joseph Bensman once told me that he thought Art Vidich was the best fieldworker of all the anthropologists and sociologists of his generation. And Art Vidich once told me that Joe Bensman was without peer in analyzing field materials. Here, in ideal-typical form, are some thoughts about fieldwork. They are based both on innumerable conversations with Art and Joe as well as on my own experiences in several fieldwork projects in different occupational and professional worlds, all inspired by Art's work in Palau and in Springdale, New York, for his and Joe's classic community study *Small Town in Mass Society*.

Fieldwork begins with framing a significant intellectual problem that—appropriately reframed as necessary—is amenable to empirical research. Thus, for example, in 1980, I set out to address the intellectual problem: How does bureaucracy shape moral consciousness? I chose to study corporate managers because they are the quintessential bureaucratic work group: they both make the bureaucratic rules of their organizations and, except at the very top layer of bureaucracies, they are bound by those rules. In order to study this occupational group, I reframed my larger focus on how bureaucracy shapes moral consciousness to ask: What are the occupational *moral rules-in-use* of corporate managers? Thirty-six corporations refused my requests to study their managers. In the end, however, I gained access to a giant chemical company, a small chemical company, a large textile firm, and a medium-sized public relations firm. Over six years, I interviewed more than 140 managers, a great many of them multiple times. And I found that yet another re-framing of my question took me immediately into the most morally fraught area of corporate managers' occupational lives. That question was: Who gets ahead around here? The struggle to survive and flourish is always foremost in the minds of denizens of bureaucracies. And that question readily prompts statements about the habits of mind and moral rules-in-use valued in a given organization. This fieldwork produced *Moral Mazes: The World of Corporate Managers* in 1988 and a 20th anniversary edition with an additional chapter commenting on the Great Recession.

Once one has framed an intellectual problem, and reframed it as necessary, fieldwork requires good eyes, good ears, and a desire to enter into and understand the worlds of others from the inside out. It requires the ability to elicit and then listen patiently to others' fits and starts of descriptions, accounts, and explanations of their worlds. It requires an adeptness at the kind of easy informal conversation that invites trust and disclosure. And it requires the recognition that each métier has its own language, metaphors, and lore. Corporate managers, for instance, are typically very organized in responding to a fieldworker's queries. One can go back to one's interview notes with managers and find clear A, B, C, D paragraphs. By contrast, in fieldwork with Janice M. Hirota during a comparative study of public relations practitioners and of advertising "creatives"—the men and women who actually write the copy and illustrate or film the commercials that surround us—we found two worlds filled with colorful often boastful stories and, in advertising, ostentatious showings of reels of one's commercials, sometimes plagiarized from others' work, essential résumés against one's inevitable firing. Moreover, the practitioners in both fields evince a faint contempt both for their clients and especially for the audiences that they address in their work. One example must suffice. A public relations practitioner had a rich financier's trophy wife as her client. The financier was about to give a mega-gift to a famous museum to use in building a new wing named after himself and his bride. The problem was that his bride, though ravishingly beautiful, was a wholly unlettered Brooklyn girl who didn't know a painting from a sculpture. The practitioner's job was to fabricate a reputation for the young woman as an expert in the arts. To do this, the practitioner began by planting an article with a journalist declaring that the woman had graduated from Smith College with a degree in art history. This was followed by seeding a series of articles about the young woman's admiration for the Impressionists and even a piece ghostwritten for her about her special love for Renoir's work. One day I was in the practitioner's office when she received a phone call from the young woman who was exceedingly angry that an article about the forthcoming new museum wing did not mention her. I listened on speakerphone as she shrieked at the practitioner: "How can they disregard me after all that I've accomplished?" As it happens, clients almost always come to believe the fictions created for and about them by public relations practitioners. And practitioners' best friends are lazy journalists. This fieldwork produced, in 2000, *Image Makers: Advertising, Public Relations, and the Ethos of Advocacy.*

Fieldwork is grounded in the premise that the basic unit of human society is meaningful action by individuals and that the meta-problem of all social analysis is: How, in what ways, and why have particular individuals come together to construct particular social worlds and concomitant worldviews? Fieldwork requires therefore a deep interest in individuals' personal biographies, the intersection of biographies of different people, and the mapping of both against the historical trajectory and convergence of trends that produce particular social structures. This, in turn, requires an appreciation of the multiple levels of consciousness possessed by every individual and instituted in every social situation. Most of all, fieldwork demands the relentless curiosity and personal skill to plumb those levels of consciousness until the "commonsense" worlds of others become clear. Doing fieldwork in an unfamiliar social world closely resembles a boyhood experience of mine. I visited a high-school friend, Hap Hathaway of happy memory, at his home in Woodstock, Maryland. After devouring Hap's home-made strawberry ice cream, we went to the Sylvan Dell Pool, a former granite quarry. As we finished undressing, I asked Hap how deep the quarry's waters were. Suddenly, he pushed me from behind over the ledge and I plunged feet-first into the clear, deep-green waters. I sank rapidly and kept going down and down, unable to gain a purchase. Eventually I landed on the rocky bottom of the quarry and thrust myself up to the surface. I had learned the hard way the depth of the quarry's waters. Fieldwork in an unfamiliar social world mirrors the experiences of surprise, apprehension, bewilderment, and, finally, firm footing that I had at the quarry.

One must also cultivate an awareness that allows one to penetrate the public faces both of individuals and organizations and to recognize the differences between publicly expressed and privately held views. Concealment, secrecy, fakery, deception, double-think, and double-speak are constituent parts of all social realities, perhaps particularly of modern bureaucratic organizations. More than one corporate manager cautioned me that whenever someone in the corporate world says to a fieldworker "Now I'll be perfectly frank with you," one should realize that a curveball is on its way.

Perhaps the greatest challenge that fieldworkers face is the task of writing up their carefully taken down and organized field materials. This demands the intellectual openness that allows the very concepts, terms of reference, and organization of one's analysis to emerge directly out of one's field materials. The discipline to let one's field materials guide, ground, inform, and limit one's interpretations is what both Art Vidich and Joe Bensman called "letting your data speak to you." In the 1990s, I did several years of fieldwork with police detectives in New York City, first with the New York Police Department's (NYPD) Midtown North precinct, then with the Robbery Squad of the New York City Transit Police (NYCTP), which was, until October 1994, an independent police authority, and finally with the detective squad at the NYPD's 34th Precinct in upper Manhattan.

The project began with an epistemological query. In the 1980s, I had developed a core course for our joint Anthropology & Sociology department entitled *Ways of Knowing* as an intellectual response to the rampant postmodernism that beleaguered and continues to beleaguer the academy.

The motivating question of the course was: How do men and women of affairs—such as medical doctors, public health officials, epidemiologists, prosecutors, and homicide detectives, charged with the grave responsibility of ascertaining the *truth* of matters in their respective fields—reach their judgments?

The worlds of detectives are organized by specific cases that they themselves "catch." In a busy squad, such as the old Three-Four, each detective in a squad of twenty regularly carried scores of cases, including several homicides. Detectives worked assiduously to "clear" their cases either by making an arrest or through exceptional clearance, meaning they had proof of a culprit's responsibility for a crime, but were unable to arrest the person for some reason, often because the culprit had fled to a country, such as the Dominican Republic, that at the time did not extradite its nationals to the United States. Such clearances were the principal measure of detectives' work for promotion from third-grade to second-grade detective and, if a detective was exceptionally able, eventually to first-grade detective.

If one asks detectives a general question such as: "How do you get suspects to talk with you?" they invariably respond with detailed recitals of particular cases that always remind them of still other cases on which they worked. The result is a vast, often bewildering, names-and-aliases-filled interlocking set of stories. To make sense of this world, I read and took detailed notes on detectives' written investigative reports, called DD5s, required for each and every case that a detective catches. Once I had mastered the names and details of each case, I re-interviewed the involved detectives, getting their own oral histories of the cases that they had raised in our earlier conversation. Before long, I had learned the details of hundreds of individual cases and that knowledge became the basis for more general reflection on detectives' work. Moreover, each of the detective squads that I studied, after initial apprehension, came to recognize that I wasn't like other visitors to their world—such as reporters, novelists, or screenwriters. They appreciated my deep knowledge of all of their cases, not just the sensational homicides that grab headlines. As a result, they took me out regularly into the field where I witnessed first-hand both the aftermaths of the appalling events that were the stuff of their work, as well as sometimes quirky events that seem like fiction. One example must suffice. Detective Pete Moro, a stalwart of the old Three-Four squad, caught a reported homicide around 75th Street in Manhattan. By the time we got to the crime scene, the person shot had already been rushed to the Crash Room at Columbia Presbyterian Hospital. Pete, I, and others entered the Crash Room and Pete asked the covering MD how things looked for the victim. The MD slowly shook his head and pointed to the middle of his own forehead to describe the victim's gunshot wound. Pete then asked if he could take a picture of the victim to show around the street. The MD nodded. As Pete brought the squad's camera close to the victim's stretcher, the victim suddenly sat bolt upright and mugged for the camera with a big smile, all the while pinching his nurse's derrière. He then leapt off the stretcher, clothed only in a hospital sheet, and announced that he was leaving. And he marched out the door entirely on his own. Pete found out later that the victim had returned to the hospital for treatment. The bullet had circled his skull and exited his body through his lower back.

What are the habits of mind detectives bring to their work? To do their work well, detectives must become urban ethnographers, close students of the communities in which they work, with particular attention to the criminal networks in a given area. And they must be willing to embrace the moral ambiguities that they inevitably experience through their regular interaction with men and women whose own moral codes are utterly different from their own. For example, the first armed robber I interviewed with the Transit Police's Robbery Squad was Rasheed, a strapping, handsome young man. Rasheed had been the lookout (the third man in a hierarchy of four—the drop [gunman], bagman [collector of the tokens and cash], lookout [the man who stands on the subway entrance steps and prevents anyone from entering while the robbery is in progress], and the wheelman [the driver of the getaway car]) in a robbery crew that plagued the J subway line in Queens. The subway token-booth clerk at the Norwood Street station was afraid to look at the drop or the bagman, but he did get a good look at Rasheed on the steps and was able to pick out his photo from an array presented to him by Transit detectives. The detectives picked up Rasheed and, on the token-booth clerk's testimony, he was convicted at trial of armed robbery and sent to Sing-Sing. After four years or so, he was given work-release (time out of prison on weekends) and he returned to the same Norwood Street station, this time with a gun, and robbed $5,000 worth of tokens and cash from the exact same token-booth clerk. He bought a car and lots of crack at $5.00 a bottle and went to South Carolina where he sold the crack for $20.00 a bottle and then bought handguns there for $50.00 apiece. He then drove back to New York City where he sold the guns for $250.00 each, bought more crack, and returned to South Carolina to continue his entrepreneurial career. Eventually, he was arrested in South Carolina for selling the crack and his New York warrant "dropped," that is, showed up in the nationwide National Crime Information Center. Transit detectives brought him back to the City to process him. After the detectives had finished interrogating him, I got to speak with him. When I came into the room, Rasheed confronted me:

> Professor, what you want? You wants to know why I does what I do? Am I right, Professor? Does you have any idea at all of how much I was makin' when we was riding' high on the J line? Professor, I was third man down and I cleared eight grand a week! And I had gold sleeves for all my teeth, jus' like the rappers, and I had me a Mercedes Benz, and fur coats for all my women, and I could fuck at will. And you wants me to get a regular job? Professor, that wooden make no sense at all.

He then turned to the two Transit detectives in the room and said: "Now, boys, I been straight wit' you and I wants a favor. I wanna be sent back to Sing Sing." The detectives said: "Why there, Rasheed? That's the toughest house in the system." Rasheed laughed and said:

> Boys, you can git anything you wants on the yard at Sing Sing. It just like bein' in Queens!! And 'sides, there's a little girl Correction Officer there who take the young boys upstairs for a ride at $100 a toss, and I wants to get me some of that again.

Detectives not only have to tolerate guys like Rasheed, but they also must learn to appreciate their insights into a different moral universe. More specifically, detectives distinguish between "homocides" and "streeticides." A "homocide" almost invariably involves sexual intimates or family members, narrowing the list of suspects dramatically. But detectives can solve a "streeticide" only by engaging with and extracting information from other denizens of the street, often criminals themselves, with moral codes similar to that of Rasheed.

The detectives introduced me to key prosecutors at the District Attorney of New York (DANY) and at the Office of Special Prosecutor for Narcotics for the City of New York, later headed by Bridget Brennan. I underwent Early Case Assessment training in Trial Bureau 50 at DANY under the aegis of Chief Warren Murray. I was able to observe first-hand the always complex negotiations between uniformed police officers, detectives, and prosecutors about the proper charges to bring in criminal cases. And because the old Three-Four was the hub of the drug trade for the entire Eastern seaboard, Special Prosecutor Brennan's tutelage of me over the years was invaluable. My fieldwork with detectives and prosecutors produced two books: *Wild Cowboys: Urban Marauders & the Forces of Order* in 1998 and *Street Stories: The World of Police Detectives* in 2005.

Currently, I am interviewing American intelligence officers whose work in the world of espionage consists of collecting and unraveling others' secrets, all the while fending off disinformation campaigns from rival spy agencies. The recruitment of "assets," that is, spies with access to valued information, closely resembles sexual seduction. Men and women become spies for many reasons—money, revenge against superiors who they think have slighted them, a loathing of their own countries' politics, adventure and excitement, and aid for their own families such as medical care, among many other reasons. Among their tasks, intelligence officers must first carefully discern that their targets do indeed have access to valued information and then what motivates their targets' willingness to spy, that is, to commit treason against their own country. The moral hazards of this world emerge directly out of its central task—the willingness to put others and their families in jeopardy in order to obtain secrets. Moreover, as with police detectives, intelligence officers must interact with men and women whose own moral codes are frequently utterly unlike their own. For instance, I interviewed at length one intelligence officer who, for years, handled Yasser Arafat's right-hand man, Ali Hassan Salameh, who provided the CIA with invaluable glimpses into the inner workings and thinking of the Palestine Liberation Organization. As it happens, Salameh was the mastermind behind the massacre of Israeli athletes at the 1972 Munich Olympics and he was eventually assassinated in Beirut by Mossad in 1979, in the second phase of its Wrath of God operation.

I am also examining the fantastically complicated world of counterintelligence, the ongoing search for spies in one's own organization. James Jesus Angleton, the CIA's brilliant and obsessive long-time counterintelligence chief aptly characterized his world as a "wilderness of mirrors," borrowing the phrase from T.S. Eliot's 1920 poem *Gerontion*. As Michael J. Sulick amply demonstrates in his 2013 book *American Spies: Espionage against the United States from the Cold War to the Present*, America's intelligence establishment has been remarkably vulnerable to domestic spies. And hardly a month passes without attempts by the intelligence apparatuses of the Chinese and of the Russians to penetrate our intelligence agencies.

Fieldwork so conceived, practiced, and written-up is the antithesis of most bureaucratically organized survey research, at least of the kind that dips into the swirling eddies of public opinion to "test" a predetermined hypothesis. And it is as well the antithesis of what passes for fieldwork today by many anthropologists and sociologists, including researchers in other disciplines who have borrowed aspects of the methodology. Here are some examples:

- One regularly sees fieldwork done or, much more often borrowed, to gather a collection of examples to illustrate an already worked-out thesis. For instance, Marianna Torgovnick's *Gone Primitive: Savage Intellects, Modern Lives* rummages through the history of modern art, many literary works including novels, and classical anthropological ethnographies to target Western thinkers, artists, and novelists for making the "primitive" a funhouse mirror of essentially modern fears and anxieties.
- In the last two decades, especially in the field of sociology, one sees fieldwork, as well as other kinds of social research, conducted as a vehicle for "social justice" advocacy. Indeed, the 2019 American Sociological Association (ASA) meetings in New York City are organized around the theme of "Engaging Social Justice for a Better World." ASA's new president, Professor Mary Romero of Arizona State University says in her statement of the meetings' purpose:

> Embracing a sociology that challenges social injustices and sustains scholar activists is pivotal in this time of increasing social inequalities. Sociologists possess the analytical tools and empirical data necessary to support communities fighting against injustices in many realms. These areas include: racial inequality, environmental degradation, immigration restrictions and law enforcement violence, housing segregation, unequal educational opportunities, disparate health outcomes, mass incarceration, and precarious violence against women and LGBTQ. Sociologists who partner with community groups, human rights

organizations, civil rights lawyers, and other social justice advocates can make significant contributions to promote scholarship that can facilitate progressive social change.

In facing the growing normalization of racism, nationalism and xenophobia, many sociologists are critically examining the concept of objectivity and its role in maintaining hierarchies of power within the discipline. In exploring steps toward a more epistemologically sound construction of unbiased methodological processes in sociology, the following questions emerge: What does 'objectivity' mean? What is the role of objectivity in our field? Are objectivity and detachment the only routes to scientific validity? Can the linkage between sociology and public engagement lead to a sounder science and weaken status hierarchies within the discipline? Does the reification of objectivity and detachment in the discipline serve to reinforce status hierarchies more than produce sound science? Does a sociology that converges scholarship with applications to social equality create meaningful opportunities to shape social and economic policies? How significant is public sociology and purpose-driven-science in connecting empirical work to social justice scholarship?

[www.asanet.org/annual-meeting-2019/2019-theme]

- Professor Romero's theme statement for the 2019 ASA meetings evinces many pervasive habits of mind exhibited in contemporary sociology and anthropology: that is, the postmodern notion that there is no such thing as "objectivity" and therefore no possibility of attaining "truth" in the Aristotelian sense of that word, meaning a correspondence between a stated proposition and some reality external to the mind of the person stating it. Everything is subjective and wholly relative, except, of course, one's fervent commitments to "progressive" causes. As George Orwell characterized Oceania in his prescient *1984*: "Not merely the validity of experience, but the very existence of external reality was tacitly denied by their philosophy. The heresy of heresies was common sense." The implication of Professor Romero's critique of objectivity is that inconvenient realities, such as the grossly disproportionate homicide rates among American blacks, both as victims and as perpetrators, or the grossly disproportionate suicide rate of LGBTQ youth must be blamed on something external to blacks and external to LGBTQ youth themselves, such as "white racism" or "homophobia," or the inconvenient fact that so-called "transgender" people have and will always have either XX or XY chromosomes in every cell of their bodies, whatever "sexual identities" they claim.

- In this time of ferocious identity politics, a whole new genre of work called "autoethnography" has emerged where one claims to be able to make general statements about the world by writing about one's own personal experiences or problems. This seems particularly true of work on race, sex/gender, homosexuality, or gender dysphoria. Similarly, one finds fieldwork data interpreted by imposing ideologically driven frameworks on one's data, whether Marx-ist, feminist, homosexual, third-world revolutionary, right-wing reactionary, or simply cheerful robotism.

- As part of the postmodern turn, some sociologists and anthropologists are turn-ing away entirely from fieldwork to focus on textual or discourse analysis. At times, this becomes a focus on narrow disciplinary issues instead of attempting to explain the social world. Sometimes it is motivated by the supposition that language alone actually constitutes social reality and that one can plumb the depths of social structures or trends by analyzing how people talk about them. So, a young sociologist studies: "What do we talk about when we talk about 'terrorism?'" instead of examining, for instance, the vast record of Islamist ter-ror against Westerners and the West itself. Related to this is the adoption of an empty notion of "culture," wherein one analyzes the vast array of images that inundate modern societies wholly divorced from any understanding of the occupational and professional groups that create and propagate those images. Here, sociologists and anthropologists can learn a great deal from two occu-pational groups mentioned earlier in this chapter. The epistemological habits of mind exhibited by both the best police detectives and intelligence officers could not be more different from those one finds in most of the humanities and social sciences in the contemporary academy, corporations, public relations, and advertising. The best detectives and intelligence officers eschew entirely the faux "realities" conjured up by men and women who have been captured by the Circes of postmodernism. Instead, the very tasks that they must perform make them into Aristotelians in a postmodern world.

Fieldwork done right shapes the self of the fieldworker in decisive ways. The true fieldworker is the compleat observer, the documenter, the man or woman who poses an important intellectual problem, but aims only to record honestly and understand deeply the accomplishments, the successes, the failures, the triumphs, the explanations, the insights, the fears, and the foibles of others well-positioned to address that problem. As Art Vidich and Joe Bensman point out, he or she is ulti-mately a eunuch in the world of affairs, a role that he or she must accept to order to carry out fieldwork and analysis properly and well. At the same time, one might add, nothing is more necessary in our day and age, than men and women wholly ded-icated to seeing the world *as it is* and being unafraid to state clearly what they see.

Acknowledgements

My thanks to Janice M. Hirota, Joshua Wakeham, and Duffy Graham for their close readings of this chapter and their many helpful suggestions. Special thanks to the Willmott Family Professorship in Sociology & Public Affairs at Williams, which provided funding for many of the field projects mentioned in this chapter.

27

WITHDRAWAL PAINS AND GAINS

Exiting from the Field[1]

John Van Maanen

Prologue

Exiting the field or, more prosaically, "getting out" is little talked about in the ethnographic literature(s) despite the fact that we ethnographers are these days supposed to be both deeply reflexive and epistemologically precise about our work. Problems of access or "getting in" is perhaps over-specified and written about fairly extensively but my claim here is that exiting is methodologically and theoretically under-specified yet can and should be problematized. Opening up this line of inquiry will, I think, prove revelatory – particularly of ethnography's relational nature and its ever changing contextuality and temporality.

All is not dark however. There are of course some references to withdrawal from the field and, in a way, they are revealing of the epistemological concerns of the era in which they were written. Thirty-five years ago David Snow (1980), for example, wrote some about "unwinding" from the field, contending that the relative inattention to the exiting process in fieldwork was due to the separation ethnographers maintained between their personal and private lives from their professional concerns, with the personal and private viewed as "extraneous" to the work and hence glossed over in their writings (if mentioned at all). Some years later, in 1995, John and Lynn Lofland argued – while still holding that disengagement warranted more attention – that our relative silence about exit stems in part because of the close and personal ties ethnographers often maintain with those they have learned from in the field and their consequent desire to keep the door open to the possibility of a return to a fieldsite (and, I would add, a return to one's friends in the field). Recently, Snejina Michailova and colleagues (2014), again noting the relative dearth of commentary about leaving the field, attributed much of this to the idiographic, open-ended character of ethnographic research. Since there are few if any prespecified algorithms for producing ethnography, exiting the field is usually a long, drawn out process of disentanglement rather than a single act and hence difficult to specify, given its often incomplete, provisional, unfinished character.

There is of course the possibility of "no exit" whatsoever, such that one is more or less always "in the field." There are many exemplars to draw from. The work of urban sociologist Elijah Anderson (1990, 1999) is an example of an approach that is "on-going" by design. Recently, Michel Anteby (2013) explored the faculty socialization process at the West Point of capitalism while himself undergoing the lengthy tenure process at the Harvard Business School and writing and publishing his monograph while still at the school (but no more). Indeed, long-term engagements in the field are not hard to find in the ethnographic literature. Hirokazu Miyazaki (2013) spent nearly 15 years following the lives and professional careers of a small group of Japanese arbitrageurs and is apparently still at it. Robin Nagel (2013) put in almost a decade as the "honorary anthropologist" at the New York Sanitation Department examining how those in this rather reviled occupation maintain their pride and dignity while keeping the city clean, navigable, and safe. Karen Ho (2009) has spent years untangling the work and careers of Wall Street traders. And most vividly, Alice Goffman (2014) for six years lived and worked closely among those "on the run" in a poor, largely Black neighborhood in Philadelphia and, in her words, left the neighborhood only "when my funding ran out and I had to write a dissertation and get a job" (p.205).

We often assume that ethnographers with anthropological training choose fieldsites – like choosing mates – for life and some of them do. Even when not true – as is, I suspect, most often the case although I have no data to support this suspicion – site switching rarely breaks the link readers associate with the ethnographer and his or her "tribe" and most admired (typically early) work – for example, Clifford Geertz being forever tied to the Balinese just as Malinowski is linked to the Trobrianders. Ethnographers with sociological backgrounds too, while perhaps engaging in a bit more site switching across studies than anthropologists (for whom return visits are proforma and may well extend across an ethnographic career) also have lasting ties with their respective groups of interest – Howard Becker with jazz musicians or Bill Whyte with his street corner confederates of Boston's North End or Rosabeth Kanter's long time engagement with up-town corporate executives here, there, and everywhere. The point being that long-lasting, cyclical involvement – full of repeated engagements in the field, replete with zooming in and zooming out of the field, rounds of attachment and detachment each marked by intensive engagement then taking a break and pulling back, staying away for a spell and then returning to the field – is hardly unknown and marks a good deal if not most of ethnography. Even the rather flexible notion of "the ethnographic interview" carries with it the idea that such interviews are open-ended and long lasting with the ethnographer returning to the same "key informants" time and time again, creating, in practice, a continuing dialogue that may span years (Spradley, 1979).

Exiting is most often a process not an act and ethnographic fieldwork may entail a number of exits (and returns). My own work with police has stretched over a 40-year period and has entailed numerous entries and exits (and re-entries and re-exits). It began with a year in the field in the Seattle Police Department in 1969 to which I returned (and left) numerous times over the next 25 years as my cohorts – fellow recruits in my training academy class – played out their respective police careers. In addition, I spent a year with detectives in the Metropolitan Police in London in 1985 and have been in and out for brief periods in a number of other police agencies in the U.S. from coast to coast. Exiting, however, even when but a pause in the work, does of course entail something of a loss of role, a change of focus, a concern for writing and theorizing, and perhaps a rather sharp shift of social and personal identity. These are matters I wish to take up in this talk but first, as a way of setting the stage, a few brief words about my take on what ethnography is and is not.

Ethnography as a Social Practice

My view is that ethnography is a logic – a stance if you will – rather than a given method or any particular type of study. It names an epistemology – a way of knowing and the kind of knowledge that results. It is anything but a recipe. It involves fieldwork, headwork, and textwork and results typically in a written representation of cultural understandings held by others – meanings about life, about work, about the past and imagined future, about problems both mundane and acute routinely encountered – that are tied closely to a specific context, often contested, and, these days, usually put forth in text in a far more provisional and partial way than in the past. As a process, it is both dynamic and recursive and the encounter with the "foreign" is the very essence of ethnography (Agar, 1980). We spend, for instance, a few days in the field, meander about the scene, hang out, talk to few people quite different from ourselves who hold ideas that in various ways differ – often spectacularly – from our own. We learn what we can and then alter the questions we ask or the way we ask them and spend a few more days in the field and talk to more people. And on and on and on it goes – and where it stops exactly, nobody knows, at least at the outset. Those who revere standardization break out in hives when ethnographers hold forth about their craft.

Ethnography is improvisational, not procedural. It is path-dependent because we learn more about the subjectivity and intentionality of those we encounter in the field well after our work is begun and, the longer we are at it, the more we learn about what we need to learn next. Our knowledge accumulates and changes over time as we come closer to understanding the perspectives – points of view – of the people from whom we are learning. Knowledge accumulates in large part because surprise – in some sense the Holy Grail of ethnography – is inevitable and taken seriously. When people do or say what we least expect, explanations are called for, however limited and tentative they may be at the moment. It is the imaginative reaction to surprise that fuels ethnography, such that the early days in the field are often the most exciting and the most creative periods of study since the learning curve for the ethnographer is rapidly accelerating. Yet, as I've discovered in all my work, cultural learning curves rarely if ever flatline – in part because culture itself is hardly static. There is always more to learn and surprise is just around the bend. Exit is then largely arbitrary, having little to do with either theoretical or empirical saturation.

Ethnography, properly speaking, is a social practice concerned with the study (fieldwork) and representation (textwork) of culture – these days with a distinctively small 'c'. It is a practice many claim to be the most humanistic of the sciences and the most scientific of the humanities. It exists somewhere in an academic limbo, an interdisciplinary pursuit and storytelling institution possessing a good deal of scholarly legitimacy with works commissioned, approved and published by the leading scholarly institutions of the day and carries the NSF stamp of approval (and usually an IRB license to commit ethnography as well). It claims a sort of documentary status by the fact that somebody actually ventures beyond the ivory towers of learning (and comfort) to, with qualifications, "live with and live like" those from whom one is learning. And these matters are not up for grabs.

One becomes an ethnographer by going out and doing it and coming back to write it all up. This is both the rite of passage into the trade and a strongly held occupational norm. The central idea is to develop a narrative about what it is like to be someone else. It requires a removal from one's usual routines, usual haunts and everyday social relationships such that the world one is studying becomes "home" (if only temporarily) on which survival in the field is itself premised on coming to see the world as others who live in it day in and day out do – maybe not with great subtlety at first but deepening with time and exposure. Nothing much can prepare you for intensive fieldwork. If you can't figure out how to get close to the community, organization, occupation, neighborhood or any odd group you want to study, if you can't figure out what to ask the proverbial natives, if you can't figure out how to build a certain type of rapport with often recalcitrant and always suspicious others, then it's time to think about a nice career in economic sociology or experimental social psychology where the so-called "data" are unlikely to be quite so cagey, to talk back, to question you, the questioner.

On Coming "Back"

It seems to me to be an open secret among those who have done lengthy, away from home, fieldwork that "coming back" is as difficult and tough – if not tougher – than "going out." When you return, you're not you anymore but those left behind – colleagues, advisors, fellow students in the groves of academe as well as friends and family in one's wider spheres – are still them (or so we believe). While in the field, your brain is churning away. Your days are full. You're trying to figure things out, to be accepted as a regular presence in what is to you an altogether novel, highly unpredictable and strange setting. The pace is hectic – new things to see, do, hear, dig out and explore; new relationships to court and, counting on the kindness of strangers, friendships to establish as a way of learning the ropes in an unfamiliar setting. And once, if you are fortunate and more or less accepted and at least moderately comfortable in the field, the work to do expands in ever-increasing waves as new and unanticipated problems and puzzles are discovered that insist on investigation. And toward the end of any given field stay, the pace again picks up as one is frantic to leave as few stones unturned in the field as possible.

Coming back however – the proverbial return of the native – much of this comes to a screeching and grinding halt. Things slow to what seems a snail's pace. Nor is home as familiar as it once was when you left nor, I would add, as you expected it to be. My first exit from the police – a transition from a most active, collective (if self-designed) research role as an apprentice police officer to the relative quiet, passive and autonomous academic grad student role was jarring – like a chugging chain saw hitting a steel spike. The return to the university was marked by a kind of reverse socialization that was informal, individualized, gray, disjunctive and called for a divestiture or dismantling of my more or less assumed adventurous fieldworker persona. Who am I now? What am I to do now? The field was rich with activity and excitement and my days were packed with things to do, people to talk to, research leads to explore (and if they were not, there were always more fieldnotes to work up).

My reception back home from those I knew – faculty as well as fellow grad students – fell roughly into three forms. First, the majority of my colleagues either didn't know or didn't really care that I'd been away. Second, some knew I'd been away for a while but were quite skeptical of whatever it was I learned from the field and sharply critical of my ethnographic approach. The halting, blundering and ill-formed tales of the field I told were merely grist for their own theories and something of a ready excuse for some of them to tell me about their own storied dalliance with qualitative work in the past (and usually why they gave it up for something more "rigorous"). Third, a few – but a precious few – were curious and seemed genuinely interested in what I'd been up to for the past year and what I might have learned. But even here attention was limited. My guess is that I got about three solid hours of serious attention during my first couple of months back from the field. When I'd start talking about what I thought I had been – and still was – learning, someone would invariably say: "Save it for the thesis." A talk I organized for my fellow students in the department about six months after returning had four people show up, most of them there no doubt for the free lunch I supplied.

In retrospect, I fully understand this state of affairs. I hadn't finished (and some might say I hadn't even begun) the ethnography. I'd only been to the field – all the text work lay ahead. I discovered of course that the scholarly community such as it was then at the University of California, Irvine had not been waiting with bated breath for the results of my expedition into the Seattle Police Department in the far northwest. The return of John Van Maanen was just another grad student coming back to school, not grounds for a university-wide day of rejoicing and celebration. Not that I expected such a reception but what I had hoped was that I would be able to lay out my field and analytic notes on the proverbial table and sit with some very smart people who would help me figure out all the things that I'd not figured out but only identified in the field – things like "deserving victims," "horns," "duck ponds," "racial profiling" (although we didn't use the phrase then), "kiss up, kick down," "rule following, bending and breaking" and so forth.

To some extent, this occurred but glacially and only after I began to develop a narrative (and narrative snippets) of what I thought I had learned that I could pass around as written drafts and précises. Writing these was (and continues to be) painful. In the field, I was busy, busy, busy and it was fun compared to the rather dreary post exit acts of composition, formulating arguments, sorting through and tinkering with various theories, reaching back to my field materials and memory for empirical support, and trying to come up with comparative analogies and persuasive examples. My early drafts were not only slow in materializing but careless, sloppy, poorly reasoned, and entirely cringe-worthy. The advice I got from the least helpful faculty members with whom I conferred was that I was to make a "contribution" to the field. And the people who told me so made it seem like such a "contribution" was an easy thing to do, like making a contribution to National Public Radio, the Salvation Army, or Oxfam. Thankfully however they were not the only ones on the academic scene for I did manage with more than a little help from my friends to complete my thesis – two years in the writing – and not only graduate but land a good academic job – that in those days of yore were remarkably plentiful compared to today's scarcity of decent positions.

Coming back then was a harsh and somewhat jolting reality shock. There was no honeymoon and my expectations of such on returning from the field have long ago vanished. What I had then (and now) was all this endless time stretched out in front of me – to write chapters and a thesis, later, to write a book, to get articles out. In short, to make the fabled contribution but I now have a far better sense of how this is done. And much of it in fact depends, unsurprising to me now, on exiting the field.

Revelatory Matters

While trying to reestablish myself as a member of good standing in my respective academic community, I also became aware that a good deal of what was hidden or appeared trivial during my fieldwork was in fact rather critical to my work. Certain things suddenly stood out that were not apparent to me while in the field – although recognizing them and figuring out how they fit in my work was a gradual and long drawn out process. Let me mention just three.

First, I had to a degree seemingly internalized a rather grim and skeptical perspective on society. Many of the cops I had come to know held with almost unerring conviction the view that the future will be different than the present, namely worse. In their view, there is always a fresh catastrophe just around the corner. There was of course a "golden age" of policing for them – although not many were around to testify as to its veracity – when restrictions were few, supervision benign, and the public supportive. But that was, alas, long gone. One of my close friends on the force, David, a crusty character full of acid commentary that cut through hypocrisy with biting and astute observations on the police was fond of quoting on an almost everyday basis a *bon mot* he attributed to Brendan Behan: "I have never seen a situation so dismal that the police couldn't make it worse." My humor and taste in jokes came to mirror my police friends and what I found amusing was rather out-of-touch with my academic peers. The police were indeed a cynical bunch and I had inadvertently absorbed a good deal of this stance, as my university interlocutors were only too happy to point out.

Second, my body felt different. I quickly discovered that I felt rather naked without my gun. I missed the weight and characteristic way of holding myself when armed (and cops rarely go anywhere on-duty or off without a weapon or sometimes two). Prior to entering the police academy, I had never even fired a gun let alone owned or carried one. But, I learned how to do so, and as such began to feel the symbolic and identity-bestowing power the gun has for the police while absorbing a sense of safety and comfort – probably entirely false – the gun provided. I learned also something of the associated paranoia that accompanies such ownership – Where can I safely store the damn thing? Where did I last put it? Is the safety on or off? I found also that I couldn't sit comfortably in a café or bar unless seated with my back to the wall and a pretty fair view of my surroundings. As a passenger riding in the front seat of a friend's car I keep my eyes curbside looking for something odd or out-of-place in the passing scene.

Third, I was annoyed and a bit taken aback now surrounded by all these "prissy professors and grad students" who knew nothing of what it was like "out there." I had come to believe and feel the police on the whole were terribly misunderstood and their work-a-day lives and problems dramatically misconstrued.[2] The police are characteristically sharp and short with people they don't know and so was I. They are a distrustful lot, skeptical of what others tell them and so too was I, questioning the motives and looking for the hidden agendas of those around me who I didn't know well. I had in some fashion absorbed the police view of the world as composed (excluding of course the police themselves) of "assholes, villains and know-nothings." Here, at home, I was surrounded by them. Even reading the newspapers I found myself channeling the police: "Why are the victims of homicide seemingly always described as outgoing, happy, fun-loving sorts with hordes of friends, a great future in store, and pillars of their respective communities? Don't hateful, miserable people get murdered too?"

Little of this appears in my fieldnotes – what Jean Jackson (1990) calls the "Saint's Bones of ethnography." My return however was making apparent the consequences of fieldwork *on* the ethnographer. For me and perhaps other ethnographers as well this resembles something akin to the Stockholm Syndrome or Hostage Mentality that results when one begins to slowly and often unconsciously identify with their captors. While I was definitely free to leave at any time during my fieldwork, I also had identified – perhaps over-identified – with the street cops who were my teachers (and had my back) in the field. I had become as close to them as I could as a way of staying in their world but my problem on exit was to get as far away from them as I could without leaving the planet.

What is required of course is to recognize and shake off the "insider's" point of view for something akin to an "outsider's" perspective that doesn't naturalize the culture. Easier said than done. And there are certainly examples of lengthy field-work that lead to "going native" – where one is so embedded in the social world they study and identifies so completely with those they have lived among that an outsider's perspective cannot be regained or imagined. If they do manage to write a research report, such writing will be designed most likely to please and generate good feelings among those written about.

This is not what I wanted to do of course. And as I readjusted to the university life I slowly began to write. The answer to establishing some distance is through writing and counting on the close reading of one's work by at least a few others you trust, others who may well be unfamiliar with the culture you are representing but otherwise knowledgeable and more or less supportive of ethnographic aims. My fieldnotes were still a comfort nonetheless if not exactly a guide. Read long after their inscription, they were revealing on many fronts. In them, for example, I discovered that about six months into my work I thought I had a good grasp of the police life. This was a delusion. Later entries, closer to my exit, suggested despair of ever understanding anything. But I also discovered that I could recall from reading about the events I described in my notes the feelings those events generated and many of the contextual details that at the time I didn't think important enough to write down.

There is a good deal made of the angst fieldworkers express on their return being chock-full of stories but not knowing much of what to do with them. This has certainly been true for me. But, as I sorted through my memories and materials, I begin to look for what I now call my "delicious ironies," my "strange quarks," my "VSTs" – "Very Special Things" – and began writing about these features of the police life. These are features, not bugs, that represent those curiosities, paradoxes, surprises that one inevitably brings back with them from the field. To me, this is a list of the things that had most puzzled and perplexed me in the field and I felt almost instinctively that they cried out for analysis. George Stocking (2010) writing about his historical research on ethnography calls such things "juicy bits" and defines them as those "revealing incongruities" that cannot be left dangling. Two examples will have to suffice here. Both are around the labeling practices of the police.

The police hold a paradoxical view that there are "deserving victims" and "unde-serving" ones. The latter of course soak up empathy, respect, support, and under-standing from the police who try to lessen their burdens and sense of victimization. Deserving victims are those who, to the police, simply have whatever misfortune they experience coming to them and receive little if any sympathy or help from the police. Sorting out who is and who is not deserving is a cultural matter and a rather complex and highly contextual one at that but this, as a VST, provided focus, a stack of examples to sort through and, most critically, something concrete to write about. Another VST of mine – a product of a field visit some five years after my original foray into the department – is the notion of "the asshole," a highly specific, relatively refined yet situational-constructed label the police – then and now – use to designate (and act toward) a class of characters they routinely encounter in their work world. And the asshole to the police turns out to show up as a rather stock but recognizable character in accounts of other careers from the humble to the proud.[3]

VSTs do not make a thesis or a book or very often even an article. But, for me, they are a way to start writing. In the field, trying to sort out, for example, how the asshole category worked was mindboggling. I would ask why is this guy now sitting handcuffed in the back of our patrol car an asshole and be told by my partner that it's because he's a jerkoff and doesn't know what the hell he's doing. When I would press why this guy is a jerkoff and doesn't know what he's doing, I was told it was because he is an asshole. I could take only so much of this circular reasoning in the field before I began to feel that my head would explode. It's a little like asking cultural members why they do what they do and getting back a blank stare of incomprehension or be told simply that it is just the way we do things around here — about as useful as asking a plumber why he uses a wrench. At any rate, by wrestling with these VSTs, I've come to the view that whatever narrative interpretation or argument I've been able to formulate is done so *a posteriori* — in the nature of an afterthought — and emerges for me primarily although not exclusively during the composition process taking place out of the field. This is the process by which I try to work out and propose a suggestively contextual — rather than authoritatively causal — explanation that at least aspires to be ineluctable such that a careful reader cannot casually dismiss my interpretation. This is basically craftwork.

This of course leaves open the kind of narrative explanations one is able to formulate. Culture does not explain itself. Here I've made use of three rather general explanatory strategies (and there are no doubt more). One of them is essentially historical or temporal and consists of building a case for how a cultural Practice X developed (or was learned and used) over time and how it now suits — or doesn't — members on the scene. Another is analytic in the sense that my explanations draw on other established scholarly work that locates Practice X as a way cultural members cope with rather fundamental human conditions surrounding power, status, survival, failure, accomplishment (or lack thereof) and so on. While it may be true that when the narrative pleasures of ethnography are great enough — meticulous detail, drama, surprise, irony — no one asks for conceptual niceties and the analytic frames, aims and implications are overlooked by readers (although surely not absent). But, following the analytic strategy involves something of a grand dive into the disciplinary dumpsters currently full and overflowing with I think more theory than we need or can ever use. The trick is finding one or several that seem to fit your ethnographic materials.[4] A third strategy follows Everett Hughes's classic notion of the locating the general in the specific (and hinted at above) in the sense that my explanation of Practice X depends on Practice X showing up (or likely to show up) somewhere else, taken up by other groups faced with similar problems. This is a way of "familiarizing" or "normalizing" what may appear to be a strange, idiosyncratic, and exotic practice by demonstrating how it comes into play in other places, times, and with other groups.

I've at various times used all three of these strategies in coming to terms with my field materials – including, especially, my VSTs. However, I haven't made these leaps in splendid isolation sealed off in my writing nook. I've written about textual practices at some length elsewhere but there remains a rather common and altogether misleading assumption held by many that writing is largely a solo act – the writer who writes alone (Van Maanen, 2011). Suppressed by this image are all the contextual and social aspects of writing that on a short list would include such matters as the substantive and thematic choices we make, the analytic guides we follow as noted above, our reading of other writers; discussing our ideas of content and style, method and theory both in passing and seriously with fellow students or colleagues, the vital roles played by others who read our drafts (polished or unpolished) including critics, friends (and foes), relatives, (dreaded) thesis advisors both past and present. And through this highly social process we come to write in a language, tone, grammar, voice, genre, and figures of speech on topics that literally encode collectivity. We place our field materials in frameworks that seem to emerge out of an ongoing series of endless negotiation processes between ourselves and those others – including reviewers and mentors, both real and imagined – whom we grant the authority to help shape our work. We are perhaps remiss in acknowledging such sources – so numerous are they – but we surely do not write alone. If an unwritten ethnography is no ethnography at all, so too is an unread one.

Little of this goes on while one is in the field. Pulling back and exiting if only for a while is a precondition, promoting a good deal of soul-searching, critical reflection, and continual learning. Often the end result is that we learn our cultural representations are at best incomplete, mere approximations, oversimplifications for there are always deeper levels of understanding to be achieved (which then takes us back to the field). Yet, sigh and alas, we have to leave the field once in a while to simply make some sense of what we've seen, felt, heard, experienced. If not, we'd be left only with piles and piles of stories and notes and no understanding. Exiting is hardly closure however, for I have come to realize there is no such thing as a finished ethnography.[5]

In Closing …

To bring this pondering on theory and exit to a close, let me rehash some of the broader aims and characteristics of ethnography that I think make such work so distinctive and valuable. I have four in mind.[6]

First, high quality ethnography is relatively free from technical jargon and highwire abstraction. While polysyllabic postmodernism is not altogether absent from contemporary ethnographic circles, it is infrequent. It is worth remembering that ethnography in sociology was being challenged when Everett Hughes first went to the University of Chicago some eighty years ago in the mid-1930s to revive and sustain the immersive fieldwork tradition that was then being treated as "old fashioned" by hypothesis-chasing, statistically minded, theory-obsessed colleagues. He succeeded brilliantly. But it is worth noting too that ethnography is still often treated as old fashioned. This is I think not so bad and represents a pretty good run for ethnography in the scheme of things. Indeed, in what I would label the mainstream realism of ethnography, concepts are still being borrowed with telling and persuasive effects largely from broad public discourse and, for better or worse, an anti-theory bias remains apparent. Representation by what anthropologist Richard Shweder (1991) calls the "merchants of astonishment" rather than generalizations by "human nature experts" remains a primary authorial pose in the trade where surprise, frame breaking, and exceptions to the norm shape the analytic domains of ethnography. A logic of discovery remains favored over a logic of verification. Abduction, not induction or deduction, continues to be the name of the game.

Second, because of this relative freedom from a thoroughly specialized vocabulary and a privileged conceptual apparatus, ethnography continues to carry a slight literary air compared to other forms of social science writing. It remains I think a less congealed, passive-verb, congested form of discourse, thus suggesting that a textual self-consciousness has been with us for quite some time. This perhaps keeps the non-specialist interested in what we do and occasionally pushes certain forms of ethnography into the trade or general reader domains, bringing the seemingly distant and alien or more proximate and familiar but still puzzling worlds we study to readers beyond the pinched warrens of our own research guilds.

Third, ethnography maintains an almost obsessive focus on the "empirical." The witnessing ideal – the "I witnessing" famously celebrated by Clifford Geertz with its intense reliance on personalized seeing, hearing, experiencing – continues to generate among ethnographers something of a hostility to generalizations and abstractions not connected to immersion in situated detail. Other forms of data are acceptable of course and responsible scholarship requires a sort of interdisciplinary contextualization of the settings in which we work – multiple and rather de-territorialized these days. But these other forms of evidence and argument are acceptable only as a concession to practicality. In the end, it is the writer's ability to convince readers that what they are reading is an authentic tale written by someone deeply familiar and knowledgeable about how things are done in some place, at some time, among some people that counts. Everything else that ethnography tries to do – to edify, amuse, challenge, annoy, surprise, critique and, yes, theorize – rests on this; thus signaling the struggle various forms of critical, historical, and analytic ethnography have had over the years, a struggle that continues today despite a recognizable broadening of ethnographic topics, tropes and genres.

Finally, there still is not much of a technique attached to ethnography beyond "being there." Ethnography it appears cannot and will not be made safe for science, leaving it immune to a standard methodology that would effectively neuter or perhaps destroy the still present Columbian spirit that marks the trade as broadly inquisitive, curious, and open-ended. "Bringing back the news" of what particular people, in particular places, in particular times are doing – whether at the far ends of the earth or just across the street may indeed be "old fashioned" but it certainly governs a good deal of contemporary ethnographic work. There remains then among many ethnographers, myself among them, a general indifference if not disdain for the seemingly endless efforts of social scientists to develop methodological or theoretical rigor. In this respect, ethnography continues to welcome a relatively artistic, improvised and highly situated model of social research where the lasting tenets of research design or theory construction have yet to leave their mark.

And, this, you will be unsurprised to learn, is the way I think it should be.

Notes

1 The paper was initially prepared for the Presidential Panel on "Finding our Way: Making Sense of Ethnographic Data" (American Sociological Society Annual Meetings, San Francisco, August 18, 2014).

2 The times are relevant here. On coming back to the university, many of my fellow students and faculty regarded the police as akin to malevolent storm troopers, "pigs," intent on crushing protest and racist to the core. To me, the police I came to know in Seattle became "family" in the sense that our personal lives were for quite some time closely intertwined and marked with a good deal of socializing together – dinners, social outings, parties, mutual visits to one another's homes, and so forth. I came back therefore holding a far more nuanced and differentiated view than my university colleagues as just who the police were and the complicated sources of the public actions in which they engaged. In general, I felt the city police I knew were (with a few exceptions of course) rather good and admirable people doing difficult and often dirty work. A large percentage of my police friends were returning Vietnam Vets who needed a job to support their young families and the police were hiring at the time. Another recognizable cluster of recruits (sometimes overlapping) were second or third generation policemen for whom the career was a family tradition to be carried on with a good deal of pride.

3 See, Van Maanen (1978). The notion of "the asshole" (and what to do about them) has become a bit of a cottage industry of late. Bob Sutton, an organization and management student, recently had a best-selling track called *The No-Asshole Rule* (2010); Geoffrey Numberg, a linguist, has a treatment called *Ascent of the A-Word* (2012) and Aaron James waxes philosophical in *Assholes: A Theory* (2012)

4 This is certainly in keeping with pragmatists such as John Dewey and Charles Pierce who favor fallibilism and theoretical pluralism when trying to work up accounts for how a part of the world might operate. They suggest that some theories work better than others depending on the particular problems addressed and the equally particular situations and times in which they are used. This is not a claim that all theories are equally valid or that research questions are themselves pre-theoretical. It is simply the recognition that one need not stake out a theoretical claim on how the world is before beginning a research project.

5 By this I mean ethnographic projects typically have beginnings but no clear endings. Even – gasp – the demise of the fieldworker doesn't conclude the enterprise, given the inevitability of restudies in the future conducted usually by younger ethnographers out to check on their elders and add a new wrinkle or two to the existing ethnographic base.

6 These points were put forth previously as a partial way to assess the quality and impact of ethnographic writings in an essay devoted to Alice Goffman's widely read and still controversial ethnography *On the Run*. See, Van Maanen and de Rond (2019).

References

Michael Agar 1980 *The Professional Stranger*. New York: Academic Press.

Elijah Anderson 1990 *Streetwise: Race, Class and Change in an Urban Community*. Chicago, IL: University of Chicago Press.

Elijah Anderson 1999 *Codes of the Street*. New York: W.W. Norton.

Michel Anteby 2013 *Manufacturing Morals: The Values of Silence in Business School Education*. Chicago, IL: University of Chicago Press.

Alice Goffman 2014 *On the Run: Fugitive Life in an American City*. Chicago, IL: University of Chicago Press.

Karen Ho 2009 *Liquidated: An Ethnography of Wall Street*. Durham, NC: Duke University Press.

Jean Jackson 1990 'Déjà Entendu': The Liminal Qualities of Anthropological Fieldnotes. *Journal of Contemporary Ethnography*. 13, 1: 8–43.

Aaron James 2012 *Assholes: A Theory*. New York: Doubleday.

John Lofland and Lynn Lofland 1995 *Analyzing Social Settings: A Guide to Qualitative Observation and Analysis*. Belmont, CA: Wadsworth.

Snejina Michailova, Rebecca Piekkari, Emmanuella Plakoyiannaka, Tina Ritvala, Irina Nihailova and Asta Salmi 2014 Breaking the Silence about Exiting Fieldwork: A Relational Approach and Its Implications for Theorizing. *Academy of Management Review*. 39, 2: 138–161.

Hirokazu Miyazaki 2013 *Arbitraging Japan: Dreams of Capitalism at the End of Finance*. Berkeley, CA: University of California Press.

Robin Nagel 2013 *Picking Up: On the Streets and behind the Trucks with the Sanitation Workers of New York City*. New York: Farrar, Straus and Giroux.

Geoffrey Numberg 2012 *The Ascent of the A-Word: Assholism, the First Sixty Years*. New York: PublicAffairs.

Richard A. Shweder 1991 *Thinking through Culture: Expeditions in Cultural Psychology*. Cambridge, MA: Harvard University Press.

David Snow 1980 The Disengagement Process: A Neglected Problem in Participant Observation Research. *Qualitative Sociology*. 3: 100–122.

James P. Spradley 1979 *The Ethnographic Interview*. New York: Holt, Rinehard and Winston.

George W. Stocking 2010 *Glimpses into My Own Black Box; An Exercise in Self-Deconstruction*. Madison, WI: University of Wisconsin Press.

Robert Sutton 2010 *The No Asshole Rule: Building a Civilized Workplace and Surviving One that Isn't*. New York: Business Plus.

John Van Maanen 1978 The Asshole. In Peter K. Manning and John Van Maanen (eds.) *Policing: A View from the Street*. New York: Random House. 221–238.

John Van Maanen 2011 *Tales of the Field: On Writing Ethnography Field* (2nd ed.). Chicago, IL: University of Chicago Press.

John Van Maanen and Mark de Rond 2019 The Making of a Classic Ethnography: Notes on Alice Goffman's 'On the Run'. *Academy of Management Review*. 42, 2: 396–406.

INDEX

Page locators in *italics* and **bold** refer to illustrations and tables, respectively.

Printed in the United States
by Baker & Taylor Publisher Services